Building a Speech

FOURTH EDITION

Building a Speech

FOURTH EDITION

Sheldon Metcalfe

Community College of Baltimore County, Catonsville Campus

Harcourt College Publishers

Fort Worth   Philadelphia   San Diego   New York   Orlando   Austin   San Antonio
Toronto   Montreal   London   Sydney   Tokyo

Publisher	Earl McPeek
Acquisitions Editor	Steve Dalphin
Market Strategist	Laura Brennan
Developmental Editor	Diane Drexler
Project Editor	G. Parrish Glover
Art Director	Garry Harman
Production Manager	Christopher A. Wilkins

Cover photography: Justus Hardin & Associates

ISBN: 0-15-506809-1
Library of Congress Catalog Card Number: 00-102807

Address for Domestic Orders
Harcourt College Publishers, 6277 Sea Harbor Drive, Orlando, FL 32887-6777
800-782-4479

Address for International Orders
International Customer Service
Harcourt, Inc., 6277 Sea Harbor Drive, Orlando, FL 32887-6777
407-345-3800
(fax) 407-345-4060
(e-mail) hbintl@harcourtbrace.com

Address for Editorial Correspondence
Harcourt College Publishers, 301 Commerce Street, Suite 3700, Fort Worth, TX 76102

Web Site Address
http://www.harcourtcollege.com

Harcourt College Publishers will provide complimentary supplements or supplement packages to those adopters qualified under our adoption policy. Please contact your sales representative to learn how you qualify. If as an adopter or potential user you receive supplements you do not need, please return them to your sales representative or send them to: Attn: Returns Department, Troy Warehouse, 465 South Lincoln Drive, Troy, MO 63379.

Printed in the United States of America

9 0 1 2 3 4 5 6 7 8   066   9 8 7 6 5 4 3 2 1

Harcourt College Publishers

To my mother, who gave me the values,
and my father, who gave me the vision
to write this book.

Contents in Brief

UNIT FIVE

Considering Different Types of Structures   345

Contents

Chapter 8   Conducting Research   151

UNIT FIVE Considering Different Types of Structures   345

Chapter 15 Speaking to Inform   347

Preface

Public speaking is a building process, wherein students gradually acquire skills in speech research, organization, and delivery. Students learn these skills step by step from their own experiences, by observing the presentations of others, through peer criticism, and from the guidance of effective instructors. This book establishes a caring environment for the learning process through a conversational style that aims to both interest and motivate students, while conveying encouragement through topics such as apprehension and listening that will help students to realize that they are not alone in their struggles. It is grounded in the philosophy that students can master the steps of speech construction if provided with a caring environment, clear blueprints, and creative examples.

Plan of the Book

The five units in this book organize skills in a sequence that is meaningful and understandable to students.

Unit I, "Surveying the Territory," presents the classical origins of public speaking as well as the modem theories of communication. In addition, it considers audience analysis, listening, ethics, and apprehension; and it introduces students to their first speaking assignment.

Unit II, "Preparing the Foundation," describes how to select topics, write purpose statements, conduct research, and choose supporting materials for speeches.

Unit III, "Creating the Structure," discusses outlining and speech introductions and conclusions.

Unit IV, "Refining the Appearance," describes the refinements necessary to complete speech construction. It helps students build skills in delivery and language, and it explains the use of visual aids to support a topic.

Unit V, "Considering Different Types of Structures," describes informative, descriptive, and demonstration speeches; persuasive speaking, with sample convincing and actuating speeches; presentations for special occasions, including the after-dinner speech; and speaking in group situations.

Features of the Fourth Edition

Building a Speech, Fourth Edition, retains all of the successful features of previous editions. It is written in a conversational style that appeals to students, and it presents a flexible arrangement adaptable to a variety of instructional approaches. It continues to offer chapters and guidelines for ma or informative and persuasive speaking assignments, present information about recent technologies in research and audiovisual aids, and provide interesting sample speeches. This edition also retains the expanded discussion of issues related to gender and cultural diversity, group-related exercises, detailed cases and illustrations for classroom analysis, sample speeches, and updated examples throughout. It continues to include the early speaking chapter, the popular chapter on apprehension, the important chapter on ethics, and the helpful presentation of alternative introductions and conclusions. In addition, *Building a Speech* now includes some important new features.

NEW SECTION ON LISTENING THEORY AND MODEL

Because listening is so important in the process of communication and public speaking, a new section titled, "The Process of Listening," has been added to Chapter 4, "Improving Your Listening Skills." This section introduces students to the theoretical listening model developed by Andrew Wolvin and Carolyn Gwynn Coakley and presents a detailed discussion to help students connect the model to their own experiences. The chapter also includes a diagram of the Wolvin-Coakley listening model to help students acquire a more comprehensive understanding of listening theory.

ADDITION OF GUIDELINES FOR SEARCHING THE INTERNET

The Internet has made speech research as well as many library data bases more accessible to students at home, in a dormitory room, or at work. It is important, however, for students to assess the reliability of web sources and determine when a brief trip to the library can yield more credible and more efficient results. Accordingly, Chapter 8, "Conducting Research," now includes "Guidelines for Searching the Internet" to help students critically examine the strengths, weaknesses, and limitations of the Internet.

ADDITION OF A GLOSSARY

Many of our Catonsville students who have used *Building A Speech* in their courses have suggested that the text include a Glossary of Terms at the end of the book. Reviewers for the fourth edition unanimously supported our students' recommendation. Accordingly, the end of the text contains a Glossary which defines key terms presented at the opening of each chapter.

ADDITION OF NEW SPEECH

The appendix includes Senator Edward M. Kennedy's eulogy of his nephew, John F. Kennedy, Jr., who died in a tragic plane crash in July of 1999. The appendix also retains speeches by Elizabeth Glaser, Garry Trudeau, Jesse Jackson, and Christopher Reeve. In addition, the text includes all of the informative and persuasive student speeches of the previous edition, including the popular "Computer Virus" informative speech with alternative introductions and conclusions, and the "Auto Repair" convincing speech with two sample organizational sequences.

OTHER FEATURES

The fourth edition also contains other revisions. Many chapter introductions have been revised or updated. Additional information is presented on digital video in Chapter 12, "Using Audiovisual Aids." A more precise discussion of opposition and rebuttal arguments appears in Chapter 17, "Speaking to Persuade." And many new examples and illustrations have been included throughout the text.

Ancillary Package

The ancillary package for *Building A Speech,* Fourth Edition, contains an instructor's manual complete with learning activities, a test bank, transparency masters, a computerized version of the test bank, and a videotape which includes both professional and student speeches.

ACKNOWLEDGMENTS

A writing project of this scope cannot be accomplished without the assistance of many individuals. My thanks goes to the reviewers whose comments helped in the revision of the third edition: Judy Deisler, Pasco Hernando Community College; Linda Grote, Shelton State Community College; Nedra Johnson, Grambling State University; John LaHoud, Ulster County Community College; Clarissa Piercall, Technical College of the Low Country.

I also wish to thank the Harcourt team who provided advice and assistance for this new edition: Steve Dalphin, Acquisitions Editor; Diane Drexler, developmental editor; Laurie Bondaz and Parrish Glover; project editors; Garry Harman, art director; Chris Wilkins, production manager; and Caroline Robbins and Cheri Throop, photo researchers.

Kathryn Allen, developmental editor for the first edition, continues to be a good friend and encourager. I am also indebted to many outstanding colleagues at the Catonsville Campus of the Community College of Baltimore County, including a superb library staff who were important resources for numerous areas of the book. And my wonderful public speaking students deserve special praise for their continued help, creative examples, and energetic suggestions. Finally, Howard and Betty Metcalfe have continued to provide encouragement and support throughout this time-consuming process.

Sheldon Metcalfe

Surveying the Landscape

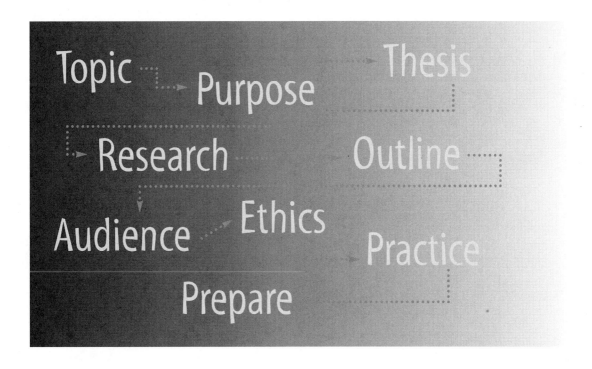

Chapter 1

INTRODUCING THE STUDY OF PUBLIC SPEAKING

"Talking and eloquence are not the same; to speak, and to speak well are two things. A fool may talk, but a wise man speaks."

Ben Jonson

CHAPTER OBJECTIVES

After reading this chapter you will be able to:

1. Recognize the importance of communication in the modern world;

2. Discuss the classical origins of public speaking;

3. Describe the communication process;

4. Apply the communication model to public speaking;

5. Describe three overall objectives for studying public speaking.

The latter 1990s have been characterized as a time of economic prosperity and one of the best times for college graduates to get good jobs. For some positions such as computer engineers, computer programmers, database administrators, and computer support specialists, job recruiters have offered starting salaries of $40,000 and signing bonuses of between $3,000 and $6,000.[1]

In spite of the booming economy, the job outlook has not been so rosy for other graduates. In 1999 about one in five graduates did not secure a position that was equivalent to the applicant's major field. Graduates in fields such as banking, journalism, advertising, and law experienced greater competition for jobs. With 1.38 million annual college graduates and only 1.1 million college-level jobs, almost 250,000 graduates worked at positions that didn't require college degrees.[2]

Even in an era of economic prosperity, it is clear that effective communication is just as important as ever. Successful communication helps us compete for new positions or maintain present ones. Active listening enables us to acquire additional job skills or to build networks with colleagues. Clear organization allows us to convey our ideas logically. Understanding the techniques of delivery gives us the ability to adapt our messages to different listeners and settings. While the application of communication skills cannot guarantee us a job or a career, a knowledge of these building blocks can at least help us to compete giving us a better chance.

Chapter 1 considers the importance of communication in today's world, and presents historical perspectives about communication. In addition, it describes a contemporary communication model and applies its components to public speaking.

COMMUNICATION IN THE MODERN WORLD

Imagine that you have two job interviews. The morning interview is for a position as a computer programmer with a nationally known company; the afternoon interview, for a similar job at a smaller firm. You are a little nervous, but you feel confident that you will make an impression.

When you arrive at the mirrored office complex on the twenty-first floor, you are ushered through a maze of work modules into a conference room where twelve people are seated in swivel chairs around a long table. At the opposite end is someone named Frank who stands and introduces himself as the division director. He asks you to take about five minutes to describe your education, work experience, and other pertinent skills. You begin:

Well, I, uh, uh, I, uh, I've heard a lot about this company, and I wanted to tell you about my experience. I had another job with a company—I was a

A job interview is one of many speaking situations requiring effective communication skills.

computer programmer with UNISYS, but uh, uh, . . . Oh wait! Before I talk about that I wanted to show you some stuff I brought. Uh, uh, I have it right here—it's got to be here somewhere—I had it this morning. Uh, uh, oh well . . .

The interview is terminated quickly. You are crushed. You had not expected the interviewer to ask you to give a five-minute presentation about yourself. You did make an impression: You were disorganized and unprepared.

You recover from the morning disaster and regroup for the afternoon appointment. You grab lunch and jot down four principal areas you want to emphasize about yourself. After writing an outline, you practice your speech, discarding irrelevant points and mentally weeding out verbal distractions such as "uh, uh."

Arriving at the small computer business, you are welcomed into the outer office. "Barbara" introduces herself and invites you into a lounge area where you begin your presentation:

I'm really glad to meet all of you. You appear to have a growing business here. As I came in, I noticed that people seemed to have enthusiasm and energy, but I also noticed that they appeared relaxed. These are qualities in a prospective working environment, which I think are important. I also noticed that you have both Macintosh and IBM-compatible equipment. I've trained on both platforms and I've had experience working with many Macintosh and IBM-compatible software programs. So what I'd like to do, if it's okay with you, is to describe my education, job experience, and some special skills I possess that I think could be helpful to your organization.

Although the preceding examples are hypothetical, they are realistic life situations that may remind you of similar experiences. In the first interview, the applicant rambled and hesitated due to lack of preparation; in the second, the prospective employee presented introductory remarks with clarity and precision. We can't categorically state that the disorganized interview destroyed the applicant's chances, nor can we say that the well-prepared interview produced immediate success. But the well-organized applicant has a much better chance of making a positive impression and of achieving successful results.

While a job interview is one type of speaking situation we all must face, effective communication skills are needed in many additional situations, for example:

- Giving a friend some simple street directions to a party.
- Proposing a toast at a wedding.
- Demonstrating the 24-hour money machine to new customers.
- Conducting a tour of a historical landmark to recent immigrants.
- Hearing a doctor describe a surgical procedure she must perform on a family member.
- Expressing feelings of sympathy to a colleague over the loss of a close friend or family member.
- Motivating a church group to donate canned food and clothing to the needy at Thanksgiving.
- Persuading an IRS tax auditor that a deduction was a legitimate business expense.
- Listening to the boss explain reasons for not granting the promotion.
- Convincing a police officer not to write a parking ticket.

This list includes speeches that provide information, reinforce feelings, and demonstrate a process. It also includes speeches of action and speeches of conviction. Each situation requires effective speaking and listening skills.

We are also affected by communication beyond our own territory. We are touched when ex-basketball star Earvin "Magic" Johnson comforts a little girl who is infected with AIDS. We send food, clothing, and medical help when we see hundreds of Americans who have suffered a loss because of a hurricane, flood, or terrorist attack. We donate food when we hear the pleas of starving families in Somalia or Ethiopia. We feel angry when we see the mass graves and displacement of Albanians as a result of ethnic cleansing in Kosovo. We examine our living standard when the

President tells us that the economy is booming and unemployment is at an all-time low. We weigh the arguments as U.S. senators debate the pros and cons of a controversial nomination to the Supreme Court. We laugh when we hear a comedian do an impression of a famous politician or actor. We become silent when an ex-soldier reads the names on the wall of the Vietnam Memorial.

Every day of our lives, we apply principles of communication. We inform, we shape, and we move others; we are equally informed, molded, and moved by others. Our success in these everyday situations often depends upon how effectively we speak and how carefully we listen.

Success will take some energy on your part. But if you are willing to spend the time, you can improve your speaking skills and be more successful in each situation you encounter. Remember that your goal is not to be Jesse Jackson, Mark McGwire, Maya Angelou, Michael Jordan, LeAnn Rimes, Tom Cruise, or Whoopi Goldberg. Your goal is to be you: a more confident and effective you.

CLASSICAL ORIGINS OF SPEAKING

In ancient times, public speaking was called *rhetoric,* which meant "the art of the orator."[3] Classical rhetoric specifically dealt with skill in persuasive oratory, or the ability to convince and to move an audience to a specific point of view.

Corax is considered to be one of the founders of rhetoric. In the fifth century B.C., a tyrant subjugated the citizens of Sicily and confiscated their property. When the dictator was overthrown and democracy was restored to the island, the courts were jammed with people trying to reclaim their lands. Corax influenced judicial oratory by developing a method of speaking that helped the common people argue their court cases more successfully.

Gorgias (483–376 B.C.) was a brilliant speechmaker and a highly influential teacher in Athens. He tended to emphasize an ornate style, figures of speech, and emotionalism in his speaking. Those, like Gorgias, who taught oratory and charged a fee to their students were called *sophists.* At first sophists were respected teachers, but later a number of con artists took over the schools and exploited students for financial profit. The word sophistry came to have a negative connotation, implying the use of deceitful methods and faulty reasoning.

Isocrates (436–338 B.C.) was a more influential rhetorician in Athenian society than Gorgias. In addition to teaching many Greek orators, Isocrates wrote a number of manuscripts and an autobiography describing his ideas. He believed that a speaker should be well educated in the liberal arts and of good moral character, and he emphasized that a speaker must possess freedom and independence, yet demonstrate self-control. He adapted the ornate style of Gorgias into a more fluid prose style of writing and speaking.

Plato (428–348 B.C.) had little regard for rhetoricians such as Gorgias and Isocrates. He described his concepts in "dialogues," which were actually stories written in play form. In his dialogue entitled *Gorgias,* Plato attacks the methods of the sophists and claims that rhetoric is not a useful pursuit. In his dialogue *Phaedrus,* Plato charges that sophists corrupt young people and that rhetoricians are more interested in dishonesty, style, and opinion than in truth. While he conceded that rhetoric could deal with truth, he continued to insist that rhetoric was "not a true art."

Plato's famous student, Aristotle (384–322 B.C.), wrote *The Rhetoric* and challenged many of Plato's negative opinions about oratory. To Plato's charge that rhetoric lacks truth, Aristotle responded that objective truth exists only in science and math. Plato wrote that rhetoric is flawed since men base their reasoning on opinions and beliefs. Aristotle replied that belief is the highest degree of certainty in the world of human beings. Aristotle introduced what he called three methods of proofs: *ethos,* the ethical appeal; *pathos,* the emotional appeal; and *logos,* the appeal to logic and reason. Aristotle's work helped to elevate public speaking to a respected place and has influenced thinkers and speakers to the present day.

Among those influenced by Aristotle were Cicero and Quintilian, two Roman orators who also added to the literature of rhetoric. Cicero (106–43 B.C.) was a skillful orator and a respected teacher who thought that the speaker should be educated in the liberal arts.[4] In his book *De Oratore,* he discusses topics such as writing, audience analysis, anxiety, evidence, and argument. Quintilian (35–95 A.D.) was a famous Roman lawyer who stressed that the "true orator must be, above all, a good man . . . skilled in speaking."[5] In his book *The Institutes of Oratory,* he describes the speaker's purpose when he writes, "There are also three objects which an orator must accomplish: to inform, to move, to please."[6]

Classical rhetoric involved real human beings who persuaded, who moved, and who influenced nations and civilizations. The writings of Aristotle, Cicero, and Quintilian were read by thinkers during the Renaissance, by reformers in England, and by revolutionaries in America. Men such as Patrick Henry, Tom Paine, Thomas Jefferson, and James Madison applied many of Aristotle's speaking techniques and energized the spirit of a new nation. Throughout our history, speakers like Abraham Lincoln, Sojourner Truth, Susan B. Anthony, Theodore Roosevelt, Franklin D. Roosevelt, John F. Kennedy, and Martin Luther King Jr. have applied the ancient speaking principles to move an often-reluctant nation into a more ethical or progressive course of action.

The classical Greeks and Romans influence *our* communication as well. When you arrange a speech into an introduction, body, and conclusion, you are applying Aristotle. When you research your topic, Cicero smiles. When you practice the delivery, Quintilian nods knowingly. When you apply moral principles, Isocrates sheds a joyful tear. We are indebted to these individuals for their contributions, and we continue to employ their speaking principles in our contemporary lives.

THE COMMUNICATION PROCESS

When we speak in any given situation, most of us take communication for granted; sometimes we succeed and sometimes we fail. But communication is not just a haphazard, trial-and-error occurrence. Often there are very good reasons for our success or failure. The more we understand about the process of communication, the more we can improve our skills.

A great many experts have written about communication and have developed theories called *communication models.* In the 1940s, Claude Shannon, an engineer at the Bell Telephone Company, and Warren Weaver, a mathematician, wrote *The Mathematical Theory of Communication,*[7] which became a classic in the field. Shannon and Weaver stated that in order for communication to take place, there must be a *source,* a *message,* a *channel,* and a *receiver* (Figure 1.1).

While this model was helpful in understanding communication, it was later criticized for its lack of flexibility. The communication model was often illustrated as a flat line with a source at one end, the message and channel in the middle, and the receiver at the other end. The model tended to give the inaccurate impression that communication is a static activity that does not change or develop. The model may accurately simulate mechanical transmission of signals over a telephone line, but it does not describe the fluid interaction of human beings.

More recent theories have emphasized the idea that communication is dynamic: It is always changing, growing, and developing.[8] These communication models can be illustrated by a circle rather than a line (Figure 1.2).

FIGURE 1.1

Claude Shannon and Warren Weaver, The Mathematical Theory of Communication, copyright 1949 by the University of Illinois Press. Used by permission.

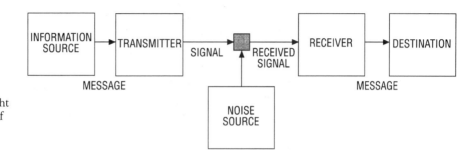

FIGURE 1.2

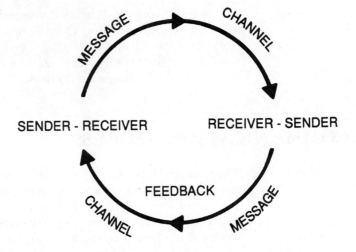

Senders can receive messages as they are sending them; receivers can like-wise send and receive at the same time. Human communication can be ad-justed to new feedback and influenced by the environment. Communication changes and unfolds on the basis of ever-changing human experiences.

A Communication Model

A model helps us understand the dynamic process of communication. We will consider seven aspects: sender, message, channel, receiver, feedback, setting, and noise. To explain each part of the model, we will use a simple example: a job interview between two people.

THE SENDER: ENCODING IDEAS INTO SYMBOLS

The *sender* originates communication. Within the sender are the ideas, thoughts, feelings, and intentions that begin the process of communica-tion. Suppose, for example, that you are the sender in a two-way conver-sation. The idea–thought–feeling "employment" has just popped into your brain. You reflect upon the idea for awhile until you encode it. *En-coding* is simply the thought process and motor skill of the sender, which changes an idea–thought–feeling into an understandable symbol. *Symbols* are verbal and nonverbal expressions or actions that have meaning. In this case, words such as *job* or *applying* symbolize the verbal meanings, and a handshake and an application form would symbolize the nonverbal meanings.

THE MESSAGE

Even though symbols have meanings, they must be arranged in some kind of logical structure. If you said "job, applying . . ." there would be meaning, but the verbal symbols would lack organization and might be confusing. If you smiled and said the word "I . . ." , the nonverbal coupled with the word symbol would still be incomplete. You must have a *message,* that is, a set of structured symbols. So you decide to encode your ideas into the message "I'm applying for the job . . ." You, the sender, have now taken the idea–thought–feeling from inside your brain, encoded or changed the idea–thought–feeling into a set of word symbols *(applying, job, I'm),* and arranged these symbols into an organized structure called a message, "I'm applying for the job . . ." Your message is clear, precise, and understandable: It has meaning to you, and potentially to someone else. However, while you have organized the appropriate message, you have not yet been able to communicate to the other person.

THE CHANNEL

The next step in the communication process is the selection of a channel. *A channel* is the means of transporting the message. The channels we use to transmit messages are sensory: We convey our messages through sight, sound, smell, taste, and touch. To communicate, you must now choose one or more of these sensory channels to convey the message "I'm applying for the job . . ." You could simply state the message. You could present a résumé, you could shake the interviewer's hand, or you could smile. You could even wear a stylish suit and apply some appropriate cologne or perfume before the interview. Each decision presents you with a different combination of sensory channels. You therefore make the decision to use all the techniques in order to employ as many senses as are desirable.

THE RECEIVER: DECODING SYMBOLS INTO IDEAS

At this point in the process, there is a sender (encoding the ideas into symbols), a message, and several channels. However, communication is still incomplete because no connection has been made to the receiver. The *receiver* is the destination, the goal of communication. When you come face to face with your interviewer, you now have the potential for communication since you have a destination for the message. You verbally state "I'm applying for the job . . ." Nonverbally, you smile, shake the individual's hand, and present your résumé.

Immediately, the process that occurred to generate communication within the sender now occurs in reverse within the receiver. The receiver *decodes* or changes the symbols in your organized message into ideas—

thoughts–feelings that the receiver can use to give meaning to the message. While we now have a receiver and decoding to add to the communication model, we still need a response to complete the communication circle (Figure 1.3).

FEEDBACK

Feedback is a verbal or nonverbal response. Feedback can tell you whether communication has occurred, how it has been received, and whether it has been understood. Feedback is a reaction from the receiver to the sender: It can be positive and negative, verbal and nonverbal. Feedback provides dimension and transforms communication from a one-way into a two-way process.

The most obvious feedback is from the receiver. Having gone to all the trouble you just took to send your multichannel message, you would hope for positive feedback, such as, "I'm happy to accept your application. You have a good chance for the job." You could also receive additional sensory feedback, such as a pat on the back or an invitation to lunch. We hate to mention this, but negative feedback can occur as well. The interviewer could conceivably respond by throwing your résumé on the floor, pointing to the door, and stalking out of the room.

However, the wonderful thing about feedback is that it can transform senders into receivers, and receivers into senders; in other words, we can

FIGURE 1.3

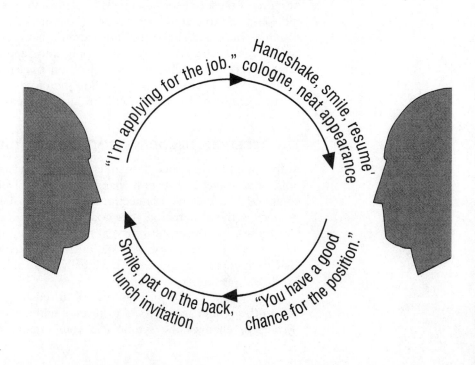

send and receive messages simultaneously and alter our messages based upon the responses that occur. As you are sending your "employment" message, you become aware that your interviewer is smiling. Upon receiving this information, you modify your message. You return the smile, move toward the interviewer, and say, "I really like this company—everyone seems so friendly." Messages continue to change on the basis of new information sent and received. Feedback circularizes communication, provides dimension, and allows us to adapt to new circumstances.

SETTING

The communication process does not exist in a vacuum. Instead, it occurs in a *setting*, which includes occasion, environment, space, and time. A speaker must consider how the occasion influences the message. The physical and psychological conditions differ for a business meeting, an anniversary, a marriage proposal, a birthday, or a Christmas party. When the occasion is clearly understood beforehand, the speaker selects an environment that is appropriate for the message.

An administrator arranging a job interview could imitate the opening example of this chapter and choose a formal conference room with a long table. This intimidating environment could be designed to convey rigidity and control to the prospective employee. On the other hand, an interviewer might use the second approach and select a lounge area with comfortable chairs and background music to convey informality and cooperation. The employer might consider spatial factors by seating individuals at a round table in front of a bright window with hanging plants. The interview could be scheduled during the lunch hour, a time when messages could be communicated in a relaxed and unhurried manner.

You can see the importance of setting in supporting the communication process. When thinking through any speaking situation, you need to consider the aspects of occasion, environment, space, and time so that the setting will support your communication successfully.

NOISE

We have established that in order for communication to take place there must be a sender, message, channel, receiver, feedback, and a setting. Noise, however, is a factor that can cause disruption or disturb the flow of communication. *Noise* is a distortion or a distraction to communication: It interferes with the process and reduces the effectiveness of communication (Figure 1.4). There are three types of noise: external, internal, and semantic.

External Noise. External noise is any interference that can be perceived by the senses in the speech setting. It is important to emphasize that the

FIGURE 1.4

Cartoon by George Goebel.

word *noise* can, but does not always, refer to sound. If you try to deliver your employment message and your interviewer suddenly glimpses the arrival of specially ordered equipment, chances are that your message won't be completely communicated. If the interviewer is interrupted by the intercom buzzer every five seconds, your message is not likely to be received clearly. Or the location of the interview may be so chilly that your potential employer is concentrating on shivering rather than on listening to you.

If the external noise is too great, communication will be lost. For communication to occur, either the interference must be eliminated or the sender must adapt to the situation. If the room is too cold, you can diplomatically suggest that the heat be turned up or that the meeting move to another room. If there are numerous interruptions in the conversation, you can try to condense your presentation or make a comment or a joke about the situation.

Internal Noise. While you can usually sense the source of external noise, you cannot always perceive the cause of internal noise. Internal noise is any interference or disruption to communication that occurs within the receiver. You may have just said "I'm applying for the job and I have a résumé and a portfolio for you to see," and you discover that your interviewer isn't listening at all. The facial expression of your prospective employer may reflect tension. There may be any number of internal distractions that act as barriers to you. The interviewer may be ill, worrying about a personal problem, or feeling stress from a confrontation with an employee. As a speaker, you cannot always know what internal problems are causing distractions within listeners, but unless the distractions are removed, little communication can occur.

Finding the source of the negative feedback is sometimes a way to understand the disruption and restore communication. If you are sensitive to the tense facial expression of the interviewer, you might carefully ask, "Have I come at a bad time?" or "Is there something wrong?" and begin to explore the reasons for the disruption. Once you have worked through the problem you can try your message again.

Semantic Noise. One other type of noise that creates a barrier to communication is semantic noise. Semantic noise is any barrier to word or other symbol meanings because of differences in environment, nationality, pronunciation, values, or experiences. If your interviewer is Japanese and speaks little English, there is an obvious language barrier to communication. If the interviewer is a Boston native and tells you, "I'm sorry I'm late for the appointment—I had to 'paahk' the 'caah,'" the accent might create a semantic barrier. If the interviewer asks, "Can I get you a soda?" the word *soda* could mean anything from "soft drink" to an ice cream-and-syrup concoction. Or your "I'm applying for the job" message could be suddenly interrupted by a stern reprimand from your interviewer: "Don't use the word 'job'—this isn't a 'job'—you are applying for a *professional position*." You would immediately become aware that perception, values, and occupational experiences have caused the interviewer to view the word *job* with negative meanings. You would need to refrain from mentioning the word and adjust to the new situation.

Semantic noise interferes with communication. To be a more effective communicator, you must become aware of these disruptions and begin to adapt to the semantic noise that exists between sender and receiver.

The Communication Model Applied to Public Speaking

You employ the communication model automatically in your daily life; now it is important that you apply the process successfully to public speaking situations as well. The following graduation speech demonstrates some of the pitfalls of communication.

The ceremony was held in a huge gymnasium where about a thousand graduates' parents, faculty, and administrators had assembled on a hot day in June. Since the auditorium was not air-conditioned, students and faculty sweltered in their black academic gowns. Every speaker's voice echoed because of poor acoustics. In addition, planes from a nearby airport took off directly over the gym. In this environment, the speaker began:

> Distinguished administrators, members of the faculty, platform dignitaries, parents and relatives, honored guests and friends, and members of the class of 2000:

> Today we gather within these sacred halls of learning to acknowledge the rite of passage—for all graduations can be considered rites of passage—we gather here to honor those of you who have aspired to higher goals, higher dreams, and higher hopes. And so we are proud to honor you today at this very special time. All of you have had the advantages of an education. And all of you are on the way to achieving your dreams. But there are many who have had higher dreams and higher goals who did not enjoy the advantages of an education at a university. They learned from the university of life. So I'd like to spend considerable time this afternoon talking to you about some of those people who succeeded in spite of their circumstances.

The speaker went on and on. Members of the audience became noisy and fidgety. Some graduates, dripping with perspiration, unzipped their academic gowns and used the commencement programs for fans. Every now and then, a low-flying jet would drown out the speaker's voice. A few faculty members dozed off in their chairs.

The speech was a disaster. The speaker falsely assumed that he would deliver his address to a receptive audience under ideal conditions. When faced with the difficulties of the speech setting, he did nothing to adapt his speech. He simply plodded along with his intended material as if nothing were wrong.

The speaker should have considered all aspects of the communication process. Audience members sent clear verbal and nonverbal feedback that they were hot, tired, and inattentive. The speaker paid no attention to the external noise of the jet, the heat, the audience chatter, or the internal noise of audience exhaustion and fatigue. Had the speaker researched the setting, he could have discovered the problems in the environment. To make matters worse, the speaker created further problems for himself when he told listeners that he would spend "considerable time" developing

A SEMANTIC PROBLEM

The real estate broker met the couple who were interested in looking at a house. After everyone had fastened their seatbelts, the Realtor headed her car toward the small development outside of town.

Realtor: "I'm going to show you a house that you're both going to love. It has three bedrooms, two-and-one-half baths, a spacious living room, family room, eat-in kitchen, screened-in porch, and a two-car garage."

Couple: "Sounds really good."

Realtor: "It's situated on almost an acre across from a beautiful river. . . ."

Wife: "I can hardly wait to see it."

Realtor: ". . . and a really nice feature is that the house comes with a wonderful FROG."

Husband: "A frog?"

Realtor: "A FROG! You'll see. Very nice."

There was silence. The husband and wife exchanged glassy stares and other pointed nonverbal expressions.

Wife *(sarcastically):* "Oh, a, a frog. Very, very nice. I've always wanted a frog with my house."

Realtor *(turning the corner to the house):* "Here we are. Everybody out."

Wife: "The first thing I've got to see is that frog."

Realtor: "Fine. You'll be impressed." *(She enters a hallway beside the garage and leads the couple upstairs.)* "Well here we are. Isn't this great? It's so spacious don't you think?"

Husband: "I don't see any frog. Where is it?"

Realtor: "You're standing in it."

Wife: "Come on. Where is the little green thing?"

Realtor *(Laughing hysterically):* "Oh, I'm sorry. I thought you knew what I meant. That's right, you're not from around here. In our part of the country, FROG means *finished room over garage!*"

Couple *(Laughing):* "And all this time we were wondering why anyone would ever want a frog in their house!"

his points. This phrase implied that the speaker was immune to the heat, insensitive to the audience, and would do nothing to shorten his speech or otherwise adapt to the situation. Therefore, the audience became equally insensitive to the speaker.

You might be thinking that this example provides so many communication problems that even the best speaker would have difficulty handling it successfully. The situation is certainly bad, but it is not impossible. Notice how this speaker has adjusted to the problems:

> Good afternoon ladies and gentlemen. It's almost hotter than purgatory in here, isn't it? I wonder if we could have the ushers open up a few doors so we could get some kind of cross-ventilation. Good. Okay. Thanks. Now I just want to tell you that I had prepared some remarks of celebration, which I believed were appropriate to this event.
>
> But I've shortened my speech so we all can go somewhere else to recover from the heat and humidity. So let me just briefly tell you about some dreams, goals, achievements, and one or two people who achieved those dreams against great odds.

This speaker has acknowledged the problems of the setting, attempted to make audience members more comfortable, and emphasized his intention to be brief. If you were a member of this audience, you would make the effort to listen simply because the speaker communicated that he was sensitive to the situation, cared about you, and was willing to modify his plans. The speaker has also done himself a big favor. Even though he has discarded some of his speech, the speaker knows that the audience will be more receptive to what remains.

Applying the Communication Model to Everyday Life

To build successful speaking skills, you should apply the communication process in daily speaking experiences. As a sender, you should be aware of your own strengths and weaknesses. You must be able to send and receive messages effectively, and you must realize that much of the responsibility for success in speaking rests with you. If a friend asks you to give an entertaining speech at a bachelor party, think of a topic that not only interests and challenges you but also involves your audience. If you develop a speech about congressional term limits for a culturally diverse audience, be sensitive to those who may not be completely familiar with the American governmental system. If you must speak against new high-rise construction at a zoning board investigation, prepare a message with a clear purpose, thorough research, and logical organization.

If your employer asks you to present a detailed financial report, be aware of the various channels of communication. Create interest by employing verbal channels (such as vocal inflection, volume, and emphasis), as well as nonverbal channels (such as facial expression, gesture, dramatic pauses, and visual aids).

Gear your message to the audience. Will women perceive the topic differently from men? Do listeners from different cultures understand American expressions and jargon? Will listeners from other geographical areas recognize specific references to places and events within your city or community? Will bachelors enjoy the humorous topic? Are zoning board members for or against new construction? Can fellow employees understand and interpret complex financial data? Be able to accurately interpret and effectively adapt to audience feedback. Is the lack of eye contact from some audience members a result of cultural differences or distractions? Are the listeners in the back row yawning because of your speech or simply because they are tired? Do perplexed audience faces indicate confusion about your ideas or a misunderstanding about your vocabulary? Do you need to alter any portion of your speech based upon audience response?

Acknowledging the noise created by a disruptive latecomer, the audience sneezer, or the distracting lawnmower helps you regain attention. You may need to define terms where cultural or semantic experiences of speaker and audience differ. You may need to check out in advance the location of the speech to determine the available resources. Is there an electrical outlet, chalk, or easel? Is there a speaking lectern, microphone, or table? Is the room adequately ventilated, lit, or heated? Does the setting contain any elements that could create problems for your speech?

DESIGNING A PLAN

You now find yourself in a course where you will be required to present speeches to an audience. This experience is important to your growth and development as a communicator. Learning from your classroom successes and failures should help you in communication situations beyond the course. While we will discuss many concepts and principles, there are three overall objectives we want you to achieve:

1. *You should be able to critically evaluate speaking situations.* Be able to understand and evaluate the speaking situation. What makes a "good" speaker? What constitutes a "good" speech? What are some aspects of the audience you need to consider when preparing a speech? What are some factors of the occasion you should know before making a presentation? When you can survey the landscape and answer some of these questions about any speaking situation, you are well on your way to delivering successful speeches.

2. *You should be able to plan, prepare, and organize speeches.* To speak effectively, you must prepare effectively. An architect draws a set of blueprints with clear specifications before a builder can erect a house. And while it may seem time consuming, a speaker must structure ideas into a coherent plan before presenting a speech to an audience. While effective planning takes effort, the process is not necessarily difficult. In fact, if you have put sufficient time into researching and outlining your speech, you may find that speechmaking is a lot easier than you thought.

3. *You should be able to deliver speeches in front of an audience with ease.* How well do you communicate your ideas in public? Do you appear confident, knowledgeable, and enthusiastic about your topic? Are you able to deliver different types of speeches in different speaking situations? Are you able to progress logically from one idea to another? When you look at members of the audience, do you actually "see" them? Do you concentrate on what you are speaking about at a given moment, or does your mind wander? Do you employ gestures and facial expressions, or do you have nervous mannerisms? Do you rehearse the speech before presenting it to the audience?

Build your speaking ability block by block. Survey the landscape, prepare the foundation, create a skeletal structure, refine the appearance, and finally, develop different types of structures. Learn from your mistakes, profit from your achievements, and effectively communicate to benefit yourself and others. When you develop the speech step by step, block by block, you will build a functional, pleasing structure.

SUMMARY

Public speaking, so important in our society, is grounded in the rhetoric and oratory of ancient times. Modern theories include the classic Shannon and Weaver communication model, as well as a more recent communication model comprised of seven components: sender, message, channel, receiver, feedback, setting, and noise. You must understand the communication process and apply the process to speaking situations. Three objectives of this course are to help you: (1) evaluate speech situations; (2) plan, prepare, and organize speeches; and (3) effectively deliver speeches in front of an audience.

SKILL BUILDERS

1. How effectively do you communicate? Write down some of your strengths and weaknesses. Decide upon areas you'd like to target for improvement.

2. Think back on some of your own communication experiences. What experiences do you feel were successful, and which ones would you characterize as unsuccessful? What elements in your communication caused success, and what elements caused failure?

3. Divide into several small discussion and work groups. After reading the example of the ineffective commencement speech described in this chapter, discuss and then answer the following questions. Report the results of your analysis to your classmates.

a. If you were the commencement speaker, what different decisions would you have made about the problem of noise?

b. What is the purpose of a graduation address? Are these speeches inherently boring, or can they be rewarding experiences for everyone involved?

c. Can you think of any commencement speeches you have heard that will be remembered by an audience? Be specific and explain your answer.

d. Develop a short graduation speech that would be interesting and meaningful to the graduates at your college or university.

4. In your class, set up a variety of role-playing situations and have the class and your instructor judge how effectively you communicate your purpose. Here are a few role-playing situations:

a. A foreigner who can barely speak English has asked you to explain the best route to take to the airport. You must give the individual directions that are clear and simple.

b. You are in the process of a tax audit and an IRS agent is questioning several costly items under "business lunches," which you have taken as a deduction. You must explain why these are justifiable expenses.

c. You are asking your boss for a raise, and you are trying to provide as many reasons as possible to support your objective.

d. You are standing at a traffic light, and you are trying to get motorists who are stopped for a few seconds to donate money to the American Cancer Society.

e. You have been asked to propose a toast to the bride and groom at a wedding reception.

f. You have smashed the front end of the family car. You must explain the problem as calmly as possible to a member of the family.

NOTES

1. Jeff Harrington, "Florida College Graduates Find Plenty of Tech Jobs," *Knight-Ridder/Tribune Business News,* June 8, 1999.

2. Ibid.

3. Edward P. J. Corbett, *Classical Rhetoric for the Modern Student* (New York: Oxford University Press, 1971), p. 31.

4. Lester Thonssen, ed., *Selected Readings in Rhetoric and Public Speaking* (New York: H. W. Wilson, 1952), p. 65.

5. Thonssen, p. 156.

6. Thonssen, p. 102.

7. Claude E. Shannon and Warren Weaver, *The Mathematical Theory of Communication* (Urbana: The University of Illinois Press, 1949).

8. C. David Mortensen, *Communication: The Study of Human Interaction* (New York: McGraw-Hill, 1972), p. 14.

Chapter 2

BUILDING YOUR FIRST SPEECH

As a vessel is known by the sound, whether it be cracked or not; so men are proved by their speeches, whether they be wise or foolish.

Demosthenes

CHAPTER OBJECTIVES

After reading this chapter you will be able to:

1. Create a blueprint of nine building blocks for constructing a speech;

2. Identify four styles of delivery;

3. Think critically about constructing a speech.

Kathleen DeSantis was a student at Catonsville Community College who successfully completed the basic course in public speaking several years ago. Her speeches were challenging and creative, and listeners always looked forward to hearing what she had to say. We asked Kathleen how she chose her topics and what she did to prepare for her speeches. She offered her blueprint:

> First of all, I think about a topic a lot. I ask people questions. I get feedback from everybody I know, and I try to get an idea of what they'd be interested in—something different, something relevant—not the same old subject they've heard again and again.
>
> When I have a topic, I ask knowledgeable people where to get material. For example, when I researched my persuasive speech on literacy, I talked to my parents who are both educators. My mom teaches at the Maryland House of Corrections in Jessup, Maryland, and she spoke to one of the tutors at the Reading Academy who gave her a poster and a newspaper article that I used in the speech. I also did a telephone interview with Janet Dent in the office of Adult Education who told me about the VIP—Volunteers in Partnership—Program. I wanted to get the audience to sign up and volunteer for literacy, and I remembered seeing a 1-800 number on TV where they could get more information about "Project Literacy"—so I copied it down and used that in my speech too.
>
> I do more research when I go to the library. What I find most valuable is the magazine index on computer—it's called "Info Trac." You just type in the subject and it gives you the titles of magazine articles that deal with the subject.
>
> Then I gather everything from the library and sort through all of it, throwing out the things that are irrelevant or don't support what I'm trying to say. I write a specific purpose so I don't go off on a tangent. And from there I do the speech in my mind. I try to see myself in front of the class. I work on an outline, always referring back to my specific purpose. Then I type it, I go back, reedit, and change my mind. I get large note cards and write down my outline. I write key words—I use a lot of red ink and different colors to underline or make notes to myself.
>
> And then I go back and practice, and practice, and practice, and practice; then I do it one more time on the morning of the speech. Then, I'm ready. If you don't do something a lot, it's hard; but the more you do it, the easier it gets.[1]

Kathleen was a hard worker who followed the basic steps of speech preparation. This chapter provides you with nine general guidelines to help you build your first speech. It also presents a plan for thinking critically about speech construction. If you are willing to work, you can be just as successful as Kathleen.

PRELIMINARY SURVEYING

Think back to the last time someone asked you to prepare and deliver a speech. It may have been in relation to a job activity, community gathering, social organization, or church group. What was your response? Did you hesitate, and finally say "No, I'm sorry—I'm not very good in front of a lot of people"? Or did you mutter a reluctant "yes" and then worry that you didn't have enough experience to be really effective?

If you have ever felt insecure about presenting speeches, you now have an opportunity to change. Public speaking is a rewarding experience that can contribute to your development as a person. It can help you improve your skills in organization and research, refine your abilities in delivery, and increase your sensitivity toward others.

You will be interested to know that many people are nervous when they deliver speeches. As a matter of fact, speech apprehension ranks among the top two fears of most Americans. While you may never be able to eliminate your apprehension completely, you can learn to cope with your anxiety in order to deliver a speech successfully.

You are about to construct your first speaking assignment. You may still feel somewhat hesitant, but you've got to start somewhere. Try not to think about the structure as a whole. Rather, build the speech, piece by piece, carefully considering each principle and clearly understanding each step in the process. Before you know it, you will have completed the construction and mastered the art of speaking in public. Remember Kathleen's last piece of advice: "If you don't do something a lot, it's hard; but the more you do it, the easier it gets."

CREATING A BLUEPRINT

To assist you in building your first assignment, nine guidelines are provided as a blueprint for speech construction. While these guidelines are presented in sequence, not all speeches will follow this arrangement. In some presentations, the steps may overlap or even reverse. You might select and narrow a topic while you are conducting library research, or you might analyze the audience before you write the specific purpose. The process is similar to constructing a building; some steps—such as preparing the foundation and erecting the walls—occur in a prescribed order. Other steps, however, are more flexible. The guidelines are presented as a suggested sequence for you to follow.

Guidelines to Speech Construction

1. CHOOSE AN INTERESTING, WELL-DEFINED TOPIC

The first step in building your speech is to choose a topic that is interesting to you, has potential interest to your audience, and is limited in scope. As you think about the topic, examine some of your past experiences and present concerns—areas which challenge you and stimulate your enthusiasm. Review your life experience, professional expertise, practical knowledge, or unique interests. Your chosen topic should also challenge your listeners and relate to their needs or curiosities. Audience members tend to be motivated by issues that involve their personal survival or their physical and emotional well-being. Finally, *narrow* the topic to a specific area that you can develop in some detail within your allotted time limit.

2. UNDERSTAND THE GENERAL PURPOSE

Once you have chosen your topic, you must clearly understand the general purpose of the speech. A *general purpose* represents the direction of the material presented: General purposes are either informative, persuasive, or entertaining. *Informative* speeches enlighten and educate audiences. These speeches can define concepts, demonstrate procedures, or describe people, events, and experiences. *Persuasive* speeches influence and alter the beliefs, feelings, or behavior of listeners. In persuasive presentations, speakers seek to convince audiences to change beliefs, move people to action, or intensify listeners' feelings. The goal of the *entertaining* speaker is to gain a humorous response by poking fun at people, places, or events. While entertaining speeches may contain biting satire or convey serious underlying messages, the material itself should be lighthearted and enjoyable rather than persuasive or seriously informative.

3. CONDUCT EXTENSIVE RESEARCH

Your next step is to find interesting, factual materials to support the topic and to establish your credibility as a speaker. Thorough research involves finding books and periodicals in the library that contain testimonies, examples, and statistics relating to the topic. Your research may also require you to conduct interviews with experts on the topic, or to gather information from institutions, businesses, or specialized organizations. The research process helps you to gain the respect and trust of your listeners; audiences tend to believe speakers who are knowledgeable about their topics and back up their ideas with facts or documented evidence.

4. WRITE SPECIFIC PURPOSE AND THESIS STATEMENTS

When you have researched the topic, you need to determine the specific purpose and thesis statements of the speech. The specific purpose represents the main objective that joins all ideas to one common theme and enables the speaker to keep on target. The specific purpose statement includes the general purpose (or its paraphrase) and one topic idea stated in clear and concise language.

> **Specific purpose:**   To inform listeners about my interest in parachute jumping.

The *thesis statement,* often called the central idea or the central objective, expands the specific purpose and tells the audience exactly what main points the speech will develop.

> **Thesis statement:**   I'll tell you how I became interested, what happened on my first fearful jump, and why parachute jumping is an enjoyable hobby.

This thesis clearly indicates that the speech is organized around three major headings.

5. WRITE A COMPREHENSIVE OUTLINE

Once you have determined your purpose and thesis, structure your thoughts by writing a *logical outline.* The outline will help to keep you on track throughout the presentation and still maintain contact with the audience. A speech has three basic parts: an introduction, a body, and a conclusion.

The *body* is the longest portion of the speech and contains the main headings that were identified in the thesis statement. For example, the speech about parachute jumping identifies the following three headings:

BODY

   I. How I became interested
  II. My first fearful jump
 III. Parachute jumping as an enjoyable hobby

Each numeral is then reinforced by subordinate points containing the examples, testimonies, and/or statistics you collected in your research. Your time limit will often dictate the number of main points that the body should develop. Generally, the shorter the speech, the fewer the main points. A one- to two-minute speech would probably contain no more than two or three main points, while a speech of six to seven minutes could expand upon as many as four headings.

Although the introduction and conclusion are much shorter than the body, they must also be carefully organized. The *introduction* should get attention and promote curiosity as well as prepare the audience for the topic and thesis statement. You can generate listener curiosity by beginning with a catchy quotation, shocking statement, thoughtful case study, or stimulating question that relates to the issue. The conclusion resolves the ideas you have presented in the speech. You can summarize the main points, appeal to the emotions, cite a quotation, or use an illustration. What is important is that your audience senses a finality and a resolution to the topic.

6. BE SENSITIVE TO AUDIENCE MEMBERS

As you organize the speech, consider carefully the needs and feelings of your audience. Present the topic at their intellectual level without talking over their heads or beneath them. Use language that they understand and define any terms that may be unfamiliar. Be sensitive to the diverse backgrounds and experiences of your listeners. Does your audience include individuals from different countries or geographical regions? Will men or women view your topic with contrasting attitudes? Could age differences or marital status affect listeners' perceptions? Are the values and ideals of your listeners shaped by their religious, ethnic, or cultural heritage? Be aware of the values and ideals that motivate the members of your audience. Avoid statements or examples that stereotype individuals and stay away from offensive language. Let the audience know that you are genuinely interested in them, responsive to their differences, and concerned about their welfare.

7. UNDERSTAND YOUR ETHICAL RESPONSIBILITIES

Whenever you present a speech, you are claiming to have knowledge about a topic that could benefit the audience. At the same time, you have an ethical responsibility to convey this knowledge fairly and accurately without misleading your listeners.

Speakers who plagiarize or steal information without giving proper credit, withhold or distort facts, engage in name-calling, or advocate harm are employing unethical practices designed to deceive or manipulate their audiences. These tactics demonstrate a lack of respect for individuals and will eventually destroy the speaker's credibility.

As an ethical speaker, you want to gain the confidence of your listeners; be reliable and fair when you report information, and avoid deceptive practices. You will earn the respect and trust of your audience if you are honest and respectful.

8. PRACTICE THE SPEECH

Success in presenting a speech requires practice. Transfer your outline to speaking notes and double or triple space between lines for easy scanning.

Good notes will allow you to maintain eye contact with your audience and still proceed logically through your material. As Kathleen DeSantis suggested (at the beginning of this chapter), go over the speech a number of times so you are confident with the order and placement of ideas. If you can, rehearse in the setting where you will deliver the presentation. Work to eliminate distractions such as fidgety mannerisms, standing on one foot, or vocalized pauses like "uh, uh, um." Convey words and sentences so listeners can hear and understand you easily. Be accurate and descriptive in your use of language and know how to pronounce difficult terminology. Let gestures and facial expressions flow spontaneously from your natural enthusiasm. If circumstances do not allow you to rehearse in the speech setting, look over your speaking outline and conduct a mental review of your presentation. Remember that your goal in speech rehearsal is to unite all of your research and organization into a coherent, unified construction.

9. BE CONFIDENT AND PREPARED

On the day of the presentation, arrive at the speech location early enough to avoid any last-minute scramble. Look through your notes to see if they are in the proper order. Relax, and take a few deep breaths as you wait for your turn. When it is time for your speech, walk calmly to the speaker's stand, placing your notes securely in front of you. Don't start the speech while you are still on the way to the lectern or while you are arranging your material. Take your time, and don't rush. Make certain that you are ready to begin. Look at the audience, and then state the first line of your speech with conviction.

Project confidence when you speak. Avoid making excuses or apologizing for mistakes. Speak clearly and distinctly. Try to make eye contact with all segments of your audience between brief glances at your notes. Stand up straight, and show the audience that you are prepared and ready to make the presentation. When you finish, don't pack up your notes while you are still talking or walk off in the middle of a concluding line. Wait until you have completed every part of the conclusion. When the last line of the speech is over, collect your notes, and walk calmly to your seat.

SELECTING A STYLE OF DELIVERY

Whenever you make a speech, you will need to choose a style of delivery that is appropriate to the speech setting. The style of delivery refers to your method of presenting the material—that is, whether the speech is manuscript, impromptu, memorized, or extemporaneous.

In situations where precision and detail are extremely important, speakers often choose to read word-for-word *manuscripts* to audiences. A scientist reporting on the results of fusion research at a convention, or a physician describing new treatments for AIDS victims to medical professionals, would write out the entire speech in advance. President Clinton employs manuscript delivery because his words are analyzed and interpreted by millions of people around the world.

You may already have had to present an *impromptu* or "surprise" speech without any notes or prior preparation. If your supervisor requested you to "say a few words" about your current work project at a division meeting or a friend asked you to propose a toast at a birthday party, you were required to organize your thoughts and ideas on the spur of the moment. An impromptu speech is good to experience occasionally and helps you to develop the ability to think on your feet.

In situations where constant eye contact and accurate timing are necessary, speakers frequently use *memorized* delivery. Tour guides, stand-up

An extemporaneous delivery allows a speaker to combine spontaneity with careful research and clear organization.

Hal Rummel Photography

comics, after-dinner speakers, and individuals presenting or receiving awards are often more effective if they memorize their material. In a Jay Leno–style monologue, for instance, the speaker wants to convey the punch line smoothly without distractions from notes. In this setting, memorization can help a speaker to respond quickly to audience feedback and to judge the right moment to deliver the humorous line.

While these approaches can be effective in a number of speaking situations, they have some clear disadvantages. In manuscript delivery, speakers often use their notes as a crutch and forget to look at the audience. These speakers may also tend to sound mechanical, forced, or monotone when they read material that is written out word for word. Audiences rarely like speakers to read to them; they enjoy being acknowledged with eye contact in a spontaneous and conversational manner.

Speakers often use memorized delivery to promote the secure feeling that they have it all down in their heads. In practice, however, memorization causes speakers to spend large amounts of time concentrating on word, phrase, and sentence order rather than on ideas. This style of delivery can even contribute to fear and insecurity about forgetting some crucial portion of the speech.

While an impromptu speech works in a surprise setting, it is not advisable to create this type of speech when the situation requires a carefully researched and structured presentation. You can't make up a speech as you go along when you must show research and preparation.

As you build your first presentation, you will find that the *extemporaneous* type of delivery is the most helpful to you. An individual using this style researches a topic, prepares an outline, and employs speaking notes—the method we suggest in this chapter and describe throughout the text. Extemporaneous delivery allows the speaker to develop eye contact with the audience, adapt to feedback, and concentrate on the sequence of ideas rather than on word or sentence order. Speakers in business and industry select this approach to help them project confidence and credibility to their listeners. An accountant presenting a quarterly report to corporate executives or an office manager training new employees wants the freedom to look at listeners, yet the security of a clear, well-organized outline. With an extemporaneous delivery, these speakers can be relaxed, spontaneous, and well prepared.

THINKING CRITICALLY ABOUT SPEECH CONSTRUCTION

Unfortunately, when we hear the word *criticism,* we often think in negative terms, such as tearing down the ideas or arguments of others. Critical thinking should not be destructive; rather, it should be a constructive process in which we examine and evaluate facts and ideas in order to make more rational decisions and improve our understanding.[2] As you progress through the guidelines to speech construction, you can think critically by testing information, being organized, listening to different perspectives, and thinking for yourself.

Be Willing to Test Information

Critical thinking implies asking relevant questions. When you are researching a topic or choosing supporting materials, evaluate the information carefully. If you find a shocking statement or startling statistic, cross check the material with other sources for reliability. If you are conducting an interview, don't be afraid to ask questions or ask for concrete verification of information. If you are listening to a speaker describing a new cure for a disease, examine the evidence presented and analyze the quality of the research. One speaker presented "constructive thought therapy" as a cure for cancer. While the topic was interesting, listeners were skeptical as the speaker expressed her opinions on the issue. One audience member commented, "I've heard of this kind of therapy, but I mistrusted the speech—there seemed to be no evidence." The speaker did not test the information and was too willing to rely on her own opinions and upon the hearsay of others. You can avoid this kind of difficulty by conducting a thorough analysis of your data and research materials.

Be Organized

Critical thinking is organized thinking. When you encounter difficulties in the process of building a speech, view them as challenges to be overcome rather than as obstacles to be avoided. Think of logical strategies for attacking problems. Define and understand the problem, seek solutions to the challenge, and then select a clear plan of action. If you discover that your audience disagrees with your controversial persuasive topic, find creative methods of appealing to their interests and needs. If you can't find material on your topic in the library, develop alternative resources by asking individuals, experts, or other institutions for information. If you have difficulty presenting the speech in front of an audience, analyze your problems and make changes by being more prepared, engaging in additional speech rehearsal, or requesting more feedback from your class and instructor. Identify problems, develop strategies, and be systematic in your approach to the speech process.

View Ideas from Different Perspectives

When we think critically, we learn from our own experiences as well as the experiences of others. As a speaker, remember that your point of view is not the only perspective on an issue. Be open to other ideas and be willing to learn from different viewpoints. If you find that facts do not support your idea, don't hang on to it, stubbornly refusing to give in. One student enjoyed the music of the late Jim Morrison (of the Doors) and collected the rock singer's music on compact disc. For his informative speech, the student wanted to describe the life of Morrison and play samples of his music for the audience—older part-time students with families. The instructor suggested that he choose a more suitable topic for audience members. Feeling insulted, the student rigidly insisted that he could make the topic interesting to anyone. Unfortunately, the student learned the hard way. After hearing the music samples and little evidence, listeners repeated the earlier suggestions of the instructor.

In a speaking situation, the composition of the audience requires that a speaker listen carefully to others. A speaker making a presentation to an audience of different races, religions, genders, or ages needs to demonstrate sensitivity and skill in responding to diverse perspectives and opinions. One student presented an informative speech about the dangers of skin cancer. The speaker had researched the disease and had developed some helpful information and advice for many of her listeners. Difficulties occurred, however, when the speaker suggested that skin cancer causes problems for "people with light skin." Members of the audience, which included Oriental, Middle Eastern, and African Americans, did not agree with the speaker's assumption and reported contrasting information once the speech was finished. Many audience members argued that facts and experience suggest that almost everyone is susceptible to skin cancer and individuals must take different precautions depending upon skin pigmentation. Listeners concluded that the speaker needed further research and more extensive analysis of her audience and should discard the erroneous information. Had this speaker been able to view her topic from her listeners' perspectives, she would have understood the need for more analysis and could have eliminated the false assumption that troubled her audience. A sign of maturity is profiting from the experiences of others, and growing as a result of other views.

Think for Yourself

Thinking critically means coming to your own conclusions after weighing the evidence. It does not mean believing everything that is handed to you. It is easy for us to point accusing fingers at those German people who

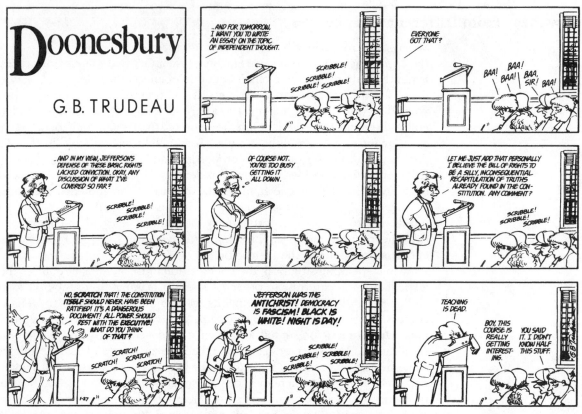

DOONESBURY copyright 1988 G. B. Trudeau. Reprinted with permission of Universal Press Syndicate. All rights reserved.

blindly accepted government propaganda and helped to perpetuate state-sponsored crimes in World War II. But ask yourself how many times you have accepted and believed someone else's opinion without question. For instance, imagine that you are on your way to class the first day of the new term and a friend sees you going into the lecture hall. She stops you at the door and insists, "Don't take that class because the professor *never* gives As or Bs." Do you immediately drop the class, do you ignore the comment, or do you proceed with extreme caution? This situation calls for critical thinking. Perhaps your friend is a chronic alarmist or is having difficulty in some of her courses. Possibly your fellow student had some kind of conflict with the instructor and holds a biased viewpoint about the situation. It is also possible that your friend is entirely credible and is giving you helpful advice. Whatever the case, the situation probably calls for more investigation and more information before you make a decision.[3]

Although it is necessary to ask for help, it is equally important to arrive at your own decisions. Don't let advertisers, salespeople, or indifferent parties tell you what to think by quoting ambiguous "facts" or subjective opinions. Examine the evidence yourself and arrive at a systematic conclusion.

SUMMARY

Nine general guidelines may assist you in constructing your first speech:

1. Select a topic that is interesting to you and to your audience and is sufficiently limited in scope.
2. Be aware of the three general purposes or directions of a speech:
   a. The *informative* enlightens the audience.
   b. The *persuasive* alters the beliefs, feelings, or behavior of listeners.
   c. The *entertaining* gains a humorous response.
3. Conduct research into your topic to obtain appropriate testimonies, statistics, and examples to support your ideas.
4. Write a clear, specific purpose or speech objective followed by a thesis statement that states the two, three, or four main points the speech will include.
5. Write a comprehensive outline of the introduction, body, and conclusion to develop your ideas in a logical sequence.
6. As you construct the speech, be sensitive to the needs and motivations of your audience.
7. Be ethical and credible when speaking.
8. Transfer your outline to speaking notes, and practice the speech to develop a conversational, extemporaneous delivery.
9. Project confidence in yourself and in the material when you deliver the speech.

There are four styles of delivery: manuscript, impromptu, memorized, and extemporaneous. One of the most effective styles is extemporaneous delivery, which requires research and organization but enables the speaker to use a brief outline and maintain eye contact and spontaneity.

Think critically as you construct your first speech by testing information, being organized, listening to different perspectives, and thinking for yourself.

SKILL BUILDERS

1. Following the guidelines provided in this chapter, prepare a one- to two-minute informative speech introducing yourself to the class. Select a topic from the following areas:
   a. Unique interest or experience
   b. Career objective
   c. Personal ambition
   d. Brief autobiography

2. Break up into pairs and exchange biographical information. Once you have learned some interesting facts about each other, develop a two-minute speech introducing your colleague to the class.

3. From a list of topics provided by your class or your instructor, select one topic for a one- to two-minute impromptu speech to inform.

4. Identify a problem you have recently solved. Describe the process you used to:
   a. Define the problem.
   b. Research and understand the problem.
   c. Seek solutions.
   d. Choose a final solution.
   e. Implement a plan of action.
   Evaluate your effectiveness in making the decision.[4]

5. Analyze two current movies you have watched. Describe one that stimulated critical thinking. How does the movie contribute to analysis and thought? Describe another movie that did not stimulate thinking. Why wasn't this movie successful in developing skills in critical thinking?

6. Read two editorials in the newspaper and carefully analyze them using the following questions:
   a. What claims are made?
   b. What evidence is used to support the claims?
   c. What do the editorials ask readers to believe?
   d. What is your analysis of the claims, arguments, and evidence?

7. Describe examples from your experience where you made uncritical decisions fitting the following situations. Describe the consequences of your decision making. Describe why the decision lacked examination and analysis. For example:
   a. You were disorganized.
   b. You failed to test information.
   c. You didn't listen to different viewpoints.
   d. You failed to think for yourself.[5]

N O T E S

1. Interview with Kathleen DeSantis, Catonsville Community College, Catonsville, MD, May 18, 1989.

2. Based on a definition used in John Chaffee, *Thinking Critically,* 3rd ed., (Boston: Houghton Mifflin, Co., 1990), p. 37. Much of this section on critical thinking is based upon chapter 2 of Chaffee's book and chapter 1 of Richard D. Rieke and Malcolm O. Sillars, *Argumentation and Critical Decision-Making,* (New York: HarperCollins, 1993), pp. 1–16.

3. Chaffee, p. 55.

4. Chaffee, p. 6.

5. Exercises 6 and 7 are based upon Rieke and Sillars, p. 16.

Chapter 3

ANALYZING YOUR AUDIENCE

The public is like a piano. You have to know what keys to poke.

Al Capp

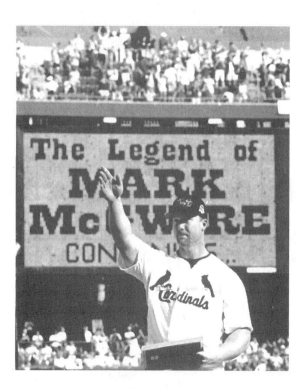

CHAPTER OBJECTIVES

After reading this chapter you will be able to:

1. Recognize the importance of audience analysis;

2. Describe five factors that can influence audience reactions to a speech;

3. Conduct an audience analysis.

Marge Schott is a successful businesswoman, owner of two car dealerships, three leasing firms, a concrete company, a sizable share of General Motors stock, and a major league baseball team. As the principal owner of the Cincinnati Reds, Mrs. Schott has worked hard to keep Riverfront Stadium's ticket and food prices among the lowest in the major leagues. But in spite of her accomplishments, Schott's public remarks often offended African Americans, homosexuals, and Jews, forcing the professional baseball community to suspend her from the game for one year in 1993. Apparently undismayed by her exile, she expressed these compassionate sentiments for Adolf Hitler in a 1996 interview: "He was O.K. at the beginning. He rebuilt all the roads, honey. You know that, right? He just went too far." In an article titled, "Heaven Help Marge Schott," *Sports Illustrated* referred to her problem as "loafer-in-mouth disease."[1]

Unfortunately Marge Schott violated an important principle of audience analysis repeated by Abraham Lincoln more than one hundred years ago:

> It is an old and a true maxim that a "drop of honey catches more flies than a gallon of gall." So with men. If you would win a man to your cause, *first* convince him that you are his sincere friend. Therein is a drop of honey that catches his heart."[2]

Our objective in this chapter is to help you analyze your audience in a speech setting. We want you to build strategies that encourage listeners to receive your messages favorably.

THE IMPORTANCE OF AUDIENCE ANALYSIS

When individuals or companies decide to invest millions of dollars developing new products or services, they conduct a *market analysis* to determine consumers' characteristics, their buying habits and motives, and their receptivity to new products.[3]

A developer, for instance, who intends to build a high-rise condominium, must determine the nature of potential buyers and what they want in housing. Will homeowners be older individuals who can afford spacious living environments with cathedral ceilings, Jacuzzis, and wraparound balconies? Or will prospective buyers be young professionals who want housing that is inexpensive, convenient, and practical?

We see the results of successful market research all around us. Automakers introduce new minivans or reinstate large luxury models. Food companies produce dietetic and low-cholesterol products for health conscious consumers. Political campaigns sway voting blocs such as senior citizens, farmers, or minorities with special-interest advertising.

This famous photograph depicts Lincoln delivering his second inaugural address in which he extended compassion even to his enemies, in the phrase "with malice toward none, with charity for all."

UPI/Bettmann Newsphotos

Like the investor, you must analyze your particular "market"—your audience. *Audience analysis* refers to the speaker's examination of audience characteristics to determine the most appropriate means of motivating them to share or participate in the speaker's concerns.[4] You need to understand your listeners' needs, their environment, and their perceptions of you as a speaker. If you understand at least some of these characteristics, you will be able to adapt your speech to gain the most favorable hearing. Knowledge of the audience helps you to choose topics which are interesting, select supporting evidence that contributes to clarity and vividness, and use language that is appropriate. Audience analysis does not mean that you must compromise your values or tell your listeners what they want to hear. The point is to adapt and adjust your presentation. The audience is your most valuable asset in the speech setting—it is the listener whom you ultimately want to inform, persuade, or entertain.

Audience analysis involves understanding five principal factors that can significantly influence listeners' reactions to a speech (see Figure 3.1):

1. Their perception of the speaker;
2. Their perception of the topic;
3. Their needs and motivations;
4. Social groups to which they belong; and
5. The occasion.

FIGURE 3.1

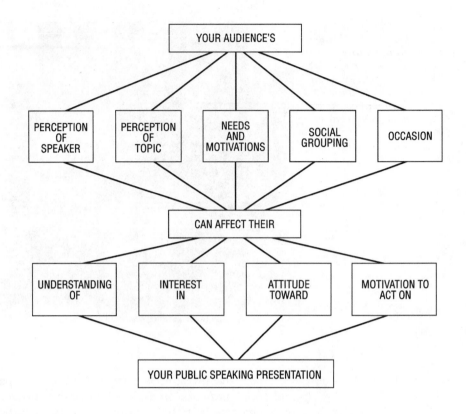

Audience Perception of the Speaker

Audiences develop very clear perceptions of speakers. They like or dislike speakers based on the content of their presentations or reputations created through past speeches or actions. We return to the same doctor, hairdresser, insurance agent, or accountant because of favorable perceptions and positive relationships we have built with them over a period of time.

Your audience will likewise develop a perception of you as a speaker. They will evaluate what they hear in your presentations, and they will form attitudes about your choice of topics and your manner of delivery. If your speeches are usually interesting and prepared well, the audience will anticipate those qualities even before you speak—they will be receptive unless you prove them wrong. At the same time, speakers who are poorly prepared, who make illogical arguments, or who use unethical methods will create negative expectations that will be hard to overcome.

A student presented a speech demonstrating shoplifting. He wore a long trench coat with large inside pockets and proceeded to tell his audience in great detail how to stuff various sizes of merchandise into the garment. He explained how to avoid discovery by store detectives and by mechanical devices. Some members of the class giggled nervously during the speech; others sat in frozen silence. After his conclusion, the speaker added, "Oh, this was only a joke; I didn't really mean it. I don't believe in shoplifting." But it was too late; the speaker had severely damaged his reputation. When he delivered his next classroom speech, his negative image still influenced listeners. It took several presentations for the speaker to earn back his credibility with the audience.

Audience perceptions are not necessarily etched in stone; they can be changed or even reversed over time. During the 1992 Democratic presidential primaries, Governor Bill Clinton of Arkansas waged an uphill battle. The media asked questions about his avoidance of military service. Tabloids ran stories about Clinton's marital infidelities and experimentation with marijuana. Opponents questioned his character and integrity, and columnists frequently referred to him as "Slick Willie." As a result of voter skepticism, Clinton did poorly in the early primaries. In New Hampshire, Clinton received only 26 percent of the vote, while former Senator Paul E. Tsongas won with 35 percent. In Connecticut, Clinton lost to former California Governor Jerry Brown by 1 percent. At the end of these primaries, Clinton as well as Tsongas were seen as "flawed candidates."[5]

In spite of the controversies and defeats, Clinton fought back. He appeared on interview programs, radio talk shows, and MTV. He ignored personal attacks and addressed major foreign-policy issues, seeking presidential stature. Declaring himself the "Comeback Kid," a term that later became a hallmark of his presidency, Clinton won important primaries in New York, Wisconsin, and Kansas, and went on to become the Democratic presidential nominee. In the general election campaign, President Bush tried to revive concerns about Clinton's character, but voters—fearful about the deficit and the economy—narrowly elected Clinton to the presidency. To effect this shift in audience perception took considerable time and effort over a period of many months; voter attitudes did not change quickly.

An audience may be unfamiliar with a speaker and feel hesitant about accepting the speaker's ideas or viewpoints. An expert in fire safety who informs listeners how to protect their homes may project interest and concern, but if the audience has never heard of the "expert," the speaker may need to increase believability by describing his or her professional qualifications and experience.

Positive audience attitudes work to your advantage in a speech. If you have developed a favorable reputation, listeners won't be resistant to your influence. If listeners believe your ideas are supported by solid evidence and sound reasoning, they will be more open to you. If you appear confident and relaxed in your delivery, the audience will relax and listen to you. The attitudes the audience forms about you play an important role in your ability to educate and influence them.

Audience Perception of the Topic

If a large company hired a computer consultant to lecture on "Innovations in Computer Technologies" to a hundred secretaries and clerks, the speaker might assume the entire audience was computer-literate. That assumption might be erroneous, however. Secretaries, like people in many skilled occupations, have become highly specialized professionals. In many companies, certain secretaries known as "information specialists" have received advanced computer training and supervise the computer and data area of an office. Other personnel, such as receptionists or clerks, may perform only data entry and possess limited computer knowledge. The consultant who assumes that every secretary is computer literate may present a speech that is far too complex for a large segment of the audience.

As you build your speech, don't make assumptions about the audience until you ask questions. If you understand the level of awareness

A successful speaker links a topic to the needs and motivations of various social groups within the audience.

about a topic, you can gear the speech toward more listeners by not isolating or losing any audience segment.

You also need to consider the attitudes of listeners toward your topic. *Attitudes* are prior inclinations people have about issues, and *opinions* are verbal expressions of these attitudes.[6] When you deliver a persuasive speech, for instance, you may have listeners who agree, disagree, or have no opinion concerning your point of view.

Suppose that you wanted to present a speech favoring capital punishment for drug dealers. You conducted judicious research. You obtained statistical evidence from the U.S. Justice Department regarding the amount of illegal drugs entering the country every year. You also included some examples of specific drug dealers who have profiteered from the broken lives of dependent addicts. You even used some emotional appeals— "Would you want these drug dealers making profits from your son or daughter, brother or sister?" But when you delivered the speech, you found yourself facing listeners with tight lips and unfriendly frowns. Once the speech ended, you discovered too late that most of your evidence and emotional appeals were irrelevant—your audience was strongly opposed to capital punishment, period. The one piece of research that was missing for this topic was audience analysis. If you don't know how your audience feels about an issue, you are less likely to use your supporting data to its best advantage.

It is crucial that a speaker ask questions about listeners either verbally or through surveys prior to a speech to determine audience attitudes in order to adjust the approach of the presentation. Generally speaking, the stronger their attitudes against an issue or idea, the harder it is to influence the audience.[7] It is unreasonable to expect individuals to move from extreme opposition to approval after a five- or ten-minute speech. With hostile audiences, the best you can do is to establish common ground and focus on areas of agreement as well as the need for change. If people are mildly against your topic, you have a good chance of changing their minds—provided that the evidence is forceful. If your listeners are neutral, you are in the best position. Neutrality often means that the audience may not know enough about the issue, or simply has not yet formed clear opinions. You have a good chance of exerting influence through strong evidence and sound reasoning. And if the audience completely supports your viewpoint, you can change the focus of your speech to motivate them to act—to contact their legislators, form political action committees, or educate the greater public about the problem.

With many issues, you will find audience attitudes ranging from strong agreement to equally strong disagreement. If you found a variety of audience perceptions about capital punishment, for example, you would focus most of your persuasive appeals on the neutral group, including those who mildly agree and disagree. You would want to maintain contact with those who favor your position strongly and, at the same time, indicate that you respectfully disagree with your extreme opposition.

Motivations of the Audience

As they are listening to your speech, the audience will ask some mental questions: "Can I use this? Will this help me? Does the topic relate to my interests?" Your answer is to appeal to the needs that are most important to your listeners. Needs and goals provide incentives to your audience to become interested and involved in your information. When you focus on significant needs, audience members realize that they can benefit from the speech, that they have something to gain by allowing the speaker to influence them.

One way to discover your listeners' strongest needs is to understand their beliefs and values. *Beliefs* are conclusions people have about the world based on observations, knowledge, and experiences.[8] The following statements would qualify as individual beliefs:

"An exercise program prolongs life."

"God answers prayers."

"Condoms help to prevent AIDS."

"Democrats are more sympathetic toward social problems."

"Censorship violates the Constitution."

Collections of beliefs, called *value systems,* cause us to behave in certain ways and to achieve goals or states of mind.[9] Most people have general values in common—physical, social, love, ego, security, and moral needs. All of us have basic physical needs, such as food, water, shelter, rest, sex, and security—which include safety and social order. One researcher who recognized that needs are strong motivating forces in human beings was Abraham H. Maslow, a psychology professor at Brandeis University. He identified five levels of basic drives, called a " hierarchy of needs," which he felt influenced our thinking and behavior: physiological, safety and security, love, esteem, and self-actualization needs. Maslow felt that people must satisfy the lowest order of needs (physiological) before they are able to progress to the next level (safety and security, then love, . . . then esteem, then self-actualization).[10]

Even though all of us have similar needs, our value systems cause us to place these drives in different priorities. Some who put a high emphasis on family-type love needs will change jobs and move long distances to be near better schools or help sick relatives. Others, who value ego needs, will uproot families and change jobs to increase status and responsibility. Those who place strong emphasis on physical needs may spend a great deal of time exercising, choosing well-balanced foods, and getting the appropriate amount of rest. Individuals who place a high priority on moral or spiritual values may cherish religious services, daily meditation, and participation in religion-centered activities. When you analyze your audience, try to determine their values so that you can connect your topic to their most significant goals.[11]

The following list identifies five principal needs and provides several examples of appeals designed to motivate listeners. Notice how speakers phrased appeals to link topics to specific audience values.[12]

PHYSICAL-SURVIVAL NEEDS

I know what you're thinking—how can a radar detector be unsafe? Suppose you're driving down the highway and you have a radar detector, and Joe Schmo who's following you does not. What's the first thing that happens when your detector goes on? You hit the brakes, and Joe Schmo is your new trunk companion!

—Scott Hipp, student speaker

Imagine. It's midnight, and you still have four chapters of sociology to study. You decide to take a break. You turn on the TV and all you see is food commercials. And what does your mind go to? Cheeseburgers? Naw. Chicken? Naw. PIZZA! Just a phone call away is a sauce-filled, cheese-covered, crisp-crusted pizza pie.

—Evan Feinberg, student speaker

SOCIAL-LOVE NEEDS

Dr. Leo Buscaglia describes intimacy as the ability to touch totally, unabashedly, unashamedly, and to lay it on the line and expose your true feelings to someone and have them tell you at every turn, that it's all right. The only way we as human beings will ever know ourselves and develop is in an intimate relationship. But doing so is difficult because intimacy is not reinforced by society.

—Ed Mincher, student speaker

Each one of us has experienced some isolation and loneliness in our lives. Well, magnify that experience and add to it the fact that this situation will never get better—and you will begin to approach the experience of many of these elderly and invalid people.

—Norma Ferris, student speaker

SECURITY NEEDS

Imagine your doctor shooting up drugs before your major surgery.

—Heather Hay, student speaker

We are being financially abused by deceptive banking practices.

—Maria Marszalek, student speaker

EGO NEEDS

David Schwartz, a professor at Georgia State University and noted lecturer on motivation, writes in his book *The Magic of Thinking Big* about the multitude of suppressive influences at work in our lives. We've all heard things like, "It's not what you know, it's who you know. Boy have you got a lot to learn—it really doesn't work like that in the REAL world. Are you kidding? You can't do that!" He calls these people "the negators," and he says they're everywhere and seem to delight in sabotaging the positive progress of others. Is it any wonder then that we trip and fall on the road to success?

—Cynthia Holley, student speaker

Not only will you feel better if you exercise, how would you like to look better?

—Kristine Ozgar, student speaker

MORAL-COMMITMENT NEEDS

If Americans reduced their intake of meat by only 10 percent—you guessed it—sixty million people could be adequately fed.

—Chris Clark, student speaker

Without the volunteer coaches, officials, and huggers, the Special Olympics would not be able to operate. These Special Olympians would not be gaining the physical exercise and emotional support that is crucial to their self-esteem. As I've listened to your speeches over the last two months, I know that many of you are interested in athletics. Volunteering would be a great way for you to continue your love of athletics, and in turn you'd be helping others.

—Colleen V. Deitrich, student speaker

In the preceding quotations, some student speakers have used negative motivational appeals, some have been positive, and some have designed appeals that were psychologically threatening. Each approach, however, seeks to connect the topic to a *specific* audience need. Listeners' attention is aroused because speakers have motivated them to care by telling them that they are directly or indirectly involved with their topics. Be certain that you really understand the beliefs and values of your audience without making false assumptions or stereotypes about them. *Stereotypes* are fixed notions or simplistic preconceptions applied to individuals or groups. Not all Democrats are equally interested in funding social programs. Not all people emphasizing moral values are responsive to quotations and examples from the Bible. Not all people who value health want an exercise program. To develop appropriate appeals to values, analyze your audience thoroughly and know the differences in their beliefs.

Impact of Social Groups on Listeners

Audience members belong to a wide variety of groups that can influence their perception of ideas. When you build a speech, you must understand the composition of the audience and the impact of specific social groupings on listeners. Consider the following areas when you analyze the audience: age, sex, religion, cultural and ethnic origin, educational level, occupation, interests, income level, geographical location, and group affiliation.

AGE

When you prepare a speech, you will discover that your approach to a topic will change depending on the age of the audience. If you were speaking about social security to a group of people in their early twenties, you would likely find listeners concerned about social security taxes as well as the reliability of the system. If, however, your audience were in their sixties, they would be more interested in benefits, cost-of-living increases, and budget cuts affecting the system. When selecting examples, use those within the knowledge or experience of your listeners. If a speaker mentioned Watergate, the Vietnam War, or "Howdy Doody," and the audience consisted of people under the age of twenty-five, listeners would have little appreciation for the examples unless they were experts in history or whizzes at the game of Trivial Pursuit. A speaker should either clearly define the examples, or use other illustrations from their listeners' contemporary experience:

> Because of their experience not only on the job but in real life, older workers tend to have fewer accidents. According to a 1988 Bureau of Labor Statistics study, older workers account for 9.7 percent of work-related accidents while workers in your age group of twenty to twenty-four account for 50 percent of such accidents. You can see that there's no replacing life-long experience.
>
> People also age at different rates. There are neither biological nor psychological reasons to connect a number, such as sixty-five, to the onset of old age. Every one of you in this room is aging at this very moment and will

face retirement sooner or later. When you face that time, retirement should be a decision that you make for yourself.[13]

Colleen Deitrich knew that her speech against mandatory retirement could be potentially uninteresting to her younger listeners in their early twenties. But she connected the topic to them by comparing accident rates of older workers to younger wage earners. Colleen also confronted her listeners with the issue by saying that they were aging "at this very moment."

Avoid alienating members of your audience by ridiculing their age or insulting their intelligence. Put-downs of any age group create animosity. A young speaker who referred to an audience of senior citizens as "you old people" would be met with anger and resentment. At the same time, if an older speaker were to describe a person under twenty-five as "just a twenty-two-year-old kid," listeners in the twenty-year-old category would probably react with equal hostility.

Eliminate false assumptions and stereotypes about age. Older people are not necessarily wiser, and younger people do not necessarily lack experience. As an effective speaker, you want to influence rather than to alienate listeners. You can acknowledge generational differences yet bring people together and appeal to the audience by establishing a common ground.

GENDER

The gender of your audience is an important factor to consider when you prepare a speech. With the changes in roles that men and women have experienced in the past two decades, it has become increasingly difficult to identify "women's" or "men's" topics. Women may be doctors, Army captains, truck drivers, airline pilots, or devoted homemakers. Men may be chefs, florists, kindergarten teachers, or nurses. You can no longer assume that male and female audiences will be interested only in certain subjects.

An effective speaker should be sensitive to the subtle differences in women's and men's perceptions. While much research concerning gender appears to be inconclusive, there are a few generalities that present interesting implications for speakers. In a 1985 study, Patricia Andrews discovered that women often prefer more complexity while men frequently like simpler procedures and criteria. Faye Crosby and Linda Nyquist's research indicates that women tend to correct the grammatical or language use of others. In 1979, Janet Sanders and William Robinson found that men and women often differ in their discussions of sexuality, and Judy Pearson, Lynn Turner, and William Todd-Mancillas observed the existence of a "general pattern" that women tend to engage in more self-disclosure than men. Christiane Hoppe concluded in a 1979 study that males tend to be more aggressive than females, but according to Pearson, Turner, and Todd-Mancillas, research is mixed as to whether men or women use more assertive language patterns. Although it has often been assumed that women are more empathetic, research by Eleanor Maccoby and Carol Jacklin in 1974 indicated that there is no significant difference between men and women regarding the ability to empathize. While the preceding statements are based on research, it must be emphasized that such generalities have numerous exceptions, and speakers need to be aware of the unique qualities of gender in every audience situation.[14]

One classroom speaker defended the persuasive proposition that mothers who kill their babies as a result of postpartum depression should be given more lenient sentences. The audience listened carefully as the speaker provided evidence that postpartum psychosis is a psychological imbalance requiring treatment and understanding. During the discussion, listeners were polarized based on gender. Men generally felt that a woman who killed her own baby should be severely punished to the limit of the law. Women, however, were much more sympathetic and agreed that the offender should be given a program of treatment and rehabilitation.[15]

Another speaker described date rape, informing listeners what it is, how it happens, and what to do about it. While audience members appeared to listen intently to the horrifying examples, expert opinion, and statistics, reactions were mixed. Women felt that the topic was helpful and caused them to be more aware and enlightened. But males in the audience argued that they were left out of the speech and treated as if they were being implicitly linked to the criminal behavior. Both examples indicate the need for speaker sensitivity. In the first, the speaker needs to examine audience perception of the topic *before* the speech to understand potential polarization according to gender. In the second, the speaker should take a more inclusive and less hostile approach to connect to men as well as to women in the audience.

When presenting a speech, avoid stating prejudicial generalities or false stereotypes that anger your listeners. To make sexist remarks such as "A woman's place is in the home," or "All men are potential rapists," would arouse hostility in any audience. Carefully consider the sensitivities of your listeners and demonstrate that you care about them.

RELIGION

Even in an audience of twenty people, there may be adherents of several religious attitudes and beliefs—Christians, Jews, agnostics, atheists, Buddhists, Muslims. Religious beliefs are a matter of deep personal conviction and must be taken into account if a speaker is going to touch upon religious subject matter:

> The book of Genesis advocates a vegetarian diet of fruits, grains, and nuts. Buddha commands, "Do not indulge a voracity that includes the slaughter

of animals." The Hindu *Mahabharata* reads, "Those who desire to possess good memory, beauty, long life with perfect health, and physical, moral, and spiritual strength should abstain from animal foods." The Islamic *Koran* prohibits the eating of "dead animals, blood, and flesh." The ancient Greeks, led by Pythagoras and supported by Socrates and Plato, believed vegetarianism was natural and hygienic and necessary for healthy living. The Romans conquered the world with an army fed on vegetables, porridge, bread, and wine. These examples were gleaned from Gary Null's *The Vegetarian Handbook* and they illustrate how history has attempted to teach the philosophy and practice of vegetarianism in order to have a long, prosperous, and healthful life.[16]

After researching his audience, Jim Kilduff decided to identify a variety of religious philosophies to build an argument for a vegetarian lifestyle. Unlike Marge Schott's offensive remarks, Jim's diplomatic approach helped to win enthusiasm for his topic by bringing philosophically diverse listeners together.

In any audience, avoid religious slurs that reflect prejudicial attitudes. These statements will arouse hostility and promote dissension among your listeners. It is important to unite the members of your audience and establish a sense of community.

CULTURAL AND ETHNIC ORIGIN

We live in a racially charged society where thoughtless words or actions can not only injure feelings but can arouse animosity serious enough to ignite violence. Inappropriate ethnic humor, questionable examples, or a hostile delivery can alienate listeners and ultimately backfire on a speaker. Unfortunately, individuals sometimes convey ideas and exhibit behavior that are considered to be *ethnocentric:* that is the belief that one culture or environment is superior to another. A speaker with this attitude usually feels, "My culture is better than yours."[17] Such arrogant attitudes may be openly expressed or implied. A speaker from one culture who repeatedly refers to listeners of another culture as "you people" may be exhibiting ethnocentric attitudes that will alienate the audience. Speakers who engage in constant put-downs about the superiority of city dwellers over rural residents, Greeks over Turks, blacks over whites, whites over blacks, American citizens over immigrants, and so forth, are expressing ethnocentric attitudes that offend audiences. To gain an effective hearing, speakers must avoid such ideas and expressions and exercise extreme sensitivity to listeners from diverse backgrounds and cultures.

One of the strengths of our society is its cultural diversity. The traditional Anglo-Saxon domination of America is rapidly changing and it is predicted that during the latter twentieth and early twenty-first centuries the white majority will continue to decline and African American, Hispanic, and Asian cultures will steadily increase in numbers. Demographers predict that by the year 2060, these three minority groups combined could actually become the majority.[18]

Because of this increasing diversity, speakers face interesting challenges when presenting messages. An effective speaker must not simply acknowledge, but must really *understand* the cultural and ethnic background of the audience. Speakers must recognize that culture and ethnic background influence language patterns, vocabulary, word meanings, dialect, accent, nonverbal delivery, and even listening behavior of an audience. An American speaker making a presentation to an Asian audience might interpret a lack of eye contact from listeners as evasive or disrespectful. But because of their cultural background, many Asians would consider such indirectness more polite and considerate than straightforward stares. Some American slang expressions or regional dialects are difficult to understand and translate. Imagine a Scandinavian hearing the slang term *Jeet,* a Mexican encountering the Pennsylvania Dutch expression *it makes down,* or an Australian trying to understand the Cajun words *gumbo z'herbes* for the first time. Unless these listeners hired the services of a good American guide or linguist, they might not realize that they are being asked *Did you eat?,* told that *it is raining,* or being offered a bowl of *green gumbo.* Similarly, some English words do not have equivalent terms in other languages. For example, the manufacturers of Pet milk advertised their product in French-speaking countries and didn't realize that the word *pet* is a French term that means to break wind.[19]

Don't take your audience for granted and don't assume too much or too little. Analyze your listeners' background, experiences, and knowledge and know how they are different and alike. At the same time, recognize your cultural differences as a speaker and be able to acknowledge or interpret these differences when it is necessary to help listeners understand you, your topic, or your speech more completely. In addition, it is important to avoid conclusions and opinions that *stereotype* your listeners. Just as there are many similarities within cultures or groups, there are also tremendous differences. Not all Asians are polite and bow when greeting another. Not all Southerners are friendly, not all Italians are extroverts, and not all Californians are "laid back." Recognize that your audience is comprised of individuals who have unique life experiences, cultures, and knowledge. Choose your words, illustrations, and concepts carefully. Exercise good judgment when you refer to unknown events or unfamiliar places to involve people of diverse backgrounds and help them connect as fully as possible to your speaking message.

Addressing an audience of public school science teachers in Hughesville, Maryland, Benjamin H. Alexander used the outmoded term "colored people," then said:

Shocked? No, because you are scientists and you know you are not white—but people of color. Were you the color of this white sheet of paper that I am holding up, you would be void of melanin, and the ultraviolet rays from the sun would burn you up. Nor am I or any other so-called black person in the world, black. Again, you are scientists and know that were we black, we would have an abundance of melanin—and be perfect receptors of the ultraviolet rays from the sun; our body temperature would quickly rise to over 108 degrees and into a fever so severe, we too would burn up. Because you have melanin in your skin—and so do I—it is factual that all people on God's green earth are people of color. God knows what He is doing when He makes no black or white people to inhabit the earth. He knows that if He had, some of them would always be fighting on this planet and disagreeing with the other. So He made a beautiful flower garden of people of all colors ranging from a pleasing cream to an exquisite sable.[20]

Alexander, a research chemistry professor at the American University, succeeded in shocking audience members by employing the term "colored." But having carefully analyzed the audience, the speaker quickly translated his message into scientific terminology that listeners could easily understand. He not only connected to his audience, he gave them a feeling of togetherness and pride by referring to them as "people of color" whom God made into a "beautiful flower garden."

EDUCATIONAL LEVEL, OCCUPATION, AND INTERESTS

When selecting a topic, a speaker must analyze the educational level, occupation, and interests of the audience. Imagine a doctor using the following language in a speech describing the pancreas to an audience of businesspeople and musicians:

The pancreas, an elongated gland situated between the spleen and the duodenum, secretes an external juice which passes through the pancreatic duct into the duodenum. It also creates an internal secretion, called insulin, which is produced in the beta cells and regulates carbohydrate metabolism.[21]

The speaker has talked over the heads of the lay audience and used terms that would be appropriate only if listeners were medical professionals. Many speakers create this kind of communication problem. But, the topic has potential interest because it involves information about good health maintenance. In this situation, however, it is advisable for the speaker to use language that is easier to understand:

The pancreas is a rather large gland located behind the stomach. It has two very important functions that are essential to the stability of our bodies. First of all, it secretes a fluid, called an enzyme, which helps in the digestion of food. Second, it produces insulin, which helps to reduce the amount of sugar in the blood and urine.

This example is superior because the speaker has used terms appropriate to the audience's level of knowledge on the topic.

The key idea in understanding audience education, occupation, and interests is *speaker adaptability.* A good speaker who talks about the "treatment of childhood illness" must interest young nonparents as well as parents in the audience. Referring to the nonparents' *future* role in child-rearing will probably help to gain their attention. If an accountant speaks to a mixed audience of medical people and air transportation workers on how to manage money, the speaker knows that there is potential for success because almost everyone is interested in personal finances. A good speaker makes topics come alive for the audience by adapting to their education, occupation, and interests.

INCOME LEVEL

A married student decided to tell his audience how to obtain a home mortgage. He talked about the preliminary steps of filling out application and credit forms, as well as obtaining income verification. He discussed the property survey, insurance policy, and the termite inspection. Finally he described settlement costs, such as points, stamps, and recording fees. He told the audience that he was especially excited about the topic because he and his wife had just purchased their first home. But when his speech was over, audience members responded negatively. One student complained, "He seemed enthusiastic about his topic, but I couldn't get into it. I'm a commuter student and I live at home with my parents. Someday I'll need to know all of this, but right now I don't have a prayer of buying my own place—I just want to graduate so I can get a decent-paying job." That critique described almost everyone's economic situation in the class.

This example graphically portrays the problems that occur when a speaker does not consider the income level of the audience. In this instance, even the speaker's enthusiasm could not motivate the class. He would have been more successful if he had chosen a topic such as taking out a car loan, which would have enabled him to adapt to the needs of his audience.

Another key term for a speaker to remember is *audience sensitivity.* If you talk about joining a country club, or about gourmet cooking, to low-income people who can hardly afford to pay their rent, your feedback might be anything from indifference to hostility. Similarly, if you speak to a group of doctors or bankers and ridicule "rich people's fancy cars and expensive tastes," you will also find your audience switching you off quickly.

GEOGRAPHIC LOCATION

Effective speakers take time to research the geographic location of an audience. When a speaker demonstrates knowledge about the audience's community, the speaker gains the admiration and respect of the listeners:

> It's an honor to address the Executives' Club of Chicago. Over a half century ago, the English writer G. K. Chesterton visited Chicago and recommended that everyone interested in the future should do the same. As Chesterton put it, "Although I won't venture a guess about the shape of things to come, if you wish to feel the pulse of things to come, go to Chicago." Chesterton's observation is still true. Despite the delays getting in and out of O'Hare [Airport], Chicago has the pulse of tomorrow.
>
> New Yorkers, of course, like to make a similar claim for their city. And while I'm a loyal resident of the metropolis, who cheered when the Giants took on the Bears and will cheer again when the Mets beat the Cubs, I refuse to let civic loyalty get in the way of truth.[22]

The speaker N. J. Nicholas Jr. (co-chief executive officer of Time-Warner, Inc.) demonstrated respect for his hosts by using a complimentary quotation that put his Chicago audience in a receptive mood. A listener who is approached in this manner tends to think, "He's really interested in me," or "I'll listen to him because he's really gone out of his way to refer to my community."

SOCIAL ORGANIZATIONS

Audiences appreciate speakers who take the time to research some of the characteristics of their organizations. Notice how former Chrysler Corporation chairman Lee Iacocca refers to attorneys at a convention of the American Bar Association:

> Let me just say that it's an honor to be asked to be here. And a little bit of a surprise, to tell you the truth. When I got the letter from Mr. Thomas last December, it said "It is my privilege to invite you . . ." and ended by wishing me "Happy New Year." Most of the letters I usually get from lawyers start out with "You are hereby summoned," and wind up with "Ignore at your peril." So this is a treat. And I'm glad to be here. I'm also a little curious because I've often wondered just what lawyers do when they have a convention. I know what *car dealers* do! I noticed, for example, that as soon as I sit down you're scheduled to get into something called "The Statement of the Assembly Resolutions Committee." Now, that sounds like *serious business:* Last year at our convention, my speech was the warm-up act for Willie Nelson![23]

Iacocca's remarks were carefully designed to make good-natured fun of the legal profession as well as of his own automotive industry. You can be sure that the attorneys appreciated his personal references to them.

Whenever you speak to a group or organization, there are certain identifiable catchwords and customs that will gain positive feedback from your audience. Knowing something about the PTA, the Longshoremen's Union, the Future Farmers of America, the Sierra Club, or the

Young Republicans will help you use terms and phrases that will get the attention of your listeners.

TARGETING SPECIFIC GROUPS

One way you can arouse interest is to target segments of your audience. *Targeting* is the process of identifying selected groups of listeners and designing specific appeals to motivate them. Political candidates target urban voters, minorities, or senior citizens and appeal to their concerns about crime, drugs, or social security. Cosmetic companies market their products to teens worried about acne and to older consumers interested in hiding wrinkles.

You can also employ targeting in your speeches by using examples, statistics, or quotations that appeal to specific interests of listeners. If your topic is about proper nutrition and there are joggers in your audience, you can specifically refer to them as you explain the benefits of a healthy diet. You can formulate appeals to specific interest groups such as business-people, young parents, part-time wage earners, church members, suburbanites, or inner city residents. Targeting helps you to motivate listeners in very personal ways to become involved with a topic. Notice how this speaker targeted listeners and related their topics to his speech:

> Several class periods ago, each of us had the opportunity to share something personal about ourselves. I'd like to take a moment to revisit that night and review some of the topics we spoke about. Karen, you described your passion for art. Jennifer talked about sailing and Tom spoke about scuba diving, the final frontier. Madalen presented a speech about insurance rates and George explained what it's like to be a member of the state police SWAT team. Donna, you shared your feelings about returning to school—the pursuit of your dreams. Kelly described her passion for jigsaw puzzles, and George discussed rollerskating for exercise. Bob presented his thoughts about friendship and Elizabeth described her feelings about coming to the USA, and we're glad you did. Jean, you talked about Girl Scouts, truly an American tradition. Jagdish introduced medicine. Shannon, you described your college roommates, giving new meaning to the term "private property." Beth introduced skiing and Michelle talked about playing the guitar. Lastly, and appropriately so, Rustin spoke about procrastination.
>
> Is there a common link to these passions? I would say yes. Actually, there are three: a man, a date, and a piece of paper. The man's name is Thomas Jefferson, the date was the Fourth of July 1776, and the piece of paper was the Declaration of Independence. This document laid the foundation for the Constitution of the United States, allowing each of us the freedom to follow our dreams and pursue our passions.[24]

Dan Callahan listened closely to the topics presented by other classroom speakers and used this personal approach to motivate the audience. After the speech, listeners commented that Dan's strategy of identifying their names and topics encouraged them to become involved with his topic.

Impact of the Occasion on Listeners

The occasion is a major influence on the audience, and a speaker must know how the environment will affect the speech. An audience subject to the antiseptic odors of a hospital will perceive a speech differently from an audience at a spring flower festival. Listeners on Christmas Eve display a contrasting mood from an audience on New Year's Eve. People have certain expectations of speakers; they want a judge to convey wisdom, a doctor to project confidence. No analysis of the audience is complete unless you understand the impact of the speaking occasion on listeners: the purpose, location, and expectations of the speaker.

THE PURPOSE OF THE OCCASION

People exhibit a variety of moods and feelings depending on the purpose of the occasion. Listeners are festive at a ballgame or a Fourth of July celebration, and more serious at a professional convention or a lecture. Jokes and humorous sketches would be entirely appropriate at a retirement banquet but (usually) out of place at a funeral or memorial service. Listeners are also influenced by upcoming holidays or by events of local and national significance. A reference to a tragedy in the community or to a special occasion such as Christmas, Veteran's Day, or the Great American Smokeout can help to make your speech more timely and meaningful to the audience. Notice how John M. Scheb, judge of the Second District Court of Appeals in Lakeland, Florida, referred to the occasion in a speech commemorating Presidents' Day:

> As we reflect on the meaning of this Presidents' Day, our individual thoughts may focus on a particular president of the past. We all remember our history lessons about our early presidents—Washington, Jefferson, Lincoln, and the others who led our country up to the twentieth century. And then we have our own personal memories of more recent leaders. I can remember my parents speaking of President Hoover, and I have vivid memories of serving in the military under Presidents Roosevelt and Truman during World War II. Most of us recall Presidents Eisenhower, Kennedy, Johnson, Nixon, Ford, and Carter. And of course, we have fresh memories of Ronald Reagan and George Bush.
>
> Our presidents over the years have differed philosophically, emotionally, and culturally. But each wove a thread of love of country into his leadership. And although those threads have been different in strength

and design, together they have formed a tapestry displaying cherished values of country and a willingness to serve. This tapestry is patriotism.[25]

Judge Scheb's references to past presidents helped listeners to reflect on the significance of Presidents' Day and prepared them for the theme of patriotism.

THE PHYSICAL LOCATION OF THE EVENT

The physical location of a speech can affect both the audience and speaker. An audience shivering in a drafty auditorium in the middle of winter will not listen effectively. A speech presented in the New Orleans Superdome requires a huge TV screen to project visual aids. A craft demonstration at a senior citizens center might require close proximity to listeners rather than a remote speaker's lectern. A speech given outside, at the local county fair, may be subject to a sudden downpour.

An effective speaker carefully examines the physical location of the speech to anticipate and adapt to as many problems as possible. Below are some questions to ask when you are investigating a speaking site:

1. Is the event inside or outside?
2. What is the size of the room?
3. How many people will be present?
4. Is there a stage or raised platform for the speaker?
5. Will there be a speaker's stand or lectern?
6. Does the room have adequate heat, air conditioning, or ventilation?
7. Does the room have good acoustics?
8. Will there be a microphone, or will the speaker need to rely on strong vocal projection?
9. Could any possible external noise in or near the speaking area cause a distraction?
10. Will props or visual aids need to be set up before the speech?
11. Are adequate electrical outlets, thumbtacks, extension cords, chalk, erasers, easels, tables, or other devices needed for the speech available?

THE EXPECTATIONS OF THE SPEAKER

Audiences attending events have certain expectations of speakers. They expect a graduation speaker to be warm and congratulatory. They expect a minister or priest to reinforce beliefs and include references to moral and spiritual values. They expect politicians to be responsive to social and governmental concerns.

Audiences even have expectations regarding the speaker's appearance. During a televised speech on energy early in his presidency, Jimmy Carter wore a sweater as he told Americans to turn down their thermostats to reduce dependency on foreign oil. In this "honeymoon" period, public and press reaction appeared favorable to the speech. Over time, however, the public returned to more traditional expectations regarding presidential appearance. Most Americans expect that the president of the United States will deliver an official speech "in proper attire"—meaning a conservative suit and tie.[26] President Carter never wore his cardigan again for a major address.

Whenever you present a speech, you need to know the expectations of your audience. To avoid "speaking surprises," ask questions. Here are points to cover when determining your speaking role on a particular occasion:

1. Do your topic and general purpose suit the occasion?
2. What is the order of speaking, and where is your speech in that order?
3. What time of day do you speak—morning, afternoon, or evening?
4. What is the time limit of the speech?
5. Who is the featured speaker?
6. Will you be introduced to the audience, or must you introduce yourself?
7. How is the ceremony organized?
8. Is someone clearly in charge of the event?
9. Are there any customs or traditions associated with the event that you will be expected to know or to perform?

Once you have gained as much information as possible about the purpose, location, and expectations regarding the event, you will be more confident that your speech will be appropriate to the occasion.

CONDUCTING AN AUDIENCE ANALYSIS

As a speaker you should conduct a thorough analysis of your audience in order to develop strategies that will help your speech to receive a favorable hearing. We suggest three steps to assist you in gathering, processing, and assessing information about your listeners.

Collecting Demographic Data about the Audience

Demographics refers to the science of gathering social and statistical information about any group of people. You can collect demographic data by surveying audience opinion or knowledge, circulating questionnaires, or by conducting personal interviews.

SURVEYS

One way to determine the attitudes of your listeners is to survey the relative strength and weakness of their opinions. You can accomplish this by constructing a scale like the one below.

AUDIENCE ATTITUDE SURVEY

>   **Proposition:** The practice of cloning cells to reproduce exact copies of humans and animals should be stopped.

Do you agree, disagree, or are you neutral? Please place a check mark at the appropriate place on the scale that describes your attitude about the above specific purpose:

−10	−5	−1	0	+1	+5	+10
opposed			neutral		favor	

This survey helps you to determine audience attitudes about controversial issues prior to a presentation. Circulate the survey to audience members while you are preparing a speech. When you get the results, carefully analyze how many in the audience agree, disagree, or are neutral. The range of audience attitudes will help you decide the types of supporting materials to use and even influence your persuasive approach.

Another type of survey can help you determine the degree of knowledge your listeners possess concerning your topic.

AUDIENCE INFORMATION SCALE

>   **Topic:**   America's new space station

How knowledgeable are you about the topic listed above?

1	2	3	4
I know a lot about it	I have some information about it	I've only heard about it	I've never heard of it

This scale is especially useful with informative speech topics. When you add and then average the score, you will have a good indication of how to gear your speech. A low audience average of 1.6 would indicate that listeners are quite knowledgeable about the topic. Your speech could then include examples and terms with a degree of depth and sophistication. On the other hand, a higher score of 3.4 would imply that your audience lacks knowledge and your speech should include definitions of unfamiliar terms and examples that are easy for listeners to absorb.

QUESTIONNAIRES

Another way to get demographic information is to circulate a questionnaire. You can develop a list of open-ended questions about age, gender, religion, income range, nationality or ethnic origin, education, occupation, social groupings, experiences, and interests. You can then have the questions distributed to audience members well before your speech to collect the needed information. Data obtained through questionnaires can help you to determine the significant values, beliefs, and interests of your listeners and assist you in preparing motivational appeals that stimulate audience receptiveness.

INTERVIEWS

Personal interviews with audience members provide more flexibility than surveys or questionnaires and allow you to ask in-depth and follow-up questions.[27] In a personal interview, you also have the advantage of observing the listener one to one: You can watch an individual's reactions to questions, evaluate the person's use of language, and observe the audience member's appearance. One disadvantage is that a personal interview can be time consuming. If you have more than a hundred people in the audience, you may have difficulty interviewing each one. It might be more efficient to interview a cross-section or sample of the group.

There are occasions when speakers are not able to survey or interview members of an audience. Speakers traveling long distances or presenting speeches on short notice might not have the time to conduct comprehensive audience research. If you find yourself in this situation, you can still get information from individuals who know your listeners well. Ask questions of the host or organizers of the speaking event. If they are unable to provide satisfactory answers, ask them for the names of individuals who might be more knowledgeable. While a complete analysis may not be possible, a brief investigation that obtains the answers to some critical questions about listeners may provide information that is extremely beneficial.

Processing the Data with a Computer

One effective way to process and organize demographic information about an audience is by using a computer. Speakers in government, business, and industry use a computer program called SPSS—Statistical Package for the Social Sciences—to assess demographic information and to develop profiles of audiences. This powerful program can process data according to key words or command names such as age, sex, occupation, or interest area. You can determine if there are relationships between audience interests and geographical region, or correlations among race, age, income, education, and social grouping.[28] If you have access to a personal computer and a statistical program, you can also enter demographic data and develop profiles using specific commands or key words. For more information about computer programs that include demographic profiles, you may want to contact your college or university sociology, mathematics, social sciences, or computer programming department.

Evaluating the Audience Profile

When you have a printout of your data, analyze and evaluate the information. Make some assessments about the audience and be able to understand some of the most significant qualities that could affect their perceptions of your speech. Develop specific appeals that relate to the most important interests and needs of your listeners.

SUMMARY

When building a speech, you need to understand some of the major influences on your listeners and how these factors will affect your presentation:

1. Be aware of listener perceptions toward you as a speaker.
2. Assess audience perceptions of the topic.
3. Understand audience beliefs, values, and value systems. When you know the motivations of your listeners, you can develop specific appeals that link your topic to their needs.
4. Determine the composition of your audience according to age, gender, religion, ethnic origin, educational level, occupation, interests, income level, geographical location, and group affiliation. You can target specific groups of listeners by creating appeals that relate to their concerns.
5. Know how the occasion of the speech influences the audience and speaker. Analyze the purpose of the occasion, the physical location of the event, and audience expectations of the speaker.

You can conduct an audience analysis by gathering demographic information, processing the data with a computer, and evaluating the audience profile.

SKILL BUILDERS

1. Divide your class into several small groups. Choose several topics for an informative or a persuasive speech. Depending on the type of speech, develop an Audience Information Scale or an Attitude Survey

for the selected topics. Circulate the scales or surveys to the audience. Assess audience perceptions and attitudes about the topics and report the results to your class.

2. Divide your class into several small groups.

   a. Develop a comprehensive questionnaire that gathers demographic information about the members of your audience. Circulate the questionnaire and analyze the results. Present the profile to your class. Compare your results with those of other groups.

   b. Develop a list of questions that would be appropriate for gathering demographic information from personal interviews of your audience. Divide the questions among the members of your group and interview each member of your class. Pool the responses you have received and develop a profile of the audience. Compare your results with the profiles of other groups.

3. Analyze the elements of the speaking occasion that will affect your classroom speech. Are there any factors regarding the purpose, location, or expectation of listeners that could influence the speech in a positive or negative way? Will any of these influences cause you to make adjustments to your speech?

4. Once you have chosen a topic for a persuasive or an informative speech, survey the audience to determine their knowledge or attitude about the issue. What do the results of this survey imply about your choice of supportive materials and your delivery?

5. If you have already presented at least one speech, assess audience perceptions of you as a speaker. Gather information by reading and/or listening to critiques from your classmates and instructor. What are their expectations of you? Have they made any preliminary evaluations that you might want to change on the next speech?

NOTES

1. Rick Reilly, "Heaven Help Marge Schott," *Sports Illustrated,* May 20, 1996, p. 77; 72–84.

2. Roy P. Baster, ed., *Collected Works of Abraham Lincoln,* Vol I. (New Brunswick: Rutgers University Press, 1953), p. 273.

3. William J. Stanton, *Fundamentals of Marketing* (New York: McGraw-Hill, 1981), pp. 35–55, 155–156.

4. This definition is partially based on a contribution from E. Joseph Lamp, professor of speech, Anne Arundel Community College, Arnold, MD.

5. Compare an early analysis of the presidential primaries in "This Was the Least Desirable Outcome for Us," *Business Week,* March 2, 1992, pp. 28–29, with a later description in "The Survivor," *The New Republic,* April 27, 1992, pp. 15–20.

6. Stephen W. Littlejohn and David M. Jabusch, *Persuasive Transactions* (Glenview, IL: Scott, Foresman, 1987), p. 54.

7. Lawrence W. Hugenberg and Donald D. Yoder, *Speaking in the Modern Organization* (Glenview, IL: Scott, Foresman, 1985), p. 182.

8. Littlejohn and Jabusch, *Persuasive Transactions,* p. 46.

9. Littlejohn and Jabusch, p. 56.

10. Abraham H. Maslow, *Motivation and Personality,* (New York: Harper & Row, 1970), pp. 46–47.

11. For this section on audience needs and motivations, we used Paul D. Holtzman, *The Psychology of Speakers' Audiences* (Glenview, IL: Scott, Foresman, 1970), pp. 50–63, and Abraham H. Maslow, *Motivation and Personality* (New York: Harper & Row, 1970), pp. 46–47. Both authors identify specific needs and both discuss hierarchies of needs or values. The authors differ in their approaches, however. Holtzman examines multiple values, while Maslow uses a five-level hierarchy of needs. Holtzman believes that audiences set priorities based on their goals; Maslow believes that people cannot achieve higher needs until they have fulfilled lower levels of needs.

12. I am grateful to the following students who gave permission to use their motivational appeals as examples in this section: Scott Hipp, Evan Feinberg, Ed Mincher, Norma Ferris, Heather Hay, Maria Marszalek, Cynthia Holley, Kristine Ozgar, Chris Clark, and Colleen V. Deitrich.

13. Colleen V. Deitrich, "Mandatory Retirement Should Be Illegal," speech to convince presented in speech class, Carroll Community College, Westminster, MD, 1991. Used by permission.

14. Research cited in this section appears in Judy Cornelia Pearson, Lynn H. Turner, and William Todd-Mancillas, *Gender & Communication,* 2nd ed. (Dubuque, IA: Wm. C. Brown, 1991), pp. 36, 113, 110, 177, 182, 108, and 41 (in order of citation).

15. Debbie Bosley, "More Lenient Sentences for Postpartum Moms," speech to convince presented in speech class, Carroll Community College, Westminster, MD, 1992. Used by permission.

16. James Kilduff, "Vegetarianism Is a Healthier Lifestyle," speech to convince presented in speech class, Carroll Community College, Westminster, MD, 1989. Used by permission.

17. Carley H. Dodd, *Dynamics of Intercultural Communication,* 4th ed. (Madison: Brown & Benchmark, 1995), p. 69.

18. Martha Farnsworth Riche, "We're All Minorities Now," *American Demographics,* October 1991, pp. 26–33, and Brad Edmondson, "American Diversity," *American Demographics Desk Reference,* July 1991, pp. 20–21.

19. D. Ricks, *Big Business Blunders: Mistakes in International Marketing* (Homewood, IL: Dow Jones-Irwin, 1983), p. 41, cited by Ronald B. Adler and Neil Towne, *Looking Out/Looking In,* 9th ed. (Ft. Worth: Harcourt Brace College Publishers, 1999), p. 219.

20. Benjamin H. Alexander, "The Uncritical Acceptance Today," *Vital Speeches,* July 15, 1992, p. 605.

21. Adapted from *Dorland's Illustrated Medical Dictionary,* 25th ed., s.v. "Pancreas."

22. N. J. Nicholas, Jr., "The Boob Tube Gets Smart," *Vital Speeches,* June 15, 1991, p. 535.

23. L. A. Iacocca, "In Order To," *Vital Speeches,* October 1, 1987, p. 745.

24. Daniel Callahan, "Thomas Jefferson," speech to inform presented in speech class, Catonsville Community College, Catonsville, MD, 1990. Used by permission.

25. John M. Scheb, "The American Patriot," *Vital Speeches,* April 1, 1991, p. 377.

26. The Carter "cardigan speech" received much favorable reaction, although there were news accounts that reported some negative feedback to the sweater. Compare "Warm Words from Jimmy Cardigan," *Time,* February 14, 1977, p. 18, to "Pleasures and Perils of Populism," *Time,* March 21, 1977, p. 25.

27. Stanton, *Fundamentals of Marketing,* p. 45.

28. I wish to thank Marie Skane, associate professor of mathematics at Catonsville Community College, who provided me with information about the SPSS computer program.

Chapter 4

IMPROVING YOUR LISTENING SKILLS

To listen is an effort, and just to hear is no merit. A duck hears also.

Igor Stravinsky

CHAPTER OBJECTIVES

After reading this chapter you will be able to:

1. Recognize the significance of listening;

2. Understand the process of listening;

3. Identify five types of listening behavior;

4. Recognize seven barriers to listening;

5. Describe how to become an active listener;

6. Identify your listening strengths and weaknesses.

An advertisement for the Sperry Corporation showed a photograph of a little boy in a classroom. The caption read: "How can we expect him to learn when we haven't taught him how to listen?" The ad went on to discuss the need for education and training in listening at all levels of society and referred to research indicating that adults listen at only a "25 percent level of efficiency."[1]

The Sperry Corporation correctly identified the significance of effective listening in the communication process. Often our success depends upon how effectively we listen to directions and data, how carefully we evaluate and weigh information. Lives depend upon a pilot's ability to listen to flight instructions from the control tower, or upon a surgeon's ability to listen to other doctors or patients.

This chapter presents four kinds of listening and introduces the concept of active and passive listening, identifies seven behaviors that create barriers to effective listening, and discusses a four-point program to build better listening skills.

THE SIGNIFICANCE OF LISTENING

We spend much of our lives listening. In fact, research indicates that most communication activity is listening activity. A classic study conducted by Paul Rankin in 1928 examined the time spent in four communication-related behaviors: listening, reading, writing, and speaking. Rankin found that listening outranked all other communication activities. Listening took place 42.1 percent of the time, talking 31.9 percent. Reading accounted for 15.0 percent of communication behavior, and writing 11.0 percent.[2]

A 1977 study supporting Rankin's findings was conducted at Auburn University. Researchers surveyed 645 students and found that listening occurred 52.5 percent of the time, speaking took place 16.3 percent of the communication day, while 17.3 percent of the time was spent reading, and writing occupied 13.9 percent of the communication day.[3]

Although we may spend the majority of our communication time listening, we don't always do it well. Poor listening is a fact of life in all professions and at every level of our society (Figure 4.1). Examples abound of problems created because individuals or groups refused to listen, didn't listen carefully, or listened only to information they wanted to hear. A few concrete examples will illustrate the magnitude of the listening problem.

On January 25, 1990, Avianca Airlines flight 025 ran out of fuel and crashed in Cove Neck, Long Island (New York), killing 73 of the 158 passengers aboard. The jetliner had missed an instrument approach to John F. Kennedy International Airport, and was attempting to make a second attempt at a landing. After investigating the accident, the National Transportation

HOW CAN WE EXPECT HIM TO LEARN WHEN WE HAVEN'T TAUGHT HIM HOW TO LISTEN.

It's ironic.

We teach children how to read, write and do arithmetic, but don't teach them the skill they need most to learn them.

How to listen.

(The bulk of a child's listening education consists of admonitions like "Pay attention!", "Open up your ears!", "Listen!")

And listening <u>does</u> need to be taught.

It's a difficult, intricate skill. And like other skills, it requires training. And practice.

In the few schools where listening programs have been adopted, listening comprehension among students has as much as doubled in just a few months.

We at Sperry are concerned about the listening problem. As parents. And as businessmen.

Denied a proper listening education as children, adults listen—according to research—at a pathetically low 25% level of efficiency.

And as a worldwide corporation with more than 87,000 employees, that's simply not efficient enough for us.

Which is why we've taken listening education into our own hands.

Listening has been a part of many Sperry training and development programs for years.

And we've recently set up expanded listening programs for Sperry employees worldwide. From sales representatives to computer engineers to the Chairman of the Board.

These programs are making us a lot better at listening to each other. And when you do business with Sperry Univac, or any of our other divisions, you're going to discover that they're making us a lot better at listening to you.

We understand how important it is to listen.

Sperry is Sperry Univac computers, Sperry New Holland farm equipment, Sperry Vickers fluid power systems, and guidance and control equipment from Sperry division and Sperry Flight Systems.

Test your listening skills.
Write to Sperry, Dept. 4B, 1290 Avenue of the Americas, New York, New York 10019 for a listening quiz that's both fun and a little surprising.

FIGURE 4.1

Based upon copyrighted material of Dr. Lyman K. Steil, president, Communication Development, Inc. St. Paul, Minnesota, for the Sperry Corporation. Reprinted with permission of Dr. Steil and Sperry Corporation (now Unisys).

Safety Board stated that "the flight crew did not adequately communicate its increasingly critical fuel situation to airport controllers." The board also noted that one controller had not heard a portion of the pilot's transmission identifying the nature of the problem with the words ". . . we can't do it now, we will run out of fuel now."

In its conclusion, the safety board criticized the flight crew for not using the word "emergency" when referring to their critical fuel situation. However, the report also stated that one probable cause of the accident was the "lack of standardized understandable terminology for pilots and controllers for minimum and emergency fuel states."[4]

An engineer supervising the manufacture of the space shuttle booster rocket repeatedly warned NASA officials that the booster rocket's "O-ring" seals might not function properly in subfreezing temperatures. Four senior

NASA officials did not listen to the warnings, and the fatal decision was made to launch the space shuttle *Challenger* on January 28, 1986, in sub-freezing temperatures. The O-ring couplings failed to seal properly, causing the explosion that killed six astronauts and one schoolteacher. The Rogers Commission investigating the disaster concluded that "NASA's decision-making process was clearly flawed."[5]

At the time of the Watergate scandal, even a good listener could be deceived by the smoke screen of words and mangled concepts emanating from the Nixon White House. In 1974, historian and former presidential assistant Arthur Schlesinger presented a speech to the National Education Association advising his hearers to listen critically to the vague words and phrases used by the Nixon administration to describe Watergate activities. Phrases such as "toughing it out," "stroking sessions," "stonewalling it," "the limited let-it-all hang out," and "how do you handle that PR-wise?" were frequently used by Nixon and his appointees to manipulate language and to deflect criticism. Schlesinger also accused the President of manipulating meaning when Nixon released the transcripts of his tape-recorded conversations about the Watergate affair:

> The presidential speech preceding the release of the expurgated transcripts was grammatically correct, but it proclaimed in tones of ringing sincerity that the transcripts show exactly the opposite of what in fact the transcripts do show. "He unveils a swamp," as the *New Yorker* well put it, "and instructs us to see a garden of flowers."[6]

Sometimes listeners must work extremely hard to detect hidden meanings behind distorted and manipulated language. In Jonestown, Guyana, on November 24, 1978, the Reverend Jim Jones persuaded 900 of his followers to commit suicide by swallowing a grape soft drink laced with cyanide. How could these people be so tragically manipulated? Part of the answer lies in understanding the dynamics of cults, charismatic speakers, and brainwashing techniques. However, part of the answer also is explained by listeners' desires to hear what they wanted to hear and to deny the truth of what was actually occurring. In the following excerpt from Jones' suicide speech, notice the varying reactions among the listeners:

Jones: What these people gone and done, and what they get through will make our lives worse than hell. . . . But to me, death is not a fearful thing. It's living that's cursed. . . . Not worth living like this.

First Woman: I think there were too few who left for twelve hundred people to give them their lives for those people that left . . . I'm not ready to die. I look at all the babies and I think they deserve to live.

Jones: But don't they deserve much more? They deserve peace. Please get some medication. Simple. It's simple. There's no convulsions with it. Don't be afraid to die. You'll see people land out here. They'll torture some of our children here. They'll torture our people. We cannot have this.

Second Woman: There's nothing to worry about. Everybody keep calm and try to keep your children calm. . . . They're not crying from pain, it's just a little bitter tasting.

Jones: Please, for God's sake, let's get on with it . . . This is a revolutionary suicide. This is not a self-destructive suicide. So they'll pay for this. They brought this upon us. And they'll pay for that. I leave that destiny to them. (Male voices praise "Dad" [Jones]. Applause.)[7]

The first woman, who had absorbed the impact of what Jones was advocating, clearly protested his suicide solution. The second woman's supportive comment helped Jones carry out his aims, and the other listeners who expressed themselves exerted peer pressure by praising "Daddy Jones" and by applauding his words. Perhaps the first woman became involved in Jones's cult by hearing what she wanted to hear—a promise of a better life. Perhaps, too, she began to listen more effectively only when it was too late. The second woman, brainwashed into believing that suicide actually offered a better life, heard what she wanted to hear instead of probing or questioning the ideas.

While these examples are extreme, they remind us of what can happen to an individual, a group, a nation, or an entire civilization if people don't learn to listen critically.

THE PROCESS OF LISTENING

In chapter 1 we discussed the fact that communication is a dynamic, ever-changing process that can be understood through a communication model that includes a sender, message, channel, receiver, and feedback. Listening, a critical component in communication, is also complex and involves its own dynamic process of receiving stimuli, assigning meaning, and formulating responses. Listening is so interesting to human beings that entire books have been written, numerous definitions have been proposed, and special college courses and curricula have been developed to help us understand this often elusive subject more completely. We have selected the definition and model developed by Andrew Wolvin and Carolyn Gwynn Coakley[8] to help you gain a deeper insight into the exciting process of listening.

Wolvin and Coakley define listening as "the process of receiving, attending to, and assigning meaning to aural and visual stimuli."[9] The listening model in Figure 4.2 indicates that the receiver decodes the stimulus through the aural (hearing) and visual senses. The listener first receives a stimulus, let's say, "Do you want some ice cream?" The upper funnel is called the *listening cone* and is wider at the top, indicating that receivers can interpret a stimulus in many different ways. The bottom of the cone is

FIGURE 4.2
Wolvin-Coakley model of
the listening process.

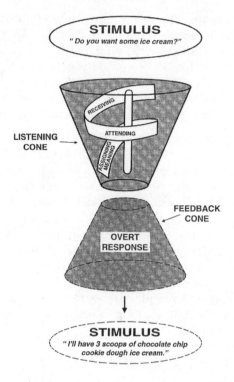

narrower to indicate that an individual makes choices to limit meaning and
interpret stimuli according to the receiver's own personal criteria. Between
the wide and narrow portions of the cone are three overlapping elements
that are critical to listening: receiving, attending, and assigning meaning.
The long oval cylinder linking the three components refers to the process
of remembering and responding covertly as the listener uses the three elements to decode the stimulus and make limited choices against the back-
drop of remembered experience, perception, and many other variables.

So the listener receives the stimulus "Do you want some ice cream?,"
pays attention to it, and begins to interpret the question and assign meaning. The receiver may covertly think, "Ah, ice cream: soft serve, hand
dipped, store bought, home made; mmmmmmm." The listener continues to
make selections. "Butter pecan; death by chocolate, mint chocolate chip,
rocky road." The receiver makes further choices. "Some ice cream. Could
that be a small scoop? Three scoops? A quart?" The listener then provides
additional limits to the meaning of the stimulus based on her own remembered criteria. "I'm on a diet. Can't do three scoops. Maybe I'll be good
and order just one teeny dish." The receiver has now begun to finalize her
choices and assign meaning as the process nears the narrower bottom of

the listening cone. She thinks: "I'll probably get three scoops of chocolate chip cookie dough ice cream. I'll worry about the diet tomorrow!"

The lower funnel in Figure 4.2 is known as the *feedback cone*. Unlike the upper listening cone, it is narrower at the top and wider at the bottom. The lower cone and the stimulus are surrounded by dotted lines to indicate that a listener may or may not choose to make an overt response to a received stimulus. The narrow top indicates that a receiver limits the meaning of a stimulus according to personal criteria. The wider bottom demonstrates that the feedback message or stimulus formulated by the listener can be interpreted many different ways by receivers. Thus, the listening process repeats the cycle through different perceptions and choices made by various receivers. So our listener has decided that she wants some ice cream and has decided to make an overt response: "I'll have three scoops of chocolate chip cookie dough ice cream." And the ice cream store attendant responds, "Will that be in a cup, or in a cake or waffle cone?" Now the process must be repeated because the listener didn't narrow her choices quite enough. Notice that throughout both the upper and lower funnels are diagonal lines representing perceptual filters that receivers use to decode stimuli and feedback senders use to encode messages when they respond covertly or overtly to stimuli.

You can see that the process of listening is complicated. There are many other variables involved such as the efficiency of the visual and hearing mechanisms, numerous stimuli competing for attention, and the dynamics of memory. Listening scholars are still theorizing and conducting experiments to determine if the process can be more precisely defined and the elements of listening more clearly identified. Although the process is complex and could require many pages of discussion, the Wolvin-Coakley model serves merely as an outline to give you a brief introduction into the interactive process of listening.

KINDS OF LISTENING

Just as speakers have general speech purposes for sending messages, listeners also have goals for receiving them. We will examine four kinds of listening: discriminative, evaluative, appreciative, and empathic.[10] In addition, we will briefly describe the concept of active and passive listening.

Discriminative Listening

When we listen discriminatively, we listen to learn, to be instructed, and to test theories. Discriminative listening can occur in formal settings such as in class, at work, or in a business meeting. If you are taking notes at a history class lecture, receiving instructions on how to operate a new computer program, or hearing a committee report, you are acquiring instructional information for future use. Discriminative listening also occurs informally in the process of daily conversation. When you hear your lunch friends describing a new restaurant, the service manager explaining what is wrong with your car, or an insurance agent providing details of a policy, you have applied discriminative listening. Whether formal or informal, discriminative listening helps us to make distinctions, and to differentiate in order to be enlightened, informed, or educated.

Evaluative Listening

Evaluative listening is our response to a persuasive message. We listen to convincing, actuating, or stimulating messages, and formulate reactions based upon our needs and the strength of the persuasion. We are bombarded with persuasive messages daily. Advertisers on television, radio, and in magazines actuate us to buy products; family members persuade us to run errands, purchase gifts, or plan vacations; supervisors encourage us to use new strategies to enhance the company image or to improve sales; a colleague urges us to buy candy to help her daughter raise money for a class trip. Persuasion is often difficult because listeners have built up resistance as a result of the constant barrage of competing stimuli. Listeners ultimately evaluate persuasive messages and decide to agree or disagree based upon the credibility of the speaker and the material, the logic of the speaker's reasoning, the extent of the commitment exhibited by the speaker, and the need of listeners to buy into the speaker's goal.

Appreciative Listening

If you have ever been to a movie, listened to a favorite recording, taken a long walk in the woods, or just enjoyed hearing the sounds of the ocean at the beach, you have participated in appreciative listening. We listen appreciatively to hear the power and beauty of words, images, music, or environmental sounds. We may enjoy hearing the variety of instruments in an orchestral symphony; we might respond with strong emotion to the vivid language of an eloquent speaker; we may listen in passive contentment to the delicate trickle of a waterfall or to the patter of rain on a roof. We might hear the call of an owl at night, or the hiss of an alley cat springing off a garbage can. We learn appreciative listening as we become sensitized to new sounds and experiences. When we learn to listen appreciatively, we establish an emotional bond by responding to the works of others and we enhance our sensory enjoyment of life.

Empathic Listening

The primary goal of discriminative, evaluative, and appreciative listening is to benefit ourselves and contribute to our understanding, decision making, and personal fulfillment. The goal of empathic listening differs, however, in that the objective is to understand and facilitate the needs and feelings of someone else.

We use empathic or therapeutic listening when we are responding to the needs of a close friend, work associate, or family member who is sharing personal joy, anxiety, or concern. We could be hearing a friend who is describing a failed marriage, a family member who is sharing pride about a successful promotion, or a relative describing a struggle with alcoholism.

Numerous businesses, professions, and volunteer organizations require their employees to possess skills in effective therapeutic listening. Lawyers assist clients in developing the best defense or offense after hearing the nature of the charges against them. Educators are required to plan strategies for growth after listening to the needs of students. Psychiatrists must provide therapeutic progress toward mental health when responding to the anxieties of patients. Volunteers often spend hours on hotlines listening to distraught individuals who describe suicidal feelings, spouse abuse, or rape. Hospice workers listen with love and devotion to the last cries and wishes of the dying. Empathic listeners must pay attention completely without giving in to distractions, without making irrelevant comments, and without ignoring the sender's message.

Active and Passive Listening

Most listening behavior is either active or passive. Active listening is attentive and involved behavior. Active listening is the kind of listening we should be using at work, in a meeting, or in class. Active listening is hard work—it represents complete mental commitment on the part of the hearer. Passive listening is relaxed or "easy" listening. Often when you listen to your stereo or watch a movie you are listening passively. Passive listening helps us escape from the pressures of everyday life. Most of us, however, are already accomplished in passive listening and probably not attentive enough to the demands of active listening. If you have ever received a poor grade on a test because you didn't take good notes in class, you have experienced the results of passive listening.

BARRIERS TO LISTENING

We all need to become better active listeners. But in order to improve our listening, we need to understand and analyze some of the poor listening behaviors we often practice. Seven barriers to effective listening are:

1. Yielding to distractions,
2. Blocking out communication,
3. Failing to concentrate,
4. Piecemeal or selective fact listening,
5. Over-criticizing the speaker,
6. Faking attention, and
7. Avoiding difficult listening situations.[11]

Yielding to Distractions

We've already discussed "noise" as a barrier to the communication process in chapter 1. As a listener, you have a constant battle with distractions that result from external, internal, or semantic noise. If a speaker has a broken pair of glasses held together at the nose by tape, you are going to have difficulty listening to the speaker's remarks because of the external distraction. Equally distracting are your own internal "noises," such as anger at a person or situation, fatigue from staying up all night, or anxiety about an upcoming conflict, court appearance, or final exam. You also might not understand several of the terms that the speaker is using, or you might react negatively to an outdated word or phrase the speaker employs.

Blocking Out Communication

Sooner or later, most of us can be accused of "blocking out" information and of not listening. One of the most common stereotypes of blocking behavior is the husband who reads the newspaper and mutters "uh huh" while his wife is trying to talk to him. We've probably all watched an exciting TV program and blocked out the phone talk or other conversation around us.

Sometimes blocking behaviors are purposeful, and sometimes they are habits acquired as a result of pressure, stress, and overstimulation of the senses. Even conscientious, active listeners can be so bombarded by competing stimuli that they are forced to adopt blocking behavior as a survival mechanism. For example, you wake up in the morning and hear on the radio that several hundred people have been killed in an earthquake; at noon you hear about a fellow office worker's sudden heart attack; coming home you hear of another terrorist attack in the Middle East, and the evening news reports that violent crimes in your community have doubled in the past two years. At home, you discover that your little sister has broken her finger and there has been another family crisis. In these circumstances, you might well choose to block out information for a while.

The problem occurs, however, when normally active listeners become so saturated by what they hear and see that blocking out stimuli becomes habitual, and they can no longer pay the necessary attention to *real* crises. When a husband and wife begin to block each other out in their marriage, or children cannot get through to their parents, serious communication barriers can be created.

Blocking can also result when a listener who disagrees turns off immediately when the topic of the speech is announced or when certain catch words are stated. Instead of giving the speech a fair hearing, a listener with an extreme bias will have a mental fight with the speaker about each point. A biased individual might not be able to get around the mere mention of the names Gore or Bush, the terms tax cut, national health insurance, or the labels *Republican* or *Democrat*.

Sometimes an individual will block out the opposing speaker so that mental time can be spent storing up all of the verbal ammunition to fire back. The listener is not hearing the speaker, but is blocking out any opposing views so that the listener's position does not have to be examined.

Failing to Concentrate

Our society puts great emphasis on relaxation. Ads tell us to go on a vacation, take a coffee break, eat a candy bar, buy a VCR, or go to a movie. We are not condemning the practice of listening to relax. Listening to a good recording or watching a comedy can do wonders for your mental health. But many of us are very good at passive television listening and not very good at active listening, which requires energy and work. Often the more time we spend in passive listening, the lazier we become in our active listening patterns.[12] It becomes easier and more fun to daydream and let our minds wander than to concentrate on more difficult information.

Piecemeal or Selective Fact Listening

Often we create a listening barrier when we try to listen for all of the details, and we don't catch the overall point of the information. An equal problem is the desire within all of us to hear what we want to hear, or to listen only to information that supports our own thinking:

Loan Counselor: Now there are several types of mortgages you and your wife should consider before making your final choice.

Mortgage Applicants: Could you explain the different mortgages for us?

Loan Counselor: Well, there is the fixed-rate fifteen-year mortgage, the fixed-rate thirty-year mortgage, and several types of adjustable rate mortgages, called ARMS for short.

Mortgage Applicants: Well, we really don't know anything about any of these, but all we know is that we want the best deal, and the cheapest mortgage with the lowest monthly payments.

Loan Counselor: Well, you can always choose the fixed-rate mortgage, which is 9 percent. Of course, your monthly payments are going to start high and stay the same for the life of the loan. Now you can take any one of the ARMS that allow you the advantage of initial low monthly payments and don't really increase for several years. One of our ARMS, which I really think you'd both be interested in, starts at the low rate of 6¾ percent for the first two years, then increases to only 8¾ percent in the third year. For the remainder of the loan the rate is set by the lender. *Imagine*, being able to have monthly payments of only 6¾ percent for two whole years!

Mortgage Appliants: Sounds good to us!

The applicants in this example have unfortunately listened selectively when they should have been listening critically. The couple, clearly interested in "the cheapest mortgage with the lowest monthly payments," has focused on the loan counselor's enthusiasm and vocal emphasis on "Imagine, being able to have monthly payments of only 6 and ¾ percent for two whole years!" These home buyers think they have agreed to favorable mortgage rates, but because they only listened partially, they did not hear the "catch" to the agreement—that after three years, the mortgage rate will be set by the lender for the remainder of the life of the loan. Our mortgage applicants have not asked if there is any ceiling placed on the mortgage rate after the initial three years. It is possible, then, that for twenty-seven years these people could be paying monthly mortgage rates as high as 13, 15, or even 16 percent, which will be set by the lender. Our buyers have now become victims.

Overcriticizing the Speaker

We can criticize a speaker to such an extent that we can destroy any possibility of hearing the speaker's intentions or purposes. The speaker's appearance may be wrong, the speaker may lean too much on the lectern, or the speaker's tie may be the wrong color. Maybe we think the speaker shouldn't wear a tie, or the speaker's voice is too soft or too loud, or the speaker is too emotional or too logical.

Many listeners feel that communication is solely the responsibility of the speaker. If the speaker isn't exciting enough, attractive enough, funny enough, emotional enough, or logical enough, these listeners switch mental channels and perform their own mental activities.

The responsibility for effective communication must be *shared* between the speaker and listener. The speaker is responsible for encoding the feelings into symbols, structuring the message, and selecting the channels of communication. The listener is responsible for decoding the message and for providing clear feedback, which signals to the speaker if communication is taking place and how effective the communication has been.

An individual who overcriticizes a speaker often assumes that it is solely the speaker's responsibility to convey a message. Often these listeners develop the attitude that "Okay—here I am sitting in front of you. Do something to me. Interest me. Get my attention. Humor me." Not only is this poor listening behavior, it keeps the individual from shouldering his or her part of the communication transaction—to listen.

Faking attention

Many of us are very good at faking attention. When we're involved in a boring conversation, we can smile, look interested, and nod our heads as if we are giving our complete attention. But in our minds we are performing some other activity, such as planning our weekend or finalizing the grocery list.

Students are very good at faking attention. A student can look straight at the instructor, smile and frown at all the appropriate times, lean forward and take notes (doodles on the paper), and generally appear to be involved in the class. The problem occurs, of course, when a question demands a specific response, or a pop-quiz is given on material just discussed. The faked response can quickly turn into embarrassment with an inattentive listener angry at being taken by "surprise."

Faking attention is a bad habit that creates a barrier to communication. The faker loses, wasting valuable time that could have been spent growing in the sender-receiver communication process.

Avoiding Difficult Listening Situations

Sometimes we avoid listening situations we feel are too demanding. We feel insecure, and our lack of experience makes us dread the situation.

A poster in a college math department reads: "Mathophobia can cost you a career."[13] Underneath the caption is a list of careers such as commercial flying, dental technology, and engineering, which are inaccessible to individuals without skills in mathematics.

We could expand the caption in the poster to state, "Avoiding difficult listening situations can cost you enlightenment, growth, and fulfillment." Imagine someone canceling a trip to the Greek Islands or the Spanish Riviera due to insecurity about foreign languages. Think of individuals passing up free tickets to a symphony concert because they don't "understand" classical music. Imagine an individual not learning how to use the computer because it appears too complicated. Unfortunately, these situations can and do occur when individuals fear difficult listening circumstances.

Sometimes listening is a matter of rethinking and overcoming inner fears. Whatever you do, don't avoid situations that you think may be difficult. Overcome the difficulty by facing it directly. Open your mind to the situation and allow yourself to receive communication. Take on the listening circumstance as a challenge: Gain perspective by exploring an unfamiliar culture; develop sophistication from an aesthetic experience; gain satisfaction by acquiring a new skill. You will be surprised at your growth and achievement in a constructive environment.

BECOMING AN ACTIVE LISTENER

We now need to work toward the development of a program to become better active listeners. Here is a simple four-point program to help you increase your awareness of the way you listen:

1. Withhold judgment about the speech and the speaker.
2. Provide the speaker with honest, attentive feedback.
3. Eliminate distractions.
4. Evaluate the speech when it is finished.

Withhold Judgment about the Speech and the Speaker

Keep an open mind. Don't turn off when you hear the speaker's name, the statement of the topic, or the purpose of the speech. Wait until the speaker has finished before you begin to evaluate the speaker or any portion of the speech. In withholding judgment about the speech and the speaker, do the following:

1. Avoid the appearance trap,
2. Don't be easily swayed by delivery and style,

3. Give all topics a fair hearing, and

4. Avoid extraneous mental activity during the speech.

AVOID THE APPEARANCE TRAP

We are easily influenced by a speaker's physical appearance. It is easy to misjudge a sloppily dressed person, or to feel that someone who is neatly dressed in the latest fashion is more worthy of our time.

While it is important for a speaker to do everything possible to support the speech nonverbally as well as verbally, we must recognize that not all speakers share the same ideas about what constitutes effective speaking. "Dressing for success" may be important to some speakers, but others might care very little about appearance. Recognize your own attitudes and standards about appearance, and try not to impose these attitudes on the speaker.

DON'T BE EASILY SWAYED BY DELIVERY AND STYLE

Don't allow yourself to become seduced or alienated by delivery and style. A speaker who has a soothing voice could be advocating ideas harmful to the audience, while a speaker with an irritating voice could be well-organized and coherent in logic and ideas. Work hard not to let a speaker's hesitations, vocalized pauses, or monotonous delivery affect your judgment unfairly. Don't be too easily impressed by a speaker's ability to use big words and flamboyant phrases that send you on a hunt through the dictionary. Recognize that every speaker has limitations in delivery. Try to accept the speaker and learn as much as you can without mentally trying to change the speaker.

GIVE ALL TOPICS A FAIR HEARING

We all like some topics more than others. Don't let your own attitude for or against an issue prejudice your receptivity to a speech. You have nothing to lose if you keep your mind open to an issue. If you still disagree with the topic at the conclusion of the speech, you will have learned something—even if it is about the speaker's organization or research.

Force yourself to listen to ideas you oppose. Listening to different beliefs develops your active listening capacities and helps you grow as a communicator.

AVOID EXTRANEOUS MENTAL ACTIVITY DURING THE SPEECH

Some books and articles on listening advise people to take mental notes, make mental summaries, or write mental outlines while listening. Such mental activity is said to help the listener concentrate on what is being discussed, and more effectively retain the main points of the presentation. One author rejects these ideas and feels that such advice causes listeners to become distracted.[14] Some research indicates that when people are still thinking about a speaker's previous point (or making mental summaries), they are usually not listening to what the speaker is currently saying.[15]

It is important that listeners concentrate on what is being said and not think behind or ahead of the speaker. When you give the speaker a complete hearing, all of your mental activity will be focused on the speaker, and you will postpone all other evaluation, summarizing, or inference-making until the speech is over.

Give the Speaker Honest, Attentive Feedback

Work hard to listen actively to the speaker. Provide clear signals that show the speaker you are paying attention. Sit up straight. Make eye contact with the speaker. Nod your head to let the speaker know you understand what is being said. Show interest in the speaker and in the speaker's topic. Give the speaker a smile when the speaker tells a joke. Try to support the speaker as much as you can. If you don't understand a part of the speech, give the speaker a puzzled expression to indicate that you don't follow what is being discussed.[16]

Don't fake attention. Don't pretend to listen when you really aren't. In chapter 3, we talked about credibility and the necessity of trusting a speaker. It is equally important that a speaker be able to trust an audience. The speaker needs to know that the speech is being actively heard and that the listener is providing clear, accurate, and sincere feedback to the speech.

In your speech class, you could conceivably deliver speeches exclusively to your instructor without class members present. In such a situation, your only concern would be to direct your speech to your audience of one (your instructor) and to get a good grade on each presentation. You could also conceivably deliver speeches to an audience commanded to fake pleasant facial expressions, giving you the false impression that whatever you said was positively received. But your speech instructor does not want a one-person audience or a fake audience. Your instructor wants every speaker to communicate to a "live" audience that is sincere, receptive, and attentive. Your position as a listener in your classroom is just as important as your position as a speaker. How well you listen can affect the learning atmosphere of the class as well as the success of each individual speaker.

Active listening is hard work and requires complete mental commitment on the part of the hearer.

Eliminate Distractions

Be conscious of the disruptions caused by external, internal, and semantic noise, and work hard to overcome them. You must continually remind yourself that your role as a listener requires you to share in the communication process and to be active in relation to the speaker. Don't allow yourself the luxury of daydreaming, making up the grocery list, or studying for an exam during a speech. Avoid the pitfalls created by these distractions. Remind yourself that, as a listener, you have the same responsibility of keeping to your task as does the speaker. Learn to block out the distractions—not the speaker.

Evaluate the Speech When It Is Finished

When the speech is completed, evaluate the presentation. Begin to ask questions, make mental summaries, and try to recall the main points of the speech. After you listen to the presentation, analyze both the content and the delivery. Speech *content* refers to the research, organization, and logical development of the topic. The *delivery* refers to the style or presentation of the speech. Here are some questions about content and delivery to use when you analyze speeches presented in your course:

CONTENT

1. Was the speech well organized?
2. Did the speech reflect the existence and development of an outline?
3. Was there a clear specific purpose and/or a thesis statement in the speech?
4. Was there an introduction, body, and conclusion in the speech?
5. Were the main points in the body of the speech easy to follow?
6. Was the introduction interesting? Was the introduction designed to gain the attention of the audience?
7. Did the speaker use credible sources to support the main points of the speech?
8. Did the speaker use examples, case studies, illustrations, or other supportive materials to explain some of the major points in the speech?
9. Did the speaker use statistics? Were these clear and easy to understand? Were the statistics logical, and did they support the main points in the speech?
10. Was the speaker's information accurate and up-to-date?
11. Was the topic appropriate to the audience?
12. Did the speaker attempt to adapt the topic to audience interests and needs?
13. Did the speaker define any unfamiliar terms?
14. Was the content of the speech generally well-prepared?
15. Was the conclusion interesting? Was the conclusion designed to wrap up the speech effectively?

DELIVERY

1. Did the speaker use eye contact?
2. Did the speaker use supportive facial expressions?

3. Did the speaker use gestures for emphasis and clarity?

4. Was the speaker's posture and body position appropriate?

5. Did the speaker use note cards effectively?

6. Was the speaker spontaneous and conversational?

7. Was the speaker's voice easy to hear?

8. Did the speaker make use of vocal inflections?

9. Did the speaker appear to be enthusiastic and energetic about the subject?

10. Did the speaker's vocal tone, vocal inflections, and verbal emphasis indicate a commitment or belief in the topic? Was the speaker's articulation effective? Did the speaker have an understanding of English usage?

11. Was the language appropriate to the topic and the audience?

12. Did the speaker use external transitions to mark the main points of the body? Did the speaker make use of internal transitions within main headings?

13. If visual aids were used, did the speaker use the visuals effectively? Were the visuals easy to see, neat, clear, and were they an asset to the speech?

14. Did the speaker have any mannerisms that created external noise?

SUMMARY

Research indicates that people spend the majority of their communication time in listening-related activities. Problems occur when people don't listen effectively.

Listening can be identified as discriminative or instructional, evaluative or persuasive, appreciative or emotional, and empathic or therapeutic. Active listening is an attentive and involved activity, while passive listening is a relaxed behavior.

Barriers to listening include: yielding to distractions, blocking out communication, failing to concentrate, piecemeal or selective fact listening, overcriticizing the speaker, faking attention, and avoiding difficult listening situations.

To become a more active listener, withhold judgment about the speech and the speaker, provide the speaker with honest, attentive feedback, eliminate distractions, and evaluate the speech when it is over.

Content deals with the research, organization, and logical development of the ideas in the speech, and delivery represents the style or manner used to present the content.

SKILL BUILDERS

1. Ask every person in your class to state his or her name and major. After you have finished hearing from the entire class, try to recall (in sequence) the names and majors from memory to assess how carefully you listened to each class member.

2. Keep a journal of your daily listening activities for two weeks. Write down the type of event you listened to, the amount of time spent listening to that activity, the kind of listening behavior you experienced, and your overall evaluation of how well you listened. In your journal, discuss any aspects of the listening situation that made it easy or hard to concentrate on the speaker.

3. By looking over your listening journal, write down those situations that really interested you, list the situations to which you had difficulty listening, then list all the situations that bored you.

4. Look through your journal and make a list of any of the distractions (external, internal, or semantic noise) that made it difficult for you to listen. Did you give in to any of the distractions and allow them to take you away from active listening? Did you daydream, or did a speaker's comment trigger any extraneous mental activity on your part?

5. Go back through the journal and select the listening situations that you consciously or unconsciously blocked out. Ask yourself why you blocked out communication and what your emotional state was at the time. Were you tired, worried, under stress, or were you experiencing conflicts? Did you disagree with the speaker? Did you dislike the speaker, the speaker's style, or the way the speaker was dressed? Did something the speaker said make you angry?

6. Look over your journal and select a situation you listened to only partially. Why did you listen selectively? Did your lack of attentive listening cause you any damage in the situation? If so, explain.

7. Make a list of the subjects you find it hard to discuss or listen to. After looking over the list, try to find some areas for improvement.

8. Make a chart in a notebook to summarize your listening experiences during any one day. Put down the following information:
   a. The date.
   b. The type of listening activity.
   c. The amount of time you spent in that activity.
   d. Whether you listened actively or passively in the situation (in some cases, you might have listened *both* actively and passively at various times during the listening experience—therefore, you would check *both* active and passive).
   e. Write a brief description of your listening behavior.

9. Take the listening test provided in this chapter.

Assessment of Listening Behavior

In the following test are fifteen statements that can help you determine how well you listen. Answer each statement by checking the box at the right under the word which BEST describes your behavior. The following five-point scale will be used to assess your total score:

Always = 5, Often = 4, Sometimes = 3, Seldom = 2, and Never = 1.

	ALWAYS	OFTEN	SOMETIMES	SELDOM	NEVER
1. I wait until a speech is over before I evaluate it.	❏	❏	❏	❏	❏
2. I keep an open mind when I hear a speaker's topic.	❏	❏	❏	❏	❏
3. A speaker's appearance does not influence my thinking.	❏	❏	❏	❏	❏
4. A speaker's delivery or style of speaking does not influence or affect my feelings about a topic.	❏	❏	❏	❏	❏
5. I keep my mind focused on what the speaker is saying at the moment rather than daydreaming about something else.	❏	❏	❏	❏	❏
6. I don't let distractions take away my concentration.	❏	❏	❏	❏	❏
7. I give the speaker some kind of honest and appropriate feedback while the speaker is talking.	❏	❏	❏	❏	❏
8. I work hard at listening to people.	❏	❏	❏	❏	❏
9. I don't block people out when they are speaking.	❏	❏	❏	❏	❏
10. When a speaker has finished, I find that I can mentally recall the main points of the presentation.	❏	❏	❏	❏	❏
11. I seek difficult listening situations that require a lot of effort.	❏	❏	❏	❏	❏
12. I don't fake attention when someone is talking to me.	❏	❏	❏	❏	❏
13. I don't mentally critique the speaker when the speaker is talking.	❏	❏	❏	❏	❏
14. I don't tune the speaker out if I hear a word, phrase, or idea that I don't agree with.	❏	❏	❏	❏	❏
15. I find that I listen completely and not selectively or in a piecemeal manner.	❏	❏	❏	❏	❏
Subtotal from each column	❏	❏	❏	❏	❏

Grand total from all columns _____

Scoring:

65–75 Total score indicates you are a good listener.

55–64 Total score indicates you listen sporadically and need to change weak areas.

45–54 Total score indicates you need to improve your overall listening behavior.

NOTES

1. Sperry advertisement, *Business Week,* February 4, 1980. Based on copyrighted material of Dr. Lyman K. Steil, president, Communication Development, Inc., St. Paul, MN, for the Sperry Corporation. Reprinted with permission of Dr. Steil and Sperry Corporation (now Unisys).

2. Paul T. Rarlkin, "The Importance of Listening Ability," *English Journal,* 17 (1928): 623–630.

3. Larry Barker, Karen Gladney, Renee Edwards, Frances Holley, and Connie Gaines, "An Investigation of Proportional Time Spent in Various Communication

Activities by College Students," Journal *of Applied Communication Research,* 8 (1980), pp. 101–109.

4. National Transportation Safety Board, *Aircraft Accident Report, Avianca, the Airline of Columbia, Boeing 707-321B, HK 2016, Fuel Exhaustion,* Adopted. April 30, 1991, pp. 6, 74, 75, 76.

5. Commission Finds Flaws in NASA's Decision Making," *Science,* March 14, 1986, pp. 1237-1238.

6. Arthur M. Schlesinger Jr., "Watergate and the Corruption of Language," *Today's Education,* September–October, 1974, pp. 25–27.

7. "Don't Be Afraid To Die," *Newsweek,* 26 March, 1979, p. 53. From *Newsweek,* March 26, © 1979, Newsweek, Inc.

8. Andrew D. Wolvin and Carolyn Gwynn Coakley, *Listening,* 5th ed. (New York, NY: McGraw Hill, 1996, pp. 69–96.

9. Ibid., p. 69.

10. Two sources were used as the basis for "Kinds of Listening": Florence I. Wolf and Nadine C. Marsnik, *Perceptive Listening,* 2nd ed. (New York: Holt, Rinehart and Winston, 1992), pp. 88–103; and Andrew D. Wolvin and Carolyn Gwynn Coakley, *Listening,* 5th ed. (New York, NY: McGraw Hill, 1996), Part II, pp. 151–380. The authors of *Perceptive Listening* present five kinds of listening that include "self listening." In *Listening,* the writers identify five areas, but include a different type they call "comprehensive listening." We believe that the four listening types presented in this chapter are most commonly identified throughout the literature.

11. This list of common barriers to listening is synthesized from two sources: Robert O. Hirsch, *Listening: A Way to Process Information Aurally* (Dubuque, IA: Gorsuch Scarisbrick, 1979), pp. 36–41; and Ralph G. Nichols, *Are You Listening?* (New York: McGraw-Hill, 1957), pp. 104–112.

12. Peter Conrad, *Television, the Medium and Its Manners* (Boston: Routledge & Kegan Paul, 1982). Conrad makes some devastating and thought-provoking attacks on the invasion of television into our lives. "Talk on television isn't meant to be listened to. The words merely gain for us the time to look at the talker. The talk shows are theatres of behavior, not dialogues" (p. 48).

13. Used by permission of the Mathematics Department, Toronto Board of Education.

14. Charles M. Kelley, "Empathic Listening" in Jimmie D. Trent, Judith S. Trent, and Daniel J. O'Neill, *Concepts in Communication* (Boston: Allyn & Bacon, 1973), p. 270.

15. Robert W. Norton and Loyd S. Pettegrew, "Attentiveness as a Style of Communication: A Structural Analysis," *Communication Monographs,* 46 (March 1979):13–16.

16. Ralph G. Nichols, *Are You Listening?* (New York: McGraw-Hill, 1957), p. 105.

Chapter 5

UNDERSTANDING AND REDUCING YOUR APPREHENSION

Courage is resistance to fear, mastery of fear—not absence of fear.

Mark Twain

CHAPTER OBJECTIVES

After reading this chapter you will be able to:

1. Recognize that speech anxiety is common;

2. Be aware of research into stress and communication apprehension;

3. Adopt an eight-point plan for reducing speech apprehension.

- When former first lady Barbara Bush began her public life, she was so nervous that her knees would knock as she tried to deliver a speech. But she eventually overcame her fear and became a seasoned professional speaker. During her career, Barbara Bush accepted honors and awards, presented commencement addresses, represented the United States at international conferences, and spoke on behalf of numerous humanitarian and social causes from literacy to leukemia. Years later, Barbara made these comments about her shyness: "For someone who has an open mouth on every subject now, it seems amazing."[1]

- American pianist Van Cliburn became a nationwide sensation when he won the 1958 Tchaikovsky Competition in Moscow. The twenty-three-year-old classical musician was welcomed back to the United States with a ticker-tape parade in New York and an invitation to the White House from President Eisenhower. After years of touring and hundreds of successful concerts, Cliburn went into a retirement that lasted for sixteen years. But the musician staged a comeback that began with a performance at the Hollywood Bowl in July of 1994. As he was playing Tchaikovsky's First Piano Concerto, his trademark piece, Cliburn experienced a memory loss that contributed to numerous errors and made the Moscow Philharmonic orchestra scramble to follow the wildly inconsistent performance. After leaving the stage for more than twenty minutes, Cliburn returned and told the audience of 14,000 that he felt faint and was unable to continue. Later, he confided to friends that he was "too paralyzed by fear" to perform some of the more difficult music in the program.[2]

- Superstar Barbra Streisand is adored as a singer, actress, writer, and Hollywood producer. But this well-known entertainer was so terrified of live audiences that she did not perform in public for twenty-seven years. During a free concert in New York's Central Park in 1967, Streisand forgot the lyrics to three songs. "I forgot the words in front of 125,000—and I wasn't cute about it or anything. I was shocked; I was terrified. It prevented me from performing for all these years."[3] After returning to the stage in a successful New Year's Eve concert in Las Vegas, the singer admitted that she is still nervous at live concerts. She explained to *Newsweek* reporters that she is unable to eat before performing and listens to meditation tapes to calm down and "think of positive things."[4]

These well-known personalities have one shared experience: a fear of speaking or performing in public. As you will see in this chapter, public speaking anxiety is a condition that affects many Americans. But if you understand speech apprehension, you can begin to develop a program that helps to reduce its affect on your speaking presentations. This chapter surveys the territory of speech anxiety: public speaking fears, research about anxiety, and ways to reduce your nervousness as you build your speeches.

SPEECH ANXIETY IS COMMON

A student began his first classroom speech. His voice trembled, his mouth seemed parched, and his hands visibly shook as he presented the introduction. At one point, he tried to control his quivering hands by placing them into his pockets; but he started to rattle his change, calling even further attention to his stage fright. When he decided to make a gesture, he suddenly withdrew his hand from his pocket, sprinkling change all over the floor.

Another student came to the instructor at the beginning of the semester with these worried comments: "I am so nervous when I get up in front of people that I freeze up—I can't remember what I am going to say, and I start to fumble with my words. I live in fear that I will try to open my mouth and nothing will come out. I'm really good speaking in one to one situations, and I would do fine if I could just give my speeches to you in an empty classroom or in your office."

If you have ever felt this kind of anxiety, or if you have ever lost sleep because you had to give a report in class or in front of an organization, you are normal. A number of researchers have conducted studies to determine some of the greatest social fears among Americans. In a 1986 study of about 1,000 individuals, researchers discovered that people identified public speaking as their number-one fear. Public speaking anxiety even outranked such fears as going to the dentist, heights, mice, or flying.[5] In a study conducted in 1984, investigators asked 3,000 people to list situations that caused the most anxiety.[6] Individuals ranked fear of public speaking as their second greatest anxiety and attending a party with strangers as their first social fear. A summary of the fears identified in the survey is on page 90.

Almost everyone experiences some type of anxiety about public speaking. Many famous or professional speakers have also experienced anxiety about public speaking. John F. Kennedy was one of the most effective presidential speakers in this century. Yet even President Kennedy could be nervous about delivering a speech. William Manchester cites a specific incident:

> The President [Kennedy] laughed, apparently relaxing. But he wasn't relaxed. In press conferences he could be at ease, despite the size of the television audience. Question-and-answer sessions were a challenge, a test of intellect. He had never learned to enjoy formal speeches, however, and his casual appearance was a triumph of the will. Unlike Lyndon [Johnson, then vice-president], he was not an extrovert. To his audiences his easy air

	SITUATION	PERCENT (%)
TABLE 5.1	A party with strangers	74
Ten Social Situations Causing Greatest Anxiety	Giving a speech	70
	Asked personal questions in public	65
	Meeting a date's parents	59
	First day on a new job	59
	Victim of a practical joke	56
	Talking with someone in authority	53
	Job interview	46
	Formal dinner party	44
	Blind date	42

seemed unstudied. Very few knew how hard he had toiled to achieve it. On a rostrum the illusion of spontaneity was almost perfect; only his hands would have betrayed him, and he was careful to keep them out of sight . . . they were . . . vibrating so violently at times that they seemed palsied. Now and then the right hand would shoot up and out, the index finger stabbing the limelit air to make a point. The moment it dropped the trembling would begin again. Several times he nearly dropped his five by seven cards. *Why, the President's nervous . . .*[7]

RESEARCH INTO STRESS AND COMMUNICATION APPREHENSION

As you begin to deal with your anxiety about public speaking, it is helpful for you to understand some of the research that has been done in the field.

In 1936, Hans Selye conducted research which has become a classic in the field of stress-reduction. From his laboratory experiments, Selye concluded that the human body reacts to stress in stages known as the general adaptation syndrome.[8]

The initial *alarm reaction* is a physical "call to arms" for the body to release a number of chemicals in response to the "fight-or-flight" situation. When you deliver your first speech, you will probably experience some of these physiological alarms:

PHYSICAL SYMPTOMS OF NERVOUSNESS

1. Increased heart rate
2. Thickening speech/decreased flow of saliva

3. "Butterflies" in the stomach
4. Increased sweating
5. Tiredness or yawning
6. Jumpiness or jitteriness
7. Tightening of muscles
8. Shaky hands and legs, twitching in some body muscles

The body's alarm reaction is often the extra special shot of adrenaline that enables you to face your audience or allows individuals to perform super-human feats of strength in times of emergency.

During the *resistance stage,* the body reduces the general physiological alarms and channels energy to those organs that are most capable of handling the tension. The body stabilizes, maintains itself, and begins to adapt to the stress. For instance, once you have been speaking for a minute or two you may notice that your physical symptoms begin to decrease.

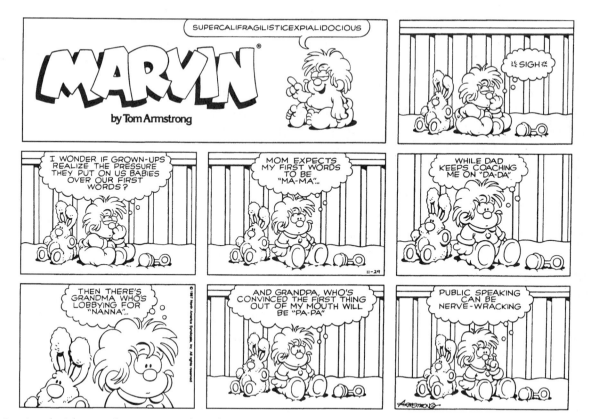

Reprinted with special permission of North American Syndicate, Inc.

In the final *phase of exhaustion,* the body systems that were summoned to cope with the stress are depleted. The body can endure tension for only so long; when tension is chronic and continues for a period of days or years, serious damage can result. People who are under severe pressure can develop ulcers, hypertension, and heart disease. Your public speaking class will not create any prolonged anxiety—only relaxation and mild fatigue after you have finished your speeches.

While Selye's conclusions represent a classic contribution in understanding tension, there is more recent research that is related to public speaking. In the 1970s, James C. McCroskey, a university speech instructor, used the term *communication apprehension* to describe an individual's anxiety about speaking to another person or a group.[9] McCroskey found that most college students experience some level of apprehension about public speaking, and he also determined that at least twenty percent of these students experience high levels of anxiety.

McCroskey also found that apprehension can be reduced. Many people who experience normal levels of anxiety can actually decrease apprehension and build self-confidence by taking and successfully completing a public speaking course. For instance, the two anxious students mentioned in the opening examples were able to overcome many of their

SUCCESS IN A CAREER REQUIRES EFFECTIVE PUBLIC SPEAKING SKILLS

"Everyone needs to be able to get his or her ideas across, but try moving up in management without being able to speak out at meetings," says Wicke Chambers, co-owner of the Atlanta speech-training firm, Speechworks.

Or if you're a salesman, it's one thing to make a one-on-one pitch, but don't expect to close hot deals if you freeze up in front of executive committees. It's effective speakers, the experts say, who are perceived as leaders—and perceptions can be more important than reality. Put another way, you may be an Einstein, but you're not going to get anywhere unless you can get your ideas across with ease.

The fear of public speaking, Ms. Chambers points out, has killed many a promising career. And many a manager has ended up answering to the trusted subordinate he delegated to attend a meeting or make a speech, says David Greenberg, owner of another training firm, Simply Speaking.

From *The Sun* (Baltimore), "Sadly most people would rather not talk about their speech phobias," December 10, 1992 sec. F, p. 17.

fears as they progressed through their speech classes. McCroskey also found that individuals who experienced high apprehension levels could lower anxiety through behavior modification techniques known as systematic desensitization.

In *systematic desensitization,* a trainer administers a test to determine individuals with high levels of communication anxiety. Subjects chosen for treatment are seated comfortably in a quiet room where they are told to close their eyes while a relaxation tape is played. When the tape is finished and individuals are relaxed, the trainer reads the first item on a list of anxiety-producing situations (such as presenting a speech, being interviewed for a job, conducting a meeting). There is a fifteen-second silence while subjects mentally visualize the stressful situation. If no anxiety is indicated, the trainer reads the next item from the list. If trainees report anxiety, they are asked to put the situation out of their minds while the trainer conducts additional relaxation exercises. The trainer then returns to the situation producing stress, repeating the process until no tension is indicated. McCroskey found that after five to seven fifty-minute sessions, almost all subjects had responded favorably to the process and reduced or overcome their apprehension.[10]

While you may not have severe apprehension, you will probably experience normal levels of speech anxiety. Here are eight areas that, if practiced, will help you to reduce your fear and build your self-confidence.

REDUCING COMMUNICATION APPREHENSION

Accept Anxiety Honestly and Face It

Try to understand your apprehension and determine your specific fears. Write down a list of things you fear about speaking in public. Here are some examples of common performance anxieties that students often express in speech classes:

I'm afraid I'll fall flat on my face.

I'm afraid I'll babble like an idiot.

I'm afraid that people will see my knees knocking together.

I'm afraid that people won't like me.

I'm afraid I'll make a mistake.

I'm afraid I'll forget everything I'm trying to say.

I'm afraid I'll make people angry.

I'm afraid I'll get sick.

When you've completed your list, take a good long look at each statement and analyze it carefully. You will probably discover that you are creating irrational fears and that most of your anxieties have no basis in fact. Anxieties are often worst-case scenarios. You will never literally fall flat on your face; and yes, you will probably make a mistake every once in a while. But who told you that you have to be perfect? A standard of achievement that is perfectionistic is unrealistic, irrational, and will probably cause you a lot of unhappiness. While you are very aware of your own nervous symptoms, many people in your audience will not detect your apprehension. So if your knees knock, you are probably the only one who knows it.

In a group such as a speech class where you have a supportive group of people with a common purpose, the fear of people disliking you is also irrational. There will always be someone who disagrees with you and a few who may not like the speech. No one can, or should, try to please everyone. And you probably won't become sick unless you eat something that upsets your stomach.

Two well-known psychotherapists, Albert Ellis and Robert Harper, refer to the dread of the future as the concept of "awfullizing."[11] The future is *awfullized* when people worry that something terrible will happen to them. These fears about tomorrow usually have no basis in fact. Awfullizing causes people to paralyze themselves with anxiety, to avoid situations thought to be unpleasant, and to stop performing constructive activities important to their growth.

Whatever you do in this speech class, don't run away from your fear or from your speaking experiences. Don't use some of the lines stated by students who try to avoid giving speeches:

I've lost my notecards, so I can't give my speech today.

I didn't have time to prepare my speech last week, so I just can't go through with it.

I've developed a severe headache—May I be excused from the speech?

I've been having car trouble all week and I'm terribly upset, so I don't think I'm in any condition to present a speech.

I have a terrible case of laryngitis, and there is no way I can talk today.

While we're not trying to ridicule legitimate problems that people may experience, it is a human tendency for people to create excuses to avoid fearful and unpleasant situations. If you run away from apprehension, you are simply creating a greater problem for yourself. In addition to postponing your performance, you will turn anxiety into a monster, which will be more difficult for you to conquer the next time. Don't run away—face your fear. Stare down anxiety; you will discover that you can control the monster so that it won't control you.

Develop a Positive Attitude

When you begin to face your fear, you may also need to examine the attitudes you have about public speaking. Psychologists and speech instructors alike have discovered that many people fail at public performance simply because they think negatively and develop negative self-talk:[12]

I'm really not smart enough to speak in front of people.

I don't do well speaking in groups.

I seem to have bad luck.

I can't finish a coherent sentence in public.

I say some really ridiculous things at times.

Researchers have discovered that if people can transform their negative self-talk into positive self-talk, anxious people can unlearn old patterns and reeducate themselves into thinking more constructively.[13] Monitor the way you talk about yourself. Keep a journal or diary of the feelings you experience before every speech in your course. When you find yourself talking negatively about yourself, consciously begin to change your attitudes by writing down positive statements to replace the old negatives. The previous negative attitudes would become *positive self-talk:*

I'm intelligent and I usually have something to contribute to people.

I can do well speaking in groups if I try.

Good things happen to me all the time if I look for them.

I can finish my thoughts and my sentences if I'm patient with myself.

While I know I'll make mistakes at times, I know I'll also say some important things in my speeches.

In addition to thinking positively about yourself, begin to develop positive attitudes about your speech course. Look at this course as a challenge—an opportunity for you to grow from other people's experiences as well as from your own. You can even develop a positive attitude about the opportunity to make mistakes in a helpful, constructive climate. When your communication is critiqued in a supportive environment there is much less anxiety than in a competitive atmosphere such as your job. In your class, communication mistakes mean simply that you try to improve when you speak again. In your job, communication mistakes may mean that you lose your livelihood.

Begin now to replace negative self-talk with positive self-talk. By reeducating yourself in this fashion, you can start to think more rationally about yourself, and you can open yourself up to good experiences that will help you to grow.

One student placed these words of encouragement at the beginning of his speaking notes:

Calm yourself.

Look at them.

They are not vicious!

Take deep breath.

You can always do better next time.

Begin.[14]

Adopt Constructive Behavior

Once you begin to think more positively about yourself, start doing something constructive related to your speaking assignment. Jot down speech topics when they pop into your mind. Think about some of your interests and abilities and ask yourself a few questions: *What ideas would I like to share with an audience? At what activities am I successful? What do I feel*

Almost everyone is apprehensive about public speaking. Research indicates, however, that speakers can reduce anxiety and build confidence by successfully completing a speech course.

confident about? What subject areas would I like to know more about? Go to the library and leaf through some magazines that interest you. Write down some ideas under a few different subject headings. Look at these rough outlines and decide which areas you want to pursue.

But whatever you do, *do something.*[15] Distract yourself from apprehension by performing constructive activities. Even if you do something that you may think is insignificant—sketching a rough list of ideas or doing a few deep breathing exercises to relax—you will help yourself. Remember that apprehension is circular; it feeds on itself and defeats your growth. Develop an active program that helps you to make progress toward your goal. When you adopt constructive behavior, you will begin to forget your worries and start advancing toward your objective of successful speech-making.

Maintain a Healthy Body

Exercise can help us to relax and reduce stress. If you jog, lift weights, do aerobics, participate in team sports, or have a consistent exercise program, you are already aware of the tremendous physical and mental benefits you gain from these activities. The night before giving a speech it makes a lot more sense to exercise so that you can relax, feel tired, and get some sleep rather than to drink five cups of coffee in order to stay up all night cramming for the presentation.

Occasionally in speech classes a student will say: "I think I need a couple of tranquilizers to relax before the speech," or "I think I'll fix a good stiff drink to loosen me up." The worst thing you could possibly do is to cloud your head with artificial "remedies" before you perform in public. You can learn to relax naturally rather than chemically. Remember that the body has its own unique chemicals that will give you the shot of energy you need.

In order to speak clearly, you need a clear head. There are even a few exercises you can do to help control your breathing and to relax. Remember that Barbra Streisand listens to relaxation tapes before a performance in order to calm down and "think about positive things." (Two relaxation activities are described at the end of this chapter.) If you don't have an exercise program, this is your excuse to start one. Physical activity can relieve tension and help you to maintain a healthy body.[16]

Be Thoroughly Prepared

One of the best ways to reduce anxiety is to be completely prepared for a speech. Being prepared means that you have worked on every aspect of the speech as much as you possibly can: the research, the outline, and the delivery. When you have selected a subject, you need to thoroughly investigate it. The more research you put into your topic, the more confident you will be when you speak about it. You must also prepare a clear and well-organized outline. When your thoughts are structured into a coherent and logical format you can relax, because you know where you're headed in the speech. It is also important that you practice the speech several times before you deliver it to an audience. While practice doesn't always mean you'll be perfect, it does mean that you will feel more comfortable with the wording of the speech when you're in front of an audience.

Many bright and capable college students do poorly in public speaking simply because they don't take the course seriously enough. The student who rushes into class late, or scribbles an outline down on paper five minutes before the speech, is not respecting the audience or his or her own abilities. If you fail to research your topic, the audience will detect that you are delivering an impromptu rather than a prepared speech. If you don't outline your thoughts, you will be disorganized and rambling. If you don't practice the delivery, you will create unnecessary external noise such as vocalized pauses (and ah's), stumbling over words or sentences, and mannerisms.

There is no substitute for preparation; one thing you can control in a speech is the amount of time you are willing to invest. The more time you spend, the more confidence you will gain; the less time you spend, the more insecurity you'll experience. Careful research, clear organization, and a prepared delivery will help you to build confidence and security in each speaking assignment.

Reward Yourself

One public speaking student was a chronic worrier. She always sat in the front row, taking furious notes on every detail of classroom discussions. After presenting a speech she would focus on her negative points and never give herself credit for doing anything well. During the critique, the instructor would begin to point out some of the positive improvements in her speaking. She would react by saying, "Yes, but I know I did poorly—I just know it! My eye contact was rotten, I had all kinds of mannerisms, and I didn't state my purpose—how much worse can you get? Now I'm really going to have to work doubly hard to improve on the next speech."

It is important to take your public speaking course seriously, but not so seriously that you destroy the educational value of learning. This student was trying so hard that she was actually defeating herself and causing more anxiety.

When you have finally arrived at the night before the speaking assignment and you have done everything you possibly can to prepare, don't create more apprehension by dreading the assignment. Do something nice for yourself. Go out to a movie, go to dinner, or treat yourself to a hot fudge sundae. If it makes sense to prepare thoroughly for a speech, it also makes sense to relax so that you can take your mind off the event. Speaking shouldn't be drudgery—it should be enjoyable and positive.

However, you should reward yourself only if you've worked hard and deserve it. If you have neglected some aspect of preparation or if you have waited until the last minute to cram for the speech, don't reward your negligence. If you have been successful, reward the success and you'll look forward to the next speaking event.

Let Go of Mistakes

You must face the fact that sometimes you will make mistakes when you speak in public. When you make a mistake, analyze it, understand it, and then let go of it. Life goes on. You'll have another chance to improve.

Even presidents make speaking mistakes that they'd like to forget. In a 1976 televised debate with Governor Jimmy Carter, President Ford mistakenly stated that there is "no Soviet domination of Eastern Europe." Four years later, President Carter said in a debate with Governor Ronald Reagan, "I had a discussion with my daughter Amy the other day [to ask her about] the most important [governing] issue . . . She said she thought it was nuclear weaponry and the control of nuclear arms." Even President Reagan also had his share of speaking errors. While campaigning in the northwest United States, Reagan made the mistake of saying, "Trees cause more pollution than people." And in the 1988 presidential campaign, Vice President Bush misstated the date when he said: "On this day, September 7, 1941, the Japanese attacked Pearl Harbor." (It was in fact December, unfortunately.)

All these speaking mistakes were costly. Ford's and Carter's gaffes contributed to their election losses, and Reagan's error caused his political support in northwest states to falter for a while. Political cartoonists enjoyed ridiculing Bush's brief lapse.

If seasoned professionals can make speaking errors, remember that you are human as well. Don't dwell on the past or on your failures—just try not to repeat them. Whenever you prepare for a new speaking situation, try to profit from both the positive and negative aspects of your past efforts. Don't place too much importance on any one speaking event; each will benefit you in some way if you let it. Life will not end if you make an error—pick yourself up and keep going. Letting go of mistakes helps you to keep your mind on improvement and makes room for success.

Accept Constructive Criticism

You are in a classroom situation where you will probably be asked to evaluate other people. In these evaluations you will critique both positive and negative elements you have found in the speeches. You will be expected to be honest in your critiques but not personal or vindictive. Your classroom instructor wants to build a supportive atmosphere where every student can feel comfortable. You can help in this process if you accept constructive criticism from others. It is important that you listen to each critique as objectively as possible so that you can improve.

Sometimes people block out criticism by being defensive or by exhibiting hostile behavior. Here are a few common statements that block out criticism, create tension, and inhibit growth:

Criticism in this class is destroying me.

I don't have poor eye contact—I don't care what anybody says.

I've seen good speakers slouch in public, and it doesn't bother me at all.

Politicians read their speeches word for word so why can't I?

I already know enough about public speaking and I'm not going to learn much of anything in this class.

Speaking is a snap—all you have to do is throw a few things together.

People in this class don't know anything anyway, so why should I pay any attention to them?

Who do these people think they are, telling me what's wrong with my speeches?

I'll just sit here and let everybody say what they please. It doesn't matter anyway.

These types of comments can cause tension in a classroom and can be harmful to the individual who states them. Individuals who cannot accept constructive criticism cannot look at themselves honestly and cannot grow—they are held captive by their fear.

Help yourself and your class by allowing yourself to hear and absorb constructive criticism. Remember that criticism is meant to promote success and to help you overcome failure. Criticism might be hard to absorb at first, but you'll learn to develop the ability to bounce back and improve after hearing critiques of your speeches. If you accept constructive criticism you will help to create a positive classroom environment, and you will also help to reduce tension within yourself.

TAKING RESPONSIBILITY TO REDUCE APPREHENSION

Begin to adopt this eight-point plan (summarized below) to reduce apprehension as you prepare to build your first speech. This approach can help you to overcome your anxiety by getting your mind on other issues related to the speech. When you use this plan actively, you'll begin to feel more confident. Recognize that reading theory is easy, but making theory work is totally up to you.

SUMMARY

Most people fear public speaking, as several studies and McCroskey's research into communication apprehension have concluded. You must understand your fear and utilize the eight-point plan to help control and reduce your apprehension:

1. Accept your fear honestly and face it.
2. Learn to develop positive attitudes.
3. Adopt constructive behavior.
4. Maintain a healthy body.
5. Be prepared for your speaking experiences.
6. Reward yourself when you succeed.
7. Let go of mistakes.
8. Accept constructive criticism.

It is important for you to take responsibility for yourself and your own growth in public speaking by putting this program into effect.

SKILL BUILDERS

1. Here are two breathing exercises that can help you to relax.

   EXERCISE 1

   a. Place your hand over your abdomen (diaphragm area).
   b. Take a deep breath—you should feel your diaphragm expand as you inhale (if you are breathing properly).
   c. Now hold the breath for just two or three seconds.
   d. Exhale very slowly, vocalizing on the word "who" until your breath is almost extinguished.
   e. Repeat this cycle once again.

   Do the exercise two or three times before you rehearse a speech. This exercise helps to develop breath control and also helps to relax the stomach muscles.

EXERCISE 2

a. Breathe in and focus on one specific area of body tension.

b. As you breathe out, relax that specific area.

c. Progress through each muscle group of the body until your entire body is completely relaxed.

Muscle groups of the body to incorporate in the exercise:

Face and neck

Shoulders and arms

Chest and lungs

Stomach area

Hips, legs, and feet

This exercise helps you to relax the entire body.[17]

2. Keep a journal of your feelings as you progress through your speech course. After each major speaking assignment, compare what you've written with the previous assignment and determine if there has been any positive change.

3. Make a list of all of the fears you have about giving a speech. Take a close look at your "fears list" and then write a counter list of positive ideas that represent opposites to the fears. Put this positive list in the cover of your text or notebook and take a look at it before every speech, or every time you get ready to develop a speech.

4. Go to the library or ask your instructor for several suggested books that provide you with a number of stress-reduction exercises. Develop a breathing exercise, a mental exercise, and a physical exercise that will help you to cope with tension before every speech.

5. Divide up your class into groups of two individuals. Interview each other to find out some facts that each of you considers to be significant. Each person should prepare a two-minute speech that will acquaint the classroom audience with the individual.

6. Prepare a two-minute speech about one of your own interests, hobbies, or experiences. Write a rough outline on notecards, then practice the delivery so that you are confident before you present it to your class.

7. Divide your class into two teams. Play the game "Win, Lose, or Draw" using speech terms, famous historical or contemporary speakers, and current events as the topics.

NOTES

1. Donnie Radcliffe, *Simply Barbara Bush* (New York: Warner Books, 1989), pp. 157–158.

2. See the following articles that describe this event: Stephen Wigler, "When Memory Fails, Great Musicians Have Ways of

Coping," *The Evening Sun* (Baltimore), July 17, 1994, "Features," p. 3H, and Stephen Wigler, "There's No Comeback in Van Cliburn's Tour," *The Evening Sun* (Baltimore), August 21, 1994, "Features," p. 1H.

3. Jean Seligmann, Tessa Namuth, and Mark Miller, "Drowning on Dry Land," *Newsweek,* May 23, 1994, p. 64.

4. Ibid.

5. "Fears." Conducted by Bruskin Associates for Whittle Communications, Inc., 1986.

6. W. H. Jones, "Situational Factors in Shyness." American Psychological Association, Toronto. Used by permission.

7. William Manchester, *The Death of a President, November 20–November 25* (New York: Harper and Row, 1967), p. 85.

8. Hans Selye, *Stress Without Distress* (Philadelphia: J. B. Lippincott, 1974), p. 38.

9. James C. McCroskey, "Oral Communication Apprehension: A Summary of Recent Theory and Research," *Human Communication Research* 4 (Fall 1977), pp. 78–96.

10. James C. McCroskey, "The Implementation of a Large-Scale Program of Systematic Desensitization for Communication Apprehension," *The Speech Teacher* 21 (1972), pp. 255–264. This article provides a detailed description of the process that McCroskey followed to help people who experienced high levels of communication apprehension.

11. Albert Ellis, and Robert Harper, *A New Guide to Rational Living* (Englewood Cliffs: Prentice Hall, 1975), pp. 102–112.

12. Susan R. Glaser, "Oral Communication Apprehension and Avoidance: The Current Status of Treatment Research," *Communication Education* 30 (October 1981), p. 330.

13. Maxie C. Maultsby Jr., "Emotional Reeducation," in *Handbook of Rational–Emotive Therapy,* ed. Albert Ellis and Russell Grieger (New York: Springer Publishing, 1977), pp. 231–247.

14. James Elliot, from speaking notes used in speech class, Carroll Community College, 1989. Used by permission.

15. Claire Weekes, *Peace from Nervous Suffering* (New York: Hawthorn Books, Inc., 1972), pp. 69–73.

16. Dorothy Dusek-Girdano, "Stress Reduction Through Physical Activity," in *Controlling Stress and Tension,* ed. Daniel A. Girdano, and George S. Everly Jr. (Englewood Cliffs: Prentice Hall, Inc., 1979), pp. 220–231.

17. This exercise is based on a relaxation activity provided in Edward A. Charlesworth's and Ronald Nathan's *Stress Management—A Guide to Comprehensive Wellness* (Houston: Biobehavioral Publishers, 1982), p. 89.

Chapter 6

CONSIDERING THE ETHICS OF PUBLIC SPEAKING

"Honesty is the first chapter of the book of wisdom."

Thomas Jefferson

CHAPTER OBJECTIVES

After reading this chapter you will be able to:

1. Recognize the need for ethics in society;

2. Evaluate a speaker's ethics;

3. Develop and apply ethical standards in speech analysis.

K EY   T E R M S

Code of ethics
Ethos
Elements of virtue
Hidden agenda

"I want you to listen to me. I'm going to say this again. I did not have sexual relations with that woman, Miss Lewinsky. I never told anybody to lie, not a single time—never. These allegations are false. And I need to go back to work for the American people." These words, uttered by President Clinton at a news conference on January 27, 1998, were a factor in a painful process that led to the approval of Articles of Impeachment in the House of Representatives and an impeachment trial against the President in the Senate.[1]

The impeachment process raised numerous ethical questions for almost everyone involved on all sides of the issue. Should the President resign because of his private actions and public denials? Should a President's personal actions be subjected to the same careful scrutiny as his or her public behavior? Was the forty-million-dollar investigation conducted by Special Prosecutor Kenneth Starr overzealous and vindictive? Should politicians such as House Speaker-elect Bob Livingston and Judiciary Chair Henry Hyde who were forced to confess past marital infidelities be allowed to sit in judgment on the same kind of indiscretion?[2]

The ethical turmoil surrounding the impeachment process prompted Sanford Ungar, dean of the School of Communication at American University, to make these observations: "There's virtually no zone of privacy left for any public official. And there are many co-conspirators in creating that situation—politicians themselves, the media, the Internet. . . . This town has gone nuts."[3]

Although there may not be clear-cut answers to all these questions, it is critical for the speakers and listeners to consider the ethics of public speaking. We will examine the need for ethics, suggest ways to evaluate a speaker's ethics, and recommend some choices as you develop your own speaking standards.

THE NEED FOR ETHICS IN SOCIETY

Interest in ethics and in ethical codes has been around for a long time. Centuries ago, Aristotle referred to character, which he called *ethos,* as "the most potent means of persuasion."[4] He also identified "elements of virtue" as "justice, courage, temperance, magnificence, magnanimity, liberality, gentleness, prudence, and wisdom."[5] These elements defined a clear code of ethical conduct for speakers in Greek society. Centuries before the Greeks, according to the Bible, God gave Moses the Ten Commandments on Mount Sinai. They were not, as TV commentator Ted Koppel has humorously observed, the "Ten Suggestions"; they were, in fact, a guide for living.[6] In Roman times, the emperor Justinian revised the law for his empire. He was the first to incorporate ethics into the legal system and establish schools to educate lawyers concerning ethics, morality, and law. Medieval Germanic tribes recognized the need for ethical conduct and enacted the Salic Laws to codify common law and guide relationships. Following Justinian's example, Napoleon simplified French law and established a code of thirty-six statutes based on the concept that all citizens, regardless of circumstances of birth or social stature, should be treated fairly and equally. One of the most famous and widely respected documents is the American Bill of Rights, which identifies and guarantees our basic democratic freedoms. Indeed, every civilization has recognized the need for establishing laws and codes to guide human relationships and behavior.[7]

As we look at contemporary American life, however, it is often difficult to comprehend our ethical heritage. The 1970s, for instance, were labeled by the writer Tom Wolfe as "the Me Decade." As the economy prospered in the 1980s, scandals seemed to plague almost every aspect of society. Cincinnati Reds hero Pete Rose was ejected from baseball for gambling activities, and then sentenced to five months in jail for tax evasion. Washington Redskins defensive end Dexter Manley was banned from football for life as a result of his drug abuse. Wall Street stockbroker Michael Milken, who became wealthy trading in "junk bonds," was sentenced to ten years for insider trading. TV evangelist Jim Bakker was convicted on twenty-four counts of diverting monies from his "Praise The Lord" ministry to private use. Advisors to President Reagan were investigated for supposedly violating congressional laws in an arms-for-hostages deal. Senator Joseph Biden withdrew from a presidential campaign because of accusations he had plagiarized a speech, and Senator Gary Hart dropped out following a sex scandal.

Ethical questions continued to haunt public figures in the 1990s. Representative Dan Rostenkowski, former chairman of the powerful House Ways and Means Committee, was accused of a "pattern of corruption that spanned three decades."[8] He pled guilty to two counts of mail fraud and was sentenced to seventeen months in jail. Congresswoman Enid Waldholtz of Utah was not reelected because of alleged illegal campaign contributions and other financial difficulties, which she publicly blamed on her husband.[9] House Speaker Newt Gingrich was forced to return a $4.5 million publishing advance because of the appearance of a conflict of interest.[10] Benjamin F. Chavis was fired as executive director of the National Association for the Advancement of Colored People for secretly paying $332,000 in NAACP funds to settle a potential sex discrimination lawsuit.[11] William Aramony, president of United Way of America, had to resign because of his extravagant spending and questionable management practices of the well-known charity.[12] Organizers who successfully won the 2002 Winter Olympics for Salt Lake City were accused of using bribes to influence the International Olympic Committee's decision.[13] And at the beginning of this chapter, we mentioned House Speaker-elect Bob

Livingston who resigned because of a previous marital indiscretion and President Clinton who withstood an unsuccessful attempt to remove him from office because of his personal actions and misleading public statements about the Monica Lewinsky scandal.

The trend in decision making where self-interest is emphasized more than right and wrong inspired writers of *Scholastic Update* to explore ethics in a 1999 article entitled, "Values in America."[14] It is clear that ethics continues to be an issue.

EVALUATING A SPEAKER'S ETHICS

It is apparent that the speaker and audience have special commitments regarding ethics in public speaking. It is the speaker's responsibility to practice ethics in every aspect of speech development, and it is the listener's obligation to determine whether the speaker lives up to ethical standards. Our purpose is not to prescribe rules or behavior, but to raise important issues pertaining to ethics and suggest areas for your consideration. We begin by analyzing a speaker's honesty, reliability, motivation, and policies.

Honesty and the Speaker

Our society places strong emphasis on honesty at all levels. The Constitution requires that the president swear to a thirty-six-word oath of office to "preserve, protect, and defend the laws and Constitution of the United States." Courtroom witnesses must swear to tell "all the truth, and nothing but the truth." Contractual agreements are signed and sealed before notaries to reinforce the truthfulness of statements contained in the documents. Similarly, wedding ceremonies include vows of mutual love, loyalty, and fidelity, which couples pledge for a lifetime.

Too often, however, speakers violate these standards causing devastating consequences. Speakers who mislead or lie to the public not only undermine their own credibility but also contribute to the erosion of public confidence in national offices and institutions as well. When probing the break-in of Democratic Party headquarters, Watergate investigators asked, "What did President Nixon know, and when did he know it?" The sad answer was that Nixon engaged in a conspiracy to cover up the burglary. The House Judiciary Committee approved articles of impeachment, and Nixon was forced to resign from office. Upon assuming the presidency, Gerald Ford observed, "Truth is the glue that holds governments together. . . . Our Constitution works."[15] Unfortunately, the Watergate scandal seriously eroded public confidence in government, and it was years before this trust was restored.

This hypothetical example, based on a factual experience, demonstrates how dishonesty can affect the lives of human beings with tragic results:

> A manufacturing plant is in full compliance with local laws concerning the emission of toxic substances. One of the company's own scientific experts, however, has discovered new research indicating that the cumulative effects of plant emissions could pose serious health hazards to the public. Furthermore, if public officials knew about the information, they would enact stricter laws that would force the company to close in order to make drastic changes costing almost $1 million. Arguing that a plant shutdown would contribute to severe economic loss for the company, employees, and community, executives decide to say nothing to local government officials about the new research. In addition, they demote their scientific expert, reprimand him for insubordination, and arrange for him to be transferred to another state. Still complying with local laws, the plant continues to emit toxins, now posing potentially devastating effects on the unknowing citizens of the community.[16]

The unethical speaker, like these executives, often rationalizes dishonesty on the basis of protecting the welfare of the community or another individual, when in fact the lie is self-serving. In this example, the temporary hardship of the plant shutdown was of little significance when weighed against the long-term health effects of poisoning the community. Here, inaction and lack of truthfulness served the convenience of the executives and led to serious consequences.

There are occasions, however, when decisions pertaining to honesty are not so clear-cut. In 1976, Governor Jimmy Carter ran for president on the slogan, "I will never tell a lie."[17] Is this a realistic slogan in a presidential campaign? Are there times when presidents must choose between two evils to protect the lives of American troops or even ordinary citizens? Are there occasions when the president must withhold information, or give partial answers to questions from journalists, for national security reasons?

Situations we face in our personal lives can also pose ethical dilemmas When a family member is hospitalized with a terminal illness, what information should the patient be told? Should the patient be fully informed as to the extent of the incurable disease? Should the doctor or family withhold some data, thereby giving the individual false hope? Might the bad information help the patient to resolve emotions and relationships—or instead contribute to further deterioration?

Here is a hypothetical situation where the speakers made personal decisions about communication that led to devastating results.

> When Benjamin turned sixteen, his parents adopted an infant they named Eva. After much discussion, the parents decided that it would be in the best interest of their little girl never to tell her about the adoption. They swore Benjamin to secrecy and advised him that family silence was necessary to protect his sister, allowing her to live a more secure life. Many years

later, at the age of fifty, Eva became seriously ill with cancer and was informed by her doctor that she would need a life-saving bone marrow transplant from a close family member. Eva approached Benjamin, who delivered the astounding news that he could not be the donor because they were not biologically related. Eva was now forced to deal with anger over a lifetime of dishonesty in addition to her pain over the catastrophic illness.[18]

The speakers in this case may have had the best of intentions for withholding information. But the conspiracy of silence created a situation that led to long-term emotional consequences for the individual.

While honesty is the best policy, you can also see that in some situations, there are no easy answers. Each speaker has the ultimate responsibility of choosing an ethical choice; but it is vitally important that the speaker think carefully and critically about the overall consequences of the choice.

The Reliability of the Speaker

One important standard for ethical evaluation is examining the reliability of the speaker. Audiences make judgments about speakers by measuring actions against words. What is the speaker's record? Does the speaker keep promises? Is the speaker committed to the ideas presented and willing to practice the deeds advocated?

Unfortunately, our political leaders are not always models of reliability. In 1988, Vice President Bush ran for president on the now famous slogan,

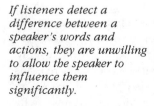

If listeners detect a difference between a speaker's words and actions, they are unwilling to allow the speaker to influence them significantly.

"Read my lips, no new taxes." Four years, a flat economy, and one tax increase later, voters held President Bush accountable for breaking his promise by removing him from office. Pledging to restore ethical standards in government, President Clinton nominated Zoe Baird to be the first female attorney general. At her Senate confirmation hearings, however, the nominee acknowledged that she had hired two illegal immigrants and failed to pay their Social Security taxes. While Baird apologized for her actions, public opinion was strongly against the nomination. Committee senators asked whether an attorney general who had broken the law would be ethically able to enforce the very laws that she had violated. Baird ultimately withdrew her name from nomination.[19] Surgeon General Jocelyn Elders was fired because of her remarks about teaching masturbation in public schools, [20] and New York Senator Alfonse D'Amato had to apologize for his remarks making fun of Judge Lance Ito's Japanese ancestry.[21]

The individuals in these examples are fine Americans, and all have served government or business with distinction. However, these instances indicate the high ethical standards that are expected of many public figures. There are even more blatant examples of speaker unreliability. The Reverend Jimmy Swaggart preached against sin, yet solicited sexual favors from a prostitute. Washington, D.C., Mayor Marion Barry advocated a drug-free city, but was caught using crack cocaine. TV evangelist Jim Bakker asked for sacrificial offerings from loyal viewers, but spent the money on extravagant homes and an air-conditioned doghouse. In Louisiana, David Duke ran for governor pledging to serve all citizens, but his job experience included serving as the Imperial Wizard of the Ku Klux Klan.

When an audience sees that a speaker does not abide by his or her own standards, many listeners are no longer willing to allow the speaker to have a significant influence over their lives.

Reliability once destroyed is difficult to rebuild. However, under certain circumstances, audiences can be forgiving after a period of time. Charles W. Colson, a special assistant in the Nixon administration, was charged with obstruction of justice in a case involving Daniel Ellsberg, a Nixon adversary and an antiwar advocate. Colson, a born-again Christian, pleaded guilty and served almost a year in prison. To many cynical observers, his religious conversion and truth-telling seemed sudden and self-serving. But over a period of years, Mr. Colson has helped hundreds of prison inmates and has established himself as a credible writer, speaker, and director of prison ministries. Colson's experience demonstrates that a "tainted" speaker can regain his credibility in another context.[22]

Even in a public-speaking class, a speaker's words are measured by actions. One student presented an informative speech about the dangers of secondhand smoke. While the material was enlightening, audience members had difficulty taking the topic seriously because sticking out of the speaker's shirt pocket was a pack of cigarettes. Another student delivered an impassioned plea for the homeless. The speaker urged listeners to bring donations of food and clothing to a subsequent class period and assured them that she would distribute the goods at a local shelter. Class members faithfully brought their donations at the appointed time, but the speaker never came to pick them up. Commenting that they felt betrayed by the speaker's lack of commitment, listeners returned home with their gifts. When assuming the role of speaker, you have the opportunity of showing your commitment to an idea. While you are spending time and energy presenting your speech, remember that your audience is also devoting considerable effort to this experience. You can build trust and generate reliability if you are willing to live by your words.

The Speaker's Motivations

One area of ethics that is more difficult to assess is the motivation of a speaker. While the stated purpose may be obvious to an audience, there may also be an unstated objective, often called a *hidden agenda*. These internal agendas are present in all of us and they can be positive motivators. We take notes, study for exams, and maintain constructive relationships with faculty in order to pass courses and obtain degrees. We work hard, form positive relationships with supervisors, and present a neat appearance in order to advance in a company. We seek advancement in our position to provide greater psychological and financial benefits to ourselves and our families.

Problems occur, however, when the agenda is deceptive and would significantly alter audience attitudes if stated openly. Consider this hypothetical example:

> The new boss constantly praises the quality of your work and does everything possible to reward you with special opportunities and quick promotions. Several months down the road, however, you discover that the compliments have become more personal in nature, and eventually develop into inappropriate behavior. You begin to realize that the boss's initial favorable actions prepared the foundation for sexual harassment.

Here, the hidden agenda led to the exploitation and manipulation of the employee. Companies now have policies against such detrimental behavior, yet this deceptive practice still occurs too often in the American workplace.

The following true story occurred several years ago:

> The Sundstrand Corporation, a company known for its high quality of manufacturing, is a major military and engineering contractor for the federal government. A few years ago, the company developed and adopted a code of ethics, which set high standards for pricing, qualitative performance, and

accounting procedures. An investigation into company practices revealed, however, that the corporation engaged in a network of financial conspiracies that included charging the Pentagon for cost overruns, funding executive perks, and providing illegal gifts to government officials. In addition, Sundstrand channeled costs from its commercial business to the government, duplicating those costs in separate accounts, and billing the government. The company pleaded guilty to fraud, conspiracy, and criminal mischarging. It was fined $227.3 million in payments and contract concessions.[23]

The deceptive practices were in direct opposition to the published code of ethics that had been designed to make the company look good to the government and public. Sundstrand's new management succeeded in restoring a degree of trust, but the dishonesty caused the company severe damage.

Agendas are not always so hidden, and often members of an audience can easily assess a speaker's motivation. When hurricane Andrew devastated south Florida, over 100,000 people were left without homes, food, or clothing. Immediately after the storm, unscrupulous entrepreneurs sold water at $10 a gallon, exploiting the disaster.[24]

In this situation, the entrapped victims had no choice but to pay the high prices to survive. When a reputable business encourages its employees to give to worthy charities, such as the American Cancer Society or the Red Cross, the company is demonstrating its social responsibility. But if company officials tell workers that there will be "unpleasant repercussions" for not making donations, the organization is openly engaging in exploitive tactics.

The Unabomber, who published a 35,000-word manifesto claiming to be concerned about technology's exploitation of society, used the same technology to make pipe bombs that killed three people and injured twenty-three others over a seventeen-year period.[25] In 1986 millionaire stockbroker Ivan Boesky publicly declared that "greed is good," but later pleaded guilty to filing false statements with the Securities and Exchange Commission, including insider trading and stock manipulation.[26] So too, did real-estate millionaire and hotel queen Leona Helmsley openly proclaim that "only little people pay taxes." Such obvious motivations are no less harmful than hidden deceptions.

Analyze a speaker carefully. Listen actively to stated objectives and read between the lines. Go beyond verbal pronouncements and evaluate the speaker's reasons for making a presentation. Examine the relationship between a speaker's public declarations and personal activities. Are the public and private actions the same, or is there a difference between what the speaker says and what the speaker does? Know the speaker's background and proceed with caution before trusting information or submitting to persuasion.

The Speaker's Policies

A good indicator of a speaker's ethical standards are the policies and actions the individual recommends. Does the speaker exhibit concern for the welfare of the audience? Does the speaker advocate choices that are helpful to listeners? Does the speaker propose solutions that benefit society?

Unfortunately, America has its share of extremist groups such as neonazis, skinheads, antigovernment militia, Klansmen, and street gangs who openly preach and practice hatred, fear, and violence. An equally dangerous problem exists with groups who claim to be fighting for justice but encourage prejudice and engage in damaging behavior. Some extreme anti-abortionists condone the bombing or burning of abortion clinics "to save the lives of the unborn." Some speakers who believe homosexuality is a sin engage in gay-bashing and advocate discrimination in housing and employment. Racial violence is sometimes viewed by minorities as a justifiable remedy for past wrongdoing or present injustice. Speakers who advocate prejudice, hatred, stereotypes, law-breaking, or violence are not promoting ethical solutions to problems and show little compassion for the welfare of human beings.

A student presented a persuasive speech actuating audience members to buy radar detectors. He reasoned that "radar detectors will help you to avoid speeding tickets, get you to your destination more quickly, and allow you to enjoy driving at whatever speed your heart desires!" Another speaker demonstrated how to make fake identity cards. The student explained how to copy false information, forge signatures, and laminate the phony document, making it appear realistic. She concluded her speech with the lines, "So remember, if you're underage and you want to get into that really neat club, you've got a solution—a fake I.D. You'll be able to drink as much as you want because nobody will be able to throw you out!"

These speeches are extremely unethical because the speakers are asking the audience to violate laws. In the first example, the speaker failed to mention that radar detectors are illegal in many states and seemed unconcerned that in using them his listeners could seriously injure themselves or others. The second speaker displayed similar disregard for her audience. Not only did she advocate making a counterfeit identification card, she also avoided describing the possibility of fines or jail sentences as penalties for possessing such a document. Finally, she seemed unconcerned about the physical consequences of drinking "as much as you want . . ." Both speakers lacked a sense of social responsibility and were indifferent to the potentially damaging results of their recommendations.

Examine the policies that a speaker promotes. Think about the results of ideas or actions that a speaker recommends. Observe whether the speaker is interested in the well-being of the audience and analyze the extent to which the speaker demonstrates concern for the well-being of society.

APPLYING ETHICAL STANDARDS

We have explored several ethical issues and examined some examples of unethical practice. It is now up to you as a speaker to formulate your own ethical standards. We suggest that you consider the following areas: honesty, concern for the audience, your motivations for speaking, and a personal code of ethics.

Be Honest

When you are building a presentation, be straightforward in every phase of speech development. Research information thoroughly, making sure that your material is accurate. Be sure that your research is complete and that you have taken the necessary time and energy to examine all the relevant sources. As you outline, be fair in reporting the data. Don't withhold portions of examples, statistics, or quotations if they are unfavorable to your ideas or viewpoints, but present these supporting materials in context. Stay away from twisting, distorting, or fabricating evidence if you can't find information to back up your issues. When you deliver the speech, give proper credit for direct quotations, and paraphrase information in your own words to avoid plagiarism. Here are some examples of quoted, paraphrased, and plagiarized material.

DIRECT QUOTATION

"According to Paul O. Sand, Executive Director of the National Conference of Christians and Jews (quote), 'Very real ethical issues can also be found in reports about persons rifling through the desks of their in-house competitors searching for something to be used against them.' "[27]

PARAPHRASED PASSAGE

"Paul O. Sand, Executive Director of the National Conference of Christians and Jews, mentions an example of unethical behavior when employees rummage through the desks of their colleagues looking for damaging information which can discredit or betray them."

PLAGIARIZED PASSAGE

"Ethical issues are found in reports about people who rifle through the desks of their competitors searching for something to be used against them."

In the direct quotation, the speaker gives credit to the author and restates the exact words by setting up the passage with the word "quote." In the paraphrase, the speaker uses different words to convey the intention of the author. The plagiarized passage merely eliminates a few words, but retains the original wording of the author. Notice also that the speaker presents no reference to the source of the material. The audience is led to believe that the words originated with the speaker. However, the passage would still be considered plagiarism even if the speaker added the name of the author to the last example. We emphasize that *a passage is plagiarized when the original wording is not changed or altered enough to recap the ideas in the speaker's own language.*

Be willing to take the necessary time to develop your speech. Avoid cutting corners or taking shortcuts that are unethical and dishonest. Give credit to the appropriate sources or individuals for materials, handouts, and audiovisuals used in the speech. At all times, provide honest information and present information honestly.

Advocate Ideas That Benefit Others

There are numerous topics and many points of view that are appropriate for speeches. Many controversial issues will generate a variety of opinions among listeners and often strong disagreement. We would expect such diversity of ideas in a free and open democracy. We have already examined how public speaking can be used as a weapon to promote hatred, injustice, and law-breaking. As you approach topics and strategies for speeches, ask yourself some questions:

Do you have any hidden agendas or ulterior motives for speaking?

How would you feel if a particular strategy or topic was used on you as a member of the audience?

Do your ideas and recommendations benefit society?

Do the actions you promote help people to work together toward solutions?

Are you careful to avoid stereotyping groups, individuals, or cultures?

Do you stay away from tactics that include name-calling or offensive language?

Do you respect the needs and values of your audience?

Do you care about people and do you demonstrate that concern in your speech?

Evaluate Your Motives for Speaking

All of us need to present positive images to gain acceptance from others. But as a speaker, you have more encompassing needs to meet than simply your own ego fulfillment. Before approaching the setting of your speech, carefully examine your motives for making the presentation. Determine whether or not your principal objectives are entirely self-serving, or if your motivations include interest in others.

Speakers are often tempted to exploit difficult situations for profit. Convicted felons who have been prominent politicians, religious leaders, sports figures, or entertainers often earn huge salaries on the lecture or talk-show circuit discussing their latest books or escapades. Such behavior is questionable and demeaning to the speaker-audience relationship unless the speaker can demonstrate that the objective is to educate others to avoid similar criminal activity.

Be willing to stand for principle rather than compromise your values to gain quick audience approval. Recognize that resisting opposition is often difficult and assumes a great deal of a speaker's energy. When you are in the right, there are benefits to both speaker and listeners. In the spring of 1992, Los Angeles exploded into a riot after a jury found four white police officers "not guilty" in the beating of an intoxicated, speeding driver named Rodney King. During this riot, Reginald Denny, a white truck driver, was stopped while hauling a load of sand and gravel through an intersection in south-central Los Angeles. He was pulled from his truck by several black males, and severely kicked and beaten. Other black citizens who had been watching the incident on television came to Denny's assistance and rushed him to the hospital.[28]

These heroic individuals looked beyond color to risk their lives for a fellow human being. Their actions took great courage, yet became a reassuring symbol to millions of Americans who anguished over racial tensions. Such speakers suffer initial setbacks, but often reap psychological rewards and satisfaction as a result of their bravery. Take responsibility and be true to yourself. Avoid the hypocrisy of disguising questionable motives with superficial appeals. Make sure that your stated objectives and internal goals are in harmony. Constantly ask yourself, "What have I to give," rather than, " What have I to gain?"

Develop a Speaking Code of Ethics

According to a study by the Conference Board, more than 75 percent of the companies surveyed have now enacted codes of ethics for their employees.[29] While these codes are not necessarily the Ten Commandments, they are standards which act as guides for ethical behavior and practice.

In a speech to a conference on business ethics, Richard R. Capen Jr., vice chairman of Knight-Ridder, Inc., a publishing company, related his recommendations for an ethical code in business.[30] They are reproduced here *verbatim:*

1. *Build trust.* Getting along in today's pluralistic world starts with trust. Trust is an ultimate value that protects an orderly, civilized society from chaos and anarchy. Trust in marriage. Trust at work. Trust among friends. Trust in public life. Trust is never guaranteed. It must be constructed carefully, nurtured vigorously and reinforced daily.
2. *Be optimistic.* Attitude in the process of serving others is important. Often what happens in our lives comes down to the way we look at life. If we believe it will be a lousy day, it will be. If we believe there is no hope, the chances are there will be no hope. . . . On the other hand, if we believe we can win, the chances are we will. If we think we can make a difference in life, we will. The difference between such success—and failure—is usually a matter of attitude.
3. *Be an encourager.* Each week, dozens cross our paths crying out for help, for love, for encouragement. For them, it's a challenging, lonely world, and such people desperately need our love. In my business, I'm surrounded by special opportunities—big and small—to be a thoughtful listener, an enthusiastic encourager, a caring advisor, a special friend.
4. *Lead by personal example.* To be the best, leaders must be truthful and candid. They must be decisive and courageous. They must keep promises and be loyal to their family, friends, employees, clients, and country.

We present these ideas as only a suggestion as you think about a speaking code. Whether you adopt Capen's model, the Golden Rule, or another viewpoint, begin to develop an ethical framework to guide you through the process of building your presentations. Remember that it is up to you as a speaker to set a responsible standard as you convey ideas and recommend actions to the members of your audience. Good speaking means good ethics.

The Right Way: A Matter of Principle

James E. Perrella presented the following speech to business students at the University of Illinois in Chicago. As an executive vice president of the Ingersoll-Rand Company, a construction manufacturing business, Perrella demonstrates his knowledge of business and ethics as he raises some important issues for the audience. In this edited speech, the speaker conveys a concern about his topic and an interest in the ethical choices of America's future business leaders.[31]

A Persuasive Speech

JAMES E. PERRELLA

1 To create suspense, the speaker avoids stating the topic until the last line of the introductory paragraph. The speaker identifies his topic.

1 Good afternoon. Professor McLimore's invitation to participate in this course with you today stirred a great deal of reflection as to the best subject for discussion. The number and variety of possible subjects seemed endless. Many subjects. Many ideas. Many possible directions. In this sea of subjects, one topic surfaced. It is a topic much in the news, a topic that affects our attitudes, a topic that touches our lives: Business ethics.

2 The speaker cites two instances and refers to an article.

2 Think about it for a minute. If you approach the subject, business ethics, in terms of Ivan Boesky or Dallas's J. R. Ewing, you may believe that "business ethics" is an oxymoron, or, as an article in *The Wall Street Journal* suggested, that "business" and "ethics" are mutually exclusive. Today, we need to ask: Are they?

3 Perrella uses the humorous quote to support the point that fact and fiction suggest businesspeople are unethical.

3 Certainly, in fact and fiction, there is much that says business is not ethical, and stories that even suggest that businessmen cannot operate ethically. Consider the case of Daniel Drew, a New York cattleman of the early nineteenth century. Stuart Holbrook tells the story in *The Age of The Moguls,* Mr. Drew "seems never to have denied his most celebrated piece of knavery, which he used for many years in his cattle business. As a big herd of anywhere from six hundred to a thousand head of Ohio beef approached New York City, Drew had his drovers salt them well. Then, just before reaching the marketplace, he let them drink their fill. Cattle were sold liveweight. Drew's processing with salt and water added many tons

to the average herd. 'Watered stock' soon became a term on Wall Street."

4-5 The speaker draws a conclusion from the story and relates it to today's business world.

4 Mr. Drew seemed a follower of a nineteenth-century parody of the Golden Rule: "Do unto the other feller the way he'd like to do unto you, an' do it fust."

5 Mr. Drew's motives and actions can fit well with motives and actions prevalent in today's business world, or should I say, in today's world.

6 We seem to put ourselves first. Or try to. At almost any cost. The extreme of this "me-first" attitude is the drug addict who will take advantage of anyone and anything to satisfy his insatiable craving.

7 The speaker uses a series of interesting hypothetical examples which successfully connect to listeners.

7 Think, for a moment, about every-day situations as well: The driver who tries to move ahead of other cars at every traffic light. The green grocer who puts the reddest strawberries on the top of the basket. The person who insists always on having the last word in any domestic argument. The doctor who prescribes more and more tests, not necessarily for the patient's benefit, but for protection against a possible malpractice claim. The salesman who thinks more of his commission than of his customer's needs. The student—certainly not anyone here— who cheats on an exam to gain a higher grade or rank. The politician who steals another's speech to make himself sound better or wiser. The individual who pays a tip to the maitre d' to get preferred seating. In every case, the action is a me-first action.

8 Me first. A likely, or as many would say, the source of ethics problems.

9 Perrella poses a question to stimulate thinking.

9 In your career development, as you become our nation's business leaders, you will face the question: May business people use any means, fair or foul, to make a sale, to insure success, to take advantage of a customer, or to do a competitor in? In other words, to put themselves first.

10 He mentions two examples of unethical business "shenanigans."

10 In business, the Ivan Boesky/Drexel Burnham Lambert shenanigans keep reappearing in the nation's headlines. A recent lawsuit charges that Boeing used bogus misbranded bearings in commercial and military aircraft.

11 Does the speaker

11 While all sorts of special situations of this type have arisen, many people, I am pleased to say, still do things the

adequately support these generalities?

old-fashioned way. In fact, many people still depend on a handshake to seal an agreement. A man's word is his bond. In many negotiations people trust each other completely. Even in complex business transactions. In today's business world, handshake deals have not disappeared. They are fewer, however, as people depend on written warranties and guarantees and exclusions and warnings in the most confusing language and in the tiniest type. In fact, "put it in writing" is a common request, accompanying the purchase of anything—from a baby buggy to a used car.

12 **The speaker makes a good point, but does it require more evidence?**

12 Lawyers love it. They sue people and companies. They defend. They challenge. They appeal. They seem to relish new opportunities in every business transaction. They try to put their clients, and themselves, first.

13 **Again, the speaker uses questions to get listeners to think.**

13 At the same time, they pose a new question for businessmen. They replace the question about business activity: "Is it right?"—with "Is it legal?"

14 This trend, developing over years, as attorneys try to protect their clients in an ever more complex business world, has created a division between morality and legality, weakening, if not dissipating, the strength and significance of once-prevalent handshake agreements.

15 **The speaker continues to employ questions as a technique to involve the audience.**

15 In our Western civilization, laws and morals have strengthened each other since the time of Moses. Until now. Our question of today should be, What's the right thing to do? The right way to behave? The right way to conduct business? Don't just ask, Is it legal?

16 **He uses two hypothetical situations to promote critical thinking.**

16 Let me be the first to admit that the choice is not always easy. Consider, for instance, these questions from Scruples, a Milton Bradley game: The garage forgets to charge you for a six-dollar oil filter. You think the labor charge is too high, anyway. Do you mention the undercharge? In a parking lot you accidentally dent a car. Do you leave a note? You are applying for a job requiring experience you don't have. Do you claim you do?

17 **The speaker describes a simple ethical standard.**

17 Questions of this sort reach beyond legality. They raise the question or right versus wrong, not legal versus illegal. The answers require no legal knowledge. They required only common sense and the sense of fair play that we all learned as

youngsters. You remember. I remember. Don't cheat. Don't steal. Don't lie. Don't take advantage of anyone's weakness. The Golden Rule. Do unto others the way you would have them do unto you. In other words, treat the other guy fair. That's the way to solve all ethics problems.

18 The speaker uses gender to connect to listeners. He resolves his earlier hypothetical examples, showing the positive results of ethical behavior.

18 Have you considered what business would be like if we all did it? If every businessman (and businesswoman) followed the Golden Rule? Ripe, red strawberries would fill a box from top to bottom. Barrels would not contain a single rotten apple. My company would not have to file a complaint with the Federal Trade Commission charging dumping of other bearings in United States markets. Congress would not have to tighten curbs on insider trading. Companies would not have to require employees to sign codes of conduct or establish strict guidelines for purchasing agents to follow. The Harvard Business School would not have to require that each entering student take a three-week course on business ethics. Drexel, Burnham, Lambert would not have to pay a $650 million fine.

19 Many people, including many business leaders, would argue that such an application of ethics to business would adversely affect bottom-line performance.

20 I say nay. The ideas we are considering today go far beyond the bottom line.

21 The speaker uses three concrete examples of companies that have provided ethical leadership.

21 If we do things right, because that's the way to do things, just imagine the effect we will have on customers. Mr. Iacocca showed the beginnings of the possibilities when he led Chrysler in new directions. Johnson and Johnson set a solid example when it pulled Tylenol off the shelves immediately during the crisis of a few years ago. H. J. Heinz and Squibb established a high standard of ethical excellence when they supported our nation's Pure Food and Drug laws early in this century. In these situations, the businesses and their leaders put the public and their customers first.

22-23 He uses repetition to make a case for "good ethics." In his conclusion, the speaker challenges the audience. He points out that their actions can lead

22 I ask you to imagine the effect on the bottom lines of tomorrow if business were to follow these examples today. Good ethics, simply, is good business. Good ethics will attract investors. Good ethics will attract good employees. Moreover, good ethics will attract and retain customers, employees, investors, and build a quality reputation.

23 As you begin your careers, please remember that you set your own standards. Your actions can lead to a Chrysler turnaround or to a Wedtech.

to positive
or negative busi-
ness ethics.

24 While his point
of view is clear,
he allows the
listener to make
the final, "crit-
ical choice."

24 In a real sense, the future is up to you. You can change the way things are done. You can make the critical choice. You can do what's right. Not because of conduct codes. Not because of rules or laws. But you know what's right. I will applaud your decision.

The Tobacco Hearings

Brenda Little was given an assignment by her speech instructor to present a three- to five-minute speech on an ethical issue. As Brenda searched for a topic, she came across several news articles that reported the proceedings of a congressional hearing about tobacco addiction. Brenda, a former smoker, became more involved in the topic as she read the testimony of tobacco executives and then recalled her personal struggles with cigarettes. She developed the following brief speech, which contrasts the testimony of tobacco executives with some of the facts regarding cigarette addiction. As you read the speech, notice how the speaker arranges the evidence to support her thesis. Ask yourself these questions: Why is the speech informative or persuasive? Why does the speaker use so many direct quotes in the presentation? Would the speech be more effective as a longer presentation, or would an audience be sufficiently influenced by the speech as it is?[32]
Brenda Little

1 The speaker
begins with
a quote from
tobacco offi-
cials. Brenda
presents a two-
point thesis
statement.

1 "Cigarettes are not addictive and we do not manipulate the nicotine content of our tobacco products." These were the statements made by seven leading tobacco company executives. Because of allegations that cigarette manufacturers manipulate the levels of nicotine in their products, the House Subcommittee on Health and the Environment held a hearing on April 14, 1994. I'd like you to know what some of the tobacco executives said at that Congressional hearing and then describe some of the facts about nicotine addiction.

2 To support the
first numeral of
the body, the
speaker uses di-
rect quotations
as her principal
supporting

2 The following excerpts are from testimony given by several executives and reported in April and June '94 issues of the Baltimore *Evening Sun* and a May 1994 issue of *Science News*. Listen to James W. Johnston, chief executive officer of R. J. Reynolds Tobacco, Inc., who stated: "We do not do anything to hook smokers or to keep them hooked. We no more manipulate nicotine in cigarettes than coffee manufacturers manipulate

materials. Her quotations are from presidents and CEOs of tobacco companies.

caffeine." He went on to say, "There is a world of difference between the irresistible need of the hard-drug addict and a 'strong urge' of a smoker to engage in a pleasurable behavior." And finally he said "Smoking is no more addictive than coffee, tea, or Twinkies."

3 The speaker continues to cite the statements of other tobacco executives. Notice that Brenda uses a quotation from a researcher who was employed by Philip Morris and who supports the views of tobacco executives.

3 Another executive, Thomas E. Sandefur, chairman of Brown and Williamson Tobacco Corp., charged that the government was making false allegations that companies use nicotine to hook smokers. He said, "Dr. Kessler suggested that cigarette manufacturers 'commonly add nicotine to cigarettes to deliver specific amounts of nicotine.' Brown and Williamson has never done that . . ." After dismissing the allegations, Mr. Sandefur said that nicotine is only important for taste. "Without nicotine," he said, "you don't have tobacco. Without nicotine, cigarettes simply would not taste like cigarettes." Also present at the hearing was William I. Campbell, president of Philip Morris who stated: "Smokers are not drug users or drug addicts, and we do not appreciate or accept being characterized as such because yes, Mr. Chairman, I am one of the 50 million smokers in this country." In addition, Kathy Ellis, pharmacologist at Philip Morris testified to the fact "that the strict pharmacological definition of addiction involves three criteria. They are intoxication, physical dependence, and tolerance. And to my knowledge there is no evidence that nicotine or cigarette smoking plays in any of these definitions."

4 The transition clearly indicates the end of Numeral I and the beginning of Numeral II of the body.

4 These were brief quotations from the tobacco executives' testimony at the Congressional Hearing. Now let's hear some other facts about nicotine addiction

5 To support the contrasting views about nicotine and addiction, the speaker cites testimony from a scientific expert at the Addiction Research Center and statistics

5 Jack E. Henningfield is chief of clinical pharmacology at the National Institute on Drug Abuse's Addiction Research Center right here in Baltimore. He contends that James Johnston of R. J. Reynolds is "out of touch" with three decades of research on nicotine effects. "What's more," he says in the May 14th issue of *Science News*, "no major pharmacological society in the last twenty years has supported the criteria for addiction cited by [Kathy] Ellis." And what about the statement from Johnston that smoking isn't addictive? David A. Kessler, commissioner of the Food and Drug Administration, asks these

questions: Why is it that after surgery for lung cancer, almost 50 percent of smokers return to cigarettes? And why do 38 percent of smokers who've had a heart attack feel compelled to light up even before they've left the hospital? And why do 40 percent of the smokers who have had a cancerous larynx removed try to start smoking again?

6 Brenda uses powerful evidence from a researcher employed by a tobacco company that shows nicotine causes smokers to become addicted.

6 But it doesn't stop here. Even their own companies have evidence that nicotine is addictive. Victor J. DeNoble, a researcher at Philip Morris, appeared before the subcommittee two weeks later to discuss his nicotine studies. He pointed out that his research on self-administration of nicotine by rodents "clearly shows that nicotine is an intravenously delivered reinforcer," that, he emphasized, "is characteristic of a drug abuse." And research since 1984 verifies an "overwhelming body of evidence that nicotine does produce addiction in the human."

7 The speaker presents her own brief testimony about smoking.

7 I know personally the power of nicotine addiction. I smoked for twelve years and today my parents continue to smoke after health problems and repeated warnings from their doctors.

8 The speaker quotes the chairman of the House subcommittee as part of her conclusion.

8 Representative Henry Waxman who is chairman of the House subcommittee charged, "those who sell aspirin, cars, and soda are held to strict standards when those products cause harm. We don't allow them to suppress evidence of dangers . . . We don't allow them to ignore science and good sense. And we demand that when problems occur, corporations and their senior executives be accountable to Congress and the public."

9 Although the end question involves listeners, it clearly establishes the speaker's point of view.

9 Now isn't it time for the tobacco industry to be accountable as well?

SUMMARY

The study of ethics has been important through the centuries and is vital to the modern speaker. When evaluating a speaker's ethics, consider the speaker's honesty, reliability, motivations, and policies. When applying your own ethical standard, be honest, convey concern about others, assess your personal motives for speaking, and develop a speaking code.

1. Divide your class into groups and spend several minutes discussing the following two cases. Try to form some agreement among group members as to the actions you would take in each situation. What criteria did you use to make your decisions? What were the most important factors that influenced your actions? What were the least important elements?

   Case 1: You are the press secretary to the president of the United States. You are told that during a routine physical examination, the president's doctor has discovered spots on the president's liver, requiring further tests. The president has important trips planned to Russia and China during the next two weeks, and he doesn't want anything to detract from ceremonies that include treaty signings. The president has told you that he wants to appear vigorous and does not wish to alarm Americans; therefore, he asks you not to tell the press corps anything about the ominous medical news. At your daily press briefing, the press, knowing that the president has just completed his yearly physical exam, asks you about the president's health, and specifically whether the doctor found any irregularities during the physical. How do you respond? Explain your statements and actions.

   Case 2: You are the public relations officer for a large auto manufacturer. Your younger sister works at one of the company's assembly plants in New Jersey. She is a single parent and her assembly-line job is the sole means of support for her three children. You receive a confidential memo from company executives stating that the New Jersey plant has lost money for the past two years and is to be closed in six months. Top executives and the public relations officer are the only individuals to know about the decision. The senior vice-president has told you that "If any of this gets out now, the union will strike all of our plants all over the country, doing irreparable damage, possibly bankrupting the company." What, if anything, would you tell your sister who will be permanently laid off in six months? Explain your actions in this situation.

2. Find three newspaper or magazine advertisements that you consider to be unethical. What elements of the ads are unethical? Are the ads partially dishonest, or do they convey false implications? How could the ads be altered, making them ethical?

3. Evaluate the ethical components of a local, state, or national political campaign. Describe the ethical and unethical strategies used to "sell" the candidate and discredit the opposition.

4. Read the speech in this chapter entitled, "The Right Way." Discuss your views of Perrella's ideas. Do you think his speech is simplistic? Does

the speaker provide any suggestions or means of putting these ethical values into practice? Are the values advocated unrealistic in a complex world? If you were to give the speech, what ideas would you change?

5. Read the speech entitled "The Tobacco Hearings." Would you consider the speech informative or persuasive? Why? Why did the speaker use so many direct quotations? The speaker used tobacco executives, testimony as the first main point of the body and then introduced "other facts about nicotine addiction" as her second main point. Did the arrangement of these points and the supporting materials make the evidence more powerful? Why?

6. Divide your class into groups of three. Discuss and develop a specific code of ethics for the following areas:

a. The speaker.

b. Members of the audience.

c. The process of gathering and reporting research in a speech.

Report the results to your class when you finish.

NOTES

1. John F. Harvis and Dan Balz, "Clinton More Forcefully Denies Having Had Affair or Urging Lies" *Washington Post,* January, 27, 1998, sec. A, p. 1.

2. Howard Kurtz, "Larry Flynt and the Barers of Bad News" *Washington Post,* December 20, 1998, sec. F, p. 1.

3. Ibid.

4. Lane Cooper, (Ed.) *The Rhetoric of Aristotle,* (New York: Appleton-Century-Crofts, Inc., 1960), p. 9.

5. Cooper, p. 47.

6. As cited in Colson, "Right or Wrong in Today's Society," p. 561.

7. I thank Paul S. Cunningham, professor of history and geography at Catonsville Community College, who provided valuable assistance for this section on history and ethics.

8. See Toni Lacy, "Judge May Ask Grand Jury to Make Changes in Rostenkowski Indictment," *The Washington Post,* February 29, 1996, Section A, P. 6, and "People," *U.S. News & World Report,* April 22, 1996, p. 26.

9. James Brooke, "Congresswoman Faces Increasing Skepticism," *The New York Times,* January 22, 1996, Section A, p. 10.

10. Serge F. Kovaleski, "Gingrich to Relinquish Book Advance: Next Speaker Says He Doesn't Want $4.5 million to Distract Congress," *The Washington Post,* December 31, 1994, Section A, p. 1.

11. "A Mountain of Debt," *The Baltimore Sun,* February 19, 1995.

12. Annetta Miller, "At United Way, Charity Began at Home," *Newsweek,* March 9, 1992, p. 56.

13. Phil Sudo, "Values in America," *Scholastic Update,* February 22, 1999, p. 2.

14. Ibid.

15. Waldo W. Braden, (ed.) *Representative American Speeches,* 1974-1975 (New York: The H.W. Wilson Co., 1975), p. 52.

16. Preston Townley, "Business Ethics," *Vital Speeches,* January 15, 1992, p. 209.

17. President Carter refers to this pledge in his 1980 concession speech. See "Transcript of the President's Concession Statement," *New York Times,* November 5, 1980.

18. Josina M. Makau, *Reasoning and Communication* (Belmont, CA: Wadsworth Publishing Company, 1990), p. 126.

20. "Clinton Fires Surgeon General," *The Baltimore Sun,* December 10, 1994, p. 1A.

21. "Senator D'Amato Apologizes for Mocking Judge Ito," *The Washington Post,* Section A, p. 9.

22. Colson details these experiences in his book *Born Again* (Old Tappan, NJ: Chosen Books, 1977). Also see Colson's speech in *Vital Speeches,* July 1, 1991.

23. See Michael O'Neal and Paula Dwyer, "Sundstrand Prepares to Pay the Piper—and the Pentagon," *Business Week,* January 23, 1989, pp. 35–36, and Louis A. Day, *Media Ethics* (Belmont, CA: Wadsworth Publishing Company, 1991), p. 33.

24. Daniel Seligman, "Hurray for Avarice," *Fortune,* October 5, 1992, p. 146.

25. Jefferson Morley, "A Terrorist and His Target: A Debate Between the Unabomber and the Pro-Technology Professor," *The Washington Post,* September 24, 1995, sec. C, p. 1.

26. See the following articles: Charles W. Colson, "Right or Wrong in Today's Society," *Vital Speeches,* July 1, 1991, p. 556; William A. Dimma, "The Decline of Ethics," *Vital Speeches,* February 1, 1991,

p. 246; and "Ever So Helpful," *The Economist,* December 26, 1987, pp. 33–34.

27. Paul O. Sand, "Business Ethics," *Vital Speeches,* November 15, 1988, p. 85.

28. Seth Mydans, "Four Held in Attack at Riots, Outset," *New York Times,* May 13, 1992, p. A20.

29. Preston Townley, "Business Ethics," *Vital Speeches,* January 15, 1992, p. 209.

30. These guidelines are quoted, in abridged form, from Capen's speech to the Conference Board Conference on Business Ethics in *Vital Speeches,* September 1, 1990, pp. 686–687.

31. James E. Perrella, "The Right Way: A Matter of Principle," *Vital Speeches,* April 1, 1989, pp. 375–376. Used by permission of *Vital Speeches* and James E. Perrella, president, Ingersoll-Rand Co.

32. Brenda Little, "The Tobacco Hearings" speech on an ethical issue, Catonsville Community College, Catonsville, MD, 1994. Used by permission.

Preparing the Foundation

Topic ····▸ Purpose ········▸ Thesis

····▸ Research ········ Outline ····

Audience ····▸ Ethics   Practice

Prepare

Chapter 7

SELECTING THE TOPIC AND PURPOSE

If you have an important point to make, don't try to be subtle or clever. Use a pile driver. Hit the point once. Then come back and hit it again. Then hit it a third time—a tremendous whack.

Winston Churchill

CHAPTER OBJECTIVES

After reading this chapter you will be able to:

1. Describe how to generate ideas for a speech;

2. Identify five guidelines for selecting speech topics;

3. Describe three guidelines for developing the specific purpose;

4. Recognize the function of the thesis statement;

5. Develop a specific purpose and thesis statement on a given topic.

Peggy Noonan is an author, newspaper columnist, and professional speech-writer. She was a member of President Reagan's White House speech-writing staff and also wrote speeches for presidential candidate George Bush. In her best-selling book, *Simply Speaking,* Noonan gives novice speakers the following advice:

> You start with trying to figure out what you want to say. This sounds easy and obvious, but is not always. We're human and tend to have lots of thoughts (often scattered) and more than a few opinions, ideas, and insights. . . .
>
> You should stick to one subject—the trade deficit, the future of the Elks Club, why you support the National Endowment for the Arts. You include and expand on the points that pertain, that explain and support and illustrate your point of view on the subject at hand.[1]

Peggy Noonan is right. Deciding what you want to say and sticking to your chosen subject are vitally important parts of building the foundation to a successful speech.

In this chapter, we examine the subject, the topic, the general purpose, the specific purpose, and the thesis statement.

GETTING IDEAS

> I've listened to everything you've said in class, and I've read the book. But I just can't think of what to give my speech about. I'm not really a very unique person—I don't sky dive or bake ethnic foods, I haven't traveled much, and I don't have hobbies or keep exotic pets. I'm just your average college student trying to get a degree. Please, PLEASE give me some ideas for a speech.

The inability to think of a subject is one of the most common complaints heard in speech classes. The same people talking with other students in the lounge or the cafeteria, or after class seem to have no problem coming up with ideas for conversation. However, in a situation requiring public speaking and evaluation of abilities, the world of ideas seems to dry up.

There are a number of ways to search for speech topics. Here are some resources and techniques that can stimulate your thinking and help you to get started.

Your Own Knowledge and Experience

One of the best resources is your own knowledge and experience. When trying to think of speech subjects people often overlook their backgrounds.

After thinking and worrying for several days, a student still had no subject for her informative speech. When asked about her interests, she responded: "Well I really like to square-dance. As a matter of fact, every week I go square dancing, and my partner and I usually try to attend a square dancing contest once a month. I'm pretty good at it, but I can't talk about anything like that, can I?" When she finally realized that she could use some of her own experiences, she recognized that public speaking could actually be interesting.

Students have delivered speeches about traveling to India, climbing mountains, shearing sheep, milking poisonous snakes, studying fossils, training dogs, collecting coins, hang gliding, making theatrical masks, excavating ancient ruins, recovering from alcoholism, military duty in dangerous war zones, stomach stapling, and tattooing. These subjects were drawn from students' personal knowledge or experiences. Don't take your background for granted. Examine your unique experiences—you will often find something to expand into a topic that fits a particular assignment.

The Dictionary and the Encyclopedia

Another way you can gather ideas is to look through an encyclopedia or dictionary. In a copy of *Webster's New World Dictionary,* we searched under the letter "B." Here is just a partial listing of some of the subjects we found:

baboon	bat	blood	brass
J. S. Bach	batik	bloodhound	breast cancer
backgammon	Beaumont	blueberries	breaststroke
Badlands	beaver	boats	Brazil
badger	Bedouin	bobby	Britain
bagel	Beirut	bobcat	Buddha
bagpipes	Bermuda	Boise	buffalo
bail bondsman	Berlin	Bonaparte	bugle
Bahamas	Bible	Book of Mormon	buggy
Baltimore	bicycle	boomerang	Bull Run
baseball	Bill of Rights	Bordeaux	burlesque
bald eagle	biofeedback	Boston	butcher
banana	Bismark	Boy Scout	butter
balloon	blackjack	Braille	buzzard
barrier reefs	blindfish	brain	Byzantine

When you choose a topic from your own interests or experiences, you are more likely to project vitality and enthusiasm to listeners.

This list of sixty subjects was compiled in about fifteen minutes. These ideas can easily be subdivided into numerous speech topics. We caution you against copying material from dictionaries or encyclopedias; these are resources to help you get ideas and general background. You may find a subject that genuinely interests you and will fit your assignment.

Brainstorming

One technique to help generate many subjects in a short period of time is brainstorming—the rapid and unrestrained listing of ideas. Take a pencil and paper and jot down anything that comes into your mind. Don't try to judge or evaluate the ideas when you list them—the goal of this exercise is to stimulate your thoughts and imagination. After a few minutes, you will have a long list of subjects on a wide variety of issues. Naturally, some of the subjects will seem ridiculous; but the purpose of the exercise is to generate a lot of ideas quickly. You can easily eliminate the irrelevancies later.

Periodical Abstracts Ondisc, the *Readers' Guide,* Newspaper Indexes, and the Vertical File

Additional places to look for subject matter are library computer software programs such as *Periodical Abstracts Ondisc* or *InfoTrac,* which contain lists of magazine titles and summaries, called "abstracts," describing the content of the articles. (See chapter 8 for a more extensive discussion.) The *Readers' Guide to Periodical Literature* also lists magazine titles by subject, but without abstracts. Most libraries have the *Readers' Guide* bound in large green volumes, and some include this helpful index on computerized CD-ROM programs for easy searching. In addition, many libraries have indexes of major national newspapers, such as *The New York Times,* in both bound volumes and computer programs. Most libraries also have a vertical file that can help you come up with ideas for subjects. Verticle files contain pamphlets and informational brochures from organizations, businesses, institutions, and self-help groups. The types of subject matter contained in the vertical file differ in each library; check your library to determine the material included.

Ask for Help

If you are having difficulty selecting a topic, ask for help from other individuals. Solicit suggestions from friends and family, or talk to your associates at work. Ask your instructor to react to several ideas or seek advice from fellow students. Talking to others helps you verbalize feelings and restore your perspective on significant interests, abilities, and motivations.

There are plenty of subjects available if you actively look for them. Get busy and do something—don't wait for inspiration. Examine your own experiences, try some brainstorming techniques, go to the library, or ask for suggestions from others.

SELECTING THE TOPIC

Once you have chosen the subject, you must narrow it down to a *topic*—the specific, limited issue that you can effectively develop into a five- to eight-minute speech. Here are five guidelines to consider as you build the speech.

It Should Be Sufficiently Narrow and Conform to the Time Limit

Most of the subjects in the dictionary list above are too general for a five-minute classroom presentation. You could sign up for entire courses on Britain, barrier reefs, or Buddha. These subjects must be narrowed to more specific topics. For example:

- British attempts at a peaceful settlement in Northern Ireland.
- The types of plant life existing in a barrier reef.
- Some of the basic beliefs of Buddhism.

Each of the above topics can be supported by several main points, and each topic can be made to conform to the time limit.

A speech on "the problem of mental health in the United States," for example, would be too broad, and could be narrowed down, as the following list shows:

Subject: Mental health in the United States.

Topics: Causes, effects, and treatments of impotence.
Common phobias experienced by "average" people.
Hyperactivity in children.
Mental illness and the homeless.
Myths about mental illness.
Personal injury claims resulting from job stress.
Problems of mental health insurance.
Pros and cons of mainstreaming the mentally retarded.
The destructive effects of perfectionism.
Treatments for Alzheimer's disease.
Unethical practices in psychiatry.

Eleven major speech topics are generated from the one general subject, and many more are possible. Your topic must be limited so that you can develop it in sufficient detail within your allotted time.

It Should Interest You, the Speaker

You must be certain that the topic interests you. A speech is not like a book report on an assigned issue; the topic you select reflects your interests, your personality, and your motivations. You cannot go to the dictionary, close your eyes, pick out a random topic, and expect to feel positive about communicating it. You need to feel confident and challenged by your choice; you must be able to use appropriate aspects of delivery—vocal inflection, gestures, facial expression—to communicate your enthusiasm to the audience.

A student in the air transportation curriculum asked his audience to play the role of passengers on a transcontinental flight. A few seconds into the presentation, the speaker, who played the pilot, stated that the aircraft was experiencing mechanical difficulty and that he would need to make an emergency landing. The "passengers" listened carefully as the "pilot" reviewed the safety precautions to take in flight and the emergency exit procedures to carry out when the plane landed. The audience was fascinated because the speaker was interested in his topic and creative in his delivery.

You may be interested in a topic, but you may not be very knowledgeable about it. Don't throw out the idea because you will have to do some additional investigation. One student, who had presented three very creative speeches during the semester, was having difficulty finding a dynamic topic for her final speech to inform. She had always been curious about ants, but didn't know very much about them. At first she thought her idea might be too trivial, but as she began to do research, she found the subject compelling. She became so involved that she even created some visual aids to support her narrowed topic, "Life in an ant colony." During the speech she was enthusiastic, animated, and extremely knowledgeable because of her extensive research. Her success started with her interest in the topic.

It Should Provide New Information

Successful speakers can make almost any topic interesting. With proper research and audience analysis, few topics are "boring." Some topics, however, can be classified as overworked or trivial, and should be avoided or altered. For example:

Toxic pollution is dangerous.

How to make a cake by following the directions on the cake box.

Drinking a beer.

Registering for a course at this university.

Transplants can help people.

To involve your audience, alter these topics and provide new or more sophisticated information.

Home carpeting can contain toxic pollution.

Secrets of making a perfect German chocolate cake.

How beer is manufactured.

Some of the most popular elective courses at the university.

Improvements in bone-marrow transplants.

These topics are not simplistic, they don't rehash information that is common knowledge, and they have the potential of providing additional knowledge.

A speaker began a presentation by identifying a process that was familiar to most audience members—decorating Easter eggs. However, as the speech progressed, listeners soon realized that the speaker was not describing the ordinary Eastertime activity. The speaker's purpose was to demonstrate "How to make Ukrainian Easter eggs"—a centuries-old process requiring skill and dedication. The speaker briefly described Ukrainian traditions and demonstrated the application of intricate designs symbolizing Easter themes. The audience was completely involved: the speaker handled an overworked topic creatively and provided her listeners with new information.[2]

It Should Be Appropriate

While setting up visual aids for a process speech, a nursing student asked the audience for a volunteer, and a male student eagerly came forward. As the speaker proceeded with her introduction, it became clear that the purpose of her speech was to demonstrate how to give a bath to a hospital patient. The face of the male volunteer turned red, and the audience began to giggle nervously. Undismayed, the nursing student instructed her volunteer to lie down on the table as she proceeded to demonstrate in great detail how a patient is bathed. The speaker's topic was appropriate in a nursing classroom, but was extremely inappropriate in a speech class.

Appropriateness is highly subjective; what is appropriate to one person is not appropriate to another. An individual speaking about personal religious convictions might be on target in a church group, but the topic would be completely out of place at a secular meeting. Use common sense when you think about a topic, and select an issue that is appropriate for as many of your listeners as possible.

It Should Conform to the General Purpose

Once you have chosen a topic, you must then consider the *general purpose* or the direction of the material presented in the speech. You need to know whether your speech assignment is to inform, to persuade, or to entertain your audience.

Ideas for speeches are often generated as a result of brainstorming, thinking about personal interests, going to the library, or asking for help from friends.

SPEECHES TO INFORM

Informative speeches are presentations that enlighten and educate audiences. In speeches to inform you can define concepts, develop personal experiences, demonstrate procedures, describe people, places, or objects, or deliver business reports or lectures on issues in which you have expertise.

If you were to define jazz, convey an experience such as life in the Marines or sky diving, demonstrate how to make clay pottery, describe the life of Irving Berlin, the principal historical sites in Boston, or the effects of elephant's disease, report to a business group about real estate projections for the year 2010, or lecture about the economic struggle in Russia, you would be contributing to audience awareness and understanding.

SPEECHES TO PERSUADE

Unlike informative presentations, your goal in persuasive speeches is to influence the beliefs, feelings, or behavior of listeners. While you must present accurate and well-researched material, you must also take a clear position regarding the information. There are three principal types of persuasive speeches: the speech to convince, which changes belief; the speech to actuate, which moves to action; and the speech to stimulate, which intensifies feelings.

Persuasive speaking is similar to taking one side in a debate. You tell your audience to do something ("plant a tree"), to believe something ("raise taxes to reduce the deficit"), or to feel something strongly ("support our football team in the bowl game"). Your goal is to build a case using logic and emotion to persuade the audience that your point of view is the correct one.

SPEECHES TO ENTERTAIN

The purpose of the speech to entertain is to promote enjoyment and to amuse and divert the audience. Entertaining speeches could include an after-dinner speech, a roast of a boss or friend, or a monologue satirizing a person, place, or event. Entertainment does not mean a lack of research and preparation; often speeches to entertain are some of the most difficult to prepare and present. The speech to entertain requires creativity, skill in writing and organization, and skill in delivery.

College speech instructors tend to emphasize informative and persuasive speeches over speeches to entertain. But developing an entertaining speech is good experience; most people have an occasion sometime in their careers or personal lives to present a humorous speech—a friend's fortieth birthday, a toast at an anniversary, an office-party spoof.

WRITING THE SPECIFIC PURPOSE

The *specific purpose* is the reason for the speech: this statement communicates the speaker's goal to the audience. When you state your specific purpose at the end of your introduction, your audience should clearly understand your topic and your intention.

Spend time developing your specific purpose so that it clearly defines and conveys your objective. Here are three guidelines to follow as you prepare the specific purpose statement:

1. Be clear, concise, and unambiguous.
2. Include only one major idea.
3. Phrase as a declarative sentence.

Be Clear, Concise, and Unambiguous

The specific purpose should be phrased in simple and concrete language. Avoid wordy descriptions and vague terminology. The specific purpose should be easy to read and easy to verbalize. Most important, your audience must clearly understand your specific purpose. Some examples:

- To inform you about the startling possibility of male pregnancy.
- To explain how you can help children afflicted with the disease called spinal bifida.
- To convince you that cosmetic surgeries are dangerous.

The first specific purpose tells the audience that they will receive information about the topic, the second asks listeners to become actively involved with the issue, and the third requests them to agree with the speaker. The first may raise some eyebrows, but it promotes curiosity. The second introduces terminology that may be unfamiliar, but spinal bifida is clearly defined as a disease, and the third takes a strong position on a persuasive issue. Each statement is clearly worded and communicates the speaker's specific intention. Now look at the following specific purpose:

Poor: To tell you of the serious implications of central and obstructive sleep apnea, and explain how these conditions impact the psyche and the physiology

This specific purpose is weak because it takes entirely too long to communicate. The sentence also introduces terminology—*central and obstructive sleep apnea*—unfamiliar to many listeners. The objective of the speech is not clearly communicated; we have the impression that the speech is about some type of sleeping disorder, but we're not exactly certain about the topic and we are not told whom it affects. This statement confuses audience members and discourages them from listening. Here's how the specific purpose can be improved:

Better: To describe the major causes and effects of a common sleeping disorder.

Here the wording is clear, and the sentence moves logically and quickly to the point. The statement eliminates technical terms and ambiguous references to "psyche" and "physiology." The specific medical terminology can be identified and explained later in the speech.

Poor: To talk about M. C. Escher.

To tell you about airline accidents.

To inform you about blacklists.

In each of these phrases, the subjects are not yet narrowed. A speaker who fails to make changes in these statements will probably speak overtime or jump from one topic to another. These are better:

Better: To describe the stylistic influences on M. C. Escher, the pop artist.

To explain how several airline crashes have contributed to stricter safety regulations.

> To convince the audience that computerized blacklists threaten individual privacy.

These statements are improved because the subjects have been narrowed and the wording is more precise.

Include Only One Major Idea

A specific purpose should contain only one principal topic. If it contains more than one topic, the speaker will be developing at least two speeches.

Poor: To describe the effects of criminal behavior on the victim and explain the merits of crime compensation plans.

To demonstrate how a dentist fills a tooth, performs a root canal, and cleans your teeth.

To explain how the United States sold technology to Iraq, encouraged Saddam Hussein to invade Kuwait, and triumphed over Iraq in Desert Storm.

To explain how computerized blacklists are compiled, and to convince you that these blacklists threaten our right to privacy.

Often beginning speakers are afraid they will not have enough material for a five- to seven-minute speech, so they include too many topics in their specific purpose statements. The first specific purpose contains at least two topic ideas. The effects of criminal behavior on a victim is at least one topic, and merits of crime compensation plans is another. The second sentence contains three separate demonstration speeches. A speaker cannot possibly demonstrate three dental procedures in six or seven minutes. In the third sentence there are numerous topics: the sale of technology to Iraq, the encouragement of the invasion, and the victory over Iraq. In the fourth statement, there are two distinct purposes. The first part of the statement is a speech to describe, and the last half is a speech to convince. Your specific purpose sentence clearly indicates whether the speech is informative or persuasive: It should not include both types. Here is how each statement can be altered to incorporate only one main topic:

Better: To describe the merits of victim compensation plans.

To demonstrate how a dentist performs a root canal.

To explain the sequence of events in the U.S. victory over Iraq.

To convince you that computerized blacklists threaten our rights of privacy.

Each specific purpose statement includes only one major topic that can be developed adequately in a five- to seven-minute speech.

Phrase in a Sentence

The specific purpose should include a declarative sentence that contains the topic, the general purpose, and an infinitive phrase such as "to inform," "to describe," or "to stimulate." The following examples are poor:

Poor: Skin disease.

Lead fishing sinkers.

African tribal body painting and how it is done.

Prayer in public schools—pro or con?

Should the United States be the peacekeepers of the world?

In each of the above statements, the speaker has not clearly identified the goal of the speech. The first example merely names a broad subject; there is no topic, purpose, or sentence. Although the second example could be an adequate topic for a speech, it is not stated in sentence form with a general purpose; it has no direction or goal. The third example still is not complete because it lacks an infinitive phrase. The fourth and fifth examples raise questions when they should make clear statements as to the intention of the speech; we are not sure if the speeches are informative or persuasive. Here are better examples:

Better: To provide the audience with an understanding of a disfiguring skin disease known as vitiligo.

To demonstrate how to make lead fishing sinkers.

To demonstrate an African tribal ritual of body painting.

To actuate the audience to support a Constitutional amendment allowing voluntary prayer in public schools.

To convince the audience that the United States should not be the peacekeepers of the world.

These five examples have the following points in common: (1) each contains an infinitive phrase that clearly describes the intent and general purpose of the speech; (2) each includes a precise statement of the topic; (3) each specific purpose is phrased as a declarative sentence, and (4) no specific purpose is stated as a question. Each specific purpose statement will provide the audience with a clear understanding of the speaker's goal.

WORDING THE THESIS STATEMENT

The *thesis statement,* often called the "central idea" or the "central objective," is the phrase that tells the audience the major points the speech will include. If a member of your audience walked in late but just in time to hear your thesis statement, the listener would know exactly what your speech was to cover. The wording of the thesis statement is important because it acts as the organizational hub of your speech; all of the major headings of the body of the speech carry out the thesis statement. Here are two effective examples:

Topic: Communication of dolphins.

General purpose: To inform.

Specific purpose: To inform the audience about how dolphins communicate.

Thesis statement: "Dolphins communicate through their sense of vision and through their sense of sound."

Topic: Meat "analogues" or substitutes.

General purpose: To inform.

Specific purpose: To inform you about the benefits of meat "analogues" or substitutes.

Thesis statement: "Meat substitutes can be high in protein, low in cholesterol, and contain less fat."

In each instance the thesis statement expands and clarifies the specific purpose; it describes what will actually be covered in the speech. In the first example, the thesis tells the audience that the speech will include two points: (1) communication of dolphins through vision, and (2) communication of dolphins through sound. In the second example, the thesis tells listeners that the speaker will describe three benefits of meat substitutes: (1) high protein, (2) low cholesterol, and (3) less fat.

A speech is confusing or hard for an audience to follow when the speaker does not have a clear thesis statement in mind.

Topic: The insanity plea as a defense.

General purpose: To convince.

Specific purpose: To convince the audience that the insanity plea should be abolished.

Poor thesis statement: Insanity shouldn't be allowed as a defense because there are just too many criminals who have gotten off with that excuse and it just isn't fair to society or to the victims at all.

This thesis statement is a prescription for speaking disaster. The statement is merely a run-on sentence that does not include the main points of the body of the speech. The speaker will probably ramble on without much logic or organization, and the confused audience will probably stop listening. Here's how to correct the problem:

> **Better thesis statement:**   Criminals can fake mental illness; psychiatrists can incorrectly diagnose criminals, and the judicial system loses control over criminals diagnosed as "insane."

This thesis clearly introduces three areas that will be covered in the body of the speech. The audience will be able to follow the speaker's organization with ease.

Problems with the Thesis Statement

If you have difficulties writing your thesis statement, it is possible that problems exist elsewhere in your speech.

> **Poor thesis statement:**   I want to describe the religious rituals of the North, Central, and South American Indians.

This thesis contains a topic that is too broad. The numerous Indian tribes with their many religious practices would require an entire series of speeches. Here is a better thesis statement:

> **Better thesis statement:**   I want to explain where and when the Sioux Indians lived, describe some of their religious practices, and explain what happened to them as a tribe.

This thesis is much improved because it incorporates a narrow topic and clearly indicates that the speech will contain three central points.
Here is another difficulty often detected in student speeches:

> **Poor thesis statement:**   I want to demonstrate how film is manufactured.

This is not a thesis statement; it is still the specific purpose sentence. If a speaker were to use this as the thesis, there would be at least ten main points in the speech—too many for a five- to seven-minute presentation. The speaker needs to write a thesis statement that expands the specific purpose and includes only a few main points.

> **Better thesis statement:**   Film is manufactured by making a plastic base, coating the plastic surface with emulsion, and cutting the film into appropriate widths.

Here is another frequent difficulty in student speeches:

> **Poor thesis statement:**   I want to describe the game board and the playing pieces of backgammon.

This thesis indicates that the topic is much too limited. The statement contains only one point—not enough for a five- to seven-minute speech. A speech given on this topic would only take about one minute. Here is how to correct the problem:

> **Better thesis statement:**   I want to tell you where backgammon originated, some of the rules of the game, and how it is played.

This thesis is better because it broadens the topic and includes three main points in the speech.

If you are having trouble writing your thesis statement, you may not have enough information and need to do more research.

PUTTING IT TOGETHER

To help you build your own speeches, here are some examples of topics, specific purpose sentences, and thesis statements other students have used in their classroom presentations.[4] A brief commentary in the margin explains why the sample speech was successful.

> **Topic:**   Collecting comic books.
>
> **General purpose:**   To inform.
>
> **Specific purpose:**   To inform you about the value of collecting comic books.
>
> **Thesis statement:**   I want to give you some basic knowledge about collecting comic books, and tell you how to protect your investment so the comics will increase in value.

Collecting comics was Dan Urton's hobby, and the audience could sense his enthusiasm for the topic. During the speech, Dan used some of his own comic books as visual aids to support key ideas. Listeners commented that the topic was "different"—many were surprised to learn how valuable old comic books can be. The specific purpose and thesis statement made Dan's speech objectives completely clear to the audience.

Professional chef John Fields showed his audience how to make a cheesecake. John went to the trouble of preparing three cheesecakes in various stages of completion. His audience watched with fascination as he skillfully used his visuals to demonstrate the details of the general process he identified in the thesis. When he finished the speech, John revealed an elegant gourmet cheesecake that he divided among his delighted listeners.

Topic: Making a cheesecake.

General purpose: To demonstrate.

Specific purpose: To demonstrate how to make a cheesecake.

Thesis statement: Making a cheesecake requires understanding a recipe and using a step-by-step method to create a beautiful finished product.

Elizabeth Crawford used quotations from the Surgeon General, references to the *New England Journal of Medicine,* and personal experience to support the three reasons stated in the thesis. She described her father-in-law's victory over cancer and

Topic: Doctor-assisted suicide.

General purpose: To convince.

Specific purpose: To convince the audience that doctor-assisted suicide should not be legalized.

Thesis statement: Doctor-assisted suicide violates the Hippocratic oath, encourages suicide, and can be abused.

acknowledged the caring physicians who had provided treatment. In an emotional statement, Elizabeth concluded: "If Dad Crawford had encountered Dr. Kevorkian as his physician, the outcome of his illness might have been entirely different." Although not everyone agreed with this controversial proposition, the audience was deeply involved in the topic.

What impressed the audience about this speech was that Kelly Burns was committed to her topic. Kelly wore a T-shirt declaring "Human Rights Now" as she described her involvement with Amnesty International. Kelly touched the feelings of love and commitment within listeners when she spoke of children stolen from their families and illegally adopted in

Topic: Amnesty International/human rights.

General purpose: To actuate.

Specific purpose: To actuate the audience to write letters to human rights violators.

Thesis statement: I want to define human rights, explain how Amnesty International works, and tell you what you can do to help those whose rights are being violated.

other countries.
"Think of your
own children, or
brothers and sis-
ters," she said,
"and be glad this
can't happen to
them." Audience
members were gen-
uinely moved, and
many offered to
help Kelly with
her cause.

SUMMARY

In your search for speech topics, explore various areas. Select a topic that is narrow in scope and will conform to the time limit, that appeals to your own interests as a speaker, is appropriate to your listeners, and conforms to your assigned purpose—to inform, to persuade, or to entertain. The specific purpose is the overall objective of the speech. The thesis statement amplifies the specific purpose and tells the audience exactly what your speech will cover.

SKILL BUILDERS

1. Pick out what is wrong with the following specific purpose statements:
   a. To explain how volcanos form, some types of volcanos, and how a volcano actually erupts.
   b. To inform you about three effects of TV violence on children and to urge your support of legislation, which requires a TV rating system.
   c. To convince you that the NCAA regulation called Proposition 42, which prevents academically "borderline" students from receiving college scholarships, is unfair, and that the NCAA should enact a fairer process.
   d. To inform you about the war in Bosnia.
2. Rewrite the following thesis statements so that they are more effective:
   a. I will describe the country of Greece and also tell you about the Greek Islands.
   b. I want to inform you about hearing ear dogs.
   c. I want to tell you how to participate in home schooling.

   d. The purpose of the speech is to inform you about radon gas: what it is, the problem it can cause in your home, and how you can test for it.
3. Divide your class into several small groups and write a topic, a general purpose, a specific purpose, and a thesis statement for each of the following subjects.

   animals

   art

   judicial reform

   lotteries

   music

   Albert Gore

   space exploration

   sculpture

NOTES

1. Peggy Noonan, *Simply Speaking* (New York: HarperCollins Publishers, 1998), p. 16.

2. Maria Marszalek, "The Art of Egg Decorating," demonstration speech presented in the Fundamentals of Public Speaking Course, Catonsville Community College, 1989. Used by permission.

3. I am appreciative of the following students who gave me permission to use their topics and specific purposes as examples in this chapter: Linda Carey, Jo Ann Dickensheets, Patricia Farquhar, Dawn Gyory, Stephen King, Lou Ann Pfister, Dwayne Mitchell, Sandra Prusin, Richard Renehan, Susan Stephan, Sherri Webb, and Tracey Weise. I also gratefully acknowledge the late Professor Stephen S. Hiten who coined the phrase "Be clear, concise, and unambiguous" in his public speaking courses at Columbia Union College.

4. Speeches in this section were presented in the Fundamentals of Public Speaking Course, Catonsville Community College, Catonsville, MD, 1987, 1988, 1989, 1990, and 1992. All used by permission.

Chapter 8

CONDUCTING
RESEARCH

*Knowledge is of two kinds;
we know a subject
ourselves, or we know
where we can find
information upon it.*

Dr. Samuel Johnson

CHAPTER OBJECTIVES

After reading this chapter you will able to:

1. Describe credible and noncredible sources;

2. Identify three general references;

3. Understand three important guidelines for using the Internet;

4. Describe the substantive sources used for speech research;

5. Develop an effective system for keeping accurate notes;

6. Recognize how to conduct an interview;

7. Know how to record bibliographic entries.

Cicero said, "There can be no true merit in speaking, unless what is said is thoroughly understood by him who says it." Cicero knew that a speaker must have an extensive knowledge of the topic in order to be effective. Without this knowledge, Cicero warned that the "volubility of words is empty and ridiculous."[1]

Cicero's thoughts about knowledge have applied in every generation. You cannot speak with confidence if you do not know your topic, and the audience will not trust you if you do not support your topic with research. The principal focus of this foundation chapter is to examine the two types of reference tools you need to research a topic: the general references, and the substantive sources. In addition, the chapter includes discussions of source credibility, the Internet, keeping accurate notes, conducting an interview, and recording a bibliographic entry.

PREPARING FOR RESEARCH

Going to the library does not have to be a boring experience, nor does it have to waste hours of your time. If you know what you are doing, you can accomplish a great deal very quickly. The key to conducting good research is knowing where to look and what to look for on a particular topic. There are also times when doing research means not going to the library at all. Even in that case, you must know the alternatives available in order to make progress toward your goal of presenting an effective speech.

ESTABLISHING CREDIBILITY

The audience must be able to trust you as a speaker and to believe what you are telling them. This confidence, known as *credibility,* is developed when you support ideas with evidence, which is verified by research utilizing sources that are respected, reliable, and relevant to the topic.

Sources exhibit varying degrees of credibility. Some, like reputable newspapers, newsmagazines, books, experts, trade journals, and encyclopedias, are extremely authoritative and reliable. Others, like some autobiographies, TV talk shows, self-help books, well-meaning friends, or condensed publications containing only excerpts of articles, have less credibility.

Noncredible sources are easily detected by audiences. A student who presented an informative speech on the positive existence of UFOs made the statement: "There have been numerous sightings of UFOs according to a recent issue of the *National Enquirer.*" Listeners tried to be polite and conceal their smiles. However, they eventually exploded into laughter because the speaker, who was entirely serious, did not perceive the credibility problem that the mention of his source had caused.

Here are some examples of other types of noncredible, hearsay, or "phantom" sources often cited in speeches:

"I got some information on diet from a muscle magazine that said . . ."

"I was talking to this guy, and he said . . ."

"Everybody knows that this is true . . ."

"Studies have proven it to be a fact . . ."

"Doctors recommend that . . ."

"I read in a movie magazine that . . ."

"There is some clinic in France, or Spain, or somewhere, that has developed a cure for AIDS."

"I was watching this TV show and it was real interesting, and it said that . . ."

"I saw this movie and it talked about . . ."

"The astrology magazine predicts a major earthquake in California by the year 2000 . . ."

"I read this book written by a lawyer who has been born eleven different times over the past 1,000 years . . ."

If you want to establish credibility with the audience, cite reputable sources in your speech. Check the reliability of authors and the authenticity of publications or so-called experts. Don't rely on hearsay, gossip columns, or fabrication for evidence. If you need a complete source, consult the original article rather than a condensed version. Be willing to spend the time researching ideas from sources that are credible and trustworthy. Cite specific sources, specific studies, and specific authorities to build confidence and believability with your listeners.

PRIMARY AND SECONDARY SOURCES

Sources can be either primary or secondary. *Primary evidence* is original, firsthand fact, or experience. For instance, if your topic were "Riding the Winning Cycle," a primary source would be a magazine article written by Lance Armstrong, winner of the 1999 Tour de France bicycle race. Primary sources, however, are often difficult to obtain or unavailable. A personal interview with Lance Armstrong is probably unrealistic and an article by him may not exist.

For many topics, secondary research may be more accessible. *Secondary evidence* is information reported secondhand by an intermediary standing between you and the original source. You may find an article in *Bicycling* magazine written by a reporter who witnessed the Tour de France or read a description of the race in *The New York Times*. These sources would be extremely helpful to your speech and they could be obtained quickly through the library. You will probably use secondary evidence frequently as you research speech topics.

USING GENERAL REFERENCES

When you go to the library, you will use the general reference sources to begin your search for information. These references help you locate books, publications, or other sources that contain the information you need. The principal research tools are the catalog and the periodical indexes.

Speakers must know how to use computerized library references to locate credible sources for presentations.

The Catalog

This index was once known as the "card catalog" because it contained drawers of index cards that provided access to all the books in the library. Today, however, most college and university libraries have computerized catalog systems that provide access to the library more quickly and efficiently. In some libraries, the catalog includes periodicals as well as audiovisual materials. Books are listed in the catalog according to author, title, and subject. If you know the author or title, it is easy to find your specific source. If, however, you are looking for a number of books in a general subject area, you will probably find a wide variety of sources to choose from.

Periodical Indexes

Periodical indexes reference a wide range of magazines, newspapers, and journals in popular subject areas as well as in technical fields of study. The *Readers' Guide to Periodical Literature,* for example, is a general reference to articles in more than two hundred popular magazines such as *Time, Newsweek, McCall's, Science Digest, Popular Mechanics,* and *Parents Magazine.* This source, often called the "average person index," is one of the most important and most helpful references for speech research. The *Readers' Guide* is a yearly index starting in 1890 and extending to the current date. It identifies a general subject, then lists the titles of numerous articles appearing in periodicals relating to the subject. After you select the titles you want to research, go to magazine collections housed in bound volumes (or stored on microfilm) to read specific articles. During the semester you take public speaking, you will probably use this index as much as the catalog.

Periodical indexes in specialized fields are organized like the *Readers' Guide* and can help you find article titles in more technical areas. Here is a partial list of some of these specialized indexes; you'll need to consult your own library reference section to see which reference tools are available to you.

Applied Science and Technology Index.   Contains article titles in aeronautics, chemistry, computer technology, the construction industry, transportation, and many other scientific and technological fields.

The Art Index.   Indexes titles appearing in a variety of art areas.

Business Periodicals Index.   Includes major business fields.

Biography Index.   An index to individual biographies, biographical collections, obituaries, letters, diaries, memoirs, and bibliographies

Cumulative Index to Nursing.   Indexes titles in the health care professions.

Education Index.   Indexes periodicals in education, counseling, and rehabilitation.

Humanities Index.   Contains titles in areas such as archaeology, literature, and philosophy.

Index to Journals in Communication Studies.   Published by the National Communication Association and indexes fourteen professional speech journals.

Index to Periodical Articles by and about Blacks.   A multivolume source that indexes thirty-two periodicals relating to black Americans.

The New York Times **Index.**   Lists all of the titles of news, editorial, and feature stories that have ever appeared in *The New York Times.*

Psychological Abstracts.   Provides summaries of articles in the principal fields of psychology.

Religion Index.   Includes 397 periodical titles in the area of religion.

Social Sciences Index.   Indexes areas such as anthropology, criminology, economics, environmental sciences, geography, and law.

Women's Studies Abstracts.   Presents brief summaries of articles in twenty-four areas related to women's issues.

Accessing the Library by Computer

The computer has made libraries more efficient and much easier to use. Many college and university libraries have computer (online) catalogs that allow students to find books quickly and eliminate lengthy manual searches. The computer also facilitates finding books by allowing more key-word entry points. In the traditional card catalog, you search for a book by locating the appropriate author, title, or subject card. With a computerized system, there are more key-word access points, such as publisher, date of publication, or a word within a title or abstract.

Many libraries also have periodical indexes like the *Readers' Guide* on computer. These are used the same way as the manual indexes, but they take less time and provide you with printouts of periodical titles related to topics. They also provide extensive search options, allowing you to focus more specifically on topics or subtopics. Most of the periodical indexes already listed are available on computer. In addition, many libraries have various computer versions of periodical and newspaper indexes that have been developed for specific markets. You may encounter some of the following software titles in your college, university, or public library:

Academic Abstracts

Academic Index

First Search

Infotrac Magazine

Article Summaries

Newspaper Abstracts Ondisc

Periodical Abstracts Ondisc

ProQuest Direct

UnCover

These software systems have no print equivalent and enhance the general reference indexes of a library. Libraries choose combinations of software systems or indexes to meet their specific needs. For example, a large university with numerous graduate programs might select an index such as *First Search,* which accesses a variety of periodical indexes as well as books. These indexes are altered and updated frequently and often networked to faculty offices, residence halls, and classroom locations. It is advisable to check with your librarian for the most up-to-date information and accurate software titles.

Many bibliographic databases are now available through the World Wide Web and can be accessed easily through a university, home, or office computer. Some electronic sources, such as *ProQuest Direct,* are available by subscription only, through your library or a local library consortium. Others, like *The Electric Library,* offer low-cost subscriptions for home users and some, such as *UnCover,* can be accessed through the Internet without an initial fee. This electronic program indexes hundreds of magazine titles such as *Newsweek, Time,* and *Flying* as well as numerous other popular titles and subjects. *UnCover* allows you to search for a person, author, or magazine by name. When you search for a periodical title you will receive a list of the contents for specific months or weeks, and you can select a particular date of publication and browse through the titles to determine if any article might be helpful. Know that if you want to read an article, you must place an order through the system and pay a fee to have the specific article sent to you. All of these databases offer full-text or full-image copies of some indexed articles, but charges for subscription services may be substantial. Find out from your college or public library what is available to you, either in the library or from your home.

GUIDELINES FOR SEARCHING THE INTERNET

The Internet is both a general reference and a substantive source that can help a speaker to find detailed materials for a speech. Millions of Americans now access billions of pieces of information from home or office computers using the World Wide Web. Any individual, institution, government agency, or business can develop and publish a computerized *homepage* describing interests, jobs, objectives, or products. Consumers can search the Internet for goods and services, download photographs and video clips, and gain access to unlimited sources of reliable (and unreliable) data. Users can also communicate by sending electronic messages, called *e-mail,* via the Internet, or participate in interactive communication known as "live chat."

As the boxed example indicates, the Internet can be a valuable source for research. However, like any research tool, the Internet has strengths, limitations, and weaknesses. If you use some of the major search engines such as *Lycos, Alta Vista,* or *Magellan,* you may spend many hours trying to locate what you need, often sifting through irrelevant junk pages and advertising that can lead to blind alleys or dead ends. In such cases, a brief ten-minute trip to the library could yield more credible information and save you valuable time. To help you become more critical in your investigation, we suggest that you consider these guidelines when you use the Internet to research supporting materials for a speech.[2]

1. Examine the Authorship or Source of the Web Site

It is important to determine the authorship of a Web site and examine the qualifications and credibility of the source. Is the source an institution, governmental agency, commercial enterprise, network, or individual? Are the authors researchers, scholars, or groups and organizations that are reliable? Are the authors' qualifications provided, can their expertise on the subject area be verified, and do they have an e-mail or other address

SURFING THE NET

Jason received an assignment from his speech instructor to prepare a 5- to 7-minute informative speech about a person, place, object, or event. As an art major, Jason was especially interested in artists and museums and he had used his Internet service to access museums all over the world. He had examined the paintings of Goya in Madrid's Prado Museum; visited the Greek sculpture room in the Louvre; gazed at the ceiling of the Sistine Chapel; and viewed some of the antiquities in the British National Museum. Jason was also interested in contemporary art and he especially wanted to learn more about avant-garde pop artist Andy Warhol, whom he chose as the subject for his speech. He decided to "surf the net" on his dorm computer to research some information. Jason clicked the computer mouse on the Internet server icon and the computer dialed the access telephone number through the computer modem to make connection to the World Wide Web. Once the link was made, the screen presented Jason with a directory of numerous *search engines* such as *Magellan, Excite, Alta Vista,* and *Lycos,* which could be used to investigate the topic. After scanning the sources, Jason decided to use *Yahoo!* for his search. He entered the term "Andy Warhol" and clicked the mouse on the window "Open this Link."

The search yielded numerous possibilities. As he explored the choices, Jason saw an entry for the "Andy Warhol Museum." He clicked on the museum and found more information. He was able to get an overview of the Warhol museum located in downtown Pittsburgh and even a summary of the Warhol collections housed on each of the museum's seven floors. As he clicked the mouse on a graphic showing each floor, Jason was able to view brilliant full-color images of Andy Warhol's paintings on the computer screen. He was even able to enlarge the color images of Warhol's *Shoe, Marilyn,* and *Campbell's Soup Can* and then print them. Each image included the title and a description of the subject matter. As he continued to explore this electronic museum, Jason went to the Museum Store and "browsed" through the T-shirts and other items. He used the convenient order form to purchase a Warhol poster of Grace Jones, which he thought would make an effective visual aid for the speech. Jason also had an e-mail address for the University of Michigan clearinghouse library, which he used to access additional information about the artist. Jason often came across material that was of questionable credibility. He did not use biographical information about Warhol appearing on "Christy's Web Page" (which contained numerous misspellings), or so-called "authoritative" material presented without verifiable sources. Even though he was able to gather several resources on the Internet, Jason wisely decided to do additional research by using some of the traditional library tools.

where you can contact them for further information? Find out who sponsors the Web page. Is it officially sanctioned by a governmental agency or institution, or does the site have an unofficial sponsor, unfamiliar alliance, or counterculture affiliation? Check the URL to see if the address includes *.gov,* for a governmental site, *.edu* for an educational address, *.org* for an organization, or *.com* for a commercial enterprise. Governmental and educational sites are often more reliable, but still require scrutiny to determine if the affiliation is legitimate, facetious, or even subversive. Commercial and organizational groups require special investigation for credibility since they are often attempting to sell products, render services, win converts, or solicit donations. Remember that anyone from a legitimate organization to an ex-convict can publish a Web page. Don't be afraid to verify, ask questions, and think critically. If you still have unanswered questions about the authenticity of the site, search for a more reliable source.

2. Identify the Purpose of the Web Site

Another area that requires close examination is the purpose of the site. Does the Web page propose to educate the public or to sell products and/or services? Is the purpose of the site clearly stated or are there hidden agendas? Examine what is said as well as what is implied or unstated on the Web page. A group or organization with a bias can often distort its conclusions or findings to fit its narrow motives. A glowing movie review appearing on a Web page of a Hollywood studio producing a film should be questioned for its objectivity. A student once took a commendable stand in a classroom persuasive speech against the killing of whales, a practice that has been banned by most countries, with some exceptions for scientific research and native populations. Unfortunately, she cited the Web page of an animal rights organization noted for its extreme positions and excessive tactics to support its agenda. The organization accused Vice-president Albert Gore of delivering a speech that encouraged the leaders of a Scandinavian country to return to the practice of killing whales in order to improve the nation's economy. When questioned about the exact words of the vice-president's address or the date of Mr. Gore's speech, the student produced the organization's Web page, which contained no direct quotations or other subsequent details of the existence of the alleged speech. Further investigation about the reliability of the Web site could have spared the student from the embarrassment and loss of credibility that resulted from her use of this questionable source. Examine your Internet sites carefully and do all you can to investigate the purpose and intention of a Web page.

3. Evaluate the Content of the Site

When you have identified the authorship and purpose of the site, your next task is to make a thorough assessment of the content. Evaluate the language, sentence structure, grammar, and spelling of the Web page. A scholarly site with credible authorship should have few, if any, grammatical mistakes or misspellings, while a nonacademic or individually sponsored site might have numerous errors. Examine the claims and conclusions made by the authors. Does the site offer explanations that describe how claims were developed or how conclusions were reached? Does the Web page include links to other Internet sites and do these links actually work effectively? Find out if there is advertising at the site and determine if such commercialization distorts the content or conclusions of the document. Determine if the content of the Web site is accurate and kept up-to-date. Look for an annotated bibliography that includes traditional library sources as well as other non-Internet sources for verification. Often a Web page of a major institution or corporation will help you assess how recent it is by clearly indicating the month and year it was last updated. It is also important to evaluate the overall design and layout of a site. A slick Web page with lavish graphics might gain significant attention but offer little substance beyond selling a product or spreading propaganda. For example, the Heaven's Gate Web page contained an eye-catching design and crisp graphics that were created by an extremely talented group of computer programmers and graphic artists. These Web designers, however, were among thirty-nine members of a cultic community who were convinced by their leader, Marshall Applewhite, to leave their earthly "containers" and die in a ritualistic mass suicide.[3] Sites that advocate violence, engage in inflammatory propaganda, or use hate speech are obviously not worth your time.

You should examine the validity of Internet sources as carefully as you would verify any library or nonliterary source. Recognize that there are few regulations governing the Internet: It can be used by anyone for any purpose. Don't be afraid to question a Web page for authorship, purpose, and content. Remember that the inclusion of an Internet source is your decision and like any source, it can help you achieve your speaking goal or cause needless damage to your credibility.

RESEARCHING SUBSTANTIVE SOURCES

Unlike general references, *substantive sources* contain subject information and help you to locate more specific information. Biographies, directories, dictionaries and encyclopedias, as well as almanacs, collections of quotations, books, and magazines, are substantive sources located in the library. Interviews with experts, as well as research using the resources of large institutions or specialized organizations, are substantive sources that require investigation outside the library.

Biographies

Biographies and biographical collections are good places to search for topics. A speech about a little-known American like John Hanson, who was technically the first president of the United States, would be interesting. Biographies can also be helpful in providing background information about a person you intend to use as an authoritative source in your speech. These collections can assist you:

Current Biography.   Includes detailed information about prominent individuals in almost every field of human achievement around the world.

Dictionary of American Biography.   Provides descriptions of important figures throughout American history.

Who's Who in America.   Contains biographies of prominent Americans who are living at the time of inclusion.

Who's Who of American Women.   Includes American women who have attained positions of responsibility or who have made significant achievements.

Who's Who among Black Americans.   Contains biographies of living black Americans who are leaders in occupations or professions and who have contributed significantly to American life.

Directories and Handbooks

Directories can be helpful if you need information about specific agencies or institutions. These directories provide names, addresses, and services of all types of groups. The government also publishes an index called the *Monthly Catalog of Government Publications,* listing the numerous booklets and pamphlets put out by the U.S. Government Printing Office. You could use this source to find the names of pamphlets written about subjects such as AIDS, fire safety, or CPR. There are so many directories and handbooks that we can't mention all of them, but here is a brief list that might be helpful:

A Handbook of Services for the Handicapped.   Helps readers to understand the difficulties of the disabled and describes resources to meet their special needs.

Civil Right Directory.   Assists people who fear various types of discrimination, and lists federal and state agencies that are responsible for handling these concerns.

Grant Seekers Guide.   Provides lists of foundations, philanthropists, and organizations that provide grants for groups seeking solutions to social or economic problems.

National Directory of Youth and Family Services.   Lists treatment centers, hospitals, crisis centers, hot lines, and professional services.

Occupational Outlook Handbook.   Identifies the major occupations and professions in the United States and describes statistics regarding employment and the projected job outlook.

The Help Book.   Lists numerous organizations and support groups that can provide assistance and intervention in difficult or crisis situations.

Dictionaries

In chapter 1 we talked about misunderstandings in the speaker-audience relationship because of varying interpretations of a word's meaning. A good way for you as a speaker to overcome semantic noise is to be very clear about the meanings of the words you employ. Consult a good dictionary such as *The American Heritage Dictionary* or *Webster's New International Dictionary.* If you need to understand technical terms in a specific field, consult a specialized dictionary. *Black's Law Dictionary, Dorland's Illustrated Medical Dictionary,* or the *Scientific Encyclopedia* are examples of sources that can provide technical definitions in specialized areas.

Encyclopedias

Encyclopedias are often good places to start when you are researching a topic because they provide you with an overview of a general subject very quickly. However, their information is not always comprehensive and, in many cases, material is not up-to-date. Be careful not to base your entire presentation on information taken from encyclopedias or your speech might be superficial.

There are encyclopedias on literally every subject. Two good general subject encyclopedias are *Collier's Encyclopedia* and *World Book*. The *Encyclopaedia Britannica* is also excellent if you need a more scholarly source.

There are numerous specialized encyclopedias on subjects such as aviation, photography, and automotive repair. We have included a brief list that is useful for speech research:

Encyclopedia of Indians of the Americas.   Contains information about the cultures of North, Central, and South American Indian tribes.

Encyclopedia of Religion and Ethics.   Describes world religions, customs, and religious beliefs.

Encyclopedia of World Art.   Includes paintings, photographs, sketches, and architectural examples of world art.

Illustrated Science and Invention Encyclopedia.   Provides information about scientific discoveries and technological advancements.

International Encyclopedia of Social Sciences.   Contains material related to anthropology, economics, law, geography, history, and political science.

International Library of Afro-American Life and History.   Emphasizes African Americans in athletics, medicine, theatre, literature, Civil War times, and the struggle for equality.

International Wildlife Encyclopedia.   Classifies the wildlife of the world and describes animal behavior.

New Grove Dictionary of Music and Musicians.   Provides definitions of music terms, describes the development of musical instruments, and includes biographies of mostly classical musicians.

Almanacs, Yearbooks, and Statistical Publications

Often you will need to find statistical information to give your speech credibility. Almanacs, yearbooks, and statistical abstracts contain numerical data on subjects such as crime, deaths, births, accidents, diseases, incomes, and budgets.

When you do statistical research, it is important to exercise care in your interpretation of the material. Be certain that you clearly understand the information as it is presented. Statistics can be presented in decimals, in percentages, in total numbers of cases, in means (averages), in medians (middle number), or in modes (number occurring with greatest frequency). Know what the statistics measure, and be able to draw clear and accurate conclusions from the data before you decide to include the information.

Some of the most useful sources for statistics are:

Statistical Abstract of the United States. Divided into subject areas representing every aspect of American life. Published by the U.S. Department of Commerce.

Vital Statistics of the United States. Presents comprehensive data in three areas: birth, marriage and divorce, and death. Published by the U.S. Department of Health and Human Services.

World Almanac and Book of Facts. Contains world statistics in many areas, including births, deaths, and population.

Information Please Almanac. Presents articles in numerous fields such as astronomy, family, and culture, and statistical information on American and international subjects.

Collections of Quotations

Many sources can provide you with the right quotation to introduce or conclude your speech. Quotations can often synthesize ideas that might take several lines for you to paraphrase. You might want to consult *Bartlett's Familiar Quotations, Morrow's International Dictionary of Contemporary Quotations,* and *The Macmillan Book of Proverbs, Maxims, and Famous Phrases.*

Books

One of the most obvious sources for a speech is an authoritative book written on your topic. Frequently you will find a collection of readings compiled by one editor or author which will be useful to your research. Be sure to notice the date a book was published. If you were researching "Latest Computer Technologies" in a book published in 1975, you would not find much current information. If your topic were "History of Computer Technology," the 1975 source might be excellent.

For some topics, using a rare book or a classic study might be more significant than a more recent source. In a speech about the *Titanic,* for example, a speaker could quote an eyewitness from a book written in 1912 by one of *Titanic*'s survivors. In this case, the speech would contain material from an excellent primary source.

Some books, like the huge selection of self-help publications in bookstores, are popular with the general public, but often, authors of these publications are not experts—they are merely lay individuals writing from their own personal experiences about divorce, jogging, or making millions in real estate. The fact that people have been enterprising enough to put their thoughts into print does not mean their words should be regarded with reverence. Analyze carefully what you read; examine how writers document and reference their material and, above all, feel free to question and even to discard information if other evidence proves data questionable or false.

Magazines, Journals, Newspapers

Newsmagazines such as *Time, Newsweek,* or *U.S. News & World Report* are excellent sources and will provide much of the information you need on current events. As you investigate these sources, however, be able to distinguish between fact and opinion. Many newsmagazines contain articles that report facts in a fairly objective manner. These periodicals also include columns, such as editorials or features, which provide opinions and interpretations of facts. Also be aware of any political or social bias of the publications, and double-check articles with other news sources for accuracy.

Quarterlies and journals contain articles relative to specific disciplines. Periodicals such as *The Automobile Quarterly, The American Journal of Psychology,* or *The Criminal Law Quarterly* can be helpful in your research, even though they are written in the technical jargon of the discipline. Be certain that you clearly understand journal articles so you are able to communicate the information easily to the audience.

Newspapers will give you some of the most up-to-date information about current events and social issues. Check the political bias of the newspaper you research. *The Washington Post* and *The New York Times,* for instance, are considered liberal publications while the *Wall Street Journal* and the *Christian Science Monitor* are more conservative. Be careful about using newspapers as comprehensive sources on issues. Since current events are constantly unfolding, one news story or article will rarely be complete. It is wise to cross-reference newspapers for accuracy.

Legal Research

You may need to cite a number of court cases to prove a point in a persuasive speech, or describe the details of litigation for an informative presentation. If so, don't be intimidated by the number of official-looking legal volumes in your library. You simply have to learn how to use these resources. If you know what information you need, a good librarian should get you to the right source.

Audiovisual Aids

In addition to books and periodicals, libraries have maps, atlases, and extensive media collections which you can research to support ideas. A visual aid, such as a map, can quickly pinpoint a physical location and make a topic more understandable to listeners. Including a brief excerpt from a *National Geographic* videotape, or playing a portion of a symphony may also add interest to particular speech topics. Audiovisual aids are effective because they help you communicate with listeners through additional channels. (Chapter 12 provides a complete discussion of the types and uses of audiovisuals in a presentation.)

Interviews with Authorities

For certain topics, your research will take you outside the library. Interviews with professionals such as physicians, lawyers, police officers, or child psychologists will yield invaluable primary source material—as long as the experts are authorities in their fields. If you are doing research about victims of rape, speak to an official in a community rape-crisis center. Your professional may be able to provide you with a wealth of supporting materials even in a brief telephone interview. Don't be content to include just a single interview—use several, so that your speech will contain a number of authoritative viewpoints.

You can also include *personal testimonies* from individuals who have actually experienced some aspect of the topic. A testimonial from someone injured by a drunk driver, or a brief quote from a person afflicted with AIDS, can vividly convey the impact of an issue.

Legislative and Governmental Research

You may have a topic that requires you to investigate specific legislation enacted by the state legislature or by the U.S. Congress. A quick phone call to the office of one of your representatives can help you to gather valuable information on a local or national legislative issue. *The Congressional Index* is an excellent source if you want to know the legislation currently pending in Congress. This index gives you the current status of legislation: that is, whether the bill is in committee, if it has been passed by one or both houses of Congress, if it has been signed into law or vetoed by the president, or if a presidential veto has been overridden by the Congress.

If you want to investigate the daily proceedings of Congress, consult *The Congressional Record,* which transcribes the floor debates and votes of the members of the Senate and the House of Representatives. (In addition, both houses of Congress now televise their daily proceedings, making a video record as well.)

When you need to understand how our Congress and the government spend our tax money, you can obtain a copy of *The Budget of the United States Government,* which can tell you how the federal government allocates more than $1.5 trillion in the current fiscal year. The budget is available in the library or through the U.S. Government Printing Office.

Institutional and Organizational Research

Many institutions and organizations have public relations or information offices that can provide you with material on specific subjects. If you need information on the eye bank, for example, contact the hospital specializing in this field. For data related to higher educational institutions, get in touch with your college or university's public relations office. If you're doing research on a foreign country, call the embassy or the foreign consulate office nearest you. Ask your state's department of motor vehicles for data regarding accident rates, insurance guidelines, or driving tests. To collect examples and statistical evidence concerning specific crimes in your community or state, consult the information office of the police department. If you need to know what people are doing to prevent drinking and driving, contact Mothers Against Drunk Driving (MADD). If you want to know what is being done to improve our nation's educational system, contact the National Education Association (NEA). Information from these institutions and organizations can provide more depth and substance to a speech topic. Here are three sources that can help you to find specific organizations or agencies:

Encyclopedia of Associations.   Lists the names, objectives, and addresses of more than 23,000 national and international organizations and associations.

The United States Government Manual.   Identifies the official names, purposes, addresses, and phone numbers of all agencies in the legislative, judicial, and executive branches of government.

State blue books, manuals, and almanacs.   A guide published by each state that lists agencies of the executive, judicial, and legislative branches of state government.

Specialized Libraries and Museums

Many cities and communities have specialized libraries in law, medicine, literature, science, astronomy, or agriculture. The Library of Congress is a comprehensive source that includes material from these libraries as well as anything that has ever been published in the United States. The Library of Congress and many other libraries have interlibrary loan services that allow you to obtain materials from other libraries at your local institution. The only disadvantage of interloan systems is that you may have to order information in advance. Check with your librarian for specific information regarding the interlibrary loan system nearest you.

KEEPING ACCURATE NOTES

When you are doing research, it is important that you have a well-organized system of note taking so that you will use your time efficiently. Often people will go to the periodical indexes, jot down a list of sources, then look up articles and forget to write down the statistics or examples they wanted to use in their speeches. They have to return to their sources a second or third time and plod through the material all over again to recall their information. A good method of taking notes can help you avoid such a time-wasting process and assist you in making substantial progress toward getting your speech organized. Get some 3×5 or 4×6 note cards. When you find a source you want to use, put a topic heading at the upper right-hand corner of the card. Then at the upper left corner put the type of supporting information you are listing on the card, such as statistics, quotation, comparison or contrast, and so forth. Then place a bibliographic entry on the next line so that you will be able to identify the exact reference for later use in your speech or in case you ever need to investigate it again. Finally, jot down the specific details of the information. Include all the necessary statistical data, illustrations, or other material you want for the speech. When you follow this system, you will be able to build an index file of supporting materials that will be easy to use and can be arranged in any order.

The following notes demonstrate how to identify the topic, the specific type of supporting data, the bibliographic reference, and pertinent details of the researched material.

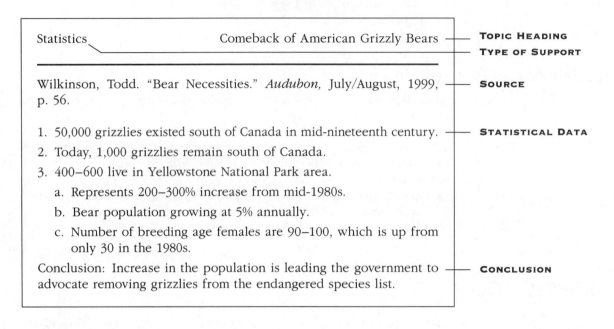

Statistics   Comeback of American Grizzly Bears —— TOPIC HEADING
                                                                            —— TYPE OF SUPPORT

Wilkinson, Todd. "Bear Necessities." *Audubon,* July/August, 1999, —— SOURCE
p. 56.

1. 50,000 grizzlies existed south of Canada in mid-nineteenth century. —— STATISTICAL DATA
2. Today, 1,000 grizzlies remain south of Canada.
3. 400–600 live in Yellowstone National Park area.
   a. Represents 200–300% increase from mid-1980s.
   b. Bear population growing at 5% annually.
   c. Number of breeding age females are 90–100, which is up from only 30 in the 1980s.

Conclusion: Increase in the population is leading the government to —— CONCLUSION
advocate removing grizzlies from the endangered species list.

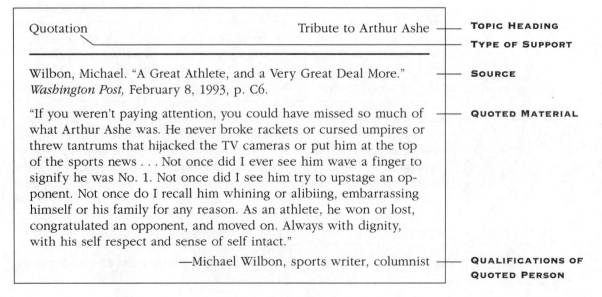

Quotation   Tribute to Arthur Ashe —— TOPIC HEADING
                                                                     —— TYPE OF SUPPORT

Wilbon, Michael. "A Great Athlete, and a Very Great Deal More." —— SOURCE
Washington Post, February 8, 1993, p. C6.

"If you weren't paying attention, you could have missed so much of —— QUOTED MATERIAL
what Arthur Ashe was. He never broke rackets or cursed umpires or
threw tantrums that hijacked the TV cameras or put him at the top
of the sports news . . . Not once did I ever see him wave a finger to
signify he was No. 1. Not once did I see him try to upstage an opponent. Not once do I recall him whining or alibiing, embarrassing
himself or his family for any reason. As an athlete, he won or lost,
congratulated an opponent, and moved on. Always with dignity,
with his self respect and sense of self intact."

                          —Michael Wilbon, sports writer, columnist —— QUALIFICATIONS OF
                                                                         QUOTED PERSON

Example	Amazing feats in advertising—bungee jumping-GMC truck	**TOPIC HEADING**
		TYPE OF SUPPORT

Bromer, Cliff. "Jumpin' Jimmy." *Popular Mechanics,* March, 1993, pp. 56–57.   — **SOURCE**

1. Bungee cord was attached to tail hook of GMC sport truck.   — **DETAILS OF EXAMPLE**
2. Bungee cord also fastened to New River Gorge Bridge, Beckley, West Virginia.
   a. Bridge is 876 ft. high and has largest steel arch span in continental U.S.
   b. Engineers determined that bridge could sustain stresses of truck bungee jump.
3. Bungee cord specially designed with 9 individual cords.
4. Launch platform from bridge required stunt engineering.
5. Jump was a success for a brief 30 to 60 sec. commercial.
6. Truck had to be "reeled in" like a fish.

THE INTERVIEW

Many of your speech topics will require you to interview people who are experts or authorities in their fields. You should know how to conduct an interview to get the material that you need from these individuals.

Preparing for the Interview

When you interview an expert on your topic, you must be completely prepared by conducting preliminary research into the topic, and developing a list of questions to ask. This kind of preparation will help you to conduct the interview more effectively and keep you from wasting valuable time.

When you have done your research and prepared your questions, call the interviewee to make an appointment. Be sure that the individual

A speaker should know how to conduct a successful interview with an expert to gather the most appropriate information.

understands your topic and knows the reason for the interview. You might even tell the individual one or two of the questions you are going to ask so that the person can be adequately prepared with answers. When you set up the interview, you may want to double-check the qualifications of the interviewee so that you are certain that you are talking to the appropriate expert. When the individual agrees to the interview, set a date and a time that accommodates the other person's schedule, and yet allows you to obtain all the information you need.

Conducting the Interview

Be sure that you are on time for the interview. Establish rapport with your interviewee by being friendly, courteous, and conversational. Demonstrate active listening skills—nod your head, sit forward, and show interest in the person you are interviewing. Let the individual know that you are easy to talk to, receptive, and noncombative.

Next, introduce your topic and state the purpose of the interview. Start by asking questions from your prepared list. As the interviewee introduces new or relevant information, think of other follow-up questions to ask. If the individual brings up ideas that are irrelevant to your topic, gently bring the person back on track by saying, "Let's go back to what you were saying before," or "Now, if you don't mind, I'd like to ask you another question." Remember that you do have a time limit, and you must gather the information you need.

Be sure that your interviewee adequately clarifies and explains material. One-word answers like "yes" or "no" will not really help when you need information in depth. Ask him or her to expand on the issue by posing open-ended questions such as, "Can you give me an example of what you're saying?" or "How do you handle that type of situation?"

During the interview make verbal summaries to help you understand the material clearly, and also to allow the interviewee to correct any misinformation or misconceptions you may have. Keep the interview moving; if it gets bogged down, ask more questions or make additional comments to get the discussion going again. Don't monopolize the conversation; give the person adequate time to formulate a response. And don't interrupt the individual unless it is absolutely necessary. This practice is not only rude, it also interrupts the individual's thought process.

Conclude the interview on time. Don't stay longer unless you are specifically asked. The person has set aside a specific time for you in a busy schedule—don't impose any further.

Taking Notes During an Interview

During the interview, you should take notes that are accurate and complete. Remember that your writing should usually be notation—not a verbatim transcript of the entire conversation. If your interview covers detailed information that requires more careful transcription, ask for permission to bring a tape recorder—but never bring one to an interview unless you ask for prior permission. There will be times when taping will not be acceptable to an interviewee. For example, if you were talking with a rape crisis counselor about specific case histories, the counselor might not allow you to tape the interview because of the need to protect confidentiality.

If you use a direct quote from the individual, make certain that everything you jot down is completely correct. Double-check the accuracy of the statement with the interviewee. Don't be afraid to ask questions to clarify an issue if you are not certain about the information.

After the interview is over, review your notes while the ideas are still fresh in your mind. Expand your notes by writing summaries and additional comments. At a later time you may want to make a follow-up call to clear up any unanswered questions.

TOPIC: AIRLINE SAFETY

Joanne had booked a flight to return home for spring break, but recent aviation accidents by commuter airlines, USAir, Valujet, and TWA had caused her to become increasingly apprehensive about the safety of air travel. Joanne thought that her concern about aviation safety might make a good topic for her five- to seven-minute convincing speech, which was due when she returned from vacation. However, she was not sure of the approach she should take. Should she arbitrarily assume that airline travel was unsafe and research the speech using that premise, or should she wait to discover what the research indicated about the issue? Joanne wisely decided to wait and see what her investigation revealed before taking a point of view.

Joanne's first strategy was to go to the library and do a computer search using *Periodical Abstracts Ondisc.* When she typed in the key words, "airline safety" Joanne was able to access seven articles. Scrolling through the list, she read the descriptive abstract of each article and chose three titles that could provide helpful information: Miller, Annetta. "How Safe Is This Flight?, *Newsweek,* April 24, 1995, pp. 18–29; "NTSB Studies Commuter Safety." *Flying,* March, 1995, pp. 28–29; and Phillips, Edward H. "Peña to Airlines: Elevate Safety Margins." *Aviation Week & Space Technology,* January 16, 1995, p. 26. Joanne printed out her selections and took them to the microfilm department where she obtained the complete articles and reviewed them on the microfilm reader. The library subscribed to several newspapers on disc and Joanne was also able to use the computer to search the *Washington Post* for more titles. Since the computerized newspaper index included the entire texts of articles, Joanne was able to read each article at the computer and print the most relevant one for her topic: Phillips, Don. "FAA Unveils New Rules For Airlines; Goal Is Safer Commuter Flights." *Washington Post,* December 15, 1995, sec. c, p. 1.

Joanne then turned to noncomputerized periodical indexes for help. She investigated the *Applied Science and Technology Index* and found numerous article titles

THE BIBLIOGRAPHY: HOW TO RECORD AN ENTRY

When you write your outline, list the sources you have used to research the topic. When you enter a book or magazine title in your bibliography, you need to use a style that is uniform and consistent. Many colleges and universities have their own style booklets that give their required bibliographic describing airline accidents. She selected "Pilots, ATC Blamed for USAir Accident." *Aviation Week and Space Technology,* April 10, 1995, pp. 32–33. She also used the *Business Periodicals Index* and found: Donoghue, J. A. "Strategy for Prevention." *Air Transportation World,* July, 1994, p. 7. Both articles required research in the library's microfilm department.

Since she wanted to find statistical information about airline safety, Joanne obtained the most recent edition of *Statistical Abstract of the United States.* Using the category, "airline accidents," Joanne was able to get a comprehensive report of accidents listed by year, but she kept in mind that the latest statistics in the current edition were actually compiled two years previously. She also thought it would be helpful to use a survey that she found in the *C Q Researcher* (formerly *Editorial Research Reports*), which rated the world's airlines according to safety.

Joanne had access to an Internet connection, and she decided to look for information using *Alta Vista* as the search engine. She was able to find the Federal Aviation Administration's homepage (FAA), which included a recent speech on airline safety by Transportation Secretary Federico Peña. She printed out the speech and began another search using *Lycos.* She came across a page that identified ten of the most recent airline accidents. Joanne thought that these incidents could be included as examples in her speech, but a disclaimer noted that these abstracts were not official government or airline reports, so Joanne decided to verify the information with additional research.

Joanne also contacted the local FAA office at the international airport nearby and made an appointment to interview the regional manager of the Flight Standards District Office about airline safety.

She now had more than enough information to begin the research process. But Joanne realized that she would need to narrow and refine her topic as her point of view emerged as a result of her investigation.

procedures. Your instructor may want you to use your college-style system or another approach.

In this text, we have used the Kate L. Turabian stylebook *A Manual for Writers of Term Papers, Theses, and Dissertations.*[4] Since you will probably be using books, magazines, newspapers, and interviews frequently, study these sample entries according to the Turabian style. Be sure to alphabetize the bibliography as you write each reference item.

BOOKS: ONE AUTHOR

Chideya, Farai. *The Color of Our Future.* New York: William Morrow and Company, Inc., 1999.

BOOKS: TWO AUTHORS

Adler, Ronald B., and Towne, Neil. *Looking Out Looking In.* 9th ed. Fort Worth, TX: Harcourt Brace College Publishers, 1999.

MAGAZINES: ARTICLE WITHOUT AUTHOR PROVIDED

"Down to Earth: Around-the-World Ballooning." *The Economist,* February 21, 1998, p. 86.

MAGAZINES: ARTICLE WITH AUTHOR PROVIDED

Marsh, Alton K. "In-Flight Emergencies: Upset Recovery." *AOPAPilot,* August 1999, pp. 59–64.

NEWSPAPERS: ARTICLE WITHOUT AUTHOR PROVIDED

"In Kennedy Plane Debris, No Hint of Trouble in Air." *The New York Times,* July 31, 1999, p. A9.

NEWSPAPERS: ARTICLE WITH AUTHOR PROVIDED

Weber, Thomas E. "Did a Web Site Foreshadow a Killing Spree?" *The Wall Street Journal,* April 22, 1999, p. B1.

THE INTERNET: ORGANIZATION (NO AUTHOR)

Reeve-Irvine Research Center. "Christopher Reeve." (20 July 1997). http://www.reeve.uci.edu/~reeve/ [15 Aug. 1999].

Organization. "Title of Document." (date revised). Web address [date accessed].

THE INTERNET: MAGAZINE (WITH AUTHOR)

Boyer, Phil. (1999, July). "Take the Time." *AOPA Online.* http://www.aopa.org [16 Aug. 1999].

Author. (Date of publication). "Article Title." *Magazine Title.* Web address [date accessed].

INTERVIEWS

Cavey, Donald R. Supervisor, Special Services, Bell Atlantic Maryland, Inc., Hunt Valley, Maryland. Interview, March 3, 2000.

SUMMARY

Sources should be credible and reliable; they may be primary or secondary.

General library references for locating sources are the catalog, the periodical indexes, and the computer. The Internet is both a general and substantive reference tool for speech research. Substantive library sources are biographies, directories, and encyclopedias, as well as almanacs, collections of quotations, books, and magazines. Interviews with experts and research into large institutions or specialized organizations are nonliterary sources. An accurate system of note taking should be used to collect research materials.

When interviewing experts, be prepared, conduct the interview skillfully, and take notes. Consult your institutional style guide or use the Turabian system to record a bibliography.[5]

SKILL BUILDERS

1. Select an individual in political life as the topic for a two- to three-minute speech to inform. The individual could be a member of Congress, or an elected official in your state or community. Gather some specific information about this person from three different sources: a biography, a news article (either in a magazine or newspaper), and an interview. Present the speech to your class. Remember that it is important for you to establish credibility in your presentation.

2. Select a current events topic for a two- to three-minute informative speech. Using the *Readers' Guide, Periodical Abstracts,* or *ProQuest Direct,* find articles in two different periodicals which support your issue. Present the topic to your class, and try to integrate your sources effectively into your speech.

3. List your sources to Exercises (1) and (2) above using your departmental style book or the Turabian system. Make sure that you are accurate in every detail of your entries.

4. Identify a speaker who you feel uses credible research in his or her speeches. Write a brief paragraph explaining the reasons you trust the speaker's sources. Repeat the same exercise with a speaker you feel does not use credible research.

5. Divide your class into groups of four. Find titles of four magazine or journal articles, four newspaper articles, and four statistical materials on the following topics using two periodical indexes, two newspaper indexes, and two statistical sources. Report your findings to the class.
   a. The flat tax.
   b. Regulation of the Internet.
   c. New treatments for multiple sclerosis.
   d. Regulation of the health care industry.
   e. Genetic engineering.

   f. Scandals involving sperm banks.
   g. Interracial adoptions.
   h. Legalizing gay marriages.
   i. Welfare reform.
   j. Cloning animals.

N O T E S

1. Lester Thonssen, comp., *Selected Readings in Rhetoric and Public Speaking* (New York: H. W. Wilson, 1942), pp. 65–67.
2. To prepare this section we were assisted by these Internet sources: Henderson, John. "ICYouSee." http://www.ithaca.edu/library/Training/hott.html [July 22, 1999] and Grassian, Esther. "Thinking Critically about Discipline-Based World Wide Web Resources." *UCLA College Library Instruction.* http://www.library.ucla.edu/libraries/college/instruct/Web/critical.htm [November 10, 1998].
3. "The Next Level," *Newsweek,* April 7, 1997, pp. 28–36.
4. Kate L. Turabian, *A Manual for Writers of Term Papers, Theses, and Dissertations,* 4th ed. (Chicago: University of Chicago Press, 1973.)
5. I want to thank Bonita J. Preston, associate professor of library science at Catonsville Community College, for her guidance and advice regarding this chapter.

Chapter 9

CHOOSING
SUPPORTING MATERIALS

A quotation in a speech, article, or book is like a rifle in the hands of an infantryman. It speaks with authority.

Brendan Francis

CHAPTER OBJECTIVES

After reading this chapter you will be able to:

1. Identify the principal types of supporting materials;

2. Describe how to use each supporting material effectively in a speech.

During his years as president, Ronald Reagan was often known as "the Great Communicator." Reagan's genius as a speaker was due partly to his ability to use supporting materials that created a strong emotional attachment with listeners. He could ignite feelings of patriotism by painting a vivid picture of the delegates to the Constitutional Convention; he could stimulate feelings of pride by describing the heroic actions of a young government employee rescuing the victim of an airline crash; and he could arouse sorrow by reading the letter of a daughter who had lost a father in World War II.

Reagan's use of supporting materials, however, has not always been accurate. At the 1992 Republican National Convention, the former president attempted to quote Lincoln to support the accusation that Democrats were trying to copy Republicans:

> They even tried to portray themselves as sharing the same fundamental values of our party! What they truly don't understand is the principle so eloquently stated by Abraham Lincoln: "You cannot strengthen the weak by weakening the strong. You cannot help the wage earner by pulling down the wage payer. You cannot help the poor by destroying the rich. You cannot help men permanently by doing for them what they could and should do for themselves."

To research the quotation, Mr. Reagan used a book entitled *The Toastmaster's Treasure Chest,* which falsely identified Lincoln as the source. Had Reagan checked the accuracy of the lines with historians or librarians, he would have discovered that the quotation was taken from a book of maxims published in 1916 by William J. H. Boetcker, a Pennsylvania minister.[1]

This final chapter on the speech foundation considers several types of supporting materials. We include examples from student and professional speakers and make suggestions for you to apply to your own presentations. While we want you to build strong connections with your audience, we want you to use supporting materials accurately and appropriately.

MAKING THE APPROPRIATE SELECTION

When you research a speech, you must look for supporting materials. If you are talking about heart transplants, a quotation from a prominent heart surgeon builds credibility. If you are asking listeners to favor bicycle helmet laws, you would use statistics from the Bicycle Helmet Safety Institute to show that wearing helmets decreases fatalities. If you are educating the audience about lupus disease, a disturbing story of a child's chronic illness obtained from an interview with a mother would paint a vivid picture. Whether your speech is informative or persuasive, you need information and credible examples to support your topic.

When you use supporting materials, it is usually advisable to mention the source for your information. While you certainly don't need to pepper your speech with "according to's," you do need to make it clear to your audience that your topic is based upon concrete evidence. If you use several facts or examples from the same source, you can make one reference that doesn't interfere with the flow of the speech. If you say "Some of my information today is taken from an article I read in the November, 1999 issue of *Consumer Reports*," you have shown your audience that your evidence is grounded in credible research.

Some of the most authoritative supporting materials are: statistics, polls and surveys; examples, stories, illustrations, and case studies; quotations and testimonies; and comparisons and contrasts. A speaker can use these materials to build a credible case for a persuasive speech or to provide verifiable support in an informative presentation.

Less verifiable, yet stimulating forms of support are: personal experience and observation, humor, anecdotes, and role-playing. Speakers use these materials to enliven speeches and to maintain audience interest and attention. It is often difficult to validate experiences, humor, or skits with sources. However, a speaker can enhance a speech if these forms of support are based upon realistic circumstances and combined with more authoritative statistics, testimony, or examples.

We will examine each type of supporting material and describe its potential use in a speech.

STATISTICS, POLLS, SURVEYS

One way to support a topic is by using statistical data. *Statistics* are a collection of facts in numerical form, *polls* are samplings of opinion on selected issues, and *surveys* are studies that draw conclusions from research.

Statistics can provide data about population, income, death, crime, and birth. You can determine the increase in the number of deaths due to heart disease by looking at statistics over a fifteen-year period. If you need to know how many people favor or oppose gay soldiers in the military, you can consult the Gallup Opinion Poll or the CBS/*New York Times* Poll. If you need to know how student performance compares in different racial or economic groups, you can investigate the conclusions provided in a specific study.

Using Statistics

You must be careful when you decide to use statistics, polls, or surveys as your supporting evidence. If you use too many complicated numbers, you'll bore your audience. Just stating that the Federal Budget in 1999 was approximately $1,730,138,492,036.29 is a mouthful. The audience would probably forget most of it by the time they heard the twenty-nine cents!

It is often advisable to round off your statistics to the nearest whole number so the audience can grasp the overall concept. Be sure that you draw conclusions from the data and relate the conclusion to your point. It is helpful to relate complicated statistics to a simpler concept. While few people could comprehend the staggering budget figure mentioned above, anyone could understand the number if it were compared to a thousand dollar bills stacked several miles high.

If you need to be more precise with statistics, you can construct a visual aid or chart to display the data so that the audience can draw conclusions at a glance.

When you cite statistics, polls, or surveys, it establishes credibility to state who conducted the research as well as when and where the research was done. When presenting a survey, you might want to mention the purpose of the research in addition to the conclusions of the study.

In the following excerpt from an informative speech about the history of Coca-Cola, Jena L. Weigel used statistics to show the amount consumed by the public:

> I'd like to tell you some startling statistics I found about Coca-Cola in the book, *Everybody's Business, A Field Guide to the 400 Leading Companies in America*. When Coca-Cola was introduced in 1886, the company sold only nine sodas a day. But almost one hundred years later in 1980, the amount of Coke sold would fill 213,000 Olympic size swimming pools. Researchers also estimated in 1980 that if you took all of the Coke ever consumed by the human race and poured it over Niagara Falls, the giant waterfall would flow at its normal rate for 23 hours and 21 minutes! That's a lot of the real thing, isn't it? Today, Coke is served more that 560 million times every day.[2]

Jena understood that raw data is not interesting unless listeners can relate to the numbers easily. The speaker made the statistics come alive by using familiar examples such as Niagara Falls and Olympic-size swimming pools. Jena also introduced a humorous note when she cited the slogan from Coca-Cola marketing campaigns. To give the data credibility, the speaker mentioned her source for the statistics.

During the presidential campaign of 1992, twenty million Americans watched with fascination as Texas billionaire H. Ross Perot used homemade charts and simplified statistics to explain the problem of the national debt:[3]

> Now we have a four trillion dollar debt. Let's look at this map here. Look at the purple, and let me tell you what, if we had the four trillion still in the bank, we could do with it . . . We could buy a one-hundred-thousand-dollar home for every family in every one of those states. We could put a

ten-thousand-dollar car in the garages of each of these houses. Then we could build one thousand ten-million-dollar libraries for a thousand cities in these states. We could build two thousand schools in these states costing ten million dollars each and have enough left over to put into a savings account. And from the interest alone in that savings account pay forty thousand nurses and forty thousand teachers an annual salary of $32,760. And finally we'd still have enough from the interest income alone to give a five-thousand-dollar a year bonus to every family in those states. That's what four trillion dollars would buy. We just can't keep throwing money out the window.[4]

For his statistics, Perot used a two-color map of the United States to show how four trillion dollars could be applied in "the purple" area representing more than half of the country. While people could not readily understand the concept of several trillion dollars, Americans could easily connect to the numbers related in personal terms.

Speaker William L. Winter, director of the National Press Institute, uses a poll from a credible source to support a point:

And finally, people are telling us that they just don't like the media very much. Poll after poll shows that readers, viewers, and listeners believe the media are biased, that they have too much power, and that they wield that power arbitrarily.

This month's *Washington Journalism Review* reports the sobering findings of a survey done by the new University of Virginia–based Thomas Jefferson Center for the Protection of Free Expression. Nearly 30 percent of those polled said that freedom of expression did not extend to newspapers. Forty percent said that they didn't believe the First Amendment protected the arts and entertainment, or that protecting such expression was not as important as protecting the spoken word.[5]

In a speech about recycling materials, David Zebraski used a survey to demonstrate the problem of wastefulness:

Dr. William L. Rathje, an anthropologist at the University of Arizona, conducted a long-term study of the residents of Tucson. In research funded by the Environmental Protection Agency and the National Science Foundation, Dr. Rathje and his students actually collected samples of garbage from different economic neighborhoods in the city. He found that, overall, Tucson's residents throw away fifteen percent of their food, wasting eleven to thirteen million dollars per year. He also discovered that middle income people throw away more food, tools, and appliances than do low or high income people. This study found that middle-class people—individuals like you and me—are the most wasteful.[6]

In addition to stating the findings of the study, the speaker mentions the name of the researcher, the place where the study was conducted, two funding agencies, and even the process used for research. The results of the study credibly support the speaker's point about the average person's wastefulness.

EXAMPLES, ILLUSTRATIONS, CASE STUDIES, NARRATIVES

When you conduct research you should look for examples, illustrations, case studies, or narratives to support your topic. An *example* is a brief, factual instance that demonstrates a point; a *hypothetical example* is a fictitious situation that has a realistic application; an *illustration* is a long example that clarifies and amplifies an idea; a *case study* is an in-depth account of a situation or a set of circumstances; and a *narrative* is telling an experience or story.

A brief example or case can often demonstrate a point more dramatically than a long description of facts. People love a good story and appreciate research, which stimulates curiosity. By combining a balance of theoretical facts with illustrations and examples, you keep your audience involved.

A speaker provides concrete support for ideas and concepts by using examples, statistics, and quotations.

Using Examples

In a speech on drunk driving, a speaker might use one or two brief examples combined with a minute-long personal narrative about driving while intoxicated. In a five- to seven-minute speech, two brief instances and one long illustration would probably be sufficient. A speaker could also cite many brief examples of drunk driving. This type of "rapid-fire" approach is effective in communicating a great deal of information in a short period of time.

You build credibility in your speech if you cite references. Let your audience know if the narrative is from your own knowledge and experience or from someone else's. State your sources for case studies, examples, and illustrations. Use a variety of sources and use a variety of instances. Don't base your speech on one personal narrative or on one brief example. Provide examples and cases that develop your topic in-depth.

In the following speech, Stanley Eitzen, professor emeritus at Colorado State University's Sociology Department, cites a series of brief examples to support his point:

> Many popular sports encourage player aggression. These sports demand body checking, blocking, and tackling. But the culture of these sports sometimes goes beyond what is needed. Players are taught to deliver a blow to the opponent, not just to block or tackle him.
>
> Coaches often reward athletes for extra hard hits. In this regard, let me cite several examples from a few years ago:
>
> - At the University of Florida a football player received a "dead roach" decal for his helmet when he hit an opponent so hard that he lay prone with his legs and arms up in the air.
> - Similarly, University of Miami football players were awarded a "slobber knocker" decal for their helmets if they hit an opposing player so hard that it knocked the slobber out of his mouth.
> - The Denver Broncos coaching staff, similar to other NFL teams yet contrary to league rules, gave monetary awards each week to the players who hit their opponents the hardest.[7]

This "rapid-fire" technique builds a strong argument, bombarding the audience with specific instances to show that many American sports teams reinforce and support the use of physical violence.

The following illustration is an example of the use of a hypothetical situation. It is a powerful tool to use in a speech because it briefly allows listeners to experience blindness:

> I'd like you all to close your eyes for a minute. Imagine that it is early morning. The alarm rings, but you must feel for it to turn it off. You get up and search for your clothes. You go downstairs to make breakfast, but you touch the food to find out what there is to eat. After breakfast, you

carefully go to the door, step outside and listen for the sound of oncoming traffic. Hearing none, you gingerly cross the street to the bus stop on the other side. You wait for the sound of the creaking brakes to stop in front of you. When the doors squeak open, you carefully make your way up the steps. You give what you hope is the correct change to the bus driver. You then feel for an empty seat. You've made it one more day! This is what it feels like to be blind. And that's what we're talking about here—a real problem that happens to human beings just like you and me. You can open your eyes now.[8]

This illustration is more effective than simply describing the difficulties of blindness because the speaker simulates the experience by cutting off the visual channel. The speaker provides clear directions to audience members as to when they are to close or open their eyes. The "you" approach has effectively placed listeners in the sightless world of the blind: The speaker has successfully communicated his point through the use of a hypothetical illustration.

The next illustration comes from the real-life experience of the speaker's family:

Three months ago, I went to my cousin's wedding, which lasted an entire weekend—Friday through Sunday. You'd be surprised though—I don't know where the time went. In India, a wedding is usually a two-day occasion, and everyone in the bride and groom's family plays a role in the wedding ceremony. The ceremony begins with the bride's and groom's parents in prayer. Heinrick Zimmer, in the book *Philosophies of India,* explains how the priest generally begins with an explanation of the union of two families with the groom present. The priest then calls to the bride, giving her one last chance to run away. Next the bride is given away by her uncle. The ceremony continues as the bride and groom walk around a fire in seven circles. During the first six turns, the groom is in the lead and the priest explains the significance: The wife will follow her husband in all the trials they go through in life, she will respect his decisions, and she will follow whatever he decides to do with the family. Then in the last turn, the bride leads, and undoes almost everything that was said during the first six circles. The groom vows to respect his wife, to love and cherish her, and always to include her as an equal in this partnership.[9]

Neha Badshah used an illustration to describe a portion of the wedding ceremony in her native India. The personal experience combined with a credible reference provided the audience with an interesting portrait of a different culture.

In the next example, Andrea Hoguet selected a case study from a local newspaper to support a persuasive speech:

It is one thing for children to have learned aggressive behavior at a young age, but it is quite another for a parent of a relative to contribute to this aggressive behavior. I read about a case in the November 13th issue of our local *Carroll County Times* newspaper. Mrs. Luella Wilson, a 91-year-old woman of Bennington, Vermont, was sued for $950,000. Here's what happened. Mrs. Wilson gave her nephew a large sum of money to buy a new car for his eighteenth birthday, knowing that he had a drug problem, and that he did not even possess a license. After drinking heavily and smoking marijuana one evening, the nephew drove the car off a bridge. The passenger riding with him was paralyzed, and finally had to have his leg amputated. The passenger sued Mrs. Wilson for negligence. She apparently knew about her nephew's problem with drugs, yet she still gave him $6,300 for a car. Should she be liable? Yes, she should! And apparently the jury agreed and awarded the victim almost one million dollars in damages. The case is currently under appeal.[10]

Andrea used this case to support the persuasive proposition that parents and guardians should be held accountable for the criminal actions of their children. The topic was controversial and some listeners disagreed with the speaker's viewpoint. However, Andrea strengthened the evidence by describing the details of the case and by citing a credible source. The speaker used gestures, vocal inflections, and emphasis to stress her conclusion to the case: "Should she be liable? Yes, she should!"

The following narrative was related by Richard D. Lamm, former governor of Colorado:

Let me begin with a metaphor. The United States fleet was on the high seas. All of a sudden a blip appeared on the radar screen. "Tell that ship to change its course fifteen degrees!" said the Admiral. The radio man did, and the word came back on the radio, "YOU change YOUR course fifteen degrees." "Tell that ship that we're the United States Navy and to change its course fifteen degrees," said the Admiral. The radio man did and the word came back again, "YOU change YOUR course fifteen degrees." This time the Admiral himself got on the radio and said, "I am an Admiral in the United States Navy. Change your course fifteen degrees." The word came back over the radio, "You change your course fifteen degrees. I am a lighthouse!" We often expect the world to adjust to our course, but alas, we find we must adjust to the realities around us. I would go further—I believe it is the duty and the obligation of each generation to perceive the realities of their times.[11]

This kind of story makes the audience sit back, relax, and listen. The narrative is interesting and has a humorous punch line. But Governor Lamm draws a conclusion from the story and relates it to his overall theme—"the need to change course." If you choose to relate a narrative such as this one, you must be certain to deliver the story smoothly so that the details and punch line retain their vigor.

QUOTATIONS AND TESTIMONIES FROM AUTHORITIES

You can also build credibility by using quotations and testimonies from experts or authorities. A *quotation* is the exact restatement of a person's words, and a *testimony* is a statement or endorsement given by an expert or an individual with a logical connection to the topic. Quotations can be used to evoke emotion, synthesize feelings, and establish the authenticity of ideas. Often a politician delivering a speech on the Fourth of July will quote George Washington or Thomas Jefferson to arouse feelings of patriotism and pride within the audience. Baseball announcers are fond of quoting baseball heroes in a tense situation. During a tie game in the bottom of the ninth inning, you might hear the announcer say, "Yogi Berra once said, 'It ain't over 'till it's over.' That sure applies here." If, for example, you are giving an informative speech on brain surgery in newborns, a brief quotation from Benjamin Carson, a pioneer physician in pediatric neurosurgery, could provide you with sufficient expert testimony.

Using Quotations and Testimonies

You need to be careful not to use too many quotes, or you may sound like a name-dropper. Select quotations with significance to your topic and use them where they will have maximum emphasis. Often, a brief quote is more effective than a long, involved quotation that has to be unraveled with a lengthy explanation.

When using testimonies, be sure that the individuals you cite are qualified through experience or expertise to comment or represent your topic. Though Tiger Woods may be a golfing professional, he is not professionally qualified to tell you which aspirin to take, or which breakfast cereal has more vitamins and nutrients. You should briefly tell the audience what qualifies the expert you have chosen to provide testimony on your topic.

When you use a quotation from someone who is not widely known, it is important to identify that person for your audience. If you are using that individual's exact words, it is a good idea to use the terms "quote" and "end quote" before and after the quoted material. A paraphrase is a general summary of the material in your own words. In that case, you would not use quotes. Be certain your quotation or paraphrase is accurate. If you use only a portion of the quotation, don't change the author's meaning or intention by taking it out of context.

In a speech about the effect of moral values on the education of the young, Myles Brand, president of Indiana University, used a quotation to inspire his audience:

> So now my question is, how do we educate our young people to create peace in a violent world? How do we teach them to respect others? As I think about this question I am reminded of the words of Harriet Beecher Stowe, whom Abraham Lincoln called the little woman who helped to end slavery. Stowe once wrote that "every human being has some handle by which he or she may be lifted; and the great work of life, as far as our relations with each other are concerned, is to lift each one by his or her proper handle." That is the challenge not only of business and of family counseling, but also of contemporary education. It is the challenge for Indiana University. I believe that handle by which we may be lifted is moral reasoning.[12]

Dr. Brand used the quote from the famous antislavery writer Harriet Beecher Stowe to help listeners think how to teach ethics and moral reasoning to young Americans.

In this persuasive speech about buying American products, Kathy Birckhead paraphrased two experts to support her topic:

> Foreign imports are taking over a larger share in almost all markets. What is the effect on our economy? I interviewed Eddie Bartee, vice president of the United Steelworkers of America, Local 2609, who told me that imported steel has virtually crippled the steel industry. I also spoke with Ted Baldwin, the public relations representative for Bethlehem Steel at Sparrows Point, who told me that in 1970 Bethlehem Steel employed 26,500 people. At the present time they employ only 9,000.[13]

Since her listeners were unfamiliar with Eddie Bartee and Ted Baldwin, the speaker supplied the necessary information to build credibility. If you provide a brief phrase identifying your authority, you can quickly establish reliability.

In the following excerpt from a commencement address, Les McCraw, president of the Fluor Corporation (an engineering-construction company), used a quotation from a baseball player to arouse emotional feelings within his audience at Clemson University:

> Jim Abbott had a dream. It takes a special kind of person to make a dream come true against all odds. Jim is the 21-year-old rookie pitcher for the California Angels. He's a left-handed pitcher. He throws left-handed because he was born without a right hand. His parents raised this remarkable man by never treating him too remarkably.
>
> "When I was growing up," he says, "I always pictured myself as a baseball player, but I can't remember how many hands I had in my dreams. I just went out and did things." And he certainly has "done things." He

earned the 1987 Sullivan Award as America's best amateur athlete, won the gold-medal baseball in the Seoul Olympics, was drafted number one by the Angels, and is pitching in the big leagues today.[14]

Notice that McCraw set the stage by describing the pertinent details of the ballplayer's story; then he used Jim Abbott's words to stir feelings of admiration and pride within his listeners.

COMPARISONS AND CONTRASTS

There will be times in your speeches when you will need to show similarities or differences in two or more things. *Comparisons* point out similarities in situations or events, and *contrasts* show differences.

Suppose you were giving a persuasive speech on the enforcement of drunk driving laws. You could contrast the enforcement of drunk driving laws in the United States with the enforcement of such laws in Scandinavian countries. In your research, you would probably find that American and Scandinavian laws are very similar, while the application of the law is very different in the two countries.

If you were persuading listeners to legalize gambling in your state, you could contrast the higher revenues in gambling states with lower revenues from nongambling states. On the other hand, if you wanted to persuade the audience not to legalize gambling, you could focus on contrasting crime rates if they were higher in gambling states.

Using Comparisons and Contrasts

Using comparisons and contrasts can be tricky. You must be careful that what you are comparing or contrasting has similar principles or characteristics. Imagine that a speaker tried to contrast gun control in the United States with gun control in England by making the following statement:

> The murder rate in the United States is five times greater than the murder rate in England. The reason for this is that England has a strict gun control law and we have a very weak one.

Although logical reasoning will be discussed more extensively in chapter 17, it is necessary to point out here that the information provided in this contrast is faulty and misleading in several areas. The United States does have a gun control law known as the Brady Law. In its first year, the law was effective in stopping 45,000 convicted felons from purchasing guns and by 1997 more than 69,000 handgun purchases were blocked.[15] In addition, the statement does not account for the numerous cities and states that have some form of gun control. It is true that in the United States the murder rate is about ten for every 100,000, and in England, the rate is two and one-half murders per 100,000.[16] However, the lower rate of murder in England could be due to other factors besides gun control. England has a homogeneous population with a lengthy common history. The British operate under different cultural rules than do Americans. British police do not wear guns, and it is rare for British police to be murdered in the line of duty. There appears to be an unwritten "agreement" between British criminals and British police that neither side will use violence when conducting "business."

In this excerpt, the speaker uses contrast to highlight the differences between Americans and Russians:

> I'd like to tell you about some of the specific differences between the American and Russian people. The statistics and examples are from *Almanac of the American People,* a Russian newspaper, which translated, is entitled *Arguments and Facts,* and my own personal experience.
>
> In America there were 6.2 strict vegetarians [for every hundred people] in 1989. This is a practice that would be just unbelievable to the Russian people. In Russia, we eat many internal organs of a cow or pig such as the tongue, tail, and brains. But according to the *Almanac,* Americans hate this type of food. In Russia, vodka is very popular and Russians drink on every occasion. But in America, only nineteen percent of men older than forty prefer vodka. Seventy percent of the American people get drunk once a year but in Russia, seventy percent of the people get drunk every day. There are also differences in exercise habits. Sixty-nine percent of Americans exercise and fifty percent enjoy walking for pleasure. Russians don't walk for pleasure—they just walk to buy things from shops. Russian people tend to be ashamed of exercise. They think bicycling, diving, and swimming are for children. You'll never see an elderly woman in tight pants on a bicycle riding through town. In my Moscow neighborhood, there was only one guy who went jogging every morning, and we all though he was crazy![17]

Olga Norko was a recent immigrant from Russia to the United States. She combined personal experience with statistics and examples to create a fascinating series of contrasts for her classroom audience. By identifying her sources at the beginning of the contrasting examples, the speaker was able to strengthen the reliability of the information.

In another example, the speaker used both contrast and comparison as supporting materials:

> I think we're all aware of the enormous differences between the United States and Japan. We're separated by geography; we're separated by language; and we're separated by culture. We go head-to-head in trade and often run up against serious frictions and conflicts. But our free and dynamic economies also afford us important shared values. No other

economies in the world are as willing as the United States and Japan to embrace new ideas, new products, and new ways of doing business.[18]

Robert McCurry of Toyota contrasts the differences between the United States and Japan, but he uses these contrasts to show how diverse and competitive cultures can share common interests and goals. In this example, the speaker skillfully transformed contrasts into comparisons. The speaker was able to find a number of areas where the United States and Japan are similar.

PERSONAL EXPERIENCE AND OBSERVATION

Personal experience and observation can help to make your speech interesting. If you are giving a speech demonstrating how a volcano is formed, you create interest if you have an experience to relate. If you are informing your audience about poverty, you make your topic personal if you describe some of the impoverished conditions you have observed. *Personal experience* is the direct firsthand knowledge of a situation. *Observation* is a judgment based upon what an individual has seen.

Using Experience and Observation

Be sure that the experience you use is appropriate to your topic. Don't use too many personal experiences, and don't base an entire speech on one elongated experience. Sometimes speakers with an abundance of personal experiences don't use enough research to support their topics, hoping their observations and experiences will make up for their lack of hard evidence.

Don't try to improvise a speech by stringing together a multitude of observations. One effective personal experience combined with some factual research can make the topic interesting and give you authority on your issue. For example:

> In June of 1973, I was diagnosed with leukemia and I had a one-in-three chance of seeing my next birthday. If I could survive that long, I had only a ten percent chance of living three years. Three years! Well, I wasn't about to buy that. There's something neat about being eighteen—you're feisty, rebellious, and out to prove people wrong. I underwent three years of intensive chemotherapy with mostly experimental drugs (which means I threw up for three years!). According to a pamphlet put out by the Leukemia Society of America, just twenty years ago there was no effective treatment for any type of leukemia. And if you had what I had as recently as fifteen years ago, the outlook was so bleak that doctors questioned whether patients should even be treated. But now this disease has a sixty percent cure rate.

Well I was still around about five years after the initial diagnosis, and the doctors started to admit that probably I was cured—which was something that my family and I knew all along. Now my oncologist brags that I have survived and have gone on to lead a "normal" life.

Well, since the day I shocked my husband Dave and my doctors by announcing that I was pregnant, my life has been far from normal. After twelve years of marriage, we have produced three healthy and active sons. Brian, Erik, and Shane's births are such rarities that they are being studied as part of a federally funded research program analyzing the offspring of chemotherapy patients. Chemotherapy does many things to you, and one of them is that it kills your good and bad cells, including your reproductive cells. One of my doctors puts it this way: "For a past leukemia patient to give birth was uncommon, because survival was uncommon." I didn't think then that having leukemia and then having children was such a big deal—I just did what I had to do. But in 1981, the American Cancer Society awarded me with their Courage Award. This prestigious award is given to just one person in the country annually.[19]

Karen Anderson's personal experience gave the audience a firsthand account of the battle with leukemia. The speaker enhanced her credibility by quoting her doctor, providing information from the American Leukemia Society, and referring to her award from the American Cancer Society.

Audiences enjoy hearing factual experiences, and a speaker can usually maintain listener interest if the observation is told effectively, without verbal blunders or hesitations.

Gilven M. Slonim, president of the Oceanic Educational Foundation, used personal experience and observation to support a point about military readiness:

So tonight I suggest, rather than celebrate the fiftieth Anniversary of Pearl Harbor, we review what the nation is doing to prevent another Pearl Harbor.

I was there; I survived Pearl Harbor fifty years ago today. I'm here to tell you how dreadfully painful an experience Pearl Harbor was to live through. Had we been ready, for the crux was readiness, how simply it could have been handled!

Admiral Raymond Spruance, the most disciplined military leader I have ever known, wept openly, when he saw the destruction the Japanese had inflicted upon our fleet, upon returning to Pearl Harbor on the 8th of December with Halsey's Task Force. This was after their sweep of the sea in search of the Japanese fleet, they fortunately did not find.[20]

Slovin presented these remarks to the Richmond Council of the Navy League on the occasion of the fiftieth anniversary of the attack on Pearl Harbor. The "I was there" personal experience gave credence to his observation that the United States is not doing enough to prevent a similar military disaster in the future.

HUMOR AND ANECDOTES

Humor is the use of lighthearted, entertaining material in a speech to generate a reaction from the audience. An *anecdote* is a brief humorous story used to demonstrate a point.

Humor can be very effective in a speech. Telling a joke or a humorous anecdote can create a positive climate in a speaking situation. If your audience smiles and nods at your wit, you have them in a receptive mood. A humorous anecdote can frequently make a point more successfully than a long theoretical statement.

Using Humor and Anecdotes

Employing humor has some risks. There is always the possibility that the joke you tell does not get the response you might have expected. When you practice your speech, you need to be prepared for a variety of audience reactions. If listeners fail to laugh at your humor or groan at your attempts, you can joke about their response, relate "safer" humor that has worked previously, or acknowledge the response and move on. Don't let negative audience reactions destroy your confidence. You can still overcome momentary difficulties if you maintain your composure and keep to your stated objective. Your audience might also respond by breaking up into laughter. Don't let a positive response catch you off guard. Pause after the joke or story, and wait for your listeners to enjoy the moment. Don't try to resume the speech until the laughter subsides.

It is best to use humor that can be related to your topic. Using irrelevant jokes simply to gain attention can often disappoint and even anger an audience. If you've ever inquired about a brand-new car for $6,999 described in a newspaper ad, remember how you felt when you discovered that the car was a stripped-down model without tires! Audiences, too, don't appreciate the tactic of "bait-and-switch."

Despite the risks, don't be afraid to use humor. If you're good at humor, use it to your advantage and develop it as a part of your style. Even if you do not feel comfortable with humor, try a few anecdotes. You might surprise yourself. A speech is not a stand-up comic routine, but you can look for ways to use humor appropriately.

Norman Schwarzkopf, General (retired), United States Army, used humor effectively in this commencement address delivered at the University of Richmond:

> Now, first of all for those of you who don't recognize me, I am *the* General Schwarzkopf. I said that because for some reason people expect me to be wearing camouflage. If I am not wearing camouflage, I'm not General Schwarzkopf. It's amazing the perceptions people have about you.

I work out every other day as you can tell from this magnificent body that stands before you, and at the end of my workout I always go into the steam bath. True story—last summer I walked into the steam bath. I was not wearing camouflage at the time, and there was a man in there, and he turned and looked at me and said, "Did anybody every tell you that from a distance you look exactly like General Schwarzkopf?" And I thought I'd play along, and I said, "Yes, I hear that a lot." He said, "Yes, it's only when you get up close you realize you're not General Schwarzkopf." I never told him—he does not know to this day.[21]

A large, imposing figure who was almost legendary for his success in leading allied troops against Iraq in Operation Desert Storm, General Schwarzkopf was willing to poke good-natured fun at himself, making him more human to the members of his audience. In the following excerpt from another graduation speech, *Doonesbury* cartoonist Garry Trudeau used an anecdote to his advantage:

I first learned about pertinent questions from my father, a retired physician . . . [whose] own practical experience frequently contradicted his worthiest intentions. A man once turned up in my father's office complaining of an ulcer. My father asked the pertinent question. Was there some undue stress, he inquired, that might be causing the man to digest his stomach? The patient, who was married . . . allowed that he had a girlfriend in Syracuse, and that twice a week he'd been driving an old pick-up down to see her. Since the pick-up frequently broke down, he was often late in getting home, and he had to devise fabulous stories to tell his wife. My father, compassionately but sternly, told the man he had to make a hard decision about his personal priorities if he was ever to get well. The patient nodded and went away, and six months later came back completely cured, a new man. My father congratulated him and then delicately inquired if he'd made some change in his life. The man replied, "Yup. Got me a new pick-up."[22]

Trudeau presents his humor effectively and smoothly, logically developing the details of the story. The last sentence of the anecdotes served as the punch line to stimulate a response from the audience. Trudeau used this anecdote to illustrate the point that an "unexpected or inconvenient truth is often the price of honest inquiry."[23]

ROLE-PLAYING

Role-playing is a technique using an individual to act out a brief skit, assume a character, or simulate a conflict. Role-playing can be a creative way of motivating listeners to become more personally involved with a speaker's topic. A skit portraying the effect of divorce on a young child might have more impact on an audience than a verbal description. One student, playing the role of a waiter in a restaurant, used two "customers" from the audience to demonstrate the proper and improper methods of taking orders and serving food.

Using Role-Playing Techniques

Speakers can use skits they have researched or they can create their own dramas. If the situation is taken from one of your sources, give the author proper recognition. If you write a brief dramatic piece, be sure that the skit is true-to-life and based on factual information. It is helpful if the situation is brief and to the point. Long, drawn-out dramas can bore listeners with unnecessary material and detract from the speech. If you need volunteers, rehearse them in advance, making sure that they are familiar with the script and know how to respond appropriately in the roles. Remember that role-playing is one of the less factual ways of supporting ideas; it should not be used as a substitute for cases, statistics, or verifiable sources. Role-playing is most effective when combined with other types of supporting materials.

Speaker Gina Alexander created a skit to demonstrate the proper and improper techniques of interviewing for a job. The speaker portrayed the applicant while a member of the audience played the role of the interviewer.

Interviewer: Can you tell me why you're leaving your present employer?

Applicant: Well, it's like, I'm so bored there, ya know? It's like I hate to go to work there everyday—I can't stand it. Ya ever felt like that?

Interviewer: Is it the work itself, or is it your environment?

Applicant: Yeeeah, both I guess, kinda, ya know?

What can I say? You do that, and you've probably lost the job right there. No matter what college you've gone to or what fancy degree you have, it's not showing. There's a better way to display the exact same message.

Interviewer: Can you tell me why you're leaving your present employer?

Applicant: Well, I'm considering leaving my present employer to seek new opportunities that they don't offer.

Interviewer: Is it the work itself, or is it your environment?

Applicant: Actually, it's a combination of both factors that are contributing to my desire to leave.

In the first example, I was sprawling all over the chair, I didn't appear interested, and it looked as if I wasn't paying attention. I used street jargon, and it appeared as if I had few language skills. Notice that I was running my fingers through my hair. This is an action that is very distracting. In some jobs, such as a food-service position, picking your face or touching your hair could lose you the job.

In the second situation, I said the exact same thing, but I displayed some intelligence. My posture was effective. I didn't sit like a soldier, but I sat up straight, appearing as an interested, active communicator who is open to new ideas. My vocabulary was precise, thoughtful, and I spoke in complete sentences. While I didn't stare, I maintained eye contact with my prospective employer.[24]

The skit was successful because the speaker conducted several rehearsals prior to the classroom presentation. While the skit was entertaining and humorous, it successfully demonstrated the speaker's point that language, organization, and poise, make a powerful persuasive impression on an interviewer.

Out of Sight, Out of Mind

Heather Hoag was so concerned about noise pollution that she wanted to investigate the topic in greater detail. Her research revealed numerous supporting materials—surveys, quotations by experts, and specific examples—that she was able to include in this persuasive speech to actuate. Notice how the speaker uses these interesting supporting materials to develop and illustrate the organizational aspects of her presentation.[25]

Persuasive Actuating Speech

HEATHER HOAG

1 The speaker signs her name to create attention and motivate audience members to listen.

Heather uses an appropriate quotation by Helen Keller.

1 Hello. My name is Heather. (The speaker does not verbalize but uses sign language.) Well some of you have figured out that I just demonstrated sign language, but does anyone know what I just said? I said, "Hello. My name is Heather." Sign language is the way deaf individuals "talk" to one another. Could you imagine what it would be like to be deaf? Think about it! You couldn't just pick up a phone to chat with a friend or even sit there, like all of you, and listen to my speech. A quote from Helen Keller, a famous and heroic woman in history who also happened to be blind, deaf, and mute, vividly expresses what a world is like without sound. "The problems of deafness are more complex than those of blindness. Deafness is a much worse misfortune because of the loss of the most vital stimulus, the sound of the voice that brings language, sets thoughts astir and helps us in the intellectual company of man."

2 The speaker continues with the example and compares the illness suffered by Helen Keller to the daily threats that noise poses to our hearing.

2 A serious illness destroyed Helen Keller's sight and hearing when she was only one-and-a-half years old. But would you ever deliberately expose yourself to circumstances that would make you vulnerable to deafness? Well we do everyday! Blasting music from car stereos, thunderous roars from planes flying overhead, and the ear-splitting racket of construction equipment are only three ways which noise pollution jeopardizes our hearing.

3 The thesis is presented.

3 Noise pollution is an invisible danger that must be silenced by protecting ourselves in order to prevent hearing impairments.

4 The speaker begins to develop the nature of the problem of noise pollution.

The speaker presents a quotation from an expert, validated by a credible source.

4 Dangers are usually things we can see like fire or broken glass. However, those that cannot be seen are more dangerous because they often go unnoticed until it is too late. Perhaps some of you have heard the phrase, "out of sight, out of mind." Well this phrase clearly illustrates why noise pollution continues to be a dangerous problem in our environmentally conscious society because it is invisible. In a March 6th, 1990, *New York Times* article, Samuel Stempler, director of New York City's Bureau of Air Resources stated that "the trouble with noise is that it's not visible like garbage, oil spills and other pollutants. So it seems to get less attention, despite the hazards it poses."

5 Heather introduces brief examples to describe how noise affects us at work, at home, and in leisure activities.

5 A second way noise pollution endangers our society is because it is everywhere: It can be heard at work, home, and in leisure activities. Workers particularly vulnerable to dangerous levels of noise include fire fighters, police officers, construction and factory workers, and musicians. At home, landscapers can be heard descending into communities with lawn mowers and leaf blowers. Finally, leisure-related activity, including high-volume music and recreation vehicles such as snowmobiles and motorcycles threaten our communities with loud noises.

6 The speaker briefly describes how noise can damage the sensitive cells of the

6 Loud noise also damages hearing. According to a November 12th, 1989 article in the *Washington Post,* noise-induced hearing loss occurs when tiny sensory cells in the inner ear are steadily worn down and eventually depleted, never to be restored. Early warning signs include ringing in the ear called tinnitus. If you've ever left a loud concert or spent a few

inner ear and
uses an example
to describe
the symptoms
of tinnitus.

hours mowing your lawn and noticed a ringing in your ears,
you've experienced tinnitus. Another early sign of trouble is
a temporary dullness of hearing after exposure to intense
noise. If the noise is not stopped or if the individual is not
protected, then permanent hearing damage will occur.

7 Heather uses a
specific example
and a quotation
from rock star
Peter Townshend.
The example
connects to many
listeners and is
an effective
supporting mate-
rial which
reminds listen-
ers of the
dangers of ex-
cessive noise.

7 I'm sure many of you have heard of the British rock group, the
Who, and its lead guitarist Pete Townshend who performed at
Woodstock and became famous for his rock opera, *Tommy.* He was
also famous for ending his concerts by smashing his guitar in
a ferocious blast of on-stage fire and explosion. But now,
more than twenty years later, Pete Townshend is known for
something else: He is going deaf. Listen to his statement
quoted in a July 24th, 1990 issue of the *Washington Post:* "You
wake up with a piece of your ears gone. I think it's worth
saying that there is a price to pay for that: It's premature
deafness and ringing and slotty hearing."

8 Other names of
rock stars are
mentioned to re-
inforce the dan-
gers of noise.

8 Other rock musicians who have experienced significant loss of
hearing include Rod Stewart, Ted Nugent, Elliott Murphy, Jerry
Harrison, and Eddie Van Halen.

9 A hearing ex-
pert is quoted
to describe the
extent of the
danger to mil-
lions of Ameri-
cans. The source
for the quota-
tion is clearly
indicated.

Heather uses a
survey as an-
other supporting
material. The
statistics are
placed on a vi-
sual aid, making
the information

9 According to Patrick Brookhauser, head of the department of
otolaryngology at Creighton University, "more than 20 million
Americans are exposed on a regular basis, to hazardous noise
levels that could result in hearing loss," which he stated in
a February 6th, 1990 article in the *Washington Post.* In 1990
the National Institute on Deafness and Other Communication
Disorders conducted a study to look at the relationship between noise and noise-hearing loss. Results indicated that exposure to sound levels over 85 decibels was potentially
hazardous. (Uses visual aid) In order to understand what 85
decibels means, I've listed some examples here to illustrate
its magnitude. As you can see decibel levels between 50-65,
like a normal conversation, would be comfortable. However, TVs
are at 70-90 and cause damage after 8 hours; lawn mowers produce 85-90 decibels; jet take-offs are at 130 decibels and
rock concerts can range from 110-140 decibels beyond the
threshold of pain. Dr. Brookhouser also stated that most Americans spend typical days in settings where the noise levels
are about 70 decibels "and of the nearly 30 million Americans

more clear and interesting. Notice that the speaker provides the source for the study.

with severe hearing loss, about one-third can attribute the loss to exposure to loud sounds."

10 Heather briefly describes four research studies showing that noise pollution is linked to various physical and psychological ailments.

10 Noise pollution is also linked to serious physical and psychological problems including high blood pressure, ulcers, antisocial behavior, and learning disabilities. The March 6, 1990 issue of *The New York Times* reported several incidents:

–Dr. Peterson of the University of Miami found that blood pressure of monkeys and other animals increased after exposure to noise and remained high even when the noise stopped.
–A study in Poland concluded that chronic exposure to sounds between 85 and 115 decibels significantly increased hypertension and ulcers.
–Doctors discovered in a 1970 study that children living on the noisier lower floors of a housing complex next to the George Washington Bridge in Manhattan didn't read as well as children on upper floors.
–Psychology Professor Dr. Fisher of the University of Connecticut found evidence that noise alters behavior and contributes to a "sense of helplessness," which leads to poor performance.

11 The transition tells listeners that the speaker has completed the problem and will now describe some solutions.

11 Now that you have heard why noise pollution is a danger, I'd like to discuss some of the efforts to control it.

12 Heather describes the efforts of HEAR, which has attempted to convince sound engineers to lower sound levels at rock concerts.

12 Some community and governmental attempts to silence the dangers of noise pollution have historically been unsuccessful. A July 24th, 1990 article in the *Washington Post* reported how an organization known as HEAR—Hearing Education and Awareness for Rockers—has used rock musicians with hearing loss (including Peter Townshend who donated $10,000 to the organization) to educate rock fans about the dangers of loud music. In some cases HEAR has been successful in convincing sound engineers at rock concerts to lower the sound. But the *Washington Post* also reports that many sound engineers have hearing impairments and

efforts to lower the sound at many concerts were unsuccessful because to many of the engineers, the sound seemed lower even though it was not!

13 The speaker uses an example to show that state legislation and community noise ordinances have been unenforceable.

13 According to an August 14, 1990 *New York Times* article, New York state passed legislation outlawing boomboxes or cars with megawatt stereos. But noise ordinances in New York and in other states and localities are unenforceable because police are too busy dealing with drugs, violence, and other crimes and can't be bothered stopping someone for playing loud music.

14 Heather describes the Reagan budget cuts as another example showing how governmental programs have been rendered ineffective.

14 Finally, an article in *The New York Times* on March 6th, 1990, revealed that in 1981 the Reagan Administration cut all federal funding to the Environmental Protection Agency's noise abatement program. These budget cuts made enforcing the laws and regulations that controlled noise impossible.

15 The speaker uses a series of concrete examples to describe several simple, effective solutions to the problem of noise.

15 But there are some simple, workable solutions that we can take as individuals. An article in a May 9th, 1995 issue of the *Washington Post* suggests that we can turn down the sound of our car radios and home stereo systems to reasonable levels. If you go to a loud concert, you can simply take a pair of ear plugs to reduce the decibels. By the way, when you attend the concert you may discover that the ushers, sound engineers, and even the rock musicians are all wearing ear plugs to protect themselves. If you mow the lawn, use heavy machinery, or constantly work near loud noise you should wear ear protection. And if you are enjoying music in your Walkman-style headset, you can turn down the sound to a comfortable, safe level. Research reported in the July 24th, 1990 issue of the *Washington Post* found that many individuals allow sound from tiny headsets to blast into their sensitive eardrums at 115 decibels or more. For example, if you are sitting next to someone and you can hear the sound from their headset, the volume is too loud. Most of these systems have settings from one to ten and a setting of four is considered the safest for comfortable listening.

16 The transition moves listeners from the solution to visualization of the future.

16 If we don't take action, the future will be deadly silent for all.

17 The speaker uses a quotation from an expert to picture how the future will appear if action isn't taken. Younger individuals will continue to go deaf "for the fun of it."

17 Up until the 1960s most hearing loss was associated with noise in the work place or old age. But today it seems that people are going deaf for the fun of it. Dr. Maurice Miller of New York's Lenox Hill Hospital stated in a July 24th, 1990 issue of the *Washington Post:* ". . . we see the casualties in our clinic all the time—people in their thirties and forties with the kind of hearing loss that we used to see only in people past retirement."

18 The speaker motivates listeners to enjoy the pleasant sounds of music or the first words of their children.

18 As you get older, wouldn't you like to still be able to enjoy the cheerful chatter of birds on an early spring morning or listen to the soothing sounds of your favorite music and hear your child speak for the first time? If immediate measures are not taken to reduce noise, then the future will be silent for all.

19 In the conclusion the speaker asks the audience to take action by signing a letter she has written to Senator Mikulski.

19 You may be wondering what you, a college student, parent, or teacher could possibly do to alleviate this massive problem. Well, not any one person can solve this problem alone but there are actions you can take to protect yourself in the present and into the future. I've written a letter to Senator Barbara Mikulski to ask her to develop and support legislation that would improve noise reduction adaptations on machinery, to protect employees and surrounding communities from debilitating hearing impairments. Sign this letter after class—it will help to protect your future.

20 The speaker also provides a short-term action and distributes ear

20 I'm also going to hand out ear plugs to each of you. Wear them the next time you go to a concert or cut the lawn. They are a convenient and cheap way to protect your hearing right now!

plugs which lis-
teners can use
immediately.

21 The speaker
makes a
final appeal.

21 Please! Don't let the invisible dangers of noise pollution silence your life or rob you of life's golden sounds. Protect
your hearing! Sound is a terrible thing to waste!

S U M M A R Y

Gather supporting materials to create interest and to provide evidence for
your ideas. Some of the most authoritative materials are statistics, polls,
and surveys; examples, illustrations, case studies, and narratives; and
quotations and testimonies from authorities. Less verifiable, yet interesting
materials, are comparisons and contrasts; personal experiences and observations; and humor, anecdotes, and role-playing.

SKILL BUILDERS

1. Select a topic which can be supported by statistics and develop a
   one- to two-minute speech to inform. Be sure you understand the
   statistics and draw a clear conclusion from your data. After you
   present the speech in class, ask the audience to respond to the following questions:

   Were the statistics clear?

   Did the speaker understand the statistics?

   Were the statistics related in a meaningful and understandable
   way?

   Did the speaker draw a clear conclusion from the data?

2. Choose a topic for a brief one- to two-minute speech to inform.
   Choose three different forms of support to reinforce the issue. Ask
   your instructor and your audience to evaluate the success of the presentation.

3. Read Garry Trudeau's graduation address (reprinted at the back of
   the book). Divide your class into four or five groups and do the following exercises:
   a. Identify the various types of supporting materials he uses to back
   up his specific purpose.
   b. Does he use several different supporting materials and are these
   materials effective? Why or why not?
   c. Does he mention the sources for any of his information?
   d. Discuss the overall effectiveness of the speech.

4. Watch a videotape of several student speeches. Identify the kinds of supporting materials each student employs in the speech. Do the students mention their sources? Do the speeches appear to be credible?

5. Read the speech at the end of the chapter entitled, "Out of Sight, Out of Mind" by Heather Hoag. Divide your class into small groups and discuss the following issues.

   a. Are the supporting materials used in the speech sufficient to persuade you that noise pollution is a problem? If not, what additional evidence is needed?

   b. How persuasive are the quotations and research done by the experts mentioned in the speech?

   c. If you were to give a persuasive speech in which you disagreed with the premise of Heather Hoag's speech, what supporting materials would you need to provide to validate your point of view? Do a brief survey using the library to determine what kind of supporting materials are available for the opposite viewpoint.

   d. How effective is this speech? Will this speech influence you to take action to change your behavior? Why or why not?

NOTES

1. "Lincoln Never Said That," *U.S. News & World Report,* August 31–September 7, 1992, p. 27.

2. Jena L. Weigel, "The History of Coca-Cola," informative descriptive speech presented in speech class, Catonsville Community College, Catonsville, Maryland, 1991. Used by permission.

3. "Prime-Time Perot," *Advertising Age,* October 19, 1992, p. 22.

4. H. Ross Perot, paid political broadcast, October 17, 1992.

5. William L. Winter, "Putting the World in Perspective," *Vital Speeches,* March 15, 1991, p. 335.

6. David Zebraski, "Recycling Our Throwaways," persuasive speech to convince presented in speech class, Catonsville Community College, Catonsville, Maryland, 1989. Used by permission.

7. Stanley Eitzen, "Ethical Dilemmas in American Sport," *Vital Speeches,* January 1, 1996, p 183.

8. Illustration created by the author.

9. Neha Badshah, "The Indian Wedding Ceremony," informative descriptive speech presented in speech class, Catonsville Community College, Catonsville, Maryland, 1992. Used by permission.

10. Andrea Hoguet, "Parents Should Be Responsible for Their Children's Actions," persuasive speech to convince presented in speech class, Carroll Community College, Westminster, Maryland, 1989. Used by permission.

11. Richard D. Lamm, "Time to Change Course," *Vital Speeches,* October 15, 1985, p. 4.

12. Myles Bran, "Lifting Up Our World," *Vital Speeches,* April 1, 1999, p. 371.

13. Kathy Birckhead, "Buy American-made Products," persuasive speech to actuate presented in speech class, Carroll Community College, Westminster, Maryland, 1990. Used by permission.

14. Les McCaw, "Nothing Much Happens Without a Dream," *Vital Speeches,* January 15, 1990, p. 217.

15. See "Brady Law Working, Surveys Show," *The Evening Sun* (Baltimore), March 12, 1995, p. 15A and "Battle Is Expected on Gun Buying Law," *The Sun* (Baltimore), July 12, 1998, p. 14A.

16. George T. Kurian, *The New Book of World Rankings* (New York: Facts on File Publications: 1984), p. 386.

17. Olga Norko, "Differences Between the Russian and American People," speech to inform presented

in speech class, Catonsville Community College, Catonsville, Maryland, 1992. Used by permission.

18. Robert McCurry, "Competing With Japan," *Vital Speeches,* July 15, 1986, p. 593.

19. Karen Anderson, "People Can Survive Cancer," descriptive speech to inform presented in speech class, Carroll Community College, Westminster, Maryland, 1989. Used by permission.

20. Gilven M. Slonim, "Beyond Pearl Harbor," *Vital Speeches,* March 1, 1992, p. 308.

21. Normal Schwarzkopf, "Leaders for the 21st Century," *Vital Speeches,* June 15 1999, p. 519.

22. Garry Trudeau, "The Impertinent Questions," *Vital Speeches,* August, 1986, pp. 619–620.

23. Ibid., p. 620.

24. Gina Alexander, "Effective Interviewing Techniques," speech to demonstrate presented in speech class, Carroll Community College, Westminster, Maryland, 1990. Used by permission.

25. Heather Hoag, "Out of Sight, Out of Mind," persuasive speech to actuate presented in speech class, Catonsville Community College, Catonsville, Maryland, 1996. Used by permission.

Creating the Structure

Topic ····▸ Purpose ········▸ Thesis

···▸ Research ········ Outline ····

Audience ····▸ Ethics   Practice

Prepare

Chapter 10

ORGANIZING THE BODY OF THE SPEECH

Good order is the foundation of all good things.

Edmund Burke

CHAPTER OBJECTIVES

After reading this chapter you will be able to:

1. Recognize how to approach speech organization logically;

2. Describe the ten building blocks of outlining;

3. Organize the body of a speech outline.

As president of the Humphrey Group, Judith Humphrey coaches the leaders of corporations and businesses throughout the United States and Canada. She reports that one of the mainstays of her company is the Executive Speechwriting Program, which helps CEOs and business executives to build effective presentations "through learning and practice." In November of 1997, Ms. Humphrey was invited to speak to the Board of Trade in Toronto, Canada. Here is what she had to say about speech organization:

> To begin with, the structure must support the message. Too many executive presentations or speeches simply ramble on, from topic to topic. When a structure elaborates an idea, it takes on an excitement, an energy. It has a pulse to it. . . . Most speeches can be structured by one of five common patterns. First is the one we call the "Four Reasons" speech—although it might be the three reasons or nine reasons speech. It's a clear, powerful format. Second is the "Ways" speech, which demonstrates the ways or areas in which the main idea can be shown to be true. Next is "Problem and Solution." It's a good way of first addressing a problem and then showing how you'll solve it. It's great for customer presentations. There's also the "Process" or "Chronological" model. You discuss a sequence of steps. This talk with its seven-fold path to eloquence follows that model. Last is the "Present Situation/Future Outlook" talk. Annual meeting speeches often take this approach. You tell your audience that while this year's results were good, we will restructure to make the future still brighter for the company.[1]

Humphrey recognized the vital importance of logical structure and clear organization in public speaking. She also stressed the importance of using the structure of a speech to elaborate an *idea* or *message,* giving "excitement" and "energy" to a topic.

An outline is just as important to you as it is to a professional speaker like Judith Humphrey. An outline is a structured plan of your ideas: It acts as a visual guide to the main and supporting elements in your presentation. You can think of the outline as the framework of your speech: It holds the speech together, keeps you within the boundaries, and clarifies the layout for the audience.

A speech has three parts: the introduction, the body, and the conclusion. It is the middle part, or body, which represents the major portion or framework of the speech and will comprise about two-thirds of your speaking time. Once you have researched the topic, written your specific purpose, and worded your thesis, you should first spend your energies outlining the body of the speech. You can develop the introduction and conclusion after the meat of your presentation has been organized. This chapter presents ten building blocks that will help you to outline the body of your presentation.

APPROACHING ORGANIZATION LOGICALLY

The thought of outlining a speech might seem difficult at first, but if you think logically about the topic, sorting through your research will be less complicated. Some topics almost organize themselves. For example, if you were to give an informative speech on a historical issue such as the history of the telephone, your research would fall into several categories according to years or time periods. By contrast, a travelogue about Alaska could be organized using location or geography such as the Arctic, Western, Southern, and Interior areas as structural points. Research can also cluster around logical categories such as three types of clowns—straight man, joker, and character clown. Your research could also be outlined according to several major causes or effects.

What is important is that you begin to think in an organized manner. Look for key ideas, patterns, and trends in your research that are supported by examples, quotations, or testimony. Think in terms of the overall plan of your speech and don't try to fill in all details at the beginning of the process. After you develop your thesis statement, write a rough outline, making sure that the main points of the body carry out the statement adequately. Don't be afraid to adjust the major headings or thesis to make your plan more clear and consistent. Try not to be intimidated or enslaved by the process. Remember that the outline is simply a tool for structure and clarity and it should help speech construction to be more enjoyable and less complicated.

PRINCIPLES OF OUTLINING

If you carefully apply each of these ten principles, your clarity of organization and speaking effectiveness will be greatly enhanced.

In this text the term *formal outline* will refer to the body of the speech. We will use the term *informal outline* when referring to the introduction, conclusion, bibliography, and other outline preliminaries.

Building Block One: The Body Should Contain between Two and Four Main Points in a Five- to Seven-Minute Speech

The thesis statement identifies how many main points you will have in the body of a speech. In a classroom speech with a five- to seven-minute time limit, the best guideline to use is to have no fewer than two and no more than four main points. If you have only one major point, your speech will be too short because you will not have enough supporting material to develop your topic. If you have six or seven points, you have the opposite problem—a lengthy speech with too much information to cover in the allotted time. Notice that the following thesis statement incorporates three elements:

Specific purpose: The purpose of the speech is to inform the audience about three funeral customs of the ancient Egyptians.

Thesis statement: Egyptian funeral customs included embalming, the use of coffins, and a process called "dry burial."

BODY

   I. Explanation of Egyptian embalming practices
  II. Description of Egyptian coffins
 III. Explanation of "dry" burial techniques[2]

The thesis statement tells you that there will be three main headings in the body: (1) explanation of embalming, (2) description of coffins, and (3) explanation of burial techniques. The organization is tight, and there will be time enough to develop the main points in sufficient detail.

Building Block Two: Main Points in the Body Should Be Structured in an Organizational Sequence Which Is Logical, Interesting, and Appropriate to the Topic

When structuring your main points, you can select an *organizational sequence* which is appropriate to the topic and stimulates audience interest. Organize main points according to chronology, space, cause-effect, topic/natural, or other sequence.

CHRONOLOGICAL SEQUENCE

When you use *chronological sequence,* you arrange the main points according to time or order of events. For example, topics such as "Human Life from Fertilization to Birth," "How to Make Yeast Bread," or historical topics such as "American Exploration of Space" or the "Life of Salvador Dali," would be organized according to chronology. Notice the example below:

Specific purpose: To inform you about the rise and fall of the American "Muscle Car."

To build a successful presentation a speaker must be willing to spend time developing ideas, structuring thoughts, and writing a clear, logical outline.

Thesis statement: American muscle cars were introduced in 1964, increased in popularity during the latter sixties, reached a "high-water mark" in 1970, and began to decline in the early 1970s.

BODY

   I. The early years—1964 to 1966
  II. The rising popularity—1967 to 1969
 III. The "high-water mark"—1970
 IV. The decline—1971 to 1972

The topic is arranged according to chronology by the historical events occurring over a period of years.

SPATIAL SEQUENCE

Space is the structuring of main points according to geography or location. Topics relating to the description of a building, a city, or a physical object are organized using *spatial sequence.*

Specific purpose: To inform you about four principal areas in the White House.

> **Thesis statement:**   The interior of the White House includes executive offices, formal reception rooms, first family living quarters, and a kitchen complex.

BODY

I. Executive offices
II. Formal reception rooms
III. First family living quarters
IV. Kitchen complex

In the above example you can see that each main point describes a different spatial area in the White House.

CAUSE-EFFECT SEQUENCE

Another way to structure the main points of your speech is by *cause-and-effect sequence.* This sequence simply arranges the main points according to cause and effect. You could inform your audience about several causes of drug dependency and then talk about the effects on the family and the individual. Another example is:

> **Specific purpose:**   To inform the audience about the causes and effects of colon cancer.

> **Thesis statement:**   While there are several known causes of colon cancer, there are advanced treatments that have significant effects on the patient.

BODY

I. Known causes of colon cancer
II. Advanced treatments for the disease
III. Effects of the treatments on the patient

Here the first and last main point present causes and effects. Notice that numeral II is not a cause or effect, but identifies a topic area necessary for the logical development of the speech.

You could also structure the main points entirely by causes or by effects. A speech about child abuse, for instance, could expand upon three principal causes of child abuse, or describe three tragic effects of abuse on the victim.

TOPICAL SEQUENCE

Another method of structuring the main points is by logical or natural sequence. This pattern can also be called *topical sequence.* On some issues, you will find that your research clusters around natural headings, which can be earmarked for your outline.

Specific purpose: To inform the audience what it's like living in Dunoon, Scotland.

Thesis statement: During the year I lived in Dunoon, Scotland, I got to know the town, learned how to negotiate the transportation system, became acclimated to a Scottish home, and enjoyed leisure activities.

BODY

I. Brief description of the town
II. Transportation in the town
III. Life in a Scottish house
IV. Activities for leisure enjoyment

In this example, the speaker has discovered four logical headings that accurately describe her experiences and observations.

You can also create a natural sequence by identifying trends in your information. For instance, you could structure your main points from least to most important item, simple to complex, or familiar to unfamiliar. These types of arrangements not only create interest in the topic, but they also help your audience to remember your main points more easily. Consider these examples:

Least to Most Important.

Specific purpose: To convince the audience that there are four reasons why HMOs do not provide quality health care

Thesis statement: Waiting rooms are impersonal, open enrollment is limited, immediate appointments with specialists are often difficult, and patients frequently experience inaccurate diagnoses and treatments.

BODY

I. Clinical, impersonal waiting rooms
II. Limited open enrollment, requiring high premiums
III. Immediate appointments with specialists difficult
IV. Frequent inaccurate diagnosis and treatment

Simple to Complex.

Specific purpose: To inform the audience about some troubleshooting techniques they can use when their car doesn't start.

Thesis statement: Be able to read and understand the instrument panel, identify possible difficulties with the starter mechanism, and know what to look for under the hood.

BODY

I. Understanding instrument panel
II. Identifying problems with starter mechanism
III. Looking under hood

Familiar to Unfamiliar.

Specific purpose: To inform the audience about five different types of stars in the universe.

Thesis statement: Stars are grouped into five categories: stars, black holes, novas, binary stars, and neutron stars.

BODY

I. Stars—Glowing gas in the sky
II. Black holes—Collapsed, former stars
III. Novas—Exploding, bright, and diminished stars
IV. Binary stars—Revolving and eclipsed stars
V. Neutron stars—Gaseous, atomic stars

In the first example, the speaker has arranged main points from least to most important reason. Numeral I "Clinical . . .waiting rooms" is a good reason why HMOs don't provide quality health care, but it is the least important of the four statements. Numeral IV "Frequent inaccurate diagnoses . . ." deals with human life and is therefore the most important item. In the second example, "Understanding instrument panel" is the least complicated troubleshooting procedure, while "Looking under hood" is the most complex. In the last example, the speaker assumes that the audience is most familiar with I "Stars . . ." and may have some limited familiarity with "Black holes" as well as "Novas." The speaker has assumed that "Binary" and "Neutron stars" are the least familiar to the audience, and has arranged them as the last two points.

OTHER SEQUENCES

There are a number of other ways to arrange the main points of the body. Many of these organizational patterns relate specifically to persuasive speeches, which we will discuss in chapter 17. But we want to briefly mention them now.

Problem–solution order is the arrangement of main points by identifying a problem and moving to a solution. The *motivated sequence* pattern is a five-stage system—attention, need, solution, visualization, action—in order to motivate the audience to act on an issue. The *reasons* organizational pattern simply arranges main points in the body according to reasons. There is also a *comparative-advantages* sequence that develops each main point by stressing the advantages of a desired plan or idea.

Building Block Three: A System of Roman Numerals, Letters, and Arabic Numbers Should Be Combined with Indentation to Identify Main and Subordinate Levels

Begin by using Roman numerals to outline the main points in the speech body. Remember that the Roman numerals carry out all the components of the thesis statement. Then introduce the next level of subordinate points with capitalized letters such as *A, B, C,* and so forth. Supporting points under capital letters should be introduced by numbers such as *1, 2,* and *3.* If you need another level, items would be preceded by small letters like *a* and *b.*

BODY

I. _____

    A. _____

    B. _____

        1. _____

            a. _____

            b. _____

        2. _____

II. _____

    A. _____

        1. _____

        2. _____

        3. _____

            a. _____

                (1) _____

                (2) _____

            b. _____

    B. _____

III. _____

    A. _____

    B. _____

    C. _____

Each level of supporting points is indented so that the outline clearly indicates the relationship between the heading and the subdivision. Just by glancing at this outline, you can easily attach subordinate points to their appropriate headings. This is an important reason for good organization. A tightly structured outline helps to trigger your thoughts so that you can maintain eye contact with your audience.

This pattern is just a guideline of general outline procedure. The shape of every outline depends upon the topic and varies according to the number of main points and the amount of supporting items.

Building Block Four: The Outline Should Include Supporting Materials That Are Coordinated and Subordinated in a Logical Manner

Once you have written two, three, or four main points of the body, your outline still presents only claims or assertions without any factual evidence or proof. You need supporting materials, that is, examples, quotations, statistics, and/or audiovisuals to provide detailed verification of each main point or numeral. When you place supporting materials beneath the main points of the body, your outline presents the details that are necessary to inform or influence your listeners.

Specific purpose: To persuade the audience to sign up as organ donors.

Thesis statement: The lack of organ donors must be corrected by everyone's participation in order to save lives.

BODY

I. There is a critical lack of organ donors
   A. 40,000 people in the United States wait for transplants *(Health Index)*
   B. Quotation from Brigid McMenamin of *Health Index:* "Last year 3,104 patients died waiting . . ."
   C. Statistics from University of Pittsburgh Medical Center
      1. 530 patients waited for liver transplant
      2. 18%, or 95 people died waiting
   D. Public misconceptions contribute to lack of donors
      1. "People who are rich and famous are bumped to the top of transplant lists."
      2. "Doctors won't try as hard to save potential donors."
      3. "There are enough donors available."

II. Solutions to overcoming shortage of donors
   A. Public education to correct misconceptions
      1. Example of Mickey Mantle
         a. Severely ill patient
         b. Matched profile in area where liver became available
         c. Not given organ because of fame
      2. Death certificate must be signed before suggestion of transplant
      3. Statistics clearly show a lack of donors
   B. Personal commitment and participation
      1. Story of Reg and Maggie Green
         a. Vacationing in Italy in 1994 with son Nicholas
         b. Son brutally murdered
         c. Parents donated organs to seven people in Italy
      2. Personal story of my twin brother
         a. Diagnosed with complete kidney failure
         b. Endured dialysis three times a week for nine months
         c. Placed on waiting list with 500 people
         d. I donated a kidney to my twin brother

In this speech, Janis Rainer wanted to show listeners that there was a critical shortage of organ donors. In numeral I, she used two sets of statistical data, a quotation, and several brief quotations relating to public misconceptions or myths. Notice that she did not provide entire quotations or complete statistics with all explanatory information in the outline. In numeral II the speaker wanted to show that public education and personal involvement were critical to solving the donor problem. She used the example of Mickey Mantle, related the story of the Green family, and described her own involvement as a kidney donor for her twin brother. Again you can see that the entire story does not need to be written in detail in the outline. Remember that an outline is not a word-for-word account of all supporting materials, but a framework that provides an overall blueprint of the areas included in the speech.

When you write the statements in your outline you must be sure that ideas are of equal importance in each level, that subordinate ideas logically support each heading, and that statements do not duplicate each other. *Coordination* refers to the placement of equal ideas within the same level of an outline and *subordination* refers to the placement of secondary or lower ranking ideas beneath higher order items. Look at the following *incorrect* outline:

Specific purpose: To provide information that helps the audience to define and understand mental retardation.

Thesis statement: I will define mental retardation, explain how it is classified, and identify some common misconceptions about it.

INCORRECT

I. What it is
   A. A definition of mental retardation
   B. Public myths about the mentally retarded
   C. Public fears of the mentally retarded
   D. Mental retardation vs. mental illness
      1. Mental illness conditions
      2. Mental retardation conditions

II. Classifications of mental retardation
   A. Factors determining mental retardation
      1. Mental ability
      2. Adaptive behavior
      3. Physical development
   B. Degrees of mental retardation
      1. Mild to moderate
      2. Severe to profound

III. Common misconceptions about mental retardation

This outline is incorrect for the following reasons: Under Roman numeral I, item A (definition) is not equal to other items in the same level: It is identical to the heading and must be eliminated. Items IB (myths) and IC (fears) are overlapping points that should be combined. If you take an overall look at the outline, it appears that I contains points that are not supportive. *Fears* really belongs under III (Common misconceptions) and ID1 (mental illness conditions), which does not define retardation, can also be categorized under III. Here is a more effective outline:

CORRECT

I. Definition of mental retardation

II. Classification of mental retardation
   A. Factors determining mental retardation
      1. Mental ability
      2. Adaptive behavior
      3. Physical development
   B. Degrees classifying mental retardation
      1. Mild to moderate
      2. Severe to profound

   III. Common misconceptions about mental retardation
      A. Confusion with mental illness
      B. Fear of "different" behavior
      C. Inability to function in society
         1. Failure to have relationships
         2. Failure to be employed
         3. Failure to perform survival tasks

This outline now contains main and subordinate points that are arranged in their appropriate relationships.

Building Block Five: Every Subdivision Must Contain at Least Two Items

Under the concept of division, it is assumed that elements have been divided into two separate but equal categories. If there is only one item, there has obviously been no division. If you have only one supporting point under a heading, you have two choices: You can either look for a second item, or eliminate the one point and include it with the heading.

Specific purpose: To demonstrate how to juggle three objects.

Thesis statement: I will explain the selection of objects, the process of juggling, and provide a brief demonstration.

INCORRECT

   I. Selecting the objects
      A. Between four to six ounces
         1. Must not be too heavy

   II. Explaining the process
      A. Display visual aid describing steps
         1. Pick imaginary points
         2. Toss ball to points and catch
         3. Use opposite hand to throw ball
         4. Use steps B and C together
         5. Repeat the process

   III. Demonstrating the art of juggling

Under Roman numeral I there is an A but no B and only one point under the A. In II there is again only one A, but there are five items under the A. Here's how to correct these problems:

CORRECT

I. Choosing the objects
   A. Should weigh four to six ounces
   B. Should not be slick
   C. Should be able to bounce

II. Explaining the process (using visual aid)
   A. Pick imaginary points
   B. Toss ball to points and catch
   C. Use opposite hand to throw ball
   D. Use steps B and C together
   E. Repeat the process

III. Demonstrating the art of juggling

Under I item 1 (Must not be too heavy) has been eliminated because it can be included with the A *Between four to six ounces.* An additional B and a C have also been created to further complete the subdivision. In II the original A (Display visual aid) was eliminated because it can be incorporated with the heading. That change eliminates the need for numbers 1 through 5, which have been upgraded to the next level—A through E. The main and subordinate points are now correct.

Building Block Six: Each Statement Should Include Only One Thought or Idea

Here is an outline that violates this principle:

Specific purpose: To inform the audience about preventing teenage suicide.

Thesis statement: I will identify the warning signs of teenage suicide and explain how to help the individual.

INCORRECT

I. Warning signs of teenage suicide
   A. Direct suicide threats
   B. Indirect statements revealing desire to die
   C. Previous suicide attempts and sudden changes in behavior
      1. Social withdrawal
      2. Variable moods
      3. Severe depression and impulsive behavior

   II. Getting help to the individual
      A. Talk to the teen
      B. Show interest in the person
      C. Be certain teen can reach adult
      D. Solicit help from professional

Under I, item C, (Previous suicide attempts and sudden changes in behavior), is clearly two ideas. The numbers under C seem to support *changes in behavior,* but they do not clearly support *previous attempts.* Item 3 also includes two separate thoughts—*depression and impulsiveness.* When ideas are mistakenly clumped together like this, the audience makes a brief attempt to put the pieces together, but often stops listening in confusion. The outline should be revised as follows:

Correct

   I. Warning signs of teenage suicide
      A. Direct suicide threats
      B. Indirect statements revealing desire to die
      C. Previous suicide attempts
      D. Sudden changes in behavior
         1. Social withdrawal
         2. Variable moods
         3. Severe depression
         4. Impulsive behavior

   II. Getting help to the individual
      A. Talk to the teen
      B. Show interest in the person
      C. Be certain teen can reach adult
      D. Solicit help from professional

Notice that a new item D, (Sudden changes in behavior), has been added, as well as a new item 4, (Impulsive behavior), to separate the ideas. The outline is now accurate. The audience will be more capable of sorting out one idea at a time.

Building Block Seven: Main Points and Supporting Items Should Be Mechanically Parallel

The sentence structure and wording in each level should be similar. For example, if your first main point begins with a noun plus a prepositional phrase (causes of pollution, effects on streams,) or an infinitive phrase (to enjoy freedom, to participate in democracy), then other main points should begin in a similar manner. Subordinate points should also have parallel language structure: for instance, sub-letters A, B, C should be comparable, and sub-numbers 1, 2, 3 should show similarity.

> **Specific purpose:** To demonstrate how to creatively use the Halloween pumpkin for decoration and for delicious food.

> **Thesis statement:** You can carve the pumpkin into a Jack O'Lantern and toast the seeds.

INCORRECT	CORRECT
I. How to carve a pumpkin	I. Making a Jack O'Lantern
A. Beginning the process	A. Initial preparation process
1. Cut	1. Cut top
2. Removing seeds	2. Remove seeds
3. Creativity with the face	3. Cut out face
4. Flashlight vs. candle	4. Use flashlight—not candle
5. Placing in window	5. Display pumpkin
B. Final preparation process	B. Final preparation process
1. Removing flashlight	1. Remove flashlight from pumpkin
2. Foil and plastic	2. Wrap pumpkin in foil or plastic
3. Refrigerate	3. Place in refrigerator
II. Toasting pumpkin seeds	II. Toasting pumpkin seeds
A. Initial preparation process	A. Initial preparation process
1. Washing	1. Wash seeds in warm water
2. Soak	2. Soak overnight in solution
B. Cooking process	B. Final cooking process
1. Draining	1. Drain in colander
2. To bake in oven	2. Bake in oven
3. Storage	3. Eat (or store in cool place)

In the incorrect example, none of the main headings or supporting points are parallel. Notice the different wording and structure of the two main points: I begins with an adverb followed by an infinitive phrase and II begins with an action verb ending in "ing" followed by a noun. Notice also that subordinate items are not mechanically parallel.

The incorrect example demonstrates improper outline form. These mistakes may actually impede the speaker's progress. The speaker is forced to read and decipher each item in detail while delivering the speech. This improper outline can then reduce eye contact and hinder the flow of ideas.

Now look at the correct example. Each main point begins with an action word ending in "ing" followed by a noun or modified noun. Subordinate items are also parallel with each other. Notice that it is not necessary that all levels be identical in sentence structure: for example, the items under IA are grammatically different from the items that support IB. You will find, however, that each level maintains internal structural consistency.

This parallel outline will be easier for the speaker to read, and will facilitate the speaker's eye contact and thought process.

Building Block Eight: The Outline Should Be Expressed in Either Sentences or Topics

When you write the formal outline of the body, you should use either complete sentences or topics—never mix the two forms. If you begin using complete sentences for numeral I in the body, you must continue employing sentences throughout all main and subordinate levels to keep the outline consistent. If you begin with topics, again employ topics throughout the outline. Some speakers use a *topic outline* because they feel it keeps them from reading their outline word for word. Others use *sentence form* because they can get a more precise idea of the wording in the speech. Use either sentences or topics—whichever is most helpful.

Here are examples of the two types of outlines:

Specific purpose: To inform the audience about the increasing emphasis on sex in advertising.

Thesis statement: Sex is increasingly used in advertising because of the economic benefits to advertisers.

SENTENCE OUTLINE

I. Sex has invaded contemporary advertising.
    A. More men are shown as sexual objects.
    B. Women are now shown to be aggressors in sexual encounters.

TOPIC OUTLINE

I. The use of sex in advertising
    A. Men as sex objects
    B. Women as sexual aggressors

SENTENCE OUTLINE	TOPIC OUTLINE
C. More nudity of both sexes is shown.	C. Increased nudity of both sexes
II. Provocative advertising benefits the advertiser.	II. Benefits of provocative ads to advertiser
A. Receive positive feedback from consumers.	A. Positive feedback from consumers
B. Advertisers experience increases in their sales	B. Increases in sales revenues

Even though one is a sentence and another is a topic outline, each form is consistent throughout. The topic outline uses phrases—not just one or two words—to make each heading and subheading as clear as possible. Either form would be a useful tool to help the speaker successfully communicate to the audience.

Building Block Nine: The Body of the Outline Should Identify the Sources for Major Supporting Materials

Portions of the outline that include significant examples, statistics, or testimonies drawn from your research should clearly identify sources containing the information. Indicating references on the outline reminds you of where you obtained the information and helps you to integrate sources more easily when you deliver the presentation.

Source notations can be abbreviated in the body of the outline since you will be including a more comprehensive bibliography at the end. Here is a suggested system you can follow when annotating your sources:

Specific purpose: To examine and explain the uses of four types of masks.

Thesis statement: For thousands of years man has used masks for religious/ceremonial, theatrical, festive, and practical reasons.

BODY

I. Religious/ceremonial
   A. American Indians
      1. Hopi tribe
         a. Katchina masks (Underhill, *Red Man's Religion,* pp. 90, 208)
         b. How masks were used

    2. Northwest Indians

       a. Half man, half animal mask

       b. How masks were used (Kondeatis, *Masks,* p. 11)

  B. Central African

    1. Northern Ba Kete mask

    2. Construction of masks (Segy, *Masks of Black Africa,* pp. 33–37)

    3. Function of masks

This outline clearly identifies sources. In heading 2b under numeral IA, the parentheses indicate that the material was researched in the book *Masks.* The abbreviated form lists only the last name of the author, the title of the book, and the page numbers. You will notice that you don't need to annotate every item in an outline; only those headings and subheadings which include specific quotations or provide extensive data necessary to the development of the speech.

Building Block Ten: The Outline Should Include External Transitions between Main Headings

External transitions are phrases that connect the major headings of your speech. These carefully crafted statements should tell listeners that one main idea is ending and another is beginning. When you build the outline, write out the complete transitional phrase or sentence, placing it at the appropriate numeral.

Specific purpose: To inform the audience about one of America's passions—chocolate.

Thesis statement: Chocolate, a sweet substance we all take for granted, has an interesting background, affects our health, and is the object of a love affair with the American consumer.

BODY

  I. General background about chocolate

    Transition: Now that you've heard about the history and background of chocolate, you need to know about chocolate and your health.

  II. Health issues related to chocolate

    Transition: In spite of the health issues, American consumers have an ongoing love affair with chocolate.

  III. American consumer's love of chocolate

Remember to make a clear distinction between external and internal transitions. External transitions are one-sentence phrases occurring *between* the major numerals of the speech and placed in the body of the outline. These "listening cues" are a guide to help audiences determine the speaker's progress through the presentation. By contrast, internal transitions are brief words such as "also," "then," "next," "in addition to," or "finally" which link the supporting materials *within* a subheading. Although internal transitions are also important to the delivery of the speech, these brief connectives are not needed in the outline.

SUMMARY

Approach the organization process in a logical manner and follow these ten principles for outlining the body of your speech:

1. The body should contain no fewer than two, and no more than five main points in a five- to seven-minute speech.
2. Main points form a sequence that is logical, interesting, and appropriate to the topic.
3. A system of Roman numerals, letters, and numbers, combined with indentation, identifies main and subordinate levels.
4. Include supporting materials that are coordinated and subordinated in a logic manner.
5. Every subdivision should contain at least two items.
6. Each statement should include only one thought or idea.
7. Main points and supporting items should be grammatically parallel.
8. Use either complete sentences or topics. Do not mix.
9. Identify sources for major supporting materials.
10. Include external transitions between main headings of the body.[3]

SKILL BUILDERS

1. From the following list of specific purpose statements, explain which method of organization you would use to arrange the main points in the body (either time, space, causal, or topical order). Be able to support your answer.
   a. To inform about the life of John Birks "Dizzy" Gillespie.
   b. To describe the interior of the Superdome.
   c. To inform about the symptoms of AIDS.
   d. To explain the origins and results of prejudice against Amerasian children.
   e. To demonstrate how to develop 35-mm color film.
   f. To describe the characteristics of the largest planets in the solar system.

g. To explain how superconductors can contribute to our lives.

h. To describe some of the myths about the homeless in America.

2. There are a number of items in the following example that are not constructed according to correct outline procedure. Identify the incorrect areas and then rewrite or rearrange any heading or subdivision to reflect appropriate outline techniques.

Specific purpose: The purpose of the speech is to inform the audience about the impact of new computer technologies upon today's music.

Thesis statement: I will describe some of the new computer technologies and explain their impact on music.

    I. New computer technologies for music
      A. Synthesizers
        1. Recorded sounds of instruments
        2. Stored within memory
      B. Micro-chips
        1. The sound is burned into the memory.
        2. When the sound is retrieved, it is exact.
      C. Traditional instruments made obsolete

    II. Impact of new technologies on music
      A. Live concerts
        1. Music electronically assisted
        2. Performer must manipulate buttons
        3. Power blackout destroys performance
      B. Synthesizer goes beyond human abilities
        1. No mistakes and can play at any speed
        2. Tune can be played in any key
        3. Music mechanical
        4. Music lacks human feeling
      C. More people will learn instruments
        1. Can be hooked to home computer, providing instruction
      D. Performers learn computer programming
        1. Stop practicing scales

3. Divide your class into groups of three or four and analyze the following nineteen items representing scrambled elements from an outline of a persuasive speech to convince. Using the thesis as an overall guide, unscramble the items into the correct three-level outline, using numerals, capital letters, and numbers. Compare your final version with that of other groups in your class.

Topic: Discrimination against divorced fathers.

Thesis statement: "Americans discriminate against divorced fathers through court decisions, legislative actions, and through the general practices of society."

1. Courts' concern with enforcement of child support
2. Punishments for noncompliance of court-ordered child support
3. Divorced dads are disposable to many women
4. Statistics on allowed visitations for fathers
5. President's proposed law on child support enforcement
6. Statistics on custody awards to mothers versus fathers
7. Economic savings for states regarding enforcement of child support
8. Discrimination of fathers by legislature
9. "Deadbeat Dads" phrase
10. Examples of visitation agreements
11. Discrimination against fathers by the courts
12. No federal visitation laws for fathers
13. Public's lack of concern for enforcement of visitation rights
14. Mandatory child support guideline
15. Court's lack of concern for visitation rights/agreements
16. Problem with much legislation
17. Discrimination against fathers by society
18. President's 1992 acceptance speech proposing legislation
19. Ease of mothers to deny visitation

NOTES

1. Judith Humphrey, "Executive Eloquence," *Vital Speeches,* May 15, 1998, pp. 468–469.

2. I am grateful to the following students who gave me permission to use their topics and to modify their outlines for this chapter: Lisa Hilton, "Ancient Egyptian Funeral Customs"; Steve Hogue, "The American Muscle Car"; Joe A. Lloyd, Jr., "Colon Cancer"; Erin Ellis, "Major Causes of Child Abuse"; Mary Holmes "Life in Dunoon, Scotland"; Richard Renehan, "HMOs and Quality Health Care"; Janis L. Rainer, "The Lack of Organ Donors"; Ralph Thompson, "Understanding Mental Retardation"; Richard Watson, "The Art of Juggling"; Tina Cerrato, "Teenage Suicide"; Deborah C. Brown, "Being Creative with Your Halloween Pumpkin"; Susan Stephan, "Sex in Advertising"; Tara Baker, "Four Types of Masks," courtesy of Mary Anne Rhoades, Associate Professor of Speech; Della Leister, "Chocolate—One of America's Passions"; David Wildt, "New Computer Technologies and Music"; and Dawn Anderson, "Discrimination Against Divorced Fathers."

3. I would also like to acknowledge Leroy Giles, Professor Emeritus of English at Catonsville Community College for his helpful suggestions as I prepared this chapter.

Chapter 11

SELECTING THE INTRODUCTION AND CONCLUSION

Everything ends that has a beginning.

Quintilian

CHAPTER OBJECTIVES

After reading this chapter you will be able to:

1. Discuss the objectives of an introduction;

2. Describe strategies for beginning a speech;

3. Discuss the objectives of a conclusion;

4. Describe strategies for ending a speech;

5. Describe two methods of outlining the introduction and conclusion;

6. Construct effective speaking notes;

7. Develop a comprehensive speech outline.

Thomas Martin, a professor of philosophy at the University of Nebraska, introduced a speech to the Mortor Board in Kearny, Nebraska, with the following remarks:

"How are you as far as sex goes, Sophocles? Can you still make love with a woman?" "Quiet, man," the poet replied. "I am very glad to have escaped from all that, like a slave who has escaped from a savage and tyrannical master." I [Cephalus] thought at the time that he was right, and I still do, for old age brings peace and freedom from all such things. When appetites relax and cease to importune us, everything Sophocles said comes to pass, and we escape from many mad masters. In these matters and in those concerning relatives, the real cause isn't old age, Socrates, but the way people live. If they are moderate and contented, old age, too, is only moderately onerous; if they aren't, both old age and youth are hard to bear." (*Republic* 329c)

These words are spoken by Cephalus in his home in Piraeus, the harbor near Athens, at the beginning of Plato's dialogue *Republic* before a group of young men and Socrates. This passage is a great ice-breaker. Most of the students who have wandered into philosophy are wondering what in the world philosophers do. What better way to capture the attention of youth than the mention of sex. No doubt many of the students are thinking, "On the first day of philosophy class we are talking about sex! Man, can I get into this."[1]

In this startling beginning, the speaker demonstrated a keen understanding of a fundamental principle of public speaking. The audience forms its first impressions of your speech while listening to your introduction. If you are going to be successful throughout your presentation, you must get your listeners' attention and stimulate their curiosity at the very beginning.

Speech introductions and conclusions are the focus of this chapter. It is important to know the purpose and structure of the opening and closing, as well as the various ways you can begin and end. Suggestions are given to help you construct your speaking notes, and an informative speech outline is provided as a model for your own presentations.

PLANNING THE INTRODUCTION

Every speech needs an entry point. The speaker does not want to start with, "My topic today is earthquakes and my purpose is to tell you how they happen—so here goes!" This type of beginning is certainly direct and to the point, but it is abrupt and uninteresting.

The purpose of the introduction is to provide a graceful entrance into your topic. You want to capture the attention of the audience, arouse their curiosity about your topic and link the topic to their needs, and introduce your specific purpose and thesis statements. The introduction is the place where the audience decides to listen or tune you out. How well you understand your listeners and how effectively you develop an introduction to connect to their unique characteristics often determines whether or not the audience will give you a hearing. Imagine a woman who presents a speech about breast cancer to an audience of mostly men, a Moslem from Saudi Arabia speaking about the religious fast of Ramadan to an audience of mostly Americans, or a speaker with strong views favoring a flat tax speaking to listeners who are strongly opposed. It is doubtful that these speakers would be successful unless they understood the differences within their audiences and developed introductory strategies that connected the topic to their listeners' background and interests. For example, the woman speaking to male listeners could develop an introduction indicating that breast cancer also afflicts men and is not just a women's issue. The Saudi Arabian speaker could begin by relating Ramadan to western religious holidays such as Passover and Christmas. And the flax tax proponent could develop an introduction that established areas of agreement with listeners about the need to save money and generate more individual income.

As you face the diverse members of your audience, use the introduction as a strategy to show how your topic relates to your listeners' interests and motivations. Understand differences in culture, ethnic background, gender, and age. Know how social affiliations or groups, educational background, occupational goals, and geographic location influence your audience and impact their perception of your topic. If you are speaking about the U.S. budget to listeners from other countries, indicate why your topic is important to them. If you are demonstrating the Heimlich maneuver to an audience of business majors, describe how the topic can assist employees in a restaurant or save a company from lawsuits. If you are talking about the financial instability of Medicare to listeners under twenty-two, describe how rescuing the program can benefit their future. Use the introduction to prepare listeners to hear and receive your ideas. Acknowledge the audience and help them to understand that your topic can be important to their needs. The introduction must be well thought out and very carefully prepared. A boring, insensitive, poorly worded, or poorly delivered introduction can quickly destroy a speaker's credibility with listeners; on the other hand, a meaningful, curiosity-provoking introduction can motivate listeners and bring your topic to life. Recognize that an introduction isn't just one or two sentences placed together; it incorporates a carefully devised technique or variety of techniques to gain your listeners' interest and goodwill. Generally, a good introduction is at least a paragraph in length.

In this section we present some examples of effective introductions and explain why they are successful. Some of these examples are taken directly from students' presentations in beginning speech classes, and some are excerpts from individuals who are experienced in delivering public speeches.

Examples, Stories, and Illustrations

You can always begin with an *example, short story,* or *illustration*. Examples make your introduction vivid, and help your audience to quickly understand the reality of a person, experience, or circumstance. Notice how the following brief story creates interest and generates concern as it moves forward.

> This is a copy of my senior yearbook. Underneath the picture of each graduate is a caption that describes our personalities or our past school experiences. I'd like to show you one picture, and I'll read the caption under it. It says, "Is there no remedy?"
>
> Is there no remedy? Jerry Shafer still asks himself that question three years later. In March of 1984 Jerry was riding on a friend's motorcycle and someone ran a stop sign and hit him. He suffered a compound fracture of his arm and lost a large amount of blood. I went to visit him right afterwards in the hospital, and I can remember seeing the plasma bottle hanging over him with a tube going into his arm. Little did I know that this would be his killer.
>
> Between the years 1978 to 1985, a lot of donated blood was HIV-contaminated—contaminated with the AIDS virus. Because of this, some exceedingly unfortunate people today are walking time bombs—and my friend Jerry is one of these individuals. AIDS—acquired immune deficiency syndrome—is a monstrous and terrifying disease which has deadly effects upon the body's immune system.[2]

This speaker could have started by telling the audience that "AIDS is a terrible disease and it afflicts thousands of people." Instead, Michael Black analyzed his listeners' perception of the topic. He understood that most members of his audience already knew that AIDS was a deadly disease affecting numerous individuals. He also understood that people often fail to place a human face on a well-known problem, so he decided to use the example of his friend Jerry and the visual aid of his high school yearbook. In addition, the speaker recognized that many listeners in the audience were not aware of the specific effects of AIDS on the body's immune system. So Michael wisely chose to present material that was unfamiliar to listeners rather than to rehash information that they already knew.

The result was an introduction to a speech that was extremely successful. The audience could sense Mike's concern and despair as he described the disease slowly seizing his friend Jerry. At the end of the speech one student said: "Mike's introduction really made me listen. He got my attention with the visual and he also made me curious—I wanted to listen to the story because I wasn't sure where it was headed. I really had a lot of sympathy for Mike and his friend. I didn't want to stop listening for a minute—I was so totally involved in the story."

Notice that the end of the introduction contains the thesis statement: "AIDS . . . is a monstrous and terrifying disease which has deadly effects upon the body's immune system."

In the next introduction, Gina Alexander uses a series of brief examples as her strategy:

- Susan's boss told her that her dress was too tight and too loud in color.
- Beth's supervisor pinched her every time she walked near him.
- Michelle was the object of many dirty jokes by her coworkers.
- John knew that making love to Norma, the vice-president of the company, was the only way to get that essential promotion.
- Ralph had to endure hugs from his professor in order to get an "A."

Degrading, counterproductive, and criminal—these words describe sexual harassment in the workplace. This is the cancer of our workplace. Sexual harassment is a problem for both men and women. These harassers want power over us, and victims are unaware of how to cut off this power.[3]

Gina Alexander understood that her listeners had probably heard a lot about this topic. Some listeners had participated in job-related seminars educating them about sexual harassment and others had heard general news reports about the issue. However, the speaker decided to present a series of brief examples to gain the attention of listeners. When developing her introduction, Gina analyzed the gender and age differences within her audience. The speaker presented instances drawn from the experiences of both men and women to indicate that sexual harassment can victimize either gender. She also used examples such as the student-professor situation that could connect to younger listeners as well as instances that were more typical of older listeners who were already pursuing their full-time careers. As audience members listened, they were able to connect the examples to their own environments and realize that the issue affects everyone. This rapid-fire technique is effective because the speaker conveys several examples quickly in order to motivate listeners.

An example, story, or illustration helps to create immediate interest, because an audience can empathize with a vivid situation or specific experience.

Shocking Statement or Situation

A *shocking statement* or situation that shocks the audience is also an effective method of creating interest. In the following introduction to a speech on tornados, Michael Gerber used the first line to startle his audience:

> It's raining toads and frogs. This may seem impossible, but it is only one of the many astonishing feats of a tornado. Yes, toads and frogs have been sucked up by a tornado and poured out by a cloud. A railroad coach with one hundred and seventeen passengers aboard was carried aloft by a tornado and dumped into a ditch twenty-five meters away. A schoolhouse was demolished and eighty-five students were transported one hundred meters. Amazingly, none of these students was killed. Chickens have lost their feathers and straw has been driven into metal pipes. These are only a few examples of the meanest and deadliest wind of all—the tornado.[4]

Mike could have started by saying: "My topic today is tornados. They are very dangerous and I'm sure you've heard stories and maybe seen movies about them." He realized, however, that a more creative way of getting the attention of listeners was by referring to the unexpected. Audiences tend to be more involved and responsive when they are surprised or startled by an idea. The one-liner combined with the brief examples effectively set up the entire speech: Listeners were completely receptive and anxious to hear other pertinent information about the tornado.

Here is another way to use a shock technique in the introduction. Before his speech began, Stephen King got the attention of his listeners by distributing a small white cup to each of his classmates. He then held up a "memo" that he began reading to his audience.

> I'd like to read you a memo from the dean of the university, which is dated today. "It has come to the attention of the administration and faculty that an increasing number of students have been abusing alcohol and illegal drugs on campus. In response, the university has adopted a policy of mandatory drug testing for all students. Since this is a serious problem— one that could cause the university to lose its state funding—all students, full-time and part-time, must submit to a witnessed urinalysis by the medical staff of the university by November 30. Should any student fail to comply with this test, he or she will be immediately dropped from class rosters. Moreover, any student who tests positive will also be immediately dismissed from the university and no longer allowed to attend class."
>
> Now I've passed around some paper cups, and I'd like you to fill out your name and social security number on the labels provided, and make note if you are taking any prescription drugs. In the hall, stationed outside both restrooms, we have members of the medical department to witness your test. Now, I'd like to start at the rear of the room. One at a time please.
>
> The memo I have just read is not real. But I'd like you to think for a minute how you would feel if it were. Would you be insulted, embarrassed, outraged? Would you say "What right do I have to ask you to do this? Who the hell do I think I am?" Well get prepared, because it's happening all across America. Sooner or later, don't be surprised if someone wants you to urinate in a cup like this. These drug tests violate our Constitutional rights and invade our privacy.[5]

Steve understood his student audience extremely well. He recognized that they would listen carefully to the contrived memo from the "dean" of their university. When developing the document, the speaker used words such as "moreover," "comply," and "class rosters" as well as bureaucratic sentence structure that sounded authentic and appeared to have been issued by a university official. This method of using a startling situation was overwhelmingly successful. One student said, "I thought this was all true. The memo that he read sounded official, and I was going to take my little cup to the restroom for the sample." Another listener commented, "I was incensed that anyone would try something like this. It really drove the point home."

Steve used this method to get to the heart of the issue. He quickly communicated that although the situation was hypothetical, the problem was real, and he placed his audience in a situation that forced them to examine the issues involved. He had his audience sitting on the edges of their seats.

Statistics

You can begin your speech by citing *statistics* to involve the audience.

> Of the eighteen people in this classroom, nine were sexually molested as children—that's one out of every two, men as well as women according to figures from Family and Children's Services of Central Maryland. Actually, there are only eight in the audience, because I'm the ninth person. And I kept that secret for thirty-six years.
>
> I've been a rape crisis counselor for two years and I've put in one hundred hours working with sexually abused child victims. Victims of child abuse have no control over what happened to them. It is the secrecy surrounding the incident that causes significant damage. As parents and future parents, you need to know what sexual child abuse is, who the offenders are, how the victims are affected, and some preventative measures you can take to protect your children.[6]

Kathy Birckhead could have started this introduction with a simple statement of the statistic and a general comment about the unfortunate implications revealed by the numbers. Instead, she related the statistics to the audience and got immediate attention by using the numbers to threaten the physical and emotional well-being of her listeners. Since the statistics indicated that half of them were abused as children, audience members listened intently to learn more about the topic. Concern intensified when the speaker acknowledged her own abuse and established credibility as a counselor. Notice that Kathy involves the audience by connecting to parents as well as "future parents" when she states the thesis at the end of introduction.

Questions

Another way to introduce a topic is by asking a question. *Questions* can be either rhetorical or open-ended. Rhetorical questions are self answered: Listeners respond silently. In the following example, Kathleen Ward asked her listeners a rhetorical question to introduce the topic.

> What do George Washington and Cleopatra have in common? Well they are just two of the many different people who have braided their hair over the centuries. Braiding goes as far back as the Egyptians who corn-braided their hair. Braiding is not just for females. Corn-braiding for the Egyptians included the males and George Washington and many other men of his time had their long hair pulled back at the nape and braided. And according to Margot Liste's book, *Costumes of Everyday Life,* many American Indians were known for braiding their hair. This book also stated that in the twelfth century, ribbons and different colored materials were woven through the braids, and it wasn't until the 1800s that these braids hung down and were uncovered. Until then, they were piled high or coiled around the head and they were covered for a headdress. This process included both men's and women's styles. Braids have been popular in the last twenty years—I can remember seeing men wearing them in the 1970s. But today, it tends to be more of a woman's style. One of the most common braids that I see women wearing is the French braid—that's the way I like to wear my hair. To me it's great, because on a hot day like today, my hair wasn't down around my forehead, and it wasn't hanging on my shoulders or around my neck. So today I'd like to show you three variations of French braiding that I know—the inward plait, the outward plait, and the fish bone.[7]

Kathleen skillfully crafted an introduction with several audience-centered techniques. The opening rhetorical question stimulated the curiosity and interest of listeners. She acknowledged gender by presenting the brief history indicating that the topic related to men as well as to women in the audience. Kathleen documented her material with a source, stated a personal observation, and demonstrated her knowledge of the topic by wearing her hair in a French braid.

Questions can also be of the open-ended type, which stimulate a direct response from the audience. Asking open-ended questions can be effective, but you need to be careful with this method. Don't ask the audience for more than a show of hands or one word answers. If you request more complicated information, you may find them taking control of your speech. In this example, the speaker asks for a simple show of hands to gain a response:

> By a show of hands, how many people in this room are Baptists? Okay, there are a few of you. I want you to listen closely, because what I'm about to read concerns you. By order of the Governor, all Baptists have been

proclaimed enemies of the state and must be exterminated, or driven from the state, if necessary, for the public good.

This sounds crazy doesn't it? It's the 1990s and we live in the United States and things like this just don't happen. Well, you're kinda right, they don't happen in the '90s, but they did happen in 1838. In the state of Missouri in 1838, Governor Lillburn W. Boggs issued an order of extermination for all Mormons. Today I want to talk about the three events leading up to that extermination order, namely, the existing anti-Mormon sentiment, the election day riot, and the Crooked River incident.[8]

Michelle Allred decided to ask a question that seemed to invade her listeners' privacy. However, the question combined with the hypothetical example helped the audience to understand the results of discrimination and religious persecution. When you seek an open-ended response, you must be clear that you want an answer from your listeners. In this instance, Michelle asked the question and told her audience the type of response she wanted. She also paused a moment to let the audience know she was waiting for their answer. The introduction then proceeded in a logical manner from the example to the 1838 extermination order that the speaker used to introduce her thesis. The strategy was extremely effective and helped the audience to connect to Michelle's historical topic.

Quotation

Another good way to introduce your speech is by using a *quotation* appropriate to your topic. In a nationally televised campaign speech, 1992 presidential candidate H. Ross Perot used a quotation to introduce a speech on the economy:

> "The budget should be balanced. The treasury should be refilled. Public debts should be reduced. The arrogance of public officials should be controlled." These are not new words. Cicero said these words over 2,000 years ago but certainly they apply to our country today.
>
> Anytime we do anything, we try to learn from experience. We learned a lot from the first program from your comments. First, you wanted better charts that you can see the fine print on, and you'll have those tonight. Secondly, we had one news announcer that criticized the pointer that I used before. So, since we're dealing with voodoo economics, a great young lady from Louisiana sent me this voodoo stick and I will use it as my pointer tonight. Certainly, it's appropriate, because, as you and I know, we're in deep voodoo![9]

Perot began with the quotation from Cicero to stress the seriousness of the issue. But the speaker demonstrated that he could "learn from experience" about the needs and interests of millions of viewers. Perot interjected humor with the visual aid to motivate listeners and to connect them to a difficult subject. He also used humor as a political weapon. In the presidential primaries of the early 1980s, candidate George Bush had commented that candidate Ronald Reagan's economic plan for the country was "voodoo economics." By reminding voters about Bush's earlier comment and using the voodoo stick, Perot mocked President Bush, who was presiding over an economic recession at the time. The combination of strategies was successful: Millions of Americans listened intently to the thirty-minute speech.

You can also include a longer quotation in the introduction, such as a poem, song, or other work that is appropriate to your topic.

> I'd like to quote a poem entitled "To Santa Claus, and little sisters."
>
> Once . . . he wrote a poem.
> And called it "Chops,"
> Because that was the name of
> his dog, and that's what it was
> all about.
> And the teacher gave him an "A"
> And a gold star.
> And his mother hung it on the
> kitchen door and read it to
> all his aunts . . .
>
> Once . . . he wrote another
> poem.
> And he called it "Question Marked
> Innocence."
> Because that was the name of
> His grief, and that's what it
> was all about.
> And the professor gave him an
> "A"
> And a strange and steady look.
> And his mother never hung it
> on the kitchen door, because
> he never let her see it . . .
>
> Once, at 3 A.M. . . . he tried
> another poem . . .
> And he called it absolutely
> nothing, because that's what it
> was all about.
> And he gave himself an "A"
> And a slash on each damp wrist,
> And hung it on the bathroom
> door because he couldn't reach
> the kitchen.[10]

> This poem was written by a fifteen year old boy two years before he committed suicide. The National Institute of Mental Health recently reported that every ninety minutes a teenager commits suicide. We must know the warning signs of teenage suicide so that we can recognize them and intervene the next time a child cries out for help.[11]

In this introduction, Tina Cerrato immediately aroused the attention of her audience. They were completely involved as they listened to the poem and they were curious to find out the underlying meaning. Tina made them wait in suspense until the final sentences of her introduction when the point of the poem became entirely clear. If parents, teachers, or friends cannot recognize the obvious warning signs of teenage suicide, they will be powerless to stop an often preventable tragedy. The poem and statistical evidence, validated by a credible source, demonstrated that the issue was real, important, and required the full attention of the audience.

Suspense

In addition to using quotations or poems to stimulate interest, you can make listeners curious about a topic by using *suspense:*

> A harness locks you into place. You move slowly forward and then upward, climbing to a height of fifteen stories. Next you drop fifty-five degrees, making you feel as if you just drove off a cliff at more than sixty miles per hour. You zoom through two sixty-foot-high loops, you are turned upside down, you gyrate through a two-hundred-foot corkscrew, and you are thrown like a boomerang into a final loop. You've been turned upside down and around six times, and pressed against your seat by the force—of gravity, that is—which is nearly four times your body weight.
>
> Is this some kind of masochistic exercise or strange ceremony? No, not really. You've just experienced the Vortex, the roller coaster ride at King's Island Amusement Park in Ohio as described by Kerry Hannon in an August 1987 issue of *Forbes* magazine. Today I'd like to give you some information that you may not know about the design and safety of these wonderful, whirling thrills.[12]

Karen Leonard realized that students in a speech class would respond favorably to the element of suspense. Without identifying her topic at the beginning, Karen described a series of events designed to sustain the curiosity of audience members. The speaker painted concrete images that allowed listeners to picture the experience in their minds. The audience could "feel" the pressure of the locking harness; they could experience the sensation of the fifteen-story climb and the fifty-five-degree drop; and they could endure the gravitational forces of the corkscrew and the slinging shot of the final loop. Karen's strategy was successful even though most listeners had guessed the topic before she revealed it. After identifying her source of the descriptive statements, the speaker stated a clear thesis at the end of the introduction.

Personal Reference, Compliment, or Reference to Occasion

Another way to begin an introduction is by making a *personal reference* or by giving a *compliment* to the audience. There are occasions when speakers face audiences they do not know and places they've never been. In this kind of situation it is important for a speaker to establish a common ground. Effective audience analysis will help the speaker mention the appropriate catch words, which will build a relationship with listeners. Notice how David Archambault, President of the American Indian College Fund, used a personal reference in the following introduction:

> Thank you and good afternoon. Hau Kola. That is how we Lakota say "Greeting, Friends." I am happy to be here today to represent Native American people. I am an Ikoeya Wicaska—an ordinary man. We think of an ordinary man as not superior to anyone else or for that matter to anything else. We—all people and all things—are related to each other.
>
> We begin our spiritual ceremonies with the phrase "Oni takuya Oyasi," which means all my relations. We believe that all people are ultimately part of one nation—the nation of mankind, but that this nation is only one of many nations that inhabit the Mother Earth. To us all living things are nations—the deer, the horses, things that crawl, things that fly, things that grow in and on the ground. All of these nations were created by the same Power, and none is superior to another. All are necessary for life. We are expected to live and work in harmony.[13]

Since he presented his remarks to an audience with few Indians, Archambault acquainted listeners with his culture by expressing warm greetings in his native language and by describing the spiritual philosophies of his tribe. The speaker's key to this effective personal reference was good audience analysis. He understood his audience members and knew the appropriate references needed to help listeners understand his background and culture.

In a speech class where you get to know everyone during the semester, you might not need to begin by complimenting the audience. But it is possible that circumstances could require you to make a personal reference. If you are from an environment or culture that is different from that of your listeners, you might find it beneficial to acknowledge this diversity and use it as a device for stimulating interest and curiosity. Like Archambault, a Turkish student once referred to his native country with its language and customs. A speaker from Zimbabwe began by presenting verbal descriptions of wild animals roaming freely over the countryside. A speaker from the Philippines asked the audience to study her facial features and attempt to guess her country of origin. These speakers used personal references as a strategy to connect to the curiosities of their listeners.

You can also begin your introduction by making a reference to the occasion of the speech. Mary Collins, associate minister for National Defense in Canada, used a reference to the occasion as an introduction:

> President Hoxie, distinguished guests, ladies and gentlemen: It's a great pleasure for me to be here in Washington tonight, and to take part in your symposium marking the two hundredth anniversary of the American Bill of Rights.
>
> Fifty years ago, when he established a national "Bill of Rights" day, President Franklin D. Roosevelt reminded Americans, and the world, of the cost of the rights and freedoms being celebrated. "Those who have long enjoyed such privileges as we enjoy," he said, "forget in time that men have died to win them."
>
> For Americans and Canadians, alike, democracy, human rights and freedom are our heritage, but they do not have a life of their own. They must be lived, they must be nurtured, and they must be safeguarded through constant vigilance.[14]

As a Canadian, Mary Collins realized that her American audience would feel a sense of pride in celebrating the 200th anniversary of the Bill of Rights. She greeted her audience, acknowledged the occasion, and used an inspiring quotation from President Roosevelt to remind listeners of the precious cost of freedom. Collins ended the introduction on a note of common ground, stressing the similarity of Canadian and American ideals.

In your speech class you could refer to an upcoming holiday like Christmas, Passover, or Easter, Independence Day or Thanksgiving, or a special event like Valentine's Day, Secretary's Day, or even April Fool's Day. An opening reference to the occasion can be related to the topic and simultaneously gain the attention and interest of your audience.

Humor

Humor is an excellent way to introduce a speech. Humor can establish goodwill between the speaker and the audience, and a joke or humorous anecdote can relax the audience and put the speaker at ease. Read this short introduction from a speech that Benjamin Alexander, president of Drew Dawn Enterprises, presented to the American Association of Retired Persons.

> It was twelve months ago that Mrs. Brown invited me to address this distinguished group of retired Americans. My role is to speak to you; your job is to listen. If you should finish your assignment before mine is completed, and you wish to leave—please do so. But if too many of you begin

to depart at the same time, let me know where you are going and if it sounds better than here, I will join you.[15]

The remarks are genuinely funny, yet they have a serious point. Alexander demonstrates his sensitivity to the speaker-audience relationship, and through the use of humor, tells the listeners that he intends to interest them.

When you think about using humor for an introduction, remember that it can be used as a two-edged sword of destruction. Never start an introduction with humor that can offend, insult, or hurt members of your audience. Beginning with inappropriate sexist jokes, insulting religious stories, or cultural put-downs can seriously backfire and drive listeners away. Once turned off by offensive humor, listeners will be difficult to win back.

Be certain that your humor is appropriate and gets the response you want from your audience. Recognize that humor can be tricky: A joke that flops or an anecdote that is poorly presented will defeat the purpose of the introduction. Be relatively sure that your humor will work by trying it out on friends or classmates in advance.

The Flexible Introduction

There will be times when your prepared introduction may not be appropriate. Unexpected events sometimes create difficult situations making an audience unreceptive to a presentation. A humorous introduction would not be appropriate if an audience had just heard a wrenching testimonial about drug addiction; a sad story about adoption might not be effective after rollicking humor; an introduction presented to freezing listeners might generate very little positive response. You may need to alter your prepared beginning by presenting another introduction that puts listeners in a more receptive mood.

One student, who was among several scheduled to present a classroom speech, had planned a statistical introduction into a speech about recycling. By coincidence, however, another speaker presented almost identical factual materials on the same topic. The student with the second recycling speech adapted to the unwelcome situation with the following impromptu introduction:

My topic is recycling as well. I was glad to see that someone else had an interest in the waste problem. (I was also shocked to see this!) That speech informed us about developments in recycling in different companies today, it showed that recycling is not developed as much here as in other places in the country, and it described the problems with dumping in the sea. I'll try not to reiterate the main points but rather, I'll try to reinforce the urgency and the need for recycling.[16]

Naming the topic is not the most effective way of beginning an introduction, but the situation that Rick Trader encountered demanded quick thinking. The speaker did not let circumstances destroy his confidence. He transformed a negative situation by acknowledging the difficulty, by joking about the coincidence, and even by restating the previous speaker's thesis. He then reassured listeners that he would provide new information in addition to material already presented. The impromptu introduction worked. Rick's listeners were positive and supportive, and appreciated his different perspective on the same topic.

Combination of Methods

You will often find that it is useful to combine a variety of methods in your introduction. Chris Koeppen used a combination of approaches to stimulate his listeners' interest.

> When you were a kid did you ever play with building blocks like this? Well I used to enjoy them as I'm sure you did. I found blocks to be fun and educational and I used to create all kinds of structures, like the one I've made here. Building these objects helped me to imagine larger structures. Consider, for example, that there are only six little blocks in my pyramid. Imagine that you had to put together two and one-half million of these blocks. Furthermore, instead of small blocks, imagine that each one of them weighed about five thousand pounds. That's the type of project that the ancient Egyptians undertook when building the Great Pyramid. What is equally amazing is that the exact reason for its existence remains a mystery. Thus the intrigue of the Great Pyramid stems from the facts about its construction, and the theories on why it was built.[17]

The speaker asks the audience a rhetorical question and uses a visual aid to remind audience members of their childhood. The opening statements create suspense and the small pyramid provides an effective comparison to the Great Pyramid of Egypt. Finally, Chris mentions some startling statistics and ends with his thesis statement.

If you combine a question with a quote, or a statistic with a startling statement, you can develop an introduction both interesting and meaningful to your audience.

OUTLINING THE INTRODUCTION

The introduction is part of the informal outline of a speech. Remember that the purpose of the outline is to help you communicate the content of your introduction. While it is never advisable to mix sentences and topics in the formal outline of the speech body, it may actually be helpful to adopt this practice in your introduction. We are providing two different outline styles you can choose for your introduction. The examples below outline the story of Michael Black's friend who had acquired AIDS.

STYLE 1	INTRODUCTION
(First sentence)	I. "This is a copy of my senior yearbook."
(Strategy)	II. Story of my friend, Jerry Shafer
(Specific purpose)	III. To inform the audience about the disease AIDS
(Thesis statement)	IV. AIDS—acquired immune deficiency syndrome—is a monstrous and terrifying disease that has deadly effects upon the body's immune system.

This style of outlining is short, but it is adequate if you know your introduction thoroughly. Numeral I includes the first sentence of the speech. It is important to write out the first line of your speech word for word so that you will be able to begin with confidence. Numeral II simply describes the strategy (or strategies) you are using for the introduction such as story, case study, quotation, or statistics. In this instance, the story mentioned in II will trigger the speaker's personal experiences. Numeral III identifies the specific purpose and numeral IV provides the thesis statement. Numerals III and IV remind you to state the purpose and/or thesis at the end of your introduction.

Here is a more detailed outline of the same introduction:

STYLE 2	INTRODUCTION
(First sentence)	I. "This is a copy of my senior yearbook."
	A. Caption describes experiences
	B. One picture with caption—"Is there no remedy?"
(Strategy)	II. Story of my friend, Jerry Shafer
	A. Hit in a motorcycle accident in 1984
	B. Received AIDS-contaminated blood transfusion
	C. Has become walking time bomb
(Specific purpose)	III. To inform the audience about the disease AIDS
(Thesis statement)	IV. AIDS—acquired immune deficiency syndrome—is a monstrous and terrifying disease that has deadly effects upon the body's immune system.

You can see that this outline has the same numerals as Style 1, but there is more detail. The detail obviously helps to keep you on track if you feel you need more information to guide you through your introduction. Use whichever style your instructor recommends to suit your particular needs.

PLANNING THE CONCLUSION

Just as a speech requires an introduction, a speech also needs a conclusion. We've often heard endings like this:

Well, uh, I guess, uh, that's about it!

And now in conclusion I'd just like to say that I hope you've learned something about holograms.

And now for my conclusion, I'll leave you with a quote: all's well that ends well.

And so finally, in conclusion, I'd like to end by telling you that my last point is that you might want to pick up a kit to test radon gas the next time you're in the supermarket. Thank you.

These are not successful ways to end speeches. The "techniques" are abrupt, trite, awkward, or repetitious. Sloppy conclusions increase the speaker's apprehension and make the audience equally uncomfortable.

An effective conclusion gives finality to a speech. The speaker must choose a clear method or device that tells the audience that the topic has been resolved. A speaker must also clearly demonstrate in his delivery (voice tone, slower rate of speech) that the speech has ended.

You should not introduce new material in the conclusion; rather, you should choose a method which reinforces the information and ideas you have already presented. We will provide brief explanations and examples of a conclusion—summary, quotation, reference to the introduction, challenge and appeal, humor, question, story, and statistics.

Summary of Main Points

A *summary* of the main points can be an effective way to end a speech on complicated or difficult subject matter. Summaries help to remind your audience of the major points and leave them with a sense of order. Meredith Kreczmer summarized her demonstration on creative photography and used a visual aid as reinforcement.

The key to a good picture is not the number of lights or the quality of your camera and lens, but it is your ability to "see" and "think" in terms of pictures. Remember the simple steps on this poster:

First, get to know your camera—

the viewfinder

shutter release

aperture

shutter

Second, remember the key techniques—

Less is more.

Move around your subject.

Look at your background.

Close in on the subject.

Simplicity is never wrong.

So snap away, and maybe someday you'll see your picture in *National Geographic!*[18]

The speaker used several visuals and described a number of techniques during the body of the speech. An ordinary verbal summary would have been adequate; instead, Meredith used words and cartoon sketches on a visual aid to remind her audience of important ideas stressed in the speech. The summary included both main and supporting points, since the body of this presentation included only two numerals. In longer, more complex speeches, however, speakers might tend to recap only the numerals.

Don't use a summary conclusion simply because you can't think of any other approach. Remember that a successful speaker has a good reason for the type of conclusion he or she selects. Summaries are good with complex material in informative speeches, but they are not effective when you need to be persuasive and appeal to the audience or challenge their thinking in another way.

Quotation

A *quotation* is often an excellent way to end a speech. A quote can express feelings eloquently and reinforce the speaker's ideas.

Kim Jones combined an example with a quotation to end a speech commemorating Sojourner Truth, a famous African American orator and reformer:

Sojourner Truth fought for increased education, Negro rights, world peace, and women's rights. But some did not give her the respect that she deserved. According to William Jacobs' *Great Lives,* the newspapers started a rumor. Because she was six feet tall, they said that she was probably a man disguised as a woman. In order to prove her womanhood, they asked her to show her breasts. With quiet dignity, she opened her blouse before the stunned crowd and declared softly: "It is not my shame, but yours, that I must do this."

Sojourner Truth died in 1883. A quotation in the Jacobs book presents a fitting tribute to the life of this great African American. "With her arms outstretched, and her eyes aflame, she argued in a deep voice about women's rights: 'If the first woman God ever made was strong enough to turn the world upside down, all alone, then together we ought to be able to turn it back and get it right side up again and now they are asking us to do it, the men better let them.' "[19]

Kim cited this vivid example to demonstrate the courage and regal dignity that Sojourner displayed in the midst of degrading and humiliating circumstances. The end quotation resolved the speech effectively by painting an elegant portrait of a strong, compassionate, yet determined woman. Listeners experienced feelings of rage, empathy, and pride as Kim delivered the quotation slowly, with strength and emotion.

Quotations can also be used to provide authoritative support for the speaker's viewpoint. Notice how the following speaker integrated a quotation into her conclusion:

> Now that I've presented some information about the insanity defense, I'd like you to hear a story found in the book *Crime and Madness* by Thomas Maeder. In 1882 Roderick Maclean tried to shoot Queen Victoria. At the trial, he pleaded not guilty by reason of insanity and he was acquitted of the charge. When the Queen heard about the result of the trial, she said, quote, "Insane he may have been, but not guilty he most certainly was not. If that is the law, then the law must be changed." As a result of this trial, the insanity law in England was altered. Under the changed law, jurors were directed to declare the defendant insane but also guilty of the crime. I think the Queen had a pretty good idea.[20]

Stacey Solesha found a quotation from Queen Victoria that supported her view that the insanity plea should not be allowed as a defense. While the brief story put the quotation in its historical context, the speaker brought the incident up to date with her closing line, "I think the Queen had a pretty good idea."

Reference to Introduction

One good way of concluding a speech is a *reference to the introduction*. This strategy can be used successfully with any type of introduction to promote unity within a presentation. Earlier we mentioned an introduction in which Stephen King shocked his audience by reading an administrative memo requiring drug tests for all students. Steve ended that speech with this conclusion:

> I want you to think about the urine cups you have in front of you. How does it feel to be looked upon as a drug user until you can prove your innocence? Suppose that your test came back positive and you were dismissed from college because of an inexperienced lab technician. Let's stop treating people as if they're being spied upon. Let's keep our Constitution strong and never relinquish our right to privacy. Let's stop drug testing—now![21]

Stephen King effectively referred to his introduction and drew his listeners' attention back to the injustice of the opening situation, reminding them of his specific purpose. He ended by challenging the audience to uphold the right of privacy granted by the Constitution.

Challenge or Appeal

In some speeches, especially persuasive speeches, you may need to conclude by issuing a general challenge or a specific appeal to the audience. A *challenge* is usually a broad, generalized summons to the audience to make some kind of effort to support the topic. A speaker telling the audience "We need to preserve liberty," or "We must protect our children," is using a general challenge in the conclusion.

Notice how Jacquelyn Shields ended her persuasive speech about increasing the length of the school year:

> Last week I received notification of my eligibility to become a member of Phi Theta Kappa, the national honor society for community colleges. It's extremely ironic that I received this announcement while I was researching this speech. If I could walk into a Japanese classroom with my Japanese counterpart, a college sophomore, and be tested on my pool of knowledge, I would come up short. Each one of you must also consider how you would compare to your counterpart in Japan. And if you feel that you also would come up short, then you must remember that you are a product of the American educational system.
>
> If you don't want your children to suffer in the future, I urge you to think about changing the system. Let's improve our educational process by lengthening the school year. Let's regain our economic and technological leadership by helping our children to compete with other nations on an equal footing.[22]

Jackie's reference to her membership in Phi Theta Kappa gave her credibility as an honor student. The comparison of American and Japanese educational systems motivated listeners to think. In the final paragraph, she directly challenged the audience to improve American education. The challenge is general rather than specific; she allowed listeners to decide for themselves how to carry it out.

You can also end a speech by using a specific *appeal* to the audience. Unlike challenges, appeals are usually well defined for the audience. When a speaker asks you to vote for someone, give to a specific cause, or support a philosophy or issue, he or she is using a direct appeal.

Notice how Shelley Snyder used appeals to conclude a persuasive speech on racism:

> I hope all of you can admit that there still remains a problem of racism and that you can commit to taking a stand against it; that you evaluate

yourselves, your preconceptions, your prejudices, and yes, your racist views. I really never thought of myself as a racist. I abhor violence. I abhor blatant discrimination and all the inequities I see. But in researching for this speech, I found that, in too many instances, I am racist. But my personal appeal, and the appeal I put before you is to understand where our attitudes come from, and to ask ourselves for a change of heart—to defend the victims of racism, to work to improve legislation for equal justice for all. I am going to hand out a test from a book entitled, *The Day America Told the Truth.* I want you to take it in the privacy of your own home and assess yourself—honestly.

Again, I ask you: take a stand against racism. For in the words of Martin Luther King Jr., "To ignore evil is to become an accomplice to it."[23]

The speaker employed several appeals in this conclusion. Shelley asked listeners to stop racism by honestly evaluating their own views. However, she did not simply make an accusation to the audience: The speaker was able to refer to her own racism, making the persuasion even more powerful. Shelley urged listeners to take action by answering questions about racism and she combined her final appeal with a forceful quotation from Martin Luther King Jr. The appeals were highly successful with audience members. One listener commented: "Shelley really persuaded me to take a look at my own attitudes." Another observed: "I'm going to take the test, and if I don't like what I see, I'm going to do all I can to change. I guess we can't solve racism until we solve it within ourselves."

Humor

Humor that is appropriate to your audience and the topic can be a good way to end a speech. Telling a joke or brief anecdote can leave your audience in a good mood and can stimulate a spontaneous positive response at the end.

Kimberly Kittle informed listeners how to use substitute remedies for household problems when the appropriate products were too expensive or unavailable. She advocated using hairspray to remove ink stains, mayonnaise as a cure for brittle hair, and vegetable oil to keep car doors from freezing in winter. She ended the speech on a light, but cautionary note.

Even though these alternative remedies can work wonders, remember that nothing is one hundred percent foolproof, and one always has to be moderate and cautious. While some products can be used to solve common household problems, they can create even worse nightmares. For example, a man who thought he'd found the perfect way to absorb unsightly motor oil in his driveway, spread kitty litter on every inch of concrete outside his house. The remedy worked and the oil disappeared, but the poor man ended up creating a monstrous cat litter box which attracted every happy feline in town![24]

The audience was enlightened by Kim's helpful hints and enjoyed laughing at the humorous punch line.

Your humor must be entertaining; stories from joke books, or worn-out anecdotes tend to backfire. Be certain that your humor is fresh, spontaneous, and appropriate.

Question

You can also conclude by asking the audience a *rhetorical question.* This approach tells the audience to "think about it" for a while.

Ernestine Cooper presented a convincing speech about the dangers of aerobic exercise. After providing statistics, examples, and a personal experience to support her point of view, the speaker delivered this conclusion:

> If you are thinking about getting into aerobics, listen to your body's signals. Check out your health clubs. Check out the floors. Wear the appropriate shoes. And most important, check out the instructors. Ask to see those credentials. Where did they receive their training? Will they address your needs on an individual basis? Remember, it is your body, your limbs that need to be protected. You have a right to know. Ask yourself, are the health benefits from aerobic exercise worth the pain? Do you want to wind up as a statistic in the next survey of aerobic injuries?[25]

Because of Ernestine's impressive evidence and the questions posed in her conclusion, the audience was persuaded to think seriously about the potential harm of aerobic exercise. The final question stimulated a silent "no" response within her listeners.

Story, Illustration, and Example

Once you have provided your audience with extensive information about a topic, you can end with *a story,* an *illustration,* or a brief *example* to keep the audience interested and at the same time drive home your point. Notice how Norma Ferris concluded her speech about the Meals on Wheels program.

> But we often think, "Well there're so many problems in the world, and I'm just one person, what could I do?" With the Meals on Wheels program, there's no question that you can do something. You—just one person—can make a difference in someone's life—someone who would otherwise be forgotten.
>
> Let me tell you about one woman on my route who was a childless widow. It was Eastertime, and while I was delivering her meal I saw someone selling flowers. So I picked up just a small hyacinth and brought it to her. She was so taken with it, she said, "No one but the Meals on Wheels

people have treated me kindly in so long—I'm so grateful—I just wish there was something I could do for you." She thought for a minute, and she went back into her bedroom and she came out with an old mink stole—it must have been thirty years old. She said, "My husband gave this to me. Would you take it? Because I appreciate what you've done so much—I'm very grateful." Well, I couldn't take it. But it just goes to show you how important you can be to someone. With the Meals on Wheels program, you can make a difference.[26]

This brief story was drawn from the speaker's personal experience and gave the topic a powerful sense of credibility. The emotional quality of the story maintained audience interest and attention to the very end of the speech. Norma communicated the idea that the Meals on Wheels program was not just another charity begging for money. Listeners could see that their involvement would benefit the elderly, and would give those volunteering personal satisfaction and reward.

Statistics

A speaker can state or re-emphasize an alarming *statistic* to get the audience to think seriously about an issue. Statistics are often effective when

In his famous speech "I Have a Dream," Martin Luther King, Jr., made skillful use of his conclusion, which included the ringing words, "Free at last! Free at last! Thank God almighty, we are free at last!"

© Bob Adelman/Magnum Photos, Inc.

combined with other types of conclusions. In a speech about battered women, a speaker combined two approaches:

> We need to help these battered women. Often we overlook the problem just because it's not happening to us. Sometimes we overlook the problem because we don't want to get involved. Twenty women were beaten as I was giving this speech. I hope you all understand the importance of getting involved by hearing, seeing, or assisting someone in need of help. It's not okay. Don't let it happen. Help—please.[27]

Tresse Bailey asked her audience to provide volunteer help to shelters for battered women. She ended her actuating speech with an appeal and a simple, but powerful statistic. The speaker was careful not to bombard listeners with complicated numbers; she simply related the one statistic to the time it took her to deliver the speech. The statistic was a dramatic reminder of the extent of the problem.

OUTLINING THE CONCLUSION

You can outline the conclusion in almost the same way you outlined the introduction. Here are two outline styles of the conclusion to the Meals on Wheels speech.

STYLE 1	CONCLUSION
(First sentence)	I. But we often think, "Well, there're so many problems in the world and I'm just one person, what can I do?"
(Strategy)	II. Story of an elderly lady
STYLE 2	CONCLUSION
(First sentence)	I. But we often think, "Well, there're so many problems in the world and I'm just one person, what can I do?"
	A. Involvement in Meals on Wheels helps
	B. Volunteers remember forgotten people
(Strategy)	II. Story of an elderly lady
	A. Woman given a flower
	B. Woman expressed overwhelming appreciation
	C. Woman offered volunteer mink stole

In both examples, I is the first sentence of the conclusion and II describes the strategy that the speaker employs for the conclusion (quote, story, question, summary, etc.). Style I is the abbreviated form that can be used if you really know your conclusion well. Style II provides more detail to help you progress through each major idea in the conclusion. As we suggested when describing the outline of the introduction, use the style that is most helpful to you.

USING SPEAKING NOTES

Your speaking notes will include the introduction, the body, and the conclusion. Speaking notes are important because they are the tools that help you to communicate to your audience. You should construct your notes so that you can see where you're headed in one brief glance.

Select either $4'' \times 6''$ or $6'' \times 9''$ notecards and number them at the upper right-hand corner. On the first card, write the outline of your introduction. Write legibly, use large lettering, and double-space between the lines. You may want to underline or occasionally use all caps for emphasis. You may even want to use different colors to highlight specific examples, statistics, or quotations. Use a reasonable number of notecards; don't cram too many phrases on two or three cards, and don't use too many notes. You don't want to squint as you read, and you also don't want to be flipping a card every few seconds. When you transfer your outline to notecards, remember that your objective is ease of communication; you want notes that help you communicate quickly and effectively.

Here are some notecards that represent an example of a clear, readable speaking outline:

INTRODUCTION   1

I. "On Nov. 2nd, 1988, at around 9:00 P.M., Robert Tappan Morris, a 23-year-old computer science student at Cornell University, pushed a single button on his computer keyboard and launched an attack."

II. A case study presented in a suspenseful manner

Thesis: "Participants of the top secret meeting in Fort Meade, Maryland, discussed the nature of an electronic virus, the threat computer viruses pose to universities, businesses, and the U.S. government, and what might be done to safeguard potential victims."

(more)

2

Transition 1: "When we think of a computer and the programs that run it, we usually think in terms of what it can do to help us, as an aid in gathering and sorting data. So what makes a computer virus different from other types of computer programs?"

BODY

I. General information on computer viruses

  A. Virus defined

  B. Two classes of viruses described

    1. Example of nuisance virus (*Time,* Sept. 26, '88, p. 64)

    2. Example of destructive virus (*Business Week,* Aug. 1, '88, p. 64)

  C. Virus redefined for clarity

(more)

10

Transition 4: "Experts point out that computers, by their very design, must somehow exchange information in order for them to be a useful tool to mankind."

CONCLUSION

I. "Because of this, we will continue to be afflicted with computer viruses as long as some computer programmers continue to develop and distribute viruses."

II. Summary with dramatic quotation for impact (*Time,* Mar. 20, '89, p. 25)

  A. No safety measure is completely foolproof

  B. Computer must continue to transfer data

  C. Computer systems will remain vulnerable to virus creators

  D. Military expert compares threat of computer viruses to most devastating military weapons available.

(end)

SAMPLE OUTLINE

Here is a complete outline of a speech to inform, presented by Christopher B. Kavanaugh:

Notice that the speaker has chosen a cryptic title that educates and enlightens.

The speaker has identified the topic area and provided the general purpose.

The specific purpose describes the overall objective of the speech, and the thesis identifies the three main points in the body.

Each part of the speech is clearly labeled as introduction, body, or conclusion.

Numeral I describes the first sentence—the very first line the speaker will say. Numeral II determines the strategy of the introduction. In this instance, the strategy is a case study followed by specific

The Computer Virus: Disease of the Computer Age[28]

CHRISTOPHER B. KAVANAUGH

Topic: Computer viruses

General purpose: To inform

Specific purpose: To tell the audience about computer viruses

Thesis statement: "Participants of the top secret meeting in Fort Meade, Maryland, discussed the nature of an electronic virus, the threat computer viruses pose to universities, businesses, and the U.S. government, and what might be done to safeguard potential victims."

INTRODUCTION

I. "On November 2nd, 1988 at around 9:00 P.M., a twenty-three-year-old student of computer science at Cornell University by the name of Robert Tappan Morris pushed a single button on his computer keyboard and launched an attack."

II. A case study presented in a suspenseful manner

III. To tell the audience about computer viruses

IV. "Participants of the top secret meeting in Fort Meade, Maryland, discussed the nature of an electronic virus, the threat computer viruses pose to universities, businesses, and the U.S. government, and what might be done to safeguard potential victims."

examples of re-
search centers
that were shut
down. "Suspense-
ful manner" tells
the reader that
examples under II
will be arranged
to create ex-
pectancy. While
the specific
purpose in nu-
meral III is not
stated, the the-
sis (numeral IV)
is taken directly
from the speech.
The introduction
is an informal
outline: it in-
cludes both
sentence and
topic form.

Transition 1 con-
nects the intro-
duction with the
first numeral
of the body.

The body of the
speech represents
the formal out-
line. Unlike the
introduction, the
body does not mix
topics and sen-
tences. This out-
line contains
only topics.
Parentheses pro-
vide abbreviated
sources. Here
notation indi-
cates that B1 and
2 are taken from
Time and
Business Week.

Transition 1: "When we think of a computer and the programs that run it, we usually think in terms of what it can do to help us, as an aid in gathering and sorting data. So what makes a computer virus different from other types of computer programs?"

BODY

I. General information on computer viruses
   A. Virus defined
   B. Two classes of viruses described
      1. Example of nuisance virus (*Time*, Sept. 26, '88, p. 64)
      2. Example of a destructive virus (*Bus. Week*, Aug. 1, '88, p. 64)
   C. Virus redefined for clarity

Transition 2: "Now that you are armed with a general description of this electronic scourge, let's examine its *modus operandi* and why it's such a devastating threat to our technological way of life."

II. Characteristics of a computer virus

    A. Comparison and contrast with a biological virus (*Discover,* Jan. '89, p. 64)

    1. Comparison of virus multiplication

    2. Contrast in virus origin

    3. Comparison of virus transmission

    B. Common means of virus movement

        1. Hypothetical example of disk infection from shared computers

        2. Electronic transference of computer virus

          a. Electronic transfer described

          b. Telephone modem described

          c. Electronic bulletin board explained

    C. Effects of the Morris virus

        1. Morris' original intention (*N. Y. Times,* Nov. 6, '88, sec.A, p. 30)

        2. Morris' terrible mistake

        3. The financial damage (*Personal Computing,* May, '89, pp. 85-86)

        4. Expert quote on implications of similar viruses (*Time,* Mar. 20, '89, p. 25)

Transition 3: "*Scientific American* magazine reported in a March, 1989 article that future efforts to improve computer security are helped by examining the viruses that have struck in the past."

III. What can be done for protection from viruses

    A. Change computer passwords (*Business Week,* Aug. 1, '88, pp. 66-67.)

        1. Make passwords more complex

        2. Make passwords more confidential

such as statis-
tics, examples,
cases, compar-
isons and con-
trasts, and
definitions.

The final transi-
tion connects
the end of the
body with the be-
ginning of the
conclusion.

Like the intro-
duction, the con-
clusion is
informally out-
lined. Numeral I
identifies the
first sentence of
the conclusion.
Numeral II states
the type of
strategy used; in
this case the
speaker will use
a summary fol-
lowed by a quote
from an expert
conveying the po-
tential harm of
the virus.

The speaker has
used a wide range
of supporting
materials from a
variety of
sources.

References are
listed alphabeti-
cally and each
source is entered

  B. Close trap doors
    1. Specific example given
    2. Trap doors defined
  C. Install anti-virus programs (*Personal Computing*,
     May, '89, p. 91)
  D. Take other precautions
    1. Making back-up diskettes regularly
    2. Not using untested "foreign" software

  Transition 4: "Experts point out that computers, by
     their very design, must somehow exchange informa-
     tion in order for them to be a useful tool to
     mankind."

CONCLUSION

  I. "Because of this, we will continue to be afflicted
     with computer viruses as long as some computer pro-
     grammers continue to develop and distribute viruses."

  II. Summary with dramatic quotation for impact (*Time*,
      Mar. 20. '89, p. 25)
    A. No safety measure is completely foolproof
    B. Computers must continue to transfer data
    C. Computer systems will remain vulnerable to virus
       creators
    D. Military   expert   compares   threat   of   computer
       viruses   to   most   devastating   military   weapons
       available

BIBLIOGRAPHY

Hafner, Katherine, et al. "Is Your Computer Secure?" *Busi-
    ness Week*, August 1, 1988, pp. 64-67, 70-72.
Markoff, John. "Virus in Military Computers Disrupts Systems
    Nationwide," *The New York Times*, November 4, 1988, sec.
    A, p. 1, 21.
Markoff, John. "The Computer Jam: How It Came About." *The
    New York Times*, November 9, 1988, sec. D, p. 10.

according to cor-
rect biblio-
graphic form.

Rasch, Mark. Prosecuting Attorney, Fraud Division, United
States Department of Justice, Washington D.C. Telephone
interview, August 27, 1989.
"Spreading a Virus; How Computer Science Was Caught Off
Guard by One Young Hacker." *The Wall Street Journal*,
November 7, 1988, sec. A, pp. 1, 6.

(The complete bibliography appears in the Appendix.)

SUMMARY

The introduction gains the attention of the audience, creates interest and links the topic to the needs of listeners, and introduces the topic. There are a variety of ways to introduce a speech: (1) example, story, or illustration, (2) shocking statement or situation, (3) statistic, (4) question, (5) quotation, (6) suspense, (7) personal reference, (8) humor, (9) a flexible introduction, and (10) a combination of approaches.

The conclusion gives finality to the speech and communicates that the topic has been resolved. Types of conclusions are: (1) summary, (2) quotation, (3) reference to the introduction, (4) challenge and appeal, (5) humor, (6) question, (7) story, illustration, and example, and (8) statistics.

To outline your introduction, numeral I should be the first sentence, numeral II should identify the strategy you intend to use, numeral III should present the specific purpose, and numeral IV should identify the thesis statement. You can outline the conclusion in the same manner without numerals III and IV. As opposed to the speech body, the outlines of the introduction and conclusion are considered informal: They often combine sentences and topics.

SKILL BUILDERS

1. Read the informative speech on "The Computer Virus: Disease of the Computer Age" in chapter 15. Evaluate the different introductions and conclusions provided with the speech. Are some more effective than others? Are there any other approaches you feel would be appropriate for this speech? Be specific in your answer.
2. Divide your class into small groups. Read the persuasive actuating speech in chapter 9 entitled, "Out of Sight, Out of Mind" by Heather Hoag. Develop different introductions geared to the following audiences:
   a. An audience of high school teenagers.
   b. An audience of parents.
   c. A college-age audience from eighteen to twenty-two.
   d. An audience of senior citizens.

  e. An audience which includes younger college-age students, parents, a senior citizen, and a priest.

  f. An audience of rock musicians.

3. After you have developed the body of your speech, write three different introductions and three different conclusions. Deliver just the introductions and conclusions for a classroom exercise.

4. Go to the library and do some research in *Vital Speeches* or *Representative American Speeches.* Look at a number of speeches and find an example of each type of introduction and conclusion that has been discussed in this chapter.

5. Read the following two speeches from *Vital Speeches:*

  Kelly, Rex. "Speakers and the Bottom Line." *Vital Speeches,* November 1, 1987, pp. 47–50.

  Rackleff, Robert B. "The Art of Speech Writing." *Vital Speeches,* March 1, 1988, p. 311.

  Write an analysis of the approach that each speaker uses to begin and end. Do the speakers use just one method to introduce and conclude their presentations, or do they use a combination of methods? Are the approaches used successful? Be able to support your answer.

N O T E S

1. Thomas Martin, "Life Lessons," *Vital Speeches,* January 1, 1999, p. 187.

2. Michael Black, "Is there No Remedy?," informative speech presented in speech class, Catonsville Community College, Catonsville, Maryland, 1987. Used by permission.

3. Gina Alexander, "Sexual Harassment," speech to actuate presented in speech class, Carroll Community College, Westminster, Maryland, 1990. Used by permission.

4. Michael Gerber, "Tornados—The Deadliest Wind of All," speech to inform presented in speech class, Catonsville Community College, Catonsville, Maryland, 1989. Used by permission.

5. Stephen M. King, "The Right to Privacy," speech to convince delivered in speech class, Catonsville Community College, Catonsville, Maryland, 1987. Used by permission.

6. Kathy Birckhead, "Child Sexual Abuse," speech to inform presented in speech class, Carroll Community College, Westminster, Maryland, 1990. Used by permission.

7. Kathleen Ward, "Braiding Your Hair," speech to demonstrate presented in speech class, Catonsville Community College, Catonsville, Maryland, 1989. Used by permission.

8. Michelle Allred, "The Anti-Mormon Campaign," speech to inform presented in speech class, Carroll Community College, Westminster, Maryland, 1990. Used by permission.

9. H. Ross Perot, Paid Political Broadcast, October 17, 1992.

10. "To Santa Claus and Little Sisters" from *A Cry for Help,* by Mary Giffin and Carol Felsenthal. Copyright © 1983 by Mary Giffin, M.D., and Carol Felsenthal. Reprinted by permission of Doubleday, a division of Bantam, Doubleday, Dell Publishing Group, Inc.

11. Tina Cerrato, "Detecting Warning Signs of Teenage Suicide," informative speech delivered in speech class, Catonsville Community College, Catonsville, Maryland, 1987. Used by permission.

12. Karen Leonard, "Roller Coasters," informative speech presented in speech class, Carroll Community

College, Westminster, Maryland, 1990. Used by permission.

13. David Archambault, "Columbus Plus 500 Years," *Vital Speeches,* June 1, 1992, p. 491.

14. Mary Collins, "The Responsibilities of the New World Order," *Vital Speeches,* May 15, 1991, p. 457.

15. Benjamin H. Alexander, "Before You Lambast This Generation," *Vital Speeches,* November 15, 1987, p. 70.

16. Rick Trader, "Participating in the Nationwide Movement Toward Recycling," speech to actuate presented in speech class, Carroll Community College, Westminster, Maryland, 1989. Used by permission.

17. Chris Koeppen, "The Intrigue of the Great Pyramid," speech to inform presented in speech class, Carroll Community College, Westminster, Maryland, 1991. Used by permission.

18. Meredith M. Kreczmer, "How to Take Interesting Pictures," speech to demonstrate delivered in speech class, Carroll Community College, Westminster, Maryland, 1990. Used by permission.

19. Kim Jones, "Sojourner Truth," speech to inform presented in speech class, Carroll Community College, Westminster, Maryland, 1992. Used by permission.

20. Stacey Solesha, "The Insanity Defense," speech to convince presented in speech class, Carroll Community College, Westminster, Maryland, 1989. Used by permission.

21. Stephen M. King, "The Right to Privacy," speech to convince delivered in speech class, Catonsville

Community College, Catonsville, Maryland, 1987. Used by permission.

22. Jacquelyn V. Shields, "Increasing the Length of the School Year," speech to convince delivered in speech class, Carroll Community College, Westminster, Maryland, 1990. Used by permission.

23. Shelley Y. Snyder, "Let's Take a Stand Against Racism," speech to actuate delivered in speech class, Carroll Community College, Westminster, Maryland, 1992. Used by permission.

24. Kimberly L. Kittle, "Helpful Ways to Use Everyday Products," speech to inform presented in speech class, Carroll Community College, Westminster, Maryland, 1992. Used by permission.

25. Ernestine D. Cooper, "Aerobic Exercise Can Be Harmful," speech to convince presented in speech class, Catonsville Community College, Catonsville, Maryland, 1989. Used by permission.

26. Norma Ferris, "You Can Make a Difference," speech to actuate delivered in speech class, Catonsville Community College, Catonsville, Maryland, 1987. Used by permission.

27. Tresse Bailey, "Helping Battered Women," speech to actuate presented in speech class, Catonsville Community College, Catonsville, Maryland, 1989. Used by permission.

28. Chris Kavanaugh, "The Computer Virus: Disease of the Computer Age," speech to inform delivered in speech class, Catonsville Community College, Catonsville, Maryland, 1989. Used by permission.

Refining the Appearance

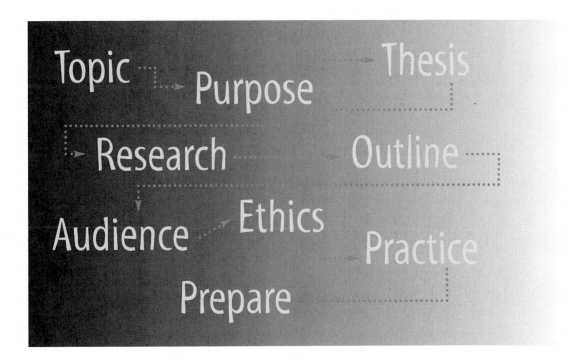

Chapter 12

USING
AUDIOVISUAL AIDS

If you use words to rebut a visual image, we know the visual image is dominant.

Kathleen Hall Jamieson

CHAPTER OBJECTIVES

After reading this chapter you will be able to:

1. Discuss the importance of audiovisual aids;

2. Describe the types of audiovisual aids;

3. Recognize the role of computers in developing audiovisual aids;

4. Describe the guidelines for using audiovisuals effectively in a speech.

Amy had just ended the introduction to her visual aids speech by telling everyone that she would "demonstrate how a dentist makes a porcelain crown." The audience settled back for a new learning experience.

Amy unrolled three large posters identifying important stages of the process. When she rested the first poster on the base of the chalkboard, it quickly rewound, fell to the floor, and bounced into a corner. Amy giggled nervously as she sensed audience reaction.

She picked up the poster and tried again. This time she climbed onto a chair she had scooted against the wall. As she stood on tiptoes, she inserted the upper edges of the poster into two sliding metal hooks atop the chalkboard. She steadied the poster with one hand, unraveled it slowly with the other, and climbed down from the chair, propelling it out of the way with her foot, which sent it tumbling across the room. As she rushed to rescue the runaway chair, Amy let go of her chart, which quickly rewound from bottom to top, snapping loose from the metal clips. Sailing through the air, it hit the forehead of a listener seated on the front row.

While audience members didn't learn much about porcelain crowns, they did have a new learning experience: Everybody discovered how not to handle visual aids.

This first chapter of Unit Four—"Refining the Appearance"—helps you to avoid some of Amy's problems. Principal types of audiovisuals are identified and their effective use in a speech is discussed. Visual aids can be used in almost any type of speech to promote interest and clarity.

THE IMPORTANCE OF AUDIOVISUAL AIDS

Newsmagazines picture members of the U.S. Women's Soccer team embracing after winning the World Cup at the Rose Bowl in Pasadena, California in the summer of 1999. The United States government publishes a pie graph to explain how the $1.7 trillion budget is spent. A guest actress on *The Late Show with David Letterman* brings a brief film clip to plug her new movie. The League of Women Voters uses a scale model or a sample punch card to teach first-time voters how to operate the voting machine or mark ballots. Supermarkets play relaxing music to put customers in a receptive mood. VCRs at department store perfume counters play glitzy commercials describing the merits of a particular fragrance. And the real estate supplement to the Sunday paper uses a line graph to display the upward or downward trend in home sales. People in every kind of institution or business understand the value of visual aids in communicating feelings, conveying information, and selling products.

Visual aids are also vitally important to the public speaker. During the 1962 Cuban Missile Crisis, United States Ambassador Adlai Stevenson displayed large aerial photographs at a United Nations Security Council meeting to verify the existence of Soviet missiles in Cuba. In 1977, President Jimmy Carter wore a sweater as he sat by a crackling fire and asked Americans to conserve energy. In his 1988 State of the Union speech, President Ronald Reagan lifted forty-three pounds of congressional documents to demonstrate the unnecessary red tape contained in many legislative actions. General Norman Schwarzkopf used a diagram to illustrate the military offensive against Iraq in Operation Desert Storm. Research indicates that visuals such as these increase the ability of listeners to remember information.[1] When you use a picture or an object to convey ideas, your audience will not only have a more concrete mental image, they will also recall your speech more completely.

TYPES OF AUDIOVISUAL AIDS

This chapter introduces you to the types of audiovisuals that can help you to communicate ideas more effectively. When we use the term *audiovisual aids,* we are referring to devices which may appeal to sight and to other senses as well: graphs, drawings and photographs, posters or chalk boards, mechanical media, physical objects, or some aspect of the speaker.

Graphs

Suppose that you needed to show your audience how murders have decreased over a four-year period in the United States. You could simply relate the statistics: 24,530 murders in 1993 decreased to 19,650 in 1996.[2] The audience might hear you, but they would also soon forget the information. Another way to present the information is by constructing a graph to display the data visually. Graphs are helpful in explaining trends, showing comparisons, or indicating portions of a whole. We will consider three basic types of graphs that can reinforce information in a speech: the bar, the line, and the pie graph.

BAR GRAPH

A bar graph is helpful when you want to compare and contrast several causes or categories, such as the major causes of divorce or the main causes of heart disease. Bar graphs allow your audience to visualize similarities or differences among categories at a glance.

The bar graph in Figure 12.1 displays the number of people incarcerated in federal and state prisons from 1970 to 1996. By looking briefly at the graph, listeners can learn that during a twenty-six-year period, the number of federal prisoners tripled while the number of state prisoners increased sixfold.

A bar graph like this one is relatively easy to construct. You can use black on white with gray shading to indicate different categories or you can highlight specific categories with color. Notice that the upper right corner contains a shading key that helps listeners interpret the black and gray areas of the chart. Your bar graph must be clear and understandable so that listeners realize how it supports your point.

LINE GRAPH

The line graph displays upward or downward trends over a period of time. Speakers use these graphs to show an increase or decrease in topics such as crime, disease, teenage suicide, income, inflation, or interest rates.

FIGURE 12.1

Federal and State Prisoners: 1970 to 1996

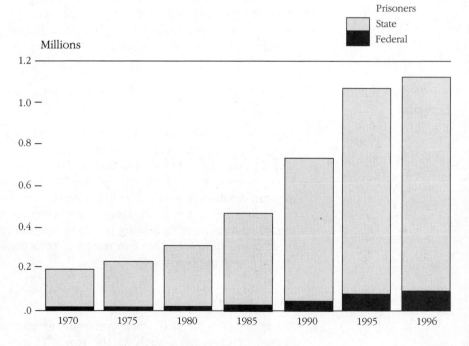

Source: Chart prepared by U.S. Bureau of the Census

The line graph in Figure 12.2 indicates the trend in numbers of consumer complaints against U.S. airlines over an eight-year period. The audience can easily see that complaints declined sharply between 1989 and 1991 and then began to increase slowly starting in 1995. Notice that brief explanatory notes add clarity to each line of the graph.

PIE GRAPH

The pie graph displays portions of a whole sum. Pie graphs are helpful to speakers who want to show percentages. Where our tax money goes, how individuals spend their income, or the racial make-up of the U.S. population are among the many subjects that lend themselves to pie graphs.

A speaker can use the pie graph in Figure 12.3 to display the percentage of American households contributing specific amounts to charities. The audience can easily see that more than twenty-four percent contribute $1,000 or more, almost fifteen percent give between $500 and $900, twenty-five percent donate more than $200, and about thirty-six percent of American households give up to $200.

FIGURE 12.2

Consumer Complaints Against U.S. Airlines: 1989 to 1997

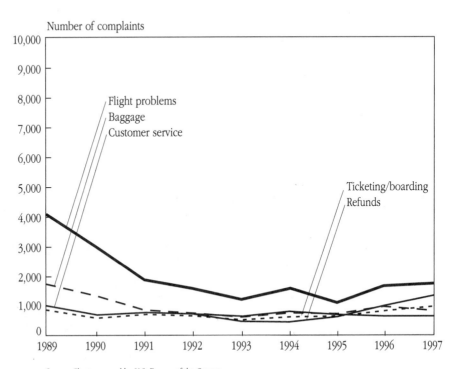

Source: Chart prepared by U.S. Bureau of the Census.

FIGURE 12.3

Percent Distribution of Housseholds Contributing to Charity by Annual Dollar Amount: 1995

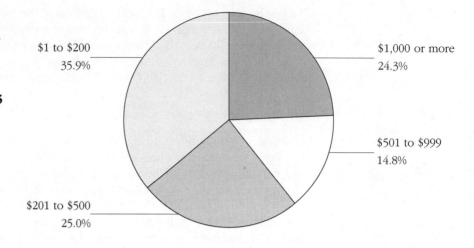

$1 to $200
35.9%

$1,000 or more
24.3%

$501 to $999
14.8%

$201 to $500
25.0%

Source: Independent Sector, Washington, D.C.

DEVELOPING GRAPHS

Before you construct any of these graphs, make sure you clearly understand the information and the statistics in order to report the data accurately. The *percentage* of crimes, for instance, is a far different concept from the *number* of crimes. Know what your data is saying in order to choose a graph appropriate for displaying the information.

When you understand the data, construct graphs that are simple and easy to read. Don't make the charts busy by drawing too many lines or numbers that can confuse listeners. Use color to emphasize different categories and bold lettering to convey meaning. Label the graph with direct and uncomplicated wording. Many computer graphics programs can help you design line, pie, or bar graphs that are of professional quality and can enhance your speaking presentation. These programs allow you to select different fonts or printing styles and make choices regarding the size and color of letters, numbers, and images. Remember that the purpose of a graph is to help the audience understand concepts quickly.

Illustrations, Photographs, and Pictures

Imagine a speaker trying to explain how to use a computer keyboard without a diagram or attempting to describe the Statue of Liberty without a picture. Without visuals, the audience would not understand the impact of the speaker's message. Topics like these require communication on visual as well as verbal channels of communication. Drawings, photographs, and pictures enable listeners to visually complete their understanding of events and procedures.

Illustrations can be used to explain complicated topics such as the AIDS virus or to portray elementary procedures like the basic tennis serve.

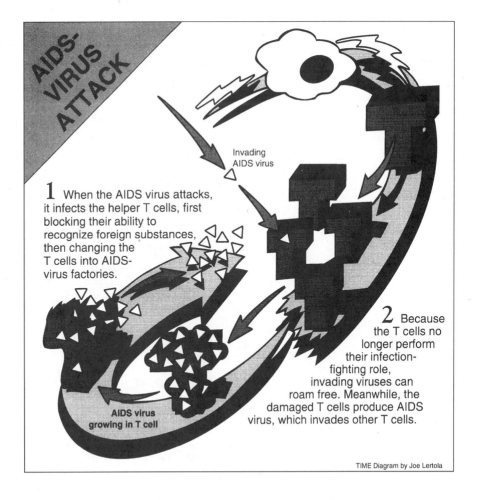

Figure 12.4 describes in a simple diagram how the AIDS virus attacks the T cells of the body's immune system. Figure 12.5 points out how one student identified facial bones with a simple crosshatching system keyed to an index. And in Figure 12.6, a speaker used very elementary sketches to demonstrate the seven basic body positions in the tennis serve.

You don't have to be an artist to draw effective illustrations like these. The principal ingredient that contributed to each drawing was not talent, but time. Be willing to spend the hours necessary to create similar visuals that are neat, simple, and clear.

Photographs and pictures also provide listeners with vivid images. A speaker who describes starvation can generate more sympathetic feedback

FIGURE 12.5

Used by permission of Michelle Collins.

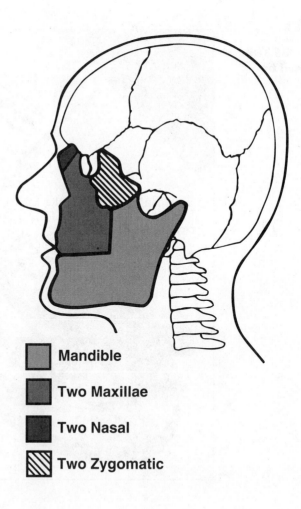

Mandible

Two Maxillae

Two Nasal

Two Zygomatic

FIGURE 12.6

Illustration by George Goebel.

by showing a photograph of a hungry child. One student who delivered a speech about sex in advertising displayed several magazine ads that used strong sexual images to sell products. And a student who described several types of drive-in businesses showed the audience a photograph (reproduced on page 276) of a drive-in funeral home.

During an informative speech about drive-in businesses, a student used this photograph of a "convenience" funeral home to stimulate interest and curiosity among listeners.

Photo by Bruce Dale © 1981 National Geographic Society

USING PICTURES

While pictures and photographs promote curiosity and interest, they must be large enough for the audience to see. Wallet-size pictures or tiny magazine photographs will not support a speech unless you make some adjustments. You can have the visuals professionally enlarged, a process which is often expensive, or you could have them photographed and made into slides. If an opaque projector is available, you can use the original picture or photograph with no additional expense. Be willing to take the trouble to communicate these important visuals so that all members of your audience can view them easily.

Posters and Chalkboards

Posters and chalkboards are also useful tools to help you convey ideas. Posters can support the steps of a process, reinforce main headings of a speech, or explain unfamiliar concepts. The poster in Figure 12.7 identifies three symbols used in weather forecasting. This visual is simple yet it is eye-catching because the speaker used different colors to coordinate symbols with the appropriate explanations.

FIGURE 12.7

**Used by permission
of Michael E. Gerber.**

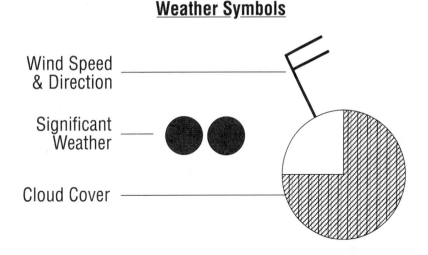

Weather Symbols

Wind Speed & Direction

Significant Weather

Cloud Cover

Unlike prepared posters, the chalk board provides you with a great deal of flexibility as you are speaking. You can quickly write down unfamiliar terms, list the principal steps to a process, or draw a simple explanatory sketch.

USING POSTERS AND CHALKBOARDS

If you decide to use posters, prepare them carefully. Lettering should be neat, large, and bold for easy reading. If you present the speech in a room that is 25 to 30 feet long, it is a good idea to use letters on your poster that are at least one inch high.[3] You also need to leave plenty of space next to words and between lines of print so that listeners can see the entire poster in a glance. Know where you are going to place your posters—taped to an easel, tacked to a bulletin board, held by a volunteer—so they will be easy to use during the presentation.

Even though you can be more spontaneous with a chalkboard, you still need to know how to employ it effectively. We've all suffered through the class where the teacher scrawls numerous concepts on the board with one hand, and erases everything with the other asking, "Did you all get that?" Avoid this problem by practicing with a chalkboard. Don't scribble down random ideas; write phrases neatly. If you need to draw a diagram, make sure it is clear and precise. Take the necessary time to plan your visuals by placing information on the board *before* you speak, or writing ideas carefully *while* you are speaking. Also, allow the audience time to absorb the material before you erase it.

We've described the chalkboard in case you need it for brief or incidental use in a speech. We don't recommend, however, that you use it in a presentation such as a demonstration or a descriptive speech, which is primarily dependent upon visuals. Visuals in these speeches require a great deal of time to plan effectively. Don't use the chalkboard as a shortcut for preparation; be willing to spend the time needed to create worthwhile visual aids.

Mechanical Media

The term *mechanical media* refers to any type of electrical device that can be used as audiovisual aids. We'll consider two categories of media: projection and recording equipment.

PROJECTION EQUIPMENT

An *overhead projector* is useful if your visuals require you to add information as you speak. One speaker used the overhead to demonstrate how to fill out a tax form. The overhead allowed the student to add and subtract numbers to show listeners the steps involved in tax preparation. Another speaker used a series of interesting "overlays" to demonstrate the progressive stages of a corneal transplant. When you use the overhead, remember that you will need to transfer all of your information to acetate transparencies. Before the speech, it is a good idea to inspect the overhead and practice with the transparencies to be sure that everything is in working order.

The *slide projector* can support a presentation if you use it with consideration for your audience. One speaker employed a slide projector to demonstrate how to bake chocolate-chip cookies. The student spent a great deal of time preparing and photographing the various stages of the process from mixing and baking to the finished product. The speech was interesting, well organized, and kept to the five-minute time limit. The speaker had to be certain that she allowed enough time to photograph the process and to develop the film in order to adequately prepare in time for the scheduled speech.

There are pitfalls to the use of slide projectors as well. Slides can be inserted upside down or backwards, bulbs can burn out easily, automatic focusing devices can malfunction, or changing mechanisms can be jammed. Problems can also occur if a room does not have a screen or proper surface for projecting slides, or the room can't be adequately darkened. Sometimes slide shows themselves are boring due to poor photography, needless repetition of scenes, or lengthy explanations. If you intend to use slides, rehearse your speech with the projector. Examine the

equipment carefully and test the projector in the room where the speech will be presented. Choose slides carefully, using enough to support your ideas, but eliminating those which are unnecessary.

If you need to display information from a computer monitor onto a larger surface such as a projection screen, you can use a device known as a *liquid crystal display* unit (LCD). The LCD is connected to a computer and then placed on an overhead projector, allowing an audience to see an enlarged version of the computer screen. The LCD is an excellent tool for projecting computer graphics, labels, procedures, or any type of computer program. Like so many media systems, LCDs vary in complexity and operation. In order to make refinements to the enlarged projection, many LCD units have their own controls which allow color, contrast, and frame adjustment. An LCD must also be connected properly to a selected computer in order to operate effectively. In addition, LCD units often require nonstandard overhead projectors that are more powerful in order to allow computers to appear brighter on projection screens. To avoid any problems or unforeseen complications, it is vitally important that you check with a media specialist for instructions and help before using an LCD in your speech.

A *laser disc player* projects photographs, video, or text onto a large monitor or screen from a ten- to twelve-inch laser disc that is similar in appearance to a smaller audio CD. Unlike VCRs that require a time-consuming process of rewinding or fast forwarding to reach appropriate segments, the laser disc player is almost immediate because it does not need to be viewed in a linear manner. A speaker can access a media clip with a number or bar code at any time and in any sequence during a speech to present a concept or an issue. A light pen is used to scan a bar code for a particular sequence and the clip is projected onto a screen in just a few seconds after a button is pressed. This instant access saves time and allows a speaker to reinforce ideas and work quickly from one set of projections to another. Currently, laser disc players can only be used for projection and unlike VCRs, cannot be used to record images. Laser disc players are easy to use and can be operated with remote control devices similar to VCRs. But you should be sure to get some instruction from a media specialist if you have never used this type of equipment before.

Digital video equipment, or DVD, operates on the same principle as the laser disc player, but with smaller discs that are the size of audio CDs. DVD systems allow speakers to project video on to a larger screen or monitor and switch quickly among clips with just the press of a button. In addition, some DVD players are now capable of recording video and audio in addition to merely replaying media.

The *opaque projector* can display a small drawing, photograph, or a picture from a book onto a large screen. This device usually has a built-in "arrow" you can employ as a pointer to refer to portions of the visual aid. But the opaque projector is large and somewhat bulky and we advise that it not be used unless there is no other device available for enlarging images.

Although film projectors aren't as popular as they once were due to VCRs, they can still be helpful in a speech. One student used a 1945 film clip to illustrate the destruction the atomic bomb caused to the cities of Hiroshima and Nagasaki. A brief segment like this can be effective; but you can't substitute a film for an entire speech. Like other visuals, a film should only amplify portions of a presentation; you must develop the substance of the speech.

RECORDING EQUIPMENT

Audio- or videotape recording equipment can generate interest among audience members. One speaker, describing the history of jazz, used tape-recorded music as a background to her introduction. Another speaker showed a videotape of a diving experience to explain scuba gear.

USING MEDIA

When you use recording equipment, your audio- or videotape should be properly cued to each segment of your speech. If you want to play a tape or a video while you are speaking, be certain you turn the sound down so that the audience can hear you comfortably. If the tape or video is the focus of the presentation, adjust the volume to reach all areas of the room or auditorium. A well-chosen tape or video can add interest to a portion of your presentation, but media can also present problems. A speaker brought an extension cord that was too short to reach from the single outlet at the back of the classroom to the lectern at the front. Another student who failed to inspect a VCR, discovered later in the speech that he was not able to operate the complicated VHS system supplied by the media department. A speaker who jammed a sluggish slide projector by banging it repeatedly finally gave up, saying, "Well, it worked at home, I can't understand why it doesn't now." One student confused an overhead with an opaque projector and placed a small photograph on the glass surface of the overhead only to find that nothing happened on the screen.

Most of these disasters can be avoided by careful planing. Practice the speech with your visuals. Know how the equipment operates. Examine the room for electrical outlets, projection screens, or tables for stationing equipment. If you use audio or videotape machinery, pay attention to set-up procedures. Check out batteries or extension cords; allow extra time to carry in and to place heavy VCR equipment. Try to anticipate problems like burned-out bulbs, unplugged cords, or inadequately darkened rooms.

Models and Objects

As a speaker, you can generate interest and stimulate curiosity with scale models, parts of objects, or the actual objects themselves.

SCALE MODELS

Scale models reduce large objects or complicated procedures for easy visualization. College instructors use models of the eye or the heart to help students understand vision or circulation. A student once used a model of a miniature volcano to explain how an actual eruption occurs.

While scale models create interest, they must be large enough for the audience to see. A speaker attempted to demonstrate a new trash removal system that had been selected by several cities. Problems surfaced, however, when the speaker took out three tiny toy trucks from her handbag and pointed to the rear-end loader, the wheels, and the cab. Listeners leaned forward and squinted in an effort to follow the process, but they soon gave up because of the inadequate visuals. Don't use scale models that are too small or too intricate; make sure that objects are large and practical enough for the audience to see and to comprehend easily.

PARTS OF OBJECTS

When it is impractical to bring the actual object, you can use a sample or a cross-section. A student demonstrated how to refinish furniture by displaying several pieces of wood in various stages of completion. Another student used a small cross-section of a studded wall to inform listeners how to wire an electrical outlet. And another speaker used pieces of shrubbery and small fir branches to explain how to do professional landscaping. Since it was not possible to bring in a china cabinet, half a house, or a nursery each speaker sensibly chose to use parts of the object that could be managed easily in a classroom.

ACTUAL OBJECTS

When listeners see a life-size visual aid, they are quickly motivated to listen. One student explained the process involved in decorating a wedding cake. Towards the end of the speech, she revealed a perfect three-tiered

Displaying objects can help speakers to convey ideas quickly and motivate audiences to listen.

cake complete with a miniature bride and groom on top. The cake was an aromatic visual appealing to the sense of smell as well as to sight. A sky diver showed listeners his parachute to demonstrate how to fold it before a jump. An antique gun collector brought out several muskets to explain how American colonists used these firearms during the Revolutionary War.

Each of these speeches was interesting. But the life-size visuals required a great deal of advance planning. The fragile wedding cake had to be transported to the classroom. The sky diver had to ask listeners to sit in a large semicircle to provide enough space to fold his parachute. And the collector had to use a special gun rack to display the large muskets effectively.

If you want to use life-size objects, you must realize they will take some added effort to the standard organization of a speech. Don't exhaust your energies in the visuals alone; research, structure, and delivery remain the focal point of a public speech.

You as a Visual Aid

Your own body movements, gestures, and actions can serve as visual aids in a speech. Imagine how body movements could simulate aerobics or weight lifting, and how gestures could illustrate sign language or skin care. One student demonstrated how actors apply theatrical makeup to enhance their appearance under intense stage lights. The speaker's face and hands were the visuals. He came prepared with a small mirror that allowed him to put on layers of makeup while he explained the steps to the process.

While gestures and movements may seem easier to convey than other visuals, they require preparation. If you are demonstrating a detailed process such as a golf swing or a karate move, your gestures and movements need to be precise and well-defined. These actions should communicate so well that audience members could repeat them if necessary. Avoid sloppy gestures or vague actions that lack clarity and create confusion. Run through the speech several times with the movements you intend to use. Refine and improve these actions until you feel confident that they will communicate effectively to your audience.

In addition to the speaker, a volunteer from the audience can also be a visual aid. For example, administering the Heimlich maneuver, bandaging an arm, dancing an Irish jig, or throwing a curve ball are procedures that could require another person. When you work with an assistant, be sure that the volunteer knows exactly what to do. Rehearse the speech several times so that both speaker and assistant are comfortable with planned actions and motions. Don't call on a volunteer from the audience unless you want a cold response. This uninformed assistant could actually be a detriment to you. Be sure that the "volunteer" really wants to help you, is adequately prepared, and will contribute positively to your speech.

USING COMPUTERS TO CONSTRUCT VISUALS

In today's business world, computers have become essential in the development of high-quality visual aids. Workers using desktop publishing systems, for example, can make most decisions regarding the design and layout of visuals at computer terminals. They can employ a tool called a *mouse* to draw illustrations or to write labels on computer monitors. If they are unable to create *original* designs, computer operators can work with lettering and graphics already provided with programs. Employees can also develop graphs or charts, and make choices regarding the appropriate size of numbers, letters, and images. A student used a desktop publishing system to design the visual in Figure 12.8 for a speech demonstrating "The Proper Techniques for Giving Injections."

Computers are helpful in producing visuals because of their tremendous versatility. They can generate large posters through a process called

Speakers can use computers as tools to create visual aids and to explain concepts clearly and effectively to listeners.

© *Joel Gordon*

FIGURE 12.8

Used by permission of Sherry Blye.

Angle of Insertion for Parenteral Injections

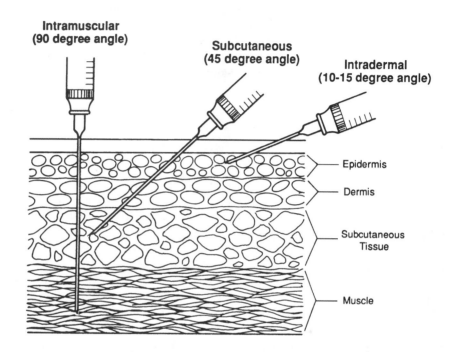

"tiling" or reduce data for small brochures. They can copy photographs with the aid of special *scanning* equipment for use in reports or in company handouts. Data for visuals can be sent by a *modem* (a device connecting a computer to a telephone) to a facility for processing into slides or transparencies. Computers that have *fax* capability can send and receive data that can be used as visual aids. Some computers can be used like slide projectors to convey data and images in timed sequence.

Although you may not have a computer with the capabilities of a desktop system, you can develop first-rate visuals if you have access to a computer with a graphics package and a copy machine. You can design a graphic or chart on a computer monitor, print out the data, and then photocopy the material onto sheets of acetate instead of paper. The result will be high-quality transparencies that can be used on overhead projectors.[4]

USING A LAPTOP, AN LCD, AND AN OVERHEAD

Shirley Goscinski was a speech student who had been a systems engineer with a local company in Baltimore, Maryland. Her position required her to understand and diagnose computer programs and systems and Shirley had become an expert in her field. Since she had been assigned to develop a five- to seven- minute demonstration for her speech class, Shirley decided to select a topic from her expertise and experience with computers. She realized that her listeners had varying levels of understanding about this topic: Many of her classmates owned computers and knew how to operate word processing programs but most students had little comprehensive knowledge and some were even intimidated by computers. After analyzing her audience, Shirley wisely decided to explain the three parts of a computer system by describing input devices, the central processing unit (or CPU) and output devices.[5]

After organizing the body of her speech, Shirley wanted to create attractive visuals to make her presentation clear and understandable. She selected a graphics program, entitled *Freelance Graphics,* published by Lotus, Inc., to design visuals that looked professional. Next she needed to select an effective means of presenting the visuals and she thought about using transparencies, posters, or photographs to support the speech. Since her topic dealt with computers, Shirley decided that a laptop would be the most effective visual aid for her presentation. The graphics package that Shirley used to create visuals also had a system which allowed her to program and time each visual aid so that listeners could view them on the computer in a predetermined sequence. But since a computer screen is too small for eighteen listeners to view in a classroom, the speaker needed to enlarge the visual aid. Shirley decided to use an overhead projector and an LCD unit to project the computer on to a large pull-down screen mounted in the classroom.

On the day of the speech, Shirley arrived in class early to set up and test her visual aids. She connected the LCD unit to the computer and placed it on the overhead projector. She checked cords, plugs, and connections to make sure all systems were functioning correctly. She turned on the equipment and conducted a test of her program and visuals for smooth operation. Finally, she focused the overhead and checked the placement of her visuals to make certain that everyone in the audience could see the projection screen easily.

Everything was now ready for the presentation. Since she knew that her listeners routinely used bank teller machines for deposits and withdrawals, Shirley began by relating her topic to ATM systems. Then she developed the main points of the thesis as each visual aid appeared, supporting her explanation in timed sequence. The speaker provided an overview of a computer system as a graphic showed the components of a PC (Figure 12.9).

She described the internal aspects of the computer and a projection displayed a computer chip, package, and a circuit board (Figure 12.10). She spoke about types of external input/output media and a diskette and a CD-ROM came into view (Figure 12.11). She introduced binary codes and the American standard code for information interchange (ASCII) was projected onto the screen (Figure 12.12). The presentation continued with visuals showing the CPU and output devices.

The speech was entirely successful. Listeners enjoyed the sophisticated visual aids and also learned a great deal about computer systems. One listener commented: "Shirley's speech helped me realize that computers don't need to be so intimidating. I think she encouraged me to learn more about computers and use them as tools in more areas of my life."

FIGURE 12.9

PC Personal Computer

FIGURE 12.10

Computer Internals

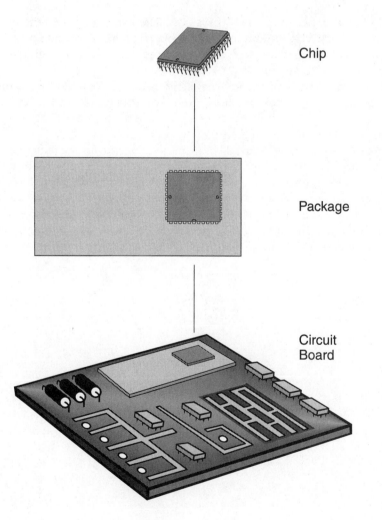

Chip

Package

Circuit Board

FIGURE 12.11

**External Input/
Output Media**

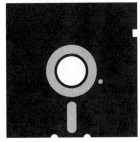

5¼" Diskette (Floppy)

3½" Diskette

CD-Rom

FIGURE 12.12

	Ascii Code	Binary Number		Ascii Code	Binary Number
A	65	01000001	N	78	01001110
B	66	01000010	O	79	01001111
C	67	01000011	P	80	01010000
D	68	01000100	Q	81	01010001
E	69	01000101	R	82	01010010
F	70	01000110	S	83	01010011
G	71	01000111	T	84	01010100
H	72	01001000	U	85	01010101
I	73	01001001	V	86	01010110
J	74	01001010	W	87	01010111
K	75	01001011	X	88	01011000
L	76	01001100	Y	89	01011001
M	77	01001101	Z	90	01011010

FIVE GUIDELINES FOR USING AUDIOVISUAL AIDS

1. Talk to the audience, not to the visual aid.

Some speakers become so involved with their visuals that they quickly forget to look at listeners. One classroom speaker turned her back on the audience and talked entirely to her poster for the majority of her speech. If you have practiced adequately, you shouldn't need to look at your visual. Remember that visuals reinforce main ideas; they won't speak for themselves, and they are not substitutes for communication. Your job as a speaker is to present visuals to your listeners and to help audience members understand them. Use a pointer, easel, table or some other device that helps you to communicate your visuals effectively. Maintain frequent eye contact with listeners and, above all, talk to your audience—not to the visual.

2. Don't pass objects around during the speech.

A student who collected fossilized rocks described each specimen and then passed them to listeners during his presentation. The speaker had about twenty-five different examples, and listeners concentrated on looking at each rock and handing it to the next person. The problem, of course, was that the speaker lost listeners' attention because of the numerous interruptions. Develop other ways to convey visuals. The fossil collector, for instance, could have taken photographs of his examples and used a slide projector to describe the objects. Keep the attention of the audience focused on you, the speaker, and avoid circulating materials that could be distracting.

3. Be sure that the audience can see your visuals.

Although it may seem obvious that visual aids need to be large enough for everyone to see, well-intentioned speakers sometimes take audience members for granted and neglect this important rule. Unprepared speakers often use photographs, objects, or scale models that are too small, posters with thin or tiny lettering, or visuals that are obstructed. One speaker who explained how to make baklava, a Greek dessert, placed all the materials and ingredients directly in front of the mixing bowl, blocking the entire demonstration. The hard work that went into researching and structuring the speech was wasted because of the poorly executed visual aids.

   In addition to these problems, listeners may not be able to see visuals because of the angles of the speaker's stand, the easel, TV monitor, or the room arrangement. If even one or two people in the audience can't see comfortably, the speaker should have done more careful advance planning. Depending on the setting, the speaker may need to readjust the visual aid, rearrange the seating area, or ask listeners to move forward.

It is the speaker's responsibility to prepare visuals and to plan an environment in which listeners can easily see everything a speaker wants to communicate.

4. Use visuals at the right psychological moment.

If you have a lot of audiovisual aids, you may need to set them up before the speech so that you don't cause unnecessary disruptions during the presentation. However, there will be times when you can wait to reveal your visuals at the right psychological moment, that is, when the audience will be most interested.

For example, if you had three different charts, you might decide to tape all of them to the chalkboard prior to the speech. The problem with this arrangement, however, is that the audience will read the visuals before you want them to, and they may not listen to your speech because of the visual distraction. It would be more effective to develop a flip chart that allows you to reveal each poster as you actually talk about it. This method generates curiosity and helps to control the attention of your audience. Speakers can apply the same principle to a single poster by covering all of the information and then removing one portion at a time. Both techniques motivate your audience to listen.

What is important is that you carefully think through how and when to use posters, charts, and objects during a speech. Talk about objects when you display them and, as a rule, don't reveal visuals before you verbally refer to them. Equally important, it is usually more effective to remove visuals when you have finished referring to them. If you keep objects in front of listeners, you'll have a hard time directing their attention to other visuals or back to your speech.

5. Be clear at all times.

Although audiovisual aids can support a presentation, they cannot speak for you. You will need to use clear explanations and precise descriptions to integrate them successfully into a speech. Explain the purpose of posters or charts: Point out relationships, show comparisons, or indicate contrasts in data. Draw conclusions from graphs or informational lists and relate audiovisuals to your ideas. Describe objects precisely and reinforce physical actions or motions with verbal clarifications. When you employ photographs and pictures, integrate them smoothly by emphasizing significant areas or details. If you use a VCR or other mechanical media, set up the audiovisual segment with appropriate verbal descriptions. Provide brief explanations of slides and transparencies to amplify concepts and ideas. Your goal in using audiovisuals is to help listeners understand how they support your presentation.

SUMMARY

The term *audiovisual aid* refers to a device that may appeal to any of the senses: graphs, (line, pie, and bar); drawings, photographs, and pictures; posters and chalkboards; mechanical media; physical objects; and you, the speaker. Posters are popular visuals, and the chalkboard is effective if you use it for brief or incidental support of your speech. Mechanical media—such as overhead, LCD, opaque, slide or film projectors, as well as audio and video tape-recording equipment—are useful in different situations. You can also include scale models, partial objects, or life-size objects in a speech. As a speaker, *you* are also a visual aid. You can incorporate your own body movements and actions into a speech, and you can ask someone to help you. The computer can help you to develop visuals quickly and efficiently.

Observe five general guidelines to use visual aids effectively:

1. Talk to the audience, not to the visual.
2. Don't pass objects around during the speech.
3. Be sure listeners can see your visuals.
4. Use visuals at the right psychological moment.
5. Be clear at all times.

SKILL BUILDERS

1. Divide the class into several small groups. Select a topic from current events that can be enhanced by the use of several visual aids described in this chapter. Topics that are appropriate to this exercise can be drawn from areas such as crime, divorce, finances, immigration, drunk driving, and so on. Find several interesting visual aids related to the selected topic by researching newspapers and periodicals such as *USA Today, Time, Newsweek, National Geographic,* and *Audubon Magazine.* Present the group topic and visual aids to the class for discussion and analysis.

2. Choose a topic for a two-minute informative speech that can be supported with statistics. To get some ideas, consult sources such as *Information Please Almanac, The World Almanac,* or *Statistical Abstracts.* Plan and prepare a graph that is appropriate for displaying the data. Be sure to employ the visual aid effectively in your presentation.

3. Prepare a five- to seven-minute demonstration speech (See chapter 16) using any of the visual aids described in this chapter. Follow the suggestions we've provided for preparing and handling your visuals.

N O T E S

1. Charles R. Petrie Jr., "Informative Speaking: A Summary and Bibliography of Related Research," *Speech Monographs* 30 (June 1963): 82.

2. The statistics regarding the increase of murders were obtained from the *World Almanac and Book of Facts,* 1999 Edition.

3. Donna Kirkley, "Visuals Help Communicate," videotape, 1975.

4. I want to thank Hal Rummel, Associate Professor of Communication and Visual Communication at the Community College of Baltimore County, Catonsville Campus, who provided valuable information about the use of computers in developing visuals.

5. This example is based on a demonstration speech by Shirley Goscinski, "The Parts of a Computer," presented in speech class, Catonsville Community College, Catonsville, Maryland, 1995. The speech and the visual aids are used by permission.

Chapter 13

CONSIDERING
LANGUAGE

Eloquence is the power to translate a truth into language perfectly intelligible to the person to whom you speak.

Ralph Waldo Emerson

CHAPTER OBJECTIVES

After reading this chapter you will be able to:

1. Recognize language that is clear and concrete;

2. Describe figures of speech and stylistic elements;

3. Discuss the importance of appropriate language usage;

4. Know how to make ideas meaningful and interrelated.

Imagine that one of the most famous speeches in American history began like this:

> Eighty-seven years ago our ancestors came to this land to build a new country dedicated to liberty and equality. But at the present time, we are in the process of a conflict which will prove if this new country or any new country founded on such principles can live on.

This passage may sound simple and straightforward enough. But listen to the way it was actually written:

> Fourscore and seven years ago our fathers brought forth on this continent a new nation, conceived in liberty and dedicated to the proposition that all men are created equal. Now we are engaged in a great civil war, testing whether that nation, or any nation so conceived and so dedicated, can long endure.

Abraham Lincoln chose his words carefully and refrained from using commonplace language in "The Gettysburg Address." He realized that the words "Fourscore and seven years" were more effective than "eighty-seven years ago." He also recognized that a metaphor could be effective in communicating the nation's origins. Instead of an impersonal reference to the nation's "ancestors," Lincoln humanized the reference to "our fathers" and continued the metaphor with the words "brought forth, conceived, and dedicated." Lincoln conveyed the image that our fathers "brought forth" or "gave birth" to a child, thereby implying struggle, labor, pain, and hardship. The words "conceived in liberty" extended the metaphor and revealed the sanctity of the new nation's purpose and ideals.

Lincoln's speeches demonstrate the power of language. In your own speeches your language can remain plain and ordinary, or it can elevate the mind, stimulate thought, and connect to the diverse members of your audience. In this chapter we consider language which conveys your ideas with clarity, concreteness, style, and appropriateness. We also include a brief discussion of how language can make ideas more meaningful and interrelated. Choose language carefully to refine the appearance of your speech.

DEVELOPING CLARITY

One of the most important rules of language usage is to say what you mean. Use precise words to create mental pictures for your listeners, and use clear terminology that your audience will understand. Speeches that include obscure terms and flowery words may sound impressive, but aren't effective if they don't communicate to the audience. Former Vice President Spiro Agnew referred to Nixon administration critics as "nattering nabobs of negativism," "an effete corps of impudent snobs," or "pusillanimous pussyfooters."[1] While his idiosyncratic style attracted public attention for a while, audiences soon tired of searching through the dictionary to find out what he meant.

Another speaker who enjoys using large words and complicated syntax is conservative columnist William F. Buckley, editor of the *National Review*. He demonstrates these qualities in this excerpt from a speech to the Ethics and Public Policy Center in Washington, D.C.:

> There is much room left over for argument, even as there is room left over, under this roof, for divisions about the impermanent things. But I tender you, Dr. Lefever, and your distinguished board of directors, and associates this challenge. Deliberate the means of saying it in our public philosophy, saying that however much respect we owe to those who hold other ideas than those that are central to Judaeo-Christian postulates, we mustn't confuse any respect for the preternatural dignity for the fruit of their reason. How at once to do both these things—to respect a difference of opinion without undertaking a respect for different opinions? It is a searing challenge, in a world sensitive to cultural condescension, a world inflamed by the notion that one man, one vote presupposes one culture, any culture; one philosophy, any philosophy; one God, any God.[2]

It is possible that Buckley's audience knew what he was talking about. However, it is more probable that they would need a dictionary and an interpreter.

Contrast the Buckley speech with this example:

> Mr. Chief Justice, my dear friends, my fellow Americans: The oath that I have taken is the same oath that was taken by George Washington and by every president under the Constitution. But I assume the presidency under extreme circumstances never before experienced by Americans. This is an hour of history that troubles our minds and hurts our hearts.
>
> Therefore, I feel it is my first duty to make an unprecedented compact with my countrymen. Not an inaugural address, not a fireside chat, not a campaign speech, just a little straight talk among friends. And I intend it to be the first of many. I am acutely aware that you have not elected me as your president by your ballots. So I ask you to confirm me as your president with your prayers. And I hope that such prayers will also be the first of many.

When Gerald Ford assumed the presidency on August 9, 1974, he took the oath of office under the most difficult circumstances. For many months President Nixon and the Congress had been engaged in a Constitutional crisis because of the Watergate scandal. When the House Judiciary Committee voted articles of impeachment, President Nixon resigned and Gerald Ford, his appointed vice president, was sworn in as the thirty-eighth president of the United States. President Ford used simple language to express his ideas. He touched the hurt feelings within Americans, acknowledged his appointment to high office, and appealed for the goodwill and prayers of his fellow citizens.

Ford correctly realized it would be inappropriate to deliver an eloquent address filled with high-sounding phrases. He knew that after the Watergate cover-up Americans wanted to hear the truth conveyed in a "little straight talk among friends." The introduction and the speech indicate that the President analyzed his audience accurately and used language effectively.

Avoiding Euphemisms

Sometimes people avoid saying what they really mean by employing nonoffensive terms or phrases called *euphemisms*. We tend to think that these veiled terms and phrases will soften the blow of the underlying meaning. Often euphemisms are so vague that the essence is lost. Look at the following euphemistic words, phrases, or sentences used in a variety of occupational and social situations, and then read the "translation."

THE FOLLOWING EUPHEMISM . . .	REALLY MEANS . . .
The government was engaged in disseminating disinformation.	The government was spreading deceit and propaganda.
I misspoke.	I lied.
She has a great personality.	She's ugly.
He's intelligent.	He looks like a nerd.
The Art Index can be found in Library, Media, and Telecourse Services.	The Art Index is in the library.
I'm going to the Physical Development Center.	I'm going to the gym.
She experienced a cerebral infarction.	She had a blood clot in the brain.
I need to consult the custodial engineer.	I'll get the janitor.
Your child needs help learning to use his leadership abilities more democratically.	Your kid is a bully.
Let me help you select a fitting memorial for the beloved.	Do you want to pick out a tombstone?[3]

The vague language seems ridiculous when matched with the intended meaning. While many of these examples may seem humorous, they are realistic.

Language is degraded and misused when people don't say what they mean. While bureaucratese and nonsense jabber will probably never disappear, public speakers should be careful in their choice of generalized expressions. Eloquence doesn't mean using elaborate words and obscure phrases; it is more often composed of simple and direct language.

Now read these excerpts from a speech delivered by Lieutenant Commander Drew Brown, an attack pilot with the United States Navy. Commander Brown visits inner city schools plagued with drugs and gang violence. He represents a positive role model to young black teenagers who must stand up to the daily pressures of their surroundings. In this emotional presentation to students in a Los Angeles high school patrolled by police, Brown made his points emphatically:

Michael Jackson goes around here saying he's bad. Mike Tyson thinks he's bad. You've got these gangs called the Bloods and the Crips and they think they're bad. They ain't bad—I'm bad. I'm bad because I can fly 550 miles an hour fifty feet from the ground and I can carry twenty-eight 500 pound bombs under my wings. I have the expertise, the know-how, and the technology not to just take out this school, but to take out the whole neighborhood. But the point I'm trying to make is, you know what makes me bad? I'm bad because I have a college education! . . .

You want to get high? You go to med school after college. You learn how to be a doctor, you save somebody's life. You watch the gleam in their eyes as they hand you a check for forty-eight thousand dollars when you can go and buy your big Mercedes that nobody can take from you—and you are toasted! . . .

There is no black and white. But the bottom line is, black and white is in your mind, so if you blame your color on somebody else's color or somebody else's origin on your success or your failures, you are a loser![4]

Brown did not hide behind obscure language. His point was loud and clear; don't give in to your surroundings—get an education. The audience might not have listened to the speaker had he used imprecise words or complicated sentence patterns. Brown was successful because he understood the kind of direct language and clear examples that would communicate his message to his teenage audience. Your speaking will be far more successful if your words and phrases convey your feelings and objectives clearly. And you will be effective if you analyze your audience well enough to understand the kind of clear language that will motivate them to listen.

USING CONCRETE LANGUAGE

When you use language, it's also important to be concrete. If you've ever had a friend tell you to "Bring me the things when we get together tomorrow" you were probably puzzled if your friend didn't tell you what he or she meant by "things." Speakers who use vague language sound as if their vocabulary consists of no more than a few hundred words. Look at the wording used in the following demonstration speech:

> Okay. The first thing you want to do is to find out how much of this stuff you need. You measure the wall longways, and then this way, and then you come up with how much paper you need. Go behind the door or somewhere else where you can't see if you mess up. Take this baby here, and measure twenty inches from the edge like so. Then just mark a line up and down. With the same gizmo, go from the bottom to the top of the wall and add four inches onto everything so you can adjust it.

If you read between the lines, you may have understood that the speaker was demonstrating how to paper a wall. It was the vague language—"stuff," "longways," "this baby," "like so," "gizmo"—that made the demonstration sloppy and ambiguous. The speaker needed concrete words to describe materials and actions. Now read the more precise wording of the process:

> You need to know how much paper you need. It's very simple. You measure the height of the wall by the length of the wall, and you multiply them together and that gives the square footage. Do this on all four walls, add this together, and divide by sixty. That's the number of double rolls that you'll need. If this is your first job, I'd suggest that you get prepasted paper.
>
> Start with an inconspicuous corner, such as behind the door. With a metal ruler, measure twenty inches from the corner. The paper is twenty and one half inches. With the extra half inch, you will paper around the corner. Then take a pencil and a level, and at the twenty inch mark, draw a vertical line on the wall. Take the same metal ruler, measure from the floor to the ceiling, and add four inches. The extra inches give you two inches at the top and two inches at the bottom to allow for adjustment of the pattern.[5]

Denotation and Connotation

Knowing the difference between denotation and connotation can help to make your language more concrete and vivid. *Denotative* meanings are the dictionary definitions of words, while *connotative* meanings are their more personal and subjective meanings. For instance, a speaker who wanted to present an objective informational report about a proposed handgun bill might want to use words that generate denotative meanings within audience members:

> According to the Justice Department, eighty percent of the small handguns that are manufactured in the United States are produced in the Los Angeles

area. A measure proposed by the members of the city council in West Hollywood, California, would ban the sales of these weapons.

In this example, words like "small handguns," "ban," "manufactured," "sales," and "weapons," are general terms which can generate denotative meanings. It is possible of course, that depending on the type of audience, the statistics could stimulate strong feelings.

But suppose this speaker strongly opposed the unregulated sale of handguns and wanted to persuade listeners to support a strict handgun law.

> According to the Justice Department, eighty percent of the small handguns that are manufactured in the United States are produced in the Los Angeles area. These sinister little weapons, referred to as 'Saturday Night Specials,' are cheap, dangerously inaccurate, and easy to hide. Many thugs prefer these badly made guns because they can be concealed in the palm of the hand like a straight-edge razor. As a matter of fact, one mini-derringer is no longer than four inches and fits inside a carrying case that looks like the electronic paging beepers which people carry on their belts. Would you want these instruments of destruction in your community? Well they certainly don't want them in West Hollywood because all five members of the city council have endorsed a law which would ban them.[6]

Words such as "sinister little weapons," "Saturday night specials," "thugs," and "instruments of destruction" are chosen to evoke strong subjective meanings within listeners. The speaker can then suggest that members of the audience who feel strongly about the issue can support a law prohibiting the sale of handguns. Obviously the effect of these connotative meanings depends upon the audience. The above passage could be very effective in many audiences but could backfire in other groups. As in any speech setting, you must analyze your audience well enough to know the type of language that will best evoke your desired response. Here are a few examples of how a speaker can transform denotative or dictionary meaning into more subjective, connotative meaning.

WORDS FROM THEIR MOST DENOTATIVE TO MOST CONNOTATIVE MEANINGS

tall building	*steel skyscraper*	**towering deathtrap**
runner	*fleet-footed racer*	**Olympic-class sprinter**
dog	*puppy*	**adorable furball**
homeless woman	*bag lady*	**pitiful pauper**

As you move from left to right, the meanings become more connotative and precise. If you want listeners to respond to your speech with strong mental images, use connotative words that have the capacity of stimulating concrete feelings and specific pictures.

BUILDING A UNIQUE STYLE

Style refers to the distinctive manner in which a speaker uses language to convey ideas and feelings. A speaker develops style with unique phrases, memorable lines, and technical devices designed to make language colorful, forceful, and dramatic. You can build an expressive style by including figures of speech like similes and metaphors, and devices such as alliteration, amplification, antithesis, repetition, and mnemonic phrases.

Similes

A *simile* is a figure of speech in which the words "like" or "as" are used to show comparison. Here are some examples:

> Our current tax system is like an old inner tube that is covered with patches. We must replace it with a new, fair, simple tax system.
>
> —H. Ross Perot, from a televised political broadcast

> Thank you very much. Inviting a physician to talk about the United States Constitution is a little like inviting James Madison to do an appendectomy. However, only one of us is going to be guilty of malpractice tonight.
>
> —Harvey Sloame, from "Jefferson, Madison, and Franklin"

> The fat cells are in your body just waiting, like Mr. Pac Man, to start eating . . .
>
> —Vickie Chester, student speaker

> As for annexing the island, I have about the same desire as a gorged boa constrictor might have to swallow a porcupine wrong-end-to.
>
> —Theodore Roosevelt, from a letter to a German diplomat

These speakers used similes to make comparisons that were colorful, vivid, and interesting.

Metaphors

In the introduction to this chapter, we identified the "birth" metaphor that Abraham Lincoln employed in "The Gettysburg Address." Like a simile, a *metaphor* is a comparison, but without the use of the words "like" or "as." Here are some other examples:

> In order for any type of plant to grow, it must first have a healthy root system. But then it must be continually maintained in water to blossom. The same theory of growth holds true for our major cities today. In order for

them to grow, they too, need healthy root systems, and these roots lie in their downtown districts.

—Edward L. Bokman, student speaker

You remember the story of Chicken Little. She ran around the barnyard proclaiming that the sky was falling, and for a while she had all the other animals in a state of alarm. Today, we have the Chicken Little theory of economics. This time it isn't the sky that's falling. Rather, America's middle class is disappearing; vanishing before our very eyes. And, guess whose fault it is? Yours, and everyone else engaged in a service business. Imagine that. You are performing magic tricks with the economy and don't even know it.

—Paul Laxalt, from "Chicken Little Is Wrong Again"

Epilepsy is a thunderstorm in the brain.

—Brad Piern, student speaker

The Student Government Organization is the sun and the clubs, organizations, and committees are the planets which revolve around it.

—Bonnie J. McGrew, student speaker

Metaphors can add life to the language of your speech. Don't be afraid to experiment with comparisons, but be certain that the comparison you make is sensible and consistent. Avoid mixed metaphors that shift comparisons midway through a presentation. A speaker who says "The Ship of State is on the five yard line, ready to go in for the touchdown" ought to stick with either the nautical theme or the football comparison.

Alliteration

Alliteration refers to the repetition of the same sounds to emphasize ideas in a speech. We've already referred to former Vice President Agnew's alliterative "nattering nabobs of negativism." Some speakers have the ability to use this device with great effect.

Today when we *debated, differed, deliberated, agreed to, agree, agreed to disagree,* when we had the good judgment to argue our case and then not self-destruct . . .

—Jesse Jackson, from "Common Ground and Common Sense"

We are here, not only to *keep cool with Coolidge,* but to do honor to Alexander Hamilton.

—Will Rogers, from "Wealth and Education"

> Provided that every effort is made, that nothing is kept back, that the whole *man power, brain power, virility, valor and civic virtue* of the English-speaking world . . . is bent unremittingly to the *simple but supreme* task . . .

> —Winston Churchill, from "Address Before United States Congress"

> A firm fruit is a friendly fruit.

> —Carol Denise Manis, student speaker

Alliteration is a creative way to develop a vivid style but it is wise to use it sparingly.

Amplification

A speaker who employs *amplification* arranges words or phrases in order of importance to emphasize an opening or closing statement. For example:

> I am in earnest—I will not equivocate—I will not excuse—I will not retreat a single inch—and *I will be heard*.

> —William Lloyd Garrison, from *The Liberator*

> We shall not flag nor fail. We shall go on to the end. We shall fight in France, we shall fight on the seas and oceans; we shall fight with growing confidence and growing strength in the air. We shall defend our island whatever the cost may be; we shall fight on the beaches, we shall fight on the landing grounds, we shall fight in the fields and in the streets, we shall fight in the hills; we shall never surrender.

> —Winston Churchill, from "Dunkirk"

In the first example, abolitionist editor William Lloyd Garrison used an ascending order of ideas to emphasize the final, most important line of his antislavery message: ". . . I will be heard."

Winston Churchill also used amplification (as well as alliteration) in a speech defending British withdrawal from the city of Dunkirk in World War II. Even though British troops had suffered a defeat by the Nazis, Churchill wanted to rally the nation by repeating ideas that emphasized British determination "not to flag nor fail" and ending with the strong, emotional phrase, "We shall never surrender."

Antithesis

When using *antithesis,* a speaker combines contrasting ideas or qualities to convey a concept. Two examples are:

The race of man, while sheep in credulity, are wolves for conformity.

—Carl Van Doren, from "Why I Am an Unbeliever"

Not often in the story of mankind does a man arrive on earth who is both steel and velvet, who is as hard as rock and soft as drifting fog, who holds in his heart and mind the paradox of terrible storm and peace unspeakable and perfect.

—Carl Sandburg, from "Address Before Congress
on the 150th Birthday of Abraham Lincoln"

Carl Van Doren effectively combined opposite metaphors to describe the gullibility and like-mindedness of human beings. Carl Sandburg, speaking to Congress on the occasion of Abraham Lincoln's 150th birthday, used contrasting metaphors as well as similes to characterize the "paradoxes" of our sixteenth president.

Repetition

Repetition of words and phrases is an effective way to emphasize key ideas, to increase interest, and to convey vivid images. Speakers throughout history have employed this colorful literary device to strengthen emotion and to summon courage. Here are two excerpts from the well-known speeches of Martin Luther King Jr. and Franklin D. Roosevelt, who employed repetition to intensify the feelings of their listeners.

Let freedom ring from the snowcapped Rockies of Colorado!
Let freedom ring from the curvaceous slopes of California!
But not only that; let freedom ring from Stone Mountain of Georgia!
Let freedom ring from Lookout Mountain of Tennessee!
Let freedom ring from every hill and molehill of Mississippi.
From every mountainside, let freedom ring.

—Martin Luther King Jr., from "I Have a Dream"

Last night Japanese forces attacked Hong Kong.
Last night Japanese forces attacked Guam.
Last night Japanese forces attacked the Philippine Islands.
Last night the Japanese attacked Wake Island.
And this morning the Japanese attacked Midway Island.

—Franklin D. Roosevelt, from "For a Declaration of War Against Japan"

In his famous "I Have A Dream" speech delivered at the Lincoln Memorial during the 1963 March on Washington, King repeated the words "Let freedom ring" from the song "My Country, 'Tis of Thee." King used this repetition at the conclusion of the speech to summarize his dream that every part of America serve the cause of liberty and equal justice.

Franklin D. Roosevelt used repetition to energize his audience to support a different cause. After the bombing of Pearl Harbor on December 7, 1941, the President asked members of Congress to declare war on the empire of Japan. The repeated instances of Japanese military aggression quickly made an overwhelming case for the declaration of war.

Mnemonic Phrases

Speakers often develop ear-catching *mnemonic phrases,* which summarize main ideas and help people to remember significant themes. We tend to remember phrases like "I have a dream," or "All we have to fear is, fear itself." Some of the greatest speeches in history have contained phrases that summarized the speaker's philosophy.

> If the British Commonwealth and Empire last for a thousand years, men will still say, "This was their finest hour."
>
> —Winston Churchill, from "Their Finest Hour"

> With malice toward none, with charity for all, with firmness in the right as God gives us to see the right.
>
> —Abraham Lincoln, from "Second Inaugural Address"

> I know not what course others may take; but as for me, give me liberty, or give me death!
>
> —Patrick Henry, from "Give Me Liberty, or Give Me Death!"

> When this is done, I will go to the king, even though it is against the law. And if I perish, I perish.
>
> —Queen Esther, from Esther 5:16

> Let us never negotiate out of fear. But let us never fear to negotiate.
>
> —John F. Kennedy, from "Inaugural Address"

> I have always been fond of the West African proverb: Speak softly and carry a big stick; you will go far.
>
> —Theodore Roosevelt, from a letter to Henry L. Sprague

Each of these mnemonic phrases was effective because it captured the essence of the speaker's intention. In your own presentations, think of creative phrases that sum up your ideas. Recognize that memorable lines, if used sparingly in a speech, can stimulate thought and heighten audience feeling about your point of view.

BEING APPROPRIATE

Speech students often ask, "What exactly is inappropriate language? Shouldn't that decision be left up to the individual speaker?" Certainly each of us uses a different standard to define inappropriateness. But a speaker cannot simply make decisions in a vacuum. A speaker who wishes to have an impact must make perceptive decisions about the language he or she uses based upon the diverse members of the audience. Here are some suggestions that can help you to be more aware of your listeners and avoid words, terms, phrases, and expressions that listeners might consider ineffective or improper.

Be Aware of Cultural Differences

In most public speaking situations you encounter, there will probably be enormous differences in the cultural backgrounds of listeners. An audience of twenty people could include Hispanics, Caucasians, African Americans, Russians, Asians, southerners, westerners, or northeasterners. If you want to educate or influence individuals of such diversity, you need to understand the impact of culture upon language. Consider these examples. The word "submarine" is used throughout many parts of the United States to describe a large, overstuffed sandwich on an Italian roll. But terminology changes

Speakers and audiences alike must be aware of the enormous impact of culture and ethnic background on language and speaking practices.

based upon geography. Bostonians may call it a "grinder," New Yorkers may order a "hero," Philadelphians might ask for a "hoagie" and residents of New Orleans may want a "poor boy." Imagine the misunderstandings that can occur when individuals whose second language is English attempt to define "submarine," "hero," or "grinder" literally. An American asks, "Can I give you a lift," but a British citizen defines the word "lift" as an "elevator." In the Eskimo language there are numerous words to describe varieties of snow such as "wet snow," or "fluffy snow;" and in Brazil, there are dozens of terms referring to the word "coffee."[7] When several American car companies decided to use the term "Body by Fisher" as a selling point in foreign advertisements, they discovered in horror that in some foreign markets the term was translated as "Corpses by Fisher."[8] And General Motors learned that one of the reasons their Chevrolet Nova models failed to sell in many Latin American countries was that *no va* means "does not go" in Spanish.[9]

If regional and ethnic differences can affect simple words and concepts, imagine how culture can influence more complicated language structures. In America individuals with more knowledge about a topic tend to be direct and assertive, speaking in a straightforward manner. However, in a country such as Japan where people are concerned with saving face, those with greater knowledge tend to speak more indirectly and avoid direct statements that would appear dictatorial.[10] Americans enjoy talking and initiating conversation, but many Chinese use more silences within their language patterns.[11] Some Hispanic, French, and Italian Americans complain that English does not allow them to express feelings as comprehensively as their own "romance" languages.[12] The native Hawaiian language includes only five vowels and seven consonants,[13] and there are some American Indian languages that contain no past or future tenses.[14]

As you discover how profoundly culture influences language, you can develop speaking practices that convey greater sensitivity to the diverse members of your audience. Use language that is inclusive and avoid using "in-group" terms, jargon, and shorthand speech that excludes another individual's background or experience. Be clear and carefully define terms that listeners may not understand. Recognize that accents are not "wrong" or "bad," but speak slowly and distinctly and be aware that people of diverse backgrounds may need to listen to your dialect or accent at a more comfortable speaking rate. Make an effort to understand the language of your audience. If you are speaking to listeners of another culture, take the time to learn greetings or important words that help you link your topic more successfully to them. Most important, respect the diversity of your audience. Avoid patronizing statements that insult or embarrass listeners and refrain from inappropriate humor that pokes fun at their culture or language. Recognize that the differences in language and culture can be a positive source for learning. As an effective speaker, you want to connect diverse cultures and languages by building bridges of understanding.[15]

Recognize Differences Due to Gender

Do women talk more than men? Are men more direct than women? Are there distinct men's and women's languages? The answers to these questions may surprise you. Before discussing differences in language, we must emphasize that the concepts being considered are based upon researched conclusions that have numerous exceptions. The language used by men and women can be influenced by family, education, or cultural socialization. Men and women can communicate differently or similarly based upon occupation, experiences, relationships, interests, needs, or social groupings. As men and women differ in size, color, age, shape, or interests, so can they vary in vocabulary, sentence structure, grammar, and language patterns.

First of all, it is a myth that women talk more than men. Studies indicate then men not only talk more, but control conversation and maintain their dominance by interrupting others more often.[16] Men seem to be less concerned with grammatical errors and tend to use vocalized pauses to occupy center stage. Men use competitive and task-oriented language to take charge and get things done. Men will frequently issue orders and directives such as "You need to fax this report," or "Let's get to the bottom line." Men have greater technical vocabularies and tend to be more fact-oriented than women. Men's language is more intense, and the language of some males includes more curse words and profanity. Men like to talk about topics such as sports, business, or current events. While they enjoy conversations with other men to escape, to share interests, and to experience "freedom," men seldom call each other simply to talk.[17]

There are interesting differences in the language used by women. Women tend to speak with more qualifying words such as "possibly," or "maybe," and more disclaimers such as "this might be silly, but . . ." Unlike men, women don't interrupt conversations and use more polite forms for giving orders—"If you don't mind . . . ," or "If it isn't too much trouble . . ." Women tend to use more "tag" questions such as "That's the way it is, right?" and more descriptive words like "exceptionally," "adorable," "precious," and "lovely." Women use more complex sentence structures, prepositional phrases, and adverbs than men, and ask questions three times as often as men. Women also use more words and convey more comprehensive details than do men. Women tend to use more tentative phrases such as "I guess," or "I think," employ language that is less assertive than men, and make statements that express negations by describing what things are not. Unlike the more dominant males, women try to support conversation and help to keep it going. Women are more comfortable disclosing personal information and expressing emotional needs and psychological states. Women talk with other women to express empathy, to share feelings, or "just to talk."[18]

What can we learn from some of these conclusions and what are the implications for the speaker and listener? We must remember that differences in language patterns can depend upon the situation, place, and environment. A businesswoman presenting a training lecture to new employees could use language that is direct, task-oriented, and to the point. At the same time, a man recounting a spectacular scuba diving experience in the Caribbean could use numerous details and include descriptive adverbs. Much has been made about "the battle" of the sexes, and much has also been written about the dominance of one gender or the vengeful role reversal of another. If we recognize that the rhetoric of confrontation is harmful, we can begin to listen honestly and genuinely learn from one another. We should enjoy the unique speaking patterns of women who can convey the depth and richness of language with expressive shades and images. We can also appreciate the directness of men who contribute power, intensity, and technical depth to language. If we avoid making judgments and understand that the language of one gender is not wrong and the other right, we can appreciate that our differences can actually complement each other. We can be more open when women or men need to alter their language patterns in response to different environments or roles. We can also be more accepting of the unique perspectives that each gender offers.[19]

Avoid Offensive Terms

When James Watt was Interior Secretary during the first Reagan term, he told an audience that he had appointed a commission made up of "a black . . . a woman, two Jews and a cripple."[20] His remarks caused a controversy that eventually led to his resignation. Former Arizona governor Evan Mecham described some reactions of Japanese businessmen by saying that "their eyes got round."[21] He was removed from office by the Arizona State Legislature because of alleged illegal business deals as well as his controversial statements. The late Jimmy "the Greek" Snyder, a noted TV sports odds-maker, stated on national television that blacks have "been bred" to be superior athletes to whites.[22] The CBS Television Network immediately severed his employment contract. And Governor Jesse Ventura of Minnesota upset many church members and religious leaders when he told a *Playboy* magazine interviewer that "organized religion is a sham and a crutch for weak-minded people who need strength in numbers."[23]

These speakers all had one thing in common; they each employed language that significantly offended large groups of Americans. Whenever a speaker uses racist or sexist language or words that attack an individual's religion or nationality, the listener will react with hostility. As a speaker, you want to win listeners and open their minds to your ideas.

You should also avoid obscene words and phrases that can offend some listeners. During the latter part of the 1960s and early 1970s, many younger Americans discovered that they could gain public attention to their causes by shouting obscenities during rallies and protest demonstrations. While demonstrators got attention, their language also helped to polarize listeners. Commentators often referred to "the generation gap" or the "age gap." In your own speeches, it is good to remember that you are being evaluated by your audience. If you utter four-letter words for their shock value, you will probably get many listeners to take notice, but you will also discover that many will be offended. Those who are insulted will judge you negatively and switch you off mentally. You may find your credibility damaged and reduced.

The guideline is to avoid language that offends your audience. Analyze your listeners, understand their backgrounds, and respect their differences. Use positive language that wins them over to you, builds your credibility, and generates constructive feelings about you as a speaker.

Eliminate Irrelevant Language

It's a good idea to avoid unnecessary verbiage or linguistic clutter. A speaker who constantly repeats words and phrases like "you know," "and so," and "well," or vocalized pauses like "um" creates external noise interfering with communication and frustrating the listener. Dr. Nicholas Christenfeld, a psychologist at the University of California in San Diego, has studied what he calls the "um phenomenon." He reports that most people use several hundred vocalized pauses every hour and some individuals use as many as nine hundred verbalized pauses in one day. From his research, Christenfeld concludes that speakers who use irrelevant vocalizations are trying to buy time in order to struggle for the next word or phrase. He observes that "people don't admire people who um."[24]

It's also a good idea to avoid irrelevant details that are not important to the speech. In this example, a speaker attempts to explain the tools needed for professional painting but loses sight of the specific purpose:

> First, you set up a flat table for your materials where you want to do th‚
> painting. I set mine up in the family room. You know, my wife and childr‚
> spend a lot of time there—they enjoy watching TV, playing games, or ‚
> reading. We find that the family room is a nice place to escape from ‚
> It's also a great place to have parties with friends.

This speech began as a demonstration of the steps involved in painting a room but soon deteriorated into a trivial description of "Life in the family room." Listeners will lose interest in presentations that get sidetracked.

Avoid Trite Expressions

Our vocabulary frequently suffers from underuse due to peer pressure, lack of knowledge, or just plain laziness. Imagine how disruptive it would be for a speaker to constantly repeat slang phrases, such as "Like, I don't know," "It's bad," "He's real awesome," "She's outta sight," or "Gag me with a spoon!" English Professor Patricia Skarda of Smith College in Northhampton, Massachusetts, counted the use of the word "like" in a conversation between two students. She reported that one used the word forty-eight times and the other mentioned "like" thirty-seven times. Such trite language is referred to as "Mallspeak" or "Teenbonics," which Smith College president Ruth Simmons characterizes as "repetitive," "inarticulate," and "imprecise."[25] To counteract mallspeak, colleges such as Smith, Mt. Holyoke, the Massachusetts Institute of Technology, and Wesleyan University have instituted speaking-across-the-curriculum and speech mentoring programs to help students organize logical arguments and express themselves with more verbal competence and confidence.[26]

Audiences also become tired of hearing trite expressions such as "The moral of the story is," "To each his own," "The bottom line is," or "And now, in conclusion I'd like to say . . ." It is better to avoid these phrases and use language indicating that the speaker is capable of thinking creatively and independently.

We aren't suggesting that you never use familiar expressions or slang in your presentations. The speech delivered by Lieutenant Commander Brown suggests that there are speaking situations where the use of slang can appeal to specific audiences and reinforce important ideas. However, it's usually much more effective for a speaker to use inventive wording than to rely on clichés.

ninate Grammatical Errors

Mistakes in grammar disturb listeners and tend to raise questions about a speaker's credibility. Imagine that after conducting a physical examination your doctor said, "Your X-rays don't show nothin'. Everything come out fine." Or suppose your pilot in a cross-country flight radioed to passengers that "I seen some turbulence up here." Your confidence in the doctor or your pilot might deteriorate.

The same principle can be applied to your own speaking situations. If you go to a job interview and you claim to have a two-year or a four-year college degree, your prospective employer will expect you to communicate without major grammatical flaws. Your instructor will no doubt insist on the same standard in your speeches.

It is always possible to make a slip in noun-verb agreement as you are moving rapidly through a complicated speech in front of an audience. But it is important to avoid any consistent grammatical problems when you are delivering a speech. If you are weak in grammar, use the opportunity provided in your speech course to improve your skills. You may not be able to change all of your speaking difficulties in one semester, but you can reduce your grammatical mistakes by attending writing labs, taking a back-up course, or getting tutoring help.

You aren't expected to understand all the intricate details of the "King's English," but you should know enough about language to be aware of the difference between good and bad grammar. A basic knowledge of a few grammatical principles will enable you to use English that will build credibility with your listeners.

Build Vocabulary Skills

Do as much as you can to increase your vocabulary. Take the time to look up unfamiliar words in the dictionary. Good reference sources like *Roget's International Thesaurus* or *The Random House Thesaurus* can help you to choose effective wording for your presentation. The more varied your vocabulary, the more interesting and colorful the speech will sound to your audience.

MAKING IDEAS MEANINGFUL AND INTERRELATED

Speakers can use language to create a sense of participation within an audience and to help listeners connect ideas smoothly. To achieve these objectives, you can employ personal pronouns and transitions.

Personal Pronouns

Listeners are more interested in a speech when they feel involved with the topic. An effective way to include the audience is to use personal pronouns like *you, your, us, our*. In the following example, notice how the speaker has excluded listeners:

Not many people in this country can say that three generations ago their family was only American. Most people in this nation were originally from

> somewhere else. Whether it was Russia, France, Italy, or Ireland, immigrants came here seeking freedom—freedom of religion, freedom of speech, and freedom to contribute to this great country.

Many people and *immigrants* are vague and impersonal. The speaker does not allow listeners to feel any sense of involvement. Now read this altered example:

> How many of you can say that three generations back your family was "only American"? Almost all of our ancestors were originally from somewhere else. Whether from Russia, France, Italy, or Ireland, they originally came here seeking freedom—freedom of religion, freedom of speech, and freedom to contribute to this great country of ours.
>
> —Evan Feinberg, student speaker

With some minor changes, the speaker has made the same passage much more personal. The introductory question addresses the audience directly—*you* and *your family.* Personal pronouns such as *our ancestors,* and *country of ours* allow listeners to feel like participants. When it is appropriate in your speech, use these personal pronouns to relate to your audience. Avoid vague, third person references such as *people, individuals,* or *they.* You want your listeners to feel they are a part of your topic whenever it is appropriate.

Transitions

Suppose you have ended the first of three main headings in the body of your speech. One way to end is by saying, "I've finished my first point. Now for point two." This external transition tells the audience they are about to hear your second main idea, but the line is abrupt and jarring. Improved language would enable ideas to flow more smoothly from one point to another. Transitions are connectives between major or minor ideas in a speech. External transitions connect main points while internal transitions join subordinate ideas. Here are some examples of external transitions:

> **Specific purpose:** The purpose is to inform the audience about circus clowns.[27]
>
> **Thesis statement:** "Clowning has a history, an educational process, and famous personalities."

Possible transitions to introduce Numeral I, "History of circus clowns":

1. Let me first tell you about circus clowns and their history.
2. Circus clowns have an interesting history.
3. I found out some really interesting aspects of clown history.

Possible transitions to introduce Numeral II, "College for clowns":

1. Now that I've told you about clowns and their history, I want you to know that they also have their own college.
2. Circus clowns not only have a history: they also have a college.
3. While I found that clown history was interesting, I soon discovered that clown college was unimaginable.

Possible transitions to introduce Numeral III, "Well-known clown personalities":

1. Since I've told you about clown college, I'd like you to hear about a few well-known clown personalities.
2. But clowns are not complete without personality—and I'd like to talk about some of the most famous clown personalities.
3. After I discovered clown college, I came across some fascinating clown personalities.

Possible transitions to introduce the conclusion:

1. Now that you've heard about clown history, education, and famous clown personalities, I hope you will have a little more appreciation of this art the next time you see a circus clown.
2. In every part of the world, people of all ages have laughed at these interesting creatures called clowns.
3. I hope you've enjoyed some of the discoveries I've made about clowns.

Each external transition is a sentence that acts as a bridge to link the previous thought with the next main idea. Notice that a transition line after the thesis helps to make a smooth connection between the introduction and Numeral I of the body. Similarly, an external transition after the last main point of the body helps to bond the last point to the conclusion. Research indicates that external transitions flag main ideas and increase listener comprehension.[28] Remember that members of your audience don't have copies of your manuscript or outline; they won't be able to distinguish major or minor points easily unless you clearly indicate them.

External transitions are complete sentences that separate main points in the body of the speech; internal transitions separate minor points under main headings. Connectives such as *also, then,* and *next* can tell listeners that a subheading has several items that are linked together. Here are a few examples of internal transitions:

and	and so	in addition
then	finally	in addition to
next	first, second, third . . .	another
also	often	but

Be sure not to mix external and internal transitions. If you were to use *also, and,* or *in addition* as your only connecting transition between two main points in the body you would confuse your audience, since they would not be easily able to separate the major elements of the speech. Your presentation would sound like one long numeral I rather than a series of headings with subordinate points. If you use complete sentences as your external transitions between main ideas, then one-word connectives will work effectively for internal transitions between supporting points.

SUMMARY

You communicate more successfully if your language is clear and direct, rather than obscure or euphemistic.

Concrete language is also more effective than ambiguity. If you want to evoke subjective feelings within listeners, use connotative rather than denotative language. A colorful and forceful style can be developed by using figures of speech like similes, metaphors, and devices such as alliteration, amplification, antithesis, repetition and mnemonic phrases.

The language of a speech should always be appropriate to the diverse members of your audience. Understand how culture and gender affect the language of your listeners. Avoid offensive words and terminology and eliminate unnecessary language and extraneous verbal clutter. Avoid trite expressions and eliminate grammatical mistakes. Work to build a comprehensive vocabulary that enables your language to be more vivid.

A speech can be made more meaningful through the use of personal pronouns. Ideas can be linked together more effectively with the construction of external transitions to bridge main points, and the use of internal transitions to connect subordinate elements.

SKILL BUILDERS

1. Write an external transition sentence to separate each main point of the body in your speech. Be sure to include transitions between the introduction and numeral I, and between your final numeral and the conclusion.
2. Divide your class into small discussion groups of 4 or 5 individuals each. First, identify several cultural, ethnic, and geographical differences among the members of your group. Then describe how these differences will influence:
   a. Specific words and vocabulary used in speeches,
   b. Language patterns of speakers,
   c. Choice of topics or ideas expressed in speeches,

d. The ability of listeners to understand a speaker's ideas,

e. The ability of speakers to enlighten or influence listeners.

3. Divide the class into several groups. In each group, discuss the following issues related to gender:

a. What are the interests, majors, and career goals of the men and women in your group?

b. How should speakers connect topics to the interests of men and women in your group?

c. Are there speech topics that could be considered exclusively "women's" or "men's" topics? If so, list them. Discuss the strategies that a speaker would use to connect these topics to the audience.

d. Are there issues or topics that should be avoided in speeches because of the reaction of one gender or the other? What are they?

e. What kind of language might be considered inappropriate to the men or women in the audience? Be specific.

f. What issues or topics might be considered interesting and appropriate to both men and women?

4. Choose one of the role-playing situations listed below, and develop two skits with another student from your class. In the first skit, the individual playing the professional should communicate using the euphemistic jargon of the occupation. Then repeat the skit, this time communicating in language that everyone understands. Raise some questions with the class: Is there a place for euphemistic language? Are there times when euphemisms are unnecessary? When is it appropriate to use euphemisms?

a. A doctor describing a surgical procedure that a patient must undergo.

b. A funeral director describing the types of services offered to the family of the deceased.

c. A lawyer explaining the steps involved in a legal proceeding (obtaining a divorce, drawing up a contract, writing a will).

d. A fourth grade teacher explaining to a parent that the child is a brat.

e. A trucker explaining that there is a problem on the road ahead to another trucker over a CB radio.

f. A weather forecaster explaining tomorrow's weather.

g. An auto mechanic describing a problem with the car.

5. Prepare a one-minute presentation in which you describe an incident in neutral or "objective" language. Then describe the same incident in language that makes the same incident sound negative. Finally, use language to make the incident sound favorable. In each description use the same details, only change your language. Were any presentations more denotative or connotative? Which presentation do you think would have been most persuasive to the audience?[29]

NOTES

1. "Leaves from a Lurid Lexicon," *Newsweek,* September 28, 1970, p. 24.

2. "Buckley's Remarks at Gala," *The National Review,* December 31, 1986, p. 24.

3. Terence P. Moran, "Public Doublespeak: On Beholding and Becoming," in *Language Awareness,* 2nd ed., ed. Paul Eschholz, Alfred Rosa, and Virginia Clark (New York: St. Martin's Press, 1978), p. 54.

4. ABC, "Incredible Sunday," October 30, 1988.

5. Norma Ferris, "Papering a Wall," speech to demonstrate presented in speech class, Catonsville Community College, Catonsville, MD, 1987. Used by permission.

6. The statistics and examples used in this passage were based on two articles: "First U.S. City Nears Ban on Saturday Night Specials," *The Evening Sun* (Baltimore), November 24, 1995, p. A10, and "The Gun Law: Maryland's High-Powered Issue," *The Sunday Sun* (Baltimore), October 30, 1988, p. A1.

7. Carley H. Dodd, *Dynamics of Intercultural Communication,* 4th ed. (Dubuque: Wm. C. Brown Publishers, 1995), pp. 133–134.

8. Ibid., p. 136.

9. R. Armao, "Worst Blunders; Firms Laugh Through Tears," *American Business* (January 1981), p. 11, cited by Ronald B. Adler and Neil Towne, *Looking Out Looking In,* 8th ed. (Fort Worth: Harcourt Brace College Publishers, 1996), p. 101.

10. Dodd, *Intercultural Communication,* p. 150.

11. Ibid., p. 149.

12. Ibid., p. 148.

13. Ray Riegert, *Hidden Hawaii* (Berkeley: Ulysses Press, 1989), p. 25.

14. Dodd, *Intercultural Communication,* p. 134.

15. Some of the suggestions used here are taken from the eleven-point plan for "Developing Skills in Language and Culture" in Dodd, *Intercultural Communication,* pp. 149–150.

16. Sarah Trenholm and Arthur Jensen, *Interpersonal Communication,* 3rd ed. (New York: Wadsworth Publishing Company, 1996), p. 193.

17. Much of the information about gender differences in language was drawn from the following sources: Ronald B. Adler and Neil Towne, *Looking Out Looking In,* 9th ed. (Fort Worth: Harcourt Brace College Publishers, 1999), pp. 214–219; Roy M. Berko, Andrew D. Wolvin, and Darlyn R. Wolvin, *Communicating: A Social and Career Focus,* 6th ed. (Boston: Houghton Mifflin Company, 1995), pp. 208–212; Sarah Trenholm and Arthur Jensen, *Interpersonal Communication,* 3rd ed. (New York: Wadsworth Publishing Company, 1996), pp. 193–195; and Richard L. Weaver, *Understanding Interpersonal Communication,* 5th ed. (Glenview: Scott, Foresman/Little, Brown Higher Education, 1990), pp. 173–178.

18. Adler and Towne, *Looking Out Looking In,* 9th ed., p. 216.

19. Weaver, *Understanding Interpersonal Communication,* pp. 175, 177.

20. "James Watt's Last Gaffe?" *Newsweek,* October 3, 1983, p. 45.

21. "Inside the Wacky World of Evan Mecham," *U.S. News & World Report,* February 22, 1988, p. 29.

22. "An Oddsmaker's Odd Views," *Sports Illustrated,* January 25, 1988, p. 7.

23. "Ventura Says Religion Is for 'Weak,'" *The New York Times,* October 1, 1999, p. 22.

24. Norma Zamichow, "California Psychologist Follows the 'Ums' in Speech," *The Sun* (Baltimore), May 3, 1992, p. 2A.

25. "Like, wow, colleges include speaking class," *The Sun* (Baltimore), March 23, 1999, p. 3A.

26. Ibid.

27. Julie Balick, "Circus Clowns," informative speech presented in Speech Class, Catonsville Community College, Catonsville, MD, 1988. Used by permission.

28. Charles R. Petrie, Jr., "Informative Speaking: A Summary and Bibliography of Related Research," *Speech Monographs* 30 (June, 1963): p. 81.

29. This verbal exercise is adapted from a written exercise in Paul Escholz, Alfred Rosa, and Virginia Clark, eds., *Language Awareness,* 2nd ed. (New York: St. Martin's Press, 1978) p. 152.

Chapter 14

DEVELOPING THE DELIVERY

To be an orator, you have to use your own words and be on fire with them.

Fulton John Sheen

CHAPTER OBJECTIVES

After reading this chapter you will be able to:

1. Discuss techniques for proper breathing;

2. Describe the elements of vocal delivery;

3. Describe the elements of visual, nonverbal delivery;

4. Know how to combine vocal and visual elements;

5. Recognize how to build a skillful delivery.

K **E Y**   **T E R M S**

Appearance
Articulation
Body movement
Clavicular
  breathing
Culture
Diaphragmatic
  breathing
Eye contact
Facial expression
Gender
Gestures
Inflection
Pauses
Phrasing
Pitch
Pronunciation
Quality
Rate
Volume

Before facing each other in the 2000 presidential debates, the candidates worked feverishly to develop images that would project favorably to voters. The nominees reviewed briefing books on the principal campaign issues, and rehearsed catchy one-liners describing the failures of the opponent. Candidates also held mock debates with stand-ins to practice fielding questions and presenting rebuttal remarks. Each side worried about its candidate's appearance and delivery on camera. Campaign staffs argued about the color of the background, the height of the speaker's stand, or the intensity of lighting. Media consultants tried to improve candidates' gestures or vocal delivery, and wardrobe specialists gave advice on appropriate clothing. The candidates made every effort to create a positive, dignified presidential image to the public.

Politicians know that extensive preparation is necessary because of the impact of past presidential debates upon voters. In the 1960 Kennedy-Nixon debates, Richard Nixon's "five o'clock shadow" and sluggish performance contrasted poorly against John F. Kennedy's sharper image and energetic delivery. Kennedy's success in the debates helped to give him the edge in a very close election. In the only 1980 debate, Governor Reagan—who was older than his opponent, a tired-looking President Carter—appealed to voters by asking "Are you any better off now than you were four years ago?" In the 1988 vice-presidential debates, Senator Dan Quayle compared his age and experience to John F. Kennedy's. His opponent, Senator Lloyd Bentsen rebuked him severely with the retort, "Senator, you're no Jack Kennedy." And in the 1992 debates, President Bush appeared to be detached or bored, often looking at his watch when he was asked a question. These debates indicate that a speaker's delivery and style can significantly influence an audience.

In this last chapter of Unit Four, we identify the skills you need for an effective speaking delivery. We discuss some of the important aspects of your vocal and visual delivery, and we'll include some brief suggestions to help you develop your delivery techniques.

DELIVERING THE SPEECH

Students often ask public speaking instructors, "Is delivery or content more important in a speech?" Our usual answer is "yes." The problem with this question is that it assumes delivery and content are somehow isolated and that a speech can successfully depend upon one or the other. An eloquent delivery is not helpful, however, if the message is disorganized or poorly researched. At the same time, well-researched and clear ideas can fail to communicate if the delivery is poor.

A speaker's expressions, posture, and gestures can convey enthusiasm and interest in the listener.

You need effective skills in both delivery and content to succeed in communicating your message. Martin Luther King's famous "I Have a Dream" speech would have been only moderately interesting had it been published in a book or magazine. It was the civil rights leader's ringing style of delivery that projected King's ideas forcefully to his audience.

There are two aspects of delivery—the vocal and the visual or nonverbal. Imagine a speech that you hear over the radio. You listen to the speaker's increase and decrease in volume, quickening or slowing of the speaking rate, and emphasis on key words and phrases. Now picture a televised speech with no sound as the speaker gestures, smiles or frowns, and makes visual contact with the audience. The radio or the silent TV speech can have a degree of success, but unless the vocal and visual aspects of delivery are combined, meaning will not be fully projected over all the available channels of communication. For example, those who heard the Kennedy-Nixon debates on radio in 1960 thought Richard Nixon had been the most effective speaker. However, a majority of those who watched the debates on television thought Kennedy was the clear winner. Vocal and visual delivery are equally important when you present a speech. If one channel is blocked, communication can be significantly altered.

PROPER BREATHING FOR VOCAL DELIVERY

You need a supply of air not only to survive, but also to produce the sound needed for an effective vocal delivery. It is the diaphragm that is primarily involved in inhalation. The diaphragm is a dome-shaped muscle attached to the base and sides of the lower ribs separating the abdomen from the chest. When you inhale, the diaphragm contracts and moves downward, while the ribs move upward and out, increasing the size of the chest cavity. At the same time, air flows into the lungs filling the vacuum. As you exhale, the diaphragm slowly begins to relax, and the abdominal muscles exert pressure upward to force air out of the lungs, through the trachea, and into the larynx where the air vibrates the vocal folds producing sound.

If you gasp for air or raise your shoulders when you inhale, you are possibly using *clavicular breathing,* or respiration from the top of the lungs. Slouching or leaning over a lectern can interrupt the natural process of inhalation and contribute to improper breathing. Clavicular breathing causes unsteadiness in the air supply and creates tension in the neck and throat. If you place your hand over your abdomen and inhale, you should feel the stomach muscles move forward in *diaphragmatic breathing.* A good, steady breath from the diaphragm produces the constant supply of air needed to produce sound.[1] The following exercises can help you to breathe properly and to establish breath control.[2]

Exercise 1: Sit in a chair that is comfortable but firm and has good back support. Stretch your hands on your abdomen immediately below your ribs, with your thumbs pointing to the rear and fingers pointing forward. Sit erect but relaxed, with your feet firmly on the floor. Inhale slowly, then exhale. When you inhale, you should feel your stomach muscles push forward, and when you exhale, they should pull in. Now repeat this exercise, but this time take about five seconds to inhale. Then take ten seconds to exhale. If you run out of breath before ten seconds, try the exercise again and exhale much more slowly. Repeat this exercise several times.

Exercise 2: Stand up straight with both feet firmly on the floor. Inhale normally and then exhale on the sound *s.* Maintain the sound as evenly as possible for about ten seconds. Repeat the exercise and exhale on the sounds *sh, th,* and *f.*

VOCAL DELIVERY

We will examine the following elements of vocal delivery: volume, articulation, pitch, quality, rate, pronunciation, pausing, emphasis and phrasing.[3]

Volume

Volume is the intensity, or loudness and softness of your voice. If you have ever been approached by a person who shouts a ten-minute sales pitch at you, or if you have ever strained to hear a speaker in a large auditorium, you are already aware of the importance of volume in speech delivery. Either of these situations is irritating, and listeners will block out a speaker who fails to adjust volume to meet the needs of a particular speech setting. If you present a speech in a gymnasium without a microphone, you'd better be prepared to project your voice so the individual on the last row can hear you comfortably. Conversely, you may need to speak more softly to a handful of people in a small conference room.

In speech classes, people rarely have the problem of projecting too much volume; more often, individuals aren't loud enough. It takes experience and training to develop vocal sensitivity. Experienced actors and actresses can project their voices, even in a whisper, without amplification in cavernous playhouses or in vast open-air amphitheatres. Unless there is a physical problem, most of us have the ability to develop good vocal projection. By doing some vocal exercises and practicing diaphragmatic breathing, you can control the intensity of your voice so that the audience can hear you comfortably.

Adjusting your volume can also be an effective way to emphasize significant portions of a speech. You can increase or lower your volume for dramatic emphasis when you convey startling information or emotional examples. The late Leo Buscaglia, educator, author, and public speaker who toured the country lecturing on love and human emotions, told this story of a smiling girl "with kind eyeballs" who was a student in one of his huge lecture classes at the University of California:

> And about five weeks into the semester this beautiful young girl was not in her seat and when Monday, Wednesday, Friday, Monday, Wednesday, Friday came, I became curious and I went down and asked the people around her what had happened to her. And do you know that in something like six weeks of school, they didn't even know her name? . . . and so I went to the Dean of Women and I asked about her . . . [and she said] "Oh Leo, I'm sorry, haven't I told you? This girl went to Pacific Palisades (which is an

area many of you know of, where sheer cliffs fall into the sea), and there were people there having a picnic on the grass and they saw her drive her car up and she left the ignition running and zombie-like, she walked across the grass and without a moment's hesitation, threw herself off onto the rocks below." She was twenty-two.[4]

When he used this example, Buscaglia increased his volume on the words "they didn't even know her name" to show anger and disgust. Then he contrasted that emotion by softening his voice almost to a whisper on the line "and threw herself onto the rocks below" to reinforce the tragedy and shock of the story. Volume can be an effective device to shade meaning.

Articulation

Another aspect of delivery is *articulation,* which refers to the clarity and enunciation of words, phrases, and sentences in a speech. Americans often exhibit sloppy enunciation; we frequently eliminate vowels and consonants, run words together, and mumble sentences. The unfortunate result often sounds like some kind of verbal jumble that not even fellow English-speaking citizens can easily understand. The following exchange could take place on almost any college campus in the country. See if you can decipher some of the garbled words and phrases.

Man: "Haryadoin?"
Woman: "Fine. Whatchurnam?"
Man: "Laryowns—urz?"
Woman: "Molyilsn. Whouwerkfor?"
Man: "Blakndeckr. Wheryagodaskool?"
Woman: "Eescampus."
Man: "O. Imonweseye. Wheryagoinow?"
Woman: "I dunno."
Man: "Yasingl?"
Woman: "Yeh."
Man: "Yawannagodamyplas?"

Although the example may be humorous, it makes a serious point. In order to communicate effectively, a speaker must enunciate clearly. The audience must be able to understand words and phrases easily without having to guess at the meaning. When you speak, you should make the effort to open your mouth and use clear articulation. Remember that words have vowels and consonants, and some words must be distinctly separated in order to be understood. Try to pronounce each of the following words containing difficult sound combinations:[5]

fifths	grasped	asks
frisked	answer	fists
sixths	oaths	months
thousands	depths	twelfths
widths	lengths	hundredths

Many problems of articulation are simply a result of bad habits caused by verbal laziness. There are some serious problems, however, such as stuttering, cleft palate, or aphasia, that may have emotional or physical causes requiring extensive speech therapy. Individuals with these speaking disorders need patience, love, and understanding in addition to good speech therapy to build confidence in their communication abilities. Many articulation problems can be improved through simple vocal exercises and by opening the mouth and speaking more distinctly.

Pitch

Pitch is the vocal element that refers to the highness or lowness of sound. If you spoke in a normal voice and struck a note on a piano corresponding to your vocal note, you would find your approximate pitch. Children have high-pitched voices, women have lower voices, and men's voices tend to be still lower. Changes in pitch, called inflections, are important in effective vocal delivery. A presentation in which a speaker uses a variety of inflections sounds interesting. If you have ever had to endure a speaker who delivered an entire speech using the same monotonous pitch, you know how bored and frustrated you felt. The most interesting written material can often seem tedious if a speaker uses a monotone. Here is an exercise underscoring the contrast between the two styles of delivery. Read the following lines to a children's story using only a monotone:

> Once upon a time, deep in the forest, there lived a talkative owl, a one-legged grasshopper, and a turtle who could climb trees. One day the owl swooped down near the ground and discovered the grasshopper hobbling along.
> "Wholoo there," said the owl perched on the lower limb of a tree. "I've been very lonely lately because I've had no one to talk to. Why don't you jump up on this limb, climb on my feathers and we'll go for a ride?"
> "I can't," said the grasshopper slowly and sadly. "I lost a leg in a fierce battle with a kitten, and now I can hardly do anything at all."
> "Ha ha," said the talkative owl, "at least you're still alive!"
> "Not funny," clicked the one-legged grasshopper. "Not funny at all. At least you can fly."

"Oh yes," said the owl, "and I can turn my head all the way around, and I have sharp sharp claws, and I am very, very wise."

"I've heard enough from you," said the one-legged grasshopper who began to limp away.

"Wait," yelled the owl. "You can do all sorts of things that I can't do. You can sneak under doors and get into people's houses, you can crouch into corners and not be seen, and best of all, you have a lovely, lovely voice to sing with. As a matter of fact, why don't you sing and entertain me right now?"

Now do it again, this time using a lot of vocal variety and different voices for each character as if you were telling the story to an audience of pre-schoolers. If you let yourself go during the reading, your pre-schoolers would probably have been fascinated. Vocal variety helps you to emphasize meaning and to create interest in the material.

You will get a similar result when you use vocal variety in your speeches. If you vary your inflection, your listeners will be much more interested and involved in your topic.

Quality

Voice *quality* refers to the sound or timbre of the voice. It is the element that makes each speaker's voice unique. No doubt you have heard speakers whose voices sounded harsh, nasal, breathy, gravelly, melodious, seductive, or hollow. Think of the differences in vocal quality of Bill Bradley, George W. Bush, Jesse Jackson, Madonna, Joan Rivers, Marilyn Monroe, Chris Rock, Maya Angelou, Jerry Seinfeld, Roseanne Barr, James Earl Jones, Charlton Heston, and David Letterman. We recognize each of these individuals by their unique trademark—the sound of their voices.

Vocal quality can add to or detract from an individual's speech. If you've ever picked up the telephone and heard a nasal, "Hallow—Haw are yoooooo?" you probably had difficulty concentrating on the message because the nasal sound was so annoying. On the other hand, you probably listened actively to a speaker who greeted you in a rich, mellow voice.

The voice quality of most adults is usually established by long-term vocal habits. Frequently, however, some bad habits that are responsible for unpleasant voices can be altered through tension-reduction vocal exercises. A good voice and diction coach should be consulted for treatment.[6]

Rate

The *rate* of speech refers to the number of words an individual speaks every minute. Your speaking rate can affect the audience's comprehension of your meaning. If you rush through your speech, listeners cannot grasp your ideas or keep up with you. One student who delivered a speech too rapidly told a joke and was surprised to discover the audience laughing several seconds later when he had moved on to more serious information. A speaker needs a comfortable rate of delivery that allows ideas to sink in. The most desirable speaking rate falls somewhere between 125 and 150 words per minute.[7] Anything significantly more or less than that is either too fast or too slow. Because of apprehension, many beginning speakers unconsciously speed up their rate. If this happens to you, try to make a conscious effort to slow down so that your listeners can absorb your ideas. Use dramatic pauses to break up important thought groups and to give listeners time to think about your ideas.

Rate can also be important in the interpretation of a speech. You can increase your rate when you want to create suspense and generate emotional feelings. You can slow down at the conclusion or during climactic points in the speech to demonstrate finality and resolution. Read the following dramatic incident aloud and adjust your speaking rate to reinforce the meaning of the material.

> The woman escaped from her assailant and ran out of the house. She ran up the street and began yelling and pleading, "Will anyone help me? Please, please, protect me. Someone's trying to kill me!" She kept running and glancing over her shoulder to see if the assailant was coming after her. She ran around a corner and spotted a police car two blocks ahead. She ran the last two blocks waving her arms wildly. "Please, save me," she screamed. Finally, finally, she saw the beautiful car with the red and blue revolving light coming toward her. She slowed to a half run, half walk. Between her sobs and heavy breathing she whispered, "Thank God!"

If you followed the events in the narrative closely, your speaking rate was probably rapid at the beginning. As the pace of the story quickened, you may have increased your rate, and as the events concluded, your pace decreased. Your rate of speech is a valuable tool you can employ to emphasize and to interpret meaning.

Pronunciation

Pronunciation describes the combinations of vowels, consonants, syllables, and accents a speaker chooses to emphasize a specific word. It is important to know how to pronounce common English words and difficult terminology you employ in a speech. Stumbling over words or making frequent errors in pronunciation interrupts the flow of ideas and raises questions about a speaker's credibility. Knowing how to pronounce a word means understanding the generally accepted pronunciation. While pronunciation can differ remarkably depending upon the region of the country, a good dictionary should be a helpful guide to the preferred pronunciation.

As part of your standard speech practice, you should check the pronunciation of any difficult words or terms unfamiliar to you. Here are some common words that are frequently mispronounced. Read the list carefully, and make sure that you are able to use the generally accepted pronunciation of each word.

adjective	gesture	picture
aluminum	harassment	potato
cavalry	mischievous	pumpkin
congratulate	neither	recognize
either	nuclear	statistics
escape	particularly	tomato
exits	pecan	veterinarian

Pauses

Pauses are breaks or interruptions in speech that separate thoughts and ideas. Dramatic pauses are intentional breaks or silences between major ideas that can bring out the meaning of a specific passage. Dramatic pauses can help a listener to focus on a startling fact, or create a moment that allows a listener to experience an emotion. Notice how the following passage reads when you place dramatic pauses in strategic parts of the story:

> Melanie was a bright, seventeen-year-old girl. She was a straight-A student, she had numerous friends, and she was extremely attractive. Everything seemed to be going well for Melanie. But Melanie had one problem that few people knew about. [pause] Melanie was an anorexic [pause] and it was killing her!

You can use pauses effectively in a number of places to bring out the meaning of this passage. If you pause briefly at each punctuation mark and then use longer pauses at the brackets, the punch line to the story is dramatically emphasized. Read it several more times and experiment with different combinations of pauses. Experiment in your speeches as well. Use pausing where it is most likely to enhance and emphasize emotional examples, startling statements, and colorful quotations.

Vocalized pauses are verbalizations such as *uh,* and *um* that cause distractions in speaking. Speakers sometimes use vocalized pauses because they are nervous or because they may be uncomfortable with silence. The three Kennedy brothers all earned reputations as effective public speakers; but the late President, his brother Robert, and Senator Ted Kennedy all developed the bad habit of incorporating vocalized pauses in many of their speeches. Try to eliminate this habit from your verbal delivery. Vocalized pauses are annoying and keep listeners from concentrating on your presentation.

Remember that you don't have to verbalize 100 percent of your speaking time. Use silences to your advantage when you deliver your presentations. Dramatic pauses can help you to separate thoughts and to provide the audience with some time to grasp your ideas.

Emphasis and Phrasing

You use *emphasis* in a speech when you make alterations in your rate, volume, and pitch to highlight significant words and sentences. In *phrasing,* you group words and sentences into units of thought, which make ideas easier to understand. Both emphasis and phrasing help to make a speech interesting and clear. In the following example emphasize the italicized words by increasing your volume and slowing your rate. Use pauses wherever you see the caret.

The U.S. national debt is three point six trillion dollars.

Think of it. *Three point six trillion dollars.*
  ^   ^   ^

You can hear how emphasis verbally helps to underscore important words and thoughts, and how phrasing helps to clarify the meaning by grouping sentences into smaller thought units. The markings reflect the emphasis and phrasing each individual used to deliver the following passages.

And so my fellow Americans, *ask not* what your *country* can *do* for *you, ask*
                           ^   ^
what *you* can *do* for your *country.*

—John F. Kennedy

I have a dream that my four little children will one day live in a nation
                                   ^
where they will not be judged by the *color* of their *skin* but by the *content* of their *character.* I have a *dream* today.

—Martin Luther King Jr.

The only thing we have to fear, is *fear itself.*
                                     ^

—Franklin D. Roosevelt

The ideas are dynamic enough. However, each speaker used his unique delivery to promote an even clearer understanding of his words. The results were powerful. If you reread each quotation using different emphasis and phrasing, the meaning is altered, and the overall effect is much less dramatic.

Your ideas can be emphasized in many ways, and your words can be grouped into a variety of patterns. Choose the emphasis and phrasing which most effectively reflects your intention and which will, in turn, contribute to the audience's understanding of your meaning.

VISUAL, NONVERBAL DELIVERY

Visual delivery refers to the nonverbal aspect of communication. This aspect of speaking is important because we communicate so many of our thoughts and feelings spontaneously through facial expressions, eye contact, or body movements. One study, for example, indicates that 55 percent of meaning conveyed in conversation is expressed through the face.[8] In addition, a speaker's appearance or "physical attractiveness" can significantly enhance a speaker's persuasive influence.[9] So it is helpful to understand that your eye contact, appearance, gestures, facial expressions, body position, and movement as well as characteristics related to your culture or gender can have a significant impact on audience perceptions of your communication.

Eye Contact

Eye contact is a very important aspect of your visual delivery. Through the eyes you can reach the intellect and emotions of your audience and gauge their feedback to your ideas. Research indicates that poor eye contact may even have a negative impact on the amount of information an audience comprehends during a speech.[10] Any audience wants the speaker's recognition and awareness. A speaker who reads word for word, without ever looking up, will promote indifference and boredom:

> The teacher arrived for every class period just three minutes late. She always sat down gingerly, pulling her chair up very slowly under the desk. She tugged three times at her skirt, making certain that it was stretched over her knees. She then began the lecture, without ever once looking at her students. "Today we are going to discuss the dangling participle," she droned in a monotone, ". . . an exciting lesson in rhetorical dysfunction." One student commented at the end of the semester, "She never looked at me anytime during the whole course. I don't think she ever knew I was alive. The trouble is, I'm not sure that she was alive."

Contrast this experience with one of your most interesting instructors. You'll find that the professor who is an effective communicator uses a great deal of eye contact. The good instructor is always aware of student reactions and knows when to repeat ideas, ask questions, or proceed to new information. This instructor combines good eye contact with many other techniques of effective delivery. The communicative professor walks around, gestures, uses facial expression, and shows interest in students who respond by becoming actively involved and interested in class discussions.

When you deliver a speech, you must establish visual contact with your audience. While you aren't expected to memorize the speech, you should have rehearsed enough to free yourself from too much attention to notecards. It may take some practice and repeated experience to discover how often to glance at notes and how much visual contact to make with listeners. When you look at the audience, sustain eye contact long enough to let them know you see them and are following their reactions. Look at each area of the audience at some point in your speech. Avoid bobbing your head up and down between notecards and audience. This practice detracts from your speech and doesn't establish eye contact. If you feel insecure in front of people, find several friendly, attentive faces at the right, center, and left. Begin by looking at these supportive individuals, and gradually expand your field of vision to other audience members. Practice your speech thoroughly so that you will feel confident enough to look away from your notecards and establish rapport with your audience.

Appearance

Your *appearance* can support or detract from the communication process. A student who worked as a school crossing guard gave a speech informing the audience about the duties and responsibilities of her job. On the day of the speech she wore her school guard uniform, complete with hat, badge, and whistle. She spoke of her role as a protector and guardian of "her kids," and firmly reminded the audience that it is her job to stop traffic whenever it is in the best interests of the children. The speaker's words and feelings conveyed commitment to the topic, while her appearance communicated authority and dedication on a nonverbal level.[11]

Politicians carefully analyze speaking situations when they make decisions about their appearance for important speeches. A governor eating chicken and politicking for votes at the local county fair may wear blue jeans and suspenders. Yet the same governor will probably choose a conservative suit with red, white, and blue accessories for the inaugural address at the state capitol.

At the beginning of the O. J. Simpson murder case, prosecuting attorney Marcia Clark appeared in court each day with a distinctive, curly hairstyle. At the midpoint of the trial, however, Ms. Clark had a makeover, transforming her hairdo into a darker, straighter style. Some legal analysts suggested that it might have been unwise for the prosecutor to modify her appearance during the course of the trial because the change could have negatively affected the relationship between the attorney and the jurors.[12]

You create a positive impression when you dress appropriately for the audience, the occasion, and the topic. Avoid distracting styles: straps that fall down, skirts that ride up, jewelry that dangles noisily, hair that hides eyes or face, shoes that skid or squeak. An appropriate appearance—neat, clean, neither too formal nor too casual—lets the audience know that you care about the speech and that the occasion is important to you.

Gestures

Enhance your speeches by using *gestures* to emphasize words or phrases, to describe physical objects or events, and to point out directions or locations. In the early part of this century there was an emphasis on elocutionary speaking, which involved the study of vocal production and gesturing in speech delivery. Speakers practiced complicated vocal exercises and studied manuals containing illustrations and definitions of gestures. From this analysis, speakers learned to project their voices in large assembly halls and to use gestures forcefully in their presentations. In the early twentieth century, William Jennings Bryan, Teddy Roosevelt, and Robert La Follette were prominent elocutionists whose booming voices and animated delivery influenced millions of Americans.

Although these speakers were effective in their era, their speeches would seem overdone today. Radio, television, and microphones have enabled speakers to be more conversational and to use more descriptive gestures in speech delivery. Modern speech educators feel gestures should be spontaneous and reflective of an individual's feelings and energies.

While it's not advisable to memorize gestures like some of the elocutionists, you can increase the effectiveness of your gestures through practice. Successful gestures are precise and punctuate your words and ideas clearly. Think of the varieties of gestures you might need to describe tying a shoelace or giving directions to your home.

Beginning speakers are sometimes afraid to use gestures in their presentations. They often stand with their arms stiffly at their sides, clasped behind or in front of them, or resting rigidly on the speaking lectern. If you make a conscious effort, you will find that gestures can help you work out some of your nervous energy in a speech. Don't let yourself be controlled by nervous mannerisms such as distracting hand, arm, or body movements. Show enthusiasm and project confidence to your audience by using gestures to punctuate ideas and to describe objects and concepts.

Facial Expression

Many of us will remember the news accounts showing the senseless bombing that occurred at the Murrah federal building in Oklahoma City several years ago. The tragic image that remains in the memories of many Americans is a picture of a fireman cradling the lifeless body of a little boy who was killed in the blast. The facial expression of the fireman conveyed the feelings of compassion, tenderness, and heartbreak felt by the citizens of Oklahoma City and those watching across the country. No words were needed to describe the picture; the image alone expressed the power and the agony of the moment.

Each of us has an extraordinary set of muscles in our faces that can express a silent picture. We can smile, frown, show sadness and anger, or convey love and joy. Our *facial expressions* help to reinforce our words. If you were to say "I love you," and show anger in your expression, your listener would either be confused or interpret the message negatively. If you had a blank facial expression, your listener might wonder if you had any feelings of love at all. A student presenting a speech about the importance of seatbelts smiled broadly as he said: "If you were involved in a traffic accident and you didn't wear your seatbelt, you might die!" The audience didn't take the speaker seriously, because his facial expression wasn't appropriate.

Your facial expression should clearly support your verbal message. If you talk about parental kidnapping, your expression should reflect anger and concern; if your topic is space exploration, your face should convey adventure and curiosity; if you are speaking about chronic illness, your face should show empathy and hope. Your facial expressions cannot be mechanically planned in advance. Like gestures, they should be spontaneous and reflect your natural feelings. Practice your speech in front of a friend or, if possible, a video camera to get some clues about your expressions and determine if they support your verbal messages. A speaker who projects emotion about a topic through facial expression will tend to receive a similar emotional response from the audience.

Body Position and Movement

Your stance, posture, poise, and *body movement* can also contribute to your communication. An individual who has good posture appears to be more prepared than a speaker who slouches or leans on the lectern. Standing on both feet gives a speaker greater stability than shifting from one leg to another. Good posture also allows a speaker to breathe more effectively to produce sound.

A student was in the process of presenting an informative speech about learning disabilities. She had researched the topic well, and she had found a number of interesting examples, statistics, and testimonies to support her main points. During her speech, however, she would wrap one leg around the other the way a contortionist does at the circus. The audience was fascinated as they watched her legs tangle and unwind. It's obvious, of course, that the awkward body movement was a distraction that kept the audience from hearing the speech.

It's good speech practice to develop posture that is both relaxed and erect. Practice using your stance and body position to your advantage. A tall speaker with good posture can use height as an added means of persuasion. A short speaker can stand beside the lectern and develop greater intimacy with the audience. Be sure that your stance and posture add to your presentation and do not interfere with the message.

When you become a confident public speaker, you can develop some variations in body movement to emphasize the transitions in your speech. Here are some suggestions:

Specific purpose: To inform the audience about dyslexia

Thesis statement: Dyslexia has a several causes and effects that can be described in a case study.

BODY

SUGGESTED MOVEMENT

I. Causes of dyslexia
   Transition line 1: "I've just told you about some of the major causes of dyslexia; now I want to go into some of its effects on children."

Move to right of lectern

II. Effects of the learning disability
    Transition line 2: "Now that I've considered some of the effects, let me tell you a personal experience that happened to my family."

Move in front of lectern

III. Case study of dyslexia

In this presentation, the speaker begins the introduction and numeral I of the body standing behind the speaker's lectern. When transition line 1 is stated, the speaker moves to the right of the lectern, reinforcing the change in thoughts. Again, when transition line 2 is delivered, the speaker moves in front of the lectern, standing closer to the audience. This final action not only supports the change in ideas but also establishes greater intimacy with listeners during the presentation of the personal experience.

You may want to gain some confidence behind the speaker's lectern before you try some of these suggestions; experiment with body movement when you become comfortable with your audience.

Culture and Nonverbal Delivery

You can see that the nonverbal aspects of delivery can enhance and support a speaker's message. Although gestures, eye contact, facial expression, appearance, and body movement are important elements in presenting public speeches, we do not all use and interpret these symbols in the same way. Nonverbal messages can vary widely depending on our *culture and background.* A Caucasian American might look directly into the eyes to establish solid visual contact with listeners. But a speaker from Japan, China, or India might find such directness inappropriate, preferring instead to use only brief, peripheral glances. Even some Native American

Cultures teach individuals to use nonverbal "language" uniquely. A listener must remember to keep an open mind when encountering differences in a speaker's gestures, expressions, or other nonverbal symbols.

© *Joel Gordon*

Indian cultures interpret direct eye contact as rude or offensive.[13] A speaker from Southern Europe, Africa, the Middle East, or Latin America might decide to make a point by moving extremely close to the audience, showering listeners with a liberal supply of mouth spray. To many Americans, however, this behavior would be considered intrusive and a violation of "personal space."

Americans use the rounded "O" formed with the thumb and index finger to signify that something is "OK." But a similar gesture made by a French speaker indicates that the object under discussion is worth a zero, and the gesture to many Latin Americans is obscene. In the United States, nodding the head up and down conveys a "yes" response of agreement, but in Greece or Turkey the movement means "no." American women enjoy a great deal of flexibility in dress and appearance, but many women in the Middle East are expected to have the body, limbs, and head completely covered. In Indonesia, a speaker would not show or point the soles of the shoes to a listener because the action would signal that the listener is beneath or inferior to the speaker.[14]

Upon hearing this classroom discussion about cultural differences in nonverbal communication, one student commented humorously, "Does this mean that we should be careful not to point our shoes at listeners when we deliver our speeches?" Well not exactly, but the discussion does imply that both speakers and audiences need to make significant efforts to understand the differences in culture and be more aware of how these differences influence the speaking message or audience response. When you listen to someone from another culture, avoid making quick decisions about the individual's nonverbal "language." Take time to observe a speaker's stance and body movements. Is the speaker from a culture where there is little need for personal space, and does the speaker have less concern about "being too close" than do members of the audience? Understand differences that occur in appearance. Does the speaker wear a "sari" or apply facial dots and other markings to indicate a distinct tribe, caste, or family classification? Also notice variations in eye contact and facial expressions. Is the speaker from a culture where direct eye contact and animated facial expressions are avoided, or is the speaker accustomed to showing facial expressions and looking at listeners in a straightforward manner? In addition, notice how culture influences the speaker's gestures. Fiorello La Guardia was New York City's colorful mayor from 1934 to 1945. As a fluent speaker of three languages, La Guardia was a skillful politician. When campaigning for office in his native Italian, La Guardia used a particular set of gestures. Yet when he spoke in English, the mayor employed other gestures, and when he spoke to Yiddish audiences, he used another set of actions to support his speeches.[15] Recognize that cultures teach individuals to use gestures differently and employ codes or emblems uniquely. In some cultures gestures may be animated and energetic while in others physical actions may be much more restrained.

When you encounter different nonverbal languages, avoid making snap judgments that categorize the behavior as "right" or "wrong." Observe the behavior and make determined efforts to understand the cultural differences by keeping an open mind. If you are uncertain or confused about nonverbal symbols, don't be afraid to ask questions of the speaker and audience. Remember that your objective is to understand and interpret the differences in culture so that you can convey your thoughts, ideas, and feelings with clarity, sensitivity, and efficiency.

Gender and Nonverbal Delivery

In American society, there have been tremendous changes in the roles of men and women in recent decades. As we saw in chapter 3, occupations that were once viewed as only "men's" or "women's" jobs are now frequently assumed by the other *gender*. Even though occupational roles may have changed, women and men still exhibit more traditional differences in their nonverbal communication patterns. Women tend to be more expressive in their gestures than men. Women are more touch-oriented and show more emotion such as sadness or fear in facial expression and in the eyes. Women maintain more fixed eye contact and stand physically closer to each other than men. In addition, it is more permissible for an American woman to touch or hug another woman than for a man to hug another male. A study at the University of Pennsylvania indicates that women are able to interpret nonverbal language cues more effectively than males and read facial expressions such as anger, sadness, and fear more quickly.[16] Although women are often rewarded for showing positive emotions such as smiling, they are not encouraged to display strong or forceful displeasure and often mask their anger with tears. For women, crying is seen as appropriate and anger is interpreted as "unladylike."[17]

Men, on the other hand, tend to use more powerful and forceful nonverbal cues to support their language. Masculine gestures are larger and occupy more space and territory. Even though they are not allowed to show as much sadness or fear as women, men are given more latitude in expressing hostility and aggression, often using anger to mask pain and sorrow. Indeed, men are able to read facial expressions that indicate disgust or dislike more easily than other emotions. For males, crying is considered "unmanly," while facial restraint is thought to be more acceptable. Men stand farther apart from each other but are permitted to stand much closer to the opposite gender. Unlike women, men are permitted much less physical contact with members of the same sex. Physical contact with other men usually appears as aggressive touch like handshaking, playful jabbing, or backslapping and occurs within activities that have well-defined boundaries such as sports, occupations, or partying. In the area of male-female relationships, men are still regarded as the initiators of touch, and women are expected to be the responders.

So what can we learn about our differences? First of all, it is helpful if we don't overgeneralize about the nonverbal cues we perceive. Listeners should take time to observe patterns of behavior and interpret nonverbal expressions and gestures in context. The behavior we see may have nothing to do with gender. A woman presenting a speech with a constant smile could be experiencing speech anxiety, or a man who frequently pounds the lectern with his hand could simply have an annoying mannerism. Recognize that differences due to gender represent generalizations and should not be viewed as finalized conclusions because there are always exceptions. A female speaker can show strong anger to support a message, and a male is capable of expressive gestures. Also remember that nonverbal speaking actions can be influenced by numerous elements such as the audience-speaker relationship, the topic, or the situation. A man delivering a speech to a lifeless audience may need to use a wide variety of facial expressions, gestures, and body movements to energize listeners. A woman presenting a speech on a highly controversial issue may want to use restrained expressions for a more rational approach to the topic. A speaker delivering a presentation to a large audience may need to use more expansive gestures, and a speaker lecturing to a small group could be more subtle. Remember that effective speakers, whether men or women, should adopt styles that are relevant to the needs and requirements of particular speaking situations. Try not to read too much into a speaker's every gesture, expression, or action, and avoid interpreting nonverbal cues in isolation. Recognize that men and women can complement each other's nonverbal behavior and provide different perspectives that enrich and enlighten the listener. Above all, learn to enjoy the subtleties and nuances of nonverbal behavior and be cautious when making judgments and observations.[18]

COMBINING VOCAL AND VISUAL DELIVERY

Vocal and visual delivery are combined in the enthusiasm and vitality that a speaker projects to an audience. An enthusiastic speaker uses vocal inflection, volume, pauses, eye contact, gestures, and facial expressions to convey a feeling of involvement in his or her topic. Audience members experience the speaker's energy visually and verbally and think "This person really cares about the topic—I'd better listen."

*Effective skills in vocal
and visual delivery allow
a speaker to pro-
ject ideas with clarity,
passion, and style.*

© *Hal Rummel Photography*

In the second 1992 presidential debate, a voter asked how the national debt had personally affected the lives of each candidate. President Bush's stumbling response included the comment, "I'm not sure I get it." This reaction demonstrated the President's difficulty in communicating his concern about the economic hardships suffered by many Americans. By contrast, Governor Clinton used facial expression, body movement, and gestures to convey his emotional response: "In my state when people lose their jobs, there's a good chance that I'll know them by their names." An individual does not have to be a vibrant public speaker in order to be president, of course. America has had many presidents who have not been effective speakers, including Calvin Coolidge, Lyndon Johnson, Richard Nixon, and Jimmy Carter. However, some of our strongest leaders have been dynamic public speakers—among them are Teddy Roosevelt, Franklin Roosevelt, John F. Kennedy, and Ronald Reagan.

To be successful in a speech, show that you care about the topic. Employ good eye contact with the audience; use your facial muscles to show appropriate emotion; alter your pitch for vocal variety and adjust your volume, rate, and phrasing for emphasis; use gestures to reinforce your ideas, and reflect your commitment in your appearance. Combine all of the vocal and visual aspects of delivery into a speaking performance that is enthusiastic and energetic.

BUILDING SKILLS IN DELIVERY

Here are a few suggestions to help you develop your skills in speech delivery.

Know Your Material

One of the first principles of an effective delivery is to be knowledgeable about your material. Your research should be thorough, your sources should be credible, and your understanding of the topic should be extensive. Know how to pronounce difficult names, terms, or concepts, and be familiar with your supporting materials. One key to a successful delivery is confidence in your material, which can free you to relay the topic to your audience.

Be Well Organized

You need a good outline written on notecards to deliver a speech effectively. Make sure the outline is clear and complete. Know exactly how you are going to begin and end the speech. Be certain that your specific purpose is defined and that the main points of the body are identifiable. Check your notecards for ease in reading. Write large enough to see comfortably, and double-space between phrases and sentences. Number your notecards at the upper corner to keep them in the proper order.

Mark Your Notes

A high school instructor marked his lecture notes with phrases like "insert joke here," "use gesture now," or "show grimace." While this type of preparation can be helpful, it might promote a memorized or mechanical delivery. We don't suggest that you plan every detail of your delivery, but we recommend that you develop your own system of marking to indicate areas of verbal and visual emphasis. Use a simple system of underlining, circling, and arrows similar to this example.

We need to do something <u>now</u> about this problem. If we don't stop dumping in our oceans, <u>there</u> <u>won't</u> <u>be</u> any more beautiful beaches, <u>there</u> <u>won't</u> <u>be</u> any more coral reefs, and <u>there</u> <u>won't</u> <u>be</u> any more deep-sea fishing. We've got to get Congress to enact strict laws with
STRONG EMPHASIS
severe penalties that deter hospitals, cities, states, and corporations from dicarding their posionous wastes into the sea. [Our oceans are
SOFTLY
a fragile part of the ecological system.] We can preserve them for
                                                    PAUSE   PAUSE
ourselves and our children,∧or we can <u>destroy</u> them∧<u>forever</u>. [Think
SLOWLY
about it. What will your choice be?]

Here just a few lines and circles indicate emphasis, and some slanting lines and arrows show increasing rate and volume. You don't need complicated notations. You merely need to be consistent in order to translate your markings into effective gestures, expressions, and verbal emphasis.

Practice the Delivery

When you have organized your material and you know what you want to emphasize, practice the speech several times. Whenever possible, it is helpful to practice in an environment similar to your speech setting. Stand behind a speaker's lectern so that you can rest your notecards and practice some gestures. Rehearse the speech aloud and work on your vocal inflections, volume, articulation, and speaking rate. Rehearse your phrasing to develop pauses between the appropriate thought groupings. If you have a tape recorder, use it in your practice sessions. Replaying the speech can help you to evaluate your vocal delivery and detect vocalized pauses, improper pronunciation, and monotonous pitch.

It is also helpful if you can practice your speech in front of a friend or video camera. You can determine the success of your eye contact, facial expressions, gestures, and body movement as you deliver the presentation. Notice how often you need to look at your cards and how comfortably you manage your notes. Try to develop a visual delivery that reinforces every aspect of your material.

Situations frequently arise where speakers cannot engage in practice sessions. Executives, physicians, and business or sales people are often too busy with scheduled appointments to devote time for speech rehearsal. In such cases, it is helpful to have a "think through" session on the corporate jet or in the car on the way to the speech setting. In these brief sessions, the speaker can mentally review the main points of the presentation or jot down a few notes on a legal pad to organize the thought process.

Whether you have a "think through" session or a formal rehearsal, work to project enthusiasm and confidence during the speech. While it is appropriate to use your prepared notes, know your material well enough to maintain eye contact with your listeners without reading word for word. Concentrate on your ideas and be natural and spontaneous. Your goal is to refine all of the elements of your delivery into a smooth, unified presentation.

SUMMARY

In this chapter we have described proper breathing practices needed for an effective vocal delivery. We have also described the aspects of vocal delivery: volume, articulation, pitch, quality, pronunciation, pauses, including dramatic pauses and vocalized pauses, emphasis, and phrasing. In addition to vocal aspects, we've stressed the importance of the visual or nonverbal aspects of delivery. A good speaker maintains eye contact with the audience, dresses appropriately for the audience, speech, and occasion, and uses gestures, facial expressions, and body movement. Listeners need to recognize that differences in culture and gender can influence the nonverbal behaviors of speakers. It is important to observe a speaker carefully and avoid making snap judgments about nonverbal delivery. When you combine all aspects of delivery, you should project enthusiasm, and vitality. Four simple guidelines to help you develop delivery skills are: (1) know your material, (2) be well organized, (3) mark your notes, and (4) practice the delivery.

SKILL BUILDERS

1. Choose a selection from a favorite piece of literature such as a lyric from a song, a poem, or a prose selection and develop a one- to two-minute reading for class. Work on your vocal and visual expression, emphasis, eye contact, and gesture. Practice the selection aloud several times. Experiment with various interpretations until you feel your reading reflects the author's intended meaning.

2. Choose a situation for a two- to three-minute pantomime. Develop your facial expressions, gestures, and body movements to portray the details of the experience. Communicate all of the elements of the pantomime without props. Here are some ideas for pantomimes.

> Visiting the dentist
>
> Getting stuck in an elevator
>
> Washing windows on a skyscraper
>
> Doing acrobatics in an airplane
>
> Styling hair at a unisex shop
>
> Applying make-up
>
> Receiving an Olympic gold medal
>
> Driving a small car on a busy freeway
>
> Getting a ticket from a police officer
>
> Participating in a drug bust
>
> Walking an unruly dog
>
> Toilet training a child

3. Divide your class into several groups containing 4 or 5 members. Identify the specific cultural and/or geographical differences among group members and discuss how these differences could influence speaking delivery. Describe how these differences could affect listeners' reaction to speeches.

N O T E S

1. For this section on the production of sound, we used five sources that you can consult for more detailed information: (1) Virgil A. Anderson, *Training the Speaking Voice* (New York: Oxford University Press, 1961), pp. 21–54; (2) Jon Eisenson, *Improvement of Voice and Diction,* 2d ed. (New York: Macmillan, 1965), pp. 15–41; (3) Hilda B. Fisher, *Improving Voice and Articulation,* 2nd ed. (Boston: Houghton Mifflin, 1975), pp. 3–23, and 87–104; (4) Giles Wilkeson Gray and Claude Merton Wise, *The Bases of Speech,* 3d ed. (New York: Harper and Row, 1959), pp. 135–199; and (5) Arthur Lessac, *The Use and Training of the Human Voice,* 2d ed. (New York: Drama Book Specialists, 1967), pp. 9–16.

2. These exercises were selected from Eisenson's *The Improvement of Voice and Diction,* p. 45–47.

3. Fisher, *Improving Voice and Articulation,* p. 3–35. We have based our definitions of vocal delivery upon Hilda Fisher's definitions, which she provides in chapter 1 of her text.

4. "The Art of Being Fully Human," Public Broadcasting Company Video, Washington D.C., 1980.

5. This exercise is drawn from a longer list of words provided in Anderson, *Training the Speaking Voice,* p. 405.

6. Fisher, *Improving Voice and Articulation,* p. 67. Hilda Fisher recommends exercises that help the muscles of the larynx to relax. If you have some concerns about the quality of your voice, try some of the exercises she suggests on pp. 64 to 72.

7. Charles R. Petrie Jr., "Informative Speaking: A Summary and Bibliography of Related Research," *Speech Monographs* 30 (June 1963), p. 81.

8. Carley H. Dodd, *Dynamics of Intercultural Communication,* 4th. ed. (Dubuque: Wm. C. Brown Publishers, 1995), p. 199.

9. Shelly Chaiken, "Communicator Physical Attractiveness and Persuasion," *Journal of Personality and Social Psychology* 37 (August 25, 1978) pp. 1387–1397. This article contains some interesting research about the impact of physical attractiveness on persuasion. The author concludes that "The present research indicates that physical attractiveness can significantly enhance communicator persuasiveness." (p. 1394).

10. Ibid., p. 82.

11. Example based upon a speech delivered by Marie E. Miller, Catonsville Community College, Catonsville, MD, 1988. Used by permission.

12. See Lorraine Adams, "The Fight of Her Life; Marcia Clark—Working Mother and O. J. Simpson's Lead Prosecutor—Takes Her Place Among Other Maligned, Adored and Misunderstood Modern Women," *The Washington Post,* August 20, 1995, sec. F, p. 1.

13. Ronald B. Adler, Lawrence B. Rosenfeld, and Neil Towne, *Interplay: The Process of Interpersonal Communication,* 6th ed. (Fort Worth: Harcourt Brace College Publishers, 1995), p. 395.

14. For this discussion we selected several examples from these sources: Roy M. Berko, Andrew D. Wolvin, and Darlyn R. Wolvin, *Communicating: A Social and Career Focus,* 3rd. ed. (Boston: Houghton Mifflin Company, 1995), p. 158; Carley H. Dodd, *Dynamics of Intercultural Communication,* 4th. ed. (Dubuque: Wm. C. Brown Publishers, 1995), p. 156, 175; and Joseph A. DeVito, *Messages: Building Interpersonal Communication Skills,* 2nd ed. (New York: HarperCollins College Publishers, 1993), p. 143.

15. Berko and others, *Communicating,* p. 156.

16. Merrill McLoughlin, Tracy L. Shryer, Erica E. Goode, and Kathleen McAuliffe, "Attitude: In Politics and Management, the 'Gender Gap' is Real," *U.S. News & World Report,* August 8, 1988, p. 56.

17. For this comparison and contrast about gender differences in nonverbal behavior we used these sources: Laurie P. Arliss, *Gender Communication* (Englewood Cliffs: Prentice Hall, 1991), pp. 75–90; Sarah Trenholm and Arthur Jensen, *Interpersonal Communication,* 3rd ed. (Belmont: Wadsworth Publishing Co., 1996), pp. 195–196; and Richard L. Weaver, *Understanding Interpersonal Communication,* 5th ed. (Glenview: Scott, Foresman and Company, 1990), p. 219.

18. Weaver, *Understanding Interpersonal Communication,* pp. 175, 219–220.

Considering Different Types of Structures

Topic ┈┈► Purpose ┈┈┈┈┈► Thesis

┈► Research ┈┈┈► Outline ┈┈┈

Audience ┈┈► Ethics

Practice

Prepare

Chapter 15

SPEAKING TO INFORM

*The best way to send
information is to wrap it
up in a person.*

   Robert Oppenheimer

CHAPTER OBJECTIVES

After reading this chapter you will be able to:

1. Recognize the difference between information and persuasion;

2. Describe several types of informative speeches;

3. Know how to build a descriptive speech;

4. Be able to analyze an informative speech;

5. Be able to present an informative speech.

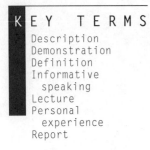

KEY TERMS

Description
Demonstration
Definition
Informative
    speaking
Lecture
Personal
    experience
Report

In this age of information, it would seem that technology rules. Travelers order airline tickets online; a Wall Street broker makes a multimillion-dollar deal from his cell phone in a restaurant; a neurosurgeon in a distant hospital provides a comprehensive diagnosis over a satellite downlink; an executive connects her laptop to the electrical outlet in her car to download office e-mail; an eighth grade class participates in live chat over the Internet with an astronaut aboard the space shuttle; the rental car driver in an unfamiliar city obeys the electronic map directions from the global positioning satellite system. Although computers, the Internet, and other machinery of the technology age contribute to our lives, they are only tools in transporting information. It is still up to human beings to research, analyze, evaluate, organize, and present information effectively—even in the computer age. When the ATM doesn't work, the cell phone breaks up, or the network servers are down, it is the human being who must exercise and maintain control of the process, relying on the human mechanism for interpreting and conveying information.

Communicating in the information age isn't easy—there is an art to being clear, accurate, and concrete. This first chapter of Unit Five helps you develop your informative speaking skills. We'll examine the difference between information and persuasion, consider several categories of informative speeches, and present some guidelines to help you build the informative descriptive speech. We also provide an analysis sheet to help you evaluate an informative presentation.

THE DIFFERENCE BETWEEN
INFORMATION AND PERSUASION

As you begin to build your speech to inform, clearly recognize the difference between information and persuasion. Some rhetoricians agree with Aristotle that all speaking is persuasive; speeches differ only in the relative strength and weakness of the persuasion. This text, however, draws a distinction between communication that is informative and communication that is persuasive.[1]

Overall, an informative speech promotes understanding, enlightenment, and education about a topic; a persuasive speech seeks to influence and alter the beliefs, feelings, or behavior of listeners. Specifically, speeches to inform can be grouped into the following categories: description, demonstration or process, definition, personal experience, the report, and the lecture.

We've listed three topics below and indicated how the specific purpose sentences would be phrased as informative and persuasive presentations.

TOPICS TO INFORM	TOPICS TO PERSUADE
To define "militia groups"	To convince the audience that militia groups are potentially dangerous to the American constitutional system
To provide a profile of a troubled teenage killer	To convince the audience that juveniles who commit violent acts in public schools should be tried as adults
To explain the process of interviewing sexually abused children for courtroom testimony	To actuate the audience to support efforts to change courtroom procedures for child witnesses

The topics on the left generally provide information on an issue, while the topics at the right seek to influence the audience to agree with the speaker's point of view. In the list of informative topics, "militia groups" would be considered a speech of definition, "profile of a teenage killer" would be a descriptive speech, and "interviewing sexually abused children" would be considered a process speech.

Some communication specialists feel that informative speeches are "factual" while persuasive speeches are more "emotional."[2] We would like to caution you, however, about making this distinction. It is true that informative speeches can contain supporting materials such as statistics, surveys, or polls, and visual materials such as graphs, maps, and charts. However, informative speeches should also incorporate emotional elements such as personal experiences, illustrations, and examples that interest the audience. While persuasive speeches should make use of strong emotional appeals, persuasive speeches should also be grounded in supporting evidence that incorporates sound logic and fact. Recognize also that speeches are not always strictly informative or persuasive.

Informative presentations often contain elements of persuasion, which modify the thinking or behavior of listeners over a period of time. In persuasion, speakers often include large portions of informative material to educate and enlighten listeners before asking them to change attitudes or take action. Speeches frequently exist on an informative–persuasive continuum, with some presentations clustering around the informative end, and others tending towards the persuasive.

Up to this point we've been talking about defining informative speeches in terms of the topic. There are also times when the audience will determine whether a topic is informative or persuasive. For example, after conducting careful research, you present an informative speech with the stated intention "to acquaint the audience with some interesting biographical data about Candidate X," a Democrat. Your listeners, however, might have different ideas. If the audience consisted of either Republicans or Democrats who favored other candidates, they might feel that your speech was subtly persuasive rather than informative.

TYPES OF INFORMATIVE SPEECHES

In this chapter, we will consider three categories of information: (1) description, (2) definition, and (3) reports, lectures, and personal experiences. A fourth informative type, the demonstration speech, will be presented in chapter 16.

The Descriptive Speech

In *descriptive* presentations, speakers choose topics related to persons, places, objects, or events. Under *objects* we are including both the animate and inanimate, and we are defining an event as an incident or occurrence. Here are a number of examples in each area:

Informative speeches can educate and enlighten listeners about places, persons, objects, or events.

PERSON(S)

To describe the personal life of J. S. Bach

To describe the feats of Wimbledon tennis champion Lindsay Davenport

To describe the culture of the Eskimo

To describe the accomplishments of Susan B. Anthony

PLACE(S)

To describe Walt Disney's-MGM studios

To describe the Baseball Hall of Fame

To describe Mackinac Island, Michigan

To describe life in Japan

To describe the largest mall in America

To describe the planet Venus

OBJECT(S)

To describe the European Chunnel

To describe the relationship of color and personality

To describe the Statue of Liberty

To describe the history of trademarks

To describe killer wasps

To describe the wonderful, wily cat

To describe repetitive stress injuries

EVENT(S)

To inform an audience about the possibility of peace in Northern Ireland

To inform an audience about the atrocities in Kosovo

To inform an audience about radon gas

To inform an audience about the effects of a hurricane in North Carolina

To inform an audience about drug education programs

To inform an audience about unusual advertising feats

To describe the benefits of the Special Olympics

BUILDING THE DESCRIPTIVE SPEECH

Since a descriptive speech is one of the major types you will probably deliver in your speech course, here are some specific guidelines to help you build this presentation.

1. **Choose an interesting topic.**
   a. Choose an innovative topic providing new information.
   b. Select a topic that is interesting to you, the speaker.
   c. Examine your personal interests, experiences, and knowledge.
   d. Avoid repeating information the audience already knows.
   e. Choose a topic that is appropriate to listeners.

2. **Conduct careful research.**
   a. Review personal experience for primary source material.
   b. Use sources that are accurate, reliable, and up-to-date.
   c. Avoid sources lacking in credibility such as "house and garden" or condensed magazines for medical or scientific facts.
   d. Conduct interviews with experts.
   e. Build credibility with accurate examples, statistics, testimony, and audiovisual aids.
   f. Check details such as events, numbers, dates, and quotations for precision and accuracy.

3. **Organize the speech in a logical sequence.**
   a. Develop a creative introduction with a clear thesis identifying the main points in the body.
   b. Choose an organizational plan appropriate to the topic.
      (1) Use external transitions to emphasize major headings.
      (2) Employ internal transitions to link supporting ideas.
   c. Construct an interesting conclusion conveying finality.
      (1) Choose a poem, quotation, or example that resolves or summarizes the topic.
      (2) Avoid providing new information during the conclusion.

AN EXAMPLE

In the following example, the speaker attempts to describe some of the highlights of Mexico City with mediocre results:

> Mexico City is a huge city in the mountains inhabited by millions of people. The city contains artifacts dating back to the ancient Aztecs, buildings constructed by the Spaniards, and structures which reflect modern Mexico.

4. **Employ vivid language.**
   a. Use clear, colorful, connotative language.
   b. Employ images that evoke mental pictures and appeal to the senses.
   c. Avoid trite phrases or vague jargon such as "to each his own," or "stuff like that."

5. **Use concrete supporting materials.**
   a. Humanize the topic with realistic supporting materials.
   b. Round off statistics for easy comprehension.
   c. Employ colorful quotations.
   d. Avoid stringing together lists of statistics or hard facts.
   e. Use audiovisual aids for variety and interest.

6. **Develop a clear, personal delivery.**
   a. Pronounce difficult names and technical terms correctly.
   b. Define unfamiliar words or phrases.
   c. Avoid extensive technical terminology, using words and phrases that listeners understand.
   d. Maintain eye contact with the audience.
   e. Use personal pronouns such as "you," "we," and "us," to include listeners.
   f. Be conversational, use extemporaneous delivery, and avoid reading word-for-word.
   g. Make effective use of your eyes, face, hands, and voice.
   h. Stimulate feedback by using humor, asking rhetorical or open-ended questions, and employing emotion.
   i. Be sensitive to audience feedback, making minor adjustments to content or delivery based upon audience response.
   j. Practice the speech to gain confidence.

In this example, terminology is only denotative. Words such as "huge," "artifacts," "buildings," or "structures" do not create mental images. The speaker employs vague generalities and uses no concrete supporting materials. This description will have little impact; the speaker has lost a wonderful opportunity to arouse interest. Notice the improvement:

> In today's Mexico City, you can sample a tasty enchilada made with white cheese; feel the rough chisel marks of an ancient Aztec pyramid; take a

leisurely stroll through the cool green palms and curving lakes of Chapultepec Park; experience the excitement of the clubs, cabarets, and outdoor cafes in the Zona Rosa; browse through shops filled with mounds of solid silver jewelry; contemplate the classic beauty of the oldest Spanish church in the Americas; navigate the flowered canals of the Xochimilco; and dance to the melodies of a hundred Mariachi groups in Garibaldi Square.

This description is effective because the words are connotative, and the speaker uses numerous sensory examples as supporting materials. Vivid language such as "tasty enchilada," "rough chisel marks," "flowered canals," and action words such as "feel," "sample," "navigate," and "dance" invite listeners to participate with all their senses. Words that identify objects in terms of color ("white cheese," "green palms"), shape ("curving lakes"), and size ("mounds of . . . silver") add to the visual imagery. Notice the foreign names that the speaker needs to pronounce correctly. The speaker has successfully created a variety of mental images.

OUTLINING THE DESCRIPTIVE SPEECH

When you develop the outline for the descriptive speech, you should follow the organizational principles suggested in chapter 10. Remember that the main points of the body should be arranged according to chronology, space, cause-effect, topic, or a combination of sequences. Here are three examples that show how these sequences can be combined.

Effective speakers convey information with clarity and precision.

In the following descriptive topic, the speaker combines chronological with spatial order:

Specific purpose: To describe the Baseball Hall of Fame at Cooperstown, New York

Thesis statement: The Baseball Hall of Fame has a unique history, and exhibits in the first, second, and third floors, which preserve the history of baseball for posterity.

BODY

I. Brief history of museum
II. First floor Hall of Fame gallery
III. Second floor history sections
IV. Third floor rooms of memorabilia

Notice that subheadings under I would be arranged according to order of events and that II through IV are arranged according to location of rooms in the museum.

In the next example, the speaker has organized main points using a combination of chronological and topic sequence:

Specific purpose: To describe the wonderful, wily cat

Thesis statement: Cats were respected in Egyptian times and feared in the Middle Ages; they are equipped for savage battle, yet make loving members of any family.

BODY

I. Cats in Egyptian times
II. Cats in the Middle Ages
III. Cats as hunters
IV. Cats as pets

The speaker uses chronology for the history in I and II then incorporates a topical sequence for the last two headings.

In the next example, the speaker combines topic with cause-effect sequence:

Specific purpose: To inform you about the dangers of steroids

Thesis statement: I want to provide an explanation of steroids, describe their intended purpose, and identify their desired effects as well as their damaging consequences.

BODY

I. General explanation of steroids
II. Intended purpose of steroids

III. Desired effects

IV. Damaging consequences

Numerals I and II are arranged in topic sequence, while III and IV characterize the issue in terms of its effects.

The Speech of Definition

In a speech of *definition,* you inform your audience about a philosophical concept such as a theory or idea, or a more concrete subject like a science or art:

SCIENCE OR ART

What is cryonics?

What is electronic music?

What is impressionistic art?

What is a phobia?

What is Romantic music?

What is vegetarianism?

THEORIES OR IDEAS

What is "ethnic cleansing"?

What is Basque separatism?

What is Shi'ite Islam?

What is evolutionism?

What is creationism?

What is libertarianism?

With any of these topics, the thrust of your information would be to explain the meaning of an unknown term to your audience. When defining such terms, follow guidelines suggested for the descriptive speech. Be concrete and accurate, use plenty of supporting materials, and work to maintain the interest of your audience. Remember that definitional speeches are not simply intellectual explanations of dry theories or complex subject matter; these speeches must be just as creative and alive as any other informative presentation.

Here are two structural examples of speeches defining terms. The first example uses chronological sequence; the second employs topical order.

EXAMPLE 1: CHRONOLOGICAL SEQUENCE

Specific purpose: To define Shi'ite Islam

Thesis statement: Shi'ite Islam is a religion having it origins in the Middle Ages and exhibiting specific characteristics today.

BODY

I. Shi'ite Islam in the Middle Ages
II. Characteristics of the movement today

EXAMPLE 2: TOPICAL SEQUENCE

Specific purpose: To define the term "vegetarian"

Thesis statement: Vegetarianism is a dietary practice that includes vegans as well as lacto-ovo-vegetarians, and has clear advantages as well as disadvantages.

BODY

I. Vegans—eliminating all animal foods
II. Lacto-ovo-vegetarians—using eggs and dairy products
III. Advantages of the vegetarian diet
IV. Disadvantages of the vegetarian diet

Notice that the Shi'ite Islam speech is organized according to chronology, and that the one on vegetarianism is structured according to the natural headings reflected in the research.

In these topics, speakers can motivate listeners by using effective supporting materials. A presentation on Shi'ite Islam could incorporate visual aids and examples relating to current events taking place in revolutionary Iran and other Middle Eastern countries. A speech about vegetarianism could relate the topic to the physical health and welfare of listeners. In both topics, speakers can provide new, interesting, and helpful information to members of their audiences.

Other Informative Types: Reports, Lectures, and Personal Experience

The *report* is often required in business or industry. You may already have had to present reports to supervisors, committees, or clients. In this important speech the quality of your presentation can improve or hinder your chances for success. Topics for reports are usually based on limited issues such as "the decrease in sales for the third quarter," "decisions of the search committee," or "marketing committee actions."

ANALYSIS SHEET FOR THE INFORMATIVE SPEECH

Introduction
Curiosity Device

Did the speech contain an effective device for building curiosity such as a case study, question, or shocking statement?

Did the end of the introduction contain a clear specific purpose and/or thesis statement?

Content
Topic

Was the topic sufficiently limited and innovative?

Was the topic appropriate and interesting to the audience?

Organization

Were main headings and supporting points structured in a clear, logical, and interesting manner?

Were main headings thoroughly developed?

Accuracy

Was the information accurate, up-to-date, and verified by credible sources?

Supporting Materials

Did the speech contain a variety of clear, concrete, and creative supporting materials—examples, statistics, quotations, audiovisuals?

Delivery
Language

Did the speaker use connotative words and vivid language to create mental images?

Was the speaker's language appropriate to the topic?

Did the speaker's language reflect good English usage?

Clarity

Did the speaker use external transitions to "flag" main points, and internal transitions to connect subordinate points?

Did the speaker adhere to the topic and keep ideas moving in a logical sequence?

Were steps in demonstrations clear and understandable?

Did the speaker define and clarify unfamiliar terms?

Vocal Delivery

Did the speaker enunciate words and phrases clearly?

Did the speaker pronounce difficult terms effectively?

Did the speaker's volume, rate, and vocal inflections enhance the speech?

Visual Aids

Did the speaker spend time and effort developing audiovisual aids?

Did the speaker know how to use visual aids?

While using visuals, was the speaker able to keep the speech moving without awkward "dead space?"

Enthusiasm

Did the speaker's voice, eye contact, facial expression, gestures, and posture reflect enthusiasm for the topic?

Emphasis

Did the speaker employ verbal emphasis and/or repetition to highlight important areas?

Did the speaker support verbal emphasis with appropriate gestures, movement, and facial expression?

Other

Did the speaker display any other effective or ineffective techniques (pauses, mannerisms, movement, appearance), which would enhance or detract from the delivery?

Conclusion
Method of Ending

Did the speech contain a clear device (quotation, summary, story, question) to provide closure to the topic?

Lectures are presented by experts in fields such as history or science for instructional or educational purposes.

In many cases, your report will summarize the work of a committee or other employee unit. You need to be completely accurate, and your comments must reflect the collective decisions of the group. Even though your report is technical, it should still be interesting, clear, and well organized. Know your material thoroughly, maintain contact with your audience, interject humor when appropriate, and use concrete examples.

Business reports often incorporate visuals: transparencies with overhead projectors, chalkboards, whiteboards with Magic Markers, and easels. Remember that effective use of visuals can create the perception among coworkers that you know what you're doing.

Lectures are presentations given by experts for instructional or educational purposes. Colleges and universities often receive grants to invite well-known authorities in science, humanities, and industry to speak on topics of national interest. Lecturers frequently read lengthy presentations from manuscripts and incorporate question-and-answer sessions at the end.

You already know from your own classroom listening experience that a two-hour lecture can seem like minutes or days depending upon the speaker's organization and enthusiasm. Some campus student groups publish evaluations rating faculty lectures according to interest, enthusiasm, and scholarship. Lectures don't have to be boring. They can be fascinating if the speaker is knowledgeable, structured, and communicates new or complicated information creatively. You will probably give a lecture, how-ever, only if you are an expert in a particular field.

The *personal experience* speech provides information about an en-counter or observation. Travelogues, harrowing adventures, or expeditions are good subject areas for personal experience speeches. These presenta-tions are often exciting and interesting; they are also potentially boring. Use good judgment in developing the topic and be sensitive to your listeners.

In your speech class, your instructor may ask you to present a brief personal-experience speech. Remember not to substitute one lengthy per-sonal experience for a major informative speech that requires a variety of research materials.[3]

The Computer Virus: Disease of the Computer Age

Constructed by an advanced public speaking student, this speech includes numerous supporting materials to describe the threat posed by electronic viruses. In addition to this descriptive presentation, Christopher Kavanaugh has developed several alternative introductions and conclusions to demonstrate the variety of creative approaches available for a single speech.[4]

Informative Descriptive Speech

CHRISTOPHER B. KAVANAUGH

1 The speaker be-gins the intro-duction with a case study to gain audience at-tention and to promote curios-ity. The events in the story are arranged to cre-ate suspense.

1 On November 2nd, 1988 at around 9:00 P.M., Robert Tappan Mor-ris, a twenty-three-year-old computer science student at Cor-nell University, pushed a single button on his computer keyboard and launched an attack. Two of his targets were the research and science centers at Berkeley, California and Cam-bridge, Massachusetts. Around 10:00 P.M. Princeton University was hit. By midnight NASAs Ames Research Center in California, the University of Pittsburgh, and the Los Alamos National Lab-oratory in New Mexico became victims. Around 12:30 A.M., Johns Hopkins University in Baltimore was struck, and by quarter after one in the morning the attack reached the University of Michigan in Ann Arbor.

2 At 2:30 that morning a frantic computer scientist in Berkeley sent out a message to computers around the country, which began with the words, "We are currently under attack . . . ." The message noted other locations around the country that had

been affected by the attack, and provided a brief description of the way the attack was taking place. At the time, the "only help" the scientist could offer to others in danger was a recommendation to shut down their computer systems in order to protect themselves.

3 Now you may be asking yourself what could attack so many locations in such a short period of time. It was neither a series of guided missiles nor a test of the "star wars" laser beam; it was a phenomenon known as a computer virus.

4 Chris carefully documents the story with a credible source.

The speaker has skillfully crafted his thesis statement at the end of the introduction.

4 The story I just described was reported in great detail on the front page of the *Wall Street Journal* on November 7, 1988. That incident prompted an emergency meeting of computer scientists and representatives of twelve government agencies, including the F.B.I., the C.I.A., the Department of Defense, the Air Force, the Army, and the National Security Agency. Participants in the top-secret meeting in Fort Meade, Maryland discussed the nature of an electronic virus, the threat computer viruses pose to universities, businesses, and the U.S. Government, and what might be done to safeguard potential victims.

5 The first external transition introduces numeral I about the nature of the computer virus.

5 When we think of a computer and the programs that run it, we usually think in terms of what it can do to help us, as an aid in gathering and sorting data. So what makes a computer virus program different from other of computer programs? Put simply, a computer virus is a type of disruptive program that someone places secretly into a computer system. Victims of computer viruses typically report that unwanted, often damaging disturbances occur in computers.

6 Throughout the speech, Chris uses specific references to back up his ideas.

The brief example of the "universal message of peace" helps the audience to visualize the symptoms of a "benign" computer virus.

6 An electronic virus can produce effects as benign as a simple picture and message on your computer screen. A September, 1988 issue of *Time* magazine reported the case of several thousand Macintosh computer users who turned on their machines on March 2, 1988 to find a picture of the earth and a "universal message of peace" on their computer screens. The message disappeared quickly and never returned, and the virus responsible for the spontaneous greeting card caused no lasting damage.

7 But a computer virus can also be sinister in nature, created with the intention of deleting some or all of the data stored within a computer system. *Business Week* gave an example of a more destructive virus in its cover story article on August 1st, 1988. A man named Donald Burleson was fired from his job as a computer programmer for a securities trading firm and decided to get revenge.

8 The case study enables listeners to understand a "sinister" virus.

8 Shortly after he was fired he wrote a virus program and secretly planted it in the company's computer system. The program was designed to wipe out all the records of sales commissions once a month. Burleson's electronic virus was discovered only two days later by the company's programming analysts, but before it could be eliminated, the virus had destroyed 168,000 records in computer's memory bank.

9 Whether the results are disastrous or merely distracting, it is important to remember that a computer virus is a foreign element—a sort of devious computer program—which secretly enters a computer system. Once inside, it activates hidden instructions that alter the performance of the computer.

10 The external transition connects numerals I and II.

10 Now that you are armed with a general description of this electronic scourge, let's examine its *modus operandi* to determine why it's such a devastating threat to our technological way of life.

11 The speaker uses an effective comparison and contrast to describe similarities and differences of computer and biological viruses.

11 The science magazine *Discover* noted in its January 1989 issue that a computer virus is similar to a biological virus, because both contain built-in instructions to duplicate themselves repeatedly. The biological virus achieves this chemically, based on genetic coding. The computer virus works electronically, using computer coding called machine language. One significant difference between the two viruses is that a biological virus usually occurs naturally, but an electronic virus must be intentionally created by someone to infect computers.

12 Both viruses need to find a way inside the "host" before infection can take place. The human body is the "host" for the biological virus, whereas the computer operating system is the "host" for the computer virus. Just as a person (without realizing it) can transmit infectious germs during a friendly handshake, a computer can also pass on its form of virus to other computers. A computer infection occurs when two or more computers share or transfer information.

13 To understand exactly how serious the virus threat is, we need only look at our increasing reliance on computers to perform everyday tasks. In the past, most records were kept on paper. Once we recognized the advantage computers provided by allowing immediate access to information, computers replaced many of our filing cabinets and typewriters.

14 Chris develops an interesting

14 Some of you use a computer as a word processor for your class assignments. It is possible that the following scenario could hypothetical example to help listeners understand how a computer virus could affect them. Because the speaker indicates that an electronic virus can pose a threat to their computers, audience members are motivated to listen.

happen to you: imagine that you have just spent eight weeks and countless hours on a major term paper. All of your research and rough drafts are stored on your computer disk and the finished paper is due tomorrow. You run into the college lab to make some last minute adjustments and as you prepare to print out the final copy, you look up to find that your computer screen has suddenly gone blank. No matter what you do, you can't retrieve your work. Now you remove your disk and take it to a friend's house so you can check it on his computer. When you place your disk in his computer, all of the data stored in his machine also disappears. Both of you are now victims of a computer virus. In this example, the lab computer, whether by accident or on purpose, had been infected with a virus. When you used the lab computer, the virus automatically copied itself onto your computer disk. Later, by inserting your infected disk into your friend's computer, you inadvertently transferred a copy of the virus into his machine. You can see how using many different machines and freely swapping computer disks increases your risk of becoming a computer virus victim.

15-16 The speaker uses the metaphor of the "mailmen" and the "envelope" to describe the computer and the computer disk.

15 Another method exists for someone to spread a computer virus. As our society demands faster ways of communicating information, many people have abandoned the old method of sending information through the mail. We can now transfer data at mind-boggling speeds by linking computers. Computers are quickly becoming our electronic mailmen.

16 For variety, the speaker poses a rhetorical question to keep the audience interested and involved in the topic.

16 The computer disk is the new envelope, and the data stored on it has replaced the document. Modern technology enables us to zip off a letter to a friend without leaving our computer keyboards. Now you may ask, "How can a computer transfer data across the country?" say, from Portland, Oregon to Portland, Maine, for example. The answer is by telephone. The same phone system which transmits your voice and the tones from your telephone push-buttons can also carry a message right out of your computer.

17 After analyzing his student audience, Chris recognizes the need to define unfamiliar terms such as "modem"

17 Computer users often exchange data by using a simple device called a telephone modem. A modem makes it possible for two distant computers to be linked electronically. A telephone modem transfers computer messages by using special frequencies and electronic pulses. If you were to listen to a computer message coming through a modem, you would hear nothing more than buzzes and bleeps. But when the telephone modem is connected to your computer, it decodes the incoming sound waves

18 The brief explanation describing the contents of electronic bulletin boards—"singles dating ads" and "techniques for treating AIDS" provide interesting concrete examples that listeners easily understand.

19 The speaker uses a simile to compare the computer virus to the ancient Greek Trojan horse.

20 The speaker explains the automatic transmission of bulletin board files by making a comparison to the Morris virus.

Chris uses statistics from the *New York Times* article to indicate the widespread effect of the virus.

so that your computer can understand them. In a matter of seconds the bleeps and buzzes are transformed into words on your computer screen.

18 Today, large networks exist so that computer users can call nationwide central computers. These massive central units are known as electronic bulletin boards, which are used to distribute information. If you used a computer to call a bulletin board you would find an amazing variety of information. The contents of an electronic bulletin board can range from singles dating advertisements to the latest medical techniques for treating AIDS—and practically everything in between. If you saw something that was particularly interesting in the vast library of information, you could easily copy that file directly into your computer with the press of a button.

19 Unfortunately, electronic bulletin boards are a prime breeding ground for most computer viruses. One of the easiest ways for a computer virus to invade your computer system is to masquerade as a legitimate program or file, known as a Trojan horse virus. Just as the ancient Greeks secretly placed soldiers inside the wooden horse, an unscrupulous programmer can plant a hidden computer virus inside what appears to be a simple file of information. Anyone who copies that file can bring the virus into their system. Computer users, like the unsuspecting citizens of Troy, are often too late in realizing their mistake—the damage has already begun.

20 Some bulletin boards even send electronic mail to thousands of machines automatically, just as advertisers send junk mail to your house. If a computer mass mailing became infected with a hidden virus, it would automatically transmit thousands of virus copies as an extra, unwanted bonus. To illustrate this point, the plague Robert Morris started began when he sent an ordinary piece of electronic mail. Even though it looked harmless, the message he sent contained an elaborate virus. His virus was automatically designed to multiply and spread to every machine linked to a national computer network. According to a *New York Times* article dated November 8, 1988, the Morris virus infected over 6,000 computers nationwide in less than twelve hours, shutting them down completely. It is the most dramatic example to date of the potential danger of computer viruses.

21 **The speaker provides further explanation and clarification of the Morris virus and the damage it actually caused.**

21 Many experts classified the Morris virus as mild when they considered the damage that might have occurred, since it did not destroy any of the files inside the infected computers. However it did cause the computers to "freeze up" so that no work could be performed on them. Friends close to Mr. Morris say his intention in releasing the virus was merely to track its growth as it spread; he was reportedly horrified by the results.

22 It appears that after he released his virus through the telephone line, he discovered he had made a terrible mistake in his math computations. The virus was only supposed to make a single copy of itself in each computer. Instead, it multiplied hundreds of times in every machine. The error caused his virus to rapidly consume all the available computer memory in the infected machines, until they were overloaded and rendered useless. The tracking system Morris designed quickly reflected that something had gone wrong, but by then he could do little more than sit and watch as the casualties mounted across the nation.

23 **The speaker has skillfully related the statistics by figuring out the hourly wages of Robert Morris and how long he would have to work to repay the $100 million damages.**

23 An article in *Personal Computing* magazine described the consequences of the Morris virus in its May, 1989 issue. It was estimated that all the costs involved with removing the virus totaled approximately 100 million dollars. Now just imagine if Mr. Morris had to repay everyone for the damage his virus created. Morris would have to earn $274 dollars an hour, working twenty hours every day without a single day off for fifty years! Keep in mind that all that expense came from what was considered to be a mild, nuisance-type virus. If the virus had been more destructive in its programming, it could have wiped out millions of files forever, and the costs could have run into the billions.

24 **A quotation from an expert is used to support the claim made about the potential threat posed by an electronic virus.**

24 In this "Age of Information" computer viruses threaten the very lifeblood of our society. Banks, universities, hospitals, satellite networks, telephone systems, law enforcement agencies, and the U.S. Armed Forces are only some of the institutions that now depend on computer information in order to function. Stephen Walker, former director of information services at the Pentagon said, "If someone at NORAD (the North American Aerospace Defense Command) wanted to do what Robert Morris did . . . he could cause a lot of damage." You can understand why computer scientists and government security experts are studying ways to protect computers from viruses.

25 **This external transition links**

25 *Scientific American* magazine reported in a March, 1989 article that future efforts to improve computer security are helped by

numerals II
and III.

examining the viruses that have struck in the past. As a result of this research, several safety measures now exist for businesses and individuals to protect their computers.

26 The speaker describes the first method of protecting computers.

26 *Business Week* magazine points out that one important measure is to do away with simple computer passwords, and to make new passwords more confidential. Basic passwords like "open" and "hello" are far too common among computer networks. Virus programs can be written to attempt entry using the most common passwords, as was the case with the Morris virus, and once inside the system the virus is free to do its programmed damage.

27 The description of the second method involves defining unfamiliar terms.

27 The *Wall Street Journal* provided another clue towards solving the puzzle created by computer viruses. When the Morris virus struck, AT&T's Bell Laboratories avoided infection because they had already closed what are known as "trap doors" in their computer programs. "Trap doors" are openings within a computer operating system which allow a programmer to make changes quickly. These "trap doors" are often built into the system because new programs need modification in the first few months, but many times a company will forget to secure the secret entry point once a program is running smoothly. Robert Morris's virus searched for and found "trap doors" in many of the machines that it infected.

28 The speaker uses a source to support almost every explanation of the alternative security systems. He states only the periodical name and avoids repeating the previously mentioned date.

28 *Personal Computing* magazine recommends the use of an anti-viral program which can set off an alarm when it detects that a new or unusual computer command is trying to enter your computer. There are now dozens of anti-viral computer programs available, and some will even automatically shut down your machine to prevent a virus from reaching your computer operating system.

29 Other practices, like making backup copies of computer disks daily, and not allowing new and untested copies of software to be loaded onto central computers, can reduce the risk and the spread of viruses. Incorporating some or all of these changes into your computer system will lessen your vulnerability to a virus attack.

30 The concluding quote from the computer expert dramatically conveys the potential damage of a computer virus. The speaker uses

30 None of these measures, however, are completely foolproof. Experts point out that computers, by their very design, must exchange information in order for them to be useful tools. Because of this, we will continue to be afflicted with computer viruses as long as some computer programmers continue to develop and distribute viruses. The current threat of computer viruses was best described by a military expert in computer security who was quoted in a March, 1989 *Time* magazine

the phrase "I would like to leave you with . . ." to set up the quotation. A better way to introduce the quote would be, ". . . a military expert in computer security who made this ominous statement in a March 1989 issue of Time magazine. He said that . . ."

Chris has made a technical topic interesting by providing meaningful examples, clear statistics, and expert testimony.

article, and I would like to leave you with his ominous words. He declared that, "The potential for offensive use of viruses is so great that I would have to view the power and magnitude as comparable with that of nuclear or chemical weapons."

ALTERNATIVE INTRODUCTIONS AND CONCLUSIONS TO THE SAMPLE SPEECH

Here are several alternative introductions and conclusions constructed by Christopher Kavanaugh. Each example is designed to demonstrate a different opening and closing technique for a speech. Every introduction ties into the speech at paragraph four, which presents the thesis statement. Each conclusion is inserted at paragraph thirty following the line, "Experts point out that computers, by their very design, must somehow exchange information in order for them to be useful tools to mankind."

Introduction 1: Shocking Statement

1 This introduction begins with a shocking

1 "We are currently under attack!" Those were the first desperate words of a message sent out to warn research facilities, universities, and military installations around the country. A

computer scientist at NASA's Ames Research Center in California, sent the emergency bulletin after struggling to control a renegade computer program that had somehow entered NASA's research computers. This was the nightmare that many computer experts had hoped would never happen, but on the night of November 2, 1988, their fears came true.

statement, which leads into the story about the computer virus created by Robert Morris. The shocking statement quickly gets audience attention.

2 An unknown computer operator had created and unleashed a terrorist program into a massive national network of over 60,000 computer terminals. In just a few hours, the terrorist program—commonly called a "computer virus"—had brought several thousand computers around the country to a standstill. Investigators frantically began searching for clues to discover who had perpetrated this unprecedented attack on the computer network.

3 The result of the investigation proved astonishing. The computer virus was not caused by agents from the KGB or the PLO, but by a U.S. college student. The virus creator, twenty-three-year-old Robert Tappan Morris, was a computer science graduate student at Cornell University. On a lark, Morris wrote what he thought was a harmless virus and then sent it out through his computer terminal.

Introduction 2: Series of Statistics

1 In this introduction, the speaker presents a series of statistics, creating suspense. The introduction has listeners wondering what could do so much damage and potentially affect their homes. The speaker satisfies audience curiosity by explaining that the problems were caused by computer viruses.

1 By September of 1988, twenty-five different types of them had been documented. Two major corporations have been terrorized by people who threatened to unleash them unless ransom money was paid. One expert estimates that 40 percent of our nation's biggest industrial corporations have been struck by them at one time or another, and in one nine month period alone, over three hundred universities, corporations, and other institutions had been victimized by them. Even homes have been attacked, with estimates soaring as high as 250,000. You may think I'm talking about bombs, missiles, or burglaries, but actually I'm talking about computer viruses. The threat of these electronic viruses is increasingly alarming.

2 The Jet Propulsion Laboratory in Pasadena, California has been infected with computer viruses four times in a single year. Computer virus attacks have been aimed at both F.B.I. and C.I.A. computer systems. The National Security Agency and the C.I.A. have even admitted that the U.S. Government had "experimented" with infecting the computer systems of other nations.

3 In 1988 a Cornell University student named Robert Tappan Morris placed a computer virus into an unclassified military

computer network with explosive results. The computer network, established in the late '60s by the Department of Defense's Advanced Research Projects Agency, electronically links over 60,000 computer terminals from all over the country. Thousands of computers on the network were brought to a halt by Morris' computer virus in a matter of hours, and the U.S. Department of Defense ordered the entire network shut down temporarily so the dangerous computer program could be completely removed from the system.

4 Immediately following the Morris virus infection, computer scientists and military security experts from twelve government agencies hastily gathered together to examine the growing problem.

Introduction 3: Rhetorical Questions

1 *This introduction begins with a series of rhetorical questions to create attention. The technique successfully generates curiosity and interest in the topic.*

1 Have you ever stopped to appreciate just how convenient your life is because of computers? Have you ever used the computer lab on campus to complete an assignment? Have you ever withdrawn money from an automatic teller machine? How many of you have placed a long distance phone call using direct dialing? Have you ever bought concert tickets over the phone, or made reservations for an airplane flight or a train trip? All of these are examples of the way in which computers influence your daily life.

2 But computers also keep track of countless other pieces of information that we rarely think about. Stocks and commodities exchanges, air traffic control systems, corporate payrolls, and strategic military bases are other prime examples of operations that rely heavily on computers and the information stored within them. Think what would happen if we suddenly lost control over the computer systems we use every day. Sound far-fetched? Not at all. In fact, there is already something in our midst which threatens to change the way that you and I do business. I am referring to the problem of computer viruses.

3 Did you know, for example, that on November 2, 1988, a college student by the name of Robert Tappan Morris wrote a computer virus and sent it into a national computer network? The network Robert Morris managed to infiltrate with his computer program connected over 60,000 computer terminals from military installations, research facilities, and universities from around the nation. In only a few hours, Morris' virus program had brought the entire network crashing down, infecting and disabling thousands of individual computers. If this example

worries you, consider this: most experts agree that the damage caused by Robert Morris was slight, and perhaps the next computer virus will be far worse. As a result of the concern raised by the Morris virus, computer scientists and military security experts from twelve government agencies held an emergency conference.

Introduction 4: Quotation

1 This quotation stimulates curiosity by revealing only a portion of the information.

1 A man by the name of Stephen Ross said, "The virus problem is potentially unlimited. The era of the firecracker virus that goes off without any purpose or gain is coming to an end, and the era of the directed virus is close upon us." Ross isn't a doctor, and he wasn't referring to a new strain of Hong Kong flu. Mr. Ross is a senior manager with Deloitte, Haskins & Sells, one of the nation's largest consulting firms, and he was talking about something called a computer virus. Computer viruses are becoming more numerous, and they are gaining the attention of corporations, the U.S. Government, and the media.

2 The *Wall Street Journal* reported a sensational example of a computer virus attack in the autumn of 1988. A Cornell University student named Robert Tappan Morris released a computer virus that infected a military network of computer terminals. The U.S. Air Force Logistics Command office at Wright Patterson Air Force Base, NASA's Ames Research Center in Moffett Field, California, the Naval Research Laboratory in Cabin John, Maryland, and the Air Forces' Electronic Systems Division at Hanscomb Air Force Base were only some of the military installations that were struck by the Morris virus. Major universities, including Berkeley, Purdue, M.I.T., Johns Hopkins, and Princeton were also infected by the computer virus that Robert Morris created. Several thousand computers were literally shut down by the Morris virus program overnight.

Introduction 5: Ineffective Strategy

1 This introduction starts by naming the topic rather than by using a well-developed strategy to connect to listeners. The vague references to "terrible

1 My topic this morning is about computer viruses. These viruses can cause terrible problems in our society. They can shut down large systems and big companies. They can affect millions of people everywhere. So basically, you can see that they are something that everybody should be concerned about. And that's what I want to focus on in my speech.

problems," "large systems," and "millions of people" lack specificity and generate few mental images. It is uninteresting and uninviting.

1 This conclusion contains a brief story, which the speaker uses to remind listeners how viruses can affect them.

Conclusion 1: Brief Story

1 Some of you may still be thinking that the computer virus problem only affects huge corporations and the U.S. Government, so let me remind you that individual computer users are equally at risk. To give you an idea of how threatening viruses can be to you, the individual, I'd like you to consider what happened to a newspaper reporter in Providence, Rhode Island. In 1988, Froma Joselow placed a computer disk into her terminal. Her disk contained interviews and notes she had compiled for articles, representing six months worth of work. As she attempted to call up files at her terminal, the message "DISK ERROR" kept flashing on the screen. Up until that moment she had never experienced any problem with her disk, yet suddenly six months of her career were irretrievable.

2 Later, while examining the disk, a computer systems engineer discovered that most of the data stored on it had been devoured by a hidden virus. Still more frightening was the discovery that the particular virus which wound up on the reporter's computer disk had been created two years earlier in Lahore, Pakistan. No one knows exactly how the Pakistani virus reached Providence, Rhode Island.

3 It is because of stories such as this that many experts are now saying that we, as a society, have reached the crossroads where our needs for convenient technology are conflicting with our needs to secure that very same technology. Most are predicting that by necessity, concern for protecting our information will eventually take precedence over the convenience we have previously enjoyed. The days of sitting down at a computer terminal and immediately beginning to work may be numbered. In the future, we may have to go through an elaborate and time-consuming ritual of confirming the integrity of our data every time we use a computer.

Conclusion 2: End Question

1 Throughout this conclusion, the speaker asks listeners several questions.

1 Throughout our investigation of computer viruses, I have given you information concerning Robert Morris and the virus he created. But there is one more thing that you should know. Remember when I mentioned that the Morris virus attacked computers connected to a large national network? How would you feel if I told you that the network that he infected, ARPANET, is controlled by the U.S. Department of Defense's Advanced Research Projects Agency and is the largest unclassified military network in the United States? Dozens of our nation's top military research facilities and even a few of our strategic installations were infiltrated by a college student who didn't even have to leave his dorm room to accomplish his deed.

2 The final question is thought-provoking and keeps the audience thinking about the impact of the virus on their own lives, even after the speaker has completed the presentation.

2 Some computer scientists say the onslaught of computer viruses like the one Morris released are the price we pay as a society that relies heavily on technology. Experts agree that it shouldn't be so easy to do what Robert Morris did. A few have even predicted that without more significant changes in computer security, we will be afflicted with viruses that, by comparison, will make the Morris infection look like child's play. In light of what you now know about computer viruses, you might ask yourself this question: "Am I prepared for the possible consequences of a virus attack in a computer that I use?"

Conclusion 3: Summary

1 The speaker develops a summary to the speech. Notice that the summary is not simply a listing of main points; it touches on some of the significant information provided in the speech.

1 In a nation where an entire generation has been raised with computers that can teach them to read and spell, to add and subtract, and even to entertain themselves by playing games, it should be no surprise that many of these same individuals have acquired a rather sophisticated understanding of computers and their operation. Due to this increase in computer literacy, we now have more people capable of creating computer viruses, and unfortunately we are seeing a steady increase in the number of computer viruses that are being written and released. In an attempt to deal with the recent surge in computer sabotage, new laws have been passed which make the misuse of a computer a criminal offense. Robert Morris became the first person ever indicted under a federal law concerning computer security, and Morris's indictment reflects a growing sentiment in our country. By holding Morris accountable for his actions, the Government has said that we,

as a society dependent on critical information systems, will no longer tolerate computer misuse, even when it is done in "harmless" fun. There is too much at stake.

Conclusion 4: Reference to the Introduction

1 This means that we will probably continue to be afflicted with computer virus programs.

2 In this conclusion, the speaker completes the story about Robert Morris, which was started in the introduction.

The reference to the introduction combined with the end quote from the prosecuting attorney, provides more information about the case study.

2 Many of you may be wondering what happened to Robert Morris. He became the first person ever indicted under a federal law dealing with the issue of computer security. The legislation, enacted by Congress and known as the Computer Fraud and Abuse Act, provides stiff penalties for the misuse of government computers. The Morris legal case may drag on for years within the court system, but if found guilty of the felony charge, Morris could be sentenced to five years in prison and ordered to repay all of the costs incurred by his virus attack. The legal action being taken against Morris signals a change in our attitude towards computer mischief. In the past, viruses like Morris's would have been celebrated for their ingenuity, but today, we recognize them as threats to our information systems. I spoke with Mark Rasch, a prosecuting attorney with the Justice Department in Washington, D.C., regarding the Morris case, and he summed up the situation with eloquent simplicity. He said, "A computer is a tool, just like a crowbar is a tool. And although a tool can be used in a beneficial manner, it can also be used to commit a crime."

Conclusion 5: Ineffective

1 This conclusion is poorly worded, trite, awkward, and has little relation to what occurred in the speech. In addition, a speaker should not begin identifying the conclusion by name nor end with "thank you."

1 And now for my conclusion I'd like to say that I hope you've learned a little bit about the computer virus situation in America. There are a lot of virus programs around in computer stores and other places and if you do a lot of work on the Internet, or generally work with computers a lot, you ought to consider investing in something that can protect all your stuff. So here's to good luck, and I hope you all don't get any serious viruses out there! Thank you.

When you deliver speeches to inform, you seek to educate and enlighten your audience—not to influence their beliefs, feelings, or behavior.

Three categories of informative speeches are: description, definition, and other informative types (reports, lectures, and personal experiences). The descriptive speech is related to a person, place, object, or event. A speech of definition identifies and explains a theory or subject area. Three other informational types are: the report, which is used primarily in organizations and institutions; the lecture, which is presented by experts; and the personal experience.

SKILL BUILDERS

1. Choose four topics and write one informative and one persuasive specific purpose for each.
2. Choose a topic and present a five- to seven-minute descriptive speech. Use a minimum of three sources and ten supporting materials to establish your credibility.
3. Divide your class into several groups. Analyze the following specific purpose sentences containing worn-out topics. Rework the topics and write new specific purposes to provide new information that motivates audience members to listen. Report your group's findings to your class when you finish.
   a. To inform you that AIDS is a deadly disease
   b. To explain the hazards of cigarette smoking
   c. To describe the benefits of an exercise program
   d. To define democracy
   e. To demonstrate how to make a cake by following the directions on the back of the Pillsbury cake box.
4. Read the informative speech, "The Computer Virus," by Christopher Kavanaugh, then divide your class into several groups of four.
   a. Identify five areas in the speech needing improvement.
   b. Discuss how you would remedy the five difficulties you identified. Provide specific examples.
5. Evaluate an informative lecture of one of your instructors. Comment on the following areas:
   a. Is the instructor clear and well organized?
   b. Does the speaker maintain the interest of the audience?
   c. If visuals are used, does the instructor incorporate them effectively into the presentation?
   d. Does the speaker have an effective delivery?
6. From your own experience, choose a term that is familiar to you but perhaps unknown to your audience. Develop a speech of definition

using this term as your topic. Make sure that your listeners understand the definition, and become interested in the speech.

N O T E S

1. Thomas H. Olbricht, *Informative Speaking* (Glenview, Illinois: Scott, Foresman and Company, 1968), pp. 15–16. Our discussion of the difference between information and persuasion coincides with Olbricht's analysis of the "traditional means of distinguishing informing from persuading" in his second chapter.

2. Ibid., p. 15.

3. I wish to thank Kara Jenkins and Tom Pfeffer for permission to use portions of their outlines and Kelly O'Connor, Joan Stark, and Tresse Bailey for topic ideas.

4. "The Computer Virus: Disease of the Computer Age" by Christopher B. Kavanaugh is used by permission.

Chapter 16

SPEAKING TO INFORM:
DEMONSTRATING PROCEDURES

A jazz performance centers upon the process of creation. The final objective is not only the finished product, but the path and process taken towards it.

David Liebman

CHAPTER OBJECTIVES

After reading this chapter you will be able to:

1. Describe several types of demonstration speeches;

2. Know how to build a demonstration speech;

3. Analyze a demonstration speech;

4. Present a process speech.

It was a monumental undertaking to move the world's tallest brick lighthouse. The Cape Hatteras Light Station in Buxton, North Carolina, had to be relocated from its original foundation because it was endanger of falling into the ocean due to the gradual erosion of the Atlantic coastline. In fact, a fierce storm in 1994 had already pushed waves to the base of the lighthouse, threatening the collapse of the structure.

Engineers from International Chimney Corporation met to discuss the process of moving the historic structure 2,900 feet from its original foundation constructed in 1868. They developed a plan which included the following process: (1) installing a temporary support system; (2) placing main beams, hydraulic jacks, and cross beams; (3) using a unified jacking system; (4) sequencing the load transfer phase; (5) resetting jacks in a three-zone system; (6) installing push jacks; (7) rolling the lighthouse; and (8) resetting the light station.[1] Once the plan was finalized, the lighthouse began its three-week journey on June 23, 1999. Park rangers described the process to tourists who were amazed at the ease with which the lighthouse inched along the steel beams on roller dollies. The lighthouse arrived at its new location on July 9, 1999, just before the fury of the late-summer hurricane season.

Even though you may not have to describe a process as complicated as moving a lighthouse, you will probably be required to present, evaluate, or participate in numerous process speeches during your occupational life. Chapter 16 helps you to develop, organize, and evaluate this type of informative speech.

THE DEMONSTRATION SPEECH

One important type of speech to inform is the *demonstration,* which usually includes a variety of visual aids to show the steps of a process. In most businesses, institutions, and professional organizations, employees at all levels are required to present or participate in programs that explain procedures and processes. Seminars are conducted to teach workers how to use new telephone systems, fax machines, laser technologies, or the Internet; how to fill out purchase orders, insurance forms, or government documents; how to confront sexual harassment, use new sales techniques, or handle consumer complaints; how to treat new diseases, implement new manufacturing procedures, or conform to safety standards. These training sessions protect the company and employee, help to maintain a company's competitive edge, and improve workers' productivity or efficiency.

No matter what your career or profession, you will probably be required to explain how something works, how something is made, how something is done, or how something happens.

An effective demonstration speech includes clear explanations, precise gestures, and careful practice with audiovisual aids.

How Something Works

To demonstrate how the eye works

To demonstrate how a computer operates

To demonstrate how a carburetor works

To demonstrate how a Revolutionary War musket operates

How Something Is Made

To demonstrate how the violin is constructed

To demonstrate how the Chinese weave rugs

To demonstrate how Greek moussaka is made

To demonstrate the art of Japanese origami

How Something Is Done

To demonstrate how to tune a piano

To demonstrate how to shear sheep

To demonstrate how to mine rubies

To explain how to rig a sailboat

To explain how to fly an airplane

BUILDING THE PROCESS SPEECH

Demonstrating a familiar process may sound easy, but when you are in front of an audience, many things can go wrong. Lack of preparation can cause misplacing or dropping a visual aid or displaying objects that are too small for the audience to see. To help you avoid these and other difficulties, here is a list of guidelines for building the process speech:

1. **Choose a topic from your experience or knowledge.**
   a. Examine your professional expertise and life experience.
   b. Choose a topic in which you teach, train, or educate.

2. **Investigate the location of the speech.**
   a. Does the room or auditorium have everything necessary to support audiovisual aids?
   b. Do you need to bring extra equipment or supplies?
   c. Can the audience see your visuals easily?

3. **Develop a logical outline.**
   a. Include all required structural elements: an interesting introduction, a purpose statement, a well-organized body, and a clearly defined conclusion.
   b. Combine information in the body of the demonstration into overall categories like "gathering materials," "preparing for the process," or "finished product."
   c. Use chronological sequence to arrange events in order of occurrence.
   d. Employ any type of conclusion, using a summary to reinforce complicated or unfamiliar procedures.

4. **Apply principles of effective delivery.**
   a. Be clear.
      (1) Verbally emphasize important points and repeat steps, key ideas, or complicated material when necessary.
      (2) Use gestures to point out significant details.
      (3) Clarify main headings in the body with external transitions.
      (4) Use internal transitions—then, next, finally—to connect steps grouped beneath main headings.
      (5) Employ simple terms, defining unfamiliar words and pronouncing difficult terms correctly.

      (6) Speak slowly enough to allow listeners to follow the steps of the process.

      (7) Relate ideas to listeners with concrete examples.

  b. Keep the speech moving.

      (1) Keep talking as you demonstrate, avoiding awkward pauses or silences.

      (2) Be prepared with additional comments if the procedure takes longer than expected.

      (3) Keep to the time limit.

      (4) Include only essential elements of the process, eliminating unnecessary detail.

  c. Know how to use visuals.

      (1) Set up visuals in advance if possible.

      (2) Use enough visuals to support the process, avoiding too few or too many.

      (3) Reveal visuals at the right psychological moment.

      (4) Avoid distractions by not passing out objects while you speak.

      (5) Be sure that visuals are large enough for listeners to see.

      (6) Integrate visuals smoothly into the speech, eliminating awkwardness.

      (7) Remove visuals quickly if there are other speakers following your presentation.

  d. Be prepared.

      (1) Rehearse with all the visuals you intend to use.

      (2) Show enthusiasm and interest through vocal variety, facial expression, and gestures.

      (3) Maintain eye contact with the audience.

5. Avoid the following problems:

  a. Long silences.

  b. Lengthy, overly complex details or terms.

  c. Visuals that are too small.

  d. Too many audiovisuals.

  e. Creating distractions with audiovisuals.

  f. Disorganization.

  g. Last-minute preparation.

  h. Going over the time limit.

Speakers who demonstrate procedures effectively maintain contact with the audience, keep the speech moving, and define terms or procedures that may be unfamiliar.

HOW SOMETHING HAPPENS

    To explain how geysers develop

    To explain how dreams occur

    To explain how pearls form

    To explain how Parkinson's disease attacks the body

An Example

Demonstrations are not simplistic show-and-tell speeches: They are sophisticated presentations that include carefully crafted visuals that support the process.

A student who was an avid mountain climber demonstrated how to do rappelling—descending a steep incline with a secured rope. He took the speech class outside to an 8-foot-high retaining wall on campus, where he described the necessary equipment and the proper procedure to descend the wall. Class members watched and listened intently as the speaker slowly lowered himself down the wall, carefully explaining each step of the process. Listeners commented that the speaker's creative approach made the speech important and "alive."

OUTLINING THE DEMONSTRATION SPEECH

Most process speeches incorporate numerous steps or phases often difficult for listeners to recall. For example, "Developing color film" would probably include more than 15 steps, and "Decorating a wedding cake" could incorporate more than 23 procedures. The body of a demonstration should never contain 15 or 23 numeral headings. In order to keep the process simple, group the steps into categories:

Specific purpose: To demonstrate how the digestive system works

Thesis statement: The digestive process includes the mouth, the stomach, the small intestine, and the large intestine.

CHRONOLOGICAL ORDER

STEPS GROUPED BY CATEGORIES	STEPS OF THE COMPLETE PROCESS
I. The mouth	A. Food enters mouth
	B. Food chewed by teeth
	C. Salivary glands secrete digestive enzyme
	D. Valves in larynx keep food from passing into windpipe
	E. Food passes through esophagus to stomach
II. The stomach	A. Sphincter prevents regurgitation
	B. Food mixed with gastric juices
III. The small intestine	A. Food enters small intestine
	B. Food mixed with bile from liver
	C. Food mixed with enzymes from pancreas
	D. Food molecules absorbed into bloodstream for transport to body tissues
IV. The large intestine	A. Food enters large intestine
	B. Receives undigested food
	C. Water absorbed from food residues
	D. Residues converted into solid mass for elimination
	E. Elimination through anus[2]

Notice at the right that there are at least sixteen separate steps in the digestive process. Like any other five- to seven-minute speech, process speeches should contain no fewer than two and no more than five numerals in the body. On the left, you can see that the digestive process can be grouped into four principal steps that incorporate all sixteen items. The four headings make the demonstration clear and easy to follow.

Notice that main points in the body of most demonstrations will be arranged according to some form of chronological sequence—by time or events. In the above example, main points are organized according to the order of occurrence. Some topics can be organized by combining chronological sequence with another arrangement. For example, Ann Foley combined topic sequence with chronology in the following demonstration of "fingerprinting:"[3]

Specific purpose: To demonstrate the science of fingerprinting

Thesis statement: Fingerprinting, an important science that identifies individuals' fingerprint types, is an interesting process used in police work.

BODY

I. The importance of fingerprints
    A. Identify fugitives
    B. Identify victims
    C. Provide unmistakable verification

II. Different types of fingerprints
    A. Plain arch
    B. Fented arch
    C. The loop
    D. Plain whorl
    E. Central pocket loop
    F. Double loop
    G. Accidental (No set pattern)

III. The process of fingerprinting
    A. Insert fingerprint card in cardholder
    B. Use small amount of ink on roller
    C. Apply thin ink coat with roller to glass inking plate
    D. Place subject approximately forearm away from fingerprint card
    E. For right hand, stand to left of subject
    F. Take right thumb and roll on inking plate
    G. Place inked thumb on fingerprint card
    H. Roll thumb from left to right for complete rounded print
    I. Continue with rolling process for other fingers
    J. Take prints of four fingers without rolling
    K. Repeat entire process with left hand

Ann chose a topic that could be demonstrated rather quickly. In order to provide more depth to her speech, she spent a few minutes explaining the importance of fingerprints and identifying the various types. Ann arranged her three main headings in a simple topical sequence. Then in III, "The process of fingerprinting," she used chronological order for the subdivisions. Because of her organization, Ann included enough material for an effective six- to seven-minute process speech.

Having a Heart

The following speech was presented by a student in the basic speech course. "Having a Heart" by Henry Humm, is a demonstration explaining the delicate heart transplant surgery the speaker experienced at age sixteen. Visual aids provided with the speech indicate how supporting materials can clarify and enhance a process.

An Informative Speech to Demonstrate

HENRY HUMM

1 While there are many ways to introduce a speech, Henry's personal story is probably the most effective method for this topic. The personal experience generates curiosity and establishes the speaker's credibility. He defined the unfamiliar medical term to keep his audience with him.

2 Both the specific purpose and

1 Three years ago, I was trying out for my high school soccer team, and I was required to have a physical examination. Little did I know that the routine physical I took would lead to the most dramatic event that ever happened in my life. Through that physical and a series of tests, I was diagnosed as having what was called a dilated cardiomyopathy. Now that may sound like a 50 cent word to you, but I want you to know that a dilated cardiomyopathy is very serious—the heart becomes globular in shape and is enlarged in size. The heart may increase as much as twice the size of a normal heart. Also, the left ventricle around the heart becomes thinner than normal.

2 Well, from this diagnosis, I was told I needed to have a very serious life-saving operation—a heart transplant—which is what

the thesis statement clearly conveyed the main point and the areas the demonstration would cover.

I'm going to demonstrate today. I'm going to tell you about matching the donor organ with the recipient, removing and transporting the heart, preparing the patient for surgery, and performing the actual transplant itself.

3 Henry clearly identifies numeral I of the body. His use of the internal transitions "first," "next," and "finally," allows the audience to follow the numeral (I) subheadings easily.

3 Let me briefly explain something about matching the donor and the recipient. First the patient must be placed on a waiting list with other heart recipients. This waiting list is based upon the severity of the illness and each case carries a rating of one to four—one standing for those with the greatest need and four representing the least. Next the blood type of the donor heart must either match the recipient's or be compatible. Finally, the donor heart must be the right size for the patient's chest cavity. As long as the heart fits it is suitable for the transplant. In my situation for instance, I was small and I could not have a large heart, so I had to wait for a donor organ for five-and-a-half weeks. I should also tell you that if a heart were too small, it would have to work twice as hard to pump blood throughout the body. So you can see how important it is for doctors to select a heart which corresponds to the patient's chest cavity.

4 He uses an effective transitional phrase to connect numeral I and II of the body.

4 Okay. I've talked about matching the recipient—Now let me tell you about removing and transporting the heart.

5 The speaker cites a primary source to provide credibility. Since listeners are not acquainted with the expert, Henry briefly provides her qualifications.

5 According to Sharon M. Augustine who is a Transplant Nurse Practitioner at Johns Hopkins, the hospital gets a call that a donor heart is available for transplant. Members of the transplant team immediately fly to the person who is brain dead to remove the organ. In order for this procedure to occur, team members hurry to the heliport located on top of the hospital and fly to the airport. Once they arrive at the airport they fly by private jet to the city where the donor heart is located. They drive to the hospital where they remove the organ. It is important for team members themselves to make this trip in order to be sure that the heart has not suffered any previous damage, or is not damaged during removal. You can imagine the incredible amount of time, energy, and resources that would be wasted if the transplant

team did not examine the heart firsthand to determine its suitability.

6 Once the organ is examined and then removed, it is placed in a Tupperware container with an iced saline solution. The saline solution keeps the organ cold, at about 4 degrees centigrade. The organ is cooled to keep the metabolism of the heart down to a minimum. The Tupperware container is then packed into sterile ice with saline and placed into an Igloo cooler—the type of cooler you take to a picnic or to the beach! Finally doctors are ready to return to the hospital of the anxious recipient.

7 The transplant team takes the heart by ambulance to the airport and flies back to the city where the transplant will be performed. State police pick up the doctors and the heart and take them back to the hospital by helicopter. Once they have returned, the special job of these team members is finished and other members of the transplant team take over to perform the actual surgery.

8 I've described how doctors transport the heart to the hospital—now I want you to know what happens to the patient right up until the transplant procedure. As the team brings back the organ, the recipient is called to the hospital. When the patient arrives, doctors take chest x-rays and do blood work to check the H.L.A.—that is, the Human Leukocytes Antigens. These antigens are checked against a panel of antibodies to see whether the donated heart will reject its new body. Doctors then give the patient an injection of a drug called Cyclosporin A, which helps to prevent rejection of the donated heart. This injection is given before the surgery so that anti-rejection drugs will already be circulating in the patient's system. When all these procedures are complete, the patient is wheeled into a room where he waits until the donor heart arrives.

9 When the heart arrives, the patient is taken into surgery where an IV is started. Once the patient is heavily sedated and the donor heart is reexamined, the chest cavity is then opened. I'd like you to look at my first poster, [Figure 16.1] which shows the steps involved in opening the chest cavity.

10 As you can see from Figure 1, surgeons must make a 9-inch incision in the skin of the chest. Then as Figure 2 indicates, they take a saw and cut the sternum. (The sternum is another word for the breastbone.) After they have cut the sternum,

---

6 Henry keeps his topic moving in a chronological sequence. He uses concrete examples (like the Igloo cooler) to make the topic come alive for his listeners.

8 Again, there is a clear transition between numeral II and III of the body.

The speaker continues to explain terms unfamiliar to his audience.

10 Each visual is simple, effective, and clearly labeled. The

FIGURE 16.1

Opening the Chest Cavity

Illustration by George Goebel

OPENING THE CHEST CAVITY

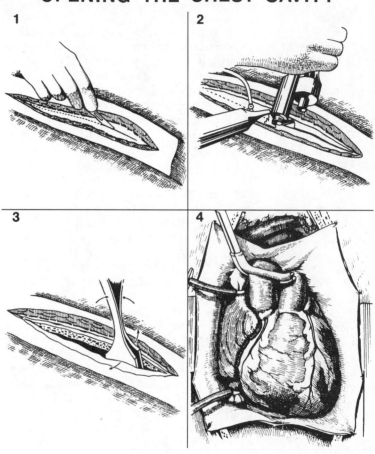

---

speaker carefully explains his visuals and uses humor to generate audience feedback.

Figure 3 shows surgeons using the rib spreader to separate the ribs in order to allow access to the chest cavity. (I hope nobody gets queasy!) Finally, they gain access to the chest cavity, and they are ready to begin the actual transplant as you can see in Figure 4.

11 Henry uses another external transition as he introduces the transplant

11 You've heard how the patient is prepared for surgery and seen how the chest is opened—now I'd like to show you the steps involved in this remarkable transplant procedure. I interviewed my surgeon, Dr. William A. Baumgartner and chief cardiologist Dr. Thomas A. Traill of Johns Hopkins Hospital who told me

process. Although the topic is based on a personal experience, the speaker has provided primary research sources such as the interviews with the doctors to supplement his own knowledge.

12 The speaker directs his

that there are basically three major steps involved with a heart transplant.

12 I'd like you to look at my next poster, [Figure 16.2] which shows the removal of the diseased heart. In the first step,

FIGURE 16.2
Removing the Diseased Heart

Illustration by George Goebel.

REMOVING THE DISEASED HEART

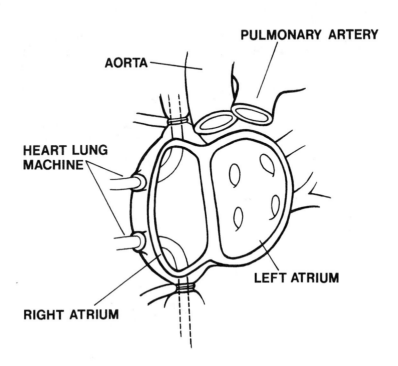

listeners to the next poster and uses the diagram to point out each step in the process. He emphasizes the section of the drawing ("I want you to notice") that he wants listeners to remember in preparation for the next illustration.

surgeons hook the patient up to a pulmonary bypass machine. Notice the tubes running from the heart to the heart-lung machine at the left. The bypass machine takes the place of the heart as the old heart is being removed. Second, the surgeons remove the diseased heart, which has already been done in this drawing; but I want you to notice that the diagram indicates that surgeons do not remove the entire heart—they have left the back of the left and right atrium along in here and parts of the pulmonary artery and aorta as you can see at the top of the drawing.

13 The speaker mentions the label of the diagram for reinforcement and for clarity.

13 Once the diseased heart is removed, surgeons can begin to surgically transplant the donated heart. The third and most delicate part of the surgery is the attachment of the donor organ to the remaining portions of the patient's heart. This step must be performed in four precise stages, which you can see in my next drawing [Figure 16.3].

14 The speaker carefully identifies each step by number, pointing out the areas which need special emphasis. His use of "here," "next," "then," and "finally" helps the audience to follow each stage in the process. The use of humor generates audience feedback, and relieves the tension of a potentially intense topic.

14   1. Here is the first step, where surgeons sew the donated heart to the left atrium, along these suture lines. (Don't try this at home!)
    2. Next they sew the heart to the right atrium, as you can see by these dotted suture lines here.
    3. Then the most important step is sewing together the pulmonary artery (along these dotted lines), which is the heart's main blood vessel that takes blood from the heart to the lungs to get oxygenated.
    4. Finally they sew the heart aorta, which you can see with the suture lines in this area.

15 Once the heart is attached in the four proper places and is checked to make sure there is no leakage, doctors can begin to close the patient's chest.

FIGURE 16.3
Attaching the New Heart
Illustration by George Goebel.

ATTACHING THE NEW HEART

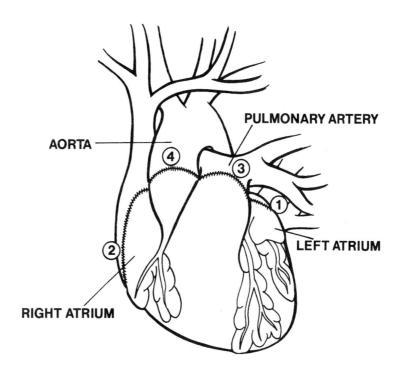

16 The conclusion effectively summarizes additional obstacles of transplant patients.

16 I hope you realize that getting a new heart does not mean everything will be easy. There are many obstacles transplant recipients face on a day to day basis. In my case, for instance, I must take medication for the rest of my life. And this medication often has unpleasant side effects. There is also the constant fear of infection and rejection of the new organ. Doctors must monitor my health closely and I'm required to return every few months for periodic checkups and heart examinations.

17 The final paragraph, revealing Henry's personal feelings, ends the speech on a powerful note.

17 But all this is a small price to pay for what I have. I've been living on my donated heart for three years, and I can honestly say I've never felt better. I would just like to someday tell the family who lost their child how grateful I am for their gift of life![4]

SUMMARY

Demonstration speeches use carefully crafted audiovisual aids to explain how something works, how something is made, how something is done, or how something happens. Demonstrations are not simplistic show-and-tell speeches; they are sophisticated presentations with detailed steps that are grouped into categories, often using chronological sequence.

SKILL BUILDERS

1. Choose a topic from your own knowledge and experience for a five- to seven-minute demonstration speech. Make extensive use of audiovisual aids to convey the process clearly. Be sure that you know how to develop audiovisuals and how to employ them effectively.

2. Watch a program on public television that demonstrates a process such as cooking, home building, or auto repair. Evaluate the effectiveness of the speaker's organization and delivery, clarity of the process, and quality and management of audiovisual aids. Describe what was successful and unsuccessful about the presentation.

3. Divide your class into groups of three or four. Choose one of the demonstration categories on pages 379 and 382: How something works, How something is made, How something is done, or How something happens. Look at the topics listed under the category your group has selected and develop a strategy for demonstrating each topic using audiovisual aids.

   For every topic:

   a. Decide what types of audiovisuals you feel would be most effective.

   b. Describe how you would make effective use of the audiovisuals during a speech.

   c. Present your conclusions to your class for discussion and reaction.

NOTES

1. Cheryl Shelton-Roberts and Bruce Roberts, *Moving Hatteras* (Norfolk: Letton Gooch Printers, 1999), pp. 3–19.

2. Information from the *Encyclopedia Americana* was used for this section on the digestive system.

3. Ann Foley, "Fingerprint Identification," demonstration speech presented in Fundamentals of Public Speaking, Catonsville Community College, Catonsville, MD, 1988. Used by permission.

4. Henry Humm, "Having A Heart," demonstration speech, presented in Fundamentals of Public Speaking, Catonsville Community College, Catonsville, MD, 1987. Used by permission.

Chapter 17

SPEAKING
TO PERSUADE

*The freedom to persuade
and suggest is the essence
of the democratic process.*
    Edward L. Bernays

CHAPTER OBJECTIVES

After reading this chapter you will be able to:

1. Discuss the nature of persuasion;

2. Describe three types of persuasive speeches;

3. Develop propositions of fact, value, and policy;

4. Describe the three means of persuasion;

5. Describe unethical persuasive practices;

6. Recognize the importance of emotion in persuasion;

7. Define and develop three types of logical arguments;

8. Describe and define fallacious arguments;

9. Understand four methods of organizing persuasive speeches;

10. Analyze a persuasive convincing speech;

11. Develop and present a persuasive convincing speech.

Justices on the Supreme Court argue whether a woman should be allowed to sue her rapist. Members of Congress debate gun control legislation in the wake of public school shootings in Jonesboro, Arkansas, West Paducha, Kentucky, and Littleton, Colorado. Government agencies, institutions, and businesses weigh the most effective tools for fixing the Y2K computer glitch. Families discuss the merits of competing Health Maintenance Organizations. Motorists consider purchasing the most desirable cell phone plans that include free weekends and no roaming charges. A preschooler pesters his mother to buy a furry blue Teletubby. Indeed, persuasion is a fact of life at all levels of a democratic society.

We use persuasion consciously and subconsciously. Whether we are asking a supervisor for a promotion, listening to a eulogy, or explaining a speeding ticket to a judge in traffic court, we are involved in persuasive activities.

We must understand and acquire the skills necessary for persuasive effectiveness. This chapter considers the nature of persuasion, the different types of persuasive appeals, and persuasive organization, and provides some guidelines to help you construct your persuasive speech to convince.

PERSUASION AND THE AUDIENCE

The Sixth Amendment to the United States Constitution guarantees that any American accused of a crime "has the right to a speedy and public trial, by an impartial jury . . ." The system was designed to provide the accused with a fair trial and to offer society a means of determining justice. Ordinary citizens hear evidence presented by two opposing sides and then debate the guilt or innocence of a defendant based upon the merits of the case. These citizens, or jurors, must then decide if there is sufficient "reasonable doubt" to acquit a defendant or whether evidence is strong enough to convict. This process requires jurors to evaluate persuasive messages,

Persuasive speakers seek to change beliefs, intensify feelings, or move listeners to action such as voting for a specific cause or candidate.

think critically about persuasive arguments, and make judgments about the credibility of testimony, events, and ultimately, individuals.

Since they know that persuasion is so important to the judicial process, prosecutors and defense attorneys strive to develop the most convincing arguments to sway jurors to accept their interpretations of the facts. In order to present the strongest cases, attorneys want to know as much about jurors as possible. Lawyers for both sides are allowed to ask questions of potential jurors to examine their attitudes about crucial issues associated with the trial. Attorneys and paralegals pour over detailed jury profiles to determine education, occupation, and life experience. In many cases, lawyers turn to professional jury consulting firms to help them analyze jurors, identify those that are sympathetic, and devise winning arguments.

The jury consulting business has become a two-hundred-million-dollar industry that has benefited defendants in some very high profile cases in America. When Lyle and Erik Menendez killed their parents with shotguns, the district attorney asked for the death penalty. However, the defense team hired a consulting firm that devised 122 questions related to the strategy of the case. Potential jurors were asked "Do you have any strongly held beliefs that a child does not have the right to kill a parent in self-defense?" and "What sort of psychological effects do you think continuous . . . sexual abuse by a parent has on the child?"[1] Individuals who didn't agree that children could kill their parents in self-defense were eliminated from the jury. The first Menendez trial resulted in hung juries, with almost half of the jurors arguing for manslaughter and the other half wanting murder convictions. In another case, attorneys for William Kennedy Smith, who was accused of rape at the Kennedy mansion in Palm Beach, Florida, hired consultants to conduct focus groups to determine what types of jurors would be more receptive to the arguments of the defense. Their research concluded that young men would be the worst jurors and older women would be the most helpful. Defense lawyers were able to keep young males off the jury and include several older women who voted to acquit Smith.[2]

Then there is the O.J. Simpson trial. Lawyers for the former football star hired jury consultant Jo-Ellan Dimitrius of Trial Logistics, Inc. Dimitrius and her colleagues developed a three-hundred-page questionnaire that was designed to help the defense select jurors that would be sympathetic to the argument that police were guilty of misconduct. The final jury included eight African Americans, eight women, no white males, and only two jurors who had college degrees. Consultant Demitrius's research found that African Americans had a higher mistrust of Los Angeles police than other demographic groups due to well-known cases such as the Rodney King beating and the acquittal of police officers charged with King's assault. Once the jury was selected, their reactions to courtroom arguments and evidence were watched closely by the consultant, who was seated in the second row of the courtroom throughout the trial.[3] Dimitrius suggested that lawyers use words such as "contaminated," "corrupted," and "cancer" when referring to the evidence. In one instance the consultant suggested that the defense shorten their cross-examinations because jurors were becoming inattentive.[4] Prosecutors in the Simpson case also used a jury consultant. Donald Vinson of Decision Quest, Inc., found that a majority of African American women were sympathetic to Simpson and felt he was unable to commit murder because of his excellence in professional football.[5] Consultant Vinson also found that more than forty percent of potential jurors "believed it was acceptable to use physical force on a family member."[6] The two sides differed significantly on how they responded to their experts' conclusions. Defense attorneys paid close attention to their jury consultant, but the prosecution, trusting instead in their "mountain of evidence," almost completely ignored their courtroom advisor.[7]

Although these examples indicate that jury analysis can be effective, it is important to stress that there are many other issues that led jurors to their decisions. The first Menendez trial may have ended in a hung jury, but a second trial concluded with a unanimous verdict of first-degree murder against the two brothers. Accusations against William Kennedy Smith were not credible to all jurors, and some evidence was inadmissible, contributing to a verdict favoring the defense.[8] And the Simpson prosecution made numerous mistakes, which included misleading the jury about the prior racial history of detective Mark Fuhrman.[9]

It is also important to emphasize that audience analysis and jury predictability is an inexact science at best. It is impossible to completely foretell how human beings will respond when presented with a unique speaker, a series of complicated arguments and emotional appeals, and the dynamics of a given setting and speaking occasion. It is clear, however, that persuasive speakers in the judicial arena use all the legal means at their disposal to understand their audiences and develop persuasive appeals that can be most influential and effective.

THE NATURE OF PERSUASION

Persuasion can be defined as communication that influences and changes the beliefs, feelings, or behavior of a listener. Persuasive speeches convince, stimulate, and actuate. To develop the correct speech for the appropriate persuasive situation, you must know how each of these types of presentation differs.

Speeches to Convince

The goal of the speech to *convince* is to alter the beliefs and judgments of an audience. As we have seen, a prosecuting attorney tries to convince jurors that a defendant is guilty. A legislator attempts to convince other lawmakers that a tax increase is the best way to solve the deficit problem. A parent tries to convince the PTA to consider adding sex education classes in elementary grades. While a convincing speech may lead an audience to take some future action, it is important to emphasize that the immediate goal of a speech to convince is to obtain mental agreement with the speaker's position. In a speech to convince, a speaker persuades an audience to believe that a problem exists, that a proposed solution is a better alternative, or that some future action may be required.

Speeches to Stimulate

In a speech to *stimulate,* the speaker seeks to reinforce and intensify the beliefs or feelings of listeners. A coach gives the football team a pep talk at halftime to generate enthusiasm and a winning spirit. A religious leader reminds the congregation about basic beliefs to strengthen faith. A political leader makes a Veterans' Day speech to rekindle patriotic feelings.

Therapeutic groups come together for mutual reinforcement. Members of Alcoholics Anonymous, drug rehabilitation centers, or parental stress organizations relate their personal experiences for empathy, encouragement, and positive change. As a rule, agreement already exists between speaker and audience about basic beliefs and goals. It is the purpose of the stimulating speech to focus on these sentiments and bring them to the surface.

Speeches to Actuate

Speeches to *actuate* motivate audiences to act. A salesperson selling a product, a candidate asking for votes, or a humanitarian appealing for donations to a worthy charity are all seeking to affect the behavior of the audience. Highly effective thirty- to sixty-second commercials motivate children, teenagers, young adults, or senior citizens to buy products designed "with you in mind." In a speech to actuate, a speaker generates curiosity, clarifies a problem, identifies a solution, and then persuades the audience to perform a specific action related to the solution. The action the speaker solicits is clear, direct, and observable.

Selecting the Persuasive Topic

When you begin to build your persuasive speech, your first task is to choose a topic with potential to influence your audience. Begin by analyzing some of your interests, concerns, and activities. You might have a concern about the pollutants in our oceans. You might be an avid hunter and resent gun-control legislation. Or you might be upset by the leniency of the courts toward criminals. Hundreds of issues would make excellent topics for persuasive speeches. The key to your success, as in any speech, is your degree of commitment to the issue, your ability to select appropriate supporting materials, and your competence in organizing and delivering your thoughts.

Wording the Proposition Statement

Once you have selected a topic, write a statement called a *proposition,* an arguable resolution phrased in a declarative sentence. The proposition acts as the focal point for your arguments and supporting materials. Like the specific purpose sentence, the proposition statement relates the overall objective of the speech at the end of the introduction. Unlike the specific purpose, the proposition reveals a clear point of view on a controversial topic.

To convince your audience that a relationship exists between TV violence and the behavior of young children, you could state several propositions:

Violence on television contributes to violent behavior in young children.

Violence in TV cartoons has harmful effects on young children.

TV violence can contribute to severe emotional trauma in young children.

You would select one of the above statements and conduct research to find supporting evidence—statistics, testimonies, and examples. You would need to be certain that the evidence did indeed back up your proposition. If it did not, you would be faced with three choices: (1) conducting a more extensive search for evidence until you found suitable data; (2) rephrasing the proposition to correspond to existing evidence, or (3) looking for another issue.

Once you had written your proposition and gathered your evidence, you would construct logical arguments to support your point of view. (We will consider logic and reasoning later in this chapter.) Thorough research and appropriate evidence are extremely important to your success as a persuasive speaker. Your speech will have a significant impact on your listeners if they feel your proposition is validated by careful research and good evidence.

PROPOSITIONS OF FACT, VALUE, AND POLICY

You can select any of three proposition statements for a persuasive speech: propositions of fact, value, or policy. In a *proposition of fact,* you develop a statement you believe is true and must be verified by evidence. Here are some examples:

PROPOSITION OF FACT

America is in decline.

Columbus did not discover America.

Victims of rape are treated as criminals by the judicial system.

Bans against controversial art exhibitions violate the First Amendment.

There will be a major volcanic eruption in Alaska within the next five years.

Global warming is a myth.

The above propositions are not actual facts, but facts as they are perceived by the persuasive speaker. If you took a survey in most audiences, you would probably find a variety of opinions about each statement. It is the speaker's job to gather evidence that persuades the audience that the perceived fact stated in the proposition is correct.

In a *proposition of value,* you are required to judge or evaluate an issue. You ask the audience to believe something is right or wrong, good or bad, effective or ineffective.

PROPOSITION OF VALUE

Home schools are damaging to children.

The practice of "Don't Ask Don't Tell" regarding the sexual preference of military personnel is discriminatory.

Athletic scholarships are beneficial to colleges and universities.

Aspartame is not the safe sugar substitute that we have been led to believe.

Research into human cloning is unethical.

Sororities and fraternities are harmful to educational institutions.

Notice that these propositions contain words like "damaging," "discriminatory," "beneficial," "unethical," or "harmful," which contribute to judgment or evaluation of the issue. If you choose a proposition of value for your persuasive speech, you must support it with appropriate evidence.

If you were to select a *proposition of policy,* you would advocate the adoption of a future action or behavior.

PROPOSITION OF POLICY

Prices for prescription drugs should be strictly regulated.

Borrowers who default on student loans should be given jail terms.

Boxing matches between men and women should be prohibited.

HMO insurance plans should be required to pay for birth control.

America should not be the peacekeeper of the world.

English should not be the official language of America.

The Internet should be strictly regulated and controlled.

Each proposition contains the word "should" and proposes an action or a change in future policy. Each issue requires extensive evidence to persuade the audience to believe that the intended policy is the correct course of action.

Spend some time developing your proposition statement. Choose simple words and clear phrases so that the statement flows evenly and conveys your viewpoint on a debatable issue regarding a fact, value, or policy.

ETHOS, PATHOS, AND *LOGOS:* THE MEANS OF PERSUASION

The Greek rhetorician Aristotle wrote that there are three means of persuasion: "The first kind reside in the character *[ethos]* of the speaker; the second consist in producing a certain attitude *[pathos]* in the hearer; the third appertain to the argument proper *[logos]*."[10] While in ancient Greece these three elements were considered as separate structures, today we view them as interrelated. Think of ethos, pathos, and logos as a pyramid that is not complete without any one of its three sides. Persuasion without ethos has no credibility; a speech without pathos generates no feeling; and a speaker deficient in logos reasons without sound argument. While we will consider each area separately, it is important to remember their interconnection.

Ethos: **The Ethical Appeal**

Ethos represents that dimension that causes us to trust and believe the individuals persuading us. We have confidence in speakers when they are sincere and knowledgeable about issues, show commitment to their persuasive goals, and demonstrate concern for the welfare of others. Ethos involves ethics, character, and credibility. To Aristotle, ethos was "the most potent of all the means to persuasion."[11]

A student remarked in class, "I believe that the most important thing in persuasion is the number of individuals the speaker is able to influence. If the speech changes the opinions or behavior of a lot of people, then it was successful, don't you think?" The problem with this idea is that it measures persuasion in terms of outcomes, without considering the means to the ends.

The success of a persuasive speech must not be measured entirely by outcomes, or civilization will continue to nurture terrorists like Adolf Hitler, Jim Jones, or David Koresh. A persuasive speech should be judged by the ethical means speakers use to influence listeners. When Saddam Hussein delivers a speech, most Americans react with hostility because of Iraq's aggressive activities in the Middle East. When South African Nelson Mandella presents a speech, however, we listen with interest because of his struggle against the practice of apartheid and his devotion to democratic reforms for the people of South Africa. Because of her unselfish service to humanity, people of all spiritual beliefs responded to the words and deeds of the late Mother Teresa. If a speaker advocates ideas that benefit others, demonstrates commitment to persuasive goals, and possesses personal actions consistent with stated beliefs, the persuader will be establishing a positive foundation for ethical appeals.

In a democratic society, citizens expect ethical persuasive practices. To help you become more aware of unethical persuasive techniques, here is a partial list including some brief explanations and examples.

UNETHICAL PERSUASIVE PRACTICES

Advocating harm.   Withholding information necessary for people's welfare, inciting people to violence; "scapegoating"; or isolating groups according to ethnicity, race, religion, or other characteristic for the purpose of assigning blame. Prior to World War II, Hitler blamed the Jewish people for all of Germany's economic problems. Scapegoating was just one sinister tactic Hitler used to prepare for the Holocaust.

Name-calling.   The so-called ad hominem argument which attacks the character or personality of an individual; the use of loaded words to attack an individual or group. In the 1950s, Senator Joe McCarthy falsely accused many Americans of being "card-carrying Communists."

Plagiarizing.   Intellectual stealing; quoting or paraphrasing words and phrases without identifying the source. During the 1987 presidential primaries, Senator Joseph Biden of Delaware was forced to withdraw from the race because he used phrases from the speeches of other politicians without giving them proper credit.

Providing False Information.   Any argument that is inaccurate, false, taken out of context, or deliberately distorts information to mislead the audience. This practice is often called "the big lie." After Chinese Communists massacred thousands of protesters in the 1989 prodemocracy demonstrations, they used "the big lie" to tell Chinese citizens that the military had fired warning shots into the air and that no demonstrators had lost their lives.

Using Offensive Language.   Language that is vulgar, obscene, or insulting; language that is offensive or injurious to any person or group. Any public speaker who uses obscenities for shock value violates the ethical standards of the community and causes most audience members to stop listening.

Card-stacking. Presenting arguments in a biased and unfair manner; arguments that unfairly stack the deck against an issue, deliberately ignoring opposite information. Here's an example of a "buy-American" sales pitch: "Americans buy more American cars than any other models; American cars cost less than foreign models; American cars have increased fuel efficiency over the past decade, and American cars have better overall performance than foreign makes." This ad ignores the fact that foreign sales have sky-rocketed over the past 15 years to more than 30 percent of the market. It also fails to mention that many foreign cars are still more fuel efficient and more reliable than their American counterparts.

Pathos—The Emotional Appeal

Pathos plays a very important part in persuasion. Speeches come alive when the speaker appeals to the heart as well as to the intellect of the listener. Without emotion, persuasive speeches would contain a lifeless collage of intellectual quotations and statistics. Think of a speech about lung

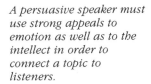

A persuasive speaker must use strong appeals to emotion as well as to the intellect in order to connect a topic to listeners.

cancer without any reference to a person afflicted with the disease, or a presentation about overcoming paralysis without any mention of an individual such as Christopher Reeve. It is emotion that helps to connect an audience to a topic and create sympathy for the speaker's point of view.

The emotions that are employed in a speech usually depend upon the topic, audience, speaker, and occasion. As you think about the use of emotion, ask yourself several questions about the speech. What emotions are appropriate to my topic? What are the characteristics of my audience and which emotions will be most persuasive to them? What feelings do I have about the topic and what emotions could I convey spontaneously and effectively? What emotions are appropriate or inappropriate to the occasion of the speech?

IDENTIFY EMOTIONS

As you are preparing your speech, identify the specific emotions you want to reach within your listeners. Do you want them to experience a feeling of empathy or should they be angry because of a problem or issue? Should they feel compassion or resentment as a result of an ongoing condition or situation? The following list and sample issues includes several emotions that you might use to influence your audience. Remember, however, that it represents only a partial listing of all the emotions and combinations of feelings that are available for persuasive presentations.

Anger	Bombings of African American churches; Bosnian war criminals; treatment of rape victims; drug-related crimes; child sexual abuse; Dr. Jack Kevorkian.
Despair	The mass murder of the people of Kosovo; famine and starvation in Somalia; public school shootings of teachers and students; enslavement due to alcoholism, cocaine and heroin addiction.
Fear	Losing health insurance, social security, or Medicare; the lack of automotive safety; credit card debt; bankruptcy; violent crime; losing a job.
Hope	The ability of people to work together to help people afflicted with muscular dystrophy, cystic fibrosis, multiple sclerosis, Alzheimer's disease, and autism.
Joy	Watching the troops return home from a war; winning the World Series or Superbowl; climbing Mt. Everest, conquering cancer; surviving paralysis; overcoming addiction; losing weight.

Love	A grandparent or parent; husband or wife; a child, friend, or pet.
Pride	Work; physical appearance; a hobby or interest; church, community, city, state, country, or flag.
Sorrow and Compassion	A victim dying of AIDS; an Alzheimer's patient and family; those dying in an automobile, train, or airplane accident; individuals losing worldly possessions as a result of a hurricane, war, flood, forest fire, earthquake, or volcano.

Heather Hoag was concerned about the lack of security within the airline industry. She became interested in this topic as a result of her own painful experience and she felt obligated to share her knowledge and misgivings with listeners. As you read this excerpt from her persuasive speech, notice how the speaker develops the example to make listeners feel uneasy:

Some of you are probably saying to yourself that if security is so bad at airports, then why do I have to walk through a metal detector or show identification in order to be allowed into the gate area? Well I'd like to share a story that may change your mind about the adequacy of airport security.

Imagine for a minute that you are a sophomore in college and you've just arrived home for Christmas break. As you open the door you are not greeted with warm smiles and happy hellos. Instead, you see your family's eyes glued to the TV. You watch and listen as a reporter frantically states that an airplane enroute to New York from England has just exploded over Lockerbie, Scotland, killing all 259 passengers and crew. Then the picture on the screen changes. You recognize it! It's your college chapel. The camera pans to a group of girls hugging and crying. You recognize them also. The reporter reveals that among the 259 killed were 35 students from Syracuse University. I was that sophomore who had just returned home from Syracuse University for Christmas break.

Investigations into the December 21, 1988 bombing of Pan Am Flight #103 revealed that inadequate security was the ultimate cause of this tragedy. In Emerson and Duffy's book, *The Fall of Pan Am 103: Inside the Lockerbie Investigation,* a former Pan Am security official testified that he had received permission from an FAA official to use less stringent procedures of x-raying bags that were unaccompanied by their owners to save time during the busy pre-Christmas rush. I don't think that the girls I knew on that flight—Linsday, Karen, and Alexis—would have minded if their flight had been delayed or canceled![12]

Heather clearly understood the emotions she wanted to reach. Beginning with a reference to her listeners' complacent attitudes, Heather quickly made the audience feel insecure and unsafe. She created suspense as she related the probable hypothetical example. By the end of the story, the audience knew that the experience was very real and had affected Heather personally. Listeners experienced feelings of sympathy and compassion for Heather and her three friends who perished in the tragedy and were dramatically named at the end of the passage.

UNDERSTAND AUDIENCE EMOTIONS

As you think about developing emotional appeals, you need to analyze your audience thoroughly in order to discover what emotional "buttons" to push. Are listeners college students who are angry at rising tuition costs and supplemental "user fees" such as parking permits, library cards, laboratory charges, and technology fees? Are they minorities who have experienced feelings of hurt and anger as a result of prejudice and discrimination? Are your listeners new parents who have experienced the joy and pain of childbirth, yet face the future with insecurity and uncertainty? If you know the motivations and needs of your audience, you will be able to develop appeals which connect to their interests and gain sympathy for your cause.

This speaker carefully analyzed the emotions of his audience. He knew that many of his listeners were parents with school-age children and he also knew that they had computers at home. Notice how the speaker combined vivid examples with concrete language to create emotional appeals that frightened the parents in his audience.

> Imagine that a child you know well is lured away from home by a pervert that he met online. Imagine that another child has a new friend that he spends countless hours with online, and that this "new friend" is not a peer, but turns out to be a pedophile. Imagine that a young girl has nude pictures of adults engaged in acts of bondage and sodomy that she has obtained online. These online services should be banned until they are child-proof because our children are being lured away from their homes and abused; our children are being exposed to explicit photos and texts, and pedophiles are cloaking their real identities.
>
> Right now, a fifty-one-year-old man is serving six years in a California prison for raping a sixteen-year-old boy. They met online. According to an article in a June 27th, 1993, issue of the *Baltimore Sun,* he lured the boy to his home by pretending to have some brand new computer software. This boy later attempted suicide. These Internet, online services provide the perfect cover for people who would victimize our children. People pose as sisterly or brother figures, motherly or fatherly figures, they masquerade as other children, and they pretend to be devoted to hobbies or subjects that interest our kids. One man went so far as to set up his own Star Trek bulletin board to attract children that he later abused.[13]

Kenneth Ruffin openly appealed to fear and anger. The speaker used the words "our children," "victimize," and "online" as tools to underscore the intensity of parental emotions and get to the heart of the issue. Following the speech a spirited discussion took place. Audience members said they often felt "violated" by the Internet and "helpless" when attempting to control these online services coming into their homes. One parent also expressed frustration at her inability to closely monitor her children's computer activities outside the home. Ken's study of the audience paid off. His research enabled him to select an issue that was vitally important to listeners.

EXPRESS YOUR OWN FEELINGS

A personal commitment to a topic is extremely helpful when a speaker wants to convey the emotional aspects of a presentation. Topics that are linked to your interests, experiences, and/or knowledge can provide the stimulus for expressing your feelings spontaneously to listeners. You have already seen how Heather Hoag demonstrated her concern about airport security by referring to her three friends who perished in the bombing of Pan Am Flight 103. Likewise, you can share your feelings more deeply if you have a personal involvement or interest in the issue.

Emotions can seldom be mechanically rehearsed or artificially staged: they are expressed more effectively when the speaker allows feelings to surface naturally during the course of a speech. A successful speaker conveys the degree and intensity of these natural emotions through the delivery of the presentation. Increased or decreased volume can communicate strength of feeling. Verbal emphasis, facial expression, movement, and gesture can reinforce important emotional segments such as stories or examples. Dramatic pauses or silences can allow time for feelings to sink in. A speaker cannot influence listeners effectively without knowing how to deliver the emotional elements needed for persuasion. This speaker selected a topic from her own painful experience with an alcoholic parent. Notice how she combined logical appeals with emotions in this brief narrative:

> Of twenty-eight million children of alcoholics in this country, the odds are that there are two within this class. Now I'm not going to survey and try to prove or disprove the odds. I will tell you that there is definitely one. Like Suzanne Somers, I too am an adult child of an alcoholic. I am in the process of learning how to talk about it, how to trust, and how to feel and own all my emotions. Suzanne's story is incredible because her entire family recovered, including those who were alcoholic. In my family there were four children. I too, like Suzanne, escaped alcoholism. But two of my siblings did not. It is my hope that, one day, my entire family will recover.

The statistic, example, and testimony comprise the logical, factual evidence. However, the evidence becomes deeply emotional when the speaker reveals her personal experience. The emotion genuinely moved the audience because the speaker used effective facial expressions, vocal inflections, and eye contact to communicate strong personal feelings. As Aristotle said about pathos, ". . . we give very different decisions under the sway of pain or joy, and liking or hatred."[14]

CONNECT EMOTIONS TO THE OCCASION

Numerous speeches are presented to celebrate or pay tribute to individuals, groups, symbols, or events on important occasions. Speakers who want to be well prepared seek to understand and acknowledge the emotions that are significant on these occasions. A supervisor might pay tribute to the loyalty of a worker who is retiring after thirty-five years of service. A religious official might refer to shared spiritual values when dedicating a new church, mosque, or synagogue. A family friend could reminisce about a couple's courtship at a fiftieth wedding anniversary. A governor might acknowledge the shared pain of citizens on the anniversary of a bombing, a natural disaster, or an assassination. No matter what the event, the speaker must understand the occasion completely in order to develop language and create images that will elicit the appropriate feelings and response.

On August 31, 1997, Princess Diana of Great Britain was involved in a tragic automobile accident in Paris, France. In just a few hours, the shocking news spread throughout the world of the car crash which killed the Princess, her companion, Dodi Al Fayed, and a driver, and seriously injured a bodyguard. The world community reacted with disbelief as the details of the accident investigation revealed facts about an intoxicated driver operating the Mercedes at excessive speeds to escape the ever-present media or "paparazzi." Several days later, a memorial service was held in London's Westminster Abbey to honor the life of the beloved Princess. It became the task of Diana's brother, Earl Spencer, to eulogize his sister in an emotional tribute witnessed by Diana's two teenage sons, her ex-husband Prince Charles, the British Royal Family, and an immense worldwide audience.

> I stand before you today the representative of a family in grief, in a country in mourning before a world in shock. We are all united not only in our desire to pay our respects to Diana but rather in our need to do so. For such was her extraordinary appeal that the tens of millions of people taking part in this service all over the world via television and radio who never actually met her, feel that they, too, lost someone close to them in the early hours of Sunday morning. It is a more remarkable tribute to Diana than I can ever hope to offer her today.
>
> Diana was the very essence of compassion, of duty, of style, of beauty. All over the world she was a symbol of selfless humanity, a standard-bearer for the rights of the truly downtrodden, a truly British girl who transcended nationality, someone with a natural nobility who was classless, who proved in the last year that she needed no royal title to continue to generate her particular brand of magic. . . .

> Without your God-given sensitivity, we would be immersed in greater ignorance at the anguish of AIDS and HIV sufferers, the plight of the homeless, the isolation of lepers, the random destruction of land mines. Diana explained to me once that it was her innermost feelings of suffering that made it possible for her to connect with her constituency of the rejected.[15]

Spencer clearly understood the intense emotions of the occasion. He acknowledged the feelings of millions who felt an emotional link to the Princess and he was candid about Diana's deep insecurities that led to eating disorders and other difficulties. Although the speech was not without controversy in its remarks aimed at the Royal Family, it honored Diana's memory and her earnest dedication to humanity.

Charisma. Some speakers possess special magnetic qualities, called charisma, that attract audiences and inspire confidence. Franklin D. Roosevelt, John F. Kennedy, Martin Luther King Jr., Ronald Reagan, and Jesse Jackson are leaders who were able to influence audiences because of these unique abilities.

No one expects you to have the charisma of these political leaders. Yet every speaker has a unique personal style that can be developed with speaking experience. Whether you use dramatic pausing, effective gestures, or vivid mental images, you can refine your personal style to communicate emotion successfully.

You can gain a better understanding of this quality by reading Jesse Jackson's speech, "Common Ground and Common Sense" in the Appendix. Remember, however, that a silent reading of the speech does not do justice to the charismatic style of Reverend Jackson. You should view the videotape to experience the feelings Jackson conveyed through his gestures, vocal inflections, and facial expressions.

A Word of Caution. Strong emotion has advantages and disadvantages. Emotion is a powerful motivator, and audiences are often captivated when charismatic speakers employ passionate examples. Emotion can be inappropriate, however, if speakers use a long string of emotional examples without appealing to the listener's intellect. While emotion can arouse curiosity and maintain audience interest for a while, strong emotion tends to fade, resulting in a shallow basis for persuasion.

Emotion and charisma can also be dangerously exploitive. In chapter 6 we discussed how a strong emotional appeal and a magnetic personality may often conceal hidden agendas of greed. Numerous charlatans have successfully contrived emotional appeals to religious feelings, humanitarian causes, or consumer needs to reap huge personal benefits. Be wary of the individual who uses only strong appeals to personal feelings. Remember that the effective persuader must appeal to ethics and logic, and use emotion judiciously.

Logos—The Appeal to Reason

Your ultimate goal in a persuasive speech is to influence the audience to consider and ultimately to accept your point of view through *logos*. Your task is similar to that of a trial attorney who builds a case based upon solid evidence and draws conclusions to persuade jurors of a defendant's guilt or innocence.

One way to achieve your persuasive objective is to follow a process called *reasoning,* in which you present logical arguments to your audience. We are familiar with arguments or disputes where we express our feelings and personal opinions about relationships, current events, movies, or fashion. Logical *arguments* in a persuasive speech, however, must be grounded in clear and correct facts, complete evidence, and accurate reasoning. A common way for persuasive speakers to develop arguments is by presenting relevant supporting materials such as statistics, testimonies, and examples and by drawing conclusions from the data to back up a point of view.[16]

A speaker wanting to support a claim that a campus parking problem exists could phrase an argument like this:

> I'm sure many of you already know that we have a severe parking problem on our campus. Statistics from the Dean of Student's office indicate that there are two thousand more commuter students than there are parking spaces. I did an informal survey of fifty students and asked them if they thought there were parking problems on campus. Thirty-nine of them said yes, six who used the bus said no, and five didn't have an opinion. The majority of the students in this survey—78 percent—felt that a parking problem exists. I also interviewed the Director of Student Activities who told me that [quote] "We have a campus parking crisis." And I want you all to know, that I was ten minutes late for this class, and almost missed my speech today because I had to "hawk" a parking place way over on the other side of campus next to the stadium. You can see that the evidence indicates that we have a severe problem—a problem that we've got to solve.

The speaker has provided a list of supporting materials that include two statistical cases, one testimony of authority, and a personal experience. The speaker cites a clear conclusion to summarize the data and to support the claim. The logical argument can be written in the form of a diagram:

Claim: There is a parking problem on campus.

Supporting evidence: A. There are two thousand more commuter students than parking spaces.

B. Seventy-eight percent of students in informal survey said there was a parking problem.

C. Director of Student Activities says there is a parking "crisis."

D. I was late for class because of parking problem.

Conclusion: Evidence suggests that there is a parking problem on campus.

When you construct arguments, be very careful how you draw conclusions from your data. Notice that this speaker states that evidence "indicates"— the speaker does not say they "prove" the conclusion. Evidence does not offer conclusive proof but rather "points to" a conclusion. Your audience will be more open to persuasion if you use terms such as *imply, signify, suggest, indicate,* or *reveal,* and stay away from terms that express absolute statements of proof.

When you use a logical argument you must avoid fallacious reasoning. A *fallacy* occurs whenever a speaker uses unclear or incorrect facts, incomplete evidence, and/or erroneous reasoning.

Biased sampling is a fallacy where statistics or examples are not representative of the entire population. For instance, were students in the informal parking survey selected by random sample, or were they deliberately chosen because they already agreed with the speaker's point of view?

A *hasty generalization* is another fallacy that occurs when a speaker draws a faulty conclusion from extreme exceptions or from limited evidence. Are there other university officials who agree with the student activity director's viewpoint, or is the director the only exception? Were the parking difficulties experienced by the speaker a normal occurrence, or were they due to a special event such as a conference or a basketball game? We've all been guilty of making hasty generalizations. The victim whose home has been burglarized declares, "I came home and discovered I was robbed. I called the 911 emergency number and it took 25 minutes for the police to respond. The cops are never around when you need them." While the victim is obviously frustrated, the one example could have been an isolated case. Much more statistical and testimonial evidence must be presented before a speaker should draw such a conclusion.

Some arguments are so frequently used that they have been classified and labeled. These arguments can help you apply general models of reasoning to your persuasive speeches. We will consider arguments based upon enumeration, analogy, and causation.[17]

ARGUMENTS BASED UPON ENUMERATION

When you employ *enumeration* in a speech, you cite a series of specific cases to support a generalization. If you wanted to support a claim that most large cities have a drug problem, you could develop the following argument of enumeration:

Claim: Most large cities have a drug problem.

Supporting evidence: A. Los Angeles, in the top 20 largest cities, has a drug problem.
B. New York, in the top 20 largest cities, has a drug problem.
C. Chicago, in the top 20 largest cities, has a drug problem.
D. Houston, in the top 20 largest cities, has a drug problem.

Conclusion: Most of the top 20 largest cities have drug problems.

In this argument, the speaker cites four different examples of large cities with drug problems, and states a conclusion which accurately reflects supporting evidence. The speaker uses the word "most" in the conclusion to indicate that "a great majority" of the largest cities have drug problems. The speaker could present a stronger argument by stating that *"All* of the 20 largest cities have a drug problem." The word *all* cannot be used, of course, unless each of the 20 largest cities has been researched and found to have these difficulties. The weakest arguments are those where the word(s) *some* or *a few* are used. If supporting evidence were to force a speaker to draw the conclusion that only "some cities have a drug problem," then the argument would lack strength and influence.

Determine the amount of evidence you need for a particular conclusion. If your conclusion is highly controversial such as for or against nuclear power plants, surrogate parenthood, or the right to die, you will need many more statistics, examples, and testimonies to construct coherent arguments and draw logical conclusions.

ARGUMENTS BASED UPON ANALOGY

When you reason from *analogy,* you are comparing two or more similar cases to show that, because of their similarity, what applies to one case can also apply to the other.[18] For example:

Claim: Baltimore is similar to other cities with new stadiums.

Supporting evidence: A. Baltimore, the Twin Cities, Jacksonville, and Indianapolis have populations of 500,000 or more.

B. These cities have a similar sports tradition.

C. The Twin Cities, Jacksonville, and Indianapolis all have built and/or planned new stadiums.

D. Further, we know that the Twin Cities, Jacksonville, and Indianapolis have been successful with their new NFL franchises.

Conclusion: Because Baltimore is similar in important ways to other cities that have been successful with their new NFL major league franchises, it is likely that Baltimore's new NFL franchise will be successful as well.

In this analogy, the speaker has cited examples to illustrate the similarity of other cities to Baltimore. The conclusion then seeks to persuade listeners that because conditions in Baltimore are similar to conditions in other cities, Baltimore will obtain a similar result.

Arguments based on analogies can be effective if the examples being compared share a number of characteristics. *Faulty analogies*

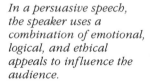

In a persuasive speech, the speaker uses a combination of emotional, logical, and ethical appeals to influence the audience.

occur, however, when examples are dissimilar. A speaker in New Jersey who wants to raise the speed limit to 70 on state highways and compares New Jersey to Wyoming and Kansas is guilty of a faulty analogy. New Jersey is an urban state with high population density, while Wyoming and Kansas are not. For an effective analogy, your examples must have a variety of similar principles or characteristics. Your audience will be persuaded if your analogy is valid in several areas.

ARGUMENTS BASED UPON CAUSATION

When you use logical arguments based upon *causation,* you identify known causes to determine unknown effects (cause-to-effect reasoning), or you identify known effects to determine the unknown cause (effect-to-cause reasoning). Here is an example of cause-to-effect reasoning:

> **Claim:** The current severe drought in the Midwest will contribute to higher food prices in the fall.
>
> **Supporting evidence:** A. People continue to buy food during droughts.
> B. Severe droughts contribute to food shortages.
> C. In the past, severe droughts have created higher food prices.
>
> **Conclusion:** The current drought will create a shortage that will cause food prices to rise in the fall.

In this argument, the speaker has used the known cause—the current drought—as well as evidence of past droughts, to predict the unknown effect—that prices will rise in the fall. So the speaker's claim that food prices will rise during the harvest is persuasive because it is based upon good evidence and sound reasoning.

Fallacies, known as *faulty causes* or *faulty effects,* can sometimes occur in causative reasoning. Effects often have more than one cause. For instance, the food shortage could have other causes, such as fewer farms producing wheat due to the grain-subsidy program and/or massive government exports that depleted grain reserves.

Also, some causes are not capable of producing the assumed effects. For example, erratic weather conditions in the United States in the latter 1990s were said to be caused by a phenomenon known as El Niño, which refers to a gradual warming of the oceans. Although this natural occurrence was a legitimate scientific explanation for many irregular weather patterns, El Niño often took the blame for anything unpleasant such as an earthquake, a downturn in the stock market, or rising food prices.

Make certain that your evidence clearly supports a single cause of the effect, and that the cause is capable of producing the identified effect.

Here is an example of reasoning based upon effect to cause:

Claim: High cholesterol contributed to Jack's heart attack.

Supporting evidence: A. Jack's doctor repeatedly warned Jack to lower his intake of cholesterol.
   B. Diets containing high cholesterol can increase blockage of arteries, which according to the American Medical Association contributes to heart attacks.
   C. Jack's cholesterol level was checked a week before his heart attack and found to be high.

Conclusion: Jack's diet of high cholesterol contributed to his heart attack.

In this example, the speaker has observed the known effect, Jack's heart attack, and drawn a speculative conclusion about the unknown cause from supporting data provided about Jack.

While it is highly probable that Jack's diet of high cholesterol contributed to his heart attack, there may be a faulty cause. Were there other possible causes of the heart attack such as Jack's weight, his lack of exercise, or his stressful lifestyle? Was his diet of high cholesterol merely a coincidental contributing factor? If Jack had lost weight, exercised, and reduced tension, would his diet have contributed to a heart attack?

Use caution when you reason from effect to cause. A woman with a black eye may not have been beaten by her husband, but might have been in a car accident. Concern about the economy may not have been the only cause of the decline in stocks; there could have been a variety of reasons, including computerized trading and a falling dollar.

OTHER LOGICAL FALLACIES

In the previous logical arguments, we have considered several fallacies—biased sampling, hasty generalizations, faulty analogies, and faulty causes or effects. Here is a chart listing some additional fallacies that you should avoid as you build your persuasive speeches.

FALLACY	EXAMPLE	EXPLANATION
Loaded Question	"Are you still using drugs?"	The question forms a no-win trap. Answering "yes" is an admission of guilt; responding "no" still admits to former drug use.
Either–or Question	"We can continue the deficits and corruption of this administration, or we can elect a new, competent, honest government."	The "choice" presents two extremes: one evil, one good. Alternatives are seldom this simplistic.
Begging the Question	Mr. A: "The United States must reduce defense commitments and spend more on social programs." Ms. B: "Why?" Mr. A: "Because it's imperative that our defense spending be reduced and our social programs be increased."	The reasoning is circular. Debater A "begs the question" by restating the issue and offering the claim as evidence. The claim remains unsubstantiated.
Complex Question	"America's strong foreign policy contributed to peace in the Middle East."	Several complicated issues are combined into one claim, making it difficult to sort through.
Irrelevant Evidence	"Joe Smith should be elected attorney general: He is a true American, a good family man, a church attender, and a friend of the poor."	The information does not support the claim. To evaluate Joe, we need to know about his experience, his skill at handling cases, and opinions of Joe from other attorneys. The "evidence" has little to do with the job of attorney general.

DEVELOPING REBUTTAL ARGUMENTS

Some persuasive issues are so controversial that audiences will listen with skepticism, raising doubts about the wisdom of the speaker's proposition. A speaker who ignores this resistance will not be taken seriously. It is crucial for a persuasive speaker to acknowledge the viewpoint of listeners who strongly disagree with the speaker's proposition and use powerful counterarguments to undermine the opposing idea. The argument that is held by audience members who strongly disagree with a speaker's proposition is called an *opposition argument.* The counterargument that the speaker uses to weaken the opposition is known as the *rebuttal argument.*

For example, imagine that a speaker who was a firm believer in the advantages of nuclear energy developed a proposition of policy stating that more nuclear power plants should be built in this country. After an effective introduction, the speaker presented a thesis declaring that nuclear power plants are safe, efficient, and cost effective. Upon hearing the speaker assert that nuclear plants are safe, many listeners would immediately recall the nuclear meltdown in Chernobyl and/or the disaster at Three Mile Island and begin to form serious disagreements with the speaker's proposition. The speaker cannot press on without ever acknowledging or answering the strong objections of the opposition; to do so would be persuasive suicide. Audience members would question the speaker's concern about their welfare, awareness of the facts, and understanding of the problem. One way for the speaker to meet this challenge would be to raise the opposition argument head-on. The speaker could say, "When you hear that nuclear power plants are safe, I'm sure many of you begin to think about the disasters at Three Mile Island and Chernobyl. I understand your concerns and I want to assure you that such tragedies must be prevented." After establishing and developing the opposition argument further, the speaker would then begin to form a rebuttal argument to undermine the opposition and provide evidence that the opposing view was flawed or inaccurate. The speaker could begin the rebuttal in this manner: "These disasters are well-publicized failures that do not fairly represent the more stringent policies and guidelines now regulating nuclear reactors." The speaker could provide additional rebuttal information about the flawed structure and regulation of the Soviet reactor or improper management and safety inspection of the Three Mile Island plant.

It is important for a persuasive speaker to carefully craft opposition and rebuttal arguments to gain the confidence of listeners and demonstrate a thorough understanding of both sides of the issue.

DEVELOPING A CONTROVERSIAL ISSUE: AN EXAMPLE

We have selected a topic from the *CQ Researcher*[19] to illustrate how a debatable issue can be developed into two opposing persuasive speeches. You will notice a clearly worded proposition, a definition, a two-point thesis on opposite sides of the issue, and supporting materials that validate each position. Recognize that these arguments represent an early stage of speech planning. More research and preparation will be necessary to develop six- to seven-minute speeches that are satisfactory for classroom presentation.

Proposition of Value: Chemical Castration is an acceptable way of treating sex offenders.

Definition: "Chemical castration" refers to drugs and medications that are given to sex offenders to reduce testosterone levels and sexual drives.

FAVOR

Thesis statement: "Drug therapy for sex offenders is effective and safe."

I. Hormone or drug therapy is very effective for sex offenders when combined with counseling.

One study of 626 patients at the National Institute for the Study, Prevention and Treatment of Sexual Trauma in Baltimore, Maryland, found that fewer than ten percent of the patients repeated sexual offenses five years later if they were receiving drugs that lowered testosterone levels and reduced their desire for sexual activity.
Gordon C. Hall, a psychologist at Kent State University, reviewed twelve recent studies of treatment programs and found that most treatment programs were effective. In an October, 1995 issue of *Journal of*

OPPOSED

Thesis statement: Drug therapy for sex offenders is not effective or safe."

I. Drug therapies as a treatment for sex offenders are not effective.

A review of forty-two studies into sex offender research appeared in a 1989 issue of the *Psychological Bulletin* and concluded: "There is as yet no evidence that clinical treatment reduces rates of sex re-offenses in general." Psychologist Vernon L. Quinsey of Queens University in Ontario, Canada, says that most studies showing effectiveness of drug treatments are weak, and study patients only a few years after treatment. These studies need to conduct research much longer because some sex offenders repeat crimes as long as twenty years later.

Consulting and Clinical Psychology, he concluded that the most effective treatment, after castration, was hormone therapy which reduced the sex drive.

"Wayne" was a respected man in a midwestern community who was an editor of a local newspaper and a coach of a youth league baseball team. Wayne was also a pedophile. He would gain the trust of boys, invite them to stay overnight at his house, show them *Playboy* magazines, and then engage in oral sex or masturbation. One of his eleven-year-old victims turned him in and Wayne pleaded guilty and was sentenced to five years in prison. He flew to Baltimore where he participated in group therapy and received weekly injections of Depo-Provera. He said that the drug helped him control his compulsive behavior and go no further with his obsessive desires.

Programs claiming success treat only the low-risk sexual offenders who may have committed only one offense and who are living in the community or are on parole participating in out-patient therapy. Lucy Berliner, research director at the Harborview Sexual Assault Center in Seattle, Washington, says that the more dangerous offenders—"the silent ones" such as the repeat criminals and those in prison—will not seek help or volunteer for these programs. Can we afford to take risks on those who commit violence such as murder and rape in addition to other sex acts? Psychologist Quinsey says: "If you're a clinician and treating these guys, you'd have to be a fool to say we should let them go. The data on effectiveness of treatment doesn't support it."

II. Unlike castration, drug therapy is a safe form of treatment that does not represent cruel and unusual punishment.

II. Drug therapy is not safe and is considered to be cruel and unusual punishment.

According to in article in a July, 1992 issue of the *American Bar Association Journal,* hormonal therapies are similar to other medications such as tranquilizers and antidepressants that are used to treat psychological

These programs are still considered experimental. According to Safer Society Foundation in Brandon, Vermont, only twenty percent of the nationwide treatment programs use them and no correctional programs

(continued)

DEVELOPING A CONTROVERSIAL ISSUE (CONTINUED)

disorders. Unlike castration, these therapies are reversible and patients can still experience erections and impregnate their wives.

According to a February 13th, 1995, issue of *Maclean's* magazine, ten percent of the sex offenders in Canada take drug medication to lower their sex drives. Jailed sex offenders in Canada are often given the choice of remaining in prison or taking injections or pills and getting out on parole. Howard Barbaree of Toronto's Clarke Institute of Psychiatry and an expert in the treatment of sex offenders said: "The patient can make an informed decision between staying in jail and off the medication, or being released on the medication. For some offenders, you want them on it."

use them. Side effects of these drugs are weight gain, hot flashes, high blood pressure, nightmares, cold sweats, atrophied testicles, and lethargy. For example, half of the patients who take Depo-Provera stop using it because of the harmful side effects.

According to a January, 1993 issue of *Health* magazine, Roger Gauntlett pleaded no-contest in a Michigan court to molesting his fourteen-year-old stepdaughter. The judge sentenced him to five years of drug therapy to reduce his sex drive. But an appeals court stated that he couldn't be forced to take medication because "it isn't widely accepted as a safe and reliable treatment for sex offenders."

METHODS OF ORGANIZING PERSUASIVE SPEECHES

Because there are different goals in persuasion, there are different methods of structuring persuasive messages. In an actuating speech, for instance, the speaker must organize the message to identify a problem that requires solution and action. In a speech to convince, the speaker uses reasons to develop a positive case in support of the proposition. In order to build a successful persuasive speech, you need to understand and be able to apply the best methods of organization for your particular assignment. You can structure persuasive messages according to reasons, problem–solution, comparative advantages, and the motivated sequence.

Reasons

Using the method of citing *reasons* is a clear and straightforward organizational approach, especially in a speech to convince. With this method, a speaker uses the three or four convincing reasons as main headings in the body of the outline. If you use this technique, be certain that your reasons are the strongest possible, that they support the specific purpose or proposition, and that they themselves can be supported with concrete evidence.[20]

Speaker David Stesch wanted to convince his audience that the Twenty-second Amendment limiting a president to two terms should be repealed. After researching his proposition of policy, David found three strong reasons that he felt would persuade the audience to agree with him. Evaluate his reasons as well as their arrangement in the outline.

> **Specific purpose (proposition of policy):** To convince the audience that the Twenty-second Amendment limiting a president to two terms should be repealed.
>
> **Thesis statement:** The Twenty-second Amendment was rejected by the Founding Fathers, it is detrimental to the executive branch of government, and it is undemocratic.

BODY

Reason 1

I. The concept was rejected by the Founding Fathers.
   A. Alexander Hamilton argued that a president should not be changed in time of national crisis.
   B. In the book *Decision in Philadelphia* historians write that the Founding Fathers felt a president should be judged by the people frequently.

Reason 2

II. It is detrimental to the executive branch.
   A. A fixed term creates a lame-duck presidency.
   B. A fixed term damages the president's ability to conduct foreign policy.

Reason 3

III. It is undemocratic.
   A. The amendment implies that people are ignorant.
   B. Many constitutional scholars say the amendment constrains the popular will.

The speaker was successful in choosing three equally strong reasons to support the proposition. Notice that he saved the strongest reason—that the amendment is undemocratic—until the last. Also notice that Dave supports reason 1 and 3 with testimonial evidence, and reason 2 with examples.

Students sometimes have difficulty coordinating their reasons smoothly with the proposition. To phrase each heading of the body more clearly, place a mental "because" in front of each reason. This method is an effective organizational tool for both speaker and listener. It helps a speaker to be logical and clear in supporting the proposition, and it enables the listener to follow the speaker's principal arguments.

Problem–Solution

The *problem–solution* method is also useful in structuring a speech to convince. This method reflects the problem-solving techniques developed many years ago by educator John Dewey in his book, *How We Think*.[21] The problem–solution method is most often used for propositions of policy, and is easy to incorporate into a speech outline. In the following outline about the automotive repair industry, Karen Anderson made effective use of the problem–solution structure.

> **Specific purpose (proposition of policy):** To convince the audience that the auto repair industry should be strictly regulated.

> **Thesis statement:** Incompetent and unnecessary repairs must be corrected by strict regulations.

BODY

Problem

I. Americans taken advantage of
   A. 40% of consumer auto repair spending wasted on unnecessary repairs.
   B. Sears scandal demonstrates company fraud
   C. "Gypsy" parts are purposely inferior
   D. Small, everyday scams rip off public
   E. Incompetent service affects consumer

Alternative solutions

  II. Several means exist to rectify problem
     A. Voluntary certification
     B. Industrywide control
     C. Consumer awareness

Selected solution

 III. Regulation can help consumer
     A. Mediate disputes
     B. Detect fraud
     C. Protect consumer

The body of the speech contains three main headings that identify the problem, explore alternative solutions, and present the desired solution. The speaker uses a combination of statistics and examples as evidence to support her three headings.

One variation of this method is *problem–cause–solution* in which the speaker includes a section identifying principal causes of, or reasons for, the problem. Here's how the preceding outline can be adapted to this method:

Thesis statement: Incompetent and unnecessary repairs, caused by lack of control, must be corrected by strict regulations.

BODY

Problem

  I. Americans taken advantage of

Cause of problem

  II. Lack of control contributes to negligence
     A. Anyone can claim automotive expertise
     B. ASE sets only voluntary standards
     C. Consumers are uneducated
     D. Most states don't regulate

Alternative solutions

 III. Several means exist to rectify problem

Selected solution

 IV. Regulation can help consumer

In this outline, only one additional heading was needed to include the reason for the problem. You can see that the problem–solution method is adaptable to a variety of arrangements. You don't need to let any of these methods constrict your topic; adjust the approach to the unique demands of the topic, developing your speech in logical sequence.

BUILDING THE PERSUASIVE SPEECH TO CONVINCE

We've discussed the nature, means, and organization of several persuasive speeches. Here is a list of guidelines to help you build your persuasive speech to convince:

1. **Choose a controversial topic.**
   a. Examine your attitudes and the opinions of others.
   b. Select a topic that is appropriate to listeners.
   c. Explore current events topics.
   d. Avoid overworked issues.
   e. Provide new insights into familiar topics.

2. **Conduct extensive research.**
   a. Examine library sources for testimonies, statistics, and examples to build your case.
   b. Be certain that sources are accurate and up-to-date.
   c. Interview experts on the topic.
   d. Research specialized institutions and organizations.
   e. Develop visual aids for variety.
   f. Be willing to change or modify the topic if evidence does not support your viewpoint.

3. **Phrase a clear proposition.**
   a. Know the difference among fact, value, and policy propositions.
   b. Make sure that the proposition is controversial.

4. **Analyze the audience.**
   a. Determine prior attitudes about a topic through interviews, surveys, or questionnaires.
      (1) Agreement implies the opportunity of using evidence as reinforcement of audience attitudes.
      (2) Neutrality indicates the necessity of employing strong evidence to influence listeners.
      (3) Opposition to the topic suggests the need to present extensive supporting evidence.
   b. Develop persuasive appeals linking your topic to audience interests and motivations.
   c. Make the audience the central focus of speech development.

5. **Develop sound arguments and coherent organization.**
   a. Present well-defined claims supported by good evidence and sound reasoning.
      (1) Use evidence in the context of its intended meaning.
      (2) Include materials which are relevant and up-to-date.
   b. Avoid subjective phrases such as "I think," or "in my opinion."
   c. Identify research sources to build credibility.
   d. Avoid unethical practices.
   e. Use a balance of logic and emotion.
   f. Choose an appropriate organizational method for the topic.
   g. Use external transitions to emphasize major arguments.

6. **Construct a sophisticated introduction.**
   a. Choose a strategy to generate curiosity and establish rapport.
   b. Present the proposition and thesis statements at the end of the introduction.
      (1) Avoid opinionated statements such as "I'm going to convince," or "prove," alienating the audience.
      (2) State the proposition in a straightforward manner.
      (3) State the thesis clearly, creating receptiveness among listeners.

7. **Develop a forceful conclusion.**
   a. Use a challenge in the convincing speech to stimulate thought or ask listeners to change their minds.
   b. Use the challenge in combination with most types of conclusions.
   c. Avoid summary conclusions in convincing speeches.

8. **Build an effective delivery.**
   a. Maintain eye contact with listeners when conveying emotional examples.
   b. Report statistics accurately without stumbling.
   c. Use gestures to emphasize arguments and facial expressions to express emotion.
   d. Express feelings through enthusiasm, verbal emphasis, and vocal inflections.
   e. Practice the speech in order to project confidence in the topic.

Comparative Advantages

The *comparative-advantages* method is helpful in organizing convincing speeches about problems with many solutions. A speaker compares the advantages of a proposed solution with the advantages and disadvantages of other solutions. Politicians who support the death penalty for drug dealers often use the comparative-advantages method to convince voters that capital punishment is more effective than other solutions.

> **Specific purpose (proposition of value):**   To convince the audience that capital punishment presents the best alternative for dealing with drug kingpins.
>
> **Thesis statement:**   The death penalty is a severe punishment, which has a greater chance of deterring drug kingpins.

BODY

I. Capital punishment is the most severe of all penalties.

II. Capital punishment has a greater chance of deterring drug kingpins than lesser sentences.

Each main heading in the body presents a comparison of the proposed solution with alternatives. Numeral I compares the severity of various punishments, and II compares the merits of each penalty as an effective deterrent. The comparative-advantages method is useful when you want to persuade your audience that your solution is superior to other approaches to the problem.

Motivated Sequence

The motivated sequence is an organizational method that is used in speeches to actuate. This strategy is composed of five steps: attention, need, satisfaction, visualization, and action. We present a detailed discussion of this important technique in chapter 18.

Let's Stop Auto Repair Rip-Offs!

This persuasive speech was developed by an advanced student who was a committed consumer advocate. Karen Anderson researched the topic extensively and found powerful supporting materials to appeal to listeners. Convincing speeches can be organized by using reasons or a problem-solution sequence.

The body of this speech is arranged according to the reasons organizational sequence. An alternative body, arranged according to the problem-cause-solution structure, and an additional introduction and conclusion appear in the Appendix.[22]

Persuasive Speech to Convince

KAREN ANDERSON

1 The speaker arouses audience curiosity by starting with an example.

1 A man, who worked the night shift, got off work one morning and drove his Cadillac into a repair shop for servicing. He had a repair order written up, went back to his car and for some unknown reason crawled in the back seat and fell asleep. When he woke up, much to his surprise, he realized that it was now afternoon and no one had been out to service his car yet. He returned to the service desk and a cashier handed him a repair order which was completely filled out listing, in detail, all parts used and labor performed on the vehicle. The cashier then demanded full payment before the owner could get his car keys back. Does this story about auto repair fraud sound incredible or far-fetched? Well after you hear what I have to tell you today, you may not find an example like this so hard to believe.

2 The speaker states the proposition of policy followed by the thesis, which contains three reasons. The reasons represent the core of the speaker's persuasive argument and identify the three numerals of the body.

2 The auto repair industry should be strictly regulated because of unnecessary repairs, incompetent work, and because regulation will help to protect the consumer.

3 Karen establishes support for the first reason by citing a statistic from the U.S. Department of Transportation

3 Americans are being ripped off by unnecessary repairs. Consumer advocate Ralph Nader writes about the U.S. Department of Transportation's study of the auto repair industry in the foreword of a book entitled *Auto Repair Shams and Scams*. The survey indicates that today approximately 40 billion dollars a year associated with auto repairs are unnecessary. The major reasons: "Unneeded repairs due to inadequate diagnosis; faulty

and using a quotation from Ralph Nader, a well-known consumer advocate.

repairs for which owners did not get their money back; unneeded repairs sold with possible fraudulent intent; accidents due to faulty repairs." Mr. Nader further comments that this sector of the auto industry has done little to reduce fraud and incompetence over the last ten years.

4 The speaker poses a question to threaten listeners' safety and security. The example from a credible source is further support that consumers are being taken advantage of.

4 Think it won't happen to you? An article in a June, 1992 issue of *Business Week* reported in what is now a much publicized case, that Sears Auto Centers in California had "systematically ripped off customers." According to the article, Ruth Hernandez of Stockton, California went to Sears for new tires. The auto technician who serviced Ms. Hernandez's Honda "insisted" the car also needed new struts with a hefty additional cost of $419.95. Ms. Hernandez went for a second opinion and was told the struts did not need replacing. Furthermore, according to the article, Sears consistently charged consumers an average of $235.00 for unnecessary repairs.

5 The visual aids add interest and provide concrete examples of attempts to defraud consumers.

5 Here are two ways that consumers pay for unnecessary repairs. You can unknowingly purchase a so-called "gypsy part," that is, an inferior auto part such as a common oil filter which is repackaged in a box with a well-known brand name and passed off to you as a quality product. Here is an example. [Shows a slide that displays two oil filters: One is a "gypsy part" and the other is the legitimate filter.] One has less paper, which provides less filtering capability. The other contains more paper and will last longer. Upon close examination, the difference is obvious. Or what about the technician who deliberately sabotages your car for profit and whose favorite weapon is an ice pick? (Holds up an ice pick.) Now although these instances are rare, they happen to out-of-state motorists who set themselves up as easy targets by leaving their cars with attendants while they grab snacks or make necessary pit stops. Returning to the car, the unsuspecting motorists are informed by attendants that a leaking tire must be patched or, better yet, replaced with a brand new tire.

6 The speaker wisely uses this example as the last supporting element for reason one. The emotional incident is verified by a credible primary source. Notice

6 Then there is the blatant fraud. I conducted a telephone interview with Tom Hopkins, a lead investigator for the Bureau of Automotive Repair in California, who related the following despicable crime. An elderly California couple took their motor home in for repairs. The disabled wife remained in the motor home while the vehicle was raised on the lift in the repair shop. Employees removed the suspension system, brakes, and wheels. The disabled woman was literally held hostage in the air until her husband paid the demanded fee to get the wheels and other equipment put back on their vehicle.

the speaker uses concrete language—"despicable crime," "held hostage"—to elicit an emotional response from the audience.

7 Although she is careful not to indict the entire auto repair industry, the speaker clearly indicates that listeners could be at risk.

7 The incidents represent a minority, and I want to stress that the majority of the auto repair industry is caring and reputable, but these cases are real and they could happen to you.

8 The external transition connects reasons one and two (numerals I and II) of the body.

8 Not only do Americans experience unnecessary repairs; we are also subjected to incompetence.

9 A survey and quotation from a verifiable source present early supporting evidence for reason two.

9 In his book *From Bumper to Bumper*, Bob Sikorsky did a remarkable survey of the auto repair business across America. Posing as an average driver, Mr. Sikorsky pulled into 225 repair shops with a simple problem: a loose spark-plug wire. He reported fair and competent repairs in only 28 percent of the stops, a satisfactory repair only 44 percent of the time, and in Sikorsky's own words, "I was victimized by incompetence, cheated, sold unnecessary parts . . . overcharged, and lied to."

10 Another quotation and a detailed example provide further evidence that consumers are often victims of incompetence.

10 Sal Fariello states alarming information regarding brake repairs from his twenty-year involvement with the automotive industry. Fariello explains that brake discs often require machining on a lathe to correct vibration or noise. But the likelihood of incompetent work is high. He advises that if a brake shop tells you that your brakes need to be machined, ask them to measure the final thickness. If they resist, it may be because they can't read a micrometer, which means they shouldn't be in the brake repair business. He concludes by saying: "I've seen some incredible butcher jobs come out of these places as far as brake work is concerned. For the sake of your own safety, make sure you are doing business with a competent brake mechanic."

11 Incompetence is not always intentional. It is often a result of the sophisticated high-tech machines we all drive and the failure of some technicians to keep up with the technology. A service assistant may be able to change the oil in your car but lack the more advanced skills to diagnose a problem in the engine, emission system, or transmission.

12 **The computer-generated visual aid introduces humor, stimulates interest, and also makes the point that anyone can go into the auto repair business.**

12 One important factor which contributes to incompetence is the lack of regulation. Let me explain. (Holds up sign saying, "Karen's Car Center—Unlimited Major and Minor Repair Service Major Credit Cards Accepted) Pretty impressive, huh? Listen, I'll even adjust your brakes for half-price, and I'll throw in a complete diagnostic muffler analysis for free—but I don't do windows! Trust me! Anyone with a computer and a graphics program can make a sign like this as I did, call themselves an auto technician, and open up a shop. Nothing stands in their way. How could I get away with this, you ask? Well, there is no mandatory licensing or certification program. There is an organization called Automotive Service Excellence, or ASE which, according to their newsletter, is designed to help consumers "to distinguish between competent and incompetent mechanics." ASE administers an excellent voluntary certification program through paper and pencil testing in conjunction with two years' automotive repair experience. But the key word is "voluntary." Anyone can hang out a sign as long as they don't use the term "certified mechanic."

13 **The external transition links reason two with reason three of the body (numerals II and III).**

13 Since it is clear that incompetence occurs in the auto repair industry, let's consider how regulation will help to protect the consumer.

14 **Karen uses an extended example to explain how regulation can protect the consumer. She returns to the Sears example stated earlier in the speech and describes how the California BAR is used to resolve complaints and**

14 California is one example of a governmental control program that benefits the consumer and the auto repair industry as well. Remember Ms. Hernandez from California who didn't have confidence in what Sears was advising her to do? She had a place to file a complaint and was assured that a remedy would be found. This is an excellent example of mandated control through the California Bureau of Automotive Repair, or BAR. (Displays slide describing information about the BAR) Kate McGuire, Public Information Officer for the BAR provided me with information about this agency. It was established in 1971 to prevent abuses in the auto repair industry. With a staff of 600 working in 36 field offices, the BAR operates on an annual budget of $70 million which is funded by the smog check program and a $200.00 registration fee paid by auto repair businesses.

abuses in the industry. The speaker uses a slide projector to display factual information that reinforces the narration. The speaker indicates that the information is verified by a source.

It provides consumers with mediation centers that handle over 40,000 formal complaints a year. This agency also sends representatives to assist and support consumers at hearings in small claims court. And money—some 4.6 million alone was returned to consumers from auto repair shops in 1991-92.

15 The quotation from a primary source is powerful support for reason three.

15 In addition, the Bureau conducts undercover sting operations to snare dishonest technicians or detect fraudulent repair shops. BAR investigator Hopkins said that they can't inspect all of the repair shops. But he explained: "We have sophisticated means of intelligence gathering. We have field offices, consumer complaints and field investigators—we know what's going on. We want to put the bad guys out of business. We want to revoke their licenses so that no one goes to them." Talk about protection!

16 The speaker presents the principal argument of opponents to acknowledge objections to regulation. The argument is supported by a credible source. Here the speaker refutes the opposition with a clear rebuttal argument, which is also supported by a source.

16 Now there are many in the auto repair industry who feel that the government or state should not be involved in overseeing the industry. Rick Glenn, the Auto Service Technology Professor I interviewed commented that many technicians feel that government or state regulation would impose a cumbersome layer of bureaucracy which could only make matters worse. But investigator Tom Hopkins told me that, in California, the auto industry is not hostile to the Bureau. In fact, he said that honest auto repair businesses welcome the BAR because it helps to keep a level playing field and put the dishonest shops out of business. So you can see that regulation does not need to be antagonistic to the repair industry.

17 Karen returns to the Sears example to provide additional reinforcement for her rebuttal argument.

17 Had the BAR not existed, we may never have discovered the Sears scandal. It was the chief of the BAR who launched an investigation after noticing a pattern of consumer complaints against Sears Auto Centers. The Bureau conducted 38 undercover runs at 33 Sears shops statewide in California. The investigation exposed Sears' unethical practices, and forced the company to change its ways.

18 **To begin the conclusion, the speaker refers back to the example she used in the introduction.**

Karen ends this convincing speech with a hard-hitting challenge to the audience.

18 Do you remember the man with the Cadillac I referred to in the opening of my speech? Well that true story was told to me by Dré Brungardt, an Automotive Consultant on a WTTR radio show in Westminster, Maryland. That example is known as a "wall job" in the auto repair industry, because when you return to the auto shop, you find your car parked next to the same wall, untouched, where you left it, but with a repair invoice attached. We don't have to take this type of behavior. We don't have to be at the mercy of fraudulent or incompetent auto repair companies. The vast majority of men and women in this business are decent and hardworking. But we need to ensure this same high standard of decency throughout the industry. Let's apply the brakes. Let's require strict ground rules.

SUMMARY

Persuasive speakers influence audiences by altering beliefs, reinforcing feelings, or generating action. Speakers phrase persuasive topics into arguable propositions of fact, value, or policy. To persuade an audience, a speaker must construct ethical appeals to build trust and confidence; emotional appeals to deepen feeling; and logical arguments based upon correct facts, complete evidence, and accurate reasoning. At the same time, a speaker must avoid unethical practices, extreme emotionalism, and fallacious reasoning.

Persuasive speeches can be structured according to reasons, problem–solution, comparative advantages, and the motivated sequence.

SKILL BUILDERS

1. Choose a controversial topic for a persuasive speech. Phrase the topic into propositions of fact, value, and policy.
2. Using the Attitude Survey provided in chapter 3, find out the strength and weakness of audience attitudes toward each proposition. Use the survey to help you decide what type of persuasive speech to present—convincing, stimulating, or actuating.
3. When you have selected your proposition and type of speech, develop three emotional and three logical appeals. Be careful to avoid fallacious reasoning.
4. Turn to the Appendix and read the speech delivered by Reverend Jesse Jackson at the 1988 Democratic National Convention. Divide your class into groups of three and use the speech as the basis for analysis and discussion of the following areas:
   a. Identify specific examples of logical and emotional appeals.
   b. Does the speech contain any fallacies? Be specific in your answer.

    c. What was Jesse Jackson's reputation as a speaker at the time? As a politician?

    d. Were there positive or negative ethical factors that helped or hurt Jackson's persuasive influence?

    e. How did Jackson connect to his audience? Did Jackson target any groups within his audience? If so, which ones?

    f. What type(s) of persuasive speech did Jackson present? Consider your answer carefully.

5. For the following topics, write outlines for persuasive speeches using the reasons, problem–solution, and comparative-advantages methods.

Foreign trade restrictions

Frivolous lawsuits

Overcoming racism

Rebuilding our inner cities

Reducing the federal deficit

Reforming the judicial system

Reforming the welfare system

The significance of fraternities and sororities

The campus parking problem

The health care system

The national speed limit

NOTES

1. Joel Achenback, "Jury Selection Could Be Key for Simpson; Consultants Helping Both Sides Seek Edge," *The Washington Post,* September 26, 1994, sec. A, p. 1.

2. Ibid.

3. Lorraine Adams and Serge F. Kovaleski, "The Best Defense Money Could Buy; Well-Heeled Simpson Legal Team Seemed One Step Ahead All Along," *The Washington Post,* October 8, 1995, sec. A, p. 1.

4. Ibid.

5. "Simpson Jury Data Reportedly Ignored," *The Washington Post,* October 9, 1995, sec. A, p. 16.

6. Ibid.

7. Adams and Kovaleski, "The Best Defense," *The Washington Post,* October 8, 1995, sec. A, p. 1.

8. Lannis Waters, "Palm Beach Lessons," *Newsweek,* December 23, 1991, pp. 30–31.

9. Adams and Kovaleski, "The Best Defense," *The Washington Post,* October 8, 1995, sec. A, p. 1.

10. Lane Cooper, *The Rhetoric of Aristotle* (New York: Appleton-Century-Crofts, 1932), p. 8. [Brackets two and three ours.]

11. Ibid., p. 9.

12. Heather Hoag, "Flying the Unfriendly Skies," speech to convince presented in speech class, Catonsville Community College, Catonsville, Maryland, 1996. Used by permission.

13. Kenneth Ruffin, "On-line Services Should Be Banned," speech to convince delivered in speech class, Catonsville Community College, Catonsville, Maryland, 1996. Used by permission.

14. Cooper, *The Rhetoric of Aristotle,* p. 9.

15. These excerpts are taken from the complete speech. See "Earl Spencer's Eulogy: Farewell to a Princess," *The Sun* (Baltimore), September 7, 1997, p. 27A.

16. Stephen W. Littlejohn and David M. Jabusch, *Persuasive Transactions* (Glenview, Illinois: Scott,

Foresman, 1987), p. 54. I want to thank James L. Koury, Professor of Philosophy at Catonsville Community College, who gave me valuable help and advice in the logic section of this chapter.

17. For the purposes of this section on the appeal to reason, I used a system of argumentation similar to Hugenberg and Yoder's section entitled: "Use Logical Proof: Appeal to Logic and Reason," pp. 188–191 in *Speaking in the Modern Organization*. However, I have made alterations in terminology, examples, and numbers of logical proofs. For a more traditional approach see Ross and Ross, *Understanding Persuasion,* pp. 155–168.

18. Lawrence W. Hugenberg and Donald D. Yoder, *Speaking in the Modern Organization* (Glenview, Illinois: Scott, Foresman, 1985), p. 190.

19. The supporting materials and references used for the topic, "chemical castration," were paraphrased or quoted from "Punishing Sex Offenders," January 12, 1996, *The C Q Researcher,* vol. 6, no. 2, pp. 25–48. *The C Q Researcher,* formerly *Editorial Research Reports,* is published by the *Congressional Quarterly* and is an excellent source for analyzing controversial issues. This publication selects a different topic each week and presents arguments and provides bibliographies on both sides of the issue.

20. The following speeches used in this chapter were presented in the Fundamentals of Public Speaking class, Catonsville Community College: a speech where the name was withheld to protect privacy; David Stesch, "The Twenty-second Amendment Should Be Repealed," 1988. Used by permission.

21. John Dewey, *How We Think* (Boston: D.C. Heath, 1933), pp. 102–118. Read chapter 7 to understand the five phases of "reflective thinking." You will discover that there is a great similarity to some of the problem–solution models presented in this persuasive speaking chapter.

22. Karen Anderson, "Let's Stop Auto Repair Rip-offs!" Persuasive speech to convince, Carroll Community College, Westminster, MD, 1993. Used by permission. For more information about the Sears issue you may read the following articles: Kevin Kelly, "How Did Sears Blow This Gasket?" *Business Week,* June 29, 1992, p. 38; Julia Flynn, "Did Sears Take Other Customers for a Ride?" *Business Week,* August 3, 1992, pp. 24–25; and "Sears Gets Handed a Huge Repair Bill," *Business Week,* September 14, 1992, p. 38. Sears denied any intentional wrongdoing or liability and CEO Edward A. Brennan stated that an internal investigation revealed that there was no "pattern of misconduct" or "systemic problem [which] led to cheating in the auto centers." However, Mr. Brennan did acknowledge "isolated errors" and eliminated commissions for its auto center employees. Sears also agreed to settle complaints by paying $8 million. [Brackets ours.]

Chapter 18

SPEAKING
TO PERSUADE:
MOTIVATING AUDIENCES

*To know what has to be
done, then do it,
comprises the whole
philosophy of practical life.*
Sir William Asner

CHAPTER OBJECTIVES

After reading this chapter you will be able to:

1. Develop strategies for motivating listeners;

2. Describe the motivated sequence;

3. Analyze a persuasive actuating speech;

4. Develop and outline a persuasive actuating speech using the motivated sequence.

Looking thin and pale in a jacket, black pants, a T-shirt, and a baseball cap, Mickey Mantle faced reporters and cameras at a news conference. During his career, the former slugger had hit 536 home runs, helped the Yankees win twelve American League pennants, and set World Series records. Mantle now confronted a different kind of challenge after an emergency liver transplant brought about by forty years of alcohol abuse. "You talk about a role model, this is a role model: Don't be like me. God gave me the ability to play baseball and I wasted it. I'm going to spend the rest of my life trying to make up. I want to start giving something back."[1]

Mickey Mantle was determined to use his unfortunate situation to help promote organ donations. And although his life lasted only one more month, Mantle's emotional appeal was credited for heightening awareness about the need for organ donations and even increasing requests for donor cards by almost twelve percent at one organ bank.[2] This chapter helps you understand strategies for motivating audiences, presents Monroe's motivated sequence, and identifies guidelines for constructing the persuasive speech to actuate.

STRATEGIES FOR MOTIVATING LISTENERS

As a persuasive speaker, you can influence listeners to believe in your message, feel more deeply about an issue, or act upon a proposal. It is difficult to be effective, however, unless you find specific ways of motivating your audience. We suggest several strategies: appeal to needs; appeal to beliefs and values; provide incentives; and involve emotions.

Appeal to the Needs of the Audience

In chapter 3 we discussed some of the basic needs that all human beings have in common and we briefly described how one psychologist, Abraham H. Maslow, organized these drives into five levels called a "hierarchy of needs." When you connect a topic to these drives, your persuasive speech will have more impact upon listeners. For example, if you wanted to persuade your audience to plant trees to improve the environment, you could conceivably develop persuasive appeals that progressed through each level of Maslow's hierarchy. Here are some examples:

Physical. Trees remove the carbon dioxide out of our air and give us oxygen. One acre of trees can keep fifteen people breathing for one year. Unfortunately, we are losing this valuable resource at the rate of 3,000 acres per hour.

Safety and security.   Trees keep us warm in the winter, and they cool us with their shade in summer. Trees hold large amounts of soil, which help to control erosion and filter out nitrogen and phosphorous contained in run-off. When trees are cut down a chain reaction is started that not only harms the ecology but affects us as well. When too much nitrogen and phosphorous enter the water system, algae grows and shades aquatic grasses, which are nurseries for fish. When aquatic grasses are shaded they die, and there is no food for fish. When the fish die, our food supply is depleted, the fishing industry is affected, and the economy is damaged.

Love.   Trees provide wildlife with habitat, from the tinniest little microorganism, to the largest elk. Trees are the oldest living things: there's a bristlecone pine tree in California that is more than 4,600 years old.

Esteem.   The governor has officially declared this month to be "Tree-mendous" month. So why don't we all pitch in and help plant a tree to make our community better? If you plant a tree, you can return this application to the agricultural department and you will receive a certificate identifying you as a "Tree-mendous Marylander."

Self-actualization.   Teddy Roosevelt established the national park system in order to preserve the beauty and wonders of nature for future generations. Today, there are over 200 million acres of forests in these national parks for all of us to enjoy.

The speaker reminds listeners that trees provide the oxygen necessary to physical survival. She also describes how the lack of trees can lead to a chain reaction that is harmful to the safety and economic security of the audience. Next the speaker uses the elk and the bristlecone pine to appeal to her listeners' love of wildlife and respect for antiquity. She introduces esteem by referring to the governor's program and awarding certificates to those who plant trees. In a final appeal to self-actualization, the speaker asks listeners to "enjoy" and "preserve" the wonder and beauty of these forests.[3]

Not all persuasive topics can be linked so comprehensively to audience needs. But you will be more effective motivating your listeners if you can develop persuasive appeals that involve several of these basic drives.

Appeal to Listeners' Beliefs and Values

As you develop motivational appeals, it is important that you understand the specific beliefs and values of your audience. What beliefs do listeners have in common? What goals are important to audience members? What

Effective persuasive speakers move audiences to action by identifying problems and proposing workable solutions.

characteristics or qualities do your listeners most admire? You can influence listeners by explaining how your proposal is in harmony with their beliefs and value systems.

Some of the most common examples of appeals to values and beliefs are found in media advertising campaigns.

AT&T used a creative strategy to promote its long distance service to businesses who value high productivity and efficiency. The company developed a black-and-white TV ad showing anxious office workers who had lost long distance telephone service from a competing company due to a malfunction. The use of jerky, amateur-looking video footage made the scene appear even more frantic and dysfunctional. The sales pitch attempted to frighten businesses into buying the "reliable" long-distance service of the advertised company to avoid such a calamity.[4]

In the 1980s, Coca-Cola discontinued its traditional soft drink and marketed a product known as "new Coke" which was poorly received by the public. People wanted their traditional, familiar product and resented any change to a new version. Capitalizing upon the controversy, Pepsi developed an attention-getting TV ad showing a spaceship "beaming up" Coke and Pepsi vending machines from earth. The alien creatures rejected the new Coke, of course, and heartily embraced Pepsi. The slogan clinched the appeal at the end of the commercial: "One has changed; one is chosen."

The ad clearly linked Pepsi to consumers who valued stability, reliability, and tradition. Perhaps the unfavorable reactions to the new soft drink persuaded Coca-Cola to return Classic Coke to the market.[5]

Appeals to beliefs and values can also be successful in a negative sense. The R.J. Reynolds Tobacco Company created a magazine ad picturing a hip cartoon character named Joe Camel enjoying a cigarette. The ad attracted the attention of numerous children, who are fascinated by cartoons and caricatures. Armed with studies from the *Journal of the American Medical Association,* health groups protested the ad campaign and accused Camel of devising strategies that persuaded children as young as twelve to smoke cigarettes.[6] The tobacco company denied the allegations, and continued the ad campaign using the Joe Camel character until a lawsuit filed by forty states forced tobacco companies to stop cartoon and billboard ad campaigns.[7]

These strategies were effective because the advertisements connected products to the values of listeners. If you are interviewing for a job, you can sell yourself by linking your qualifications to the goals of your prospective employer. If you are presenting a classroom speech, you can relate many topics to the specific interests and values of your listeners. If you are required to promote your company's products at a trade convention, you can look for creative ways of appealing to the beliefs and values of prospective customers. Remember that it is the speaker's responsibility to analyze and understand the values of a specific audience in order to develop appeals that are successful.

Provide Listeners with Incentives

When you are presenting a persuasive speech, you need to be aware that listeners will silently ask themselves how they will benefit from your proposals. An effective persuasive speaker clearly communicates the advantages of a proposal by providing long- and short-term incentives for the audience. *Long-term incentives* are benefits that listeners gain over a period of time after agreeing to a speaker's proposal. One speaker advocated a tax deduction for responsible pet owners. She provided statistics showing that county governments are spending significant tax funds to maintain animal shelters for stray pets. The speaker provided two long-term incentives for those who agreed with her plan: (1) deductions would provide financial assistance to individuals who adopted stray animals; and (2) increased pet adoptions would save taxes by reducing the number of strays in animal shelters.[8] Another speaker who urged listeners to research their family genealogy identified these specific incentives: (1) researching family history can help individuals discover genetic illness; (2) understanding genealogy can encourage people to alter previous family lifestyles and prolong life;

and (3) enlightenment can lead to actions that improve the health of future generations in families.[9]

In these examples speakers explained that listeners would benefit by saving money or improving their health. If audience members are told that a proposal will help them to look or feel better, protect their families, save money, improve their safety, be wiser consumers, or live more successfully, they will see the long-term advantages of supporting the plan.

Speakers can also include *short-term incentives* to motivate listeners and provide immediate reinforcement of ideas. A speaker who advocated courteous driving practices handed out buttons with the slogan "Please be patient: God isn't finished with me yet."[10] Another student who suggested that listeners improve their nutrition passed out carrot sticks at the end of a speech. A speaker who urged audience members to bring toys for tots at Christmas presented a carnation with a friendly reminder to each listener. Bumper stickers saying, "I brake for animals" were given out to support a speech on animal rights. Speakers have used pamphlets, seeds, T-shirts, pens, sugarless cookies, refrigerator magnets, and pins as short-term incentives to reinforce messages. Remember that these items should not detract from the speech, but should be handled in a manner that enhances the presentation.

Present listeners with long- and short-term incentives. Let members of your audience know how their lives will be improved by agreeing to your proposal, and provide immediate incentives to encourage them.

Involve the Audience Emotionally

A persuasive speaker cannot be completely successful unless listeners experience an emotional connection to the topic. Speakers make these connections by using colorful language, stirring examples, and an expressive delivery.

Pat Masimore, a speaker of Indian descent, believed that professional teams should not adopt Native American names because the practice is insulting and disrespectful. She described how sports fans who wear costumes made from chicken feathers unknowingly ridicule the Indian ceremonial headdress of eagle feathers. She used this quotation from an editorial in *Sports Illustrated*[11] to express her strong emotional feelings about Indians:

> An anthropologist was studying Indians in the mid-1800s when he came across an old, old tribal chief. He asked the chief what America was called before the white man came. The old Indian looked at him and said, "Ours."

The speaker used vocal emphasis and a dramatic pause to stress the emotion in the line containing the Indian's response. Audience members got the message.

Another speaker conveyed sympathy for the homeless by asking listeners to hold small plastic bags filled with ice cubes during a portion of a speech. When audience members became uncomfortable with the subfreezing temperatures, Becky Meyers asked listeners to briefly express how they felt. One listener commented: "My fingers were so numb that I could hardly concentrate on what you were saying." Another observed: "If I had difficulty holding ice cubes for two minutes, imagine how a homeless person feels, existing in these temperatures for an entire winter." Becky had succeeded in using emotion to link members of the audience to her topic.[12]

Ashley Pettis wanted listeners to volunteer for Movable Feast, an organization that distributes one meal a day to AIDS sufferers. At one point in the presentation, the speaker played a videotape of her interview with a patient who had benefited from the program. In simple but emotional words, the AIDS victim appealed to Ashley's audience: "I don't know what to say, but I know it's a great organization and I certainly couldn't have done without it. I didn't realize it existed until I needed it. They're beautiful people."[13]

These speakers understood the importance of relating their topics to the emotions of audience members. Similarly, you can employ emotional examples, vivid language, and expression in your persuasive speeches. Recognize that listeners will be more likely to accept your ideas if you touch their emotions.[14]

THE SPEECH TO ACTUATE

The persuasive speech to actuate is an excellent presentation to build if you want to motivate listeners to perform a specific action. This speech often incorporates an organizational method known as the motivated sequence, which was developed by Alan Monroe, a professor of speech at Purdue University in the 1930s. Monroe used this method successfully to train sales personnel by combining problem–solution techniques with motivational approaches.[15] The motivated sequence consists of five steps: attention, need, satisfaction, visualization, and action.

Attention Step

The attention step is the introductory phase of the speech which arouses the curiosity and stimulates the interest of the listener. Any of the types of introductions we discussed in chapter 11 (shocking statement, quotation, narrative) would be appropriate techniques to get the attention of your audience in a speech to actuate.

Actuating speakers must connect to beliefs, motivations, and emotions in order to persuade listeners to "buy into" recommended actions to solve problems.

Need Step

Next, a speaker must persuade the audience that there is a need or problem that remains unsolved. Issues such as "Our oceans and beaches are being polluted," "Our nation is going bankrupt," or "Our educational system is at risk" can be appropriate choices for actuating speeches. When you identify a problem, use statistics, testimony and examples that persuade the audience that there is a real problem, and that the problem affects them. For example, if you show pictures of polluted beaches and cite instances of ocean-dumping, you are providing supporting evidence for the problem. If you tell your audience about unpleasant vacations at the ocean, where hospital waste has washed ashore, your listeners will begin to see that the problem affects them directly.

Satisfaction Step

When you have identified and developed the problem, you must provide a solution. It is helpful if you have evidence that indicates that the solution has worked in similar situations, and that a number of authorities and experts have supported it. If you advocate that "Congress must adopt a strict law that regulates dumping in our oceans," you need to supply statistics, testimonies, and/or examples which persuade the audience that this solution is sensible and workable.

Visualization Step

In the visualization step, you must "picture" in vivid words and examples what will happen in the future if your listeners adopt your proposed solution and the negative results if they do not. A speaker tells the audience, "We can continue to watch as more used needles, syringes, and vials containing the AIDS virus wash up on our beaches, or we can support the bill in Congress imposing strict fines on ocean-dumping." While this statement must be supported with specific evidence, it is an effective visualization because it portrays both positive and negative results. Visualization is a crucial step in the actuating speech—audience members learn how supporting the solution will benefit their future.

Action Step

The action step is the how, where, and when of the motivated sequence. The speaker tells audience members exactly what they are to do if they support the solution. The action should be as specific as possible—"Give blood next Wednesday"; "Register to vote"; "Sign a petition to support the bill outlawing ocean dumping"—so that listeners can take an active part. The action step is placed near the conclusion and can be combined with an appeal, personal testimony, or experience. If your action is clear and specific, your audience will be able to demonstrate their agreement with your solution by performing the action you advocate.

APPLYING THE MOTIVATED SEQUENCE

Here are five excerpts from a speech to actuate by Kara Jenkins entitled "Feeding the Hungry Here at Home."[16] Notice how the speaker develops each phase of the motivated sequence to reach her ultimate goal of action.

Specific purpose: To actuate the audience to bring cans of food for the hungry.

Thesis statement: If the homeless are provided with nourishing food, hope can be restored to these deserving Americans.

Attention Step. In her introduction, Kara gets attention by combining her personal testimony with a series of brief examples. She uses repetition of the words "A place where I saw . . ." for emphasis and dramatic effect:

> Not long ago, my older brother took me to a place that I will never forget. A place where I saw people who were homeless and poor and hungry. A place where I saw old women who carried trash bags with everything they owned in them. A place where a man begged me for one more piece of bread. A place where I saw a mother sit down with her four tiny children. This place is not on TV or in the movies—this place is not in Ethiopia. This place is Our Daily Bread—a soup kitchen right here in Baltimore.

The examples were short but powerful. Kara conveyed strong emotion as she related her personal testimony. The "I was there" approach achieved the purpose of the introduction and aroused the attention of her audience.

Need Step. Kara uses testimony from two experts and her own observation to develop the problem:

> I talked to Mrs. Johnson, a food coordinator for Social Services, and she told me that there are about thirty-one soup kitchens in Baltimore. I also talked to one of the workers at the soup kitchen, Raleigh Lemon, who said that anywhere from 350 to 500 people eat at Our Daily Bread in one day. The center is run by Catholic Charities and serves one meal between 11:00 A.M. and 1:00 P.M. Since this center is a private, nonprofit organization, it depends on volunteers and donations to keep it running. I remember when I was there they were having a shortage of rye bread, so we could only give one slice to each person. I remember one very shy old man whispering to me, "Please Hon, could you just get me one more slice of bread?" More food is needed so people don't have to beg for another slice of bread. We need to develop some solutions to this problem.

The speaker used statistics as a logical appeal to help listeners understand how many people must be fed at the soup kitchen every day. She then quoted the old man to appeal to each listener's emotions and to convey the human dimension of the problem. Kara's use of logic and emotion was successful; listeners were deeply touched as they heard about the tragic consequences of hunger in their city.

Satisfaction Step. The speaker tells the audience what other people are doing to help the homeless. The variety of solutions allows the audience to choose their degree of commitment to the issue:

> Let me tell you what others are doing to help. Sue Thompson, an assistant director of Our Daily Bread, said that business groups sponsor breakfasts on Monday, Wednesday, and Friday mornings. Church groups, private organizations, and concerned individuals sponsor one main meal a month for the 350 to 500 hungry people. If that is too much for a small organization,

they can sponsor just the juice, salad, or dessert portion of the meal. There are also many volunteers who donate their time to serve the food and help with the cleanup afterwards. And some who can't donate a meal or their time donate canned goods, clothes, socks, or toothpaste—anything that a homeless person could use. So while we may not be able to take 500 people into our own warm homes, the least that we can do is make sure that these people have some nourishing food.

Even though she lists a variety of solutions, notice that the speaker's easiest alternative—"some who can't donate their time can donate canned goods"—is the last in the list. It is this solution which will be the requested action. Notice that the testimony from the assistant director provides valid evidence that businesses, churches, and "concerned individuals" are an important part of the solution.

Visualization Step.   The speaker provides both negative and positive visualization. She tells the audience what will happen if the audience "just sits and does nothing," and she explains how adopting her solution will answer the immediate need:

> We've all driven past a bum or a bag lady, and most of us feel sorry for them and wish that we could do something. Today, I'm giving you all a chance to make a difference in their lives. We can just sit back and do nothing and that bag lady will miss another meal and those children I mentioned earlier won't get a second helping to fill their stomachs. Or we can provide more food so that all of these people can have nourishing and fulfilling meals. We can tell our friends, relatives, and neighbors about the ongoing need for food and keep providing these lifesaving meals.

Notice how skillfully Kara connects the solution to her listeners' motivation or wish to help the hungry. Also notice the effective use of language ("filling their stomachs, and "fulfilling meals") to visualize the results of supporting or of not supporting the solution.

Action Step.   In the conclusion, the speaker requests a clear, direct, easy-to-follow action:

> I hope that you all care about this problem and really want to help. I'm not going to ask for a big portion of your time or your money. All I want you to do is to reach into your pantry and pull out a couple cans of corn or green beans and bring them to class on Tuesday, May 17th, and I will take them down to Our Daily Bread. Remember when your mother said, "Eat all your food—there are starving people in Ethiopia"? I think she forgot that we don't need to go as far as Ethiopia—there are people starving right here in Baltimore. I know that the people who eat your canned food may not know your name or who you are, but they will know that there is a light at the end of the tunnel—there is someone out there who cares. Please, won't you take a few minutes of your time and be that light for these people?

BUILDING THE PERSUASIVE ACTUATING SPEECH

We've described several strategies for motivating audiences and presented the organization of the speech to actuate. Here is a list of guidelines to help you build this important persuasive message:

1. **Choose a topic requiring audience commitment.**
   a. Examine your attitudes and the opinions of others.
   b. Explore topics from current events.
   c. Avoid overworked issues.
   d. Provide new insights into familiar topics.
   e. Choose a topic that allows listeners to perform a specific action.
   f. Be certain the topic is appropriate.
2. **Conduct extensive research.**
   a. Examine library sources for testimonies, statistics, and examples.
   b. Interview experts on the topic.
   c. Research specialized institutions and organizations.
   d. Be certain that sources are accurate and up-to-date.
   e. Select audiovisual aids for variety.
   f. Be willing to change or modify the topic if evidence does not support your viewpoint.
3. **Phrase a clear specific purpose and thesis.**
   a. The specific purpose contains the specified action, but is not stated in the introduction.
   b. The thesis includes the need, satisfaction, and visualization steps of the body and is stated at the end of the introduction
4. **Analyze the audience.**
   a. Make the audience central to speech development.
   b. Determine prior attitudes about a topic through interviews, surveys, or questionnaires.
   c. Develop persuasive appeals linking your topic to audience interests and motivations.
   d. Plan alternative strategies if the audience resists solutions or suggested actions.

5. **Develop sound arguments and coherent organization.**
    a. Present well-defined claims supported by good evidence and sound reasoning.
        1. Use evidence in the context of its intended meaning.
        2. Include materials that are relevant and up-to-date.
    b. Avoid subjective phrases such as "I think," or "in my opinion."
    c. Identify research sources to build credibility.
    d. Avoid unethical practices.
    e. Use a balance of logic and emotion.
    f. Be able to apply the five stages of the motivated sequence.
    g. Use external transitions to emphasize major arguments.
6. **Construct a sophisticated introduction.**
    a. Employ a creative strategy for gaining audience attention.
    b. State a clear thesis at the end of the introduction.
        (1) Avoid stating the specific purpose containing the specified action.
        (2) Avoid opinionated statements such as "I'm going to actuate," or "prove," alienating the audience.
        (3) State the thesis in a straightforward manner, creating receptiveness among listeners.
7. **Develop a forceful conclusion.**
    a. Employ an appeal in the actuating speech to seek a specific commitment from the audience.
        (1) State the action clearly.
        (2) Provide listeners with all necessary details of the action.
    b. Use the appeal in combination with most types of conclusions.
    c. Avoid summary conclusions in actuating speeches.
8. **Build an effective delivery.**
    a. Maintain eye contact with listeners when conveying emotional examples.
    b. Report statistics accurately without stumbling.
    c. Use gestures to emphasize arguments and facial expressions to express emotion.
    d. Express feelings through enthusiasm, verbal emphasis, and vocal inflections.
    e. Practice the speech in order to project confidence in the topic.

In one brief sentence, the speaker has told audience members the what, where, and when of the action step—"bring cans to class Tuesday, May 17th." She has also taken the familiar motherly admonition of "Eat your food because of the starving in Ethiopia" and related it to the solution and action she advocates. Kara ends the speech with an earnest appeal to "take a few minutes of your time."

Outlining the Motivated Sequence

It is easy to incorporate the motivated sequence into the traditional speech outline. This brief outline of the following speech on current events can help you structure the introduction, body, and conclusion of the speech to actuate.

> **Specific purpose:** To actuate the audience to become better informed about current events by reading the newspaper.

> **Thesis statement:** Our lack of knowledge must be overcome by educating ourselves in order to avoid ignorance.

INTRODUCTION

Attention Step

   I. "Let's take a little quiz."
  II. Ask audience series of open-ended questions
      A. How is Japan overcoming U.S. distrust?
      B. What nation won World Soccer Championship?
      C. Whose mother and aunt are suing *National Enquirer?*
      D. Which major university is losing athletic director?
      E. What are effects of human growth hormone on body?

BODY

Need Step

   I. Americans grossly uninformed, according to survey
      A. Under 30 ages read less than in prior decades
      B. 18–29 ages less likely to follow news events
      C. Newspaper readership in decline
      D. 1980s compare poorly with 1960s statistics
      E. Over 35 ages exhibit decline in news interest

Satisfaction Step

  II. This problem is solvable
      A. Listen to radio news
      B. Watch TV news broadcasts
      C. Read evening paper

Visualization Step

III. We can blindly follow, or gain knowledge
   A. Ignorance creates easy target for manipulation
   B. Being informed leads to knowledge and awareness of society

CONCLUSION

Action Step

   I. "You never know what you can find in the newspaper."
  II. An appeal.
   A. Don't miss news such as ad in local paper
   B. Use gift of quarter to buy paper
   C. Don't contribute to knowledge decline
   D. Read, learn, enjoy

Ignorance Is Not Bliss

The following speech was presented by a journalism student who was extremely concerned about the lack of awareness exhibited by many younger Americans regarding news and current events. The speaker makes effective use of the motivated sequence and builds creative motivational appeals into her presentation. Although some of the introductory facts are now dated, Jessica raises some important issues for us to consider and put into practice.[17]

A Persuasive Speech to Actuate

JESSICA GREGG

1 Jessica used a series of open-ended questions about current events as her attention step. The audience participation stimulated curiosity, yet prepared the way for the topic.

1 Let's take a little quiz. If you know the answers to these questions, you can just call them out. What is the Japanese government doing to overcome what they feel is a sense of mistrust in this country towards their nation? Anyone know? The answer is that they are undertaking a 330 million dollar effort to make Americans more familiar with Japan's cultural and social life. Question number 2. Which nation won the World Cup soccer championship? West Germany? Yes, you're correct. I knew we had a soccer fan. Whose mother and aunt are suing the *National Enquirer* for publishing unauthorized photographs of this model? The answer is Marla Maples. And the athletic director of which major university is leaving for a job at the University of Connecticut? The University of Maryland, correct. And the final question: What effects have scientists discovered a human growth hormone to have on the body? No one

knows? Well scientists have discovered that a human growth hormone reverses the effects of aging. This has interesting implications for the future, doesn't it?

2 Many listeners did not know the answers to these questions. Jessica related this lack of knowledge to her topic.

2 If you did not know the answers to these questions, you are not alone. Despite the fact that we have entered an information age, a majority of the public remains uninformed and uninvolved when it comes to current events.

3 The thesis includes the three numerals of the body, but avoids identifying the action.

3 Our lack of knowledge must be overcome by educating ourselves in order to avoid ignorance.

4 The speaker uses statistics from a study and an article from a newspaper as support for the need or problem.

4 According to a new study, "The Age of Indifference," released two weeks ago by the Times Mirror Center for the People and the Press, the under 30 generation knows less, cares less, and reads the newspapers less than any other generation in the past five decades. The survey also states that persons between the ages of 18 and 29 are 20 percent less likely to follow important news stories such as events in Eastern Europe and they are 40 percent less likely to identify newsmakers like West German Chancellor Helmut Kohl. There are two exceptions to this. People in this age group show a high interest in sports and in issues like abortion. According to an article in the *Baltimore Sun* entitled "If You're Under 30 You'll Likely Skip This," the survey's most dramatic revelation is the decline in newspaper readership. Only 30 percent of Americans under the age of 35 said they had read a newspaper the previous day. This contrasts with figures in 1965 when 67 percent under 35 said they had read the previous day's newspaper. What is surprising is that TV has not filled the gap. The percentage of people viewing television newscasts is down as well. This then is truly the tuned out generation.

5 Jessica recognized that her audience included older as well as younger listeners. She developed appeals to both groups.

5 If you're over 35 and you're sitting there relieved that none of this seems to affect you, think again. According to the Times Mirror survey, the percentage of all of those reading newspapers and watching TV newscasts has declined in general. In other words, Americans don't have the information need to be good consumers, make good business decisions, vote, or understand the current issues of today.

6 A transitional sentence introduces numeral II, the satisfaction step.

6 We don't have to stay this way however; there are options.

7 The speaker provides alternative solutions to satisfy the need.

Jessica refers to an interview with an expert to support a statistic.

7 For example, we can listen to radio news. Most radio stations have a news program every hour and some have them as often as every half hour. There are some good news programs around. WTTR-1470 AM has a good program and National Public Radio-88.5 FM has excellent news. You can also watch TV news. This is possibly one of the easiest and most accessible options for everyone. On the average weekday, there are 56 news programs on television, and this does not include cable channels, business programs, talk shows, or interview programs like *20/20,* which do stories about current events. I interviewed Sherri Parks, a Professor of Radio, Television and Film at the University of Maryland who told me that 99 percent of American households have TVs. In other words, more people have television in their homes than have running water. So it shouldn't be too hard for someone to find a television to tune in to.

8 The speaker presents her third solution in detail, which is later connected to the action.

Jessica educates the audience about the inverted pyramid style.

8 But just in case television isn't possible, there is a third option. For twenty-five cents which is less than the price of a candy bar, you can buy the weekday edition of *The Baltimore Sun* or even *The Washington Post.* Many people shy away from newspapers because they feel they're too time-consuming or boring. Well the secret to reading a news article is understanding how it is written. Most news reporters use what is called inverted pyramid style. That is, they place the most important details or facts at the beginning of the article and work their way down to the least important. So in order to understand an article, you only need to read a short way to get the main idea. Sometimes this means you only have to read the headline. Other times you must read the entire article. Now the inverted pyramid style does not apply to features or sports. As you can see, reading the newspaper does not have to be a chore. None of these options are. They are easy as well as important.

9 A transitional phrase introduces numeral III, the visualization step.

9 You may wonder why this is so important. What does it matter if you choose not to be informed?

10 The speaker visualizes the negative consequences of choosing not to be informed. She appeals to safety and security, telling listeners that ignorance can lead to exploitation and "blind following."

10 Well, according to the Times-Mirror Survey, the fact that the under 35 generation is so uninformed makes them an easy target of manipulation. We know of powerful speakers such as Martin Luther King who used his influence for the common good to get people involved in the civil rights movement. And we also know of Adolph Hitler, one of history's worst manipulators who was also a powerful speaker. Do we want to get caught in that trap of blind following? Ignorance is bliss; but then again, ignorance is still ignorance.

11 Here the speaker visualizes numerous positive results and long-term incentives if listeners educate themselves. There are appeals to love, esteem, and self-actualization.

11 We can avoid being uninformed and ignorant by following one of the three options. For example let's look at reading the newspaper. By reading the paper you can learn much more about world events. You can learn about national events, happenings within the state and county. You can read the sports, the weather, stock figures, the foreign report, and the classifieds. You can find out the opinions of your favorite columnist as well as those individuals from your community who have written letters to the editor. You can read stories about real people like you in the features section. Plus there's all the fun stuff like horoscopes, comics, and crossword puzzles.

12 To begin the conclusion, Jessica used a creative motivational appeal. She placed an ad in the local county newspaper, which no one in the audience had read. The paper was dramatic visual evidence that listeners needed to become more informed.

12 You never know what you can find in the newspaper. For example, if you happened to have read today's classifieds in the *Carroll County Times,* you might have seen this message that I left for our class. It says, "Speech 101. We made it through the semester!" So you see, newspapers are truly a fun and enjoyable way to learn what is dramatic visual evidence going on in the world.

13 The speaker used another creative motivator

13 Since it's so important for us to learn about the world, I'm going to ask you to follow through with that last option and to read the paper this week. I'm going to give you all a

quarter so you don't even have to go to the library and borrow a copy. Buy a newspaper. Read it, learn, and enjoy. We don't want to be a nation in trouble because of our lack of knowledge.

for the action step. She provided a short-term incentive by giving each listener a quarter to buy the evening paper. Jessica demonstrated her willingness to "invest" in the education of her audience.

FIGURE 18.1

Carroll County Times

Thursday, July 12, 1990

18 Gorsuch Rd. July ... Childrens clothes, ... benches, records, ffed animals, dishes,

family yard sale. Fri, ... pm; Sat., July 14th, shine. 4033 Rineha... Rd.).

'12 Old Westminster ... 8 a.m. -?. Quality ... lies clothes, teaching ore.

19 Fairfield Ave., Fri. Sears cartop carrier, scooter, clothes, toys, tc.

19 Gahle Rd. Multi-

great music- GREAT TIMES! Radio professionals with music variety for your occasion. 848-4596.

NEED A DISC JOCKEY for your next party, dance or celebration? For reasonable rates, call Scott Young, 848-6433 after 5 pm.

SPEECH 101

We made it through the semester!

YOUNG MAN, age 24, 6'5", happy, out-going good looking sincere type person. Loves to live life to the fullest. Would like to meet female of same for a happy relationship. Not into bar scene or smoking. Send photo and letter to: P.O. Box 1543, Westminster, MD. 21157.

BLACK LAB, 3 year o... shots, neutered, exc... needs room to run. Call 876-6613.

CAT, 4 year old, ne... white. Good outdoor... home, 876-6613.

DESPERATELY NEEI... farm kittens: 4 black... friendly, 8 week old b... Please call 833-2107...

FIREWOOD. Large... Already down. You ... Easy access along har... 756-4062.

FREE 3 CAR METAI... firewood inside. You...

| **SUMMARY** | A persuasive speaker must find ways of motivating audiences. Strategies of involving listeners include appealing to needs, values and beliefs, providing incentives, and involving emotions. |

The persuasive speech to actuate is an excellent motivational presentation. It is organized using Monroe's motivated sequence, which includes five steps: attention, need, satisfaction, visualization, and action.

SKILL BUILDERS

1. Select a topic and develop an outline for a speech to actuate using the five steps of the motivated sequence.
2. Select five magazine or newspaper advertisements that appeal to different levels in Maslow's hierarchy. Identify the specific appeals, and state how they connect to audience needs.
3. Most TV commercials and magazine ads use the motivated sequence to sell products. Divide your class into several groups and select two television commercials for discussion and analysis. Bring in a video copy of the commercial and present your analysis to the class.
   a. Identify each step in the motivated sequence. Be specific.
   b. Which commercial is more effective?
   c. Do the commercials clearly target specific audiences?
   d. Is the persuasive approach employed in the commercial effective?
   e. Are any unethical tactics used?
   f. Can you find any research that indicates what kind of marketing tactics are successful for particular groups?
4. Find an advertisement in a magazine or on television that uses strong appeals to emotion, and provides long- and short-term incentives to listeners. Identify the emotional appeals, and name the specific incentives that are presented.
5. Read the speech by Elizabeth Glaser in the Appendix. Identify the various types of appeals the speaker develops to relate to members of the audience.

NOTES

1. "Don't Be Like Mick, says Mantle," *The Sun* (Baltimore), July 12, 1995, p. 5C and Peter Schmuck and Jim Henneman, "Baseball Mourns Lost Legend," *The Sun* (Baltimore), August 14, 1998, p. 1A.
2. "Don't Be Like Mick, says Mantle." Ibid.
3. Examples used for the five stages of Maslow's hierarchy were taken from two speeches: Cecelia Broos, "Deforestation," and Kimberly Warhime, "Chesapeake Bay Pollution," persuasive speeches to actuate, Carroll Community College, Westminster, MD. 1991 and 1992. Used by permission.
4. Bob Garfield, "AT&T Refines Fine Art of Selling Long-Distance," *Advertising Age,* May 27, 1991, p. 38.
5. Katherine Schofield, vice-president, Division of Strategic Planning, W.B. Doner, Inc. Interview, March 1, 1993.
6. "Old Joe Must Go," *Advertising Age,* January 13, 1992, p. 16.

7. See Schofield interview, and Scott Shane, "Maryland to Join Tobacco Settlement," *The Sun* (Baltimore), November 21, 1998, p. 1A.

8. Gina Alexander, "Pet Owners Should Receive a Tax Deduction," persuasive speech to convince, Carroll Community College, Westminster, MD, 1990. Used by permission.

9. Karen Mundell, "Research Your Family Genealogy," persuasive speech to actuate, Carroll Community College, Westminster, MD, 1990. Used by permission.

10. Cathy Manzer, "Highway Etiquette," persuasive speech to actuate, Carroll Community College, Westminster, MD, 1990. Used by permission.

11. Rick Really, "Let's Bust Those Chops," *Sports Illustrated,* October 28, 1991, p. 110, as cited by Patricia Masimore, "Sports Teams and Racism," persuasive speech to convince, Carroll Community College, Westminster, MD, 1991. Used by permission.

12. Becky Meyers, "People in Need in Carroll County," persuasive speech to actuate, Carroll Community College, Westminster, MD, 1990. Used by permission.

13. Ashley V. Pettis, "Have a Moving Experience," persuasive speech to actuate, Catonsville Community College, Catonsville, MD, 1992. Used by permission.

14. Suggestions for incentives and appeals to emotions are based upon Rudolph F. Verderber, *Essentials of Persuasive Speaking* (Belmont: Wadsworth Publishing Co., 1991), pp. 114, 116–119.

15. Bruce E. Gronbeck, Douglas Ehninger, and Alan H. Monroe, *Principles of Speech Communication,* 10th ed. (Glenview, IL: Scott, Foresman, 1988), pp. 272–285. Reprinted by permission of Scott, Foresman and Company.

16. Kara Jenkins, "Feeding the Hungry Here at Home," persuasive speech to actuate, Catonsville Community College, Catonsville, MD, 1988. Used by permission.

17. Jessica Gregg, "Ignorance Is Not Bliss," persuasive speech to actuate, Carroll Community College, Westminster, MD, 1990. Used by permission.

Chapter 19

SPEAKING FOR SPECIAL OCCASIONS

Ceremony keeps up all things.

John Selden

CHAPTER OBJECTIVES

After reading this chapter you will be able to:

1. Identify twelve types of speeches for special occasions;

2. Describe the purpose of each special occasion speech;

3. Develop speeches for special occasions.

Eulogies
Keynote speeches
Testimonials

On April 19, 1995, the Alfred P. Murrah Federal Building in Oklahoma City was the target of the worst terrorist attack in American history. A powerful bomb placed inside a rental truck erupted in a violent explosion, blasting the structure apart and hurling concrete and steel floors to the ground. One hundred sixty-seven people lost their lives, and many others were wounded in the attack.[1] Among the dead were federal workers as well as children who were playing in a daycare facility on the ground floor. Five days after the bombing, 20,000 people attended a memorial service at the Oklahoma State Fairgrounds where President Clinton delivered a moving tribute on behalf of a grieving community and nation:

> Today our nation joins with you in grief. We mourn with you. We share your hope against hope that some may still survive. We thank all those who have worked so heroically to save lives and to solve this crime, those here in Oklahoma and those who are all across this great land, and many who left their own lives to come here to work, hand in hand, with you. . . . We pledge to do all we can to help you heal the injured, to rebuild this city and to bring to justice those who did this evil. . . . You have lost too much, but you have not lost everything, and you have certainly not lost America, for we will stand with you for as many tomorrows as it takes.
>
> If ever we needed evidence of that, I could only recall the words of Governor and Mrs. Keating: "If anybody thinks that Americans are mostly mean and selfish, they ought to come to Oklahoma."
>
> If anybody thinks Americans have lost the capacity for love, and caring, and courage, they ought to come to Oklahoma.[2]

In these excerpts, the president expressed compassion for the victims and their families, gratitude towards the rescue teams, the need for healing, and a fierce determination to bring the terrorists to justice.

The tribute is one of many speeches prepared for special occasions that this chapter considers.

During your lifetime, you will probably be called upon to deliver speeches for a variety of special events or social occasions. A friend may ask you to propose a toast at a birthday party; your employer might request that you present an award or certificate to a deserving employee; your civic or social group might want you to introduce an important community leader.

While these presentations may appear uncomplicated, effective speeches for special occasions require careful planning and a clear understanding of the speech setting. You need to know the purpose of the occasion as well as the mood of the audience. If you deliver a eulogy, for instance, you need to include material that is appropriate to an audience experiencing grief; if you present a commencement speech, you need to know that listeners in a celebrating mood will not listen to a lengthy, intellectual discourse.

This chapter helps you to build speeches appropriate to a variety of occasions. We include the following types: tribute, presentation, acceptance and dedication speeches; speeches of welcome and introduction; keynote, nomination, farewell, and commencement speeches; the after-dinner speech and the toast.

TYPES OF SPECIAL OCCASION SPEECHES

The Speech of Tribute

Speeches of tribute recognize distinguished careers and contributions of either the living or dead. The tribute may be a *testimonial* presented at a retirement or other going-away ceremony, or a *eulogy* delivered at a memorial service or funeral. The speech of tribute seeks to stimulate and reinforce feelings people share about a person (or group) admired within a community. In this presentation, the speaker's goals are to acquaint the audience with the individual's life, remind listeners of the person's significant contributions and virtues, and leave people feeling positive and hopeful for the future.

CONSTRUCT A BRIEF BIOGRAPHICAL SKETCH

Clearly identify the individual who is the subject of your tribute. Conduct accurate research to collect interesting anecdotes and incidents amplifying the individual's character and personality. Present a biography or life-sketch providing insights into the individual's family background, role models, education, and occupation. Be brief: Include information that promotes understanding, and avoid insignificant details that interrupt the flow of the speech. Be sensitive to the setting of the presentation. If you are delivering a eulogy, recognize that your audience will be grieving at the loss of a family member, friend, or business associate; choose examples and quotations that contribute to the healing process. If your speech celebrates the current life of a distinguished person, you may have greater latitude in the use of supporting materials such as colorful vignettes and humorous anecdotes. In both cases, however, choose materials honoring individuals, and avoid negative incidents or hostile satire revealing unsavory qualities. Construct a positive and hopeful tribute celebrating a unique personality.

ACKNOWLEDGE SIGNIFICANT ACHIEVEMENTS AND VIRTUES

Speeches of tribute focus upon achievements and virtues. Speakers recount examples of heroism in battle, contributions in science, religion, or sports, or charitable service to humanity. These examples often identify and praise high moral values—qualities that serve as models for others.

Speakers presenting tributes frequently include comments such as "She was the best athlete in her category," "He worked tirelessly in the cause of equality," or "He kept going in spite of extreme adversity." The intention is to remind the audience of the qualities that contributed to the significance or greatness of the individual.

CONVEY HOPE AND ENCOURAGEMENT

Effective tributes link past virtues and achievements to present times by encouraging listeners to continue similar struggles or to embrace the values of those they admire. Audiences experiencing separation from loved ones as a result of retirement, relocation, or death should not be left with a sense of despair or futility. It is appropriate to use biblical quotations, citations of individuals being honored, or testimonies from others to reinforce feelings and to inspire listeners to grow from difficult experiences.

In a tribute presented at the funeral of Robert F. Kennedy in 1968, Edward M. Kennedy praised his brother's values and quoted one of his brother's speeches to encourage listeners to "shape" America with reason and principle:[3]

> Our future may lie beyond our vision, but it is not completely beyond our control. It is the shaping impulse of America that neither faith, nor nature, nor the irresistible tides of history, but the work of our own hands, matched to reason and principle, will determine our destiny.
>
> There is pride in that, even arrogance, but there is also experience and truth, and, in any event, it is the only way we can live. That is the way he lived. That is what he leaves us.
>
> My brother need not be idealized or enlarged in death beyond what he was in life. He should be remembered simply as a good and decent man who saw wrong and tried to right it, saw suffering and tried to heal it, saw war and tried to stop it.
>
> Those of us who loved him and who take him to his rest today pray that what he was to us, and what he wished for others, will some day come to pass for all the world. . . .
>
> As he said many times, in many parts of this nation, to those he touched and who sought to touch him:
>
>> Some men see things as they are and say why. I dream things that never were and say, why not.

The Presentation Speech

Speeches of presentation are given to honor specific achievements of individuals in institutions, occupations, or in community organizations. The president awards the Medal of Freedom to distinguished Americans; the

Pro Football Hall of Fame inducts sports personalities into membership; the Academy of Motion Picture Arts and Sciences annually selects a best actor, actress, director, and best picture; public school systems award certificates to outstanding teachers, and universities award scholarships to deserving students; businesses give away trips and prizes to employees with distinguished service records.

Since these speeches often take place in public ceremonies, they must be carefully crafted. The speech of presentation must be brief, accurate, and clear. It should identify the nature or type of award, provide brief information about the recipient's life or career, and acquaint the audience with the individual's specific achievement or service. The speech often includes adjectives like *most, best, first, last, greatest,* to describe the individual's merits and accomplishments. The speaker usually ends the speech by formally presenting the award to the recipient.

The speech of presentation should exhibit polish and show evidence of rehearsal. The speaker must know how to pronounce the recipient's name correctly and deliver phrases smoothly. During the presentation, the speaker should avoid embarrassing actions such as dropping framed certificates, or handing out plaques upside down. The award should be presented carefully, without unnecessary fumbling. A speaker will often follow the presentation with a handshake or hug (if appropriate), and then step aside to allow the recipient to deliver the acceptance speech.

During the July 3, 1986, celebration marking the 100th anniversary of the Statue of Liberty, President Reagan awarded the Medal of Liberty to twelve distinguished American immigrants—among them, comedian Bob Hope and song writer Irving Berlin. ABC newsman Ted Koppel narrated the televised ceremony and made the twelve speeches of presentation.

Here are two of these speeches—one honoring educator Hannah Holborn Gray, and another saluting author Elie Wiesel.[4] Because of the number of awards, each presentation had to be brief, yet each speech effectively acquainted listeners with the recipient, describing the individual's contribution to American life.

> When Hannah Holborn Gray was four years old, her father was dismissed from his teaching position in Heidelberg for opposing the Nazi party. He moved to New Haven, Connecticut, where Hannah pursued her education, becoming the first female provost at Yale University and eventually being chosen in 1979 to be the first woman president of the University of Chicago. The Medal of Liberty is awarded to this outstanding educator, Hannah Holborn Gray.

> Elie Wiesel was born in Rumania, and as a boy he lost both parents and a sister in the concentration camps. When the Americans liberated Buchenwald in 1945, they found the fourteen-year-old boy who had cheated death. He vowed to dedicate himself to bearing witness to what had happened during the Holocaust in the hope of preventing that dark history from ever

being repeated. He has become, through his writings and teachings, the foremost voice of warning and remembrance. The Medal of Liberty is awarded to Elie Wiesel.

The Acceptance Speech

The acceptance speech is the response to the presentation. The recipient gratefully acknowledges an award, gives proper credit to those who have assisted in or been part of the achievement, and states personal values and convictions that led to the accomplishment.

The speech should be well-prepared. In many ceremonies, individuals know in advance if they will receive awards; in others, individuals may know only that they have been nominated. In either case, potential recipients should have acceptance speeches prepared to deliver if called upon.

The speech should be brief. The recipient should thank the presenter and organization for the honor and identify colleagues who have contributed to the achievement, as well as personal friends or associates who have given emotional support. The speaker should exercise care, however, with the number of acknowledgments given. If you've ever watched the televised Academy Awards ceremony, you have seen embarrassing speeches where Oscar winners have thanked everyone from the obstetrician to the usher opening the theater door. Such problems can occur when recipients attempt to deliver impromptu speeches or ramble on without considering the needs of their audiences.

The recipient should exhibit poise in delivery. The speaker should receive the award graciously, possibly holding up the plaque, statue, or certificate to allow the audience to see it easily. The speaker can then place the award on the lectern (if available) to allow freedom of gesture and movement. The recipient should try to avoid distractions such as wiping the forehead or clearing the throat. While agitated mannerisms or brief references to human feelings ("I'm really nervous tonight") might generate some empathy from the audience, listeners expect a speaker to show competence and demonstrate the qualities being honored.[5]

Dr. Benjamin Carson, Director of Pediatric Neurosurgery at Johns Hopkins Hospital, was honored at the Tenth Annual American Black Achievement Awards for his accomplishments in neurosurgery and for his success in the separation of West German Siamese twins joined at the head. Dr. Carson's remarks, accepting the Award in Business and the Professions, conveyed humility and gratitude, acknowledged emotional and spiritual support, and demonstrated the values that led to the achievement:

> I'd like to take this opportunity first of all to say that I'm tremendously honored. I don't feel, particularly after listening to the accomplishments of the other nominees, that I should be the one to receive this award. I'd also

like to say how much I appreciate, as the representative of the business and professionals, the fact that Hollywood is recognizing that, in the Black community, achievements in intellectual fields are important.

I'd like to thank my wife; and I'd like to thank my mother who, when I was in last place in my fifth-grade class, turned off the television set (believe it or not), said I had to read two books a week, and made the big difference in my life when I learned to appreciate learning; and lastly to my Father, who is the Owner of the universe, and anyone who knows my story, knows that I'm talking about my Father above. Thank you all very much.[6]

The Speech of Dedication

The speech of dedication is presented to commemorate the completion of a project such as a national monument, a museum, church, ship, or hospital. The speaker refers to the sacrifice and service of individuals who fostered the project and moved it to completion. Effective dedication speeches acknowledge the symbolism of the venture and convey its meaning to the community. Speakers often remind listeners of their values and emphasize the way the finished project will meet individual or collective needs. Dedication speeches usually include phrases revealing the purpose of the project: "This is a place where families can receive help," or "This building will be a house of culture and creative thought." Dedication speeches can bring the members of a community together by reacquainting listeners with their shared interests and common goals.[7]

On November 11, 1984, the Vietnam Veterans Memorial was presented to the United States Government in a special dedication ceremony in Washington, D.C. One of the principal speakers at the event was Jan C. Scruggs, a Vietnam veteran whose commitment to the memory of his colleagues moved him to raise the $8 million needed for the monument. In his dedication speech, Mr. Scruggs acknowledged the bitter dissension caused by the war. But he also described the memorial as a symbol of national reconciliation: a "sacred" site where the sacrifices of young soldiers could be remembered, and where national healing could take place:

> But before we give the Vietnam Memorial away to the Government, I have a few things to say. At age eighteen I was among the thousands who volunteered for combat in Vietnam. We returned home scorned as the nation was too divided over that war to honor those who served and only wanted to forget those who died. In 1979 I decided to remind America of our patriotic service and to make certain that the names of the 58,000 who died would never be forgotten.
>
> So today the memorial is to be given to the United States Government. Vietnam veterans are giving this beautiful statue and the wall of names to America. It seems ironic. Indeed, it seems that rather than Vietnam veterans building a memorial for the government, that the government should

have built the memorial for the veterans. But Vietnam was that kind of war.

My fellow veterans, because of this memorial, we now have our recognition. And we can now say that we have honored our dead. All of this has been a long time in coming, and is a time for America to be proud again.

Yet this Memorial has given America far more than that. Out of the bitter divisiveness of Vietnam has come a symbol of national unity. This is a memorial to heal the wounds of the veterans and to heal the wounds of a nation.

People will always debate that war—and let them. But this site is sacred ground where Americans have shown their honor and their respect for the sacrifices made by a generation of young soldiers who answered the call to duty. . . .

Today we also thank those who gave the funds for the memorial: locals from the AFL-CIO, school children, veterans' posts, anti-war protesters, conservative businessmen, retired people. From across America, compassionate people responded to the need for funds. Thank you America.[8]

The Speech of Welcome

Welcoming speeches extend greetings to new or returning members of organizations. University officials welcome incoming students, company representatives say hello to new employees, religious leaders greet new converts, and convention organizers extend warm regards to delegates. The speaker giving the welcome should express pleasure at seeing new as well as familiar faces, mention the goals of the group or organization, briefly identify problems to be solved, and convey best wishes to the audience members for success. The speech of welcome should be concise, communicate warmth in its tone and message, build trust and support, and establish common ground.

This welcome, presented to a group of public-speaking students on the first day of class, uses questions to build a sense of community, identifies general course goals, and emphasizes positive achievement:

I want to give all of you a special welcome to this class. First, I'd like to ask a couple of questions. How many of you have ever had any type of speech or communications course before, either in high school or in some other college class? A few of you—fine. Now for another question. How many of you have ever participated in a theatrical production or in a debate, given a report in a class, or been asked to deliver a talk in church or at your job? Well that's almost all of you. You can see that almost every one of you has had some experience with public speaking in your lifetime. And certainly all of you had to present a series of mini-speeches as you went through the registration line to sign up officially for the course.

No matter what your background, your experience, or your knowledge, this course will help you. You'll get to know people you've never met before, you'll be confronted with a variety of ideas—some unfamiliar, some unconventional—and you'll participate in a number of learning situations that will contribute to your growth. If you're willing to work, listen, and participate, you should succeed.

The Speech of Introduction

The speech of introduction acquaints the audience with a speaker or lecturer. The introduction should help to establish speaker credibility by relating the speaker's occupation, experience, and expertise regarding the topic. The introduction might include descriptions of personal qualities—"He is a family man," or "She is an avid gardener"—and brief anecdotes providing insights into the speaker's personal life. The speech of introduction also describes values the speaker has in common with the audience.

The introduction should be concise and well-organized. Lengthy or flowery introductions can exhaust audiences and defeat speakers before they are able to establish credibility on their own. The goal of the introductory speech is to enlighten the audience about a speaker and to prepare them positively for the speaker's remarks.

Dr. Paul Hardin, president of Drew University, gave the following introduction of actor Alan Alda, who delivered the commencement address at this small Methodist-affiliated institution in Madison, New Jersey. The university had originally invited Jesse L. Jackson to be the commencement speaker, but because of illness, he was replaced by Mr. Alda. This excerpt from Dr. Hardin's speech demonstrates an effective verbal transition from Jackson to Alda, conveys familiar as well as unknown information about the speaker, and describes some of Alda's important qualities and virtues:

> We are, of course, very sorry that Mr. Jackson became ill and most regretful that he cannot be with us today. We wish him a speedy recovery. I would have been proud indeed to present him to you.
>
> I am equally proud, I assure you, to present to you the man who on just thirty-six hours notice, gracefully and unselfishly agreed to rescue us from a terrible predicament, and to speak from this platform today. Oh, I might say, Hawkeye to the rescue!
>
> MASH is an acronym. MASH stands for Mobile Army Surgical Hospital. It also is the title of what has been called the most literate comedy series in the history of television. Probably everyone in this audience knows the series and loves its leading character, Captain Benjamin Franklin Pierce, better known as "Hawkeye." Hawkeye and his fellows are constantly fighting the insanity of war, even as they fight to save the wounded victims of war. They instruct as they entertain.
>
> The talented actor who plays Hawkeye was a hard-working and much traveled and successful veteran of stage, screen and television, long before he made the role famous. This distinguished actor is the son of another

distinguished actor, Robert Alda, who taught him much of what he knows. He is also a graduate of Fordham, an army veteran, a writer, producer, at times a television critic, an impassioned supporter of good causes, including the Equal Rights Amendment; and our speaker is justly respected as one of our nation's foremost family men. Happily for Drew on this occasion, our speaker, his wife Arlene, and their three daughters, love their small town in New Jersey.

Will you please give a very generous welcome to Hawkeye, to the very distinguished and humane actor and writer, Mr. Alan Alda![9]

The Keynote Speech

Keynote speeches are presentations given at the beginning of major conferences or conventions. Democrats and Republicans invite nationally known speakers to address their conventions every four years. Teachers, lawyers, physicians, automakers, and chefs are among the many groups who ask experts to focus on specific issues at regional or national conferences.

Keynote speeches can be lengthy, sometimes as long as forty-five minutes to an hour. Keynote speakers highlight challenges and obstacles to goals such as divisiveness, inferior working conditions, unknown cures, or inequality. To help members face these challenges together, speakers remind listeners of unifying principles and values within party platforms, bylaws, or creeds. Portions of keynote speeches identify solutions the group must accomplish—overturning Supreme Court decisions on abortion, defeating opposing candidates, or building better cars. Keynote speeches should convey emotion, reinforce feelings about organizational values, and inspire commitment to group goals.

On July 12, 1976, Barbara Jordan became the first black woman to deliver a keynote address to the Democratic National Convention. In her remarks, the congresswoman from Texas called for strong ethics in government, asked party faithful to provide America with a "vision for the future," and appealed for a sense of community and participation. As this excerpt reveals, Ms. Jordan's ideas are as applicable today as they were in the 1970s:

> And now, what are those of us who are elected public officials supposed to do? We call ourselves public servants but I'll tell you this: We as public servants must set an example for the rest of the nation. It is hypocritical for the public official to admonish and exhort the people to uphold the common good if we are derelict in upholding the common good. More is required of public officials than slogans and handshakes and press releases. More is required. We must hold ourselves strictly accountable. We must provide the people with a vision of the future.
>
> Now, I began this speech by commenting to you on the uniqueness of a Barbara Jordan making the keynote address. Well I am going to close my

speech by quoting a Republican president and I ask you that as you listen to these words of Abraham Lincoln, relate them to the concept of a national community in which every last one of us participates: As I would not be a slave, so I would not be a master. This expresses my idea of Democracy. Whatever differs from this, to the extent of the difference is no Democracy.[10]

The Nominating Speech

Nominating speeches present the names of individuals for consideration to elective office before a group. The nomination should identify the qualifications necessary for the job, state the values and achievements of the nominee, and discuss how the group will succeed under the nominee's leadership.[11]

An effective nominating speech is accurate, brief, and optimistic. The speaker should have carefully researched the nominee's background to avoid embarrassing misstatements or factual errors. The speaker should mention the nominee's experience and qualifications, but eliminate biographical details having little significance to the position sought. A nominating speech should be short: a lengthy speech can affect listeners negatively, even damaging the nominee's chances of election. The nomination can include statements of the individual's virtues, quotations from speeches, or brief anecdotes and testimonials. The speech should end positively, conveying inspiration and promise.

In this speech nominating General Dwight D. Eisenhower for the presidency at the 1952 Republican National Convention, Governor Theodore McKeldin of Maryland reminded delegates of Eisenhower's heroism as Supreme Allied Commander during World War II. He also portrayed Eisenhower as a simple man, "rooted in the soil" of the Midwest, who could unite the nation and its allies.[12]

> The Man whose name I shall present . . . has been summoned successively from one gigantic task to another in freedom's cause. His whole career as a soldier, statesman, administrator, has prepared him uniquely for the greatest office in the realm of our people's sovereignty—the Presidency of the United States. . . . Here is the man to unite our party; here is the man to unite our nation; here is a man to unite our productive forces—labor and capital—in the teamwork that is essential to the times, fully recognizing the dignity and the rights of each; here is the man to unite our allies and potential allies against communism and all threats of aggression and oppression. . . .
>
> . . . While some of us kept interparty competition alive and active in our states, the candidate whose name I shall give you was engaged in leading America's brave sons in the great, successful invasion of Normandy on D-Day. . . . This man is a true son of America's frontier. His beginnings

are rooted in the soil of our great Middle West and in the deep religious convictions of his devout, Bible reading parents. . . . He was appointed to West Point during the Administration of President William Howard Taft. . . . It is with pride that I place before this convention for president of the United States the name of Dwight David Eisenhower.

The Farewell Speech

Farewell speeches are given on the occasion of retirements, resignations, or some other change in status and position. The speaker thanks listeners for their association and friendship, conveys appreciation for their help and/or support, and expresses hope and best wishes for the future. These speeches are often emotional and moving, especially if speakers are saying goodbye after many years of association with listeners.

Some of the most celebrated farewells in history were presented by leaders such as George Washington, who advised the new nation to "Steer clear of permanent alliances with any portion of the foreign world"; General Douglas MacArthur, who identified himself with "Old soldiers [who] never die; they just fade away"; and Abraham Lincoln, who told friends in Springfield, Illinois, that he owed them "everything."[13]

In Lincoln's brief Farewell Address at Springfield in 1861, he acknowledged his friends and family origins, invoked God's blessing, and expressed almost prophetic uncertainty about the future:

> No one, not in my situation, can appreciate my feeling of sadness at this parting. To this place, and the kindness of these people, I owe everything. Here I have lived a quarter of a century, and have passed from a young to an old man. Here my children have been born, and one is buried. I now leave, not knowing when or whether ever I may return, with a task before me greater than that which rested upon Washington. Without the assistance of the Divine Being who ever attended him, I cannot succeed. With that assistance, I cannot fail. Trusting in Him who can go with me, and remain with you, and be everywhere for good, let us confidently hope that all will yet be well. To His care commending you, as I hope in your prayers you will commend me, I bid you an affectionate farewell.[14]

The Commencement Speech

Commencement speeches are given to honor the graduates of an institution, seminar, or field of study. Speakers congratulate listeners for their achievements, identify problems they will encounter throughout life, and refer to values that should guide their thinking.[15] Too often, when well-intentioned speakers become too self-absorbed, or try too hard to sound

An effective commencement speaker is clear, down-to-earth, and uses meaningful examples.

eloquent and intellectual, graduation speeches become tiresome affairs proclaiming platitudes having little meaning or interest to graduates.

Since the circumstances require the announcement of hundreds, and sometimes thousands of graduates, successful commencement speeches should be brief. The speaker should remember that the focus of the ceremony is the awarding of diplomas—not the speech. A graduation speech should contain clear ideas and meaningful examples. The "down-to-earth" speaker will often be received more favorably than the individual who attempts to create high-sounding phrases. For an example of an effective commencement address, read cartoonist Garry Trudeau's "The Impertinent Questions" at the end of this book.

The After-Dinner Speech

The after-dinner speech is usually a light, humorous presentation designed to entertain or amuse an audience. There are numerous occasions where this type of speech would be appropriate: An "over-the-hill" party satirizing a friend's fortieth birthday; a football victory celebration poking good-natured fun at the coach; a business luncheon "roasting" the boss; a graduation party lampooning teachers; or an end-of-speech-class party reviewing the memorable blunders and bloopers of the semester.

While the objective of the after-dinner speech is usually to entertain, it should not consist of a series of unconnected jokes and disjointed stories. After-dinner speakers should observe the same principles of development needed for any other speech occasion.

An after-dinner speech requires a unifying theme—a topic that generates interest and captures the imagination of the audience. Topics such as "Mind-Expanding Courses to Get You through College," "Doing Spain on One Foreign Word a Day," or "Renaming Vegetables" could be developed into successful entertaining speeches. After-dinner speeches can be lighthearted, satiric, or subtly serious.

While research for entertaining speeches often involves exploring your own imagination and creativity, these presentations require specific supporting materials such as quotations and examples to clarify ideas. The introduction should generate curiosity and include a clear thesis statement identifying the main points of the speech. The body should contain proper transitions and references to sources where necessary. The speech should conclude with a suitable quote, reference to the introduction, or interesting narrative.

One way after-dinner speeches differ from other types is in the use of humor. While your speech may deal with a light topic designed to amuse an audience, you should not try to become a stand-up comic or a professional entertainer. Develop your own natural and spontaneous style. It is more important to elicit a few genuine smiles from the audience than to force raucous laughter. Humor depends upon timing and smooth delivery. If you've ever heard a comedian stumble over a punch line, you know how verbal blunders can destroy humor. Practice the after-dinner presentation as you would any other speech. Deliver anecdotes and punch lines clearly, and wait for laughter to subside before you continue. If you feel uncomfortable with humor, evaluate some of your strengths to determine what to include in the speech. Are you a good mimic? Can you tell a good story? Are you good at facial expressions or bizarre voices? Can you write clever rhymes or catchy poems?

Toasts

Toasts are presented to honor individuals at ceremonial occasions such as birthdays, bar mitzvahs, weddings, graduations, or the conclusion of negotiated agreements and business transactions. An effective toast acknowledges past relationships, salutes the events surrounding the present ceremony, and expresses best wishes and hope for the future.

In a wedding toast, a speaker may acknowledge past relationships, relate a humorous incident, and express best wishes for the future.

Depending on the occasion, toasts can be serious or humorous. A U.S. president welcoming a foreign head of state will often use a toast to define areas of unity or disagreement between countries, demonstrate commitment to continuing association, and convey interest in solving problems. At a birthday or wedding party, a speaker can be more humorous. The toast can relate colorful incidents from past relationships to enliven the speech and to entertain the audience. The speaker usually concludes the toast by expressing sincere wishes for the happiness and future success of the individuals being saluted.

In the following wedding toast, the speaker summarizes listeners' mutual feelings, relates one humorous incident, and wishes the couple success and happiness for the future:

> Good friends, I'd like to propose this toast to Mike and Diane—the reason we're all here today. I remember when Mike came over to our house after proposing to Diane, he said, "She didn't say yes, and she didn't say no," and he asked me, "What should I do?" Now I don't usually give advice in these situations, but I said to Mike, "Why don't you just wait and call her tomorrow. Maybe Diane is testing you and she'll give you an answer in a day or two." Well, the "test" lasted for about six weeks—(you can see why I don't give advice). But we're all glad that you both came to terms and decided to make the arrangement official.

Will you all raise your glasses with me in wishing the best possible for Mike and Diane—happiness in life's joys, mutual comfort in life's sorrows, and most important, a lifelong respect and love for each other. Here's to the bride and groom.

Remarks at the Memorial Service for President Richard Nixon

On April 27, 1994, President Bill Clinton delivered this eulogy for the late President Nixon at the Richard Nixon Library and Birthplace in Yorba Linda, California. The speech for this solemn occasion presented Mr. Clinton with many difficult challenges. A tragic and paradoxical figure, Richard Nixon was the only U.S. President in history to resign his office in disgrace after a congressional committee had approved articles of impeachment as a result of the Watergate conspiracy and cover-up. By contrast, Mr. Nixon enjoyed the respect and admiration of many world leaders for establishing bold new relationships with old enemies such as China and the Soviet Union. But he was also assailed in the press and vilified on college campuses for his conduct of the Vietnam War, bombing of Cambodia, and handling of antiwar protesters. It was during the Vietnam War that a young Bill Clinton, a Democrat, had opposed the policies and programs of Richard Nixon, a Republican president. Facing an audience of grieving family, loyal Nixon friends, old enemies, four past presidents of the United States, and millions of Americans watching on television, President Clinton met the unique challenges of the occasion. In this simple, yet eloquent message, Mr. Clinton honored President Nixon's memory, soothed the family's pain, and led the nation in a spirit of healing.[16]

A Eulogy

WILLIAM J. CLINTON

1 President Clinton began by acknowledging the late president and the physical surroundings which included the Nixon birthplace, a tiny

1 President Nixon opened his memoirs with a simple sentence, "I was born in a house my father built." Today, we can look back at this little house and still imagine a young boy sitting by the window of the attic he shared with his three brothers, looking out to a world he could then himself only imagine. From those humble roots, as from so many humble beginnings in this country, grew the force of a driving dream, a dream that led to the remarkable journey that ends here today where it all began, beside the same tiny home, mail-ordered from back

home that Nixon's father had ordered by mail from a Sears Roebuck catalog.

East, near this towering oak tree which, back then, was a mere seedling.

2 Clinton establishes the central elements of his speech.

2 President Nixon's journey across the American landscape mirrored that of his entire nation in this remarkable century. His life was bound up with the striving of our whole people, with our crises and our triumphs.

3 The President pays tribute to Nixon's achievements in domestic and world affairs.

3 When he became President, he took on challenges here at home on matters from cancer research to environmental protection, putting the power of the Federal Government where Republicans and Democrats had neglected to put it in the past. In foreign policy, he came to the presidency at a time in our history when Americans were tempted to say we had had enough of the world. Instead, he knew we had to reach out to old friends and old enemies alike. He would not allow America to quit the world.

4 Remarkably, he wrote nine of his ten books after he left the presidency, working his way back into the arena he so loved by writing and thinking, and engaging us in his dialogue.

5 Clinton uses a personal reference to indicate appreciation for Nixon's advice and continued interest in government.

5 For the past year, even in the final weeks of his life, he gave me his wise counsel, especially with regard to Russia. One thing in particular left a profound impression on me. Though this man was in his ninth decade, he had an incredibly sharp and vigorous and rigorous mind.

6 In this passage Mr. Clinton demonstrates his sensitivity to the wide ranges of emotions within listeners. He honored Nixon's intelligence and resolve, acknowledged the controversies surrounding his administration,

6 As a public man, he always seemed to believe the greatest sin was remaining passive in the face of challenges. And he never stopped living by that creed. He gave of himself with intelligence and energy and devotion to duty. And his entire country owes him a debt of gratitude for that service. Oh yes, he knew great controversy amid defeat as well as victory. He made mistakes, and they, like his accomplishments, are part of his life and record.

and made a wise but brief reference to Nixon's "mistakes."

7 But the enduring lesson of Richard Nixon is that he never gave up being part of the action and passion of his times. He said many times that unless a person has a goal, a new mountain to climb, his spirit will die. Well, based on our last phone conversation and the letter he wrote me just a month ago, I can say that his spirit was very much alive to the very end. That is a great tribute to him, to his wonderful wife, Pat, to his children, and to his grandchildren whose love he so depended on and whose love he returned in full measure.

7 Again the President makes a personal reference, which he uses to encourage and sustain the members of Nixon's family.

8 Today is a day for his family, his friends, and his nation to remember President Nixon's life in totality. To them, let us say, may the day of judging President Nixon on anything less than his entire life and career come to a close. May we heed his call to maintain the will and the wisdom to build on America's greatest gift, its freedom, to lead a world full of difficulty to the just and lasting peace he dreamed of.

8 Mr. Clinton urges the nation to set aside judgments based upon the negative aspects of President Nixon's career, but rather evaluate him on "his entire life."

9 As it is written in the words of a hymn I heard in my church last Sunday, "Grant that I may realize that the trifling of life creates differences, but that in the higher things, we are all one." In the twilight of his life, President Nixon knew that lesson well. It is, I feel certain, a faith he would want us all to keep.

9-10 President Clinton ends with a quotation, an appropriate reference to his distinguished guests, and a farewell to the late president on behalf of the American people.

10 And so, on behalf of all four former Presidents who are here, President Ford, President Carter, President Reagan, President Bush, and on behalf of a grateful nation, we bid farewell to Richard Milhous Nixon.

SUMMARY

This chapter has considered speeches for special occasions. The tribute recognizes distinguished careers and contributions of people either living or dead. Speeches of presentation honor the accomplishments of individuals, and acceptance speeches are given by individuals who receive honors and awards.

Dedication speeches memorialize the completion of national or community projects, welcoming speeches extend greetings to new or returning members of organizations, and speeches of introduction acquaint audiences with speakers or lecturers.

Keynote speeches are thematic presentations given at the beginning of major conferences or conventions; nominating speeches present the names of individuals for possible election to an office; farewell speeches are given on the occasion of retirements, resignations, or other changes in status and position; and commencement speeches honor candidates for attaining degrees.

The after-dinner speech is designed to entertain, while toasts are presented to honor individuals at ceremonial occasions.

SKILL BUILDERS

1. Choose someone you know or admire, such as a friend, family member, professor, or celebrity, and develop a two- to three-minute speech of tribute. Build the speech using the guidelines discussed in this chapter.

2. Using the brainstorming technique, compile a list of topics that could be developed into entertaining speeches. Choose one topic from this list and construct a four- to six-minute after-dinner speech. Use your creativity and imagination.

3. Choose one of the following ideas for a one- to two-minute classroom speech:

   a. Propose a toast to a friend or classmate.

   b. Present a welcome to a group of freshmen, or greetings to new employees at your job.

   c. Nominate a friend or classmate to a student government office.

   d. Introduce a well-known personality in sports, in entertainment, or in politics.

   e. Dedicate a memorial in your community or state.

   f. Present a farewell to your public speaking class.

4. Divide the class into equal groups. Have each group create an award for every member in the opposite group. Each group member should develop a one-minute speech of presentation, and each recipient should be prepared with a one-minute speech of acceptance.

NOTES

1. "Rescuers Abandon Oklahoma Search," *The Sun* (Baltimore), May 5, 1995, p. 1A.

2. Bill Clinton, "We Share Your Grief . . . But You Have Not Lost Everything," *Washington Post,* April 24, 1995, p. A10.

3. Edward M. Kennedy, "A Tribute to His Brother," *Vital Speeches of the Day,* July 1, 1968. p. 547.

4. ABC, "Liberty Weekend," July 3, 1986.

5. Richard L. Johannesen and others, *Contemporary American Speeches,* p. 343.

6. This acceptance speech appears courtesy of Dr. Benjamin Carson, who gave permission for its use.

7. Richard L. Johannesen and others, *Contemporary American Speeches,* p. 342.

8. This excerpt was supplied courtesy of Jan C. Scruggs, who gave permission for its use.

9. Speech by President Paul Hardin, formerly president, Drew University, delivered at the 111th Commencement of Drew University, May 19, 1979. Used by permission of Paul Hardin, Chancellor, University of North Carolina.

10. Barbara Jordan, "Keynote Address," *Vital Speeches of the Day,* 1976, p. 646.

11. Richard L. Johannesen and others, *Contemporary American Speeches,* p. 343.

12. "Excerpts From Texts of the Nominating Speeches," *The New York Times,* July 11, 1952, p. 9.

13. Andrew Bauer, ed., *A Treasury of Great American Speeches* (New York: Hawthorn Books, 1970), p. 47 and p. 296.

14. Roy P. Basler, ed., *Abraham Lincoln: His Speeches and Writings* (New York: Grosset and Dunlap, 1962), p. 568.

15. Richard L. Johannesen and others, *Contemporary American Speeches,* p. 342.

16. Bill Clinton, "Remarks at the Memorial Service for President Richard Nixon," April 27, 1994, Yorba Linda, California.

Chapter 20

SPEAKING IN GROUPS

CHAPTER OBJECTIVES

After reading this chapter you will be able to:

1. Define and describe the characteristics of small groups;

2. Identify and develop three types of discussion questions;

3. Develop a problem-solving agenda for a discussion;

4. Describe negative, self-centered behaviors;

5. Identify group-centered behavior;

6. Describe the principal leadership theories;

7. Recognize and describe positive leadership behavior;

8. Describe five discussion formats;

9. Apply discussion theory to practical group situations.

A few years ago, Michele Wong got the idea to start a software company that she named "Synergex." Not long after workers were hired, however, the business experienced severe financial difficulties and Ms. Wong decided to handle the difficulties alone without telling her employees. But the company's problems got worse and abruptly surfaced when some workers were forced into layoffs. The remaining employees suggested that Wong hold group sessions to get ideas and assist in problem-solving. As a result of these meetings, employees made suggestions that not only increased morale, but turned the company around the following year. Synergex did so well, in fact, that Wong decided to expand the problem-solving sessions. The company instituted open forums where employees could ask questions, propose ideas, and thank workers. Team meetings were established to help workers set goals and solve problems. A learn-at-lunch program was created to allow employees from various departments to share ideas. The team approach, sharing sessions, and open forums even improved the customer service aspect of the company. Synergex, which now employs almost one hundred workers, was given an award in 1996 for the best business practices in the category of sharing knowledge. Wong summarizes her success by saying: "The company's management is convinced that when employees—especially the sales and product-support staffs—are kept up-to-date on Synergex's overall direction and product news, they can be more articulate and forthcoming with customers."

This chapter presents some of the concepts that helped Michele Wong's company to get on track. It describes characteristics of small groups, types of discussion questions, and ways to solve problems. It includes guidelines for successful group participation and leadership. In addition, the chapter presents information concerning special discussion formats. We want you to communicate and solve problems in group-centered situations as effectively as the workers did in Ms. Wong's company.[1]

CHARACTERISTICS OF SMALL GROUPS

Think of the number of small groups to which you belong. You may be a participant in a campus club or association, a leader of an advertising committee at work, or a member of a bowling league. You may have joined these diverse groups for different reasons: to develop friendships, to get a job accomplished quickly, or simply to relax. While the groups may differ, they have several similar characteristics: each has a shared goal, group interactions, a number of members meeting over a specified period of time, and a leader.[2]

Shared Goals

Groups have goals that bring individuals together. Researchers refer to this quality as *cohesiveness*—that is, the unifying element, common purpose, or mutual feelings of members. Individuals belonging to a church have similar beliefs; employees in an assembly plant share production quotas. Small groups can be classified into types based upon general goals.[3]

Task groups place emphasis on the completion of objectives or implementation of solutions. Employers form search committees to review applicants, conduct interviews, and recommend candidates for positions. Baseball teams develop athletes to play specialized positions in the effort to win games. Civic groups organize membership, nominating, entertainment, or fund-raising committees, each with a different objective. As a member of a college class, you have the task of completing certain specific course requirements for a number of credit hours.

Encounter groups contribute to interpersonal learning and to insight. Couples go away for weekend encounters to develop greater sensitivity and to improve communication. Companies sponsor retreats for employees, managers, or executives to increase self-understanding and awareness of others. Support and therapy groups such as Parents Without Partners, Victims of

In a successful group, members share tasks, maintain dynamic interactions, and work together to achieve common goals.

© *Hal Rummel Photography*

Child Abuse, or Alcoholics Anonymous provide a caring environment for individuals with similar experiences. Colleges and universities sponsor retreats for student leaders to identify leadership strengths and weaknesses.

Social groups help members to establish friendships and personal relationships. If you go to the park for a picnic with a few friends or invite a roommate to a party, you are participating in a group to fulfill social needs. A social group can be an informal gathering like the "lunch bunch" at work or a more structured arrangement like the Tuesday night bridge club.

Group Interaction

Groups usually require interaction among members to accomplish goals. Imagine construction workers trying to complete a building without speaking or a football team attempting a touchdown without signals or physical contact. Communication in groups is dynamic: It is continually active, steadily growing, and constantly changing. To maintain the dynamic energy of a group, members need personal contact with one another.

Size

A small group consists of from two to fifteen members. Six to eight individuals often makes an effective discussion—there are enough members for lively interaction, yet communication does not require limitation because of too many participants. Large groups are frequently divided into smaller work units of five or more members so that business can be conducted more easily and efficiently. The 535-member United States Congress, for example, conducts most of its business in small committees and subcommittees.

Time Period

To make progress towards an objective, a group must meet over a period of time. A schedule allows a group to develop cohesiveness and to explore issues in a systematic manner. Intervals between meetings are sometimes as valuable as the meetings themselves. Members have time to process ideas and to bring fresh insights to the next discussion. An education committee, for example, would need to schedule a variety of meetings in order to design a new computer graphics curriculum. Members would come together to share preliminary ideas and to assign tasks; the group would then schedule future meetings to assess data, to formulate alternatives, and finally to write the curriculum.

Leadership

Small groups usually require leaders to manage or to regulate discussion. In business, industry, or government, formal leaders with specific responsibilities are appointed or elected by organization members. A building foreman, a school principal, a club president, or a union negotiator are good examples of officially appointed or elected formal leaders. In groups without designated leaders, individuals with strong personality characteristics or competent management skills often become informal leaders. Leaderless gatherings such as protests, support groups, ad hoc committees, or social groups are often influenced by powerful individuals who gradually emerge as leaders during the course of group discussions.

SOLVING PROBLEMS IN GROUPS

Questions for Discussion

Issues for group discussions are usually phrased as questions. Open-ended questions tend to promote better discussions than yes-no alternatives. For example, the issue—"Should we increase tuition to solve financial problems at the university"—limits discussion because it offers only two alternatives. The question does not give members the freedom to analyze the complexities of the problem or to explore a wide range of solutions. A more effective question would be "What can be done to solve the financial problems at the university."

Discussion issues can be phrased as questions of fact, value, or policy.

Questions of *fact* explore issues where information is either unknown or disputed. For instance, when President John F. Kennedy was assassinated, the Warren Commission was established to search for answers to the question, "Who was responsible for the assassination of the President?" During the investigation of the Iran-*Contra* arms scandal in the Reagan administration, the Senate Iran-*Contra* Committee attempted to find answers to the question "What was the President's involvement in the arms-for-hostages deal?" Questions of fact require group members to research and analyze evidence in the effort to draw conclusions.

Questions of *value* require discussion members to use personal judgments or feelings to evaluate issues. Words such as "effective," "fair," "harmful," or "beneficial" are often used in the phrasing of value questions. A group might discuss "How has the women's movement improved American life?," or "Would pass-fail grading be more equitable than the current system?" The difficulty with these issues is that they are often more dependent upon personal opinions than upon evidence and research. While questions of value may be useful topics for encounter groups where personal feelings are important, these issues often have no real solution and simply generate circular discussions of members' views. Groups who want to gather facts to form conclusions or develop specific solutions to problems should avoid questions of value.

Questions of *policy* stimulate discussion about solutions or future actions. Issues such as "How should America meet its defense needs in view of the decline of world communism?" or "What should be done to reduce the possibility of oil spills?" would be effective problems for policy discussions. Questions of policy require research, analysis of facts, and discussion of possible solutions for implementation. The word *should* is frequently included in the phrasing of policy issues.

Developing a Problem-Solving Agenda

In order to discuss a problem, a group must have an agenda, or an orderly list of topics the meeting will cover. One of the most effective ways to organize an agenda is to use a process known as "reflective thinking" developed in 1910 by educator John Dewey in *How We Think*.[4] Through the years several researchers have adapted Dewey's ideas more comprehensively to the discussion process.[5] To develop a systematic approach in a group discussion, we suggest an eight point problem-solving plan similar to that described by Larry L. Barker and others in *Groups in Process*.[6]

DEFINE THE PROBLEM

Groups should clearly understand all elements of an issue under consideration. Members may need to define ambiguous terms and provide explanations of key phrases found in the discussion question. For example, in the policy issue, "How should America meet its defense needs in view of the decline of world communism?" "defense needs" could be interpreted as the total defense budget, future expenditures, or new weapons systems. "Decline of world communism" might refer to the collapse of the Soviet Union and former Soviet satellites, or the decline of current communist regimes such as Cuba and China.

NARROW THE PROBLEM

As is the case with speech topics, problems for discussion must be sufficiently limited. In narrowing topics, members should consider the needs of the group as well as the length of time available for discussion. The topic

"What should be done to reduce the possibility of oil spills?" is a broad area that might require discussion for a period of several months or years. The issue might also include areas such as "government inspections" or "cleanup costs" which may be irrelevant to group objectives. One way to limit the problem would be to develop subcategories that could be managed more efficiently:

1. New technologies for building tankers
2. Laws regulating shipping
3. Establishment of early detection systems
4. Prohibition of tankers in fragile ecological areas

The group could select the subtopics that were most important to their analysis, and gauge their discussion according to time limitations. In a one-time class discussion of fifty minutes, a group might be able to handle only two areas. A governmental group meeting over several weeks, however, might be able to handle ten or more categories.

ANALYZE THE ISSUE

The next step in problem solving is to research and analyze the issue. If the group were to consider the question, "What can be done to solve financial problems at the university," members could divide up research responsibilities according to expertise or personal interest. An administrator could interview the dean of Business Administration; an archivist could investigate the history of the financial dilemma; a faculty chair could contact other academic coordinators, a student could circulate questionnaires to fellow classmates, and a mathematician could do a statistical analysis of current fiscal difficulties. If members conduct thorough research into the problem, they will have the tools necessary to discuss the complexities of the issue and to develop workable solutions.

Set Up Criteria. Once the problem has been analyzed, the group should develop criteria or guidelines for a workable solution. This phase of problem solving keeps a discussion on track and helps a group to focus on successful results. A committee analyzing the question, "What kind of uniforms should we select for the marching band?" might set up the following criteria:

1. Uniforms should incorporate school colors.
2. Uniforms should be weather resistant.
3. Uniforms should be within budget constraints.
4. Uniforms should be eye-catching.
5. Uniforms should be comfortable and lightweight.

SUGGEST SOLUTIONS

Next, the group develops a variety of potential solutions from individual research, through spontaneous discussion, and/or as a result of brainstorming techniques. Group members discussing band uniforms might have obtained bids from several companies estimating the costs of the uniforms. Some members might have contributed new suggestions during the discussion process or thought of different alternatives as members jotted down ideas that came to mind.

APPLY CRITERIA TO SOLUTIONS

Once a group has selected alternatives, members can apply the predetermined criteria to identify the most desirable solution. This step in problem-solving enables a group to eliminate solutions that are not workable. Notice how the above criteria can be applied to select a company to manufacture uniforms for the marching band:

ALTERNATIVE SOLUTIONS		APPLICATION OF CRITERIA
Company A	Colors for uniforms come in only three combinations— beige/red, black/gold, green/blue.	Violates # 1. (School colors are maroon and white)
Company B	Uniforms come in two fabric choices—wool, and cotton.	Violates # 2 and # 5.
Company C	Uniforms are inexpensive, but the company has only two standard styles.	Violates # 4.
Company D	One-of-a-kind, designer uniforms; prices start at $300 per uniform.	Violates # 3. (Budget ceiling is $125 per uniform.)
Company E	Company carries uniforms in maroon and white; has variety of styles in lightweight weather-resistant materials. Basic costs start at $85 plus accessories.	Solution meets all criteria.

IMPLEMENT THE SELECTED SOLUTION

When group members make a final choice, their job is not complete until they actually implement the solution. In well-organized groups, members develop a plan of action and divide up responsibilities. To implement the plan for uniforms, for instance, some group participants might contact the company to sign contracts, others might take clothing measurements from band members, and some could form another group to raise funds.

MONITOR THE SUCCESS OF THE SOLUTION

A solution needs to be monitored to determine its degree of success. Is the solution working as intended? Are there problems with any aspect of the plan? Does the group need to modify the solution or reevaluate its decision in view of new information? A group might need to conduct interviews or circulate questionnaires to examine how well the solution is working. After initial observations, for example, group members might discover that the band uniforms were poorly manufactured. The group could withhold payment until satisfactory modifications were made or reject the contract entirely and choose another company. Group members might also decide to evaluate the decision by circulating a survey asking band members about the comfort, quality, and durability of the clothing.

A SAMPLE AGENDA

Here is a sample agenda to demonstrate how problem solving is applied in a group meeting. Notice that the agenda clearly identifies the time, date, and place of the meeting as well as the supporting documents included.

Meeting of the Search Committee

Wednesday, June 7, 2000
Room 201 (2nd Floor Conference Room)
2:00–4:00 P.M.

Topic: Which applicant(s) should be recommended for the position of director of Public Relations?

I. Introduction of new members

II. Approval of minutes of 5/24/00

III. Introduction of topic
  A. Discussion of decision-making process
  B. Scope of the committee responsibility
  C. Concerns of committee members

IV. Qualifications required for P.R. position

V. Review and evaluation of applications

    VI. Committee decision and recommendations
       A. Eliminate unqualified candidates
       B. Narrow choice to two to four qualified candidates
    VII. Group assignments
       A. Conduct further research
          1. Contact previous employers
          2. Interview coworkers
          3. Collect samples of applicants' work
          4. Request educational transcripts
       B. Make appointments with applicants for interviews
    VIII. Schedule next meeting

Documents Enclosed:

   1. Agenda
   2. Minutes of 5/24/00
   3. Fifteen Applications for Director of Public Relations

Keep in mind that the committee discussions are an ongoing process: Group members have made a preliminary decision to select two to four qualified applicants at the present meeting. But the committee needs to conduct further research and to meet again in order to make a final decision. The committee cannot monitor a solution at this stage, since a final choice has not yet been made.

PARTICIPATING IN GROUPS

Effective participation is vitally important to the success of a discussion and to the efficient completion of a task. Group members sometimes believe that they possess little power within an organization and that most of the authority remains with the leader. Such a view is usually mistaken. While leaders can exercise influence, success within a group is often determined by the skill and expertise of participants. One individual can exert a powerful influence to move a group towards the completion of a task, or to inhibit the decision-making process.

Self-Centered Behavior

Behavior that inhibits discussion in a group is often self-centered. A *self-centered* member uses the group to achieve personal goals and demonstrates a lack of interest in group needs or objectives. Self-centered conduct reroutes discussion and often stops problem solving. In 1948, Kenneth D. Benne and Paul Sheats studied groups extensively to determine some of the positive and negative characteristics members exhibit within small groups. Here is a list of eight negative group behaviors based on Benne and Sheats' research:[7]

NEGATIVE SELF-CENTERED BEHAVIORS		EXAMPLE
Attacking	Displaying aggressive behavior towards group members by making hostile comments (telling nasty jokes or putting down individuals), showing envy, or expressing disapproval.	"You're dead wrong—You're DEAD wrong. Where did you go to school anyway?"
Blocking	Behavior that delays the decision-making process such as being unreasonable or negative, taking positions in opposition to the group (bringing up issues already decided or postponing issues members want to discuss), or generally failing to cooperate.	"I think we should table the motion—we've got a lot more important things to do than to spend our time talking about trivia like this."
Boasting	Attempts to impress group members and to maintain a central position in the group by bragging about professional expertise, personal qualifications, or past accomplishments.	"The company president always calls upon me when he needs a creative idea . . . In fact, I had lunch with him yesterday and he thought my proposal was an excellent solution."
Clowning	Exhibiting a lack of involvement in the group by telling inappropriate jokes, expressing cynicism, advocating recreational objectives, or simply "goofing off."	"Why don't we have our next meeting in a bar?"
Confessing	Using a group as an encounter or therapy session to fulfill personal needs by relating irrelevant stories, inappropriate personal examples, or boring anecdotes.	"That reminds me of the time my husband and I were having communication problems and we tried to work them out but . . ."

(continued)

NEGATIVE SELF-CENTERED BEHAVIORS		EXAMPLE
Dominating	Attempts to display self-importance and superiority by monopolizing or manipulating group discussions.	"This problem should be no surprise to anyone who has listened carefully to my past statements—I have repeatedly predicted this situation."
Pleading	Efforts to gain constant sympathy for help—or support from group members by expressing insecurity or inadequacy.	"I've never been in charge of a subcommittee before—It seems almost overwhelming. Why don't you ask Sharon—she's more experienced."
Promoting Special Interests	Behavior that seeks to manipulate a group based upon the needs, prejudices, or interests of one member.	"I never function before 11 A.M. and I can't meet after 2:30 because of a dentist appointment. Could we plan a lunch meeting instead?"

Group-Centered Behavior

Groups cannot afford to waste time reacting to interpersonal problems caused by negative behaviors. An effective discussion requires group-centered behavior: Members need to cooperate with each other and share responsibility to help the group work efficiently towards solution. Here are six group-centered behaviors that can contribute to positive decision-making:[8]

BE AN ACTIVE OBSERVER

An effective participant carefully observes a group by listening attentively and watching intently. When you are in a group situation, observe how members approach problems, how frequently they contribute to the discussion, or how effectively they perform tasks. Ask yourself these questions: is there a difference between what members say and do? Is the group analyzing all aspects of the problem? Is the group making progress towards stated goals? Are there any contributions I can make which can move the group more effectively towards solutions? Active observation can help you to sense the right moment to make an appropriate contribution.

For example, if you were to see a heated conflict developing between two group members, you might cool the argument with the suggestion, "We can't solve all these problems at once." When discussion is at an impasse, you might recommend that members return to the issue later, or introduce a new idea to rekindle discussion. If you have listened actively, you might have the opportunity to remind participants of previous decisions that have been forgotten.

SUPPORT GROUP PROCEDURE

Discussion groups usually have a wide variety of tasks for members to perform. As an active participant, you should be willing to take on your fair share of assignments. You might be asked to chair a subcommittee; you might be placed in charge of duplicating and circulating committee pamphlets, questionnaires, or supporting materials; the group leader might even request your assistance in preparing the agenda or contacting fellow members. One job participants frequently dislike is recording minutes of committee conversations and decisions. Keeping accurate records is important, however, especially in formal organizations where documentation of past committee actions is required. If a group has no assigned secretary, it is helpful to rotate this important responsibility among group members. As a participant, you should view tasks as opportunities to help the group complete its goals.

BE RELIABLE

If groups are to function smoothly, members must perform tasks efficiently and on time. Groups are easily sabotaged by irresponsible members who are chronically late, who fail to complete assigned tasks, or who manage assignments carelessly. As a group member, take your responsibilities seriously. Be on time for group meetings and complete duties conscientiously. Take care of any arrangements that may be required for your portion of a meeting: do necessary research, notify invited guests of the time and place of the meeting, and have all handouts or other paperwork ready for circulation. Recognize that irresponsibility wastes everyone's time and energy within a group.

BE WILLING TO COMPROMISE

Group participation is not a game of winners and losers; an effective group experience should exhibit a healthy give-and-take among members. When you are a part of a discussion, you must be willing to hear other points of view and accept changes to some of your ideas and proposals. While you are not expected to compromise your personal beliefs or values, you should be able to alter your thinking if other suggestions prove to be more workable. Compromising is often viewed as watered-down or weak-willed decision making. But if a group is open to all the facts and genuinely seeks the best alternative, group members will often need to make compromises and modifications before coming to final decisions.

BE COURTEOUS AND RESPECTFUL

Groups cannot function effectively when members are at odds. Participants who constantly interrupt each other, launch personal attacks, or exhibit insensitivity are engaging in disrespectful behavior that could eventually lead to the destruction of the group. While members don't need to like each other in order to accomplish group objectives, they must demonstrate respect and common courtesy. When another member is talking, give your full attention. Wait until the individual is finished before you contribute an idea or make a suggestion. Respect the background, experience, and expertise of others and recognize that everyone does not have the same perspective as you. Be sensitive to those group members who speak English as a second language and may need help understanding difficult terms or colloquial expressions. Respect individual differences and do not discriminate on the basis of appearance, sexual orientation, gender, race, or religion. Women should not be required to bring coffee or perform secretarial duties because they are female any more than men should be assigned leadership roles or asked to empty the trash simply because they are male. Individuals should not separate or isolate themselves according to race or gender, but place themselves in seating arrangements that will assist and facilitate group procedures and tasks. Recognize that members with special needs such as individuals in wheelchairs or those who are hearing impaired may require specific arrangements such as accessibility to ramps or proximity to interpreters. Be patient with irrelevancies or inappropriate remarks. Avoid tactics such as personal attacks or name-calling, which can stimulate anger. Don't ridicule the ideas of members or jump to conclusions about their decision-making abilities. Know when to exercise silence and let the leader handle difficulties.

ENCOURAGE AND ENERGIZE MEMBERS

Groups must work together to solve problems. If an outfielder drops a fly ball, the second baseman doesn't laugh at the error; the player tries to help the team by making a face-saving play. When members must complete difficult tasks, give assistance or make helpful suggestions. Show encouragement to participants who perform competently. Compliment a member by saying, "Your idea is a good one—maybe we can use it as a basis for the solution." This type of support builds group cohesiveness and cooperation, and helps to energize members to complete assignments. Participation is not a contest of wills: individuals must be able to subordinate personal egos for the overall benefit of the group.

GROUP LEADERSHIP

Leadership Theories

There are many theories concerning group leadership. Some researchers believe that leaders possess certain powerful *traits* such as physical appearance, speaking ability, or behavior which determine leadership.[9] The trait approach suggests that leaders do not learn or acquire these skills but are born with natural abilities. It can be argued, for example, that Abraham Lincoln, Winston Churchill, Franklin Roosevelt, and Martin Luther King possessed natural leadership abilities.

Another theory suggests that power and authority are significant factors in leadership.[10] Members of a group will respond to a leader's position, expertise, or job title—"chief executive officer," "lieutenant," "heart specialist," "committee chair," "florist," "builder," or "tax accountant." According to this theory, members opposing a decision might be persuaded to comply with an argument such as, "You may not agree, but this proposal is what the president wants."

In the 1930s, Kurt Lewin, Ronald Lippitt, and Ralph K. White studied the reactions of ten-year-old boys to three different leadership behaviors over a three-month period. This research, now classic in the field, identified three leadership styles: *autocratic, democratic,* and *laissez-faire*.[11] The autocratic leader acted as the chief decision maker of the group, giving orders and commands to group members. Democratic leaders functioned more as coordinators, promoting discussion and stimulating group decision making. The *laissez-faire* style was a leaderless group where members themselves took care of managerial or administrative responsibilities. In this study, researchers found that members of democratic groups experienced the greatest degree of satisfaction with leaders and group outcomes, while autocratic group members were least satisfied with leadership and group achievements. Members of leaderless groups were pleased with mutual associations and friendships acquired within groups, but participants felt that little was accomplished. Research updating the Lewin study combines leadership style and personality. Investigators suggest that authoritarian personalities are more "object-oriented" while democratic personalities tend to be more "people-oriented."[12]

Today, some researchers view effective leadership in terms of adaptability. Arbitrary leadership styles or predetermined traits may not be appropriate in many group situations. Leaders may need to adopt a variety of approaches to meet group needs and to help members accomplish organizational tasks.[13]

Positive Leadership Behaviors

Most of us will be leaders at some time in our lives, either by choice or necessity. Whether you are a PTA president, a manager, a self-employed professional, or a committee chair, you need to know some of the skills that contribute to effective leadership. In this section, we examine four positive leadership behaviors that are necessary for successful group management.

BE PREPARED

A leader cannot simply appear and improvise an agenda for a group meeting; effective leadership requires careful advance planning. A leader must choose an appropriate location, prepare an agenda, and anticipate potential problems.

Choose an Appropriate Location.   Know the size of the meeting area; don't try to fit a large group into a tiny cubicle, or a small group into a huge auditorium. Understand the characteristics of the room and ask yourself these questions: Are there tables for discussion, are there enough chairs for participants, and can all members see each other easily? Will participants need small tables, blackboards, or screens for visual aids? Do invited guests have any special room requirements? Is the meeting located near noisy traffic areas, or can the room be closed for privacy? Is the area flexible enough to accommodate any rearrangement which may be necessary during the meeting? Is a telephone accessible for messages, and is a tape recorder available to document committee discussions and actions? Make any arrangements required for scheduling the room. Be sure that the room will be unlocked and set up for the discussion on the day of the meeting.

Circulate an Agenda.   As a leader you will need to prepare an agenda of the major topics to be covered during a meeting. Contact group participants to determine topics included in their presentations, and remind invited experts of their meeting obligations. Have the agenda and all supporting documents duplicated and circulated to the group well in advance of the meeting so that participants are prepared for the discussion and can notify you if changes are necessary. Be certain that the agenda clearly identifies the date, time, and place of the meeting. If any guests may be unfamiliar with the location, include clear directions to the meeting place.

Anticipate Potential Problems.   If you have smokers as well as non-smokers in the group, be sure that everyone understands the policies governing smoking in the building where meetings are conducted. If there are no policies or regulations, establish clear guidelines to alleviate conflicts. In order to stimulate a positive discussion, it may be helpful to place shy members near more talkative participants, or to separate members who constantly argue. Members with disabilities or special difficulties may require assistance with wheelchairs, interpreters, or readers. You may also need to handle potentially disruptive members by assigning specific tasks to keep them occupied. As a leader, you should be in contact with members a day or two before the meeting to determine if there are significant problems that could affect discussion and alter planning: Members with schedule conflicts might need to arrive late or leave early; members with extreme personal emergencies may ask to be excused or replaced; members having complicated group assignments may need extended deadlines; members discovering additional information may request further group discussion. A knowledge of potential problems and an awareness of special circumstances can help you manage a discussion smoothly.

KEEP TO TIME LIMITS

Meetings should start and end on schedule. Tardiness not only wastes everyone's time, but it also conveys disorganization and contributes to member hostility. Individuals who are angry because a meeting began twenty-five minutes late will not be in a constructive mood for decision making. Leaders should be prompt and expect members to be on time. If a meeting is scheduled to end at a specific time, the leader should do everything possible to close off discussion. When a meeting drags beyond the closing time members convey negative feedback by stacking papers into neat piles, watching the clock, or squirming uncomfortably. A leader should be sensitive enough to realize that little will be accomplished by keeping participants overtime. Keeping to schedules can increase the satisfaction of group members and contribute to efficient problem solving.

BE ORGANIZED

Begin the meeting by announcing any changes in the published agenda. Remember that agendas are not fixed in stone: They contain topic outlines designed to serve group needs. A leader who is willing to be flexible and make a few changes builds cohesiveness and improves the climate for decision making. A brief procedural comment can convey sensitivity to individuals: "We'll consider item 3 on the agenda first—Julie is here from the day-care center. Because she has to leave to supervise the children, it would help her if we could deal with day-care issues first. Do you have any objections?"

Guide group members skillfully through the agenda. If the agenda is long, set time limits for specific items so that the group will cover all topics efficiently. If issues remain unresolved, establish additional subcommittees or work units to complete analysis and problem solving.

Help members seek information and analyze problems. Promote decision making by asking questions or interjecting thoughts such as "Has that problem occurred before?" or "Maybe we need to distribute a questionnaire." Move members towards solution of issues by asking for alternatives and requesting data verifying solutions—"Has this solution been successful in other places?" Work for consensus on issues. Groups don't need to vote on everything; constant hand-raising or balloting can disrupt the flow of discussion. Reserve formal votes for final decisions or solutions.

Communicate effectively when you manage a discussion. Identify agenda topics clearly. Refer to exhibits, page numbers, or supporting documents distinctly so that members can easily follow what is being discussed. Be open to procedural questions or comments from members: let participants know that you want them to move forward toward solutions.

At the end of the meeting, clarify group tasks, summarize individual goals, and define future objectives. Set the time and place of the next meeting. Make sure the group feels a sense of accomplishment with the discussion, commitment to goals, and awareness of future responsibilities.

KNOW WHEN TO INTERVENE

No theory or rule can tell you the exact moment you should do or say something as a leader of a group. It often takes many leadership experiences for an individual to develop a group "sense" or intuition regarding appropriate leadership behavior. There are, however, several ways a leader can intervene constructively during a group discussion. A good leader can resolve conflicts, provide emotional support, clarify and summarize, and demonstrate flexibility.

Resolve Conflicts. Conflicts are inevitable when group members are involved in the decision-making process. Participants can become fixed in their attitudes or take positions they feel the group must adopt. While disagreement can stimulate debate among participants, serious conflict can damage the survival and success of a group. The leader must handle major conflicts carefully to allow the group to complete its objectives. If a serious argument develops between two members or opposing forces, the leader should identify areas of common ground. If none exist, the leader can then restate each argument, identifying its relative strengths and weaknesses. When reviewing the conflicting positions, a leader should give equal time to each argument and avoid taking sides. Being fair will strengthen the leader's position; showing partiality will compromise and undermine the leader's effectiveness. If no agreement can be reached, the leader should define areas of progress, honestly acknowledge unresolved conflict, and move the discussion to other topics. Disputes can often be settled at a later time when emotions have cooled.[14]

Provide Emotional Support.   There are occasions in a discussion when a leader must provide members with emotional support in order to maintain a positive climate for decision making. New members who are meeting with a well-established group for the first time may need reassurance and special courtesy to feel secure, comfortable, and less isolated. Group members may experience hurt feelings after engaging in disputes, suffer humiliation after losing arguments, or need encouragement when not participating. A comment such as "That's an excellent idea—but it may work better in a different situation" might help a member to save face in a discussion, or a statement like "That's a great idea—why don't you expand on it?" might encourage a member to participate more actively.

Clarify and Summarize.   A good discussion is dynamic—there is a great deal of give-and-take. While dynamism is a positive force in a discussion, a leader must occasionally summarize the comments of group members who relate incomplete information, make disjointed remarks, or draw vague conclusions. Summaries help members follow the discussion easily, keep the discussion from backtracking, and clarify group decisions. A good summary is brief and clear, providing an accurate synopsis of a participant's contribution or a group's decision. A leader who comments— "Bill, I think you're asking us to compare the data, is that right?"—is diplomatically summing up Bill's remarks, while at the same time checking the accuracy of the comment with the member. If the leader is unable to comprehend the content of a member's remarks due to language, accent, or other cultural barrier, the leader should be careful not to embarrass or humiliate the individual. A considerate leader finds creative ways of clarifying a difficult contribution such as obtaining a written outline, talking privately with the member during a meeting break, or asking for help from other members who are able to translate or summarize more easily.

Demonstrate Flexibility.   A flexible and observant leader knows when to intervene and when to be silent. If a conversation gets off track, the leader should step in to check the irrelevancies. When a participant monopolizes the conversation, the leader should guide the discussion to other members. The leader needs to quiet the group clown who constantly engages in inappropriate humor or to gently reprimand the member who frequently interrupts others. Uncomfortable group silence may require the leader to activate discussion, while a hostile exchange may necessitate leader mediation. Not all situations, however, require intervention by

THE DYSFUNCTIONAL GROUP

Task: Members of the personnel department are to write specifications for new offices in a new building complex.

Leader: Carla

Group Members: Dave, Jane, Marie, Marty

Meeting Time: 1:30 P.M.

Place: The Conference Room

Members started drifting toward the conference room at about 1:40 P.M. Marty was the first to arrive. Then came Carla several minutes later. The members found the conference room already occupied with five people from graphics who were having a departmental meeting. Marty and Carla argued as they stood in the hall outside:

Carla: "These people have stolen our meeting room. We'll just have to tell them to leave."

Marty: "I already tried that but they said they'd requested the room four weeks ago. They showed me the signed approval form. Did you screw up again, Carla?"

Carla: "Don't tell me I screwed up. You were the one who was supposed to take care of the form, weren't you?"

Marty: "I beg your pardon. That's never been my responsibility. I don't do forms, remember?" *(Jane enters)*

Carla: "Hi Jane. You're late again."

Jane: "I'm really sorry. I had lunch downtown with a friend and there was just too much traffic and I couldn't make it back in time. I'm so very sorry. Why's everybody out in the hall?"

Marty: "Dave or somebody messed up and forgot the sacred yellow form."

Jane: "Well, why don't we meet in my office?"

Carla: "Oh gosh, your office is so teeny, there's only room for two people. Mine's so much more spacious and has a better view."

Marty: "Yeah, the Dumpster looks great when the sun is shining."

Jane: *(Ignoring Marty and insisting)* "No, really, why don't we meet in my office? We can all crowd in. It's kinda cozy, I've got a coffeepot, and anyway I could use some company—I've had such a bad day. Please? PLEASE?"

Carla: "Oh, all right. But there's only room for three chairs in Jane's office. What'll we do if Dave and Marie show up?"

Marty: "Don't worry, they won't show up. And if they do, they'll just have to stand. Serves 'em right for being late."

Carla: "OK let's go."

Jane: "Shouldn't we leave a note or something on the door for Marie and Dave to let them know where we are?"

Carla: "Naw. We've waited long enough for them. They're late anyway so let them have to hunt a little to find us!"

Marty: "You're learning, Carla."

THE FUNCTIONAL GROUP

Task: Members are to write specifications for their new graphics departmental offices in the new building complex.
Leader: Stuart
Members: Dara, Dwight, Hal, Joanne
Meeting Time: 1:30 P.M.
Place: Conference Room

Stuart arrived about 1:15 P.M. to make sure the conference room was set up properly with enough chairs and work tables to accommodate group tasks. He placed folders at each member's table containing additional information needed for the meeting. Dara and Hal arrived at 1:25. Joanne came in a couple minutes later and told Stuart that Dwight had left word that he would be a few minutes late because of a child care problem. The meeting began at 1:32 P.M.

Stuart: "Well I'm glad everyone's going to be here today. Joanne, why don't we start with you, since you're the first item on the agenda. By the way, since it's after lunch, I brought dessert for everyone so please, help yourself to the cookies in the middle of the table."

Joanne: "Thanks. Gee, more calories. Everybody keeps bringing food. I'm going to have to go on a diet after these meetings are over! OK. I've got a lot of information that I want to pass around to each of you."

Hal: "Do you need some help?"

Joanne: "Sure. That would be great. Thanks."

Stuart: "If you and maybe Dara could distribute these spec sheets, then I'll circulate the rest of the documents. *(Dwight enters)* Hi Dwight. Thanks for the message. We're just getting started. Joanne is passing around some documents from her research. Take some cookies."

Dwight: "Thanks."

(There is a knock on the door)

Dara: "I'll get it. *(Answers the door to the conference room)* It's Marty from Personnel. He claims that their department has reserved this room for their meeting and they want us to leave."

Stuart: *(To Dara)* "Show Marty this yellow room confirmation form I have here in my folder. I reserved this room a month ago. Tell Marty that his group needs to send in a written request for the conference room in advance of the requested day. *(To Joanne)* Are you ready Joanne?"

Joanne: "Yes. I think everyone has five spec sheets? Alright, let's start with the first recommendation from our subcommittee."

the leader. A participant raising a point that seems irrelevant may, if allowed to continue, contribute important insights into an issue. A spontaneous joke related at the right moment can reduce tension and move an immobile conversation forward. Group silences can be necessary to help members think through ideas. A lively argument can be a productive force in solving a problem.

The style a leader adopts is often determined by the needs of the group as well as the requirements of the moment. Well-motivated participants who are experienced at discussion may require less intervention by the leader, while inexperienced members may require more guidance. A discussion that is moving along effectively may actually be impeded by an autocratic leader who tries to interject ideas or impose solutions. At the same time, members who are floundering may be frustrated with a democratic leader who provides little direction. During the life of a group, a combination of democratic, autocratic, and *laissez-faire* leadership styles may be necessary.

SPECIAL DISCUSSION FORMATS

There are a variety of groups with different formats: the forum, panel, and symposium as well as buzz groups and role-playing groups.[15]

The Symposium

The *symposium* is a highly structured group in which two to six experts reveal their views and perspectives on some aspect of a problem. Participants deliver prepared speeches to an audience but do not discuss issues informally. A chairperson usually identifies the question, introduces each member, and explains how the meeting will proceed. Participants are usually seated at a table facing the audience while one member speaks from a lectern. An example of a symposium would be a convention program in which three renowned scientists reported differing results from similar fusion experiments.

The Panel

A *panel* is an informal discussion with three to six individuals in front of an audience. One person acts as moderator, regulating participation and guiding the discussion through the problem-solving sequence. Panel members are often experts who speak from their own experience and knowledge.

In a panel discussion, participants exchange ideas, analyze issues, and explore solutions to problems with the guidance of a leader or moderator.

Participants do not deliver prepared speeches in a panel discussion; members make one point at a time, frequently interrupting each other, and commenting upon ideas presented by other individuals. Panelists are often seated in a semicircle or in another arrangement so that members can see each other during the discussion. Panels present issues and examine problems to inform and educate the audience. An example of a panel would be the nation's four chief law enforcement officers considering America's drug policy.

The Forum

A *forum* is a public discussion in which all members of an audience have the opportunity to ask questions, make statements, or deliver speeches about issues. Because so many individuals are involved, a leader is needed to set the ground rules for the discussion and to regulate participation. The seating should be arranged so that all audience members can see everyone easily. The Senate and House of Representatives function as forums. In legislative forums, participation is guided by a speaker or president who operates according to strict rules of parliamentary procedure. In more informal town meetings or council hearings, moderators might allocate specific time limits for individual contributions. Forums are often used in combination with other formats such as symposium forums or panel forums. When panelists have completed discussion or symposium participants have presented speeches, the audience becomes involved in the discussion.

Buzz Groups

Buzz groups are often used in large organizations to involve many people in the decision-making process. Individuals are divided into small units or "buzz groups" of three to eight members. These smaller groups are then given specific tasks to accomplish or issues to examine within a time limit. Groups then report the results of their discussions to the larger organization through elected or appointed leaders. For example, a company could ask its two hundred employees to discuss the topic, "What can be done to improve productivity" and divide into twenty-five groups of eight individuals each. Using this method, a large number of ideas could be generated by many people in a brief period of time.

Role Playing Groups

In *role playing* group members assume characters or personalities to portray relationships and interactions among individuals. Members act out conflicts between parents and children, criminals and victims, or supervisors and employees to reveal dilemmas and to portray inner turmoil. Role-playing experiences are used effectively in encounter groups to stimulate discussion and to help members with decision making and problem solving.

SUMMARY

Small groups are characterized by shared goals, several individuals engaged in face-to-face interactions over a period of time, and a leader. Types of groups include task, encounter, and social groups. Issues for discussion are phrased as questions of fact, value, or policy. Problem solving involves choosing a systematic agenda based upon John Dewey's method of "reflective thinking." When involved in group discussions, members should adopt group-centered behavior and avoid negative self-centered conduct. Although there are many leadership theories, recent research emphasizes the need for leaders to demonstrate flexibility in managing a group. Special discussion formats include the panel, symposium, forum, buzz groups, and role-playing groups.

SKILL BUILDERS

1. The instructor will divide your class into several small groups. When you are assigned to a group, help fellow members select a leader to manage the discussion. Choose several issues for discussion, and

write at least one fact and one policy question. With the advice of your instructor and the opinions of other group members, choose one question for analysis and presentation to the class. Schedule group meetings to make assignments, conduct research, and develop an agenda. Present the issue in a twenty-five- to forty-minute class discussion.

Here are some possible discussion topics.

1. What should be done to reform Congress?
2. What can the United States government do to encourage the development and use of synthetic fuels?
3. What can be done to eliminate acid rain?
4. Who is responsible for juvenile crimes?
5. How does the Palestinian issue affect Americans?
6. What are the causes and effects of illiteracy?
7. What are the characteristics of prison work-release programs?
8. How can our judicial system be reformed?

2. As you participate in the discussion process, keep a journal of your reactions to the group. Write down any problems or frustrations occurring in your group such as unreliability, difficulty in keeping to the task, or ineffective participation or leadership. Try to use the journal to help members overcome difficulties and to make progress towards group tasks.
3. Observe a "professional" committee or group in operation. You might watch the televised hearings of a congressional committee, a task group at your work, or a committee of volunteers in a church or social organization. Analyze the group carefully and write an evaluation of the following factors:
   a. The discussion issue
   b. The process used for decision making
   c. The nature of participation by group members
   d. The quality and effectiveness of leadership
   e. The success of the group in analyzing and in solving problems
4. Divide up into several groups and discuss the examples of "The Dysfunctional Group" and "The Functional Group." Discuss and answer the following questions.
   a. What are the elements that make the Dysfunctional Group ineffective and the Functional Group effective?
   b. What types of personalities does each group include?
   c. Identify and discuss the specific type of behavior exhibited by members in both groups.
   d. What types of leadership are present in each group? How does the attitude of the leader affect each group?

NOTES

1. Roberta Maynard, "Sharing the Wealth of Information," *Nation's Business,* September 1997, p. 14.

2. Compare the definition and characteristics of a group discussion found in Larry L. Barker and others, *Groups in Process,* 4th ed. (Englewood Cliffs: Prentice-Hall, 1991), pp. 7–10 with descriptions provided by Ernest G. Bormann, *Discussion and Group Methods* (New York: Harper and Row, 1969), pp. 3–6.

3. Compare John F. Cragan and David W. Wright, *Communication in Small Group Discussions* (New York: West Publishing Company, 1980), pp. 46–48 with H. Lloyd Goodall, Jr., *Small Group Communication in Organizations* (Dubuque, Iowa: Wm. C. Brown Publishers, 1985), p. 94. Cragan and Wright list three "generic" types of groups: task, encounter, and consciousness-raising groups, while Goodall uses Julia Wood's typology of task, social, and dually oriented groups (a combination of task and social groups). Since we believe that encounter and consciousness-raising groups can be combined into one category, we have used the labels—task, encounter, and social—as the classifications for our study.

4. John Dewey, *How We Think* (Boston: D.C. Heath and Company, 1933), pp. 102–118.

5. See James H. McBurney and Kenneth G. Hance, *Discussion in Human Affairs* (New York: Harper and Brothers, 1950), pp. 3–15.

6. Barker and others, *Groups in Process,* pp. 110–116.

7. Kenneth D. Benne and Paul Sheats, "Functional Roles of Group Members," *Journal of Social Issues* 4 (Spring, 1948): 45–46. Also see Cragan and Wright, *Communication in Small Group Discussions,* pp. 116–117, and Barker and others, *Groups in Process,* pp. 46–47.

8. For this discussion we have combined recommendations appearing in Cragan and Wright, *Participating in Small Groups,* pp. 114–116, as well as Benne and Sheats, "Functional Roles of Group Members," pp. 44–45 with some of our own suggestions.

9. H. Lloyd Goodall Jr., *Small Group Communication in Organizations* (Dubuque, Iowa: Wm. C. Brown Publishers, 1985), p. 122.

10. Cragan and Wright, *Communication in Small Group Discussions,* pp. 75–76.

11. Kurt Lewin, Ronald Lippitt, and Ralph K. White, "Patterns of Aggressive Behavior in Experimentally Created 'Social Climates,'" *The Journal of Social Psychology* 10 (1939): 271–299.

12. Lawrence B. Rosenfeld and Timothy G. Plax, "Personality Determinants of Autocratic and Democratic Leadership," *Speech Monographs* 42 (August 1975): 203–208.

13. Julia T. Wood, "Leading in Purposive Discussions: A Study of Adaptive Behavior," *Communication Monographs* 44 (June, 1977): 152–165.

14. Goodall, *Small Group Communication in Organizations,* p. 145.

15. Barker et al., *Groups in Process,* pp. 193–219.

Appendix

ANNOTATED SPEECHES BY EDWARD M. KENNEDY, ELIZABETH GLASER, GARRY TRUDEAU, JESSE JACKSON, CHRISTOPHER REEVE, AND KAREN ANDERSON

INTRODUCTION TO THE SPEECH OF TRIBUTE BY SENATOR EDWARD M. KENNEDY

It was to be a festive family gathering at a cousin's wedding in Hyannis Port, Massachusetts. John F. Kennedy Jr., a recent pilot, had decided to fly his wife and sister-in-law to the ceremony in his private airplane. Kennedy took off from Fairfield, New Jersey, at about 8:38 P.M. on a hazy summer night and intended to fly his Piper Saratoga along a northeasterly route and land at Martha's Vineyard about one hour later. The plane never reached the airport, however. The aircraft spiraled into the ocean at almost one hundred feet per second and John F. Kennedy Jr., his wife Carolyn, and her sister Lauren Bessette perished in the tragic crash on July 16, 1999.[1]

It became the sad duty of John's uncle, Senator Edward M. Kennedy, to help grieving family members make arrangements for the memorial service and burial at sea. In a bitter irony, Senator Kennedy had walked behind the casket bearing John's assassinated father, President John F. Kennedy, thirty-six years earlier. And more than three decades had passed since he had eulogized John's other uncle, Senator Robert F. Kennedy, who was assassinated while campaigning for president. The task of eulogizing another family member was again the burden of Senator Edward Kennedy who delivered this loving tribute in memory of his nephew at the Church of St. Thomas More in New York City on July 23, 1999.[2]

Tribute to John F. Kennedy Jr.

A Eulogy

EDWARD M. KENNEDY

1 Senator Kennedy acknowledges and thanks the President and his family.

2 Kennedy begins by quoting his nephew to show similarity with John's father, President Kennedy.

4 Although Kennedy cites public reaction to a famous photograph, he provides a more personal interpretation which portrayed John's early fascination with flying.

5-8 Kennedy continues to provide personal insights into his nephew's life, strengths, understanding of his legacy, and his struggle "to live with it."

1 Thank you, President and Mrs. Clinton and Chelsea, for being here today. You've shown extraordinary kindness throughout the course of this week.

2 Once, when they asked John what he would do if he went into politics and was elected President, he said: "I guess the first thing is call up Uncle Teddy and gloat." I loved that. It was so like his father.

3 From the first day of his life, John seemed to belong not only to our family, but to the American family. The whole world knew his name before he did.

4 A famous photograph showed John racing across the lawn as his father landed in the White House helicopter and swept up John in his arms. When my brother saw that photo, he exclaimed, "Every mother in the United States is saying, 'Isn't it wonderful to see that love between a son and his father, the way that John races to be with his father.' Little do they know— that son would have raced right by his father to get to that helicopter."

5 But John was so much more than those long ago images emblazoned in our minds. He was a boy who grew into a man with a zest for life and a love of adventure. He was a pied piper who brought us all along. He was blessed with a father and mother who never thought anything mattered more than their children.

6 When they left the White house, Jackie's soft and gentle voice and unbreakable strength of spirit guided him surely and securely to the future. He had a legacy, and he learned to treasure it. He was part of a legend, and he learned to live with it. Above all, Jackie gave him a place to be himself, to grow up, to laugh and cry, to dream and strive on his own.

7 John learned that lesson well. He had amazing grace. He accepted who he was, but he cared more about what he could and should become. He saw things that could be lost in the glare

of the spotlight. And he could laugh at the absurdity of too
much pomp and circumstance.

8 He loved to travel across this City by subway bicycle and
roller blade. He lived as if he were unrecognizable—although
he was known by everyone he encountered. He always introduced
himself, rather than take anything for granted. He drove his
own car and flew his own plane, which is how he wanted it. He
was the king of his domain.

9-10 Kennedy ac-
knowledges John's
achievement as
founder and edi-
tor of the polit-
ical magazine,
George. He men-
tions a humorous
incident in which
a photograph of
Cindy Crawford on
the cover of
George was sati-
rized in the
Washington Post,
showing a plump
Senator Kennedy
appearing in the
photo instead.

9 He thought politics should be an integral part of our popular
culture, and that popular culture should be an integral part
of politics. He transformed that belief into the creation of
George. John shaped and honed a fresh, often irreverent journal. His new political magazine attracted a new generation
many of whom had never read about politics before.

10 John also brought to *George* a wit that was quick and sure. The
premier issue of *George* caused a stir with a cover photograph
of Cindy Crawford dressed as George Washington with a bare
belly button. The "Reliable Source" in *The Washington Post*
printed a mock cover of *George* showing not Cindy Crawford, but
me dressed as George Washington, with my belly button exposed.
I suggested to John that perhaps I should have been the model
for the first cover of his magazine. Without missing a beat,
John told me that he stood by his original editorial decision.

11-13 Kennedy re-
calls another hu-
morous incident
in which John
told campaign
workers of his
need to share a
hotel room with
his "companion."

11 John brought this same playful wit to other aspects of his
life. He campaigned for me during my 1994 election and always
caused a stir when he arrived in Massachusetts. Before one of
his trips to Boston, John told the campaign he was bringing
along a companion, but would need only one hotel room.

12 Interested, but discreet, a senior campaign worker picked John
up at the airport and prepared to handle any media barrage
that might accompany John's arrival with his mystery companion. John landed with the companion alright—an enormous German
shepherd dog named Sam he had just rescued from the pound.

13 He loved to talk about the expression on the campaign worker's
face and the reaction of the clerk at the Charles hotel when
John and Sam checked in.

14 Throughout the
speech, Kennedy

14 I think now not only of these wonderful adventures, but of
the kind of person John was. He was the son who quietly gave

pays tribute to his nephew's virtues and achievements. Here he speaks of John's "quiet" contributions to the Institute of Politics at Harvard University.

extraordinary time and ideas to the Institute of Politics at Harvard that bears his father's name. He brought to the Institute his distinctive insight that politics could have a broader appeal, that it was not just about elections, but about the larger forces that shape our whole society.

15 The Senator acknowledges John's close family bond with his mother, Jacqueline Kennedy Onassis, and his sister Caroline Kennedy Schlossberg.

15 John was also the son who was once protected by his mother. He went on to become her pride—and then her protector in her final days. He was the Kennedy who loved us all, but who especially cherished his sister Caroline, celebrated her brilliance, and took strength and joy from their lifelong mutual admiration society.

16-18 The Senator also paid tribute to John's wife and "soul-mate," Carolyn, whom he affectionately referred to as "the new pride of the Kennedys."

16 And for a thousand days, he was a husband who adored the wife who became his perfect soul-mate. John's father taught us all to reach for the moon and the stars. John did that in all he did—and he found his shining star when he married Carolyn Bessette.

17 How often our family will think of the two of them, cuddling affectionately on a boat—surrounded by family—aunts—uncles—Caroline and Ed and their children, Rose, Tatiana, and Jack—Kennedy cousins—Radizwill cousins—Shriver cousins—Smith cousins—Lawford cousins—as we sailed Nantucket Sound.

18 Then we would come home—and before dinner, on the lawn where his father had played, John would lead a spirited game of touch football—and his beautiful young wife, the new pride of the Kennedys, would cheer for John's team and delight her nieces and nephews with her somersaults.

19 In further tribute to the Bessette and Freeman families, Kennedy acknowledges Lauren, Carolyn's sister, who also died in the plane crash.

19 We loved Carolyn. She and her sister Lauren were young extraordinary women of high accomplishment—and their own limitless possibilities. We mourn their loss and honor their lives. The Bessette and Freeman families will always be part of ours.

20 John was a serious man who brightened our lives with his smile and his grace. He was a son of privilege who founded a program called "Reaching Up," to train better care-givers for the mentally disabled. He joined Wall Street executives on the Robin Hood Foundation to help the city's impoverished children. And he did it all so quietly, without ever calling attention to himself.

21 John was one of Jackie's two miracles. He was still becoming the person he would be, and doing it by the beat of his own drummer. He had only just begun. There was in him a great promise of things to come.

22 The Irish Ambassador recited a poem to John's father and mother soon after John was born. I can hear it again now, at this different and difficult moment:

> We wish to the new child
> A heart that can be beguiled
> By a flower
> That the wind lifts
> As it passes.
> If the storms break for him
> May the trees shake for him
> Their blossoms down.
>
> In the night that he is troubled,
> May a friend wake for him,
> So that his time be doubled,
> And at the end of all loving and love,
> May the Man above
> Give him a crown.

23 We thank the millions who have rained blossoms down on John's memory. He and his bride have gone to be with his mother and father, where there will never be an end to love. He was lost on that troubled night—but we will always wake for him, so that his time, which was not doubled, but cut in half, will live forever in our memory, and in our beguiled and broken hearts.

24 We dared to think, in that other Irish phrase, that this John Kennedy would live to comb grey hair, with his beloved Carolyn by his side. But like his father, he had every gift but length of years.

bids John and
Carolyn a loving
farewell.

25 We who have loved him from the day he was born, and watched
the remarkable man he became, now bid him farewell. God bless
you, John and Carolyn. We love you, and we always will.

INTRODUCTION TO REMARKS
BY ELIZABETH LASER

Before contracting the AIDS virus, Elizabeth Glaser enjoyed a comfortable
lifestyle in California. She was married to an actor, the mother of a daughter and son, and described herself as a "well-to-do white woman." But
when her daughter was born in 1981, she received blood transfusions as a
result of complications during labor. Instead of being her lifeline, these
contaminated transfusions infected Ms. Glaser, who then transmitted HIV
to her infant daughter, and later, to her newborn son. The virus eventually
took her daughter's life and changed Elizabeth Glaser profoundly. She
became an advocate for pediatric AIDS research and traveled across the
country, raising thirty million dollars for the Pediatric Aids Foundation, an
organization she founded. Because of her efforts, millions of dollars are
now allocated for pediatric AIDS research and changes in treatment programs have dramatically reduced the transmission of the virus from pregnant women to infant children.[3] Ms. Glaser presented this speech at the
Democratic National Convention in Madison Square Garden, July 14, 1992.
She refers to her family's struggle with AIDS, criticizes the Bush administration, and delivers an emotional appeal for listeners to consider HIV as
"everyone's problem." On December 4, 1994, almost two-and-a-half years
after the speech, Elizabeth Glaser died at the age of 48.[4]

Speech to the 1992
Democratic National Convention

Persuasive Speech

ELIZABETH GLASER

1 I'm Elizabeth Glaser.

2 Ms. Glaser be-
gins with brief
references to her
personal tragedy.

2 Eleven years ago, while giving birth to my first child, I hem-
orrhaged and was transfused with seven pints of blood. Four
years later, I found out that I had been infected with the
AIDS virus and had unknowingly passed it to my daughter,
Ariel, through my breast milk and my son Jake, in utero.

3 Twenty years ago I wanted to be at the Democratic Convention because it was a way to participate in my country.

4 Today I am here because it's a matter of life and death.

4 The speaker states a clear purpose.

5 The speaker appeals to each American regardless of party or political philosophy.

5 Exactly four years ago, my daughter died of AIDS—she did not survive the Reagan administration. I am here because my son and I may not survive four more years of leaders who say they care, but do nothing. I am in a race with the clock. This is *not* about being a Republican or an independent or a Democrat—it's about the future—for each and every one of us.

6 Elizabeth Glaser refers to herself as "a strange spokesperson" for those with HIV who are fighting for their lives.

6 I started out just a mom—fighting for the life of her child. But along the way I learned how unfair America can be today. Not just for people who have HIV, but for many, many people—poor people, gay people, people of color, children. A strange spokesperson for such a group—a well-to-do white woman—but I have learned my lesson the *hard way*—and I *know* that America has lost her path—and is at *risk* of losing her soul. America wake up—we are all in a struggle between life and death.

7 The speaker uses portions of her speech to connect to the viewpoints of her Democratic audience and attack the Reagan-Bush administrations.

7 I understand the sense of frustration and despair in our country, because I know firsthand about shouting for help and getting no answer. I went to Washington to tell Presidents Reagan and Bush that much, much more had to be done for AIDS research and care and that children couldn't be forgotten. The first time when nothing happened I thought, they just didn't hear me. The second time when nothing happened I thought, maybe I didn't shout loud enough. But, now I realize they don't hear because they don't *want* to listen. When you cry for help and no one listens you start to lose your hope.

8-9 The speaker uses strong emotion to express her disappointment in America—that "most people" think HIV is "not my problem."

8 I began to lose faith in America. I felt my country was letting me down—and it was.

9 This is not the America *I* was raised to be proud of. I was raised to believe that others' problems were my problems as well. But when I tell most people about HIV, in hopes that they will help and care, I see the look in their eyes—it's *not my* problem they're thinking—well, it's *everyone's problem* and we need a leader who will tell us that.

10 The speaker describes the example of young Ryan

10 We need a visionary to guide us—to say it *wasn't* all right for Ryan White to be banned from school because he had AIDS, to say it wasn't all right for a man or a woman to be denied a

White who was not allowed to attend public school because of prejudice and ignorance toward his disease.

11-15 Glaser uses repetition of the lines, "I *believe* in America," for emphasis and dramatic effect.

11 Glaser presents a shocking statistic to illustrate the cost of her own health care. She contrasts her situation with someone without insurance who must have the same care but cannot afford the cost.

12-16 The speaker criticizes the Bush administration and calls for new leadership.

job because they are infected with this virus. We need a leader who is truly committed to educating us.

11 I *believe* in America, but *not* with a leadership of selfishness and greed where the wealthy get health care and insurance and the poor don't. Do you know how much my AIDS care costs? Over forty thousand dollars a year. Someone without insurance can't afford this. Even the drugs that I hope will keep me alive are out of reach for others. Is their life any less valuable—of course not. This is not the America I was raised to be proud of—where the rich people get care and drugs that poor people can't. We need health care for all. We need a leader who will say this, and do something about it.

12 I *believe* in America, but *not* a leadership that talks about problems and is incapable of solving them. Two HIV commission reports with recommendations about what to do to solve this crisis sitting on shelves, gathering dust. We need a leader who will not only listen to these recommendations, but implement them.

13 I *believe* in America, but *not* with a leadership that doesn't hold government accountable. I go to Washington to the National Institutes of Health and say "Show me what you're doing on HIV." They hate it when I come because I try to tell them how to do it better. But that's why I *love* being a taxpayer because it's *my* money and they *must* feel accountable.

14 I *believe* in an America where our leaders talk straight. When anyone tells President Bush that the battle against AIDS is seriously underfunded, he juggles the numbers to mislead the public into thinking we're spending twice as much as we really are. While they play games with numbers, people are dying.

15 I *believe* in America, but an America where there is a light *in every* home—a thousand points of light just wasn't enough—my house has been dark for too long.

16 Once every generation, history brings us to an important crossroads. Some times in a life there *is* that moment when it's possible to make a change for the better. *This* is one of those moments.

17-18 Glaser criticizes both the President and Congress for gridlock, creating a "crisis of caring."

17 For me, this is not politics. This is a crisis of caring.

18 In this hall is the future: women, men of all colors saying take America back. We are just real people wanting a more hopeful life. But, words and ideas are not enough. Good thoughts won't save my family. What's the point of caring if we don't do something about it. A President *and* a Congress that can work together so we can get out of this gridlock and move ahead. Because I don't win my war if the President cares and the Congress doesn't—or if the Congress cares and the President doesn't support the ideas.

19 The people in this hall—this week, the Democratic Party—all of us can begin to deliver that partnership, and in November *we can all* bring it home.

20-22 In her conclusion, the speaker returns to the personal example that she introduced at the beginning and describes her daughter's last year of life with the AIDS virus. She compares the simple love of a mother and daughter to America's potential to "do the same."

20 My daughter lived seven years, and in her last year, when she couldn't walk or talk, her wisdom shone through. She taught me to love when all I wanted to do was hate. She taught me to help others, when all I wanted to do was help myself. She taught me to be brave, when all I felt was fear.

21 My daughter and I loved each other with simplicity. America, we can do the same.

22 This was the country that offered hope. This was the place where dreams could come true. Not just economic dreams, but dreams of freedom, justice and equality. We *all* need to hope that our dreams can come true. I challenge you to make it happen, because *all our lives*, not just mine, depend on it.

22 Glaser issues a strong emotional challenge in her conclusion to persuade listeners to "offer hope" for all.

23 Thank you.

INTRODUCTION TO COMMENCEMENT ADDRESS BY GARRY TRUDEAU

Satiric cartoonist Garry Trudeau (creator of the *Doonesbury* comic strip) delivered this commencement address at Wake Forest university on May 19, 1986. Its political content may be viewed by some as dated or debatable; some economic experts trace the Soviet Union's 1991 collapse in part to the USSR's failed attempt to compete with America's SDI program. However, this speech indicates that wit and satire can convey serious underlying themes, regardless of the era. Trudeau escapes the bounds of mundane graduation speeches by mixing humor with supporting materials to challenge his listeners to become, in his words, "self-aware," "open," and "seeing."[5]

"The Impertinent Questions"

Commencement (Special Occasion) Address

GARRY TRUDEAU

1 In his introduction, Trudeau relaxes the audience with humor.

1 Ladies and gentlemen of Wake Forest: My wife [TV personality Jane Pauley], who works in television, told me recently that a typical interview on her show used to run ten minutes. It now runs only five minutes, which is still triple the length of the average television news story. The average pop recording these days lasts around three minutes, or about the time it takes to ready a story in *People* magazine. The stories in *USA Today* take so little time to read that they're known in the business as "News McNuggets."

2 To make a serious as well as humorous point, the speaker calculates the number of days that then-President Ronald Reagan has reportedly spent reading newspaper comic strips.

2 Now, the average comic strip takes only about ten seconds to digest, but if you read every strip published in the *Washington Post,* as the President of the United States claims to, it takes roughly eight minutes a day, which means, a quick computation reveals, that the Leader of the Free World has spent a total of eleven days, three hours, and forty minutes of his presidency reading the comics. This fact, along with nuclear meltdown, are easily two of the most frightening thoughts of our time.

3 There's one exception to this relentless compression of time in modern life. That's right—the graduation speech. When it comes to graduation speeches, it is generally conceded that time—a generous dollop of time—is of the essence.

4-5 Trudeau pokes
fun at graduation
speeches, refer-
ring to them as
"anesthetics."

4 This is because the chief function of the graduation speaker
has always been to prevent graduating seniors from being released into the real world before they've been properly sedated.

5 Like an anesthetic, graduation speeches take time to kick in,
so I'm going to ask you to bear with me for about a quarter of
an hour. It will go faster if you think of it as the equivalent of four videos. (If you put up with Jimmy Carter for four
years, you can put up with me for fifteen minutes.)

6 The speaker
states his spe-
cific purpose
and thesis.

6 I want to speak to you today about questions. About pertinent
questions and impertinent questions. And where you might expect them to lead you.

7 I first learned about pertinent questions from my father, a
retired physician who used to practice medicine in the Adiron-
dacks. Like all parents racing against the clock to civilize
their children, my father sought to instruct me in the ways of
separating wheat from chaff, of asking sensible questions designed to yield useful answers. That is the way a diagnosti-
cian thinks. Fortunately for me, his own practical experience
frequently contradicted his worthiest intentions.

8 Trudeau relates
an anecdote
from personal
experience.

8 Here's a case in point: A man once turned up in my father's
office complaining of an ulcer. My father asked the pertinent
question: Was there some undue stress, he inquired, that might
be causing the man to digest his stomach? The patient, who was
married, thought about it for a moment and then allowed that
he had a girlfriend in Syracuse, and that twice a week he'd
been driving an old pickup down to see her. Since the pickup
frequently broke down, he was often late in getting home, and
he had to devise fabulous stories to tell his wife. My father,
compassionately but sternly, told the man he had to make a
hard decision about his personal priorities if he was ever to
get well.

9-10 The speaker
effectively sets
up and delivers
the punch line of
his story.

9 The patient nodded and went away, and six months later came
back completely cured, a new man. My father congratulated him
and then delicately inquired if he'd made some change in his
life.

10 The man replied, "Yup. Got me a new pickup."

11 So the pertinent question sometimes yields the impertinent answer. In spite of himself, my father ended up teaching me that
an unexpected or inconvenient truth is often the price of honest inquiry. Of course, you presumably wouldn't be here if you

didn't know that already. I'm confident that your education has been fairly studded with pertinent questions yielding impertinent answers.

12 The speaker employs a transitional question to relate the anecdote to his specific purpose.

12 But how many of you have learned to turn that around—to ask the impertinent question to get at that which is pertinent?

13-16 Trudeau presents an enumerative argument by listing a series of cases to support his generalization that "the impertinent question is the glory and the engine of human inquiry."

13 The impertinent question is the glory and the engine of human inquiry. Copernicus asked it and shook the foundations of Renaissance Europe. Darwin asked it and is repudiated to this day. Thomas Jefferson asked it and was so invigorated by it that he declared it an inalienable right.

14 Daniel Defoe asked it and invented the novel. James Joyce asked it and reinvented the novel, which was promptly banned.

15 Nietzsche asked it and inspired Picasso, who restated it and inspired a revolution in aesthetics.

16 The Wright brothers asked it, and their achievement was ignored for five years. Steven Jobs asked it and was ignored for five minutes, which was long enough for him to make $200 million.

17 The speaker also uses a quote to support his argument.

17 Whether revered or reviled in their lifetimes, history's movers framed their questions in ways that were entirely disrespectful of conventional wisdom. Civilization has always advanced in the shimmering wake of its discontents. As the writer Tristan Vox put it, "Doubt is precisely what makes a culture grow. How many of what we call our classics were conceived as the breaking of laws, exercises in subversion, as the expression of doubts about the self and society that could no longer be contained?"

18 The value of the impertinent question should be self-evident to Americans, for at no time in human history has it been asked more persistently and to greater effect than during the course of the American experiment. It is at the very core of our political and cultural character as a people, and we owe our vitality to its constant renewal.

19 In another argument of enumeration, the

19 Today, the need for that spirit of renewal has never seemed more pressing. There is a persistent feeling in the country that many of our institutions have not measured up, that with

speaker relates a
series of cases
to support his
claim that the
nation is "a long
way from fulfill-
ing [its] expec-
tations." While
he does not state
a source, the
speaker presents
the findings of
an opinion poll,
which reveals
many people's
lack of confi-
dence in American
institutions.

all our recourses and technology and good intentions, we as a nation are still a long way from fulfilling our own expectations. The social programs that have failed to eliminate poverty, an educational system which has seen its effectiveness seriously eroded, the chemical breakthroughs that now threaten man's environment, the exploding booster rockets, malfunctioning nuclear power plants—these are but some of the images that have shaken our confidence. According to a recent poll, the only American institution that still enjoys the trust of a majority of college students is medicine; only forty-four percent of those polled trust educational institutions, twenty-nine percent trust the White House, twenty-three percent trust the press, and only twenty-one percent say they trust religion.

20 It's difficult to think of an institution in this country that has not had to re-examine its agenda, to ask impertinent questions about its purpose and the means of its missions. Society's leaders, whose number you join today, face a wall of public cynicism. As professionals, they have to speak more clearly about what they can do. As citizens, they have to speak clearly about what they should do.

21 Here Trudeau
introduces an ar-
gument against
the SDI program.
He cites statis-
tics involving
scientists and
professors as
his support.

21 Nowhere is the need for accountability more urgent that in what is shaping up to be the largest coordinated undertaking of your generation—the Strategic Defense Initiative. It may well become the most fiercely contested issue of your times. Already 6,500 college [-affiliated] scientists, including a majority of professors in 109 university physics and engineering departments, have declared their opposition to SDI, and have signed a "pledge of non-participation" in a project they have called "ill-conceived and dangerous." This group, including fifteen Nobel Prize winners, maintains that the weapons system is inherently destabilizing, and that further pursuit of its development is likely to initiate a massive new arms competition.

22 The actions of these scientists constitute an extraordinary repudiation of the amorality of indiscriminate weapons research. Science, since it leads to knowledge, has all too frequently led it practitioners to believe that it is inherently self-justifying; that there is nothing dangerous about splitting atoms in a moral vacuum. These attitudes are held in abundance by some of the brightest people of your generation, who are already hard at work on what nearly all of them concede is a dangerous fantasy.

23 Listen to these comments from the young Star Warriors, still in their twenties, working on particle beams and brain bombs at Lawrence Livermore National Laboratory.

24 The speaker uses testimony from young scientists working on SDI to support his contention that SDI is a "dangerous fantasy."

24 This from the inventor of the atomic-powered x-ray laser: "Until 1980 or so, I didn't want to have anything to do with nuclear anything. Back in those days I thought there was something fundamentally evil about weapons. Now I see it as an interesting physics problem."

25 His coworker, another brilliant young physicist, says he has doubts about the wisdom of SDI, but concurs that "the science is very interesting."

26 A third member of the team had this to say: "I think that the great majority of the lab's technical people view the President's [SDI] speech as somewhat off the wall and the program being proposed as being, in the end, intrinsically rather foolish. But, obviously, the lab is benefiting right now and will continue to benefit, and everybody's happy with the marvelous new work."

27 Trudeau cynically cites the conclusion to his argument.

27 Marvelous new work, indeed.

28 Does the speaker draw a hasty generalization?

28 No one in the defense industry seriously believes in a "peace shield"; in fact they're betting against it. If an American SDI is big business, then the hardware needed to overcome the anticipated Soviet response is even bigger business. The industry is further encouraged by the mindless momentum of the program, as evidenced by the recent admission of Reagan's undersecretary of defense that he pulled the $26 billion price tag out of the air.

29 The speaker uses a quote from an unnamed Pentagon official as evidence of what he considers "the mindless momentum of the program."

29 Said the official, "I tried to figure out what the hell we're talking about. Congress wanted a number and kept on insisting on having a number. Okay. [The] first year was $2.4 billion, and I figure, okay, [the] best we could handle is maybe a twenty percent—twenty-five percent—growth."

30 Another quote, from a former SDI advisory panel

30 It should not surprise us that so many in the scientific establishment find this obscene. Said computer scientists David Parnas, who recently quit an SDI advisory panel, "Most of the

member, is used to support the speaker's view that money spent on SDI is "obscene."

money spent will be wasted; we wouldn't trust the system even if we did build it. It is our duty . . . to reply that we have no technological magic [that will make nuclear weapons obsolete]. The president and the public should know that."

31 The impertinent question. We need it now more than ever.

32 And yet, sadly, healthy skepticism is at odds with the prevailing sentiment of our times. As Tristan Vox sees it, "Arguments abound to the effect that a nation does not grow great by doubting itself; indeed, that self-criticism was the trap that American democracy had laid for American greatness."

33 Trudeau compares his view of the 1980s to that of the 1950s.

33 We've been here before. It was called the [nineteen-] fifties. This supposedly conservative doctrine holds that the very qualities from which this country has traditionally drawn its strength—idealism, openness, freedom of expression—are naive and dangerous in a Cold War struggle. It maintains that American's raucous squabbles, our noisy dissent—in short, its very heritage—have weakened us as a nation and caused it to lose its unchallenged supremacy.

34 As the *New Republic* [magazine's] Mike Kinsley put it: "Talk about blaming America first."

35 Trudeau presents yet another list of examples to support his claim that many who asked "impertinent questions" were either ignored or psychologically threatened.

35 In such an atmosphere, the impertinent question comes with risks. Ask the two engineers at Morton Thiokol who protested the launch of the doomed *Challenger* space shuttle. Ask any Pentagon procurement whistle-blower. Ask David Stockman. The mere fact of the president's widespread popularity casts suspicion on the motives of even the loyalest of oppositions. There is, of course, no question that this president seems to have fulfilled a deep yearning in many Americans to feel positively about their country. And yet the Reagan presidency often reminds me of a remark made by a woman to sportscaster Heywood Broun following the victories of the great racehorse Secretariat in the Triple Crown. After the trauma of Vietnam and Watergate, she told Broun, Secretariat had "restored her faith in mankind."

36 Trudeau uses an anecdote to make a derisive analogy involving President Ronald Reagan.

36 I would submit to you that Ronald Reagan is the Secretariat of the eighties. He has restored our faith in ourselves, and for that, we are all in his debt. It does not, however, exempt his administration from criticism from concerned citizens who love their nation as much as he does. One of the things that has always distinguished this country from most others is that we've always challenged ourselves to do better. As a satirist,

I can't foresee any administration, Republican or Democratic, under which the basic message wouldn't be the same—that it's possible to do better.

37 Trudeau refers disparagingly to the 1984 Summer Olympic Games, held in Los Angeles; the metaphor of the "Caribbean golf course" refers to the island of Grenada, where, in October 1983, U.S. armed forces met, defeated, and ousted Cuban troops in combat following a Marxist coup there.

37 This is the true glory of America. This hope is what stirs me as a patriot—not a winning medal count at the Olympics, not the ability to drop nine thousand servicemen on a Caribbean golf course, not jingoistic commercials that tell me that "the pride is back, America," when for many of us the pride never left—and certainly not by the fantasy of a thousand laser rays crisscrossing the heavens in software-orchestrated precision, obliterating a swarm of supersonic projectiles.

38 The speaker again uses humor to lighten his return to the topic of SDI.

38 Skeptical? You bet. You're looking at a man who has attended sixteen graduations, at four of which, including one technical college, the microphone failed.

39 The speaker uses a quotation to relate his specific purpose to each listener. Trudeau is saying, "Examine your own thought processes; ask yourself impertinent questions."

39 The impertinent question. The means by which we reaffirm our noblest impulses as a people. But what about the impertinent question as it pertains to us as individuals? [The physicist Jacob] Bronowski had an addendum to his comments on the subject. "Ask the same kind of question," he charged [interviewer] Studs Terkel, "not about the outside, but the inside world; not about facts, but about the self."

40 Trudeau cites (without source) a figure pointing to political corruption as "the new prevailing ethic."

40 This is impertinence of the gravest sort. The inner life finds very little currency in this, the age of hustle. David Stockman has written of a leadership circle, which is intellectually inert, obsessed by television, bored by introspection and ideas of substance. Meanwhile, all across town, the sad stories of sleaze abound, one hundred and ten to date, all pointing to the new prevailing ethic of corner-cutting and

self-advancement, whose only caveat is the admonition not to get caught.

<table>
<tr>
<td>

41 Trudeau describes the need to think critically and "to see and feel . . . the connectedness among things."

</td>
<td>

41 It can seem a pretty grim picture. Indeed, as you look around you, you see very little to distract you from this narrow path. And yet that is exactly what your liberal education—with its emphasis on ideas, on inquiry, on humanist values—sought to do. As the president of my *alma mater* [Yale University] once observed, "The whole point of your education has been to urge you to see and feel about the connectedness among things and how that connectedness must be fostered so that civilization is sustained."

</td>
</tr>
<tr>
<td>

42 Trudeau presents himself as taking a strong position and as unafraid of being negatively received.

</td>
<td>

42 This won't please you, but let me share a little of what one of the more astute voices of your generation, twenty-four-year-old David Leavitt, has written about his peers: "Mine is a generation perfectly willing to admit its contemptible qualities. But our contempt is self-congratulatory. The buzz in the background, every minute of our lives, is that detached, ironic voice telling use: *At least you're not faking it, as they did. It's okay to be selfish as long as you're up-front about it.*"

</td>
</tr>
<tr>
<td>

43 He then softens his stance by complimenting his listeners as including "hundreds of exceptions."

</td>
<td>

43 This is a pretty bleak portrait of the values of a generation, and my guess is that I'm staring at hundreds of exceptions. My further guess is that the yearning for moral commitment is as intense as it always was, but that the generation with no rules—the generation that grew up in the rubble of smashed idealism, fallen heroes, and broken marriages—is deeply suspicious.

</td>
</tr>
<tr>
<td>

44 Trudeau paraphrases fellow media personality Ellen Goodman, a newspaper columnist.

</td>
<td>

44 Columnist Ellen Goodman has speculated that this is why apartheid and the soup kitchen have emerged as the causes of choice; they offer that stark unambiguous clarity that World War II offered their grandparents, that sense that there is no good news about the other side of the argument. But Goodman, being incorrigibly of her era, also believes that micro evolves into macro; that to be involved inevitably leads to decisions between imperfect options; that many of you will take risks, make mistakes, and become citizens in spite of yourselves.

</td>
</tr>
<tr>
<td>

45 In his conclusion the speaker asks listeners to apply his speech

</td>
<td>

45 I'm afraid there's simply no other way. If ours becomes a society intolerant of failure and uncompassionate in the face of suffering, then surely we are lost. With the uncertainties of the future hedging in on you, you need to assess your

</td>
</tr>
</table>

to themselves, loosely para- phrasing the Golden Rule.

commonalities. You need to say how you would treat other peo- ple, and how you would have them treat you back.

46 Trudeau returns to his stated theme, and chal- lenges listeners to become "self- aware" rather than "self- absorbed."

46 The best your college can do for you is to remind you that it's one thing to be self-absorbed, and quite another to be self-aware. It comes down to a matter of being open, of see- ing. It comes down to a matter of remaining intrigued enough by life to welcome its constant renewal. In short, it comes down to the impertinent question.

47-48 Presenting himself as a rep- resentative of the "real world," Trudeau offers warm words of encouragement and "welcome."

47 From those of us out here in the real world, to those of you preparing to enter it, may I just say, Welcome. We need you.

48 Thank you and good luck.

INTRODUCTION TO PERSUASIVE SPEECH BY JESSE JACKSON

The following is an abridged version of the speech Jesse Jackson delivered to the Democratic National Convention in Atlanta, Georgia, on July 20, 1988. At the time, the Reverend Mr. Jackson had just concluded his second bid for the Democratic nomination for the presidency. While the speech contains traditional appeals for party unity, it is organized—and was deliv- ered—in Jackson's own inimitable style.[6]

"Common Ground and Common Sense"

Persuasive Speech

JESSE JACKSON

1-2 In his intro- duction, Jackson acknowledges

1 Tonight we pause and give praise and honor to God for being good enough to allow us to be at this place at this time. When I look out at this convention, I see the face of America—red,

spiritual support, and refers (paraphrasing a hymn) to the ethnic diversity that his campaign termed "The Rainbow Coalition."

He also pays tribute to individuals who advanced the cause of civil rights, and to members of his own family who supported his political aspirations.

yellow, brown, black, and white—we're all precious in God's sight—the real Rainbow Coalition. All of us, all of us who are here and think that we are seated. But we're really standing on someone's shoulders, ladies and gentlemen. Mrs. Rosa Parks, the mother of the civil rights movement.

2 I want to express my deep love and appreciation for the support my family has given me over these past months. They have endured pain, anxiety, threat, and fear. But they have been strengthened and made secure by a faith in God, in America, and in you.

3 Jackson briefly introduces his topic in a statement of contrast.

3 We meet tonight at a crossroads, a point of decision. Shall we expand, be inclusive, find unity and power; or suffer division and impotence?

4 The speaker refers to the location of his speech and provides brief examples signifying historic change.

4 We come to Atlanta, the cradle of the Old South, the crucible of the New South. Tonight there is a sense of celebration because we are moved, fundamentally moved, from racial battle-grounds by law, to economic common ground; tomorrow we will challenge to move to higher ground.

5 Common ground! Tonight in Atlanta, for the first time in this century, we convene in the South. A state where governors once stood in schoolhouse doors. Where Julian Bond was denied his seat in the state legislature because of his conscientious objection to the Vietnam War. A city that, through its five black universities, had graduated more black students than any city in the world. Atlanta, now a modern intersection of the New South. Common ground!

6 Jackson presents the specific purpose of his speech.

6 Tonight we choose interdependency in our capacity to act and unite for the greater good. The common good is finding commitment to new priorities, to expansion and inclusion. A commitment to expanded participation in the Democratic party at every level. A commitment to a shared national strategy and involvement at every level. A commitment to new priorities that ensure that hope will be kept alive.

<table>
<tr>
<td>

7 Throughout his speech, Jackson repeats the words "common ground" for emphasis and for transitional purposes.

</td>
<td>

7 Common ground. Easier said than done. Where do you find common ground at the point of challenge? This campaign has shown that politics need not be marketed by politicians, packaged by pollsters and pundits. Politics can be a marvelous arena where people come together, define common ground.

</td>
</tr>
</table>

8 Jackson speaks metaphorically of the "plant gate," "farm auction," "schoolyard," and "hospital admitting room" as brief examples of social issues.

8 We find common ground at the plant gate that closes on workers without notice. We find common ground at the farm auction where a good farmer loses his or her land to bad loans or diminishing markets. Common ground at the schoolyard where teachers cannot get adequate pay, and students cannot get a scholarship and can't make a loan. Common ground, at the hospital admitting room where somebody is dying tonight because they cannot afford to go upstairs to a bed that's empty, waiting for someone with insurance to get sick. We are a better nation than that. We must do better.

9 This series of brief examples is supported by personal observation, enhancing the speaker's credibility.

9 Common ground. What is leadership if not present help in a time of crisis? And so I met you at the point of challenge in Jay, Maine, where paper workers were striking for fair wages; in Greenfield, Iowa, where family farmers struggle for a fair price; in Cleveland, Ohio, where working women seek comparable worth; in McFarland, California, where the children of Hispanic farm workers may be dying from poison land, dying in clusters with cancer; in the AIDS hospice in Houston, Texas, where the sick support one another. Twelve are rejected by their own parents and friends.

10 The speaker begins an analogy by referring to personal experience.

10 Common ground. America's not a blanket woven from one thread, one color, one cloth. When I was a child growing up in Greenville, South Carolina, and grandmother could not afford a blanket, she didn't complain, and we did not freeze. Instead, she took pieces of old cloth—patches, wool, silk, gabardine, croakersack on the patches—barely good enough to wipe off your shoes with.

11 But they didn't stay that way very long. With sturdy hands and a strong cord, she sewed them together into a quilt, a thing of beauty and power and culture.

12-13 In the analogy, Jackson relates his grandmother's quilt to the

12 Now, Democrats, we must build such a quilt. Farmers, you seek fair prices and you are right, but you cannot stand alone. Your patch is not big enough. Workers, you fight for fair wages. You are right. But your patch is not big enough. Women, you seek comparable worth and pay equity. You are right. But

various "patches" of economic and social groups in the country.

your patch is not big enough. Women, mothers, who seek Head Start and day care and prenatal care on the front side of life, rather than jail care and welfare on the back side of life, you're right, but your patch is not big enough.

13 Students, you seek scholarships. You are right. But your patch is not big enough. Blacks and Hispanics, when we fight for civil rights, we are right, but our patch is not big enough. Gays and lesbians, when you fight against discrimination and [for] a cure for AIDS, you are right, but your patch is not big enough. Conservatives and progressives, when you fight for what you believe—right-wing, left-wing, hawk, dove—you are right, from your point of view, but your point of view is not enough.

14 The speaker draws the conclusion that the different social and economic "patches" will bring "hope to our nation" if joined by the "common thread" of "unity and common ground."

14 But don't despair. Be as wise as my grandmama. Pool the patches and pieces together, bound by a common thread. When we form a great quilt of unity and common ground, we'll have the power to bring about health care and housing and jobs and education and hope to our nation.

15 The speaker uses statistics and examples to bolster his view that America's economic priorities should be changed.

15 I just want to take common sense to high places. We're spending $150 billion a year defending Europe and Japan forty-three years after the war [World War II] is over. We have more troops in Europe tonight than we had seven years ago, yet the threat of war is ever more remote. Germany and Japan are now creditor nations—that means they've got a surplus. We are a debtor nation—it means we are in debt.

16 The speaker uses repetition of a phrase to introduce different examples.

16 Let them share more of the burden of their own defense—use some of that money to build decent housing! Use some of the money to educate our children! Use some of that money for long-term health care! Use some of that money to wipe out these slums and put America back to work!

17 Jackson compares the investment required to "bail out" Europe

17 I just want to take common sense to high places. If we can bail out Europe and Japan, if we can bail out Continental Bank and Chrysler—and Mr. [Lee] Iacocca [of Chrysler Motors] makes $8,000 an hour—we can bail out the family farmer.

and the Chrysler Corporation with one he believes Is needed to support American farmers.

18 I just want to make common sense. It does not make sense to close down 650,000 family farms in this country while importing food from abroad subsidized by the U.S. government.

19 Leadership must meet the moral challenge of its day. What's the moral challenge of our day? We have public accommodations. We have the right to vote. We have open housing.

20 What's the fundamental challenge of our day? It is to end economic violence. Plants closing without notice, economic violence. Even the greedy do not profit long from greed. Economic violence. Most poor people are not lazy. They're not black. They're not brown. They're mostly white, and female, and young.

21 The speaker describes the plight of the poor in extended, emotional statements.

21 But whether white, black, or brown, the hungry baby's belly turned inside out is the same color. Call it pain. Call it hurt. Call it agony. Most poor people are not on welfare.

22 Some of them are illiterate and can't read the want-ad sections. And when they can, they can't find a job that matches their address. They work hard every day, I know. I live amongst them. I'm one of them.

23 Jackson refers to his own eyewitness observations to establish his credibility.

23 I know they work. I'm a witness. They catch the early bus. They work every day. They raise other people's children. They work every day. They clean the streets. They work every day. They drive vans with cabs [sic]. They work every day. They change the beds you slept in, in these hotels last night, and can't get a union contract. They work every day.

24 Here the speaker uses an ironic example—those who care for the sick but are themselves not "cared for."

24 No more. They're not lazy. Someone must defend them because it's right, and they cannot speak for themselves. They work in hospitals. I know they do. They wipe the bodies of those who are sick with fever and pain. They empty their bedpans. They clean out their commodes. No job is beneath them, and yet when they get sick, they cannot lie in the bed they made up every day. America, that is not right. We are a better nation than that. We are a better nation than that.

25 The speaker repeats one word for emphasis and as an introduction to the next section.

25 Leadership. What difference will we make? Leadership cannot just go along to get along. We must do more than change presidents. We must change direction. Leadership must face the moral challenge of our day. The nuclear war build-up is irrational. Strong leadership cannot desire to look tough and let that stand in the way of the pursuit of peace. Leadership must reverse the arms race.

26 Leadership—we now have this marvelous opportunity to have a breakthrough with the Soviets. Last year, two hundred thousand Americans visited the Soviet Union. There's a chance for joint ventures into space, not Star Wars and the war-arms escalation, but a space defense initiative. Let's build in space together, and demilitarize the heavens. There's a way out.

27 The speaker uses statistics to support his view that seven-eighths are not represented by what were then the two superpowers.

27 American, let us expand. When Mr. Reagan and Mr. Gorbachev met, there was a big meeting. They represented together one-eighth of the human race. Seven-eighths of the human race was locked out of that room. Most people in the world tonight—half are Asian, one-half of *them* are Chinese. There are twenty-two nations in the Middle East. There's Europe, forty million Latin Americans next door to us, the Caribbean, Africa's half-billion people. Most people in the world today are yellow or brown or black, non-Christian, poor, female, young, and don't speak English—in the real world.

28-29 Jackson uses a poem to express his feelings.

28 I'm often asked, "Jesse, why do you take on these tough issues?." . . A poem by an unknown author went something like this: *We mastered the air, we've conquered the sea, and annihilated distance and prolonged life, we were not wise enough to live on this earth without war and without hate.*

29 As for Jesse Jackson:

> "I'm tired of sailing my little boat
> Far inside the harbor bar.
> I want to go out where the big ships float,
> Out on the deep where the great ones are.
> And should my frail craft prove too slight
> The waves seep those billows o'er,
> I'd rather go down in a stirring fight
> Than drown to death in the sheltered shore."

30 The speaker issues an emotional challenge to motivate listeners to "dream" and "hope" to "rise above the pain." Jackson then paraphrases a line—written by playwright George Bernard Shaw—that

30 Wherever you are tonight, I challenge you to hope and to dream. Don't submerge your dreams. Exercise above all else [sic]—Even on drugs, dream of the day you're drug-free. Even in the gutter, dream of the day that you'll be up on your feet again. You must never stop dreaming. Face reality, yes. But don't stop with the way things are; dream of things as they ought to be. Dream. Face pain, but love, hope, faith, and dreams will help you rise above the pain.

was often quoted by Senator Robert Kennedy ("You see things and you say, 'Why?' But I dream of things that never were; and I say, 'Why not?'").

31 Jackson continues his emotional challenge with several figures of speech: repetition, rhyme, and alliteration.

31 Dream of teachers who teach for life and not for [a] living. Dream of doctors who are concerned more about public health than private wealth. Dream of lawyers more concerned above justice than a judgeship. Dream of preachers who are concerned more about prophecy than profiteering. Dream on the high road of sound values.

32 And in America, as we go forth to September, October, and November, and then beyond, America must never surrender to a high moral challenge.

33 Do not surrender to drugs. The best drug policy is no first use. Don't surrender with needles and cynicism. Let's have no first use on the one hand, or clinics on the other. Never surrender, young America.

34 Don't surrender and don't give up. Why can I challenge you this way?

35 The speaker concludes with a narrative drawn from his own experience.

35 I have a story. I wasn't always on television. Writers were not always outside my door. When I was born late one morning, October eighth, in Greenville, South Carolina, no writers asked my mother her name. Nobody chose to write down our address. My mama was not supposed to make it. You see, I was born to a teen-age mother who was born to a teen-age mother.

36 I understand. I know abandonment and people being mean to you, and saying you're nothing and nobody, and can never be anything. Jesse Jackson is my third name. I'm adopted. When I had no name, my grandmother gave me her name. My name was Jesse Burns until I was twelve. So I wouldn't have a blank space, she gave me a name to hold me over. I understand when nobody knows your name. I understand when you have no name. I understand.

37 I wasn't born in the hospital. Mama didn't have insurance. I was born in the bed at home. I really do understand. Born in a three-room house, bathroom in the backyard, slop jar by the

bed, no hot and cold running water. I understand. Wallpaper used for decoration? No, for a windbreaker. I understand. I'm a working person's person; that's why I understand you whether you're black or white.

38 I was born in the slum, but the slum was not born in me. And it wasn't born in you, and you can make it. Wherever you are tonight, you can make it. Hold your head high, stick your chest out. You can make it. It gets dark sometimes, but the morning comes. Don't you surrender. Suffering breeds character. Character breeds faith. In the end, faith will not disappoint.

39-40 This final emotional challenge reveals Jackson's energy, enthusiasm, and warm, charismatic style.

39 You must not surrender. You may or may not get there, but just know that you're qualified and you hold on and hold out. We must never surrender. America will get better and better. Keep hope alive. Keep hope alive. Keep hope alive. On tomorrow night and beyond, keep hope alive.

40 I love you very much. I love you very much.

INTRODUCTION TO PERSUASIVE SPEECH BY CHRISTOPHER REEVE

Since the age of fifteen, Christopher Reeve pursued a career in the performing arts. He first appeared at Massachusetts' Williamstown Theater Festival, graduated from Cornell University, studied with John Houseman, and acted with many seasoned professionals such as Katherine Hepburn, William Hurt, and Vanessa Redgrave. The public came to know Reeve through the four *Superman* movies that gave him international stardom and established him as a leading actor in romantic comedy. In addition to his professional career, Reeve was an active pilot, yachtsman, tennis player, ice skater, and horseman. On May 27, 1995, Reeve was thrown from a horse during an equestrian competition in Culpeper County, Virginia, and suffered multiple fractures of the spinal column close to the skull, leaving him paralyzed and unable to breath without a respirator. After months of rehabilitation, support from family and friends, and sympathy from concerned fans, Christopher Reeve assumed a new role as a spokesman for those suffering with spinal cord injuries. He helped to establish the Reeve-Irvine Research Center, which is charged with finding a cure for paralysis and developing more advanced therapies for the treatment of paralysis. In the following speech to the Democratic National Convention in Chicago, August 16, 1996, Reeve calls for more research, increased awareness, and greater commitment from all Americans to provide hope for the suffering.[7]

"America Is Stronger When All of Us Take Care of All of Us"

Persuasive Speech

CHRISTOPHER REEVE

1 Over the last few years, we've heard a lot about something called family values. And like many of you I've struggled to figure out what that means but since my accident I've found a definition that seems to make sense. I think it means that we're all family, that we all have value. And if that's true, if America really is a family, then we have to recognize that many of our family are hurting.

2 Just take one aspect of it, one in five of us has some kind of disability. You may have an aunt with Parkinson's disease. A neighbor with a spinal cord injury. A brother with AIDS. And if we're really committed to this idea of family, we've got to do something about it.

3 First of all, our nation cannot tolerate discrimination of any kind. That's why the Americans with Disabilities Act is so important and must be honored everywhere. It is a civil rights law that is tearing down barriers both in architecture and in attitude. Its purpose is to give the disabled access not only to buildings, but to every opportunity in society. I strongly believe our nation must give its full support to the caregivers who are helping people with disabilities live independent lives. Sure, we've got to balance the budget. And we will. We have to be extremely careful with every dollar that we spend. But we've also got to take care of our family and not slash programs people need. We should be enabling, healing, curing. One of the smartest things we can do about disability is invest in research that will protect us from disease and lead to cures. This country already has a long history of doing just that.

4 When we put our minds to a problem, we can usually find solutions. But our scientists can do more. And we've got to give them the chance. That means more funding for research. Right now, for example, about a quarter-million Americans have a spinal cord injury. Our government spends about $8.7 billion a year just maintaining these members of our family. But we spend only $40 million a year on research that would actually improve the quality of their lives, get them off public assistance, or even cure them. We've got to be smarter, do better.

---

1 The speaker begins by providing his own definition of the term "family values."

2 Reeve focuses on the specific purpose of his speech.

3 The speaker refers to the law that he feels has helped to increase opportunities for the disabled.

4 Reeve presents statistics indicating the number of Americans with injuries similar to his own. He then compares the billions spent maintaining these

disabled citizens
with the small
amount spent
on research.

Because the money we invest in research today is going to determine the quality of life of members of our family tomorrow.

5 Reeve's brief
reference to his
own disability is
a powerful re-
minder of his
commitment to
this issue. He
introduces an
emotional example
of a disabled
friend to urge
listeners to
consider their
"moral" and
"economic
responsibility."

5 During my rehabilitation, I met a young man named Gregory Patterson. When he was innocently driving through Newark, New Jersey, a stray bullet from a gang shooting went through his car window, right into his neck and severed his spinal cord. Five years ago, he might have died. Today because of research he's alive. But merely alive is not enough. We have a moral and an economic responsibility to ease his suffering and prevent others from experiencing such pain. And to do that, we don't need to raise taxes. We just need to raise our expectations.

6 The speaker
uses several
brief instances
to appeal to au-
diences. He also
refers to the
personal example
of the auto-
graphed photo
from NASA astro-
nauts who in-
spired him with
the motto, "We
found nothing is
impossible." He
then challenges
individuals to
solve this prob-
lem "together."

6 America has a tradition many nations probably envy; we frequently achieve the impossible. That's part of our national character. That's what got us from one coast to another. That's what got us the largest economy in the world. That's what got us to the moon. On the wall of my room when I was in rehab was a picture of the space shuttle blasting off, autographed by every astronaut now at NASA. On top of the picture it says, "We found nothing is impossible." That should be our motto. Not a Democratic motto, not a Republican motto. But an American motto. Because this is not something one party can do alone. It's something that we as a nation must do together.

7 Reeve again
refers to na-
tional achieve-
ments and
determination
that have helped

7 So many of our dreams at first seem impossible, then they seem improbable, and then, when we summon the will, they soon become inevitable. If we can conquer outer space, we should be able to conquer inner space too. The frontier of the brain, the central nervous system, and all the afflictions of the body that destroy so many lives, and rob our country of so

America to attain "improbable" feats. He argues that America can also solve the problems of the "inner . . . frontier."

much potential. Research can provide hope for people who suffer from Alzheimer's. We've already discovered the gene that causes it.

8 The speaker presents a series of brief examples—famous Americans who have been afflicted with incurable diseases.

8 Research can provide hope for people like Muhammad Ali and the Reverend Billy Graham who suffer from Parkinson's. Research can provide hope for millions of Americans like Kirk Douglas, who suffer from stroke. We can ease the pain of people like Barbara Jordan, who battled multiple sclerosis. We can find treatments for people like Elizabeth Glaser, whom we lost to AIDS. Now that we know that nerves in the spinal cord can regenerate, we are on the way to getting millions of people around the world like me up, and out of our wheelchairs.

9 Reeve ends his persuasive remarks with a quotation from Franklin D. Roosevelt, the disabled president who was able to "lift a nation," and an emotional challenge for his listeners.

9 Fifty-six years ago, FDR dedicated new buildings for the National Institute of Health. He said, "the defense this nation seeks, involves a great deal more than building airplanes, ships, guns and bombs. We cannot be a strong nation unless we are a healthy nation." He could have said that today. President Roosevelt showed us that a man who could barely lift himself out of a wheelchair could still lift a nation out of despair. And I believe and so does this Administration in the most important principle FDR taught us: America does not let its needy citizens fend for themselves. America is stronger when all of us take care of all of us. Giving new life to that ideal is the challenge before us tonight. Thank you very much.

INTRODUCTION TO PERSUASIVE SPEECH BY KAREN ANDERSON

Convincing speeches can be organized by using reasons or by problem-solution sequences. Karen Anderson developed the following alternative version of the speech presented in chapter 17 to demonstrate how the body of that speech could instead be arranged according to the problem-cause-solution organizational structure. The following speech is introduced and concluded by strategies different from the speech reproduced in chapter 17. It is also followed here by alternate opening and closing sections.[8]

Let's Stop Auto Repair Rip-Offs!

Persuasive Speech to Convince
(Problem-Cause-Solution Organizational Sequence)

KAREN ANDERSON

1 In the introduction, the speaker uses a strategy that shocks listeners.

1 I'd like each of you to hand over $1,500 right now! Come on, $1,500. I'll take a check, credit card, cash, or money order. What's the problem? You don't have it? I don't care if it's your car insurance, house payment, or hospital bill. Let me put it to you this way. You are driving to work and your transmission feels, you know, "funny"—it slips out of gear. Fearing for your safety more than a reprimand from your supervisor for being late, you go directly to the nearest auto repair shop. Luckily, the technician on duty has time to look at your car and determine that a faulty transmission needs, in his opinion, to be overhauled or replaced, to the tune of $1,500. Or does $25 seem a little easier to manage? Because in many cases that "slipping out of gear" problem may have been solved by a relatively simple and cheap twenty-five dollar adjustment. Because of situations like the one I just described, we are at the mercy of automotive repair shops.

2 The thesis identifies the main points of the body and clearly presents the proposition of policy.

2 Unnecessary, incompetent repairs, caused by lack of control, should be corrected by strict regulations.

3 Karen cites a study and an example, supported by credible references, to begin her explanation of the problem. Notice that the speaker connects to listeners

3 Americans are being ripped off. As reported by Sal Fariello in his book *Mugged by Mr. Badwrench*, a study done by the United States Department of Transportation indicates that as much as forty percent of the money American consumers spend on auto repairs is wasted due to fraud and incompetence. Think it won't happen to you? An article in a June 1992 issue of *Business Week* reported, in what is now a much-publicized case, that Sears Auto Centers in California had "systematically ripped off customers." According to the article, Ruth Hernandez, of Stockton, went to Sears for new tires. The auto

by asking a question.

technician who serviced Ms. Hernandez's Honda "insisted" the car also needed new struts with a hefty additional cost of $419.95. Ms. Hernandez went for a second opinion, and was told the struts did not need replacing. Furthermore, according to the article, Sears consistently charged consumers an average of $235 for unnecessary repairs.

4 Karen uses the words "Now listen to this" to maintain audience interest and to set up this credible survey and quotation.

4 Now listen to this. In his book *From Bumper to Bumper,* Bob Sikorsky posed as an average driver and did a remarkable survey of the auto repair business across America. Mr. Sikorsky pulled into 225 repair shops with a simple problem: a loose spark-plug wire. He reported fair and competent repairs in only twenty-eight percent of the stops, a satisfactory repair only forty-four percent of the time, and, in Sikorsky's own words, "I was victimized by incompetence, cheated, sold unnecessary parts, overcharged, and lied to."

5 The speaker employs two visual aids to explain how listeners can be harmed by unscrupulous auto repair businesses.

5 Here are two ways that consumers pay for unnecessary repairs. You can unknowingly purchase so-called "gypsy parts"—that is, an inferior auto part, such as a common oil filter, which has been repackaged in a box with a well-known brand name and passed off to you as a quality product. Here is an example. *[Shows slide comparing two oil filters.]* One oil filter has less paper, which provides less filtering capability, clogging sooner. The other contains more paper, is of higher quality, and will last longer. Upon close examination, the difference is evident. Or what about the technician who deliberately sabotages your car for profit, and whose favorite weapon is an ice pick? *[Holds up ice pick.]* Now, although these instances are rare, they happen to out-of-state motorists who set themselves up as easy targets by leaving their cars with the attendants while they grab snacks or make necessary pit-stops. Returning to the car, the unsuspecting motorists are informed by attendants that a leaking tire must be patched, or better yet, replaced with a brand new tire.

6 The speaker cites an interview with a credible primary source to validate this strong emotional example. Language such as "despicable" and "held

6 I conducted a telephone interview with Tom Hopkins, a lead investigator for the Bureau of Automotive Repair in California, who related the following despicable crime. An elderly California couple took their motor home in for repairs. The disabled wife remained in the motor home while the vehicle was raised on the lift in the repair shop. Employees removed the suspension system, brakes, and wheels. The disabled woman was literally held hostage in the air until her husband paid the demanded fee to get the wheels and other equipment put back on their vehicle.

hostage" are designed to evoke powerful feelings in listeners.

7 The speaker continues to connect to listeners by indicating that these incidents "could happen to you."

8 Karen uses creative metaphors ("Let's shift gears") as a transition from the problem to the cause of auto repair rip-offs.

9 The speaker uses a creative visual aid to add interest and demonstrate one cause of the problem.

Karen makes a comparison to the medical profession and asks a question that connects to listeners.

11 She employs another automotive metaphor for her

---

7 These incidents represent a small minority, and I want to stress that the majority of the auto repair industry is caring and reputable, but these cases are real and they could happen to you.

8 The issue is apparent and many of you, I'm sure have experienced auto repair rip-offs. So let's shift gears, and talk about the causes.

9 One factor that contributes to incompetence is the lack of control. Let me demonstrate. *[Holds up sign reading, "Karen's Car Care Center—Unlimited Major and Minor Repair Service—Major Credit Cards Accepted."]* Pretty impressive, huh? Listen, I'll even adjust your brakes for half-price, and I'll throw in a complete diagnostic muffler analysis for free—but I don't do windows! Do you trust me? Anyone with a computer and a graphics program can make a sign like this (as I did), call themselves an auto technician, and open up a shop. Nothing stands in their way. Nancy Tian, the communications coordinator of the Automotive Service Excellence program, made it clear that there are no federally mandated regulations. Think of a person opening up a medical practice without prior education, internship, testing or experience. Would you let such a person perform intricate open-heart surgery on you or a loved one without first checking their credentials? There's an adage in the automotive profession: Doctors bury their mistakes, auto technicians just keep having theirs return.

10 Another cause of auto repair incompetence is our own ignorance. Admit it. We expect to be ripped off, we expect repairs to be expensive, yet we put up with it.

11 Now there are some routes we can take to solve this nationwide problem.

transition from causes to alternative solutions.

12 Throughout her discussion of alternative solutions, the speaker briefly identifies the possible solution, and then explains why it is unworkable.

12 I mentioned the National institute for Automotive Service Excellence, or ASE, which was established in 1972 to improve auto repair service by testing and certifying auto repair technicians. They develop exams in automotive specialties, such as transmission, brake and wheel, and emission repair. They offer tests twice a year. It is an excellent idea, and it is the only nationwide certification program. But there are several problems. One: A technician who is certified in one area, such as suspension and steering, may not be certified in another area, such as electrical systems. Two: Certification does not necessarily mean competence. And, three: This certification program is only voluntary—and again, there is no nationwide, mandatory licensing of the auto repair industry. Remember my business sign? The only thing I could not advertise was an earned certification. This program is a start, but voluntary certification doesn't go far enough.

13 I interviewed Richard Glenn, an associated professor of Automotive Service Technology at Catonsville Community College, near Baltimore, Maryland, who suggested industry-wide regulation as the solution. This would be similar to the medical profession's self-regulation through the AMA. Licensed technicians and experienced automotive-board specialists would take matters into their own hands by assessing fees and fines to enforce regulations. But according to Mr. Glenn, the majority of technicians prefer to go with the status quo, and it has been difficult to rally enough interest or enthusiasm from auto technicians to support self-regulation.

14 The automotive metaphor is used for the final transition from alternative choices to the speaker's selected solution.

14 But there is one route we can take to help us out of the auto repair roadblock.

15 Through documented examples, statistics, and a credible interview with an expert, the speaker has

15 California is one example of a governmental control program that not only benefits the consumer but the auto repair industry as well. Remember Ms. Hernandez from California who did not have confidence in what Sears was advising her to do? She had a place to file a complaint, and was assured that a remedy would be found. This is an excellent example

constructed a persuasive case for the effectiveness of her selected solution.

of mandated control through the California Bureau of Automotive Repair, or BAR. Kate McGuire, Public Information Officer for the BAR, provided me with information about this agency. As you can see from this slide, it was established in 1971 to prevent abuses in the auto repair industry. With a staff of six hundred, working in thirty-six field offices, the BAR operates on an annual budget of $70 million, which is funded by the smog check program and a $200 registration fee paid by auto repair businesses. It provides consumers with mediation centers that handle over forty thousand formal complaints a year. This agency also sends representatives to assist and support consumers at hearings in small claims court. The bureau also conducts undercover sting operations to snare dishonest technicians or detect fraudulent repair shops. And money—some $4.6 million alone—was returned to consumers from auto repair shops in 1991-92.

16 Here the speaker presents the opposition and rebuttal arguments. Information from an interview is used to raise a major argument against governmental regulation of the auto repair industry. Then the speaker uses another interview to refute the opposition argument.

16 Now there are many in the auto repair industry who feel that the government or state should not be involved in overseeing the industry. Rick Glenn, the Auto Service Technology professor I interviewed, commented that many technicians feel that government or state regulation would impose a cumbersome layer of bureaucracy which could only make matters worse. But BAR investigator Tom Hopkins told me that in California the auto industry is not hostile to the bureau. In fact, he said that honest auto repair businesses welcome the BAR because it helps to keep a level playing-field and put the dishonest shops out of business. Mr. Hopkins also said that some of the best technicians leave the auto repair industry and work for the bureau. So you can see that regulation does not need to be antagonistic to the repair industry.

17 The speaker returns to the Sears example to provide listeners with concrete support for the recommended solution.

17 Had the BAR not existed, we might never have discovered the Sears scandal. It was the chief of the BAR who launched an investigation after noticing a pattern of consumer complaints against Sears Auto Centers. The Bureau conducted thirty-eight undercover runs at thirty-three Sears shops statewide in California. The investigation exposed Sears' unethical practices, and forced the company to change its ways.

18 In the conclusion, the speaker uses a hard-hitting

18 We don't have to be at the mercy of fraudulent auto repair companies. The vast majority of men and women in this business are decent and hard-working. But we need to ensure this same

challenge, combined with a powerful quotation, to motivate listeners.

high standard of decency throughout the industry. Let's put the brakes on incompetence and unnecessary repairs by requiring strict ground rules. I think California Consumer Affairs Director Jim Conran spoke for all of us when he said: "We are here today to send this message to the entire automotive repair industry: If you are ripping off the consumers of the State of California, we are after you. We have zero tolerance for abuse of the public trust."

ALTERNATIVE INTRODUCTION AND CONCLUSION

Here are an alternative introduction and conclusion to Karen Anderson's speech, which demonstrate additional strategies for opening and closing a presentation. The introduction ties into the thesis in paragraph 2 of the problem-cause-solution and reasons organizational sequences. The conclusion is inserted after paragraph 17 in the problem-cause-solution and reasons sequences.

1 The speaker makes a personal reference, and describes a stereotype relating to women and automobile repair. Karen destroys this myth with a study, which indicates that in the auto repair industry "there is no sex discrimination."

Alternate Introduction: Personal Reference with Statistic

1 What I know about automobiles would fit into a thimble. But don't think for a second it's because I'm a woman. In the past, females have taken a bad rap when it comes to car knowledge—like all we know is where the key goes. Of course, we are made out to be totally helpless when it comes to changing a flat tire, too. And forget any kind of repair work. We're so automobile illiterate that we will believe anything the repair person tells us. If a fan belt, carburetor, or dipstick needs replacing and we're told it'll cost $50, we have the reputation of saying, "Sure, whatever it costs, just get it done fast because I'm headed to the mall." Well, I'll clue you: When it comes to auto repairs, there is no sex discrimination—we are all at risk. According to a study done by the U.S. Department of Transportation, as much as forty percent of our money is wasted as a result of fraudulent or incompetent repairs. Well, it's time for us to stop being so vulnerable.

Alternate Conclusion: Challenge, Statistic, and End Questions

1 Karen uses a challenge and statistic to ignite listeners in this conclusion. Notice that the speaker poses questions in the final lines to get audience members to think about her persuasive proposals.

1 We no longer have to be targets of irresponsible behavior in the auto repair industry. The vast majority of men and women in this business are honest, decent, and hardworking. But we need to ensure this same high standard of decency throughout the industry. Do we really want to continue paying almost forty percent of our hard-earned dollars on unnecessary or incompetent repairs? Isn't it about time to put the brakes on this behavior by requiring strict ground rules to protect everyone?

N O T E S

1. Evan Thomas, "Final Journey," *Newsweek,* August 2, 1999, pp. 27–30.

2. Edward M. Kennedy, "Tribute to John F. Kennedy Jr.," is used by permission.

3. Nat Hentoff, "AIDS Breakthroughs and AIDS Politics," *The Washington Post,* December 22, 1994, sec. A, p. 19.

4. Elizabeth Glaser, "Speech to the 1992 Democratic National Convention," is used by permission of Paul Glaser.

5. Garry Trudeau, "The Impertinent Questions," is used by permission of *Vital Speeches of the Day,* LIX, no. 21.

6. Jesse Jackson, "Common Ground and Common Sense," is used by permission of *Vital Speeches of the Day,* LIX, no. 20.

7. See the following Internet sources: http://www.reeve.uci.edu/~reeve/ "Reeve-Irvine Research Center," University of California, Irvine, July 31, 1996, and Gregory Cerio et al., *PEOPLE Online:* "Christopher Reeve," June 12, 1995. The speech by Christopher Reeve is used from *Vital Speeches of the Day.*

8. Karen Anderson, "Let's Stop Auto Repair Rip-Offs!" Persuasive speech to convince, Carroll Community College, Westminster, Maryland, 1992. Used by permission.

COMPLETE BIBLIOGRAPHY FOR "THE COMPUTER VIRUS: DISEASE OF THE COMPUTER AGE"

Dewdney, A.K. "Computer Recreations of Worms, Viruses, and Core War." *Scientific American,* March 1989, pp. 110–113.

Elmer-DeWitt, Phillip. "Invasion of the Data Snatchers!" *Time,* September 26, 1988, pp. 62–67.

_____."The Kid Put Us Out of Action." *Time,* November 14, 1988, p. 76.

Henderson, Bruce W. and Nordwall, Bruce D. "Rapid Spread of Virus Confirms Fears About Danger to Computers." *Aviation Week and Space Technology,* November 14, 1988, p. 44.

Honan, Patrick. Avoiding Virus Hysteria." *Personal Computing,* May 1989, pp. 85–87, 89, and 91–92.

Markoff, John. "How Need for Challenge Seduced Computer Expert." *The New York Times,* November 6, 1988, Sec. A, pp. 1 and 30.

————."Computer Experts Say Virus Carried No Hidden Danger." *The New York Times,* November 9, 1988, Sec. A, p. 18.

Marshall, Eliot. "The Scourge of Computer Viruses." *Science,* April 8, 1988, pp. 133–134.

————."Worm Invades Computer Network." *Science,* November 11, 1988, pp. 855–856.

"The Worm's Aftermath." *Science,* November 25, 1988, pp. 1121-1122.

Peterzell, Jay. "Spying and Sabotage by Computer." *Time,* March 20, 1989, pp. 25–26.

Schendler, Brenton R. "Computer Security Firms Suggest Ways to Stop Viruses." *The Wall Street Journal,* November 7, 1988, Sec. B, p. 4.

U.S. Congress. Office of Technology Assessment. *Defending Secrets, Sharing Data: New Locks and Keys for Electronic Information,* 1987, pp. 3–6.

U.S. Department of Justice. "Student Who Released Computer Virus Indicted," Official press release #89–231, July 26, 1989.

Vogel, Shawna. "1988 Disease of the Year: Illness as Glitch." *Discover,* January 1989, pp. 64–66.

Wines, Michael. "FBI Begins Investigation of Computer Virus Case." *The New York Times,* November 8, 1988, Sec. A, p. 16.

Glossary

A

abbreviated sources Partial references that are included in parentheses within the body of a written outline. They usually include only the author's last name, title of the book or periodical, and page number.

abstract A brief summary of an article, study, or narrative.

action step The fifth step in Monroe's Motivated Sequence which requires the persuasive actuating speaker to provide listeners with a specific behavior to perform in order to solve a problem.

active listening Attentive, involved behavior that represents a complete mental commitment on the part of the hearer.

active listening behaviors Becoming a better listener by withholding judgment about a speaker, providing honest, attentive feedback, eliminating distractions, and evaluating the speech when it is finished.

actuate A persuasive speech which motivates listeners to action.

agenda An orderly list of topics a meeting or discussion group will cover.

alliteration A figure of speech which refers to the repetition of the same sounds.

amplification A figure of speech in which words or phrases are arranged in order of importance to emphasize an opening or closing statement.

analogy A logical argument comparing two or more similar cases to show that, because of their similarity, what applies to one case can also apply to the other.

anecdote A brief humorous story used to demonstrate a point.

antithesis A figure of speech contrasting ideas or qualities to convey a concept.

appeal A specific call to an audience to act on an issue such as vote, donate money, or volunteer for a cause. This strategy is often used in persuasive actuating speeches. (See **challenge.**)

appearance Dress which is appropriate for the audience, occasion, and speech topic.

appreciative listening Listening to hear the power and beauty of words, images, music, or the environment.

argument A logical, organized method of supporting a claim by presenting clear, correct, and complete facts and by drawing conclusions from the data to support the claim.

Aristotle Plato's famous student who lived from 384–322 B.C. and wrote *The Rhetoric,* challenging many of Plato's negative opinions about oratory. He helped to gain respect for the study and practice of public speaking as an art and a discipline.

articulation The clarity and enunciation of words, phrases, and sentences.

attention step The first step in the motivated sequence that generates audience interest and curiosity in the persuasive actuating speech.

attitudes Prior inclinations people have about issues; a spectrum of audience perception from disagreement or neutrality to agreement.

audiovisual aids Devices which may appeal to any of the senses: graphs, drawings, photographs, posters, chalkboards, mechanical media, models, and objects.

awfullizing A term coined by two psychotherapists, Albert Ellis and Robert Harper, referring to an irrational dread of the future.

autocratic A leadership style in which the leader is the chief decision maker and gives orders and commands to group members.

B

barriers to listening Poor listening behaviors such as blocking, selective listening, yielding to distractions, and avoidance.

beliefs Conclusions people have about the world based upon observations, knowledge, and experiences.

bibliography The complete alphabetical listing on an outline of sources that are used as research for a speech.

body The longest part of a speech containing the main headings which were identified in the thesis statement.

body movement Stance, posture, and poise which can support the ideas of a speech.

brainstorming The technique of rapidly and uncritically listing ideas to generate topics for a speech.

buzz groups Technique often used in large organizations of dividing the larger group into small units of three to eight members and report back to the larger organization through designated leaders.

C

causation A logical argument identifying known causes to determine unknown effects (cause-to-effect reasoning), or identifying known effects to determine the unknown cause (effect-to-cause reasoning).

cause-effect sequence   The arrangement of main points of the body of a speech according to causes and/or effects.

case study   An in-depth account of a situation or a set of circumstances.

CD   An audio CD that is used for listening to music.

CD-ROM   Computer Disc Read Only Memory. A small laser disk containing video and/or audio that is used with a computer for education, information, and entertainment.

challenge   A broad, generalized summons to an audience to support a topic. This strategy is often used to conclude a persuasive convincing speech. (See **appeal.**)

channel   The means of transmitting a message through our senses of sight, sound, smell, taste, and touch.

charisma   A special magnetic quality, possessed by some speakers, that attracts audiences and inspire confidence.

chronological sequence   The arrangement of the main points of the body of an informative speech according to time or order of events.

Cicero   A Roman orator and respected teacher from 106–43 B.C. In his book, *De Oratore,* he discusses writing, audience analysis, anxiety, evidence, and argument.

clavicular breathing   Incorrect respiration from the top of the lungs.

code of ethics   Standards of right and wrong which act as guides for ethical behavior and speaking practices.

cohesiveness   One of the characteristics of a small group representing a unifying element, common purpose, or mutual feelings of members.

communication apprehension   Coined by university speech instructor James C. McCroskey, this term describes an individual's anxiety about speaking to another person or group.

communication model   A system or plan that helps us understand the dynamic process of communication.

comparisons   Similarities in situations or events.

comparative advantages   A method of organizing the main points of the body of a persuasive convincing speech by comparing the advantages of a proposed solution with the advantages and disadvantages of other solutions.

compliment   An introductory strategy in which the speaker praises elements of the audience or speaking occasion to build a relationship with an unknown speaker or unfamiliar audience.

conclusion   The ending of a speech which resolves the ideas presented in the body.

connotation   Personal, specific, and subjective meanings of words.

content   The research, organization, and logical development of a speech topic.

contrasts   Differences in situations or events.

convince   A persuasive speech that seeks to alter the beliefs and judgments of an audience.

coordination Refers to the placement of equal ideas within the same level of an outline.

Corax One of the founders of rhetoric in the fifth century B.C. He influenced judicial oratory and developed methods that helped common people to argue cases successfully in court.

credibility Confidence listeners place in a speaker as a result of the speaker's use of verifiable research and reliable sources.

critical thinking The ability to test information, be organized, listen to different perspectives, think independently, and use self-discipline.

culture Nonverbal messages that can vary widely depending on background and origin.

D

database A computer software system such as *First Search* or *Periodical Abstracts Ondisc* that indexes periodicals, journals, and books and helps speakers to locate relevant research quickly.

decoding The thought process within the receiver that changes symbols into meaningful ideas, thoughts, or feelings.

definition speech An informative speech about a philosophical concept such as a theory or idea, or a concrete subject like a science or art.

demographic analysis Collecting social and statistical information about listeners through surveys or interviews that will help the speech to receive a favorable hearing.

delivery The style or presentation of the speech.

democratic A leadership style in which the leader functions as a coordinator, promoting discussion and stimulating group decision making.

demonstration speech An informative presentation which includes a variety of audiovisual aids to show the steps of a process.

denotation Dictionary definitions of words.

descriptive speech An informative speech related to persons, places, objects, or events.

diaphragmatic breathing Steady breathing from the diaphragm which produces a constant supply of air needed to produce sound.

digital video player (DVD) A means of viewing movies or other prerecorded video using a small laser disc the size of an audio CD.

discriminative listening Listening to learn, to be instructed, and to test theories.

discussion questions Open-ended issues that are phrased as questions and become the subject of a group discussion. Questions of fact explore issues where information is either unknown or disputed; questions of value require discussion members to use personal judgments to evaluate issues; questions of policy stimulate discussion about solutions or future actions.

dramatic pauses Intentional breaks or silences between major ideas that can bring out the meaning of a specific passage. (See **pauses** and **vocalized pauses.**)

E

e-mail Electronic messages that are sent via the Internet.

emphasis Alterations in rate of speech, volume, and pitch to highlight significant words and sentences.

empathic listening Listening to understand and facilitate the needs and feelings of someone else as in therapeutic listening.

encoding The thought process within the sender that changes ideas, thoughts, or feelings into understandable symbols.

encounter groups A type of discussion that contributes to interpersonal learning and insight.

enumeration A logical argument in which the speaker cites a series of specific cases to support a generalization.

ethnocentrism The belief that one culture or environment is superior to another.

ethos One of Aristotle's three proofs. It refers to the ethical appeal and the ability of the speaker to gain the confidence and trust of listeners.

ethics Earning the respect and trust of listeners by avoiding deceptive practices, and by being reliable, fair, and honest.

eulogy A speech of tribute delivered at a memorial service or funeral.

euphemism A vague, inoffensive term that conceals what an individual really means.

evaluative listening Listening as a response to a persuasive message.

example A brief factual instance that demonstrates a point. It can serve as an introductory or concluding strategy, or used as a supporting material in a speech. (See **illustration** or **story.**)

extemporaneous Approaching speech development with research, a prepared outline, and speaking notes. The style of speech delivery presented in a public speaking course.

external transitions Complete sentences or phrases which connect the major headings or main points of the speech.

eye contact Communicating visually to reach the intellect and emotions of the audience and gauge feedback to ideas.

F

facial expression Nonverbal signs demonstrating smiles, frowns, anger, love, or joy which can express silent pictures and support the emotions of a speech.

fallacies Illogical arguments that employ unclear or incorrect facts, incomplete evidence, an/or erroneous reasoning.

fax A computer or machine that allows letters and messages to be sent electronically over a telephone line.

feedback A verbal or nonverbal response from the receiver to the sender. It can indicate whether communication has occurred, how it has been received, and whether it has been understood.

formal outline The formal written structure that refers to the speech body. It includes the main points, subordinate elements, abbreviated sources, and written transitions.

forum A public discussion in which all members of an audience have the opportunity of asking questions, making statements, or delivering speeches about issues.

G

gender Traditional differences some women and men exhibit in their nonverbal communication patterns.

general adaptation syndrome Refers to Hans Selye's classic research in the field of stress reduction. He concluded that the body reacts to stress in stages through an *alarm reaction,* a *resistance stage,* and finally a *phase of exhaustion.*

general purpose The direction of the material presented in a speech: to inform, persuade, or entertain.

general references Library research tools such as the catalog and periodical indexes that help speakers locate books, publications or other relevant research sources for speech topics.

gestures Physical movements of the hands and arms to emphasize words, describe physical objects, or point out locations.

Gorgias A brilliant Athenian speechmaker and teacher from 483–376 B.C. He emphasized an ornate style, figures of speech, and emotionalism in speaking.

graphs Three types of graphs are the bar, line, and pie graphs that are helpful visuals for explaining trends, showing comparisons, or indicating portions of a whole.

H

hidden agenda An unstated, often deceptive speaking goal that a speaker uses to manipulate an audience.

hierarchy of needs Basic needs of all human beings organized into five levels by psychologist Abraham H. Maslow: physiological, safety and security, love, esteem, and self-actualization.

homepage A Web site developed by an institution, business, or individual and placed on the Internet for information, publicity, commerce, or entertainment.

humor A joke or humorous anecdote that is used as a strategy to introduce or conclude a speech.

hypothetical example   A fictitious situation or scenario that has a realistic application.

I

illustration   A long example which clarifies and amplifies an idea. It can be used as a strategy for the introduction and conclusion or provided as a supporting material in the body of the speech.

impromptu   A speech presented without prior notice or preparation. A "surprise" speech.

incentives   Benefits or rewards people gain by agreeing with and adopting the goals of a persuasive speaker. Long-term incentives are benefits which listeners gain over a sustained period of time. Short-term incentives are devices that provide immediate reinforcement of ideas.

indentation   Each level of supporting elements are indented under main points so that the outline clearly indicates the relationship between the heading and the subdivision.

inflection   Changes in pitch which make a speech sound interesting and avoid monotony.

informal outline   The portion of the written outline that refers to the introduction, conclusion, bibliography, and other outline preliminaries.

informative speaking   A type of speech that promotes enlightenment and education about a topic.

internal transitions   Brief terms such as "also," "then," "next," "in addition to," or "finally," which link the supporting materials *within* a subheading of a speech.

Internet   Computerized cyber system connecting offices, businesses, institutions, and homes to the World Wide Web.

introduction   The beginning of a speech that generates curiosity and prepares the audience for the topic and thesis statement.

Isocrates   A Greek orator and teacher in 436–338 B.C. In manuscripts and autobiographies he wrote that a speaker should be well educated, of good moral character, and possess freedom and independence tempered with self-control.

K

keynote speech   Presentations given at the beginning of major conferences or conventions.

L

laissez-faire   A leadership style in which no leader exists, or the leader exerts little or no influence. Group members take care of managerial or administrative responsibilities.

laser disc player   A device that projects photographs, video, or text onto a large screen from a ten- to twelve-inch laser disc.

lecture   A type of informative speech presented by an expert for instructional or educational purposes.

liquid crystal display unit (LCD)   A device that is connected to a computer and then placed on an overhead projector, allowing listeners to view an enlarged version on a projection screen.

logos   One of Aristotle's three proofs. It involves the speaker's appeal to logic and reason.

M

manuscript   A style of speech delivery that is written out and read word-for-word.

Maslow, Abraham H.   A psychology professor at Brandeis University. He identified five levels of basic drives that he felt influenced our thinking and behavior. (See **hierarchy of needs.**)

mechanical media   Any type of electrical devices that can be used as audiovisual aids.

mechanically parallel   Refers to the similarity of sentence structure and wording in each level of an outline.

memorized   A style of speech delivery that requires the speaker to commit the entire speech to memory and make the presentation without speaking notes.

message   A set of organized, structured symbols for communication.

metaphor   A figure of speech used to show comparison without the words *like* or *as*.

mnemonic phrase   A memory device used to help people remember main ideas or significant themes.

modem   A device connecting a computer to a telephone.

Monroe, Alan   A professor of speech at Purdue University in the 1930s. He combined problem–solution techniques with motivational approaches to train sales personnel. His technique, known as the motivated sequence, is a five-step system used in persuasive actuating speeches.

movement   (See **body movement.**)

N

narrative   An experience or story that is told by the speaker.

need step   The second step of the motivated sequence that identifies and develops the existence of a problem in the persuasive actuating speech.

negative self-talk   Thinking negatively about one's efforts at public performance; having a derogatory attitude about public speaking

noise   A distortion or distraction to the communication process. Noise can be *external, internal,* or *semantic.*

O

observation A judgment based on what an individual has seen.

occasion The impact of the environment of the speech. It includes the purpose and location of the speech as well as the expectations of the audience.

opaque projector A bulky device that can display a small drawing or picture from a book onto a large screen.

open-ended question A strategy that requires a clear response from the audience. It is often used in the introduction. (See **questions.**)

opinions The verbal expressions of attitudes; verbal inclinations or perceptions about topics and issues.

opposition argument A strong argument against a speaker's proposition or viewpoint.

organizational sequence The manner in which the main points of the body are organized. Informative speeches can be organized according to chronology, space, causation, or topic. Persuasive speeches can be structured by problem–solution, reasons, comparative advantages, or motivated sequence.

overhead projector A device that is used with clear acetate transparencies to enlarge images onto a screen.

P

panel An informal discussion where one person acts as moderator guiding three to six members through an interactive problem-solving process in front of an audience.

passive listening Listening that is relaxed or "easy" such as listening to a stereo or watching a movie.

pathos One of Aristotle's three proofs. It involves the speaker's appeal to the emotions of an audience.

pauses Breaks or interruptions in speech that separate thoughts and ideas. (See **dramatic pauses** and **vocalized pauses.**)

personal experience Direct firsthand knowledge of a situation that can be a valuable supporting material in a speech. Also a type of informative presentation that provides information about an encounter such as a travelogue, adventure, or expedition.

personal reference An introductory strategy in which a speaker includes autobiographical facts to help listeners learn more about the speaker. This strategy is used when an audience is unfamiliar with the speaker.

persuasion Communication that influences the beliefs, feelings, or behavior of a listener.

phrasing A vocal technique of grouping words and sentences into units of thought that make ideas easier to understand.

pitch   Vocal element that refers to the highness or lowness of sound.

Plato   Lived from 428–348 B.C. and argued that rhetoric was not a "true art" and attacked the methods of sophists in stories known as "dialogues." He described rhetoricians as individuals who were more interested in dishonesty, style, and opinion than in truth.

polls   Samplings of opinion on selected issues.

positive self-talk   Developing positive attitudes and thoughts about one's abilities at public performance.

primary evidence   Original firsthand fact or experience such as an autobiography.

problem–solution   An organizational sequence used to organize the main points of persuasive speeches by developing a problem and then proposing solutions.

pronunciation   Describes the combinations of vowels, consonants, syllables, and accents a speaker uses to emphasize a specific word.

proposition   An arguable, debatable statement that acts as the focal point for a persuasive convincing speech. Propositions of fact create a controversy out of commonly held beliefs; propositions of value seek judgment as to whether an issue is right or wrong, good or bad; and propositions of policy advocate the adoption of a future action or behavior that proposes a change in the *status quo*.

Q

quality   Refers to the unique sound or timbre of the voice.

Quintilian   A skillful Roman lawyer who lived from 35–95 A.D. and wrote *The Institutes of Oratory,* which stresses that the orator must be "a good man . . . skilled in speaking."

questions   Can be used as attention-getting devices in speech introductions or to stimulate serious thought among listeners in speech conclusions. *Rhetorical questions* are self-answered and *open-ended questions* require a verbal response from the audience. (See **rhetorical questions** and **open-ended questions.**)

quotation   The exact restatement of a person's words. Quotations can be valuable supporting materials in the body of the speech or used as a strategy for the speech introduction or conclusion.

R

rate   Refers to the number of words an individual speaks every minute.

Readers' Guide   A general reference to articles in more than two hundred popular magazines; often called the "average person index."

reasoning   The process of presenting logical arguments to draw conclusions or inferences.

reasons   A method of organizing the main points of a persuasive convincing speech by building a case using the strongest reasons from thorough research.

rebuttal argument   Diffusing possible disagreement in a persuasive speech by providing evidence that opposing viewpoints are flawed or inaccurate.

recipient   The destination or recipient of communication.

reference to the introduction   A strategy used in the conclusion to remind listeners of a point, story, or issue mentioned at the beginning of the speech. This strategy promotes unity in the speech.

repetition   A figure of speech in which a speaker reiterates key words or phrases to emphasize key ideas and convey vivid images.

report   A type of informative speaking that is required in business or industry.

rhetoric   In ancient times referred to "the art of the orator." Classical rhetoric dealt with the ability to persuade and move an audience to a specific viewpoint.

rhetorical question   A question that a speaker poses that is self-answered. The audience does not respond verbally. It is often used as a strategy to introduce a speech. (See **questions.**)

role-playing   A technique using an individual(s) to act out a brief skit, assume a character, or simulate a conflict. Also a type of group where members assume characters or personalities to portray relationships and interactions among individuals to act out family conflicts or reveal inner dilemmas.

S

satisfaction step   The third step in the motivated sequence that identifies and develops solutions to a problem in the persuasive actuating speech.

scanning   The process of copying visual aids or written documents into a computer by using a scanning machine.

search engines   Means of locating topics on the Internet. Major search engines are *Lycos, Yahoo!, Alta Vista,* or *Magellan.*

secondary evidence   Information reported secondhand by an intermediary standing between the researcher and the original source.

sender   The individual who originates communication with thoughts, ideas, or feelings.

sentence outline   Refers to a format that includes complete sentences throughout main and subordinate elements of an outline.

setting   The physical and psychological factors of the communication process that includes occasion, environment, space, and time.

Shannon and Weaver In the 1940s Claude Shannon and Warren Weaver wrote *The Mathematical Theory of Communication* describing a classic communication model as a flat line with a source, message, channel, and receiver.

similes A figure of speech in which *like* or *as* is used to show comparison.

shocking statement A situation, experience, or phrase that is used to get the attention of the audience in the introduction.

social groups Help members to establish friendships and maintain personal relationships.

sophists Teachers in ancient Greece who taught oratory for a fee. At first they were respected but later were identified as con artists who exploited students for financial profit.

sophistry A word referring to individuals in ancient Greece who used deceitful methods and faulty methods of reasoning.

source A term relating to the origin of communication. It is used extensively in the Shannon and Weaver communication model.

spatial sequence The arrangement of main points of an informative speech according to geography or location.

speaking notes A brief outline written on 4″ × 6″ or 6″ × 9″ note cards that contain a brief written outline of the entire speech.

specific purpose Includes the general purpose and one topic idea stated in clear and concise language.

statistics A collection of facts in numerical form. They can be used as credible supporting materials in the body of the speech, to gain the attention of listeners in the introduction, or to get the audience to think seriously about an issue in the conclusion. (See **surveys.**)

stereotyping An oversimplified perception and often a prejudicial opinion that all people in a group, culture, or region have the same rigid characteristics or qualities without much exception.

stimulate A persuasive speech in which the speaker seeks to reinforce and intensify the beliefs or feelings of listeners.

story A short narrative that can be used as an attention-getting strategy for the introduction or as a final narrative in the conclusion. (See **illustration** and **example.**)

subdivision Refers to the subordinate points under a heading of an outline. The elements in a subdivision should be divided into separate and equal categories.

subject A broad, general area or issue before narrowing to a limited topic for a speech.

subordination Refers to the placement of secondary, or lower-ranking, ideas beneath higher-order items in an outline.

substantive references Sources such as biographies, encyclopedias, almanacs, books, and magazines that help the speaker locate specific information for a speech topic.

summary A strategy used in the conclusion to recap the main points or thesis statement of the speech. It is especially effective when the topic involves complicated subject matter.

surveys Studies that draw conclusions from research.

suspense A strategy used in the introduction to stimulate interest or make listeners curious about a topic.

symbol Verbal and nonverbal expressions or actions which have meaning.

symposium A type of highly structured group in which two to six experts reveal their views on some aspect of a problem and deliver prepared speeches to an audience without informal discussion.

systematic desensitization A process developed by James C. McCroskey of treating and reducing high levels of communication anxiety through relaxation tapes, visualization, and follow-up exercises.

T

targeting The process of identifying selected groups of listeners and designing specific appeals to motivate them.

task groups A type of group in which the completion of objectives or implementation of solutions is emphasized.

testimonial A speech of tribute presented at a retirement or other going-away ceremony.

testimony A statement or endorsement given by an expert or an individual with a logical connection to the topic.

thesis statement Often called the central idea or central objective, it is the sentence at the end of the introduction that expands the specific purpose and tells the audience exactly what main points the speech will cover.

tiling A computer-generated process of creating large posters with a graphics program.

topic An interesting, well-defined, and limited area that a speaker selects for speech development and delivery.

topic outline A format that includes brief phrases throughout the main and subordinate elements of an outline.

topical sequence Structuring the main points of the body of an informative speech by a logical or natural sequence. Finding research that clusters around natural headings, which can be earmarked for the main points of the outline.

trait A leadership philosophy suggesting that leaders possess certain powerful characteristics such as physical appearance, speaking ability, or behavior.

transitions Connectives or listening cues between major or minor ideas in a speech. (See **external transitions** and **internal transitions**.)

transparencies Clear acetate sheets of plastic used with an overhead projector to enlarge photographs or other documents onto a large screen for easy viewing.

Turabian style A style book by Kate L. Turabian entitled, *A Manual for Writers of Term Papers, Theses, and Dissertations,* that provides speakers with uniform and accurate guidelines for writing papers, outlines, bibliographies, and footnotes.

U

unethical practices Untrustworthy behaviors in which a speaker advocates harm, provides false information, uses offensive language or name-calling, plagiarizes, or stacks the deck to manipulate or exploit members of an audience.

V

values A set of principles or standards that people consider to be important and cause individuals to achieve goals or states of mind and behave in certain ways.

visualization step The fourth step in the motivated sequence that pictures the future if a problem is, or is not solved in the persuasive speech to actuate.

vocalized pauses Verbalizations such as *uh* and *um* that cause distractions in speaking. (See **pauses** and **dramatic pauses**.)

volume The intensity or loudness and softness of the voice.

Index

Permissions and Acknowledgments

Photographs

SUGGESTED TOPIC AREAS

The following lists contain suggested topics for speeches. Some issues are general and include a wide range of ideas, while others are more specific. Topic areas can be altered easily to fit the interests of a speaker, the needs of an audience, or the requirements of an occasion. We include these suggestions to stimulate creative thinking and productive investigation.

ART, CRAFTS, AND HUMANITIES

Classic movies
Collecting: airplanes, art glass, baseball cards, bottles, buttons, cars, Civil War memorabilia, clocks, coins, comic books, dolls, fossils, guns, hats, juke boxes, linens, minerals, model trains, presidential campaign buttons, phonograph records, porcelain, quilts, slot machines, stamps, teddy bears
Costs of maintaining museums
Creating: batik, designer cowboy boots, Greek moussaka, ice sculptures, perfect diamonds, stained-glass art
Designing: a home, clothing, flower arrangements, a landscaped garden, a mall, a wedding cake, a high-rise condominium, a city, a solar-powered car, a golf course, an Olympic-standard racing bicycle, a surf board, a jet ski, a tunnel, a stadium, an airplane, a race track, a submarine, a nuclear power plant, a suspension bridge, a guitar
Famous objects: Broadway theatres, cathedrals, jewels, light-houses, museums, opera houses, palaces, prisons, ships, stadiums, streets, cities, ruins, mountains, forests, parks, trees, weapons, rivers, monuments, graves
Famous people: composers, musicians, painters, sculptors, actors, actresses, dancers, singers, authors, poets, presidents, first ladies, hall of fame personalities, Nobel Prize winners, world leaders
Fashion design and the consumer
Government funding of controversial art projects
Learning to make clay pottery
Life in a symphony orchestra
Looking for treasures at antique stores and flea markets
Major contemporary architectural styles
Manufacturing musical instruments
Re-enacting battles from the War of Independence or the Civil War
Science of restoring artworks
Understanding: Japanese origami, cubism, impressionism, Cajun cooking, the Amish, the game of cricket, soccer, lacrosse, Mexican history, Sioux tribal festivals, the festival of Kwanza, the celebration of Christmas in different countries, the feast of Ramadan, Hanukah, the Chinese New Year
Understanding ethnic food, music, or dance

BUSINESS AND INDUSTRY

Analyzing employee-owned companies
Bar owners' responsibilities to their intoxicated customers
Cleaning up industrial pollution from major waterways
Change in the United States from an industrial to a service economy
Creative packaging for increased sales
Enforcing food-industry health standards
Increasing the minimum wage
Investing in the stock market
Making U.S. products more competitive with foreign goods
Maintaining business and industrial health and safety standards
Maintaining ethical practices in business
Manufacturing American goods in foreign "sweat shops"
Overcoming the groupthink mentality in large corporations
Positive and negative impact of labor unions on U.S. business
Profitability of legalized gambling
Rating airlines' service and safety
Reducing America's trade imbalance
Regulating savings and loan institutions
Regulating the U.S. auto industry
Women and minorities in management positions

CONTEMPORARY ISSUES

Banning cigarette farming, production, and sales
Destructive nature of "designer drugs"
Effective prison rehabilitation programs
Eliminating inner-city slums
Eliminating street gangs
Endangered species
Government-supported day-care centers
Improving relations among races
Jury consulting as "legalized" jury tampering
Legality of car radar detectors
Mandating energy-efficient appliances and lighting
Most-wanted criminals in the United States
National health-care insurance
Need for judicial reform
Police roadblocks as a deterrent to drunk driving
Preventing crime and violence in public schools
Regulating auto insurance rates
Regulating Health Maintenance Organizations
Reliability of child witnesses in sexual-abuse trials
Solutions to homelessness
Solutions to prison overcrowding
Stopping frivolous lawsuits
Victims' rights

CURRENT EVENTS

Airline regulation and safety
Apprehending and sentencing drug smugglers
Automatic jail terms for child molesters
Declining role of the United States in European affairs
Detecting auto-sales fraud
Effectiveness or ineffectiveness of affirmative action
Eliminating the Department of Education
Eliminating the Internal Revenue Service
Eliminating nuclear weapons
Government effectiveness in responding to disasters
Illegal tampering with foods and medicines
Legalized gay marriages
Publishing ex-convicts' names and addresses in community newspapers
Repairing the interstate highway system
Raising versus cutting taxes
Reducing the federal deficit
Relevance or irrelevance of the vice presidency
Shutting down government offices to reduce the deficit
Solving serial murders
Success or failure of the president's economic program
Supreme Court decisions regarding: search and seizure, freedom of the press, freedom of expression, surrogate parenting, executive privilege, separation of church and state, affirmative action, illegal immigrants and social services, school prayer, cruel and unusual punishment, suing HMO insurance companies
Term limits for members of Congress
The appointment of independent prosecutors to investigate the president
The "don't ask, don't tell policy" in the military
U.S. effectiveness in dealing with foreign enemies
U.S. foreign policy (pro and con): aid to Russia, granting China most-favored-nation trade status, the United States as "the world's policeman," accepting immigrants from third-world countries, building U.S. factories in other countries for cheap labor, responsibility in feeding the world's hungry, free trade agreements
Welfare reform

EDUCATION

Creative financing for a college education
Decline of the U.S. educational system
Defining and eliminating illiteracy
Differences between U.S. and Japanese educational systems
Effectiveness or ineffectiveness of home schooling